JOAN OF ARC AND 'THE GREAT PITY OF THE LAND OF FRANCE'

JOAN OF ARC AND 'THE GREAT PITY OF THE LAND OF FRANCE'

MOYA LONGSTAFFE

AMBERLEY

To the memory of my dear parents, Jack and May
Laverty; and for the three men in my life, Richard,
Stephen and Peter

Page 1: Joan of Arc's signature.
Page 3: Statue of Joan of Arc outside the Église Saint-Augustin de
Paris, 1919. (Courtesy of the Library of Congress)

First published 2017

Amberley Publishing
The Hill, Stroud
Gloucestershire, GL5 4EP

www.amberley-books.com

British Library Cataloguing in Publication Data.
A catalogue record for this book is available from the British Library.

ISBN 978 1 4456 7304 2 (hardback)
ISBN 978 1 4456 7305 9 (ebook)

Map design by Thomas Bohm, User design.
Typesetting and Origination by Amberley Publishing.
Printed in the UK.

Contents

Prologue – Joan: A Burning Question Still   6

Part I   The Great Pity of the Land of France   11

1 France: The Most Distressful Country   12
2 The Tragedy of Civil War: Orleans and Burgundy   32
3 Henry V, the Assassination of John the Fearless
   and the Disinheritance of the Dauphin   47
4 Bedford at War, and the Uncertain Start to the
   Reign of Charles VII   61

Part II   A Girl Called Joan from Domrémy   71

5 Childhood and Growing Up in Domrémy   72
6 Joan Sets Out: Vaucouleurs   102
7 Chinon   118
8 *La Pucelle*: Joan the Maid   131
9 Orleans   144
10 After Orleans   164
11 The Road to Rheims: Coronation   187
12 After Rheims   203
13 Paris and After   216
14 Capture   236
15 The Road to Rouen   252
16 Preparations for Bishop Cauchon's 'Fine Trial'   260
17 Joan before the Judges   281
18 The Triumph of the Judges   311
19 After Joan: The War Goes On   348
20 The False Joan of Arc   369
21 The Last Victory: Forever the One and Only Joan   376

Bibliography   385
Notes   392
Index   411

Prologue

Joan: A Burning Question Still

Ô Jeanne, toi qui as donné au monde la seule figure de victoire qui soit une figure de pitié!
André Malraux, Rouen, 30 May 1964

On Wednesday, 21 February 1431, at 8 o'clock in the morning, a girl of nineteen years of age was led into the chapel of the castle of Rouen, before a tribunal presided over by the portly Bishop of Beauvais and comprising no less that forty-two eminent theologians and canon lawyers of all ages, sitting in solemn array, leaning forward and gazing at her with intense curiosity, mingled in many cases with stern disapproval, dark suspicion, and occasionally perhaps even pity. She was dressed in plain and sombre male clothing, a belted knee-length tunic over the hose of a page, but she was of average height and build for a girl of her time, not at all the strapping hoyden they might have expected.[1] Her dark hair, cut round and still short like a soldier's even during her captivity in Rouen, lent a curious pathos to her appearance, somehow underlining her present vulnerability. After passing the previous two months imprisoned in a cell in the tower of the castle, chained to a heavy wooden beam by night and by day, allowed no exercise and only meagre rations, and guarded at all times by five hostile English soldiers 'of the roughest sort', of whom three were shut in the cell with her at night and two kept guard outside,[2] she now looked pallid and very young.[3] And when she spoke, the greatest surprise of all was her voice, for it was soft and feminine, with a hint of the speech of her native Lorraine.[4]

Who was this notorious and enigmatic prisoner, on trial for her life? What had brought her to this pass? We have no portrait of her, although we know that at least one did exist, and probably more. During her trial, on 3 March 1431, she mentions having once seen a portrait of herself, in the possession of a Scotsman. There were of course large numbers of

Scots troops fighting as allies of the French. 'It showed me fully armed,' she said. 'I was on my bended knee before the king, presenting him with letters. I have never seen nor had any other portraits made.' However, she is certainly one of the best-documented figures in history. In the weighty volumes of the minutes of her trial in 1431 and the careful enquiry which was the Nullity hearings of 1452-6, every detail of her life, from childhood onwards, is recorded either in her own words or in the eyewitness accounts of her friends and her companions-in-arms. These documents and related ones were first collected together and published, in five hefty volumes, in the 1840s by the eminent historian Jules Quicherat, thus making possible for the first time a serious and informed study of her life and personality, four hundred years after her death. There are abundant other, less immediate, accounts of her drama to be found in the writings of the chroniclers and letter-writers of her time, much of which needs sifting and weighing. Yet despite this wealth of evidence, controversies have raged, historians have argued, painting conflicting portraits of her and the role she played on the international stage, ever since her brief and brilliant intervention in 1429 in the war between France, on the one hand, and England and its Burgundian allies on the other. Her time was short and she knew it, a little more than a year of warfare, then a year of captivity, finishing in her trial and terrible death at the stake on 31 May 1431.

Aeneas Sylvius Piccolomini (later Pope Pius II), who was present at the negotiations for the Treaty of Arras in 1435, which effectively closed the bitter conflict with Burgundy and signalled the end of the English enterprise in France, wrote in his *Memoirs* that they were many conflicting opinions about Joan at the time. 'It is a great shame,' wrote Étienne Pasquier already in the late sixteenth century, 'for no-one ever came to the help of France so opportunely and with such success as that girl, and never was the memory of a woman so torn to shreds.'[5] Biographers have crossed swords furiously about her inspiration, each according to the personal conviction of the writer. Among the most celebrated of earlier historians we find Siméon Luce, ascribing her visions to an imagination heightened by the episodes of war and the tribulations of her village, Henri Wallon dismissing such an argument and painting a much more peaceful picture of Joan's youth, Anatole France classifying her among the numerous petty prophets and visionaries of the time with their crazy illusions, a thesis indignantly refuted by the Scottish writer Andrew Lang, and the learned Jesuit, Father Ayroles, championing the saint.

So it has continued to this day, each biographer striving for objectivity or grinding his or her own axe, perhaps subconsciously. She has been claimed as an icon by zealous combatants of every shade of opinion, clericals, anticlericals, nationalists, republicans, socialists, conspiracy theorists, feminists, far-rightists, loony-leftists, yesterday's communists, today's *Front National* (which, by claiming her as one of their own, has managed to damage her image more than any of the rest), old Uncle Tom

Cobley and all. As Bernard Shaw said, in the prologue to his famous play, 'the question raised by Joan's burning is a burning question still.' And so it always will be, for she is for all of them a sign, but a sign of contradiction. A sign perhaps, but not a legend. There is no 'legend of Joan of Arc'. For my part, I do not intend to study her as a sign, nor to use her as a cosh with which to batter anyone about the head, but as a person, a very human, vulnerable person, against the background of her own time.

No fantastic miracles were ascribed to her, such as were plentifully heaped by the excitable popular imagination of the day upon so many genuine or fraudulent or self-deceived visionaries. She was never said to have made corpses get up and walk to confession or to have made the sun rise three hours early, folk tales such as were told about Saint Colette of Corbie, her contemporary. Her achievements crowned human effort and courage on her own part and on the part of those with her: 'The soldiers will fight and God will give the victory,' was her motto. The walls of Jericho (or any other town) did not obligingly fall down before her. The nineteenth-century historian Vallet de Viriville, sums it well up when he writes, 'The Maid appears as a profoundly religious young woman of outstanding piety, but in no way a mystic or miracle-worker.' Her history is recorded in sober factual detail both by contemporary chroniclers and above all in the legal documents of the two trials of 1431 and 1456, where we can read it and make up our own minds. In this book, I intend to put before the reader the essential material from those documents and from contemporary records and chronicles.

On that morning of 21 February 1431, Bishop Cauchon opened the proceedings of the famous trial by asking Joan to state her name and surname. 'At home, they used to call me Jeannette,' she said, adding that after she embarked on her public career she was called *Jeanne* (Joan).[6] *Jeannette*: Jeannie or Jenny, as you will. All of Joan's personality is there: a simple country girl (as indeed many witnesses would testify), maybe somewhat naive, devoid of pretention or vanity in spite of her rise to fame. Plain Jeannie, plain Jane. Or, if one must be more formal, Joan. As for her surname, she said she didn't know about that, for like most of the ordinary folk of the day, she didn't have one, or never used it,[7] although she testified that her father was called Jacques d'Arc (like Shakespeare's, his name is spelt in different ways by different people). The appellation *Joan of Arc* or *Jeanne d'Arc*, with its spurious aristocratic particle, gives a curiously remote and lofty impression, whether in French or in English, quite misleading as to the personality of the nineteen-year-old Joan. She never called herself Joan of Arc, *Jeanne d'Arc*, but wished to be known simply as *La Pucelle* (the Maid), or *La Pucelle de Dieu* (God's Handmaid), thus reminding her troops all the time that she was convinced, and wished others to accept, that she came not of her own volition or ambition, not as the tool of any clique, but at the behest of the Almighty, the girl sent by God.

Jean Guitton, the French philosopher, considered that Joan's life brings us face to face with three great moral questions:

1): The problem of justice and force: is war ever morally justified?. Is it permissible to use force to obtain justice?

2): The problem of the letter and the spirit of the law, raised by Joan's decision to wear male clothing, something forbidden by Deuteronomy as an outrage against feminine modesty, but for Joan the best way of protecting herself when obliged to live as a soldier among soldiers;

3): A very modern problem: that of the vocation versus the institution; that is to say, the right of the individual to follow a calling which appears to put him or her at odds with the current social norms and institutions. [However, since the publication of Guitton's book in 1961, this is no longer problematic, at least in Western society.].

It is in the light of these questions and her own answers to them that I wish to examine Joan's life and death. There is of course another question of a different order: what are we to think of her claim to be inspired by divine revelation? Was she deluded, unbalanced, fraudulent, or indeed a great visionary, of the order of Catherine of Siena or Francis of Assisi? And why in any case would God choose to interfere in human affairs, above all to come to the rescue of Charles VII, not the most saintly of men? These are the questions that inspired the passions of her contemporaries, enraged Anglo-Burgundians who saw her as a limb of Satan, enthused those on the French side who regarded her as a saint. However, they are not questions for the historian, since they are outside his/her remit (unless documentary evidence can show Joan to be a fraud or mentally deranged, which is not the case). As Quicherat himself wrote in 1850 (confirmed anti-clerical and rationalist though he was), 'Theologians, psychologists, physiologists, I have no solution to offer them. Let each one of them find, if he can, each from his own point of view, the elements for an explanation which is proof against all contradiction. The only thing I feel myself able to do towards such research, is to present in the most exact form those details of Joan's life which seem to be outside the sphere of human faculties.' He added, 'Whether science can make anything of it or not, we have to admit the visions and, as I shall show, the strange perceptions arising from them.'[8] All that the writer of history can achieve is to record the facts, together with Joan's own claims and descriptions of her experiences, and leave the reader to make up his or her own mind. Indeed, Joan's contemporary, the bishop and historian Thomas Basin, declared no less in his history of Charles VII's reign. His admiration for Joan is plain, but he concludes his chapter on Joan as follows:

Having recounted all these things, we leave to each and everyone the freedom to think what they will, according to their own understanding and ability, concerning Joan's mission and the apparitions and revelations which she claimed she had had.[9]

In this book I hope to present the very human person, too often hidden or distorted behind an icon, too often seeming remote, formed by and belonging to a very different age. As it has been said, the past is another country. It takes an effort of understanding. I want to place Joan's humanity in the context of the times and society in which she lived. To try to achieve some clarity in the picture of the woes of France and its people, to try to understand the climate of the times, I have found it necessary to give a fairly detailed account of what had brought about the disastrous state of political and social affairs in France in the first part of the fifteenth century. So the first section of this book has become extended, but I hope it is not without interest.

My aim is to bring Joan and those who knew her vividly to life, by putting before the reader her own words, as recorded in the first trial which condemned her, and in the words of her companions and those who knew her, as recorded in the second trial (basically an appeal) which annulled that verdict. To give immediacy to the voices of these people who lived some six hundred years ago, I have taken the liberty of giving in direct speech the testimony which, in the original documents, is recorded in indirect speech (*'the witness said ...'* etc.). All names are given in the original French, except occasionally that of a prominent figure in the story, the English version of whose name is familiar enough to us, and of course the name of the Maid. It seemed best to call her Joan, as she is so well known by that homely name in English. It is as the lively, down-to-earth and valiant *Saint Joan* that George Bernard Shaw fixed her image once and for all in the minds of the theatre-going public. Like him, I cannot do better than use her own voice to tell her tremendous story.

PART I

The Great Pity of the Land of France

1

France: The Most Distressful Country

Ô malheurée et très infortunée France pour cely temps!

Chastellain

War is the trade of kings

Dryden

Joan's life and the mission which she devoutly believed she was called to fulfil was not inspired by hatred of an invading army, nor of foreigners, nor of the Burgundian faction allied to them, it was something deeper, an immense *'pity'*, as she said, for the ordinary poor people of France, that *most distressful country* (to borrow the phrase of an Irish popular song of the century before last), pity for the victims of siege, starvation, pillage, looting, rape, expropriation, murder and all the ills concomitant with war. It was the misery caused by rampaging bands of mercenaries, by indisciplined or (in periods of truce) disbanded, unpaid and sometimes starving soldiery, whether French, English, Scottish, Gascon, Flemish or of whatever origin. It was the fields which were of necessity left untilled and the ensuing periods of famine, it was the fear of marauding bandits and the general disarray and wretchedness of whole areas of France. Guitton calls it a 'radical anarchy'. Moreover, as has been pointed out elsewhere, a military policy of devastation was a direct tool of invading armies, for 'it enriched the raiders, demoralized and impoverished their enemies and gave the people of the raided country (from bottom to top of the social hierarchy) an immediate and direct reason to desire peace', which in the last resort could only be secured by capitulation.[1]

This state of widespread devastation, wretchedness and lawlessness was not due to any lack of serious reflection on the profound moral questions which arise from the waging of war. Such preoccupations had exercised learned and acute minds from antiquity. In the fourth century Augustine had sought to define a 'just war', one which is undertaken in defence of one's homeland and in pursuit of peace and justice. That is still our legitimisation of war. War must not be undertaken for reasons of cupidity or domination. Throughout the medieval period the questions were debated and the detail refined. Theologians, ecclesiastical councils, canon and civil lawyers strove to impose limits on inhumanity and barbarism. Various councils attempted to outlaw pillage and other crimes, to invoke excommunication against those who committed them, to protect the poor, the peasants, the old, women and children against outrage, against what they termed *depraedationes et invasiones*. It was laid down that in a *just war* prisoners must not be killed, women must not be raped, pillage must not occur, churches must not be desecrated, the harvests and homes of the poor must not be destroyed, non-combatants must be respected, heralds and messengers must be sacrosanct. The Lateran council of 1139, for example, condemned the use of archery and crossbows against Christian nations, regarding these things as too indiscriminately devastating (rather as we regard the atom bomb). Later attempts were made to outlaw the use of artillery and gunpowder.

The widespread and blatant disregard of these prohibitions and exhortations do not invalidate them. The fact is simply that war, with its inevitable depiction of the enemy as hateful, its terrors and horrors and the abolition of all restraints, can bring out the worst in many of us. Even among the best, necessity can be invoked for behaviour that they would never countenance in normal life. Only those concerned about the state of their souls would feel that they had to take seriously these proscriptions. It was kings and princes who needed to assure themselves that they were not imperilling their own salvation, according to the theologians and lawyers, for it was they who bore the ultimate moral responsibility for the waging of wars. In the fourteenth century both Charles V of France and Edward III of England, at war with each other, consulted canon and civil lawyers about the justice of their causes. Naturally in both cases the lawyers decided that the monarch had right on his side. In the early fifteenth century, Henry V had early convinced himself utterly of the rightness of his cause and viewed himself as the heavenly appointed scourge of the wickedness of the French.

Voices were raised deploring the miseries of the country and denouncing the evils of the state of war. The most eminent and respected theologian of the period, Jean Gerson, was chosen by the University of Paris, of which he was Chancellor, to deliver remonstrances before the king and his Council and to make clear the duties of the monarch, together with the rights and duties of each of the three *estates*, clergy, nobles and people, while setting out forcefully the deplorable state of the kingdom. He was, like Joan, the child of pious and respected peasants, and he pulls no punches in that famous sermon of 7 October 1405, known as *Vivat rex*:

> Is it not a thing intolerable for the people, when nothing is sure, neither their physical security, nor their belongings, nor in their minds? The fearful worry, the continual anxiety about pillage by princes or

men-at-arms, causes them very grave and painful torment, very hard to bear, so much so that in our time some have fallen into despair and committed suicide. Dear God, what a horror! Some have hanged themselves, some have drowned themselves, others have driven a dagger into their hearts [...] How many families have left the kingdom because of such outrages, how many adults, children and beasts have died for lack of food? The fields are left unploughed, a thing pitiful to see, for they have not the wherewithal to sow or don't dare to keep horses or oxen for fear of princes or men-at-arms, or simply haven't the heart to plough since they have nothing left.[2]

The younger generation deserts the land, he adds, the old and feeble are left to fend for themselves, beggars starve since no-one has anything to give them. The 'loyal subjects' suffer more from the soldiery and the pillaging than from the king's enemies.

Thousands of armed men were roaming the country in bands, attacking the English-controlled areas, but also the French. They had taken to a sort of guerrilla warfare as a way of life, because they had no other, writes Quicherat in his *Aperçus nouveaux*. The bishop Thomas Basin, describing the state of the country when Charles VII came to the throne, writes that from the Seine to the Somme the peasants who had not been killed by pillagers had fled, so that for years there had been nobody to till the fields, now returned to heathland and forest. Cultivation was possible only in and immediately around towns, fortresses and castles. He claims that the very animals had learnt to heed the alarms of church bells and watchmen's trumpets, and that unyoked shire horses and oxen, together with pigs and sheep, would of themselves rush headlong to safety at the call.[3] If Joan had not experienced these horrors to any extreme degree herself, she certainly knew they were happening.

How had France descended into such a wretched state of disorder? The history of the on-going tragedy is sombre and long. However it was not until the nineteenth century that historians hit upon the convenient idea of describing as the 'Hundred Years War' that period (from 1337 to 1453) during which English troops and others supporting the English presence were to be found in France. But in fact the hostilities were on-and-off affairs, there were periods of peace and truces and changing allegiances, one might as well lump together the two twentieth-century World Wars under the title of *The (modern) Thirty Years War* – as indeed some reputable historians have done.

The fourth and last period of these wars dates from 1411 (the year preceding that in which, most probably, Joan of Arc was born), when the ailing Henry IV of England, whose government was at that point under the political dominance of his son (the future Henry V), intervened in the on-going terrible civil wars between Armagnacs and Burgundians. The Armagnac/Orleanist party was led by Bernard VII, the notoriously ferocious Count of Armagnac, and it supported the mentally unstable French king, Charles VI, while the Burgundians were led by their Duke, John the Fearless (*Jean sans Peur*). Why should the king of England have wished to entangle himself and his people in the convoluted affairs of France? Ian Mortimer and other historians describe this fourth and last period as a campaign undertaken by the Lancastrians to strengthen their position, many in England regarding them as usurpers, while their claim to the crown of France lacked a solid legal basis. A short account of the run-up to the situation may help to clarify matters.

The English Claim to the Throne of France

The Lancastrians claimed the throne of France through descent from Edward III, who, in 1338, during a period of hostile relations with France, had laid claim to the French crown through his mother's line, his maternal grandfather being Philip IV of France. The French barons, unwilling to have the powerful king of England as their overlord, rejected this claim, somewhat disingenuously invoking the Salic Law to bar succession through the female line. This law was in fact an ancient statute which, in 1317, had been confirmed, with a little tinkering round the edges, by an assembly of notables at the instigation of Philip V, in order to legitimise his claim to the throne. It prohibited women from either succeeding to the throne or passing on the succession.

Edward never in fact became king of France. In 1328, Philip of Valois, grand-nephew of Philip IV through his father, had become Philip VI on the death in that year of his cousin Charles IV. Charles was the youngest of the three sons of Philip IV, the two elder brothers being Louis X (died 1316) and Philip V (died 1322). Had Edward succeeded in his claim in 1338, there would sooner or later have appeared other claimants with pedigrees in the female line as good, if not better, than his. In the end, under the Treaty of Calais, which confirmed the Treaty of Brétigny arrived at earlier in the same year (1360), Edward abandoned his claim to the French throne in return for the renunciation by his captive, John the Good, (*Jean II*) of sovereignty over the territories which he ceded to the English crown. The treaty followed the English victory at Crécy in 1346, the taking of Calais in 1347 and Edward's victory at Poitiers (1356), which is where John II was captured.

The story of the burghers of Calais has been made famous through Rodin's celebrated group sculpture portraying the six civic leaders who accepted the king's conditions at the end of the terrible year-long siege and surrendered themselves, barefoot and with ropes around their necks, to face execution as the price of mercy for their fellow citizens. Their lives were spared at the intercession of Edward's queen, Philippa of Hainault.

The Treaty of Brétigny, signed by the Dauphin (later Charles V), by proxy for his father, still a prisoner in England, gave Edward sovereignty over more than a third of France, not only Guyenne and Gascony, but Calais (of course), Poitou (including Poitiers), Limousin (including Limoges) and more, a great slice of territory stretching from below the Loire to Bayonne, in a broad oblong with two protuberances reaching into the Limousin and to the very edge of the Languedoc. Since the marriage of Henry II and Eleanor of Aquitaine in 1154, the English kings had held the rich province of Aquitaine (Guyenne) as vassals of the king of France. Now they would hold it and all the ceded territory free of any oath of fealty.

On acceding to the throne, Charles V set out to recover a good number of the lost provinces with considerable success, but the reign of his successor, Charles VI, was disastrous, for the unfortunate king was subject, after 1392, to periodic bouts of violent insanity and the kingdom was in effect governed by a *conseil de régence* presided over by the Queen, Isabeau of Bavaria, and led jointly by Charles's younger brother, Louis, Duke of Orleans, and his uncle, Duke Philip the Bold of Burgundy.

In the twelfth century the duchy of Aquitaine had comprised a large swathe of south-west France, from the Loire to the Pyrenees. It was rich and fertile, its climate delectable, its wines famous then as now, its trade with ports such as Bristol and Southampton prosperous, its villages thriving. The palaces and castles of the aristocracy were havens of leisure and culture, of poets, of minstrels and troubadours. In Eleanor's day it was, in short, a Garden of Eden, at any rate for the rich and powerful (but then, at what period were things *not* pleasant for the rich and powerful?). By the time of Henry IV the duchy had been reduced to the region around Bordeaux and Bayonne. During the period 1404–1407, campaigns under the command of various French nobles, chiefly the Duke of Orleans and the Count of Armagnac, came near to subduing it. Bordeaux itself was seriously threatened, but the troops of Louis d'Orléans were forced to retire when they were defeated at Blaye in 1407.

Who's Who: Dramatis Personae

In England: *Henry Bolingbroke, who took the crown as Henry IV*
When, in 1399, the first Lancastrian took the throne of England by force from his cousin Richard II and was crowned king as Henry IV, the relationship between the English monarchy and France was long-standing and close. Henry was bilingual in French and English, and his sons were bought up to be fluent in French, English and Latin. However, the crown of England always sat uneasily on the head of Henry Bolingbroke, eldest surviving son of John of Gaunt, the hugely influential and deeply unpopular uncle of Richard II. As Henry IV, Bolingbroke was widely held to be a usurper. The horrified Bishop of Carlisle, protesting at Henry's declaration of intent to take the throne from Richard II, demands in Shakespeare's play, *What subject can give sentence on his king?* and goes

on to foresee that, if Henry is crowned, *The blood of English shall manure the ground!* [4] (For his pains, he is immediately arrested on a capital charge of treason). The deposed King Richard was mysteriously done to death (but probably by starvation, on Henry's orders) at Pontefract in 1400.[5]

Richard's successor had stepped into a quagmire of political intrigue and ambitions. Soon the most celebrated and troublesome of Henry's adversaries would be the Percy family. Henry Percy, father of Shakespeare's fiery Hotspur, had been created earl of Northumberland on the occasion of King Richard's coronation in 1377, but in 1399 he was the *ladder*, as Shakespeare puts it, by which Bolingbroke ascended to the throne.[6] His allegiance thereafter veered back and forth. In 1403, before his son, young Hotspur, joined battle at Shrewsbury with Henry IV's army, Northumberland had entered into an alliance with Glendower in Wales in order to oppose the king. Hotspur having been killed at Shrewsbury (July 1403) and his uncle, the Earl of Worcester (brother of Northumberland), captured and executed, there followed a brief renewal of the elder Percy's fealty to the crown, but in 1405 he reverted to the Welsh alliance. In 1408 he raised troops in Scotland for a second insurrection and met his end at Branham Moor in February of that year. Thomas Mowbray, Duke of Norfolk, and Richard Scrope, archbishop of York, had been executed in 1405 on charges of conspiring with him and raising rebellion.

The execution of the archbishop contributed to Henry IV's reputation for cruelty, blotting out the glory earned in the 1390s as a chivalrous and gallant crusader against the 'heathens' in Lithuania and Prussia and as a pious pilgrim to Jerusalem. To add to all this grief and turbulence, Henry was eventually stricken with a disease commonly rumoured to be leprosy, the ultimate allegory for grave sin, in an age fervently addicted to allegories. And what greater sins could there be than the sacrilegious execution of an archbishop or the usurpation and murder of your king? The inviolability of the king's person was sacrosanct in the eyes of mediaeval man, since royal authority having been bestowed by God, only God could deprive a king of it or condemn him for misuse of it.

No wonder then that Henry was tempted to consolidate and justify his position by a triumphant military campaign abroad, to this day a sure popularity winner. On the one hand, wars were (and are) costly businesses and he was in a considerably straitened economic situation, his treasury being depleted by the rebellions at home and the cost of keeping a colony and garrison in Calais. On the other hand, victory in France would be an indisputable proof of God's favour and hence of his legitimacy as ruler of both France and England, ensuring stability and tranquillity to his royal line. From 1408 onwards, however, he was very gravely ill. In June of that year, his courtiers thought he was dead when he fell into a coma lasting several hours. In 1410 and early 1411, during a period when his eldest son, the future Henry V, had managed, thanks to the king's dire state of health, to take control of the policy-making Royal Council, the

Duke of Burgundy, John the Fearless, entered into negotiations with a view to securing an alliance against the forces of the Count of Armagnac. In return for such an alliance, his ambassadors dangled before the eyes of the prospective ally, the young Henry, the cession of several of the duke's Flemish towns to English sovereignty, together with the hand of Burgundy's daughter in marriage. All this was very enticing, since the wool trade between England and Flanders was a major part of the economy of both countries.

Henry IV was much less beguiled by this scenario than his son, with whom he had a number of serious differences of opinion, among other things, their view of the murdered Richard II, of whom the prince had been fond. However an English military contingent set sail for France in the autumn of 1411 in support of Burgundy. With the Burgundians, they scored a notable victory in November over the Armagnacs at Saint-Cloud, near Paris, and returned home. Henry IV then reasserted himself, received envoys from the Armagnacs with counter-offers (including recognition of the English claim to the duchy of Aquitaine, without any mention of vassalage) and reached an accord with them in the spring of 1412. He bestowed the title of Duke of Clarence upon his younger son, Thomas, who was his favourite, and in August sent him into France with an army of some fifteen hundred men-at-arms and four-and-a-half thousand archers. Unfortunately for Clarence, the two opposing sides in the civil war in France concluded a truce on 8 August and the English were no longer welcome, whereupon Thomas, outraged, declared war on the Armagnacs, accusing them of treachery. Among other bloodthirsty exploits, he proceeded to sack the town of Meung on his way home. Henry IV died on 20 March, 1413, aged only forty-five. *How I came by the crown, O God forgive, / And grant it may with thee in true peace live!* are his last words to his elder son in Shakespeare's play, after he has counselled the young Henry to channel the insubordinate energies at home into the great enterprise of 'foreign quarrels'.

Henry V and His Victorious Campaign

Henry V, on succeeding to the throne, was determined to continue his father's work, and to revive the English claim to the throne of France. He immediately made preparations for an invasion. He is patriotically glorified in Shakespeare's history plays, but the cold, puritanical and ostentatiously (even if genuinely) pious side of the historical figure is nonetheless reflected in the playwright's dramatic portrayal of the newly crowned monarch's frosty dismissal of the heartbreaking salutations of Falstaff, his old roistering companion: *I know thee not, old man. Fall to thy prayers.* In the play, the dying Henry IV tells his son, the duke of Clarence, that the heir apparent is made of flint when angered. Made of cold steel too, as far as ambition is concerned. One French historian describes the reformed broth of a boy as *pieux et glacial*. Ian Mortimer chooses the words 'solemn', 'conscientious' and 'virtuous' to describe him, and stresses his acute sense of pride and deep anger when he felt in the least way offended.[7]

The campaigns in France would show, once and for all, whose side God was on, and that not only in France, but in England. Like Joan later, Henry was said to hear three Masses a day (it should be noted that an everyday 'Low Mass', that is one without sermon or music, takes no more than half-an-hour to celebrate, possibly less if the priest is a record-breaker). Henry could moreover present his campaign as a holy crusade against the promoters of schism within the Church, the French having chosen to support the claims of the anti-pope Benedict XIII at Avignon, while the English recognised Boniface IX in Rome. The Great Schism was the scandal of Christendom and at her trial Joan of Arc would be asked a very loaded question: 'Which do you believe to be the rightful pope?' Henry presented himself not only as the dispossessed but rightful claimant to the crown of France and all its possessions, but as God's scourge of French sinfulness. His was a holy war. Others see, and saw, the matter differently. Ian Mortimer writes that the French provided 'the foreign stage on which the Lancastrians attempted to prove their legitimacy'.[8]

On 22 September 1415, Harfleur fell to Henry. No conditions were allowed, the French population was expelled and all property confiscated, together with belongings which they were unable to take with them. Upon completion of this exercise, Henry piously attended Mass. Interestingly, the captain of Harcourt forced to surrender the place was the seasoned warrior Raoul de Gaucourt, whom we shall meet again at Orleans when Joan of Arc arrives to raise the siege. The population of Harfleur was soon replaced with English colonists, in a repeat of what had happened in Calais in 1347, when, after eleven months of heroic resistance, it fell to Edward III. At least, Henry did not demand the heads of six leading citizens.

A month later, on 25 October, the amazing victory at Agincourt seemed the definitive vindication of the House of Lancaster, when a small, carefully recruited army, against huge odds, defeated the flower of French chivalry, thanks to the greater professionalism of the English, the superior fire-power of their archers and the thick mud of the battlefield, which together proved disastrous for the insouciant French nobility and their motley collections of vassals and mercenaries. The French aristocracy still regarded war as basically a sport requiring little coordination. In the words Shaw puts into the mouth of Dunois in his play, 'They beat us because we thought battles were tournaments and ransom markets.' Weighed down by their heavy armour and mounted on their splendid chargers, the French were so numerous and so pressed against each other that they did not even have room to swing their swords, the muddy ground gave way beneath their weight even when they dismounted, the horses stumbled and fell, the whole army floundered.

Henry's reputation as a chivalrous adversary was blotted when, towards the end of the battle, on hearing that the French were regrouping or attempting another attack, he ordered the hundreds of prisoners taken to be executed. Only those of royal blood were to be spared. Every man was to slay the prisoners he had taken, who were now locked up in houses nearby. When their captors refused to carry out the order (whether out of humanity, or reluctance to lose ransom money), Henry sent in two hundred archers as executioners and the slaughter was obediently carried out with great brutality, some of the prisoners being simply burnt alive as the houses holding them were set alight. According to the rules of the game, the prisoners had given themselves up in full expectation of being duly ransomed. Ian Mortimer gives us an exhaustive analysis of the battle and reluctantly comes to the conclusion that 'by all the standards of the time, the killing was an ungodly act and no way to win the love or respect of the people whom Henry sought to rule as king.'[9] The episode has been justified as a necessity of war, but in fact such a crime was as much against all the rules of chivalry as it would be today against the Geneva Convention. It was not, of course, the only atrocity in medieval or later warfare. The Burgundian chronicler Monstrelet skims over the ghastly event, merely remarking that it was done because the king had been informed that he was being attacked from the rear.

Monstrelet reckons that ten thousand perished at Agincourt, more cautious modern estimates put it at around four thousand, including the massacred prisoners. It was certainly a huge number. Long pages of Monstrelet's chronicle are filled with lists of the nobility who fell, and the chronicler says that he passes over many others 'for the sake of brevity'.[10] The two brothers of the Duke of Burgundy were among the dead. John the Fearless himself, keeping all options of alliance open, had not taken part in the encounter. After the battle, Henry sent for the French and English heralds and put to them the rhetorical question: 'Who has won this battle, is it I or the king of France?' 'It is you, Sire,' they dutifully replied, at which Henry solemnly declared: 'It is not we who have made this slaughter, but Almighty God, as we believe, because of the sins of the French.'[11] On subsequent occasions he lectured the French prisoners at some length on their uniquely wicked ways.

Henry, the 'mirror of chivalry' as one near-contemporary English chronicler calls him,[12] was certainly, in the eyes of the French, henceforth a tarnished and distorting mirror. Chivalry was at an end. The next day the French casualties lying amid the blood and mud on the battlefield were despatched by Henry's soldiers, unless they were rich (so ransomable) and still able to trudge all the way to Calais, along with the victorious army. Henry reserved the most valuable captives for himself. In the case of the twenty-one-year old Duke of Orleans (who would later be the poet Charles d'Orléans) however, Henry forbade any release, since he was the nephew of Charles VI and as second in line to the throne of France after the Dauphin, an abiding threat to Henry's pretensions to the French crown. The duke did not see France again until 1440, when a huge ransom was paid, crippling the people of Orleans and his fiefs with taxes. His deliverance from captivity would be one of the four principal goals of Joan of Arc. His illegitimate half-brother, Dunois (rejoicing in the then current aristocratic title of *Bastard of Orleans*) was the captain of Orleans when Joan arrived and thenceforth one of her staunchest allies.

Following Agincourt, the towns of Normandy were left defenceless. Henry's army was backed up in the Channel by a fleet of thirty warships, the largest fleet until the reign of Henry VIII.[13] Caen fell on 4 September 1417, its French population was driven out if they refused to take an oath of allegiance to the English overlordship, their property being distributed to English colonists. Bayeux and other places surrendered. Rouen seemed impregnable with its rich merchants, its weavers, its gold- and silversmiths, its cathedral and abbeys and churches, its castle and garrison provided with abundant artillery, the whole defended by mighty walls, towers and surrounding moats or fosses. Henry considered it, after Paris, to be the second city in France. He determinedly starved it out during a seven months' siege lasting into the bitter winter, from July 1418 to January 1419, during which time food was so scarce that mice, dogs, cats and anything else that could be caught was sold for eating. The population had been swollen by thousands of refugees. As a desperate measure the old and infirm, men, women and young children, were expelled from the town in the hope that they would be allowed through the besieging lines to find refuge elsewhere, but Henry stonily refused to let them pass and watched as they died lingering deaths of cold and hunger in the ditches.

When Duke John the Fearless of Burgundy and the king decided that they were not in a position to relieve the town, the duke sent secret messengers to tell the citizens to negotiate surrender on the best conditions they could obtain. They were sorely grieved, says the Burgundian chronicler Monstrelet: 'All the citizens were sick at heart and as for most of the men-at-arms, they were greatly bewildered as to how they could survive the danger in which they found themselves.'[14] The Burgundian captain of the town, Alain Blanchart, was executed after its capitulation. This was the town in which, ten years later, Joan would be tried. We may well speculate on the degree of warmth in the relationship between the ordinary citizens and the occupiers.

Despite these apparently divinely sanctioned victories, the Lancastrian claim by descent from Edward III had no basis in law and would have had none even if the Dauphin Charles had never been born. As already noted, the Salic law proscribed succession through the female line and even in English law, Henry's own father, Henry IV, had only justified his claim to the English throne by reverting to the restriction of succession rights to the male line, which had been the legal situation before Edward I.[15] Henry V's marriage in June 1420 to the French princess Catherine changed nothing, for even if there had been no Salic law, Catherine was not Charles VI's eldest daughter. She had three older sisters.

The marriages of these royal sisters illustrate the complexities of dynastic alliances at the period. Until long after the Middle Ages such marriages were arranged from earliest childhood onwards and if both parties were children, they were sometimes reared together, living as brother and sister until both had reached puberty, the age of consent being fourteen for boys, twelve for girls. Catherine's eldest sister, Isabelle, was pledged in 1396, at the grand age of seven, to the twenty-nine-year-old Richard II, King of England. After her husband's untimely demise, Isabelle was married in 1406 to the fifteen-year-old Charles, who became Duke of Orleans in November 1407, following his father's assassination by Burgundy. She died giving birth to a daughter in September 1409. In 1410 Charles d'Orléans married Bonne d'Armagnac, daughter of the Count of Armagnac, hence the party supporting Orleans and his cousin the Dauphin became known as the *Armagnacs*. Bonne died during Charles's imprisonment in England after Agincourt. On his return he married for the third time, his choice being the daughter of the Duke of Cleves, who gave him three children, of whom one became King Louis XII in 1498. Of the other two sisters, Jeanne had married John, Duke of Brittany, in 1396, and Michelle was married in 1406 to none other than the son of the Duke of Burgundy, who would succeed his assassinated father in 1419 and be known as Philip the Good.

Charles VI, King of France

King Charles VI, who ascended the throne in 1380 a month before his twelfth birthday, was much loved by his people. From the early days of his reign he was known as *Charles le bien aimé*. He was a blond, good-looking young man, rather taller than average, athletic, good-natured, good fun and good company, well-intentioned in his government. His father had seen to it that his tutors were men of learning, valour and experience. The first, Philippe de Mezières, had travelled widely in Europe and the Near East and been chancellor to the last king of Cyprus. His only complaint about his pupil was that the prince preferred the popular *romans de chevalerie*, the romances of King Arthur and the knights of the Round Table, to his more serious studies. After 1392 and his collapse into periodic episodes of violent mental instability, the population at large seems to have regarded Charles with charitable pity and even affection.

The first of these episodes struck with unheralded fury while Charles was riding through a forest in August 1392. The king had set out from Le Mans on an expedition to Brittany, where he was convinced he would find and arrest a certain Pierre de Craon, who, with a number of accomplices, had made a near-fatal assassination attempt the previous June on the Constable of France, Olivier de Clisson. The king had not been well recently, suffering headaches and feverish temperatures, but no advice or pleas would deter him from his purpose. It was a torrid summer's day. In the forest, suddenly a ragged vagrant slipped through the escort and seizing the reins of Charles's horse, cried 'King, you are betrayed! Turn back!' The man was beaten off and allowed to flee, never to be seen again. Soon thereafter, the party emerged from the forest onto a sandy plain. One of the pages, dozing off on his horse, dropped his lance, which clanged against the helmet of the page in front of him. At that, seized with the paranoid delusion of being surrounded by traitors, Charles roared and charged at his entourage, recognising none of them and frenziedly pursuing his brother, the Duke of Orleans, with his naked sword. He wheeled about dementedly, slashing wildly at all and sundry, until, man and mount dripping sweat, he was at last unhorsed, his eyes rolling in his head, incapable of speech and knowing no-one, neither his brother nor his uncles, the dukes of Berry and Burgundy. He was carried back half-dead to Le Mans, and from there later to Creil, the doctors giving little hope for his recovery or even his life. According to the chronicler Froissart, although some of the escort were struck, no one was killed. Accounts vary on that point. The *Religieux de Saint Denis* (a cleric of the Abbey of Saint Denis), who claims to have been, not at the scene of the drama, but 'in the camp', alleges that four people were killed, but the truth of the matter is uncertain.

On his arrival back in Paris, the king's uncle, the Duke of Burgundy, Philip the Bold, who had played a leading role in government during the boy-king's minority, convoked a council and got himself declared regent. A *conseil de régence* was set up, presided by Queen Isabeau, and Louis d'Orléans became co-regent with his uncle, Duke Philip. The older and more experienced man predominated. Thus from 1392 onwards, Charles VI's younger brother, the duke of Orléans, and his uncle, Philip the Bold, were the joint rulers of France, with Philip determinedly at the helm.

Isabeau of Bavaria, Queen of France

Isabeau and Charles had been married only seven years when this disaster befell them. For a dozen years after the onset of her husband's intermittent (but increasingly frequent) bouts of violent insanity, Queen Isabeau hoped and prayed for his recovery, but the frightening outbursts of rage, the filth and squalor into which the madness dragged him, wore her down bit by bit. Isabeau, the daughter of Duke Stephen II of Bavaria and his wife, Taddea Visconti (the daughter of the duke of Milan), had been married to Charles at the age of fifteen, when Charles was seventeen, and the two young people had seemed genuinely fond of each other and happy in those early years. She was a small, dark-haired girl, resembling her Italian mother more than her Wittelsbach father, and while not considered outstandingly beautiful, in those day when only pale-complexioned blondes were in fashion, she was pretty and had charm enough to make a young king fall in love at first sight. On 13 July 1385, when she arrived at Amiens with her escort of nobles, ostensibly on a pilgrimage, she had been coached in a few *formules de politesse* in French, but apart from

German, she knew only the basic Latin which she had been taught. In fact, the real object of the long expedition from Bavaria was an encounter with the seventeen-year-old king, with a view to marriage should he find her to his liking (no question about *her* finding *him* to her liking). The minute he set eyes on her, it was a *coup de foudre*, according to Froissart. 'The king can't take his eyes off her,' as the Constable of France, Olivier de Clisson, joyfully informed another grandee.

Charles certainly couldn't wait to marry her. Instead of continuing on to Arras for a grand ceremony, as his uncle the Duke of Burgundy had arranged, Charles insisted that the wedding take place straight away in Amiens on 17 July 1385. The first child, named Charles after his father and grandfather, was born in September 1386. Unhappily, the child died in December of that year. Nonetheless, for some years the young couple seem to have been very happy, Isabeau apparently regarding as beneath her regal notice her husband's light-hearted and frequent infidelities. Even after the onset of the king's terrible malady, marital relations were resumed during his lucid intervals. For a long time, during those periods, he regained his perfect health and sense, taking up his royal responsibilities, playing tennis, engaging in all kingly sports. His appearance did not deteriorate. However, by the last decade of his reign (he died in 1422), his memory was dimming and he was increasingly slow to react to political and personal situations, appearing impervious to even what touched him most. By 1403 Isabeau had given him eleven children, of whom the latest was the future Charles VII, Joan of Arc's *gentil dauphin*. In 1407, one other child would be born, but he died immediately.

Isabeau was the darling of her father, Stephen III of Bavaria, who, on the initial approaches on the subject of his daughter's marriage to the king of France, at first refused to consider it, saying that it was too far away and that he would rather she were married nearer home. Later in her reign as queen, her lavish expenditure on clothes and jewelry and splendidly flamboyant court entertainments gave rise to resentment among the people. However, it was not she, it must be said, who introduced ostentatious sartorial opulence into France. In fact, when she arrived at Amiens, her clothes were judged too modest for a princess and she had to be decked out in something much more splendid.

The end of the fourteenth century and the early fifteenth was an era of extravagant fashion for the aristocracy, both men and women. Ladies' crowning glory was plaited and rolled around their ears and set off atop by extraordinary headdresses such as the *hennin*, which to modern eyes is reminiscent of nothing so much as an inverted ice-cream cone, excessively elongated, from the tip of which streams a diaphanous veil. In a miniature in Froissart's *Chronicles*, we can see Isabeau wearing such a confection and riding a white horse for her entry into Paris in June 1389. *Décolletés* were extreme, robes hugged the figure to the waist, from whence they flowered out into a long train behind (to be glamorous, then as now, one had to be fashionably *svelte*), jewelry was ostentatiously displayed, sometimes on girdles draped over padded stomachs for greater effect. Sleeves, on men's and women's garments, flared out from the elbows and draped themselves far below the waist. Now for the first time men wore short doublets over torso- and leg-hugging hose, in glaring colours and stripes, scandalously emphasising all the virile attributes. Ridiculously long pointed toes on shoes (*poulaines*) curled upwards, the higher the rank of the wearer the longer, often impeding movement and having to be held up by ties attaching them to the wearer's belt.

Needless to say, all this suggestive apparel called down the disapproval of preachers and moralists. The Dominican preacher Vincent Ferrier (died 1419) caricatures fashionable dress in a sermon, saying that when women kneel and incline forwards to receive his benediction, the hennin hits him over the head.[16] Even in this ambience, Isabeau's expenditure on dazzling jewelry and sumptuous clothing was considered exorbitant. Her breathtaking merry-go-round of court festivities was prodigious also. In the midst of civil war, her banquets, her entertainments and minstrels, her fabulous embroidered and bejewelled garments, were a glittering spectacle to all who beheld them. All this had to be paid for through excessive taxation imposed upon nobles, clergy and people. Little of it was spent for the public good or to finance the on-going wars, and considerable amounts were sent on occasion to Isabeau's family in Bavaria, although recent historians have found some justification for this, regarding it as payments for debts or fiefs. In 1405, the disorders of her *entourage* were forcefully denounced in a sermon preached before the court by the Augustinian monk Pierre le Grand, and repeated again at Whitsun before the king, a little over a week later. However, Pierre's criticism was directed at the dissolute behaviour of the court and there was no suggestion of disorder in Isabeau's private life.

Recent historians have come to her defence, pointing to her efforts to reconcile duke Philip of Burgundy and his rival for power, his nephew Louis of Orleans, and to her later ineffectual efforts to patch up reconciliations between Philip's son, John the Fearless, and Louis of Orleans. Her difficulties after the onset of Charles VI's madness, her lack of any real power as regent, her need for money to support her numerous progeny, all this is highlighted. She certainly had loved Charles and grieved for him in his terrible state and there is evidence that she was a good mother. Like Marie Antoinette later, she was reviled as a foreigner, that *German woman*, and made the butt of vicious propaganda, much of it after 1404 issuing from the circles around the new Duke of Burgundy, John the Fearless.

Her old age was spent miserably cooped up in the Hôtel St. Paul, detested by the populace of Paris, who blamed her as the cause of all their ills. Standing forlornly with her women at the window of the palace on Sunday, 2 December 1431, she watched the ceremonial entry into Paris of her English grandson, the not quite ten-year-old Henry VI. Mounted on his white horse, he rode in through the Porte Saint Denis, solemnly escorted by a great procession of all the city dignitaries, the streets thronged with curious crowds of sightseers. When they passed in front of the Hôtel Saint-Pol, the chronicler known as the *Bourgeois de Paris* (now identified as a University cleric named Jean Chuffart), writes,

> Queen Isabelle of France, the widow of King Charles VI, was standing at the windows with her ladies to see the young King Henry, the son of her daughter, who doffed his hat to greet her as he passed. She bowed very humbly and turned aside, weeping. [17]

When she was told that the Treaty of Arras had been signed on 21 September 1435, between the Duke of Burgundy and Charles VII, effectively signalling the end of the English venture in France, she is said to have wept for joy.[18] On that occasion, no doubt it was a joy tinged with melancholy. She died very shortly thereafter, on 29 September 1435. She was buried in Paris in the abbey of Saint Denis, but with none of the pomp and ceremony which usually accompanied the funerals of queens of France. When the Duke of Burgundy, still in Arras, heard this, says Monstrelet, he had a solemn requiem celebrated for her by the bishop of Arras, which he himself attended, dressed in mourning.[19]

One cannot but feel that, for all her faults or political inadequacies, Isabeau was a victim. The trauma of the descent of the charming *Charles le bien-aimé* into appalling bouts of madness and squalor, the constant pregnancies with their attendant high risks, the stress of living in a foreign country riven by factions, always on the brink of civil war, and whose language she had to learn laboriously, all that must have been a difficult cross to bear.

In January 1393, less than a year after the first attack of the king's madness, in the midst of court entertainments meant to stabilise his recovery (and which had seemed moreover to be having the desired effect), the terrible episode of the *Bal des Ardents* took place. In the midst of exuberant merrymaking and festivities at court, Charles and six of his nobles entered the great hall disguised as satyrs, in costumes heavy with tar and fur, and all, except the king, attached in line to each other. The hall was dark, as Charles had banned torches for the occasion for fear of fire. In the midst of their cavorting, the Duke of Orleans, unaware of the ban, entered with torch-bearers. Taking a torch to see what was going on, he bumped into the leading satyr who went up instantly in a blaze, as did those behind him. As the screams of the victims filled the ears of the horrified queen and court, Charles was saved by his aunt, the young Duchess of Berry, who pulled him away and smothered him under the train of her robe. The queen had fainted and been carried into a nearby chamber. Only one other of the merrymaking band survived, having managed to rush out ablaze and plunge into a vat of water.

Charles's mental state seemed to have been unimpaired by the disaster, He remained calm, showed himself that very evening to the people to allay alarm and rumours, and the next day proceeded with an escort to Notre-Dame, where a Mass was celebrated to give thanks for his narrow escape. He resumed his political and other activities. But in June of that year, he had an unforeseen relapse in church, suddenly attacking all those around him and having to be restrained by force. This time his mental unbalance lasted until the following January, nearly eight months. The attacks recurred at varying intervals throughout his reign, sometimes lasting only a few days, sometimes for months. In his lucid intervals he was greatly distressed, because he remembered every detail of the nightmare he had been through and was aware of the anxiety and hurt his brutish behaviour had caused, particularly to the queen. Sometimes he felt an attack coming on and asked that weapons be taken away from him. All sorts of remedies were tried, including those proposed by imposters who claimed to have the requisite sortileges and spells. All to no avail. Modern medical opinion inclines to see the case as a variety of schizophrenia. After all this trauma in her young life, Isabeau was to become very much a pawn, as we shall see, in the political rivalry between Burgundy and Orleans and in the deadly game of war with England.

The Dauphin, Future Charles VII

In appearance and character the Dauphin Charles resembled neither his father the king nor his uncle Louis d'Orléans, rumoured by the Burgundian propagandists to be his mother's lover. Ungainly and ill-favoured, he was introverted and isolated. Perhaps we should not be surprised at that, given the traumas of his childhood, his father's insane rages, his mother's fears for her very life, the early deaths of his two elder brothers. What exactly was the nature of his mother's relationship with the fascinating Louis of Orleans remains unclear. No contemporary source actually accuses her of adultery and it must be said that, apart from her rank, Queen Isabeau would hardly have been a trophy conquest. Now after a deal of sumptuous banqueting and ten births preceding that of the future Charles VII in 1403, she had lost her youthful prettiness and become obese. The historian Philippe Delorme points out that she would have had little opportunity for amorous transgression, queens of France never being alone. Even at night, ladies of the bedchamber always slept in the same room as their royal mistress. Delorme remarks also that relations between sisters- and brothers-in-law were considered incestuous in medieval theology, a sin so grave that it was regarded as a crime punishable by death.

In considering the question of the legitimacy of Charles VII, it is worth noting that his sister, the princess Catherine, bride-to-be of Henry V, had been born in October 1401, sixteen months before him, and that the mental deterioration of her son, Henry VI of England, is generally regarded as an inheritance from the unfortunate Charles VI, a guarantee therefore of Catherine's own legitimacy. Her brother Charles was born in February 1403, thus conceived only some seven months after the birth of his sister. This is not conclusive proof, but adds some weight to the view that at that date marital relations still took place at intervals between the royal couple and that Charles was indeed the son of the mad king.

The Dauphin's enemies sought to undermine his credibility by casting doubts on his legitimacy, but his date of birth pre-dates the gossip surrounding his mother's alleged dalliance with Orleans, which was noised abroad after 1404, mostly by John the Fearless's propagandists. Sometime between 1405 and 1407, an obliging (or perhaps browbeaten and terrified, no one can know) young teenage lady named Odette de Champdivers was found to share the king's bed during his periods of mental illness. During these breakdowns he had latterly become violent towards Isabeau, who was urged for her own safety to keep away at such times. It was even rumoured that in his unhinged state he didn't notice the substitution. Odette gave him a daughter in 1407, the same year in which Isabeau bore her last child. The king's young mistress came from a Burgundian family and it is said that she owed her choice 'position' to the good offices of John the Fearless. She was handsomely rewarded by him, which has given rise to some speculation as to the exact nature of her employment. Was she required to pass on information to the duke? To exercise a pro-Burgundian influence over the king?

Be that as it may, the boy, who by the end of his life would have proved himself a strong and wise ruler and had earned the nickname of Charles the Victorious, was a melancholy and unsure adolescent. 'Charles VII was one of the small number of princes who improved after they came to the throne,' wrote the great nineteenth-century historian, Quicherat.

The Houses of Burgundy and Orleans: Disastrous Rivalry
The first of the four powerful Dukes of Burgundy was Philip the Bold (*Philippe le Hardi*), youngest son of King John the Good of France. His rule was in general wise and benevolent. He was succeeded by his son John the Fearless (*Jean sans Peur*) in 1404, who was in turn succeeded by his own son, Philip the Good (*Philippe le Bon*) in 1419. The history of their ambitions, of their campaigns and those of their adversaries, the Orleanists and the party of the Count of Armagnac, who later supported the disowned and exiled Dauphin, Charles, are too long and involved to be described in any detail here. An outline will fill in the background to the drama of Joan of Arc. To start at the beginning, we have to go back to the political situation, the mental instability of Charles VI after 1492, and the murder of Duke Louis of Orleans in 1405.

Louis of Orleans, younger brother of Charles VI, was handsome, witty, daring, ambitious, prodigal, hedonistic, and most inordinately proud of his reputation as a lady-killer. His biography, says one nineteenth-century historian, can be summed up in very few words: 'much harm caused by one who could have done a great deal of good'.[20] His love of luxury and splendour and of magnificent celebrations of every variety matched the Queen's own. Louis was detested by many, particularly in Paris (thanks in great part to the propaganda war relentlessly waged against him by John the Fearless) for the enormous taxes he imposed, but, on the other hand, he retained a certain charisma. He was never wholly unpopular, his charm, gaiety, wit and courage earned him a certain indulgence. His long-suffering wife, the Italian Valentina Visconti, famed for her beauty, adored him. In 1402 he had challenged Henry IV to a duel, stating in a second letter that he did not give Henry his royal titles 'because I do not approve of the manner in which you attained them'.[21] After all, Louis was the uncle of Isabelle, the unfortunate Richard's child-widow, and therefore her proper champion, her father, Charles VI, being incapacitated. The challenge was scornfully rebuffed, Henry considering it beneath his royal dignity to duel with someone of inferior rank.

Louis was implacably opposed to the English invasion, with its men-at-arms ignorant and scornful of the French language and French ways. His eagerness to engage with the English had been held in check by his uncle Philip the Bold of Burgundy, who saw that, at the time, the interests of both Burgundy and France were best served by the truces in force, but this moderating influence was removed with Philip's death in 1404. Louis's political ambition was however unbounded, he intended to play the principal role in the government of his mentally afflicted brother's kingdom and to maximise the military and financial power of his inherited domains. A conflict with the identical ambitions of his cousin of Burgundy, John the Fearless, son of Duke Philip, was sooner or later inevitable.

Duke Philip of Burgundy possessed vast territories which rivalled those of his nephew Charles VI. He had increased his inheritance by virtue of dynastic marriages, beginning with his own marriage to Marguerite, only daughter and heiress of the Count of Flanders, and later the marriages of two of his sons and a daughter to scions of the immensely rich and powerful Wittelsbach dynasty, rulers not only of Bavaria, but of the Palatinate (Rhineland) and lands on the upper Danube. It was he who promoted the marriage of his nephew Charles VI to Isabeau of Bavaria, another Wittelsbach. He ruled over Flanders, Picardy, Holland, Zeeland, and huge fiefs in the north and east of France, where his capital was Dijon. He was a large, heavily-built man, strong-featured, with a jutting lower jaw and a prominent nose, which did not detract from a general air of benevolence. Statesmanlike and cultivated, like his brother, King Charles V, he was a lavish patron of the arts, of painters, sculptors, architects, gold- and silversmiths and jewellers. He adorned with splendid tapestries the halls and chambers of his many châteaux, he endowed his magnificent library with profane and sacred literature of every age from antiquity to his own day.

An admirer of his wisdom and prudence was the celebrated woman poet Christine de Pisan, whom Philip honoured in early 1404 with the commission to write a full and scholarly account of the reign of his brother, King Charles V, based on documents in his own possession. Christine had just finished the first part of this work, dedicated to the king whom she had, as a child, personally known and loved, when, to her great sorrow and dismay the duke was carried off on 27 April 1404, at the age of sixty-two, by a plague raging in Hainaut where he was residing at the time. She wrote an elegy for his passing, calling on all the French, great and small, beginning with the 'good King Charles VI' and his Queen, to lament the passing of the *très sage* and excellent Duke of Burgundy. He was succeeded by his son, John the Fearless, a quite different kettle of fish.

John the Fearless, *Jean sans Peur*, was born in 1371 and lived most of his life in Flanders. In contrast to his generally good-natured and physically well-built father, he was small, ill-favoured, taciturn and devious, in fact resembling his parent as little as the Dauphin would later resemble the young man his father Charles VI had been. We can ponder John's portrait in the Antwerp museum: the long, aquiline nose, the calculating eyes, a determined, pursed mouth, a firm jaw-line and chin. Clearly not a man to be trifled with. The French historian Michelet has called him a man 'sans peur des hommes et sans peur de Dieu'. He had little time for courtly manners, elegance or stylish dress, (except on state occasions, when the ostentatious display of opulence was called for). He spoke Flemish, which his father had never learned, an accomplishment which enhanced his desired image as the people's prince. This is the point in French history when public opinion begins to play an important role in political affairs. Bernard Guenée has pointed out, for example, that the early fifteenth-century *Chronicle* of Michel Pintoin, known as the *Chronicle of the Monk of Saint Denis*, gives considerable attention to the swings in public opinion at the time and to the rise of political propaganda, of which John the Fearless was a consummate master. One historian speaks of the new phenomenon of an 'urban mentality' at this period, the importance of public opinion in the increasingly populous towns, in particular Paris.[22]

The powers devolved from Charles VI to Isabeau to govern during his 'absences' were never more than a façade. Real power, after the death of Duke Philip of Burgundy, was a prize fought over by his son, John the Fearless, in competition with his cousin, Louis of Orleans. Later on, the backbone of the Burgundian faction would be the merchants and bourgeoisie of Paris, backed up by the University (from which the opposition, such men as the great theologian Gerson, had been purged), while the party of the 'Armagnacs' would find support among certain sections of the aristocracy and in the humbler population outside Paris, who resented the English invasion, groaned under the miseries of the endless wars, and felt themselves to be French.

Most say John the Fearless had earned his sobriquet '*sans peur*' when, in September 1396, he led his troops in battle at Nicopolis in Hungary, on the occasion of the crusade against the Turks, who constituted at the time a very great menace for Europe and would do so for a considerable period to come. In 1396, the apparently unstoppable sultan Bayezid (*Bajazet* to the French) with his huge army conquered the Serbs and gained control over parts of Hungary, boasting not only that he would take Rome and that his horse would eat oats on the altar of St. Peter's, but that he would attack France as well.[23] The King of Hungary called on Christendom to come to his aid and from all parts of Europe they came. Later, the Burgundian chronicler Chastellain would talk of *le grand Turc* (Sultan Mehmed II) as the 'cruel enemy of God' who has taken Constantinople from the Christians (1453), while Shakespeare, in *Richard II*, has the bishop of Carlisle praising the Duke of Norfolk for his valour in the crusades against 'black pagans, Turks and Saracens'.

The last regret of Henry V on his deathbed was that he had not had the time to go on crusade to the rescue of Jerusalem. John, at that time duke of Nevers, led the French contingent at Nicopolis. As Bayezid approached to relieve the siege, a massacre of Turkish prisoners by the French was followed by a devastating defeat for the crusaders. The French contingent was practically wiped out and the hundreds of prisoners taken by the Turks were paraded before Bayezid and slaughtered in a three-hour-long massacre in his presence, except for those few deemed rich enough to pay enormous ransoms. John was one of those and had to be ransomed by his father for the jaw-dropping sum of two hundred thousand florins.

According to the Burgundian chronicler Monstrelet, however, he earned the title much later, in September 1408 when, having hastened from Paris to the aid of his brother-in-law, John of Bavaria (a Wittelsbach, of course), that worldly bishop of whom the people of Liège wished to rid themselves, he crushed the army of the *Liègeois,* giving orders, when the butchery was at its height, to take no prisoners (very few indeed were the exceptions made). Thousands of the people's army perished under the onslaught of the archers and cavalry of Burgundy and Hainaut. The defeat was followed by a ferocious vengeance wreaked upon the opposition by the bishop and the duke. Priests and canons of the opposing party were drowned in the River Meuse, even women were executed and a tyrannical regime was installed.

All in all, John the Fearless was the antithesis of the debonair Duke Louis of Orleans. A wily politician and master propagandist, although lacking the charisma of his cousin, who was only a few months older, he nonetheless certainly knew how to impose his authority through demagoguery or terror, whichever best suited his purpose. He relentlessly sought power, exploiting the king's incapacity and presenting himself to the common people as their saviour. He set about wooing the citizens of Paris with every kind of inducement, notably by opposing the heavy taxes Louis of Orleans and Isabeau wished to levy. His enmity with Orleans would prove disastrous for France.

2

The Tragedy of Civil War: Orleans and Burgundy

Forbear to judge, for we are sinners all
Shakespeare, *Henry VI, Part 2*

Rivalry was unavoidable between the houses of Orleans and Burgundy. By the time of Duke Philip the Bold's death in 1404, the Duke of Orleans was acquiring Luxembourg and possessions bordering on the territories of Burgundy, threatening thus to split them off from Flanders. He was said also to have insulted John the Fearless by an attempted seduction of his young wife. In all things, his recklessness and policies put him on a collision course with his dangerous cousin. John of Burgundy wanted the continuation of truces with Henry IV's kingdom, in furtherance of the commercial interests of Burgundy, while Louis thirsted for war and the reconquest of French territory. John, for his own ends, set himself up as the defender of the king's subjects against the extortionate taxation which Louis and Isabeau sought to impose, although this accusation has become a subject of debate, recent historians arguing that the need for taxation was urgent and that those most affected by it were the rich bourgeoisie.

John the Fearless turned the occasion to his own advantage, demanded in full Royal Council explanations for his rival's extravagant expenditure, and declared that if new taxes were raised, he would refuse to apply them in his fiefs. He managed to secure for the Parisians the right, as a security measure, to close off their streets at night with chains, a right which had been taken away in 1382, following popular disturbances. The widespread disorders and corruption of those in positions of responsibility and power were excoriated in Burgundian pamphlets and the people of Paris were led to regard the duke of Burgundy as their champion against such scandals and their saviour from the insatiable demands of his cousin of Orleans. Dark murmurings had swirled around for some time among the populace, it was said that Louis's ambition was to replace his brother and take the crown, that he had tried to burn Charles VI to death at the *Bal des Ardents*, that his Italian wife was a sorceress, versed in black magic and the art of poisoning (like all other Italians), that the king's madness was her work or that of her husband, Louis himself. These nasty rumours reached such a pitch that Louis, profoundly grieved, had to exile his wife Valentina from Paris for her own safety.

The friction between the two dukes, Orleans and Burgundy, became open hostility in August 1405, when, in response to a convocation from Charles VI to discuss affairs of state, John the Fearless set out for Paris at the head of a large army of infantry and cavalry. This caused widespread panic in the capital. Why was the duke bringing an army? At his approach, Louis and Isabeau, fearing for their security, had precipitously left the capital for Corbeil, having to leave behind the eight-year-old Dauphin Louis who was suffering from a feverish indisposition, as well as the other royal children. Instructions were given that the children were to follow immediately and the next day, 18 August, they set out in the care of their uncle, Louis of Bavaria, and other nobles. On hearing this, Burgundy set off with a detachment of horsemen, intercepted the party and, against all protests, brought the Dauphin back to Paris, where he gave the child into the care of his own uncle (and the child's great-uncle), the nearly septuagenarian Duke of Berry, thus covering the illegality of the abduction with a veneer of care and concern. The dukes of Berry and Bourbon and other nobles came out to meet him as he made his triumphal entry into Paris, where he was greeted by cheering crowds. Soon the capital was under the control of his troops. His mansion, the Hôtel d'Artois, was transformed into a fortress. His troops, however, were in great part men from Flanders, Hainault and Artois, together with sundry mercenaries, mostly speaking dialects of German, not a thing likely to endear them to the population.

Meanwhile the Duke of Orleans, now in Melun, summoned his vassals and recruited mercenaries. While the population of Paris again waited in fear and trembling for civil war to engulf them, a propaganda battle raged, political manifestos and pamphlets flying to and fro. Burgundy ferociously denounced the misrule of Orleans (not without grounds) and demanded that the country be governed, as in former times, by the Three Estates (representatives of the aristocracy, clergy, and bourgeoisie) and that merchants and country people be assured of peace and freedom from penury and extortionate taxation. Louis sent out a manifesto to the principal towns of the kingdom, attempting to refute the accusations and accusing Burgundy of fomenting rebellion and seeking to take power away from the incapacitated king and arrogate it to himself. In October, a reconciliation was patched up, thanks to the efforts of the dukes of Berry and Bourbon and the mediation of the queen, and Louis and Isabeau returned to Paris from Melun.

Over the next couple of years the façade was kept up, the rival dukes appearing together in public and exchanging gifts. In June 1406, they attended together the lavish festivities in Compiègne on the occasion of a double marriage, that of Louis of Orleans's fifteen-year-old son Charles to his sixteen-year-old cousin, Isabelle (widow of Richard II of England), and that of Isabelle's brother, John (the seven-year-old son of Charles VI), to Jacqueline of Bavaria, niece of John the Fearless. But the reconciliation of Orleans and Burgundy was merely a façade. Louis continued to undermine the position of John. In April 1407 he got the king's Great Council reduced from fifty-one members to twenty-six, dismissing all but two of the Burgundian counsillors. John the Fearless was teetering on the edge of ruin.

The Assassination of the Duke of Orleans

On Sunday, 20 November 1407, the Duke of Berry believed he had persuaded Louis of Orleans and John the Fearless to make peace with each other. The two heard Mass together in Notre Dame and received communion, setting the seal on an oath of reciprocal love and brotherhood. But John the Fearless had already, probably as early as the spring of 1407, decided to rid himself of his rival. In June certain mysterious happenings took place. Secret negotiations were set in motion to find and rent a house near the Hotel Barbette, the queen's palace. In early November such a house was found and rented in the Rue Vieille-du-Temple. A dozen or so unknown horsemen moved in. Their appearance made the neighbours uneasy, for they never said who they were, nor indeed did they speak to anyone in the neighbourhood.

On the wintry evening of Wednesday, 23 November 1407, Louis of Orleans paid a visit to the queen at the Hôtel Barbette, where Her Majesty had given birth on 11 November to a son, Philip, her last child, who died that same day. She was still in the lying-in period and distraught. Some time after seven o'clock in the evening, one of the king's servants appeared and informed Louis that His Majesty wished to see him urgently to discuss a matter of great importance to them both. Louis, suspecting nothing, took his leave of the queen, mounted his unwarlike mule, and set off up the Rue Vieille-du-Temple with a modest escort, two young squires mounted on the same horse riding ahead of him and several valets and pages carrying torches and walking beside him.

He was his usual blithe self. As he passed, he was singing to himself and playing with one of his gloves. Suddenly a gang of armed men with covered faces sprang out from the shadows shouting 'Die! die!', and ferociously attacked him with axes. 'I am the Duke of Orleans!' cried Louis. 'It's you we're after!' they bellowed. Louis was hacked to death. One of his pages threw himself over the duke's body to protect him and was bludgeoned to death himself (Louis was capable of inspiring devotion!) A woman looking out of a window had seen the whole episode (we know her name, Jaquette Griffart) and she now shouted 'Murder! Murder!' as a tall man, his large hat pulled down over his face, came out of the rented house, looked down at the bodies, and gave the order: 'Put out the lights. We'll go. He's dead. Take heart!' The assassins threw a flaming torch into the house, shouted 'Fire!', and made off, some on horseback and some on foot, terrorising in their flight the shocked neighbours who had appeared at their doors.

The provost of Paris was called, the mangled bodies of Louis and his page were inspected in the house into which they had been carried. The dukes of Berry, Bourbon and John the Fearless and others were sent for, to meet the provost and hear his report. The gates of Paris were closed to prevent any escape of the murderers, who in fact were already safely inside the Hôtel d'Artois, the residence of John the Fearless. And throughout, John appeared as horrified as everyone else.

Louis was buried on 24 November in the chapel of the Celestines in Paris. Despite his unpopularity because of the taxes he had levied, the funeral was attended by a 'great multitude of the people', no doubt drawn to see the huge gathering of princes, dukes and all the other great figures of nobility and church who attended the ceremony. John and all his household appeared clad in deepest black. Now he wept with the best of the assembled mourners, making obeisance to the corpse and declaiming that 'Never has there been such a wicked murder in this kingdom.' The coffin was solemnly carried out of the church by Louis II of Anjou, king of Sicily (a cousin of Charles VI), together with the dukes of Berry and Bourbon and John the Fearless, each holding a corner of the pall.

The investigation ordered by the provost, a conscientious official by the name of Guillaume de Tignonville, soon pointed to the involvement of John the Fearless, who, when he heard that permission to search his residence had been obtained, realised that the truth was about to be revealed. He went to his uncle, the duke of Berry, who was with Louis of Anjou, and confessed to them that he had organised the murder 'at the prompting of the devil'. Profoundly shocked, but anxious to protect their own, Berry and Anjou disclosed nothing while John fled, as they advised, to his own duchy on 26 November. On the same day the news of his guilt was made public.

The assassination of Louis of Orleans on the covert orders of Burgundy appalled many, especially in view of the very public reconciliation and their receiving the sacrament together only two days previously in Notre-Dame. Some of Louis's followers wished to pursue the duke as soon as they heard that he had fled, but Louis d'Anjou forbade further bloodshed. The duke of Orleans's distressed widow, Valentina Visconti, arrived in Paris on 10 December to seek justice and was received by the king, but left again in January without obtaining any satisfaction. All recognised that it was extremely difficult to punish a man as powerful as John the Fearless. After all, he might, if pushed, it was argued, join forces with Henry IV of England.

Back in his own territory, Burgundy lost no time in repairing his position. The inaction of the king and court in general handed him *carte blanche* to present his case to the public. He chose attack rather than defence. After a meeting with the duke of Berry and Louis d'Anjou in Amiens in January 1408, conducted with full diplomatic cordiality, he returned as a hero to Paris on the Shrove Tuesday (25 February), at the head of eight hundred armed men, banners waving, crowds cheering, and his manifesto prepared. His return had been well paved in advance by his propagandists. His chosen apologist, or rather his counsel for the prosecution of Louis of Orléans, was the University of Paris theologian Jean Petit, whose long academic diatribe was delivered, at the duke's behest, in a public session on 8 March before the assembled court.

Under John the Fearless's direction, a whole committee of academic clerics and lawyers had helped Petit to produce one of the most notorious pieces of mendacious political propaganda in French history. Burgundy had sent out invitations to all the royals and notables. The great hall of the Hôtel Saint-Pol in Paris was packed with nobles, citizens, clerics, lawyers, those who were allowed to file past the guards and enter by the only door not closed off. The king, suffering one of the attacks of his malady, was not present. The murder organised by Burgundy was presented as 'good, licit, and meritorious',[1] being the noble, disinterested deliverance of the people from a man 'stained with every vice, a villain, a tyrant', who was aiming at the Crown. Louis was accused not only of raising outrageous levels of taxation, of traitorous and underhand negotiations with Henry IV, of laying waste the country with his bandits and looters and promoting schism in the Church (he was a supporter of Benedict XIII, the rival pope residing in Avignon during the Schism), but also of being the cause of the king's insanity and of attempting to murder both king and Dauphin by poison or sorcery. Far from condemnation, John the Fearless deserved public gratitude and reward. Petit's four-hour-long 'justification' was received in silence. 'There was none so brave as dared to speak against it,' wrote Jean Juvenal des Ursins, who had been present.[2]

The duchess of Orleans returned to Paris shortly afterwards with her sixteen-year old son Charles. In the Louvre, in the presence of the young Dauphin, Louis of Guyenne, she made a detailed rebuttal of Burgundy's accusations, demanding justice for herself and her children, but she returned to Blois defeated. Later, at Easter, 1411, the young Charles, now duke of Orleans, petitioned the king for justice for his father, but in vain.

On 9 March 1411 the Great Council issued letters patent in the incapacitated king's name, absolving the duke of Burgundy of all blame. Nonetheless, in the 1450s, during the time of Duke Philip the Good, son of John the Fearless, many years after the event, Chastellain, writing the prologue to his *Chronique des Ducs de Bourgogne*, had to admit that the crime was a grievous blot on the record of his master's father. He felt obliged to write an long apologia for it, comparing it to the unfortunate lapse of King David sending his general Uriah to his death, claiming that it was a panic reaction triggered by a threat of assassination emanating from Louis of Orleans and declaring that the later assassination of John the Fearless, in the presence of the Dauphin in 1419, was infinitely more wicked and treacherous.[3] The chronicler doth protest too much ... At least it shows that many had remained unconvinced by the efforts of Jean Petit and the Great Council.

The Career of John the Fearless after the Assassination of His Rival

John the Fearless quickly set about getting rid of those whom he found in any way inconvenient. The provost of Paris, having shown himself to be over-zealous in pursuit of his duties, was dismissed and replaced by someone more amenable to the duke, a man called Pierre des Essarts (of whom more later). Some months later, in September 1408, Burgundy went to the aid of his brother-in-law, John of Bavaria, bishop of Liège, and crushed the resistance of the people of Liège in the battle of Othée, as described above. He returned in triumph to Paris, the Parisians caring little (or perhaps knowing less) about the massacre and the brutal crushing of a popular revolt by the professed champion of the people.

The widow of Louis of Orleans died in early December 1408, reportedly of a broken heart and frustration at her inability to obtain justice, while Burgundy was said to have received the news joyfully, since he regarded her as the backbone of the opposition. Around the king, it was decided the time had come to close the chapter. On 9 March 1409, in the cathedral of Chartres, the formal reconciliation took place with great solemnity and policed by some four hundred men-at-arms and one hundred archers in the service of William of Bavaria, Count of Hainaut (another Wittelsbach brother-in-law of John the Fearless). Not only were the king and queen and all the princes of the blood royal and other great nobles present, but also the sons of the murdered duke.

Monstrelet reports that the two boys wept and the king had to repeat a second time his demand that they make their peace with the Duke of Burgundy and pardon him. They made it clear that they were taking the oath only at the royal command. The young Duke Charles of Orleans, the future poet whom Joan of Arc would dream of liberating from English captivity, was now aged eighteen. The bargain was to be sealed by the marriage of his twelve-year-old brother, Philip, to a daughter of John the Fearless. In fact, the marriage never took place.

Back in Paris, it was not long before John the Fearless found the pretext he required to start consolidating his position. Orders were given to Pierre des Essarts, who had replaced the provost of Paris, to arrest Jean de Montaigu, financier and Great Chamberlain (principal minister) of Charles VI. Montaigu had been close to the dukes of Orleans and Berry and opposed to Burgundy since the murder of Orleans. He was arrested and horribly tortured before being executed on 17 October 1409, as Monstrelet tells us, 'on the authority and by the will of the Duke of Burgundy'. On the grounds of having enriched himself at the expense of the royal Treasury, he was charged with financial malversations, felony and treason. All his goods and property were forfeit, his Parisian residence going to William of Bavaria, count of Hainaut (John the Fearless's brother-in-law) and his castle of Marcoussis to Louis of Bavaria, the queen's brother. Burgundy then saw to it that, once again, the vacant post was filled by Pierre des Essarts, who had acted as one of the judges in the case. John the Fearless was now the most powerful great lord in France.

Despite her previous detestation of John the Fearless, Queen Isabeau decided her best course of action was now to put herself and the royal children, including the Dauphin, twelve-year-old Louis, Duke of Guyenne, under his protection. The accord was signed on 11 November 1409, at Melun. The twelve-year-old Dauphin was already married to Burgundy's daughter, Marguerite de Bourbon, and in January 1410 his father-in-law became his 'governor', entrusted with his education and upbringing.

Burgundy's uncles, the dukes of Berry and Bourbon, finding themselves bypassed, left the court and returned to their fiefs, where, in April 1410, Berry, Bourbon and others formed a league of princes with Charles of Orleans. At the age of nineteen, the young man was already a widower, and now was married again, this time, to Bonne d'Armagnac, the daughter of Berry's son-in-law, Bernard VII of Armagnac, the man popularly known as the *diable en fourrure d'homme* ('devil in man's clothing'). Armagnac at once set about recruiting Gascon mercenaries, whose reputation was as ferocious as his own, while the French they spoke, the *langue d'oc* of the south, was as incomprehensible to the people of the north and Paris as the German dialects of Burgundy's Flemish and other cohorts. The country was again on the point of civil war. By the summer, the Armagnac army was reckoned at six thousand men-at-arms, eleven hundred archers and four thousand crossbow men. They pillaged their way forward, devastating and terrorising as they went. As mentioned earlier, the Orleanist party would henceforth be known as the *Armagnacs*, which quickly, and understandably, became a term of abuse in the mouths of their enemies.

In the capital, Burgundy had gathered an army of about fifteen thousand men, from Burgundy, Flanders and Artois, together with contingents from his allies and brothers. A peace was patched up in November 1410, but both sides intended war and the moment came which Burgundy had manoeuvred for, when, on 11 July 1411, Charles of Orleans sent a manifesto addressed to Charles VI and distributed to all the principal towns, calling for justice for his father. On 18 July, he sent a letter, in his name and that of his brothers, to John the Fearless, accusing him of treacherously organising the murder. Burgundy replied with insults asserting that he had had rendered service and done his duty towards 'our very great, mighty and sovereign lord', in doing to death 'as was right and proper, that false and disloyal traitor', and adding that 'you and your brothers have lied, lied wickedly and treacherously, like the false, wicked and disloyal traitors that you are'.[4] Burgundy had achieved his aim of provoking war while foisting onto the Orleanists the appearance of responsibility for the resumption of hostilities.

At this juncture, both Burgundy and Orleans had had to absent themselves from Paris, on orders from the king, in an attempt to preserve the peace. The Armagnac army, in its usual style, now pillaged and ravaged its way to Paris and succeeded in taking Saint-Cloud and Saint-Denis. Burgundy set out from Douai to return to Paris and confront them with an army of nine thousand foot-soldiers and a thousand Flemish archers. He had now, at the end of the reign of Henry IV, forged an alliance with England's crown prince, the future Henry V (as already noted above in chapter I). On 22 October 1411, he entered Paris with his army (minus the Flemish who had inconveniently and obstinately decided to go home on 26 September). The city was now reinforced by a contingent of seven or eight thousand English soldiers, including a large number of the feared archers, introduced into Paris despite the aversion to them of the artisans, Shakespeare's 'rude mechanicals'.

Burgundy was in fact, says one historian, the first prince of the blood to call in foreign aid.[5] The Orleanists would follow suit in May 1412, signing a treaty which recognised the right of the English monarch to the duchy of Guyenne, the duke of Berry even promising to hand over twenty fortresses. The outlook of the aristocracy was still feudal, loyalty to the great dynasties taking precedence over any idea of duty to a *patrie* (the word was not even in use in French at the time). On the field of battle there was no national flag to follow, only the banners of the great feudal lords and their mercenaries. Nonetheless, a national consciousness was already awake in France and had been so at least since the time of Charles V and his Constable, Bertrand Du Guesclin, hero of the campaigns against the English. Andrew Lang, the Scottish historian of Joan of Arc, long ago pointed out that even in the early twelfth century, the *Chanson de Roland* lovingly evokes *la douce France*. The people were increasingly feeling themselves to be distinctly French in tradition, language and customs, as Joan of Arc's intervention would amply show, and their king had for centuries been seen as the father of his people, bound to them by obligations of justice as they were to him by the duties which were incumbent upon them.

Pierre Tisset, the most recent scholarly editor of the documents of Joan's trial in Rouen, comments that the Hundred Years War, 'at the beginning feudal and dynastic, became a national war, notably as the result of the foreign occupation'.[6] The chronicler Chastellain, born, like Joan, in the early part of the fifteenth century, frequently refers to the woes of '*la povre France*', insists that the duke of Burgundy and Charles are '*tous deux François'* and writes of *'la très haute et noble nation françoise'*.[7] The historian Colette Beaune quotes a letter written already in 1395 by the diplomat Philippe de Mézières to Richard II of England, including a reference to a proverb: 'Lombardy will be for the Lombards, Spain for the Spaniards, France for the French and England for the English.'[8] The young nobleman who took Joan to the king asked her teasingly, at their first meeting, 'Well, m'dear, what are you doing here? Is the king to be chased out of his kingdom and must we all be English?'[9] When Bedford took over the reins of government after the death of Henry V in 1422, he was anxious to avoid giving the impression of imposing an occupying force on the French. In Paris, for example, there was only a very small English garrison.

Yet it was the great English lords with their retainers who swept through the streets of the city, it was English armies that Joan met at Orleans and Patay. By 1431, says the French historian Jean Favier, the English were no longer regarded as they had largely been at first, simply as the allies of a French duke (Burgundy), they were there 'by force of arms'.[10]

Saint-Cloud was re-taken by the Burgundians and their English allies on 9 November 1411, forcing the Armagnacs to withdraw, the soldiery pillaging and looting as they went. Mayhem reigned in the countryside, devastated by soldiers and freebooters of both parties and every nationality. On the Burgundian side, terror, repression and intimidation swept through Paris and other towns, with the worst elements of the populace hunting down mercilessly and slaughtering those thought to have Armagnac sympathies. At this point, in May 1412, the Armagnacs also approached Henry IV for help. In return the English, as we have seen, were to recover all Aquitaine and rule over it with full sovereignty. However, in July 1412, before the Duke of Clarence had even arrived in August with his army, another peace had been patched up between the warring parties at the congress of Auxerre. Both sides now rejected all foreign intervention. At this defection of his allies, Clarence marched away in high dudgeon with the soldiers he had brought over from England. They took hostages with them, the most important being the brother of Charles of Orleans. Duke Charles couldn't raise the money for his brother's huge ransom, so John of Orleans remained a hostage for the next thirty years or so.

John the Fearless had been back on the king's Council and at the head of the government since early 1412. After Auxerre, he escorted the royal family back to Paris to the acclamations of the citizens. He had taken steps to solidify his popularity in the capital, where he was the hero of the butchers' corporation (*la Grande Boucherie*), the best organised and most powerful of the guilds, which had shown itself to be quite capable of weighing in politically with brute force. It was run by rich and ambitious citizens, not themselves butchers, but nonetheless not really accepted by the affluent bourgeoisie, the bankers and merchants, in view of the indelicate lower-class associations of their trade. Burgundy courted them with expensive gifts. At another end of the social scale he flattered the intelligentsia, the University theologians and lawyers, many of whom were close to him politically in any event and shared his views on the way to end the schism in the Church. At the lowest end of the social spectrum, he wooed the rougher elements of the populace, seeking them out in the Halles (the markets), courting even the most ignorant and uncouth, the écorcheurs (the flayers, whose job it was to flay the dead animals), tanners, tripe-merchants and others handy with knives, who were entirely won over and regarded him as their champion. It was a dangerous game to play.

In January 1413, in line with the policy which John the Fearless had advocated over the years for his own ambitious ends, the States General were summoned. This was a consultative body of representatives of the nobility, clergy and the *Third Estate* (the people, or rather, the lawyers and magistrates, the bourgeoisie), presided over by the king. Their task was to find remedies for the scandalous abuses in the areas of finance and administration, to bring about peace between the warring factions, and to make provision for resistance to the English invaders. This was not a revolutionary programme, but rather an attempt to restore the customary lawful procedures of former times. In fact, only the representatives of the provinces north of the Loire, the *langue d'oïl*, were called on this occasion, the southern part of the country, the *langue d'oc*, being prudently left to organise its own assembly, since Burgundy feared their Armagnac sympathies. The Armagnac princes did not show up, fearing for their safety. In fact, it was basically a Burgundian and Parisian assembly.[11]

The deliberations of the great and the good were however too slow for John of Burgundy's lusty butchers and flayers and slaughterhouse men on the ground, and he was soon to find that he was no longer able to keep them in check. The spark for rebellion was the recall by the sixteen-year-old Dauphin Louis, Duke of Guyenne, of the former provost of Paris, Pierre des Essarts, who, although formerly John the Fearless's right-hand man for any unsavoury bit of work, had lately aroused his master's suspicions of collusion with the Armagnacs and fled to Cherbourg. On 27 April, an armed mob some three thousand strong marched on the Bastille where he had been given command. To avoid a massacre, Burgundy arrived on the scene and persuaded Des Essarts to give himself up and he was hustled off to the duke's residence. He and other prisoners were executed later. On 28 April, the residence of the Dauphin was invaded by the mob, who demanded that a large number of 'traitors' be handed over to them. In spite of the prince telling them furiously that here were no traitors in his house, in spite also of the arrival on the scene of the Duke of Burgundy, they burst into the palace and seized a number of the nobles. '*Beau père*', the young prince exclaimed, boiling with rage, to his father-in-law, Burgundy, 'this riot is your doing. You can't deny it, for the leaders are men of your household. Rest assured that you'll rue this day, for things won't always go your way!' To which the duke replied arrogantly, 'My lord, you can look into the matter when your anger has cooled.'[12]

A *cabochien* reign of terror ensued throughout the month of May. On 22 May, the royal residence, the Hôtel Saint-Pol, was invaded and the queen's brother, Louis of Bavaria, gave himself up to the rioters to avoid further bloodshed. Her confessor and others of her household, together with a number of her ladies (whose fault was that they were German) were seized and led away. The Dauphin had retired to his room and wept with frustration, the queen and her other ladies were left in tears also. To cries of *Vive Caboche!* in the days that followed, murders, violence, arbitrary executions, intimidation and bloodshed darkened the streets of Paris in what was to be remembered as the *Dictature des Abattoirs*, the dictatorship of the slaughterhouses. In the rioting and slaughter, Simon Caboche, a 'flayer of cows at the Saint Jacques butchery', led the notorious mobs to whom the name *cabochiens* was given. People suspected of 'Armagnac' sympathies were thrown into prison, had their heads chopped off by the rioters' bloodthirsty executioner Capeluche, were murdered, tortured, or sewn into sacks and thrown into the Seine. Terror reigned. The mansions of the rich were pillaged. When his house in the cloisters was attacked and ransacked by the mob, Gerson, still Chancellor of the university, was forced to take refuge in the 'high vaults' under the roof of Notre Dame. He was lucky to escape with his life and was still in his retreat in September 1413. The bourgeoisie and the University took fright at all this violence, the queen and the Dauphin sent messages to the Duke of Orleans pleading for him to come to their rescue. Peace was only restored when John the Fearless, seeing that he could not restore order on his own, came to terms with the Armagnacs at Pontoise in July and the leaders of the mobs beat a retreat out of town.

On 23 August 1413, John the Fearless left Paris for Flanders, at no notice, with a small escort, having decided it was unsafe for him to try to cohabit with the Armagnacs. Jean Juvenal des Ursins claims that he attempted to take the king with him, having proposed a hunting expedition. As there is no other evidence, this may be only hearsay. Juvenal des Ursins is drawing upon his father's reminiscences and is in any case a hostile witness.[13] The dukes of Orleans and Bourbon and other leaders of the Orleans party rode into the capital in triumph on 1 September 1413, greeted by delegations of the merchants, the magistrates and other leading citizens, who presented them with gorgeous sleeveless surcoats (*huques*) in their heraldic royal colour, purple, on which the motto *Le droit chemin* was richly embroidered with pearls. The population gave them an ecstatic welcome. Alas, this wonderful political opportunity was soon totally squandered. The reform bill of May proposed by the States General was annulled, certain notables who had supported Burgundy were banished, the dreaded troops of Bernard of Armagnac soon enforced their own rule of disorder and terror. The tide began to turn towards John the Fearless once more. The Dauphin, anxious to reach a balance between Orleans and Burgundy, made overtures to the latter, then thought better of it and retracted. A failed attempt by Burgundy to re-enter Paris with an army, after which he was declared to be a rebel, was followed by a counter-attack by the army of the Dauphin and the Orleanists, during which they took Soissons. A peace was again patched up, this time at Arras, in September 1414. Burgundy promised to abandon all negotiations with Henry V, to banish all those who had displeased the king, and not to enter Paris without royal permission. None of the promises was kept.

To understand the policy of John the Fearless, one should perhaps in fairness remember that he was not simply the grandson of King Charles V of France, but ruler of the powerful duchy of Burgundy, which included Flanders, Picardy and Artois, much of what is now the Netherlands. He and his brothers, by virtue of dynastic marriages, held sway over lands beyond the borders of the kingdom of France, territories richer than the kingdom of France and more advanced in industry, chiefly textiles and the woollen trade with England. His duchy and his sphere of influence reached right down the eastern borders of France as far as Switzerland. In 1406, his younger brother Antony became duke of Brabant, with its great towns of Antwerp, Brussels and Louvain, his brother-in-law William was Count of Holland and Hainaut.[14] Thus his concerns, in particular his commercial concerns, were not necessarily compatible with the interests of his liege lord, Charles VI of France. In his defence, Bernard Schnerb points to his piety (this he had in common with Henry V, Louis d'Orleans, and others of his time whose conduct was less than saintly); to his generosity as a benefactor of churches and of the Franciscan order of friars; to the rise, in his state, of a bourgeoisie to high positions in the army, finance and law, the chancellor Nicolas Rolin among others, whose stern appearance is known to us from the portrait by Roger van der Weyden. Schnerb sees in his programme of reform of the kingdom more than a mere instrument of propaganda.

England's Opportunity: Civil War in France

Henry V saw his opportunity in these internecine French quarrels. His army, estimated at about twelve thousand men, disembarked in Normandy on 13 August 1415. Harfleur fell in September, the French aristocracy and their ill-organized army met their nemesis at Agincourt in October. On 18 December, the eighteen-year-old Dauphin, Louis, died of a 'fever' (he probably had tuberculosis) and his seventeen-year-old brother John became Dauphin. John had had a Burgundian upbringing, having been betrothed as a child to John the Fearless's niece, Margerite of Hainaut, and reared (against the wishes of his mother) at the court of her parents, William of Hainaut and Marguerite of Burgundy. Charles VI's state of mental incapacity and apathy was worsening all the time. His youngest son, the future Charles VII, had already been appointed to the depleted royal council. Bernard d'Armagnac was recalled to Paris and became Constable of the kingdom, in place of the previous holder of the office, Charles d'Albret, killed at Agincourt.

Meanwhile, Burgundy was still trying to obtain, by negotiation with the king or otherwise, his return to Paris. He had hopes that the people of Paris might rise in his favour, but that did not happen. The population was divided between pro-Burgundian and pro-Armagnac sympathisers. Pro-Burgundian plots were followed by the execution or imprisonment of the conspirators. On 4 April 1416, the Dauphin John of Touraine died suddenly of mastoiditis at Compiègne, never having entered Paris. Bernard d'Armagnac obtained a royal *ordonnance* (decree) on 13 May to abolish the *Grande Boucherie* (the butcher's guild). John of Touraine's death was followed on 15 June by that of the Duke of Berry, who had once been Burgundy's favourite uncle and who might have made peace with him. These events put an end to John the Fearless's hopes of re-entering Paris by negotiation. The new Dauphin, Charles, was bitterly opposed to him.

Burgundy decided to act. On 25 April 1417, he launched his campaign with a thundering broadside of propaganda against the opposing party, the Armagnacs, denouncing them as murderers, traitors, perjurers, cruel, rapacious and lawless. He promised to abolish all taxes save that on salt. In August 1417, the Burgundian army, based mainly around Arras, moved towards Paris, at the very time that Henry V returned to France to complete his conquest. Henry had landed at Touques, in Normandy, on 10 August 1417. Burgundy had some six thousand men-at-arms, four thousand archers and over twenty thousand horses, but it was not Normandy that was in their sights. The suspicion of the Armagnac party was that John the Fearless had a secret agreement with the English. In fact, in October 1416 he had spent over a week parleying in Calais, where he was presented with a document asking him to recognise that all the responsibility for the war was on the French side, that he would recognise the right of Henry V and his heirs to the crown of France, pay homage to him, and *secretly* help him in his forthcoming campaigns. He should keep this alliance secret until the English victory was assured. He did not sign the agreement, but what else was agreed during the talks remains unknown and it is possible that there was indeed a clandestine pact.[15]

His army made rapid progress, and by mid-September 1417, was encamped around Paris, cutting off supplies and causing great hardship. Still there was no rising in his favour and leaving Paris under siege, he headed for Chartres and then Tours, where the queen, Isabeau, had been obliged to reside in resentful exile by the Constable, Bernard d'Armagnac. Burgundy and Isabeau had been covertly in contact, and now, on 2 November he succeeded in secretly meeting her in the abbey of Marmoutiers and spiriting her away to Troyes. On 11 November, letters signed by the queen were sent to all the 'good towns' of the kingdom summoning them to rally to the Duke of Burgundy and to herself. Burgundy was now her *'très cher cousin'* whom she loved dearly because he had 'delivered [her] from prison'.[16] He and she together set up in Troyes a rival *Parlement* to that of Paris (the *Parlement* consisted of a consultative body of lawyers and was the highest court in the kingdom). On 10 January 1418, Isabeau completed the handover to Burgundy of all the powers which the king had donated to her in 1403, appointing her to rule in his place during his 'absences'. The government of the kingdom was invested solemnly in John the Fearless by the Parlement of Troyes.

In the meantime, the English were making practically unimpeded progress. In September 1417 they took Caen, a dozen other places followed, and when Cherbourg fell in August 1417, the only pocket of resistance in Normandy still holding out was the Mont-Saint-Michel. It would valiantly hold out until the final departure of the English from France. At the same time, various efforts were made to reach a peace agreement between Burgundy and the Armagnacs, a principal negotiator being Yolande of Sicily, the mother-in-law of the Dauphin Charles. Yolande was particularly worried about her lands in Maine. The schism in the Church was finally healed on 11 November 1417 with the election at Constance of the new pope, Martin V, who sent legates to both camps, to encourage them to come to an agreement. While the queen and Burgundy, as also the Dauphin and the king, were in favour of ratifying the accord which the cardinal legates proposed, Bernard d'Armagnac and others of his party would not hear of it.

In the night of 28 May 1418, one of the gates of Paris was opened to the Burgundians by a young man named Perrinet Leclerc, who had stolen the keys from under his father's pillow, his father being a trusted supporter of the Armagnacs and holder of the keys. The Burgundian troops poured into the city and set about arresting their opponents. Some of the leading Armagnacs managed to escape. The fifteen-year-old Dauphin Charles was saved by the Provost, Tanguy du Chastel, who snatched him from his bed in the Hôtel Saint-Pol, hoisted him onto a horse in his dressing-gown, got him dressed in the Bastille and galloped off out of the city with him until they reached Melun. Poor mad Charles VI, the symbol of legitimate rule and power, was taken under Burgundian escort from his residence in the Hôtel Saint-Pol to the Louvre, in order to remove him from the possible reach of the Armagnacs who were holding out in the Bastille. Bernard d'Armagnac was arrested, along with a host of other notables. Bourgeois, bankers, magistrates, members of the royal Council, financiers in the government, all were swept up. Some time later, the Dauphin would end up in Bourges and be contemptuously dubbed by his enemies the 'Roi de Bourges'.

In June, there followed a terrible orgy of massacre and pillage. The pro-Burgundian element of the population, enraged by the efforts of the fifteen-year-old Dauphin and Tanguy du Chastel to retake Paris (they had managed to get together about fifteen hundred troops) and fanaticised by Burgundian rumours of the horrors that the Armagnacs were said to be preparing, frenetically slaughtered anyone who was even suspected of being pro-Armagnac. In the few days following 12 June somewhere between fifteen hundred and two thousand men and women perished; many, including Bernard d'Armagnac, were slaughtered in the prisons, their throats cut, their corpses abused and dragged through the filth of the streets. Even the gaolers were murdered in the frenzy. Four bishops, several hundred members of the University of Paris, magistrates, ordinary citizens, all perished. Even pregnant women and children were massacred. The houses of the rich were despoiled to the uproar of drunken merrymaking, corpses piled in the streets were pillaged of valuables, clothes. As before, the butchers and flayers were the ringleaders.

During all of this, John the Fearless was still in Troyes with Isabeau, prudently keeping his distance from the horror. They re-entered Paris on 14 July 1418, in magnificent style, being met outside the city by a procession of twelve hundred citizens. Fifteen hundred archers, a thousand men-at-arms from Picardie, a regiment of fifteen hundred Burgundian soldiers carrying lances, and a rearguard of five hundred men, soldiers of the prince of Orange, formed their escort. John the Fearless himself rode proudly alongside the carriage of Isabeau of Bavaria as they entered Paris and crossed the city to the Louvre to meet the king, all the way with cries of *Vive le Roi! Vive la Reine! Vive Bourgogne!* ringing in their ears.

Burgundy knew that the massacres had traumatised the mass of citizens. His propaganda had let loose a monster and the dregs of the population were now in charge of Paris. The 21st of August was another day of bloodletting. The prisons were again full of political prisoners, who were massacred by the sadistic Capeluche and his bands of ruffians as soon as John the Fearless turned his back. The manic frenzy was again such that the gaolers were butchered along with the prisoners. Another couple of thousand were murdered. It was in vain that Burgundy rushed to the scene and tried to stop the slaughter, even steeling himself to shake the insolently proffered hand of Capeluche. The streets again ran with blood. Passers-by, people in their own houses, whether Armagnac or Burgundian little matter, were brutally done to death, pregnant women were ripped open and left to die with the unborn child in the street, corpses were stripped, pillaged, abused. Capeluche gave himself airs and addressed the duke familiarly as *mon frère*. The mass of the citizens were terrorised. They pleaded with John the Fearless to intervene. At last he managed to get rid of the murderous throng of Flayers (*les Écorcheurs*) by appealing to them to go to the aid of his troops besieging Charenton, promising booty in abundance. They left enthusiastically and Capeluche and others were promptly executed the same day.

3

Henry V, the Assassination of John the Fearless and the Disinheritance of the Dauphin

> We will in France, by God's grace, play a set
> Shall strike his father's crown into the hazard
>
> Shakespeare, *Henry V*

Rouen capitulated, as recounted above, in January 1419, after the seven months of heroic resistance and appalling suffering. Other Norman towns tumbled like a pack of cards in the course of 1419. After the capitulation of the towns of Harfleur, Honfleur and Caen, English colonists had been brought in and were given possession of confiscated French property. The Chancellorship and other principal offices of government were held by Englishmen, extortionate taxation was levied to pay for the ongoing war. Henry V regarded himself as rightful successor to William the Conqueror. He did indeed make efforts to win over the populations by imposing discipline upon his soldiers, trying to put an end to looting and other misdeeds. He did his best to placate the places he had taken and records show that, beneath the rank of mayor *(bailli)*, the civil officers in his administrations were nearly all French. 'Scarcely an English name appears in the numerous extant documents appointing receivers, sergeants [...] money-changers, officers of the mints, surveyors of weights and measures, keepers of seals, to mention no others.'[1]

On the other hand, the military administration was almost exclusively English. While the occupiers found a compliant local second level of bureaucracy, probably people genuinely convinced that the best prospect for the end of their miseries was the establishment of Anglo-French government, the people in general were simply exhausted and cowed. The resigned acceptance of English overlordship has been compared to the attitude of Pétain's government regarding German domination in 1940, in that it must have seemed to many the only viable option. There was of course resistance, a plot to hand over Rouen to the Dauphin was foiled in 1424, guerrilla warfare was waged by dispossessed nobles, by soldiers who had escaped from defeated garrisons, by exploited peasants, all of whom were held to be brigands and hanged when caught. Mont Saint Michel alone held out against all odds as a stubborn beacon of resistance, despite the fact that its abbot, Robert Jolivet, defected to the English side after the Treaty of Troyes in 1420.

The teenage Dauphin had declared himself Regent on 26 October 1418. At the age of ten, in late 1413, the year of the terrible Caboche violence, he had been affianced amid lavish court celebrations in Paris to the nine-year-old Marie d'Anjou, daughter of Yolande of Aragon, Queen of Sicily and Duchess of Anjou. Yolande promptly removed him to her court at Anjou, to be brought up in a more calm environment on the pleasant banks of the Loire with her own children, where he no doubt spent the least unhappy years of his childhood. In 1416, after Agincourt and the death in December 1415 of his brother, the Dauphin Louis, he was required to return to his mother Isabeau in Paris. There he in turn became Dauphin after another death, that of the second Dauphin, his elder brother John of Touraine, in 1417.

It was at his mother's court of Vincennes that he first become acquainted with such corrupt and influential men as Georges de la Trémoille (who would always oppose Joan of Arc) and Pierre de Giac, popularly believed to be a Satanist and to have dedicated his right hand to the Devil. When his mother was forcibly removed, first to Blois and then to Tours, by the dreaded Count of Armagnac, who found her inconvenient, Charles, together with his father the king, became to all intents the political pawn and trophy of the Count. In 1418, as we have noted above, thanks to the swift action of Tanguy du Chastel, he narrowly escaped the clutches of the Burgundian mob that killed Armagnac himself. At the head of the troops which he and Tanguy had gathered, he showed himself to be brave in the ensuing attempts to advance on Paris. Not lacking in courage or intelligence, in his retreat at Bourges the fifteen-year-old prince lapsed into inertia and chronic indecision, deeply unsure of himself; unsurprisingly so, given the turbulent events of his childhood. He seemed like putty in the hands of those around him. His favourites were by no means the most honourable of counsellors, nor even the least vicious. Andrew Lang sums it by saying that, at this time, the adolescent Charles was surrounded by 'successive sets of violent men, who violently got rid of each other as temptation arose and as opportunity suggested'.[2]

Meantime John the Fearless was finding his potential ally, Henry V, difficult, to put it mildly. Henry was now threatening the Burgundian-held city of Paris. The pro-Burgundian (and bitterly anti-Armagnac) chronicler known as the *Bourgeois of Paris* gives a distressing account of the arrival at the gates of Paris on 31 July 1419 of terrified, starving and dying refugees, men, women and children from the town of Pontoise, which had been taken by the English that morning with great slaughter. Weeping, collapsing from hunger, fear and the great heat of that day, many had not had time to dress before fleeing, some were carrying their children in their arms. They wept for their friends left behind, for the pregnant women who gave birth and died by the wayside, they wept for the loss of their homes and families and the fate of their town.

Refugees continued to arrive for the next week from all the villages around. The authorities in Paris were incapable of providing food or lodging for so many, the city itself suffering food shortages. The people of Paris, says the *Bourgeois*, were scandalised that the Duke of Burgundy, residing nearby with all his army and the king in his keeping, made no attempt to come to the rescue of Pontoise. The 'common people' of Paris themselves had to man the walls of the city as best they could, to discourage the English from attacking. 'At that time,' writes the *Bourgeois*, 'the news was all of the havoc the English were wreaking in France, for every day they were taking towns and castles and emptying the kingdom of wealth and people and sending all back to England.'[3]

At the conference of Meulan, during the months of May to July 1419, John the Fearless and Isabeau presented the queen's beautiful daughter Catherine to Henry as a prospective bride, who would also bring with her a large dowry. Henry had been determined for a long time, and of course for political reasons, to marry, even sight unseen, a daughter of the king of France, and he was indeed dazzled by the damsel when he first saw her. However, her beauty was not enough to persuade him to modify his demands: the restoration to the English crown of all the provinces ceded at the Treaty of Brétigny (more than a third of all French possessions), plus Normandy and certain rights over the duchy of Brittany. The King of England's demands were so extraordinary, says Monstrelet, that no agreement could be reached and the convention broke up, but not before Tanguy du Chastel arrived as an envoy from the Dauphin to parley with Burgundy. A furious Henry vented his anger on John the Fearless, well aware that it was the duke, not the unfortunate Charles VI, who held the reins of power. '*Beau cousin*,' he said, 'We wish you to take note that We will have your king's daughter and everything else that We have asked for along with her, or We will throw him out of his kingdom, and you along with him.'[4]

In these circumstances the Dauphin's envoy did not find it overly difficult to persuade John the Fearless to negotiate with the Dauphin Charles. It was Charles who was to prove the difficult party, refusing to meet Burgundy in Paris, probably afraid of finding himself once more a captive and a pawn in the duke's game. A meeting between the two took place at Pouilly, near Melun, in July 1419. After bitter argument, a peace treaty was signed and it was agreed that they would join forces against the English. A further meeting was fixed for two months later. That was the fatal meeting of 11 September 1419, on the bridge at Montereau. John the Fearless and Charles approached each other from opposite ends of the bridge, Burgundy with an escort of ten armed knights and Charles with nine. According to the Burgundian chroniclers, John the Fearless was struck down without further ado as he knelt before the prince, but the French side of the story is very different: they describe a long and heated discussion, the duke insisting that the prince return with him to his parents, the king and queen. At length one of Burgundy's knights, furious and exasperated, suddenly rushed forward, seeming to draw his sword, whereupon Charles's men pulled the prince away and struck down the duke. This is basically the version which Charles gives in the letter of regret and condolences which he sent to John the Fearless's son Philip on 15 September 1419. Charles claims in the letter that Burgundy had intended to take him by force. This would indeed be consistent with the duke's insistence that he must return to his father and mother in Troyes.[5] At all events, the assassination was a mortal blow to any hope of an end to the civil war between the Burgundians and the supporters of the Dauphin and, whether premeditated or not, a catastrophe for any prospect of a united front against the invaders.

The Dauphin was certainly badly shaken by the episode, which left him with a horror of blood and of bridges for the rest of his life, but he did not take any action against those who had struck down the duke, thus lending colour to accusations of conspiracy and complicity. Who actually killed the duke is unclear, but it was believed that the ultimate mortal blow was struck by Tanguy du Chastel, the saviour of the Dauphin in the blood-drenched Paris of May 1418. Tanguy denied the accusation and wrote to the duke's son, now Duke Philip, offering to defend his innocence in combat against any two opposing champions. None took up the challenge, and in fact the last trial by combat of that sort had taken place in 1386, with solemn state and rigid protocol, in the presence of the young Charles VI and a multitude of spectators. It was already a rarity, regarded by many as a barbarous relic of the past and never again given legal sanction.[6] Duelling to assert one's offended honour continued, of course, in spite of illegality, throughout Europe until at least the end of the nineteenth century.

Charles's own long letter of regret and condolences to the duke's son, Philip (now to become known as Duke Philip the Good), was futile. Philip, some seven years older than the prince, was married to the latter's sister Michelle, but he was not prepared to accept his brother-in-law's protestations of innocence in the matter of his father's death, all the less so as he received at the same time a frenzied denunciation of her son from Charles's mother, Isabeau, who depicted the meeting at Montereau as a well-laid snare, the innocently trusting duke (an unlikely portrait!) being struck down as he knelt in homage before the Dauphin.

The twenty-five-year old new duke of Burgundy, tall, lean, lantern-jawed, with his somewhat sallow aristocratic features, his long straight nose and firm mouth, gave an impression of determination and intelligence. He had the advantage of being better-looking than his father. He also had somewhat more attractive personal qualities, it may be said, for he was less viscerally devious and murderous, although just as ambitious, arrogant and ferociously hot-tempered. A temperamental and emotional young man, enamoured of drama and splendour, he displayed inconsolable grief for the father he had lost and of whom he no doubt remembered only the better side. The magnificence of his court, the sumptuous apparel of his bejewelled courtiers, his unrivalled collection of illuminated manuscripts and splendid tapestries, his lavish patronage of Flemish musicians and artists (the most famous of them being Jan van Eyck and Roger van der Weyden), his creation of the chivalrous Order of the Golden Fleece, his brilliant entertainments, feasts and jousts, were to become the admiration of Europe.

The number of his mistresses astounded his peers. His first two wives were Michelle of Valois, daughter of Charles VI, and then Bonne d'Artois, widow of his uncle, the count of Nevers. Both died young. When he visited Paris in 1424, he enraged Thomas Montacute, Duke of Salisbury, by paying ostentatious court to the latter's young wife. He had three sons by his third wife, Isabella of Portugal, daughter of King John I of Portugal, whom he married in 1430. He went on also to have no less that eighteen illegitimate children, all of whom he provided for handsomely.

Politically Philip was always ready to change policies to his own advantage. No-one could be sure of his reliability as an ally. After his father's assassination in 1419, political pressures as well as filial grief weighed heavily upon him. Paris was pressing for peace with the English and after deliberation the ducal Council of Burgundy considered that it was better to let the English, now masters of Normandy, have a part of the kingdom of France, rather than risk losing the whole of the territory and their stake in it. In October 1419, Philip sent ambassadors, headed by the bishop of Arras and other nobles, to Henry V at Rouen (they actually found Henry at Mantes), to propose an alliance. On 1 January Henry sent an answer 'in words as cutting as a razor' says Chastellain, to say that he would not be played along as John the Fearless had sought to use him, and that with or without Philip he meant to 'proceed with my conquest and enterprise in this kingdom which is my heritage, and which I have put off for too long'.[7] No doubt gritting his teeth, Philip entered into an alliance with Henry at the end of the year.

Meanwhile, around the Dauphin Charles, his favourites seemed to have settled for keeping a cosy little kingdom south of the Loire, above all for themselves. An immense fortune had been spent on organising an extravaganza of a royal progress through the south (paid for with more taxation on the southern provinces). Cavalcades of splendidly apparelled and armed knights on magnificently accoutred chargers, banners waving, helmets and lances glinting in the sun, paraded behind Charles who rode ahead, resplendent in shining armour, red, white and green plumes waving from his helmet, pennants fluttering aloft around him, pages following him in gorgeous livery in the royal colours, while he graciously acknowledged the cheering crowds, the flowers thrown from balconies and the deputations of the bourgeoisie come to pay him homage.

At the conclusion of this jamboree, the thunderbolt struck. On 21 May 1420, the deranged King Charles VI had compliantly put his name to the treaty of Troyes, which disinherited his son and replaced him with 'the very high Prince and Our very dear Son, Henry, King of England, heir to the throne of France', who 'has become Our said Son, by the marriage contracted, in the interests of the said peace, between King Henry, and Our very dear and well-beloved Daughter, Catherine'. It is stipulated that, on the occasions when Charles VI is unable to carry out his royal duties, Henry is to reign and govern in his place (that is to say, he would in fact exercise royal power right away). Henry is to labour to 'bring into our obedience all those Cities, Towns, Castles, places, localities and persons within Our Realm who are disobedient to us and rebellious, supporting or belonging to the party vulgarly known as that of the Dauphin or the Armagnacs'. Henry thereby is committed to carrying on the war indefinitely, not only in northern France, but in order to take possession of the territories south of the Loire.[8] All lords temporal and spiritual, clergy and university, barons, nobles, jurists, citizens, communities and others are commanded to take an oath of loyalty to Henry, only after which would they continue to enjoy their current rights and privileges. The Treaty provided in fact for two kingdoms under one crown, each with its own institutions. As to the Dauphin, 'Considering the horrible and enormous crimes and offences perpetrated in the said kingdom of France by Charles, so-called Dauphin of the Viennois, it is agreed that neither We, nor Our said Son, King Henry, nor Our very dear Son, Philip, Duke of Burgundy, will in any way enter into negotiations for peace or concord with the said Charles, unless by the advice and consent of all and each of Us Three and of the three Estates of the two aforementioned countries.'[9]

The alliance of the mentally unstable King of France, of Philip of Burgundy and of Henry V was now signed and sealed. Philip hoped to find in the alliance with England the way forward to add to the already huge territories of Burgundy. Some historians have wondered whether his secret ambition was to establish a powerful kingdom, with himself no longer the vassal of the king of France, but the glorious monarch of a great country. Queen Isabeau came out of the bargain well, having allowed it to be implied that her son Charles, the *so-called Dauphin*, was illegitimate. Not only would she be the mother-in-law of the future king of both England and France, but she was to enjoy a settlement of two thousand francs a month drawn on the finances of the Parlement set up in Troyes.

On 2 June 1420, at Troyes, Henry V married the youngest daughter of Charles VI, the princess Catherine, who had wept, as did her sister Michelle, the wife of Philip of Burgundy, when she read the treaty. Instead of having the customary jousting and celebrations the next morning, Henry insisted on leaving that very day to besiege Sens, declaring that 'there is no greater prowess in the world than to exact justice on the wicked.'[10] Having taken Sens, he proceeded to take Montereau on 1 July. Next in line was Melun, which resisted bravely for four months and was starved into submission in November. In all cases Henry V showed little or no mercy to the defeated, executions and inhumane treatment of prisoners followed. Of the prisoners taken from Melun to Paris, several were thrown into the ditches of the Châtelet and left to starve to death, mocked and insulted by elements of the populace This, writes Jean Juvenal des Ursins. 'was greatly to the disgrace of the King of England'.[11] As far as Henry was concerned, all that mattered was that the future fulfilment of his ambitions was guaranteed. However, shortly after Christmas 1420, in response to a petition from the Commons in London, he returned to England, ostensibly for the coronation of his new Queen, but essentially to reassure his subjects that he had their interests at heart, despite his three-and-a-half-year absence in France, and to obtain much needed money for his costly wars. Not much more could be forthcoming in France, for Paris and Normandy had been squeezed dry by taxation.

The disinheritance of the Dauphin Charles was recognised only on the Anglo-Burgundian side. All the princes of the Blood Royal, except Burgundy himself, rallied to Charles, as did the pope. The treaty was supported by Sigismund, the Holy Roman Emperor, who had concluded a pact with Henry V in 1417 and remained an ally. As to the population at large, many in the northern half of the country accepted it resignedly as their best hope of achieving peace and stability, while others were horrified that the king should so cavalierly dispose of his crown and disinherit his son. They could only suppose that the mentally ill monarch had been exploited by those around him, principally by Isabeau herself.

1420–1421 was an exceptionally hard winter, the worst for forty years, says the *Bourgeois*. It was still snowing and freezing at Easter. It is in 1421 that the *Bourgeois* first mentions in his *Journal* famished wolves roaming the streets of Paris and unearthing and devouring corpses in the cemeteries. He describes the distress of the poor in Paris, the children dying of hunger and cold on the rubbish heaps where they were scavenging, 'and no-one could help them, for there was neither bread, nor corn, nor logs ...' All through the winter the poor were dying of starvation. The luckier better-off set up what hospices they could to shelter the orphans. When the spring at last came and they threw out what was left over from their winter's hoard of rotten apples and plums and vegetables to feed the pigs roaming the streets, the starving got there first and 'ate what the pigs disdained to eat'.[12]

In April 1421, while Henry was making his royal progress through all the principal towns in England, news of the death of his brother, the Duke of Clarence, at the battle of Baugé in March had reached him. When he returned to France in June, with fresh troops and finance (raised through subsidies and loans), Henry set about avenging the defeat. He marched first to the relief of Paris, threatened by the forces of the Dauphin, and went on to take Dreux, bringing with him on this campaign the twenty-seven-year old King James I of Scotland, who had been held a prisoner in England since 1406. Brought up and educated at the English court, James was now more English than Scottish in outlook. The presence of the young man was intended to dissuade the Scottish troops who had triumphed at Baugé under their commander, John Stuart, Earl of Buchan.

Henry consolidated his reputation for ruthlessness when he took the fortress of Rougemont and hanged every man of the garrison, later drowning any escapers who were caught. Shakespeare's 'warlike Harry' was a man of flint indeed. After an eight-month siege, he next took the town of Meaux in March 1422. The thirty or so Scots among those who surrendered were executed on the grounds that they had borne arms against their king, James I, now Henry's ally. The reprisals taken against the town's inhabitants, who had had the insolence to mock Henry with a braying donkey on their walls, were again merciless. The commander of the place was beheaded, as was a trumpeter who had made mock of Henry from the walls. More prisoners were sent to Paris and left to die of starvation in the prisons. Juvenal des Ursins asserts that some were so tortured by hunger that they were driven to cannibalism, dementedly tearing with their teeth at the dead bodies of fellow-prisoners.[13]

Perhaps, after all, not everyone – even in Henry's army – was comfortable about Henry's methods, or even about the war itself. Juvenal des Ursins tells us that many of the army besieging Meaux died, not only from the arrows and offensive sallies of the besieged, but from epidemics and sickness. There must have been a great deal of suffering, hence a great deal of discontent, for reasons ranging from the appalling conditions to soul-searching among the more sophisticated about the justness of the war itself. After the capture of Melun, says Juvenal des Ursins, Henry V's treatment of prisoners was 'very disagreeable to some of the English themselves'.[14] Moreover, war was a much more bloody enterprise in the early fifteenth century than it had been earlier, thanks to the development of more powerful cannon, the so-called the 'Artillery Revolution'. By 1420, the biggest cannon were able to fire stone balls of up to seven hundred and fifty kilogrammes.[15]

Juvenal des Ursins tells the story of Sir John Cornwall, wounded at Meaux, whose only son, 'a fine young squire' only seventeen years old, had his head blown off by cannon fire right beside his father. A grief-stricken Sir John then openly declared that 'nothing but the conquest of Normandy was decided upon in England, and now against God and all reason, we want to deprive the Dauphin of the kingdom which rightfully belongs to him.' Fearing for his life and his soul if he continued in France, he hastened back to England and swore never again to bear arms against Christians.[16] This is the same Sir John Cornwall, Henry IV's brother-in-law, who had campaigned with Clarence in France in 1412 and distinguished himself at Agincourt. He made a fortune from French ransoms, even after he ceased campaigning. Perhaps the story of his scruples is simply war propaganda, but he certainly returned to England and never left it again. Together with Henry V's insistence on his deathbed that Normandy at least should never be given up and his unease about a possible future peace treaty with Charles VII, it reveals a chink in the psychological armour of the English army and in its conviction that God was on its side.

All in all, 1422 was an eventful year. Henry's brilliant military career came to an unexpected end with his early death at Vincennes on 31 August 1422, from dysentery, or some form of intestinal haemorrhaging from which he had been suffering since February of that year. On his deathbed he voiced the desire that Bedford should be Regent of Normandy, that his youngest brother, Humphrey, Duke of Gloucester, should be Regent of England and guardian of the eight-month-old Henry VI, also that Philip of Burgundy should be Regent of France, unless he did not wish to accept the charge.[17] Bedford, seeming to have decided that Philip did not want the position, filled it very happily himself.

Henry had urged his brothers above all to keep alive and well the Burgundian alliance and never, in any future peace treaty with the Dauphin, to relinquish Normandy, which he saw as his birthright. This last exhortation reveals both his uncertainty about the outcome of the campaign and his unease that Charles might one day be in a position to enforce his claim to the throne of all France. Having given these instructions, Henry turned his face to the wall and died with his chaplains around him. Jean Chartier writing from the French point of view in the late 1430s, gives him a measured epitaph: 'In life he was a cruel and very hard enforcer of justice, greatly obeyed by his subjects, a wily conqueror, skilled in arms, and graced with various honourable qualities and virtues.'[18] His death was followed on 21 October 1422 by that of the unfortunate Charles VI, and on the 30th of that month the Dauphin was proclaimed King Charles VII. As he had not yet been crowned at Rheims and received upon his forehead the holy oil, believed to have been provided miraculously for Clovis's baptism in Rheims at Christmas in the year 496 and used ever after to anoint the kings of France, he continued to be known as the Dauphin, which is how Joan addressed him when she first met him at Chinon.

France was now, like Caesar's Gaul, a country in three parts: English-held France, Burgundian France, and the Dauphin's France. Broadly speaking, the English held sway in Normandy and the places they had taken in the north (their south-western province of Guyenne was another area of dispute), Paris and its surroundings were politically Burgundian in sympathy (a state of affairs existing since the massacres of 1418) and then there were the Burgundian fiefdoms of Artois, French Flanders and of course the Duchy of Burgundy, with its capital at Dijon. The poorer part of the country south of the Loire remained loyal to the Dauphin. There were two Parlements, one in Paris, and the other in Poitiers, which had been set up there by the French after the takeover of Paris by the Burgundians in 1418. There were also two *Chambres de Commerce*, one in Paris and the other set up in Bourges to take charge of the financial affairs of the Dauphin's kingdom.

The Dauphin's court was established in Bourges, the capital of Berry and seat of his uncle, the late Duke of Berry, whose splendid palace there was filled with art treasures, for the Duke had been above all a great patron of the arts, his seventeen palatial residences being filled with innumerable books, paintings, sculptures and tapestries. His huge menagerie of exotic animals was famous also. He is best remembered nowadays as the patron of the Limbourg brothers and that jewel of illustrated manuscripts, the *Très Riches Heures du Duc de Berry*.[19]

When Henry V died, John of Lancaster, Duke of Bedford, was a man still only thirty-three years old. As Regent, he devoted himself to the affairs of France, leaving England to his unreliable brother, Humphrey, Duke of Gloucester, as Lord Protector and to Henry Beaufort, Bishop (later Cardinal) of Winchester, of whom we shall hear more at Joan's trial. Bedford was an intelligent and well-respected man, who, like Henry V, sought to curb the excesses of the indisciplined soldiery in the territories under his control. Especially after the English victory at Verneuil in 1424, which was followed by a lull in hostilities, he was able to turn his attention to matters of law and order. Commerce and agriculture picked up. Thomas Basin, writing in the 1470s, describes him as 'diligent, humane, and just', saying that he treated the French nobles who submitted to him with respect and even friendship, so that, as long as he lived, 'the Normans and French of that part of the kingdom had a great affection for him'.[20]

Paris was nominally under English control, but its trade, economy, and all the associated employment and industries, were reliant on Burgundy and the north (hence the importance of the Seine as a trading highway). In the Church, the University, the institutions of state, Burgundian Frenchmen were in post, although Philip of Burgundy himself, eclipsed as regent by Bedford, was seen in the capital only once after 1424 and that for only a week in 1429. The English presence in Paris was discreet. The garrison numbered a paltry three hundred men. Bedford was well aware that the Burgundian alliance was vital, but he was determined to secure for his infant nephew, Henry VI, the entire kingdom of France, which meant French Flanders, Artois, and all territories held by Philip under French sovereignty, including Champagne, which officially he now administered for Henry VI. A large part of the principality of Burgundy was outside the borders of the kingdom of France (in the case of Dutch

Flanders). Holland, Zeeland and Hainaut, which Philip would before long manage to wrest from the Countess Jacqueline, lay within Philip's sphere of influence. This gave him a large measure of independence. His ambition was the greatness of Burgundy, England for him was a means to that end and if the alliance did not serve his purpose, his policy would sooner or later change. He held court, in great splendour, not at Dijon, but outside the kingdom of France, at Ghent and Bruges. There he was the *Grand Duc d'Occident*, the magnificent Grand Duke of the Western World.

The Treaty of Amiens in April, 1423, sealed a triple alliance between England, France (Burgundy) and Brittany, but Brittany was a wavering partner and moreover the interests of Philip of Burgundy and Bedford were not identical, although they were soon to be brothers-in-law. Bedford married Philip's sister Anne at Troyes, on 14 June 1423, a political marriage, but one which worked out excellently on the human plane also. At Dijon, in October, 1423, Arthur de Richemont, younger brother of the Duke of Brittany, married another sister of Philip of Burgundy, Marguerite, the young widow of the late Dauphin Louis whom Charles had been called upon to replace. Arthur de Richemont had fought at Agincourt, been captured by the English and held in England until 1420, when he took an oath of loyalty to Henry V. He then persuaded his brother, the Duke of Brittany, to sign the Treaty of Troyes, but after other vicissitudes served as Constable of France fighting on the side of Charles and Joan of Arc. We will hear of him again.

Paris was pro-Burgundian, but this was by no means synonymous with pro-English. The English had acquired in particular an unenviable reputation for drunkenness and were popularly known in France as the *godons*, a Gallic version of their favourite oath, *God damn (it!* or *you*, or *me*). The *Bourgeois of Paris* records that, after the ferociously cold winter of 1422–1423, when the Seine froze over and wolves roamed the city streets, when the fruit harvests were doomed, Philip of Burgundy and Bedford met in Paris at the end of August. While en route the English and Burgundian soldiery had laid waste all the villages around the capital, destroying the few grapes that were still to be had, 'like pigs', *comme eussent fait porcs*.[21]

Of course we do not know how many actual sympathisers with the French cause there may have been in Paris, for of necessity they did not dare voice such opinions. Bedford issued decrees forbidding anyone to speak of Charles as 'the King', or to refer to his supporters as 'French'. Charles was to be referred to only as the 'self-styled Dauphin', his followers as 'Armagnacs'. The penalties for disobedience were hefty fines, or, for those who could not pay, the piercing of tongues or branding of foreheads. The *Bourgeois* describes how, in February 1423, the whole population of Paris was obliged to take an oath of allegiance: 'citizens, householders, carters, shepherds, cowmen, pig-keepers to the abbeys, charwomen, even the monks'. The oath committed them to obey Bedford in all things and to do all they could to thwart Charles 'who calls himself king of France' and all his 'allies and accomplices'. The chronicler adds that 'some complied willingly, others very much against their will.'[22] Around the same time, fearing the French now installed in nearby Meulan, the authorities in Paris, 'day and night, for a week, arrested people suspected of having pro-French sympathies and imprisoned them'. In general, disenchantment with the Anglo-Burgundian administration would grow as the years passed. Reforms promised by John the Fearless had never materialised, a rival to the Paris *Chambre des Comptes* had been set up by Henry V in Caen. Its chief officer, the *Trésorier-Général* was always English. No less than ten conspiracies were put down in Paris and Normandy between 1422 and 1434.

After 1424, many pro-French citizens applied for *rémission*, or permission to return to Paris, where they had left behind families or their means of livelihood. They gave various pretexts for having left after 1418. The same happened in other places. Remission was frequently granted, since the exodus of large numbers of the working population was undesirable. The registers of the *Trésor des Chartes* in the National Archives in Paris contain a large number of these demands. A few examples suffice to show the difficulties in which the French population found itself; for example, on 14 June 1427, remission was granted to a 'barber/surgeon' who had been 'implicated in the treason of the canons' of the cathedral of Saint-Gervais in Sées. His excuse was that he was held prisoner by the said canons all night and threatened with death if he revealed their plot to admit the Armagnacs which he had stumbled upon and that, although when the town was retaken by the English, he left with 'our enemies', he had taken no part in any act of war.[23] Conspiracy, murderous canons, and no local support? Or take the case of Brother Laurent Anquetil, of the Abbey at Mortemer, who was granted remission on 5 June 1427.[24] Brother Laurent had taken into the abbey hostel an injured armed man brought to him by a dozen or so 'brigands'. He had subsequently given shelter to the said squire and his page for some five weeks until the young man recovered and left. Brother Anquetil of course also acted under threats of death and has no idea where his visitor headed for after he left. Other cases include that of the merchant of Rouen whose crime was that he did not report various subversive remarks made to him by certain neighbours, one of whom had expressed the wish that 'he who calls himself Dauphin were in the town', another opining that if *the enemy* (the French) had succeeded in getting into the town, they would have harmed none but the English. Our merchant incautiously repeated these remarks to someone who reported him to the authorities, since which time he had found himself sitting in the prison of Rouen, accused of covering up conspiracy.

Rémission is humbly asked for by the 'parents and friends' on behalf of various 'poor and honest' young peasants, encumbered with wives and children and suspected of various degrees of collaboration with the *enemy*. The plea is always that of *force majeure*, you can believe it if you will. Other cases involve resistance to pillaging English troops, ending in bloodshed, like that of the young peasant who fled to join the 'brigands' after killing one of the soldiers bent upon seizing a fine mare attached to his plough. These are all recorded alongside the ordinary crimes such as forging money, common robbery or drunken brawls, mostly among soldiers. Talking of Normandy, the historian Pierre Champion asks: 'Were these peasants always acting under constraint when they helped brigands across the rivers, when they accompanied them on their journeys, when they provided them with food, when they bought, bridled and saddled horses for them, when they stole the same on their account?'[25] The Anglo-Burgundian soldier and chronicler, Wavrin de Forestel, mentions that when he was given a mission by Bedford in 1429 to stop supplies reaching the besieged city of Orleans, his efforts were completely foiled by 'the local communities, which rose up against us'.[26]

In general in occupied France, the English administration played the language game, conflating the notions of resistance and banditry. Without distinction, bandits and those resisting Anglo-Burgundian rule went to the gallows or were sewn into sacks and thrown into the Seine. It was in fact sometimes difficult to make the distinction, since those who took to the woods or elsewhere were obliged to live off the land, finding their next meal usually clucking about in a farmyard. They were sometimes members of former garrisons, but hardly ever nobles (no Robin Hoods) and certainly not lawyers or academics. The aristocrats either joined the Dauphin's army or went back to their own fiefs, the lawyers and academics went to the Parlement in Poitiers or to the *Chambre des Comptes* at Bourges, while the more self-seeking joined Charles's entourage at Chinon or Bourges, courting royal favour and advancement.

In the country below the Loire, (excepting the part of Guyenne remaining to the English Crown), the English were seen and known only as raiders and plunderers, but the population suffered much from both sides. On the English side there were freebooters such as Richard Venables who gathered an army of deserters after 1428 and plundered and massacred the peasantry of Normandy. Among the most notorious captains of mercenaries were men such as André de Ribes (nominally in the service of the English), who devastated the countryside around Toulouse, or Perrinet Gressart, a former stonemason, on the payroll of Bedford, for whom he held as captain of the places Saint-Pierre-le-Moutier and La-Charité-sur-Loire. Joan would take the former town in her campaign in the last months of 1429, but failed to take La Charité. Perrinet, knowing on which side the bread was buttered, finally went over to Charles VII after the Treaty of Arras (1435), in return for the appointment as governor of the town for life.

Ribes had the misfortune to be taken and executed, but the even more merciless Spaniard, Rodrigo de Villandrando, rose to dizzy heights. He had started out in the company of the Burgundian Villiers de l'Isle Adam, then fought on the French side at Verneuil and elsewhere, subsequently terrorising the Languedoc and sowing alarm as far as Lyons. Of minor Spanish aristocracy himself, he eventually married into the family of the Duke of Bourbon, acquired châteaux, had ten thousand mercenaries (mainly English) under his command by 1433, and ended up back in Spain as a hero and Marshal of Castille. Such leaders of mercenary bands, commonly known as *routiers* or *écorcheurs* (like the slaughterhouse men of the Parisian Butchers Guild) extorted huge sums in 'protection money' from the unfortunate citizens, burnt villages, devastated the countryside, changed sides as suited them, placed their ill-gotten gains with bankers, bought land and hobnobbed with the great and powerful.

Bedford, who could at times be as stern and pitiless as his late brother, not hesitating to execute hostages, for example, when a town failed to surrender on the due date (as happened in La Gravelle in 1427), did indeed make efforts in these extremely difficult circumstances to rule justly and to improve conditions in Normandy, Paris and the occupied areas. In 1422–1423 he took measures to reform the debased currency and regulate the hours which men were expected to work, fixing them from sunrise to sundown in the shorter days of winter and from 6am. to 6pm. in summer, with breaks for meals. He issued ordinances for the supervision of the proper quality of food on sale, with the daily inspection of the meat markets and regulations concerning the slaughter of animals. Appropriate penalties were attached to the disregard of these measures. He attempted to rid the law courts of bribery and corruption. 'If he had been king of England,' writes Joseph Stevenson, the nineteenth-century collector of letters and papers from the reign of Henry VI, 'he would certainly have ranked as the wisest of our sovereigns.'[27]

4

Bedford at War, and the Uncertain Start to the Reign of Charles VII

Conquering kings their titles take
From the foes they captive make

John Chandler, 1817

The Dauphin Charles had finally married his patient fiancée Marie d'Anjou at Bourges in April 1422. They had played together as children in Anjou, on Charles's side there was affection but certainly it was not *le grand amour*. Marie was a devoted and faithful wife and bore her husband fourteen children. Their first child, the future (and very troublesome) Louis XI, was born in 1423. Marie was not blessed with great beauty, although to judge by the bust preserved now in the abbey of Saint Denis, she scarcely deserved Chastellain's ungallant remark that she had a face to frighten the English.[1] Charles may have had other *amours* of which we have no certain knowledge, with the exception, in later life, of his acknowledged mistress, the famous Agnès Sorel, the *Dame de Beauté* depicted in Fouquet's painting of the Virgin and Child (a work rather more profane than sacred). But at least he was always considerate towards Marie, with an affection which Chastellain has described as an *amour de dette*, a dutiful love.

Not surprisingly, given the violent events crowding his youth, his mother's public condemnation of him and the doubts thereby aroused concerning his legitimacy, together with his own lack of an imposing physical appearance or any form of charisma, Charles was fundamentally a melancholy and unsure young man, tortured by fears, anxieties and scruples. After the assassination of John the Fearless at the bridge of Montereau, he could never again cross a bridge on horseback. There was a tragic incident in October 1422, ten days before the death of his father, when he was holding a meeting in the Hôtel de l'Évêque in La Rochelle to settle finances. Charles was seated in an alcove above the assembled courtiers and authorities when the floor collapsed. A number of people were killed and others seriously injured. The Dauphin was very badly shaken by this event and regarded his escape as miraculous. If he seemed to have too great an appetite for the entertainments and pleasurable pursuits that court life could provide – hunting, dancing, feasting – such was his choice of escapism. No one suspected that he would one day come to a somewhat late but forceful maturity and earn himself the title of Charles the Victorious.

When Bedford took over as regent of France in 1422, the English campaign was making headway, although during Henry's six-month absence in England, his younger brother, the impetuous Thomas, Duke of Clarence, had been killed in a battle at Baugé (March 1421), in which the English were defeated by an army largely composed of the Scottish allies of the Dauphin. The Scots were led by Archibald Douglas, Earl of Wigtown, son of the great Earl of Douglas, and by John Stuart, Earl of Buchan, who was the son of the duke of Albany, regent in Scotland during the captivity in England of his young nephew, James I of Scotland. This army had been recruited in Scotland in 1418, and was transported to France in a fleet of Spanish ships, landing at La Rochelle.

The history of the Scots in the service of Charles VII and in France in general is illustrious. After Baugé, John Stuart, Earl of Buchan, became Constable of France, which made him commander-in-chief of the French army. At that time there were some six thousand Scottish soldiers (of whom four thousand were archers) in France, while later, in the famous siege of Orleans, the accounts of the French Treasurer for War record the presence of companies of Scots commanded by three knights and five squires. In 1427, another John Stuart, Earl of Darnley, had been made Count of Evreux and granted the right by Charles VII to quarter his arms with those of France. The same John Stuart soon afterwards left for Edinburgh, together with the poet, Alain Chartier, secretary to Charles VII, and the Archbishop of Rheims, Regnault de Chartres (of whom we shall hear more). They came to ask for the hand of the eldest daughter of James I, Margaret of Scotland, aged four, in marriage to the son of Charles VII, the future Louis XI, aged five. Margaret was later married to Louis, at the age of twelve, but she died in 1445, before Louis became king. The names of Scottish notables abound in the records of those fighting alongside Joan of Arc: Ogilvy, Melville, Galloway, Lennox, Hamilton, Kennedy, Wishart, Houston, Crichton, Blair. The thousands of ordinary footsoldiers and archers, like all the generations of the humble, have of course left us no names.

On 30 July 1423, the Anglo-Burgundians, under the Earl of Salisbury, inflicted a crushing defeat on a much greater Franco-Scottish force at Cravant, a town on the Yonne, not far from Auxerre. The casualty figures vary widely in the different sources, but up to three thousand Scots are said to have died and two thousand prisoners to have been taken, including John Stuart, Earl of Darnley, who was later ransomed and released. He could have been executed, since, as Henry IV had claimed suzerainty over Scotland, Scots opposing the English crown were technically held to be traitors. A fresh contingent of Scottish troops arrived at La Rochelle in February 1424, under the command of the other John Stuart, the Earl of Buchan. The release of the Scottish king, James I from long English captivity in March of that year, in return for agreeing to a seven-year truce between England and Scotland, meant that James recalled the Scottish army, although many Scottish troops remained in France under the command of Buchan and Douglas.

After Cravant, the next great disaster was to follow at Verneuil, in August 1424. On the English side, under the command of Bedford and Salisbury, there were about eleven thousand men, and on the French side about seventeen thousand, including six thousand Scots and a contingent of Italian cavalry. Bedford himself led his men into a battle in which the Earls of Buchan and Douglas perished, the young Duke of Alençon (of whom we shall hear more) was captured and over seven thousand Scots and French lay dead on the field. The Scots were practically wiped out. The English lost about a thousand men.

Monstrelet tells us that the Dauphin Charles was devastated when he received the news, and that his grief could not have been greater 'for the destruction of his princes and his chivalry'.[2] However, relations between the French and the Scots do not seem to have been altogether harmonious at the time, no doubt in part at least due to Scottish over-indulgence in alcohol (in such exploits the Scots rivalled the English). Their reputation for bad behaviour seems to have hit an all-time low around 1424, when the French regarded their allies as essentially barbaric and it was darkly rumoured that if there had been a Scots victory at Verneuil, it would have been followed up by the victors exterminating all the French nobility and seizing their women and property. Basin soberly considers that Verneuil at least saved France from such a nightmare.[3] In fact, Acts of the Scottish parliament in the early fifteenth century forbade pillage under pain of death (which is not to say that the law was always strictly observed). Be that as it may, daily Masses were said in Orleans until the Revolution of 1789 for the repose of the souls of the Scots who had given their lives at Verneuil.

The Franco-Scottish alliance spanned centuries, negotiations for such an alliance between the two countries having been ongoing since the twelfth century. There was a saying current in England, quoted by Shakespeare in *Henry V*: *If that you will France win, / Then with Scotland first begin.* The first of the elite Scots Guards had been recruited into the army of Charles V, the grandfather of Joan's Dauphin. The Scots continued to play a distinguished role in the armies of France for a very long time, up to the Revolution of 1789 and even later, after the Restoration of Louis XVIII in 1814.[4] In the *Adoration of the Magi*, from the *Livre d'Heures* of Etienne Chevalier,[5] illustrated in 1454 by Jean Fouquet and now in the Museum Condé at Chantilly, we can see Charles VII himself, in the guise of principal Mage, kneeling before the infant Jesus and surrounded by the Scottish archers of his personal guard. Scottish archers under the command of Patrick Ogilvy, Sheriff of Angus, gave protection to Joan's column on its way from Blois to the relief of Orleans. Three Scottish knights and five squires, with their men, as noted above, were in Orleans during the siege.[6] The bishop of Orleans who was elected in 1426 was also a Scot, John Carmichael, known in France as Jean de Saint-Michel. He was described in a Scottish history written in 1644 as a 'valiant and learned man'. He had come to France in 1420 as chaplain to the Douglas who became Duke of Touraine, and should not, it seems, be confused with the Sir John Carmichael (or *Kirkmichael*) who distinguished himself at Baugé in 1421.[7] There were even Scottish soldiers and archers in the garrisons of castles in the Meuse valley, not far from Joan's Domrémy. They were on the payroll of Louis de Bar, Bishop of Verdun.

An interesting footnote is that an anonymous continuator of the fifteenth-century Scottish chronicle, the *Scotichronicon*, compiled by Fordun and later Walter Bower, claims that he had followed Joan throughout her campaigns and was present at her death. All we know about him is that he was a monk of the abbey of Dunfermline, writing at the behest of his abbot. Unfortunately, the page or pages of the manuscript dealing with Joan's career are missing.[8]

Shortly after the disaster of Verneuil, however, in September 1424, the Dauphin Charles and Philip of Burgundy signed a truce (one of many short-lived truces) promising to abstain from attacking each other, a truce in which, for the first time, Philip referred to Charles as *Roi de France*. Philip's loyalty to his English ally was perpetually wavering. The chronicler Jean Le Fèvre de Saint-Rémi reports hearing him say, when he was an old man, that regardless of whether he had lived or died there, he deeply regretted not having had the good fortune to fight on the French side at the battle of Agincourt.[9] Perhaps he felt that the chance of military glory had escaped him. When John the Fearless had forbidden his nineteen-year-old only son's participation in the encounter and sent him out of harm's way to Arras, Philip had gone into his chamber and wept. Ironically enough, Le Fèvre had himself fought on the English side in that famous battle.

Charles was fortunate in having as a mother-in-law the Queen of Sicily, Yolande d'Aragon, a woman whom historians unanimously praise for her wisdom, prudence and loyalty to her son-in-law. After Verneuil, she managed in 1424 to have installed at court Arthur de Richemont, a battle-hardened soldier with a huge disfiguring scar across his face. Richemont was a great noble in his own right, the brother of Duke John V of Brittany and, at the end of his life, he became Duke of Brittany himself. His parents were John IV of Brittany and his Duchess, Joanna, daughter of King Charles the Bad of Navarre (of deservedly evil repute) and grand-daughter of John II of France. Arthur was born in 1393, and when his father died in 1399, his mother had promptly married Henry IV of England. She left for

England in 1403, after which most of her numerous children saw little of her. [10] The English title of Earl of Richmond was bestowed upon Arthur as a child. After being captured at Agincourt, he was a prisoner in England. He was allowed to reside with his mother, now imprisoned on charges of witchcraft at Pevensey. On his release in 1420, he took an oath of fealty to Henry V and offered his services to the Anglo-Burgundian party. In 1423, as already noted, he married Philip of Burgundy's sister Marguerite. With his English and Burgundian connections and changes of loyalty, it was not difficult to make Charles mistrustful of him; and his disfigured face, the mirror of his somewhat fearsome reputation, could do little to help him establish himself. Nonetheless, he it was who, in March 1425, asumed the mantle of Constable of France, after the demise of John Stuart, Earl of Buchan, fallen at Verneuil.

Richemont found himself insidiously but determinedly opposed by the clique surrounding the young Charles, who seems to have lapsed into lethargy and discouragement at this stage. There were in fact reasons to take heart: Charles was able to pay his troops, his tax office (*Fisc*) was working efficiently, his resources were not at an end, but he was despondent and demoralised. In June 1424, Richemont managed to rid the court of many of the more baleful influences around Charles. This included those suspected of having set a trap for John the Fearless at Montereau, chiefly Tanguy du Chastel, the man who had snatched the Dauphin from under the noses of the Burgundian troops in Paris in 1418. Tanguy departed with dignity, saying that God forbid he should be an obstacle to such a great blessing as peace between the king and the Duke of Burgundy. Evicted also were the President of the Council, Louvet and his friends, specialists in the art of amassing huge fortunes and trimming their sails to the winds of opportunity while the Dauphin personally was reduced to penury. But Richemont made a fatal mistake when he enlisted a certain Georges de la Trémoille for the Dauphin's party. La Trémoille came of an immensely rich and powerful Burgundian family, He was brought up at the court of John the Fearless, became Grand Chamberlain of Charles VI in 1413, was captured at Agincourt and released on payment of a large ransom. In 1416 he married the very rich elderly widow of the Duke of Berry. She conveniently died in 1423. La Trémoille was a past master in the art of diplomatic duplicity and lucrative career moves and would be all-powerful as Charles's Grand Chamberlain in 1427. He determinedly and insidiously opposed the military aims of Joan when she came on the scene, for, needless to say, he had useful connections with the Burgundian camp, which he had no wish to see jeopardised.

Two men stood in the way of La Trémoille: the Constable Arthur de Richemont, and Pierre de Giac, a handsome, sinister, greedy and murderous scoundrel who had remained in place as Charles's Chamberlain when the rest of the old guard had been paid off. Richemont agreed with La Trémoille that the man must be dealt with. Charles's court was peripatetic, travelling now to this château, now to another. In February 1427 it was in residence at Issoudun. La Trémoille and Richemont, with a small band of armed men, crept into the château at dawn, made their way up to the room in which Giac was sleeping with his second wife, seized their man and carried him off. The wife was calm until the intruders started to carry off the silver on her dressing tables. The Dauphin, awakened by her screams, summoned his guard, who were confronted by Richemont. The Constable dismissed them, saying, 'What I am doing is for the good of the king.'

Giac was taken to Bourges, where the *bailli* of the town, on orders from Richemont, put him on trial. Among numerous other crimes, he admitted the murder of his pregnant first wife, whom he had poisoned, thrown over the croup of his horse, and then galloped through the woods until she expired. Having buried her somewhere, he had returned gaily home, free to marry the second wife. Condemned to death by drowning in the river, it was in vain that he offered Richemont a large sum of money, together with his wife and family, as pledges in exchange for his life. When that failed, his last request was that his right hand should be severed and be no longer a part of him, since he had promised it to the Devil in return for satanic help. Satan himself would be out-schemed. Request granted.

A month after the execution, La Trémoille married Giac's widow, on whom he had set his sights some time previously. Now all he needed to complete his felicity was to rid himself of Richemont. He had so successfully wormed his way into the latter's confidence, that it was Richemont himself, a few months later, who proposed him to Charles as Grand Chamberlain (first minister). The Dauphin had his doubts, saying to Richemont: '*Beau cousin*, you want to give him to me, but you will regret this, for I know him better than you.' He was not wrong. Once in, La Trémoille gained supreme sway over Charles. Playing on the latter's uneasiness about Richemont and his undiplomatic bluntness, it was not long before he inspired the Dauphin with a fear and dislike of the man. The Constable realised his error too late, when he found himself deprived of his governorship of the duchy of Berry, handed over instead to La Trémoille. He withdrew from the court before the end of 1427 and all efforts thereafter to dislodge the new favourite failed. It would take Joan of Arc to persuade Charles to allow Richemont back. The Constable managed to get La Trémoille ousted from the court in 1433, after Joan's death.

After Verneuil, Bedford's French campaign, together with the whole alliance with Burgundy, was put in jeopardy by the antics of his popular but reckless brother, Humphrey of Gloucester, who in 1423 had taken it into his head to marry the Countess Jaqueline of Hainaut, widow of the Dauphin John who had died in 1416 and now runaway wife of the Duke of Brabant, cousin of Philip of Burgundy. In 1420, the spirited Jacqueline had ditched her boring and graceless young husband to whom she had been married two years earlier at the age of sixteen (he was then fourteen) and fled to England, where she was royally received and made the acquaintance of the twenty-one-year old Humphrey. The two young people made an attractive pair. Humphrey was basically an intellectual, interested in literature and the arts, but also a romantic, anxious to win chivalrous glory for himself on the battlefield.

However, the path of true love did not promise to run smooth. Apart from the small matter of Jacqueline's current husband and the refusal of an annulment from the pope (the love-stricken pair made do with one from the anti-pope Benedict XIII at Avignon), there was the inconvenience of arousing the fury of Philip of Burgundy; for by marrying Gloucester, Jacqueline would put an end to Philip's prospects of succeeding to her vast estates on the death of her husband, who had health problems and hopefully would not tarry too long in this earthly vale of tears.[11] Humphrey not only took the lady, but gave himself the title of Count of Hainault, Holland and Zeeland. This hubris was intolerable to Philip of Burgundy. Humphrey rashly landed with five thousand men at Calais at the end of 1424, joined up with troops supplied by his mother-in-law, took Mons and established himself there.

Bedford's first attempt to patch things up with Philip through a meeting in Paris, was defeated by the stubborn refusal of Humphrey to agree the terms. 'On account of these tribulations,' writes Monstrelet, 'the Duke of Bedford was exceedingly angry with his brother, fearing that because of these divisions and differences his whole alliance with the Duke of Burgundy would be completely wrecked.'[12] An enraged Philip declared that his troops would fight on the side of the Duke of Brabant against the aggressor Gloucester. Humphrey wrote to his 'very dear and beloved cousin', Philip, expressing hurt indignation at the latter's belligerent reaction to his campaign, and signing himself 'Your cousin, the Duke of Gloucester, Count of Hainault, Holland, Zeeland, Penneburg, and Lord of Frizeland'.[13] A furious Philip thereupon challenged Humphrey to a duel and went into serious training for it. The date set (at Humphrey's insistence) was St. George's Day. He failed, however, to turn up on the day, having already returned to England, where he had been on the receiving end of the disapproving sentiments of the Great Council in London. In any case, he had now changed his affections. He had fallen in love with none other than Jacqueline's lady-in-waiting Eleanor Cobham, whom he made his mistress and was finally able to marry in 1428, his marriage to Jacqueline having been declared invalid.[14]

Humphrey's next quarrel was with his uncle Henry Beaufort, Bishop of Winchester, Chancellor of England. We will meet him again as the Cardinal of Winchester at the trial of Joan of Arc. Humphrey detested Beaufort who had opposed his nomination as Regent after the death of Henry V. With Humphrey stirring up mob passions in London, Beaufort appealed to Bedford to return from France to restore order. The result was that the latter absented himself from Normandy from December 1425 until March 1427.

He needed in any case to spend a period in England in order to raise badly needed funds for the French war. This was less than popular, for the English population thought that the war should be self-financing and that the occupied French territories should bear the brunt of the on-going costs. But the populations of those territories were already drained dry. There is a detailed account of the Earl of Salisbury's expenses for the second half of 1428, for example, in a document of 24 March 1428. The exchequer had to find the money to pay the Earl, his six hundred men-at-arms, six knights *bannerets*, thirty-four knights *bachelors*, eighteen hundred archers together with all their proper equipment. The list included four 'master artillery men' (paid at more than three times the rate of the archers), ten *miners* (men skilled in the art of undermining besieged towns, paid half as much again as the archers), seventy or eighty carpenters, masons, fletchers and others, who are included among the archers. Added to this were the costs of sea-transport of the Earl and his retinue to and from France, also one thousand marks sterling to be paid to the supplier of 'cannon, balls of stone, pincers of iron, ropes' and other necessary articles. In return the king takes one third of all profits from the war, which means ransoms and booty. Kings, great captains of the blood royal, and important personages such as the Constable or Marshals of France, officers therefore of 'Charles, who styles himself King of France', were to be handed over to the King who will appropriately recompense those who have captured such prizes.[15] A great deal of taxation was necessary to cover such expenses for all the nobility leading the King's army.

Short of funds or not, when Bedford returned the English continued to advance. Humphrey's withdrawal allowed peace to be made with Burgundy and the Anglo-Burgundian alliance to be put back together again. In May, the fortress of Pontorson, not far from the Mont Saint Michel, was taken back from the French who had managed to capture it the year before. In the summer of 1427, the Earl of Warwick failed to take Montargis, an important strategic place, nearly seventy miles south of Paris and about forty-five miles east of Orleans. Surrounded by canals and waterways, it dominates the valley of the river Yonne, which flows majestically from the hills of Burgundy through Auxerre and Sens to flow into the Seine at Montereau. The six-week English siege and artillery assault on the town was raised by the twenty-four-year-old illegitimate son of the murdered Duke Louis of Orléans, known as the 'Bastard of Orleans' and later as the Count of Dunois. When the English were drawn into an attack on the approaching relief force, the townspeople, in a pre-decided strategy, opened the floodgates, washing away the bridge and engulfing the attackers in the torrent. Warwick lost about a thousand men that day (5 September 1427).

It was at Montargis that Warwick found himself confronted by several important actors in the story of Joan of Arc, foremost among them the Bastard of Orleans, half-brother to the prisoner-of-war, Duke Charles of Orleans, and to the duke's younger brother, Jean d'Angoulême, also a prisoner in England since 1412. It is as *Dunois* that we meet him at the Nullity hearings in 1456 and that English-speaking audiences meet him in Shaw's play. So he will be referred to here as Dunois from now on, since the English epithet 'bastard' is a term of abuse, which was by no means the case in French in the time of Joan, who would cheerfully shout to her comrade-in-arms in the heat of the fray: 'Bastard, do this!' or 'Bastard, do that!' As a title of nobility, it was a badge to be worn with pride. We shall meet Dunois shortly as the commander of Orleans.

At Montargis with Dunois we find others whom we shall also meet soon again at Orleans, notably the famous couple of Gascon captains, Xaintrailles and La Hire (the latter familiar to English-speaking audiences through Shaw's play) and the veteran of Nicopolis and Harfleur, Raoul de Gaucourt. La Hire was the nickname of Étienne de Vignolles, generally thought to signify his hot temper, for *la hire* in Old French is the equivalent of the English word 'ire', or anger. Other etymologies have been mooted, but that one seems appropriate. La Hire started out originally in the early 1400s, as the captain of a band of *routiers*, or freebooters, offering his services to the Count of Armagnac and then to Charles VI. By 1428 he was a veteran of Baugé and Verneuil. The *Chronique de la Pucelle* says that before Montargis he offered up a prayer to the Almighty: 'Please God, do today for La Hire what You would wish La Hire to do for You, if he were God and You were La Hire'. On 29 April 1429, he will enter Orleans with Joan of Arc.

He fought faithfully for her throughout her campaigns, and even afterwards, making an attempt to rescue her from her captivity at Rouen, but he was captured after taking the town of Louviers in 1431. He escaped the following year and continued his buccaneering career, sowing mayhem and destruction not infrequently in his wake with his mercenary army. He was made captain of Normandy in 1436 and died in his bed in 1443, as a result of his numerous injuries. The contemporary historian, Bishop Thomas Basin, called him 'a most renowned military leader among the French captains of the time'. One of his most famous exploits was the capture of the fortress of Château-Gaillard in Normandy in 1430. The place was considered impregnable. La Hire and his men approached it by night in boats on the Seine and took it by scaling the walls. They freed a famous prisoner-of-war by the name of Barbazan, who refused to leave his prison until released by the English commander of the place from his oath to remain there, which had been required of him and which he had given. The commander, a man called Kingston, duly obliged and was led away thereafter until he should in his turn be ransomed. La Hire's name was immortalised when it became, in the seventeenth century, the name given to the Jack of Hearts in the pack of cards.

La Hire's inseparable comrade, of whom occasionally we shall hear more, was Poton de Xaintrailles, a brilliant jouster who had also begun as a mercenary captain of freebooters. He had been captured by the English and ransomed a couple of times before distinguishing himself in Joan's campaigns, from her début at Orléans to Compiègne, where she was captured. He himself was captured by the Earl of Warwick in the summer of 1431 and appears as a prisoner in the castle of Rouen some months after Joan's execution. As a noble, however minor, he was considerably better treated than the peasant girl on trial for heresy and witchcraft, being invited to dine at the table of the nobility, together with other persons of rank, Joan's judge, Bishop Cauchon, for one. Joan had had to make do, as her biographer Régine Pernoud has pointed out, with her bare cell, her heavy chains, and whatever prison fare her gaolers gave her. Xaintrailles was appointed Marshal of France by Charles VII in 1454. After the king's death in 1461, he was stripped of his titles by Charles's disaffected son, Louis XI. He died two months later.

After Montargis things began to look up again for the English, with the arrival of military leaders such as Talbot, first Earl of Shrewsbury, known later as 'the English Achilles', who took Le Mans from La Hire. He arrived in June 1428 with fresh forces and took more than forty towns and fortresses, including strategic places on the Loire, Jargeau, Meung, Beaugency. The Earl of Salisbury was insistent that Orleans should be next. Its strategic importance was immense, dominating as it did the way into the centre of France and Charles VII's remaining territories. Bedford would have preferred to take as his target Angers, the capital of Anjou. The geographical position of Anjou on the lower Loire, east of Brittany, would bring the English-controlled territories in north-west France closer to the lands held in Guyenne in the south-west. Salisbury's arguments won the day. The die was cast, the fate of Orleans would decide one way or another the future course of history for both England and France.

PART II

A Girl Called Joan from Domrémy

Childhood and Growing Up in Domrémy

Mais à présent je sais la voix des immortels,
Et j'ai vu le regard des yeux inoubliables.
Charles Péguy, *Mystère de la Charité de Jeanne d'Arc*

We wove a web in childhood,
A web of sunny air

Charlotte Bronte

Eight o'clock on the morning of Ash Wednesday, 21 February 1431. First public hearing of the Joan of Arc case in the Chapel Royal of the Castle of Rouen, judge Monsignor Pierre Cauchon, Bishop of Beauvais presiding, with the prosecutor, Jean d'Estivet, canon of Beauvais, and forty-two assorted 'assessors': canons, theologians, doctors of canon and civil law, all belonging to the cathedral chapter of Rouen or the University of Paris.

All are paid by the English Treasury. As for the great University, it is still considered to be the intellectual power-house of Europe and its hubris is undented. Its authority in moral and religious spheres has no rival, given, among other things, the scandal of the Great Schism in the Church, with one pope in Rome and another claimant in Avignon, a state of affairs which had only come to an end a little over a dozen years previously, in 1417, when the Council of Constance elected Odo Colonna as Pope Martin V. To this must be added the deplorable accumulation of riches accruing to bishops and canons through multiple benefices, as well as the laxity of many of the clergy, scandals which would within a century give rise to the Reformation. From 1418 onwards, the members of the University of Paris actively support, or at least passively accept, Anglo-Burgundian rule. Its eminent chancellor, Jean Gerson, who had left Paris in February 1415, to play a major role in the deliberations of the Council of Constance, could not return in 1418, fearing the vengeance of John the Fearless; whose anger he had incurred by denouncing the immorality of Petit's oration on the murder of Louis of Orleans. The propositions of Petit's *apologia* for political assassination (which he described as *tyrannicide*) were in fact condemned at Constance, at Gerson's insistence, but in general terms, so that John the Fearless was able to claim that they had been taken out of context. Fearing for his life, Gerson took refuge in the great Benedictine abbey of Melk on the Danube in Austria and in 1419 he retired to the Celestine monastery in Lyons, where his brother was prior. Other pro-French academics and clergy had also fled Paris in 1418, in the midst of massacre and turmoil.

The Bishop conducts the interrogation. The minutes are taken during the sessions and written up in the evening by the clerks of the court, the notaries Manchon and Colles (otherwise known as Boisguillaume). From March 14, a third notary, Nicolas Taquel, secretary to the interrogator, Jean Beaupère, will be appointed to agree their minuutes. They too are all members of the clergy.

Joan is led from her cell in the keep of the castle into the chapel by Massieu, the priest whose is responsible for bringing her from the castle to the court. She has no defence lawyer. The interrogation is conducted by Jean Beaupère, right-hand-man of Bishop Pierre Cauchon on several diplomatic missions and rector of the University of Paris in 1412 and 1413.

She is asked to state her name and origins:

Beaupère: What is your name and surname?
Joan: At home they called me Jeannette (*Jeannie*), and when I came into France, they called me Jeanne (*Joan*). I don't know about a surname.
Beaupère: Where do you come from?
Joan: I was born in the village of Domrémy, which is one with the village of Greux. The main church is in Greux.
Beaupère: What are the names of your father and mother?
Joan: My father is called Jacques d'Arc and my mother is called Isabelle.
Beaupère: Where were you baptised?
Joan: In the church in Domrémy.
Beaupère: Who were your godparents?
Joan: I had a godmother called Agnès, and one called Jeanne, and one called Sibille, and a godfather called Jean Lingué, another one was Jean Barrey, and I had other godparents too, so my mother told me.
Beaupère: Who baptised you?
Joan: It was Father Jean Minet, I believe.
Beaupère: Is he still alive?
Joan: I believe so.
Beaupère: How old are you?
Joan: Nineteen, I think.
Beaupère: Who taught you your prayers?
Joan: My mother, and nobody else. She taught me the Our Father, the Hail Mary and the Creed.[1]

From this exchange, we learn that Joan is a country girl, that countrywomen, unlike their menfolk, do not in general bother with surnames. Joan gives only the first names of her godmothers. She herself was never called Jeanne d'Arc in her lifetime, that name only appears later, in the documents of the Nullity hearings, where it appears as Darc. In the fifteenth century there was no apostrophe in non-noble names and names beginning with 'd' followed by a vowel usually merely signified a place of origin. Joan's family seems to have come originally from the small village of Arc-en-Barrois, south-west of Chaumont on the Marne, in Burgundian territory, although Joan's father, Jacques, possibly came from another village, Ceffonds, but that is uncertain.[2] Simeon Luce unearthed a number of Darcs (or d'Arcs) living in that area at the end of the fourteenth century. On the documents which she signed, Joan merely wrote *Jehanne* (had she learned to write in the course of her soldierly career, or was her hand guided?). More formally, she wanted to be known as Joan the Maid (*Jeanne la Pucelle*), which would soon give rise to ribald taunts from the English soldiers and the conviction that she had worked as a chambermaid in some low hostelry, the word *pucelle* meaning in French either a maiden or a servant girl, just as 'maid' does in English.

When asked her age, Joan says that she thinks she is nineteen, which means that she was born in 1412, or possibly in 1411. Ordinary people were less obsessed with the exact passage of time than we are today. Saints' days were celebrated, not birthdays. Even the most prestigious witnesses at the Nullity hearings in 1456 are generally registered as being 'about' a certain age, Dunois is 'about fifty-one', Raoul de Gaucourt 'about eighty-five', the noble Duke of Alençon 'about fifty'. We learn too that she comes from a hamlet on the marches of Lorraine, on the border between France and the Holy Roman Empire. Domrémy was named after Saint Rémy, the Archbishop of Rheims, who had baptised Clovis, the first Catholic king of the Franks at Christmas in the year 496, in the small church on the site of which Rheims cathedral would arise.[3] But when Joan talks about coming 'into France' she is referring to what we would now regard as the Île de France, the area around Paris. When, for example, she says later during her trial, 'My own wish would have been to go into France', she means that she wanted to besiege Paris rather than La Charité-sur-Loire.

There has been some debate over whether she was legally entitled to be called '*la bonne Lorraine*', as the French poet François Villon affectionately named her a generation after her death, or if she was even in fact a French subject. To put it as simply as possible, we can say that she came from the border with Lorraine. Colette Beaune tells us that she was born within the frontiers of France, since the Meuse was by tradition the border between France and the Holy Roman Empire. In Joan's day, the River Meuse, as it snaked its way along a wide green valley bordered on both sides by thickly wooded low hills, was a frontier between Lorraine, Champagne and the duchy of the Barrois (Bar). The d'Arc family was technically on the wrong side of the river for Lorraine. However, it has been established that Domrémy, with Joan's parents' house and the village church (both still standing today, the house restored in 1481, but not reconstructed, by a grand-nephew of Joan),[4] lay in the valley on the meadowlands belonging to the *seigneurie* of the town of Vaucouleurs, less than ten miles away. Vaucouleurs belonged directly to the French crown. It was, says Georges Duby, the only stronghold north of the Loire, together with Tournai, the Mont Saint Michel and Orleans, which still held out for the 'Armagnacs' and the Dauphin, derisively dubbed the 'King of Bourges'. As for Domrémy, the fact that the king exempted Domrémy and Greux from taxation in 1429, in acknowledgement of Joan's success at Orleans, is evidence enough that the two villages came under the Crown.[5]

The legal niceties are in any case of little importance, for Joan's sympathies and those of all in her village (except one!) were fervently on the side of the Dauphin, the future Charles VII. The village lay on a strategically and commercially important route. Wines were transported along it from the vineyards of Burgundy to Flanders, the great weaving centres of Flanders sent bales of cloth along it to Dijon and beyond. Soldiers, regular and irregular, captains, knights, squires, tradesmen, merchants, envoys on business and travellers of all kinds would have been constantly passing up and down. Those living on the route would have been well aware of what was going on in the kingdom.

The next village down-river from Domrémy-Greux was Maxey. It did not belong to the French crown, but belonged partly to the duchy of Bar and partly to Lorraine. Its inhabitants were strongly Burgundian. In the trial session of 24 February 1431, Joan remembers seeing the village boys of Domrémy coming home battered and bleeding after scraps with the boys of Maxey. However, the adults of the two villages seem to have lived in a state of truce with each other, there is no talk of any fisticuffs between them.

Joan had quite a number of godmothers and godfathers. It was not until the Council of Trent in the mid-sixteenth century that the Church limited the number to one of each. At the Nullity hearings in 1456, a number of witnesses claimed to be godparents themselves or named other godparents. No doubt the number is an indication of how respected the family was in the village. Among the godparents appearing in person were Jean Morel, Béatrice (a widow), Jeannette, widow of a certain Thiescelin, who had been a *clerc* in Neufchâteau (evidently a person of some standing and education),[6] another Jeanne, widow of a certain Thievenin le Royer, and Edette, widow of Jean Barré (Barrey). Agnès, Sibille and Jean Lingué do not appear, and must have died before 1431. No wonder Joan could not recite a full list of names.

Joan's mother, known as Isabelle Rommée, was born in nearby Vouthon. She had at least one sister, Aveline, also a brother Jean, who earned his living as a roofer in the village of Sermaize. The parish priest of Sermaize, Henry de Vouthon, was most likely another brother, but possibly a cousin. Jean de Vouthon had three sons and a daughter. His son Perrinet became a carpenter, while another son, Nicolas, became a Cistercian monk in the abbey of Cheminon, a couple of miles or so outside Sermaize, and served as chaplain to his cousin Joan throughout her campaigns. These clerical connections doubtless also gave the family a certain standing. The name Rommée signified that someone in the family (if not Isabelle herself) had made an important pilgrimage. Certainly there was a strong religious culture in the d'Arc household. Relations between the cousins were close. In 1476, Henry de Vouthon, the son of Joan's cousin Perrinet de Vouthon, could remember happy visits to Domrémy when he was a child and Joan was still at home, and equally happy times when the d'Arc family used to come and spend several days in his father's house in Sermaize.[7]

Joan was probably the youngest of the five children of the family. She had a sister, Catherine, and three brothers, Jacques (known as Jacquemin), Jean and Pierre. From 1425 onwards, Jacquemin was married and settled in Vouthon, perhaps on his mother's side there were a few acres of land for him to exploit there. Joan seems to have been particularly close to her 'big sister' Catherine. Perrin Drappier, formerly churchwarden of the church at Domrémy and in 1456 a witness at the Nullity hearings, remembers that Jeanne 'often went with her sister and some others to the chapel of Our Lady of Bermont', some two miles or so from Domrémy. Catherine grew up and married Jean Colin of Greux, who appeared as a witness in 1456 at the Nullity hearings. Sadly, she died young, probably not all that long before Joan's departure in 1429, and when Joan's aunt Aveline became pregnant, Joan asked her to call her baby, if it was a girl, Catherine, 'pour la souvenance de feue Catherine' (in memory of Catherine). It was a close family.

The children were lovingly but strictly brought up. They were taught good manners and behaviour. When Joan arrived at Chinon to see Charles VII, the courtiers were astonished at the simplicity and correctness with which she conducted herself.

We know quite a lot about Joan's childhood. Joan's family were certainly among the village '*notables*'. Her father had been appointed *doyen*, an office third in line after that of the local mayor and his deputy (the *échevin*), with various administrative responsibilities concerning the welfare of the community, such as organising the watch (each family in turn supplied a member for watch duty, either by day or by night), convoking the assemblies of local dignitaries and tax collection. In 1427 he was the person chosen by the village to represent its interests in an important legal case heard before the captain of Vaucouleurs, none other than Robert de Baudricourt, whom Joan will persuade her relative, Durand Laxart, to take her to see in 1429.[8] The family home was a solid stone house with an upper story, situated in a choice central position beside the church, a dwelling well above the standard of the average village house.

Her parents seem to have been reasonably comfortable peasant farmers or *laboureurs*, a *laboureur* being not a ploughman (*un charron*) or what we might call a labourer, but someone who owned his own house and some acres of land, as well as animals, rather like a crofter in Scotland.[9] There was, as historians such as Georges Duby and Jacques Heer have shown, a hierarchy in the world of the peasantry and the Darc or d'Arc family were at the upper end of it. In 1420, Joan's father and five other villagers were able also to obtain a nine-year lease on the abandoned Château de l'Île and the land pertaining to it.[10] As a *laboureur*, her father would cultivate his land himself, with his family or with the help of hired farmhands. Joan, as the daughter of parents well-considered in the community, was certainly not a cowherd or shepherd girl. Those were not considered to be occupations for any properly brought-up young person, since they could give rise to unseemly encounters with members of the opposite sex in the solitude of the countryside. Joan strongly rejected the implied suggestion that such had been her early life.

The fact is that there were contrary images of the shepherdess in the fifteenth century. One was the earthy view fixed in the minds of the country folk, another was begotten by pastoral Biblical symbolism: the shepherds chosen by God in the Old Testament to lead His people, the Good Shepherd image of Christ in the New Testament, protector of the flocks against the wolves, defender of the poor of this world.[11] The long mystery play, *Mystère du Siège d'Orléans*, composed in verse, with a cast of a hundred and sixty characters, and revised several times in the course of the fifteenth century (the oldest section dating probably back to around 1430), depicts Joan as a poor shepherdess guarding her flocks, to whom God sends the Archangel Michael.

Then there were the innocent and dainty shepherdesses of the imagination of poets and aristocrats, an imagery inspired by the pastoral poetry of antiquity, reflected from the fourteenth century onwards in the poetry of Petrarch and the early Renaissance in Italy.[12] In that literature, all country girls were 'little shepherdesses', and this is how Joan's noble comrades and the poets of the period described her. Guillaume de Ricarville, the lord of Ricarville, for example, giving testimony on 8 March 1456, calls her a 'little shepherd girl' (*une bergerette*). Raoul de Gaucourt, testifying on 25 February 1456, says that he was present when she was granted her first audience with Charles VII at Chinon, and that she introduced herself 'with great simplicity and humility, like a poor little shepherdess'. She herself would have rejected this prettified image as forcefully as she did the demeaning one, finding it equally condescending.

The details of Joan's early life were of course of great importance. If she was in any way disreputable, her claim to a divine mission was clearly bogus. Her trial in 1431 opens with questions concerning her background.

Session of 22 February 1431, Beaupère takes over the interrogation:

Beaupère: Did you learn any skill in your youth?
Joan: Yes. I learned to sew sheets and to spin. I can hold my own with any woman in Rouen for sewing and spinning.

After this innocent boast, she took care to add: 'When I was at home, I did housework. I didn't go to the fields with the sheep and other animals.' It would seem that some insidious question about being in the fields with the animals must have prompted this reply. She was evidently aware of the implications. She was asked again two days later (24 February) about herding animals. She answered as follows:

I have already replied to that. When I was a bit older and had reached the age of understanding, I didn't usually keep the animals, but I helped to take them to the meadows and to a château called the Château de l'Île, for fear of the soldiers. I don't remember if I kept them when I was very young or not.

From this we may take it that she had occasionally been asked to take her family's turn at looking after the animals belonging to the villagers, which were guarded communally. Each villager had grazing rights for a certain number of animals and each family took it in turn to keep watch over the whole group, just as a member of each family in turn did guard duty in the church tower. If by 'the age of understanding' Joan means seven years of age (which the Church defines as the age of reason), she was probably required as a small child to keep an eye only on the sheep, one would hardly ask a young child to look after bigger animals. But just possibly she means that she didn't usually look after the animals after she had her visions, at the age of twelve or thirteen. In any case her very strict parents would no doubt have considered it improper to send a girl of that age out alone into the fields.

We learn more about her early years from the records of the 1456 revision (Nullity) trial, when twenty-two witnesses who had known Joan personally from her childhood onwards were among those called to testify. Nearly all of them were heard in Domrémy on 28, 29 and 30 January of that year. Her cousin by marriage, Durand Laxart[13] was heard in Vaucouleurs on 31 January, as was Michel Lebuin who had been one of her childhood friends. Another childhood friend, Jean Jaquard, who lived in Greux, was heard for some reason in Toul. Those who had played with her as children, their elders, the friends and neighbours of her parents, all remember her as a thoughtful, helpful and obedient child and young girl. Their testimony confirms what she had said about herself and her family. Each of these witnesses was asked to answer a list of twelve questions concerning her parentage, the character of her parents, her upbringing, her practice of her religion and her behaviour from the age of seven until her departure from Domrémy.

The first of the witnesses from Domrémy and its neighbourhood was called on Wednesday, 28 January 1456. This was Jean Morel (or Moreau) from the village of Greux, now aged 'about seventy', one of Joan's godparents, and like Joan's father, a *laboureur*, a peasant farmer. He was also, like one of the other witnesses, Perrin Drappier, one of the four *notables* of his village. This is his deposition:

> Jeannette's parents were peasant farmers in Domrémy, where they lived all their married lives. I knew them and saw them to be good and faithful Catholics, good, well-respected farming folk, leading decent lives. I spoke with them on a number of occasions. I was one of Jeannette's godparents [...]. In her childhood, as I see it, she was properly brought up in faith and morals and nearly everyone in the village loved her. Like the other young girls, she knew her Creed, the Our Father and the Hail Mary. She was well behaved, being like any young girl whose parents are not very rich. Until she left home, she helped with the plough and sometimes kept watch over the animals in the fields. She did the work that women do, spinning and all the rest.

The other witnesses testified similarly. The next day her godmother Beatrice, now 'aged about eighty' and widowed, was called, and declared:

> When the village of Domrémy was destroyed by fire,[14] Jeannette used to go every feast day to hear Mass in Greux [...] It seems to me that there was none better than her in our two villages. She did certain tasks in her father's house, sometimes she spun hemp or wool, or helped with the plough or the harvest when the time came round, and sometimes she used to keep the animals or the village's flock of sheep, when it was her father's turn to look after them.

Yet another godmother gave evidence on the same day. This was Jeannette, 'aged about seventy' and married to Thévenin, who was also a witness:

> I saw that Jeannette was a good, simple country girl, adequately instructed in the faith, like the other girls. [...] For the love of God, she often gave alms to the poor. I believe she used to go often and piously to church and to confession, for she was a good girl.

A *simple girl*, the terms nearly all the witnesses used to describe Joan, an unassuming, country girl. Like Beatrice and other witnesses, Jeannette recalls Joan spinning or helping her father. Perrin Drappier, who had been churchwarden in the Domrémy church when Joan was a girl (he is now 'about sixty'):

Joan was always a good girl, chaste, simple, reserved, never taking the name of God or the saints in vain and fearing God. She used to come frequently to the church and to confession. I know what I'm talking about, because at the time I was churchwarden in the Domrémy church and I often saw Joan coming to the church for Mass and complines. If I neglected to ring the church bell for complines, she would scold me, saying it was wrong of me, and she promised to bring me little cakes as long as I took care to ring for complines. [...] She often went with her sister and some others to the chapel of Our Lady at Bermont, and she gave a lot of alms.

Joan's visits to the chapel at Bermont are mentioned by a number of witnesses. Her dislike of profanity would be evident in her dealings with her soldiers. Bernard Shaw makes affectionate fun of that in his play. Another godmother, Jeannette, who says that Joan was named after her, confirms Perrin's comment. 'Joan never used swear words,' she remarked. 'She just said, *Par mon martin!*'[15] This Jeannette was the widow of the Thiescelin who had pursued the estimable calling of *clerc* in Neufchâteau. They would have been a respectable, reasonably well-to-do couple, and for them, Joan's parents were relatively poor folk, 'not very rich'. One of their grandsons would be granted letters of nobility and a coat of arms before the end of the century.[16]

The most touching of the depositions are those given by Joan's childhood friends, Hauviette and Mengette. Hauviette is now 'about forty-five',[17] married to another witness, Gérard de Syonne, and still living in Domrémy. She was interviewed at Domrémy on Friday, 30 January 1456. We can hear her first:

I knew Jeannette when I was a child. Her parents were Jacques d'Arc and Zabillette (Isabelle). They were honest farmers and good Catholics, in good standing. I know all that, because I was often with Jeannette and I used to sleep over in her father's house, because we were friends. I can't remember about her godparents, I only knew what people said, for Jeannette was older than me, by about three or four years, so they said [...] She was good, simple and kind. She went often to the church and to holy places, of her own accord. She was embarrassed when people told her she was too devout. The parish priest at the time said she often came to confession. She did the tasks that other girls do, housework, spinning, sometimes she looked after her father's animals. That is all I know.

Asked about Joan's departure from Domrémy, Hauviette said simply:

I didn't know she was going to go and I wept a lot when I heard it, for I loved her for her goodness. She was my friend.

Mengette was interviewed on the same day as Hauviette. Her testimony is in substance the same as Hauviette's, adding one or two details:

> Our house was beside Joan's father's. I knew her well and was often in her company and we did household tasks together during the day and in the evening. [...] She went gladly and often to church, she gave alms from what her father provided, She was so good, simple and devout, that I and the other girls used to tell her she was too pious. She worked with a will and busied herself with a lot of tasks. She spun, of course, she did housework, she helped with the harvest. Sometimes she would spin while watching the animals, when her family's turn came round. She went of her own accord to confession, I often saw her kneeling in front of the parish priest of our village.

If she could spin while keeping an eye on the animals, they must have been grazing on common land somewhere nearby, not way out in the fields. We remember that she declared that she 'didn't *go to the fields* with the sheep and other animals'. Was she sitting at her door, with a distaff and spindle?

Another witness from Domrémy, heard on Thursday, 29 January, Jacquier de Saint-Amant, also a *laboureur*, describes Joan as follows:

> Jeannette was a good girl, fearing God and going willingly to church. Every day she was busy with tasks about the house. Sometimes I saw her in the evening in my house, spinning with my daughter. I saw no harm in her. She looked after the flock when it was her turn and went to confession at Easter.

An interesting witness is Gérardin d'Épinal, some fifteen or sixteen years older than Joan. Gérardin was the only pro-Burgundian inhabitant in Joan's village, to which he had come, he says, when he was eighteen. One may wonder for what compelling reason a Burgundian came to settle in such a staunchly pro-French village, but he evidently managed to live there on reasonable terms with his neighbours, despite his political views. He even married one of them, so perhaps he had moved there for that reason. His testimony about Joan's upbringing and daily life is similar to that of the other witnesses. At her trial, Joan declared provocatively, 'I only knew one Burgundian, and I wouldn't have minded if they'd chopped his head off, God willing, of course.' As the French writer and polemicist Georges Bernanos remarked, 'Poor, poor Jeannie! she said it impishly to see the look on all those podgy faces!.'. She can't have felt so very bloodthirsty regarding Gérardin, for he was the only person to whom she gave a clue as to her intention before she left, an incident he recalls in his testimony:

> I don't know anything about her departure from the village, except that, when she was about to go, she said to me, 'Compère, if you weren't a Burgundian, there's something I'd tell you.' I thought she was talking about some lad she intended to marry. I saw her again at Châlons, with four other people from our village, and she said she wasn't afraid of anything except treason.

The teasing and friendly way Joan speaks to Gérardin is typical. She may have been pious, but she was no long-faced 'holy Joan'. That she calls Gérardin '*compère*' may surprise us, until we see from his wife's evidence that Joan was in fact the godmother of their child! *Compère* and *commère* were how godparents and parents of a child addressed each other. Joan's underlying regard for Gérardin is evident, in spite of her exasperation with his politics.

Gérardin wasn't the only person whom Joan teased with a hint about the future. Michel Lebuin, a farmer from Domrémy, interrogated at Vaucouleurs on Saturday, 31 January 1456, gave this piece of information:

> I don't know anything about her departure, except that once, on the eve of the feast of Saint John the Baptist, Joan told me that there was a girl, between Coussey and Vaucouleurs, who would have the King of France crowned, and indeed within the year the king was crowned at Rheims.

Michel describes Joan as 'unassuming and reserved', but whatever her reserve, she obviously could not resist the innocent delight of mystifying her friends a little. Michel was about the same age as Joan, and remembers going with her on pilgrimage to the chapel of Our Lady at Bermont, as Joan did, 'nearly every Saturday, with her sister'. So no doubt she was close to her sister, whose death must have been a great sorrow in Joan's young life.

As to Gérardin, perhaps he had changed his political outlook after Joan left, since he hastened later to see her at Châlons with several of his neighbours. Châlons was one of the towns taken (without bloodshed) after the relief of Orleans, on Joan's way to Rheims. What a fever of wonder, excitement and admiration must have swept over them all back home in Domrémy, when the news of the triumph at Orleans reached them! Gérardin and his four enterprising neighbours set out all agog, to look with astonished eyes at this quiet and unassuming village girl so miraculously transformed and now leading the king to his coronation. One of the neighbours was Jean Morel whom we have already met above. When he caught up with her in Châlons, she made him a present of a red robe which she had worn. She was of course wearing male clothing by then, but if it fitted him, he can't have been a very tall man. Charles VII entered the town on 14 July, 1429, with Joan riding beside him. They were welcomed by a great number of citizens led by the bishop of the place. The next day, they set out for Rheims, where Charles would be crowned in the cathedral.

Gérardin's wife, Isabellette (or, less formally, Zabillette), some ten years younger than her husband, was heard on the same day as her husband, 30 January 1456. Her testimony is in accord with that of the other witnesses, and she adds some interesting details:

> When I was young, I knew Jeannette's's parents and Jeannette herself while she was living at home [...] She gave alms generously, brought the poor into her house and gave them her bed to sleep in, while she herself slept in the kitchen. She wasn't to be seen hanging about the road, instead she was in the church, saying her prayers. She didn't join in the dancing, which often gave rise to annoyance among certain of the young people and others [...] She went frequently and of her own accord to confession, as I saw for myself, because she was a godmother to my son Nicolas.

One wonders what the reaction of Joan's parents was to her bringing beggars (or perhaps stray travellers) into the house and giving them her bed to sleep in. They must have been equally charitable, since apparently they did not make any objection.

Another witness heard on 29 January 1456 was Jean Colin, the son of Jean Colin of Greux (to distinguish him from Messire Jean Colin, canon and parish priest of Domrémy at the time). He, like Jean Morel, was one of the four *notables* of Greux. He also was a *laboureur*, aged 'about fifty', therefore, like Isabellette, some five or six years older than Joan. His testimony, like all the others, affirms the good character of Joan and her parents. He remembers how he and the other youngsters made fun of her because she was too pious, and he adds the tribute paid to her by the then parish priest:

> I heard Father Guillaume Front, parish priest of Domrémy, say that Joan was a good Catholic, he had never seen better, indeed there wasn't a better in his parish.

The last of the witnesses able to recall Joan's childhood was Jean Jaquard from Greux, who testified in Toul on 11 February 1456. Jean was roughly the same age as Joan, and his testimony is consonant with that of all the others who had known her before she left Domrémy:

> I saw her several times at Domrémy and in the fields. She was very gentle and good, chaste and modest [...] I never heard anything bad about her. Everyone thought she was a good and pious girl.

Clearly Jean was not a close friend, his opinion of Joan is based on what people said about her and glimpses of her as she went about her daily life.

What he says is interesting because it illustrates the general view of Joan as she was growing up.

Whatever the extent of her shepherding duties, Joan herself portrayed the pastoral side of life in Domrémy in idyllic terms during the course of the 1431 trial in Rouen. The judges prompted this with questions aimed at uncovering practices of superstition or sorcery which would constitute damning evidence. On Saturday, 24 February 1431, Beaupère asked her to tell the court about the remarkable tree near her village. Here is Joan's answer:

> Quite near the village of Domrémy there is a tree called the Ladies' Tree (l'Arbre des Dames). Other people call it the Fairy Tree and near it there is a spring. I've heard tell that people suffering from a fever come to drink at the spring and to take away water to restore them to health. I've seen that myself, but I don't know whether it cures them or not. I've heard also that sick people, when they are able to get up, enjoy outings to the tree. It's a big tree, a beech, and it's called the May Tree (le Beau Mai). It used to belong to Sir Pierre de Bourlemont.

The tree was a weeping beech, according to the historian Pierre Tisset. It was still standing when the aged Montaigne saw it in 1580. The theologian Edmond Richer, luminary of the Sorbonne, who died in 1631, also describes it in his *Histoire de la Pucelle d'Orléans* and claims it is over three hundred years old.

In response to more questioning, Joan gave a longer description of life in the village:

> Sometimes I used to go for walks with other girls, near the tree. We used to make garlands of flowers for the picture of Our Lady of Domrémy. I heard old people, but not anyone belonging to my family, say that the Fairy Ladies lived there. I heard a lady called Jeanne, the wife of the mayor of the village, who was my godmother, say that she had seen the Fairy Ladies, but I don't know if that was true or not.
> Beaupère: Did you ever see the fairies?
> Joan: I never saw a fairy, as far as I can tell, neither at the tree nor anywhere else.

Joan is obviously careful to stress that she and her family had no superstitious belief about fairies, keeping a fairly sceptical and open mind on the subject. On 17 March, in one of the last interrogations, she would be asked whether or not she had believed that the fairies were evil spirits, to which she replied dismissively that she knew nothing about the matter. In answer to another question on 24 February, she stated:

> I have seen girls putting garlands on the branches of the tree, and sometimes I put some on the tree with the other girls. Sometimes they

took them away and sometimes they left them there. When I realised that I had to go into France (i.e. after the age of thirteen or so, when she heard the Voices), I didn't take part very much in their pastimes, in fact as little as possible.

Beaupère: Did you dance around the tree?

Joan: I don't know whether I danced near the tree after I reached the use of reason, I may well have danced there sometimes with the children and I sang there more than I danced.

Dancing round fairy trees, claiming to have seen or had commerce with supernatural beings such as fairies, was of course to give rise to suspicions of witchcraft and the practice of sorcery. The questioning next turned to the other suspect place in the village, the ancient oak wood, the *Bois chenu*. Joan knew where the interrogation was heading and she made a fairly lengthy statement about the wood, which, she said she could see from her father's house, less than half a league away (something over a mile). She was asked if she had ever heard that there were fairies there:

Joan: I don't know, and I've never heard that there are any fairies there. But my brother has told me that people were saying in our area that I had got my instructions at the Fairy Tree. That is not true. I told him it was absolutely untrue.

Beaupère: Weren't you asked about the wood when you came to see your king?

Joan: When I came to see the king, some people asked me if there wasn't a wood called the Bois Chenu where I came from, because there were prophecies saying that a maid would come from that neighborhood who would do wonderful things. But I didn't believe all that.

In fact, such stories seem to have been rife at the time. At the Nullity hearings of 31 January 1456, Durand Laxart says that Joan quoted a prophecy to persuade him, in spite of his misgivings, to take her to see Robert de Baudricourt: 'Hasn't it been said long ago that France would be ruined by a woman and restored by a maid?' (The woman who had ruined France was of course widely held to be Queen Isabeau). As to the Fairy Tree, it was also known as the Ladies' Tree, because in popular parlance the *Fairies* were also called the *Ladies*. It was a magnificent tree: 'As beautiful as a lily! Its foliage and branches reach all around it down to the ground!' said Gérardin d'Épinal, giving his testimony in 1456. Not only the judges and assessors at Joan's trial in 1431, but also those of the Nullity hearings in 1456, were especially anxious to know exactly what went on around the tree, in case there had been superstitious and heretical practices, sorcery, orgies or other disorders. Here are some of the depositions made by witnesses at the appeal, beginning with that of Perrin Drappier, taken on Thursday, 29 January 1456:

The tree in question was commonly called the Ladies' Tree. I have seen a lady of the village, the wife of Sir Pierre de Bourlemont, together with his mother, going for walks sometimes beneath it, taking with them the young ladies of their household and girls from the village. They used to bring along bread and wine and eggs. In the spring and on Laetare Sunday,[18] which we call Fountains Sunday, it is the custom that the boys and girls of the village go to the tree and the fountains. They bring little breadrolls to eat under the tree and they amuse themselves singing and dancing. When Joan was very young, she used to go too, sometimes, with the village girls and they played and danced near the tree and the Fontaine des Groseilliers.[19]

The next day it was the turn of Joan's childhood friend, Hauviette, to give very similar evidence:

We've always called that tree the Fairy Tree. People say that in the olden days, the ladies called Fairies used to come there, but I've never heard that anyone ever saw them. The girls and boys of Domrémy are in the habit of visiting the tree and the Fontaine des Groseilliers on Laetare Sunday, which we call Fountains Sunday. They bring breadrolls with them. I myself used to go with my friend Joan and the others on Fountains Sunday. We went for walks and played and picnicked. I saw that some people brought nuts too.

That loquacious old lady, Joan's godmother, Béatrice d'Estellin, adds some picturesque details:

I've been for walks to that tree myself, with the lords and ladies of Domrémy, for it is a magnificent tree. It's beside the main road that goes to Neufchâteau. I heard people say that in the olden days the fairy ladies gathered there, but they don't come any more, because of their sins. Every year on Laetare Sunday, or as we say, Fountains Sunday, and in the spring too, the boys and girls of Domrémy and Jeannette along with them, every year, as I say, they sing and dance around the tree, and they picnic, then they go home by the Fontaine des Groseilliers and drink from it. And when the parish priest carries the crucifix through the fields on the eve of the Ascension, he walks under the tree too, and chants the Gospel, and then he goes to the Fontaine de Groseilliers and the other fountains and chants the Gospel. That's all I know about it.

The other witnesses from Domrémy all paint the same picture. Several insist that Joan never went to the tree on her own, but always in the company of the other children. Jacquier de Saint-Amance and Perrin Drappier are careful to sress that she was young (*in sua juventute*) when she took part in these rejoicings.

Joan's godmother Jeannette (Thiescelin's widow), whom we have heard already, recounts a little tale which may shed some light on the legend of the 'Fairy Tree':

> The tree in question is called the Fairy Tree because, in the olden days, they say a certain knight, Sir Pierre Granier, Lord of Bourlemont, used to meet a lady under the tree and they conversed together. She was called Fay (Fairy). That was in a book somebody read out to me.
>
> Perhaps the original Fairy was a lady of flesh and blood and perhaps Sir Pierre did more than talk to her and perhaps altogether the tree was a trysting place for more than the Lord of Bourlement … .

Domrémy was in the middle of a region devastated by pillaging freebooters, mercenaries and soldiery in the pay of one side or the other. Marina Warner says that it was more torn asunder by war than anywhere else in France except Paris and the Seine basin. It was devastated by the marauding troops of Robert de Saarbruck, on the Burgundian side and by the famous La Hire on the other side, rampaging through the pro-Burgundian villages of Champagne during the 1420s. The young husband of Joan's cousin Mengette, daughter of her uncle Jean de Vouthon, was killed during the fighting against the Burgundians laying siege to Sermaize in 1423. Joan was then about eleven and would have felt the grief of her cousin deeply, for the two families were close.

Other historians present a more soothing picture of Domrémy itself. The village was something of a haven in the midst of this havoc. It continued to produce its own wine and cereals, it had grazing for its sheep and cattle, whose products of milk, butter and wool provided the main source of income for the peasantry. The wooded hills provided fuel for the winter. There were fish in the river, honey from the beehives, pigs in the pigsties, hens and ducks and geese.

The dark shadow hanging over this idyll was the ever-present apprehension of a raid by mercenaries and brigands, not the English, in this part of the world, but bands of mercenaries of the feuding dukes of Lorraine and of Bar, or in the pay of the dreaded Robert de Saarbruck, Lord of Commercy (the *Damoiseau*) among others. The Damoiseau fought for himself or for anyone who would make it worth his while. Slaughter and arson, destruction of property and crops, the holding to ransom of any inhabitants worth the effort, harvests ruined, terrorised inhabitants put to flight, there was no end to the miseries of the peasantry. At the end of 1423, the inhabitants of Domrémy and Greux felt it necessary to agree to pay yearly protection money to Robert de Saarbruck. For Domrémy, the act was signed by the mayor, the échevin, and the *doyen*, Jacques d'Arc.[20] Perrin Drappier, who testified at the Nullity hearings of 1456, was also a signatory for Domrémy. One who signed for Greux and who later gave evidence in 1456 was Jean Morel, Joan's godfather. The mayor of Greux,

Jean Colin, whose son (also Jean Colin) had married Joan's elder sister Catherine, was another signatory. Domrémy was far from the only village to have to pay this type of forced tribute to a local garrison and of course they were then not safe from reprisal raids from the other side.

It was as a place of refuge against such incursions and cattle-rustling that Joan's father and a small group of friends had acquired, as noted earlier, a lease on the deserted castle and its surroundings on the island embraced by the two arms of the Meuse, which Joan refers to as the *Château de l'Île*.

We hear of a couple of such incidents which befell the villages of Domrémy and Greux. The first occurred when Joan was about thirteen. The historian Siméon Luce, quoting from a legal document of 1455 which refers to the event as taking place thirty years earlier, dates the episode to July 1425. A Burgundian band of men-at-arms in the service of a certain Henry d'Orly, 'a man of ill-repute, having at the time a number of scoundrels under him, causing untold misery, murders and robberies throughout the locality',[21] descended on the two villages and drove off all the cattle belonging to the inhabitants. We can well understand the terror of the villagers at the approach of a band of such soldiery and their desolation at the loss of their animals, which would have left them facing extreme hardship and ruin. Happily for them, on that occasion the cattle were recovered by the quite audacious action of a small posse of men in the service of the Count of Vaudemont, in response to the appeal of his cousin, the Dame d'Ogéviller, a member of the Bourlemont family, who had inherited the position of lord of the manor of the two villages.

The other episode was similar. In July, 1428, when Joan would have been sixteen, Antoine de Vergy, Bedford's governor for Champagne, laid siege to the town of Vaucouleurs, which had held out in stubborn and lonely fidelity to the Dauphin for as long as anyone could remember. The villages nearby feared the worst and this time Joan and her family, along with the other inhabitants of Domrémy, had to take refuge in the neighbouring town of Neufchâteau, the market town for Domrémy, on the borders of Lorraine, Champagne and Bar. The town was strongly loyal to the Dauphin. The d'Arc family were not strangers to Neufchâteau. Relations between Domrémy/Greux and the town were close. Several of Joan's godparents came from Neufchâteau, all of them respectable members of the bourgeoisie of the town. The parish priest of Domrémy, Guillaume Front (or *Frontey*), who had such a good opinion of Joan, according to the testimony of Jean Colin of Greux, was also a native of Neufchâteau. The family must have had good advice as to suitable lodgings and they took refuge in a hostelry belonging to a certain good lady called La Rousse, described by a witness at the Nullity hearings, Gérard Guillemette, as 'a decent woman' and by another witness, Husson Lemaistre, as 'a virtuous woman'. Joan was plenty old enough to help the hostess with some of the housework and she did so. When it was safe to return, the villagers from Domrémy, Joan and her family among them, went back to their homes.

Such was the life of Joan as a young girl. But at the age or thirteen or so, something very powerful and mysterious had happened to her. She did not talk to anyone in Domrémy about it, nor did she describe it later to her companions-in-arms, who knew only that she was convinced that she had a mission from God to lead them. She was asked in the second session of her trial at Rouen, on Thursday, 22 February 1431, to describe what had happened:

> When I was about thirteen, I heard a voice coming from God to help me to lead a good life. That was the first time and I was very afraid. The Voice came at about midday, in the summer, in my father's garden.

At this point, the interrogator Beaupère must have asked her if she had been fasting the previous day. No doubt he suspected, like any modern doctor or psychiatrist, that it was all an adolescent's illusion, probably brought on by the lack of a good dinner. Joan declared:

> I hadn't been fasting the day before.[22] I heard the Voice on my right, towards the church. I rarely hear it without a light. The light is on the same side as the Voice, usually there is a great light. When I came into France, I often heard the Voice.
> Beaupère: How could you see the light if it was on your right?

Joan ignored this rather idiotic question and continued:

> If I was in a wood, I could hear the Voices very well. It appeared to me that the Voice was an honourable Voice and I believe that it was sent from God. When I had heard it three times, I realised that it was the voice of an angel.

Beaupère then asked her: 'What did this Voice teach you for the salvation of your soul?' Obviously, if the Voice taught her to transgress faith or morals it could not come from God! Joan answered:

> It taught me to behave well, to go often to church, and that I had to go into France […]. It told me that two or three times a week.

It was after these overwhelming experiences that, at the age of thirteen, Joan made a vow of chastity. Such an undertaking was the traditional way of consecrating oneself totally to the service of the Divinity, as recommended by Saint Paul. Young as she was, she was not ignorant of the nature of the commitment she was making, for she took care to stipulate that it was only for 'as long as it should please God'. She felt that she did not have the vocation of a nun and she did not wish to preclude the possibility of marrying at some future date.

It was in the fourth session of her trial, on Tuesday, 27 February, 1431, that Joan named the saints who she believed had appeared to her:

> Beaupère: Was it the voice of an angel which spoke to you, or was it that of a saint or was it God Himself directly speaking to you?
> Joan: The Voice was that of Saint Catherine and Saint Margaret.
> Beaupère: What did they look like?
> Joan: They were crowned with beautiful crowns, set with precious stones. Our Lord gives me leave to tell you that much.
> Beaupère: How do you recognise them from each other?
> Joan: I know them by the salutation they give me. It is seven years since I took them for my spiritual guides and I recognise them because they name themselves.

She refused to answer various questions concerning the appearance, age and clothing of the apparitions. No doubt the experience defied description, perhaps also she was aware of the hidden intent of entrapment underlying the apparent silliness of the questions, for if her answers could give rise to suspicions of erotic or prurient imaginings she would be damned indeed. She went on however to add that Saint Michael also appeared to her:

> Beaupère: Which of these apparitions was the first to appear?
> Joan: Saint Michael was the first.
> Beaupère: Is it a long time ago that you heard the voice of Saint Michael for the first time?
> Joan: I'm not talking about the voice of Saint Michael, but of the great comfort I received.

Shortly after, she was again asked which vision came first:

> Joan: It was Saint Michael. I saw him with my own eyes and he was not alone, but accompanied by the angels of Heaven. I came into France soley at God's command.
> Beaupère: Did you see Saint Michael and the angels bodily and truly?
> Joan: I saw them with my eyes as clearly as I see you and when they left me I wept and could have wished they would take me with them.

Later in the interrogation a new question about the visions was put to her:

> Beaupère: Is there a lot of light when the Voice comes to you?
> Joan: There is a great deal of light on all sides, as is fitting. The light is not all for you alone, you know!

Joan can't resist a quip, until the relentless aggression of the trial and the brutal conditions in her prison in Rouen finally wore her down.

Two days later, on 1 March, the attack was renewed. She was asked if she saw the figures always in the same dress and how she could tell whether the apparition was a male or female figure:

> Joan: I know very well, I recognise them by their voices, they have revealed it to me. I know nothing except by revelation and God's command.

The questioning went on: do the apparitions have long, heavy hair? Does she see their arms or other limbs? Joan could only say that she saw the faces, she can describe nothing else.

Why these three saints – Michael, Catherine and Margaret? What did Joan know about them before the visions? Obviously the sudden arrival of saints she had never heard of would not have made any sense to her.

First of all, Saint Michael the Archangel, leader of the Heavenly Host and vanquisher of Satan. Everyone knew about him! He had followed Saint Denis as the patron of the Valois royal house. Saint Denis was the first bishop of Paris, martyred in Diocletian's persecutions of Christians around AD 250. The great abbey dedicated to him outside Paris had been founded in the eighth century. It was the burial place of French kings and the place of coronation of French queens. The *oriflamme*, the banner of the French kings, was kept there. Later the Dauphin would occasionally call Joan, somewhat affectionately, his 'oriflamme'.[23] When, in 1419. the royal abbey fell into the hands of the English, the Dauphin, despairing perhaps of Saint Denis's ability to help, took the archangel Michael officially as his patron saint and had his image painted on the royal standards. The cult of Saint Michael was in any case extremely popular throughout France, Charles had believed that he was under the special protection of the archangel since that day in La Rochelle in October 1422 when the floor had collapsed in the Hôtel de l'Évêque with disastrous results, while he himself had been almost miraculously spared. The following April he had ordered that a Mass should be said in thanksgiving every year in the church of the Mont Saint Michel. The rock's stubborn resistance and the breaking of the Earl of Suffolk's ten-month siege in 1425, thanks largely to the audacity of the mariners of Saint Malo, filled the supporters of the French cause with joy and admiration. Moreover, the Archangel Saint Michael was a powerful counterpart to England's Saint George, both of them victors over the powers of darkness in the symbolic form of the dragon. The Archangel, by the very fact of his angelic nature, was of course the greater and mightier.

Saint Catherine can be identified with Catherine of Alexandria, a celebrated virgin martyr of the fourth century, although her story is so overlaid with legends of the miraculous that we cannot be sure of anything about her. She is said to have been a brilliantly intelligent and beautiful young woman who converted to Christianity. Born into a noble family, she took it upon herself to remonstrate with the Roman emperor Maxentius who was violently persecuting the Christians. Meaning to confound her views and ween her away from Christianity, the Emperor sent the best of his philosophers and scholars to debate with her, but instead several were converted by her passionate and intellectually convincing arguments. They were as a result executed, as was Catherine herself. She was hugely popular in the Middle Ages, innumerable churches were dedicated to her both in France and in England, as well as elsewhere. The church in the neighbouring Burgundian village of Maxey was one of them. Young maidens were under her special protection, as were female students (some did exist in the Middle Ages!). Together with Saint Margaret of Antioch, another fourth century virgin martyr, equally bathed in legends, she was regarded as one of the 'fourteen helpers', the fourteen most powerful intercessors in Heaven. Saint Margaret resisted the lustful pursuit of the Roman prefect Olibrius who had caught sight of her watching over her flocks (hence the shepherdess theme) until finally he became so frustrated that he had her beheaded during Diocletian's persecution of the Christians. Both saints, Catherine and Margaret, were virgin martyrs.

Joan would have been well acquainted with the stories of the two saints and she would have seen statues or paintings of them in church. Many churches in France were dedicated to one or other of the two.

In the afternoon session of 17 March, which like all the later sessions took place in her prison, she was interrogated by Jean de la Fontaine, deputed as examiner by Bishop Cauchon, with only the vice-inquisitor Lemaître and six of the assessors present. She was questioned as follows about the apparitions:

La Fontaine: Did you give them garlands of flowers?
Joan: On several occasions I gave garlands in their honour to their images or representations in churches, but I don't remember ever giving any to them when they appeared to me.

The point of all these questions is to ascertain whether Joan has been guilty of idolatry, worshipping apparitions or illusions dangerous to the orthodoxy of the Church. Her answers do not admit of such an acusation.

She was very young at the time of these first visions, and the Voice does not tell her to go 'into France' immediately. Still a mere child, she kept all these overwhelming experiences, whatever they were, hidden within herself, speaking to no-one about them, neither father nor mother nor brother, neither friend nor parish priest. Did they wonder what was making her more reserved, more devout? Her parents must have asked themselves anxiously what was going on in their daughter's mind.

On Monday, 12 March, she was asked if she had not committed a sin of disobedience in leaving home without her parents' permission. She replied that she had done so by God's command:

> Joan: Since God commanded it, I had to do it. Since it was God's command, I would have gone even if I had had a hundred fathers and mothers, even if I had been a king's daughter.
> La Fontaine: Did you ask your Voices if you should tell your parents that you were going?
> Joan: The Voices didn't mind if I told them, apart from the difficulty I would have had as a result. As for me, I wouldn't have told them for anything. It was left up to me.

In the afternoon of the same day, La Fontaine asked her about the dreams the examiners had been told that her father had had before she left home. She gave a detailed answer:

> When I was still at home, my mother told me several times that my father had dreamt that I would go away with the soldiers. My father and mother kept a very close watch on me and were very strict. I obeyed them in everything, except for the lawsuit about marriage that I had in Toul. I heard my mother saying that my father said to my brothers, 'If I thought that my fears about my daughter would come true, I'd want you to drown her, and if you wouldn't, I'd do it myself.' My father and mother nearly went out of their minds when I left to go to Vaucouleurs.
> La Fontaine: Did your father have these thoughts or dreams after you had your visions?
> Joan: Yes, more than two years later.

From this answer, it is clear that Joan's father must have got wind of her intention from somewhere. Maybe Joan wasn't quite so good at keeping her experiences secret as she thought. The lonely burden of such heavy secrets must have been very hard to bear. She had dropped mysterious hints to both Gérardin d'Épinal and Michel Lebuin, as we have seen. Did Jacques d'Arc really make this threat, or was Joan's mother trying to frighten her into obedience? At any rate, Jacques clearly didn't make up his mind to drown his daughter during the uneasy time which preceded her departure. The words which Joan quotes really amount to no more than saying: 'I'd sooner see her dead than a camp follower'. And who has not, as an adolescent, heard someone say: 'My father would kill me if I did so and so'? We have absolutely no indication that Jacques Darc was ever violent with his children and certainly Joan was never a battered child. Far from drowning her, her brothers Pierre and Jean followed her to the war, joining her at Tours on her way to Orleans and thus protecting her reputation. They were lodged in the town with Nouillompont and

Poulengy, the two young men who had accompanied her on her journey from Vaucouleurs to Chinon to see Charles VII. They must have had faith in their sister, since they followed her *before* she gave the great 'sign', which was the lifting of the siege. Her other brother Jacques (Jacquemin) was married and had been living in Vouthon before she left. He, like her father, must have died sometime before the 1450s, since they are nowhere mentioned in connection with the retrial of 1456.

The lawsuit before the ecclesiastical court in Toul, which she mentioned above, was a case brought against her by a young man for breach of promise, when she was about sixteen. When questioned about it in Rouen, where she was accused of having brought the case to compel the unwilling young man to marry her, she replied: 'I didn't summons him, it was he who summonsed me and I swore before the judge to tell the truth. I never made him any promise.'

She admits that she went against her worried parents' wishes to fight her own case in Toul. It seems that they were anxious to get her married, to have her 'settle down', to put all this dangerous nonsense about running off with the soldiers out of her silly head. She won her case, as she declared the saints had promised her. As she insisted, how could she have wished to marry, since she had made a vow of chastity at the age of thirteen? At any rate, we can conclude that she must have been attractive enough to have a young man very keen to marry her. Joan was no compliant daughter, but we may be sure that, naturally affectionate and obedient as she was, she went her own way with a heavy heart.

In one of the last interrogations, on the afternoon of 17 March, the subject of the ring given to Joan by her parents with the names *JhesusMaria* (*sic*) inscribed on it was broached again. She was asked why she liked to look at it before entering battle. She replied, 'Because it comforted me, and in honour of my father and mother. Also I touched Saint Catherine, who appeared to me, with this ring on my finger.' It was obviously of great sentimental as well as religious value to her and is evidence of loving relationships within the family.

It must have caused her anguish to think of her parents' immense upset and grief if she should leave them secretly, against their wishes, without as much as a word of farewell. Was this anguish the reason why she resisted the command from the 'Voices' to 'go into France' for a time after she first heard it? Finally, however, 'Since God commanded it, I had to do it.' *Dieu premier servi*, 'God comes first' would be her constant refrain throughout her trial. It is after all the injunction of Christ in the Gospels and the constant rule of behaviour for believers thereafter. The wealthy young man Francis of Assisi, to give only one example, had not acted otherwise than the peasant girl from Domrémy, when the time came to choose between bowing to parental incomprehension and following what he considered his calling to a life of poverty.

The time was approaching when Joan would have to make up her mind whether or not to answer the call. When Salisbury arrived to set up the siege of Orleans on 12 October 1428, with his troops recruited in England and a couple of thousand more added by Bedford in Paris or recruited from garrisons in Normandy, probably towards five thousand men in all, the future of the Dauphin Charles and thus of France was hanging in the balance. Admittedly the English were not able to cut the town off completely. The total number of troops raised by Bedford and Salisbury is unclear, for both on the French and on the English side men and captains came and went, so that the fragmentary financial accounting documents which have come down to us give a confusing picture.[24] Orleans was the gateway to the Dauphin's remaining territory, the vital entry point between north and south. Charles was contemptuously nicknamed the *roi de Bourges*, as he had retreated to the ancient city of Bourges, capital of what was then the province of Berry, which bordered the Orleanais to the south-east. 'His enemies mocked and made fun of him, calling him the King of Bourges, because he had taken up his main residence there,' writes Mathieu Thomassin, writing an account of the Dauphiné for Charles's grandson, later Charles VIII, in 1456.[25]

The English, as noted earlier, had been on a progress of triumph in the summer of 1428. Salisbury, whose decision it was to campaign along the Loire, was one of the most experienced and brilliant of the English commanders. The French were well aware of this, the contemporary *Journal du Siège d'Orleans* calling him 'the most feared and renowned of all the commanders of the English army', while the *Bourgeois de Paris* describes him as 'very chivalrous, a great soldier, subtle in all his strategies', or again as 'taking towns and *châteaux* as he pleased, for he was very expert in warfare'.[26] He had played his part in the great English victories of Agincourt and Verneuil. When he arrived at the gates of Orleans, he had already taken numerous fortresses that summer as well as the strategically important towns on the Loire: Meung, less than ten miles from Orleans, was taken on 5 September, Beaugency (25 September), Jargeau (5 October), Châteauneuf (6 October), thus he gained control of the Loire both above and below the city, which was now surrounded by English-held territory. If the English could succeed in cutting off all its supplies, it could be starved, like many other places, into submission. The capitulation of Orléans would open wide the way for the conquest of Charles's remaining territory, he would be hounded out of his retreat at Bourges, possibly into exile or capture, and the victorious English forces would link up with their Duchy of Guyenne (with its capital, Bordeaux) and the troops raised in Gascony.

There was in fact an impediment to the undertaking of a siege of Orleans. The Duke of Orleans's captivity made such a proceeding unlawful, since according to the rules of war of medieval chivalry, no town should be attacked when its lord was held prisoner and thus unable to protect it. Nor could he then raise the money for his ransom. However, the days of chivalry were fast fading. Salisbury was even rumoured to have given an undertaking to Charles d'Orléans not to attack his duchy and then to have disregarded it. Whether that be true or not, these rumours are evidence of the French view of the siege as totally immoral. The immorality was compounded by the desecration of the shrine of Notre-Dame-de-Cléry, outside Meung-sur-Loire, by some of Salisbury's troops on the way to Orleans.

Orleans was, by the standards of the time, a populous city (some thirty thousand inhabitants), with many beautiful churches and convents and its own university, welcoming students from all over France and as far abroad as Germany and Scotland. The city was girded about by high ramparts and fortified gates and towers. A number of recent writers, sceptical of the importance of Joan's contribution (except as a sort of mascot) claim that the English offensive was hopeless from the beginning, given that the number of Salisbury's troops could be considered insufficient. That was certainly not the opinion of the hard-pressed French military leaders at the time, nor of the people of Orleans. Nor indeed of Salisbury, of course. He had only to sit it out and wait for the morale of the townspeople to crumble, which it did after 12 February, 1429 and the disaster known hilariously by the triumphant English as the Battle of the Herrings. But first it is necessary to look at the events leading up to that fateful day.

The governor of the town was none other than Raoul de Gaucourt, who had fought with the army of John the Fearless in 1396 against the Turks at Nicopolis and later put up such a brave defence of Harfleur before it fell to Henry V in 1415. After that he spent a dozen years in English captivity. When he was able to return to France in 1427, he was appointed Captain of Orleans by Duke Charles, who, although in captivity in England, still had the right to make this appointment. Gaucourt had been present also at Warwick's discomfiture at Montargis in 1427. He knew what to expect, and every able-bodied citizen, whether monk, student or lawyer, was conscripted to help in strengthening the defences of the city, its walls and its *boulevards*, raised earthworks outside the gates, crowned by palisades, which could only be taken with the help of scaling ladders. Horse-driven mills were constructed to grind grain and replace the water-mills outside the walls, destroyed early in the siege by the English. On the other side of the river, the suburbs were razed, churches, monasteries, also the fine houses and gardens of the wealthy, who by the fifteenth century had abandoned the cramped and unhygienic inner city with its narrow streets and filthy gutters. The *Journal du Siège* lists no fewer than a dozen churches and monasteries which were levelled, adding:

> Also they burnt down and demolished all the suburbs outside the city, very rich and beautiful to see before they were demolished, for there were many great and rich buildings there, so many that these were considered to be the finest suburbs in this kingdom.[27]

Outlying buildings of every kind were levelled pell-mell, leaving no cover for the attackers. When the attack came, even the women would rush to the walls to pour down on the assailants boiling water, oil, burning cinders or anything else available. Catapults, bombards (heavy stone-throwing artillery) culverins (long-barrelled cannon) were dragged onto the walls. The garrison at Orleans had a big *bombarde* capable of hurling stones of a hundred and twenty pounds across the Loire, but the assailants had one capable of hurling even heavier missiles right into the city centre. The *Journal du Siège d'Orleans* records how, on Monday, 14 February 1429, one such cannonball, fired across the Loire from Les Tourelles, the fortress on the left bank at the other end of the ancient stone bridge, shattered a hostelry in the Rue des Hostelleries in the centre of the city, killing three citizens as it came tumbling down.[28] After 25 October, when the English had captured Les Tourelles, Gaucourt had ordered the destruction of the last two of the nineteen arches of the bridge linking the left bank with the southern gate of the city on the right bank.

Early in the siege, on 25 October 1428, Salisbury was mortally injured by a cannonball fired from the walls of Orleans as he looked across the Loire at the town from the upper storey of one of the towers of Les Tourelles, which the English had taken earlier that day. One of his English knights was also killed by the same shot. Some said the cannon had been fired by a boy amusing himself on the battlements after the gunners had gone home for the night. The next day Dunois (still known by his title of *Bâtard d'Orléans*) arrived with the reinforcements and took over command of the defences of the city, ordering still more buildings outside the walls to be levelled.

The Earl of Suffolk, along with Talbot and Scales, was appointed by Bedford to replace Salisbury and they arrived with some two and a half thousand soldiers to take over command of the siege on 1 December. It is unclear how many of these men were replacing those of Salisbury's troops who had signed up for six months, their contracts ending in December. The assault on the town resumed and was intensified. The *Journal du Siège* says that the bombardment began in earnest on 23 December. 'During the Christmas festivities there was very heavy bombardment from each side. In particular there was in the Orleans garrison a gunner, a native of Lorraine, called Maitre Jean, said to be the best man in his profession. He proved it too, for he had a big culverin and from the pillar of the bridge near the *boulevard* of Belle-Croix, he fired across at the English and killed and wounded many.'[29] For John the Gunner (*Jean le Canonnier*), war was the ultimate game. Sometimes he pretended to have been killed and had himself carried off the battlefield on a stretcher, to the relief of his enemies, only to pop up again a little later and put the fear of God into them once more. There is news of him with Joan throughout her campaigns, until the end at Compiègne.

The siege of Orleans knew the respite of a brief truce at Christmas, when Glasdale, the captain in command of the English troops on the south side of the Loire, sent a message to Dunois asking him to send minstrels and trumpeters and buglers to provide music for the feast-day, a request with which the French duly complied. The truce lasted from nine in the morning until three in the afternoon. The musicians returned safely at the end of the festivities. *Toujours la politesse.*

Although there were skirmishes and attacks on the gates nearly every day, supplies and reinforcements continued to reach Orléans throughout January. On 3 January, nearly a thousand pigs and four hundred sheep were brought in from Blois, passing within less than a couple of miles of the besiegers in the fortress of Les Tourelles and crossing the Loire further upstream to enter the town by the Porte de Bourgogne. On 5 January, two hundred soldiers arrived following the same route. On 24 January, La Hire arrived with thirty men-at-arms, while on 8 February, a large force of fifteen hundred soldiers managed to enter the town. Meanwhile, on 16 January, the English troops had been reinforced by twelve hundred soldiers under the command of Fastolf, none other than the unfortunate knight so unfairly lampooned in Shakespeare's two *Henry IV* plays under the name of Falstaff. On 12 February, the same Fastolf, who had set out this time from Paris with supplies and reinforcement for the besiegers, would inflict a devastating defeat on the French forces who came to meet him as he approached Orleans. The encounter is derisively known as the Battle of the Herrings, since waggonloads of herrings figured largely among Fastolf's food supplies. After that, only a trickle of supplies continued to reach Orleans, eight or nine horses from time to time carrying corn or salt herrings for Lenten fare, on one occasion it was six horses laden with gunpowder. Before getting that far, we should go back and take a look at the run-up to the Battle of the Herrings.

Charles de Bourbon, Count of Clermont, son of the Duke of Bourbon captive in England after Agincourt, arrived in Orleans with two hundred men on 30 January, 1429. John Stuart, Earl of Darnley, and his brother William arrived around a week later with a Scottish contingent of captains, archers and men-at-arms. The accounts of Charles VII's treasurer for war, Hémon Raguier, lists those to whom payments were made for the wages of their men at Orleans in 1428-9. Many Scots are listed under the French versions of their names, since there were maybe as many as fifteen hundred of them in Orleans during the siege. When, over the next few months, the English had finished constructing their own *bastides* or *bastilles* (fortresses) and *boulevards*, only one gate was left unblockaded, the Porte de Bourgogne on the eastern side of the city. The besiegers had not sufficient manpower to blockade it, but it was hoped that in the end supplies would be cut off. The besiegers also dug trenches between their *bastilles*, so that, if reinforcements were needed, troops could be moved from one to another in safety and without being seen. Bedford did not present himself at the siege, but went down to Chartres and returned to Paris in January. Perhaps, being the devout man that he was, he had some scruples about the morality of attacking the city of the captive Charles d'Orléans.

Bedford's lament, in a letter of 1434 addressed to the young king, Henry VI, that the siege had been undertaken 'by God knows what advice', had the benefit of hindsight, although indeed he had wanted to advance instead on Angers, the capital of Anjou. At least he could have the satisfaction of saying 'I told you so'. But at the time there was no reason to hold back from a campaign which would have effectively dealt a knockout blow to the Dauphin's efforts to regain his kingdom. His army was demoralised by Salisbury's successes and he himself was vainly trying to get help from Scotland through a betrothal of his five-year-old son Louis to the four-year daughter of James I. But although a betrothal by proxy took place in December 1428, the Scottish princess and the promised army never arrived, James I preferring to hedge his bets and keep on reasonably good terms with England. Charles, always at that stage in his life prey to scruples and doubts, was thinking of giving up and seeking refuge in Scotland or Spain. Those around him, his Grand Chamberlain, La Trémoille, leading the band, were not averse to seeking what handsome benefits they could reap under the Duke of Burgundy.

On 10 February, Dunois, with an escort of two hundred men, left Orleans for Blois, some fifty or so miles away. He wished to agree a plan with the army there, under the command of the Count of Clermont, to capture the large convoy of supplies led by Sir John Fastolf, who had set out from Paris with the provost of that city and some sixteen hundred men-at-arms, not counting a contingent of a thousand or so Parisian militiamen, to bring four or five hundred waggonloads of armaments and provisions to the besiegers. As it was Lent, a good part of the food supply was composed of salted fish, mainly herring. On 11 February, John Stewart, Earl of Darnley, and his brother William, together with Sir Hugh Kennedy, Dunois, La Hire and Xaintrailles, left Orleans by the Porte de Bourgogne with fifteen hundred men. They were to join up with the two and a half thousand men under the command of Clermont who, that same day, had set out to meet up with them at Rouvray, some thirty miles or so north of Orleans, where the Orleans contingent spent the night. Clermont's men broke their journey overnight and arrived at Rouvray when battle was already joined between Fastolf's soldiers and the Orleans troops.

Had the Franco-Scots contingent attacked as soon as they encountered Fastolf, it should have been an easy task to vanquish an enemy encumbered with so much baggage, but Clermont sent riders with messages demanding that they await his arrival. While the Orleans troops looked on in helpless frustration, Fastolf had time both to set out pointed stakes in the ground to disembowel the opposing horses, as well as to construct a barricade with his wagons, behind which his archers could mow down their attackers. The strategic error of the French was compounded by the fury and impetuosity of Darnley, who, blazing with anger at Clermont's dilly-dallying and not willing to wait longer, rushed headlong into the attack with his troops. He and his brother William both perished in the ensuing slaughter, as did other leading captains and up to six hundred men, mostly Scots. Dunois was crippled by an arrow wound in the foot. Clermont, when he arrived, furious because the Scots had not waited for him, decided to withdraw his troops and galloped straight off again to Orleans from the battlefield, leaving it strewn with bloodied corpses, dead or dying horses and scattered herrings.

The Battle of the Herrings dealt a heavy blow to French morale. Memories of the terrible seven-month siege of Rouen ten years previously and the appalling suffering of its people were a dreadful warning of what might be to come for the people of Orleans. The Count of Clermont left Orleans, no doubt judging its situation hopeless, as did La Hire, John Kirkmichael, the Scottish bishop of Orleans, the Archbishop of Rheims, Regnault de Chartres the Chancellor of France, and a number of other notabilities. Rumours of treason added to the despair. It is true that the Porte de Bourgogne still gave entry to reinforcements and that the English did not have enough troops to take the city by assault, but whatever conclusions the modern analysts of the situation may arrive at, it is clear that the citizens and a large number of the defenders of the place did not see any reason for optimism. The French were so demoralised, says Dunois, that before Joan arrived, 'a couple of hundred English would put to flight eight hundred or a thousand men of the king's army'. The roar of the terrible English war cry, 'Hurrah!' was enough to put the fear of God into their opponents.

However, civilised norms of behaviour continued to be observed on both sides. On Tuesday, 22 February, as we read in the *Journal du Siège d'Orléans*,

> The Earl of Suffolk and the Lords Talbot and Scales sent a herald to the Bastard of Orleans with a present of a platter full of figs, grapes and dates, asking him if he would be so kind as to send to the Earl of Suffolk a length of black fur lining for a robe. This he did most gladly, by the same herald, and the earl was most grateful to him'[30]

And this was only eleven days after the Battle of the Herrings. Dunois was crippled with the wound in his foot, but, as before, war is no excuse for bad manners.

Despite such courtly interludes, such was the general hopelessness that it was decided in early March to send a delegation to the Duke of Burgundy to appeal to him to take the city under his control and protection while guaranteeing its neutrality. It seemed better than waiting for the English to receive reinforcements, cut it off completely and reduce it to a slow and agonising death by starvation before the inevitable capitulation; moreover the duke was, after all, of the Blood Royal of France. Philip was delighted, but Bedford indignantly vetoed the offer, saying that he would be 'pretty sickened to have beaten the bushes only for others to take the little birds'.[31] This led to a huge row between the two men, with Bedford accusing Burgundy of having leanings towards the Dauphin. Philip, incensed, withdrew with the troops he had had at Orleans. Once again, we do not know what the number of such troops was. It seems to have been fairly small. The work of blockading the city went on apace throughout March and April. The ruined monastery of Saint-Loup (torn down by the defenders of the city) was occupied on 10 March, allowing the besiegers a dominant position to the east of the city, new *bastilles* were built facing the gates, the first on 10 March, provokingly christened London (or even the 'Tower of London'), then Rouen (27 March) and lastly Paris (20 April). Slowly, Orleans would be strangled. But what rekindled hope and courage in the defenders was the mysterious rumour abroad, from the end of February, some time after the disaster of the Battle of the Herrings, that God was sending help in the form of a young girl on her way to meet the Dauphin. Dunois himself testified in 1456 to the state of excitement these rumours aroused in the town. Here is his testimony, taken in Orleans on 22 February 1456:

Question: Do you believe that Joan was sent by God to accomplish these feats of arms, rather than being set up by human shrewdness?

Dunois: I believe that Joan was sent by God and that her feats were divinely inspired rather than coming from human intelligence.

Question: Why do you think that?

Dunois: For several reasons. Firstly, when I was in the city of Orléans at the time it was besieged by the English, news and rumours came that a certain young girl, commonly called the Maid, had just passed through Gien and claimed to be on her way to see the noble Dauphin in order to raise the siege of Orléans and to lead the Dauphin to Rheims to be crowned. As I was in command of the city, being lieutenant general for war, and as I wished to be better informed about this Maid, I sent Messire de Villars, seneschal of Beaucaire, and Jamet de Tillay, later bailli of the Vermandois, to see the king. On their return they reported to me and declared in public, before all the people of Orléans, who were very agog to know the truth about the arrival of this Maid, that they had seen her when she met the king in the town of Chinon.

Dunois goes on to make a very long and detailed statement about the coming of Joan and the lifting of the siege, to which we shall return later. It is clear from the beginning of his account, that the mass of the people of Orleans felt that their last hope lays in this girl who claimed to be on a mission from God to help them.

6

Joan Sets Out: Vaucouleurs

Puisque Dieu le commandoit, il le convenoit faire. Puisque Dieu le commandoit, si elle eust c peres et c meres, et s'il eust esté fille de roy, si fust elle partie.

Since it was God's command, it had to be carried out. Since God commanded it, if she had had 100 fathers and 100 mothers, even if she had been a king's daughter, she would have gone.

Court proceedings, Rouen, 12 March, 1431

Joan's Voice or Voices became compelling after the start of the siege of Orleans. Again in the second session of the trial at Rouen (22 February 1431), she endeavours to make her experience comprehensible to her judges:

> The voice was telling me that I should go into France, I couldn't stay any longer where I was. It was telling me that I would raise the siege of Orleans. It told me that I should go to the town of Vaucouleurs and find Robert de Baudricourt, the captain of the place, and that he would give me people to go with me. I said that I was only a poor peasant girl who didn't know how to ride a horse or conduct a war.

The word daunting is not enough to describe the prospect for a young village girl leaving home all alone, without a word of farewell to her parents, brothers, friends, to be plunged into the unknown, fearsome world of battlefields, soldiers and powerful nobles. But as she had to do it, she refused to ponder such difficulties and concentrated only on how to go about it. Finding a way of leaving home without arousing her parents' suspicions was not an easy task. For once in her life, Joan did not divulge her whole intention to her parents, she simply asked a relative to request their permission for her to go and help his wife, Jeanne, who was pregnant. Jeanne was the daughter of Joan's aunt Aveline (her mother's sister) and married to Durand Laxart (or Lassois), whom Joan called her *uncle*, for he was about fifteen years older than herself and it was customary at the time to call older cousins 'uncle'. Durand and his wife

Jeanne lived in the village of Burey-le-Petit. There are two villages called Burey between Domrémy and Vaucouleurs and it is not certain which is the one in question.

Jean Waterin, a witness at the Nullity hearings of 1456, recalled seeing Joan leave the village of Greux, no doubt as she was going to stay with her cousin at Burey: 'She was saying "Adieu!" to people. I heard her say several times that she was going to come to the aid of France and the Royal line.' In 1456, several witnesses recalled, accurately or otherwise, bits of information they had heard concerning Joan's departure. Isabelle, or Zabillette, whom we have already met as the wife of the 'Burgundian', Gérardin d'Épinal, made the following statement:

> I heard Durand Laxart say that Joan told him to tell her father that she was going to help his wife, who was having a baby. That was so that he would be able to take her to Robert de Baudricourt.

Joan's childhood friend, Mengette, gives the same account:

> When Jeannette made up her mind to go to Vaucouleurs, she sent for Durand Laxart to come and tell her parents that she was going to his house, in Burey-le-Petit, to help his wife. When she was leaving, she said 'A Dieu!' to me and then she left. She recommended me to God's keeping, and then she went to Vaucouleurs.

Jean Colin of Greux:

> I heard Durand Laxart say that she told him he had to take her to Vaucouleurs, for she wanted to go into France, and that he should say to her father that she was going to help his wife, who was having a baby. Durand did as she told him, and then, with her father's permission, she went to Durand's house and he took her to Vaucouleurs to talk to Robert de Baudricourt.

Durand's testimony, given at Vaucouleurs on 31 January 1456:

> It was I who went to fetch Joan from her father's house to bring her over to mine. She told me that she wanted to go into France to see the Dauphin and have him crowned. She said, 'Isn't there an old saying that France would be ruined by a woman and restored by a maiden?' She told me that she would go and tell Robert de Baudricourt to send her to the Dauphin.

No doubt Joan did in fact busy herself about her cousin's home while she stayed there during the period of Jeanne's confinement. Her testimony in the second session of the trial at Rouen indicates that she only told

Durand of her desire to go to Vaucouleurs some time after she arrived in Burey:

> I went to find my uncle and told him that I wanted to come and stay with him for a while and I stayed there about a week. Then I told him that I had to go to Vaucouleurs and he took me there.[1]

Durand's recollection is that she stayed about six weeks! Here is his statement:

> Joan was good, pious, patient, she liked to go to church and to confession, she gave alms to the poor when she could. I saw that for myself, both in Domrémy and when she was with us in Burey, where she spent six weeks.

One week? Six weeks? Neither Joan nor Durand had anything to gain by misreporting the length of her stay in Burey. If after a week, she asked her cousin to take her to Vaucouleurs, no doubt he hesitated and worried for some time about the rightness of the path to take. It was a heavy responsibility and likely to lead to a deep rift between him and his wife's relatives. We do not know if or when he discussed the matter with his wife Jeanne. Moreover, he would scarcely have wanted to absent himself if the birth was imminent. When was the baby born? After that, Joan would have had no excuse for staying on. Certainly her parents would have wanted to know what was keeping her in Burey. When did Durand inform them about the situation? Joan said at her trial that her parents were sick with grief when they discovered that she had left and that she had sent a letter asking their forgiveness, which they gave her (session of Monday, 12 March). There was nothing to upset them as long as they thought she was at Burey. When did they resign themselves to the *fait accompli*?

At all events, Durand was finally prevailed upon and Joan was on her way. But when, exactly, was that? Possibly, she left Domrémy before Christmas, 1428 and went to Vaucouleurs in January or early February.[2] Witnesses heard in Domrémy in 1456 are understandably somewhat vague about exact dates for her visit or visits to Vaucouleurs in 1429.

There Joan and her uncle stayed in the house of Henri le Royer and his wife Catherine. They both gave evidence at the Nullity hearings on Saturday, 31 January 1456. What impression did Joan make on the couple? Henri: 'Joan lodged in my house at Vaucouleurs. I thought she was a good girl, sitting spinning with my wife and going to church, where she often went with my wife.'

Joan herself was proud of her spinning and sewing. Catherine mentions this accomplishment also, among other things:

> After she left home, when Joan was brought to my house by Durand Laxart because she wanted to go to talk with the Dauphin, I saw that

she was good, full of simplicity, gentle and modest and well brought up. She went often to church and she liked to go to confession. I know, because I took her to the church and I saw her making her confession to Father Jean Fournier, then parish priest of Vaucouleurs. She liked to spin and she was skilled at it. We did it together [...] She stayed altogether three weeks with me, at different intervals and during that time she sent word to Sir Robert de Baudricourt to take her to the Dauphin. Sir Robert refused.

Jean Morel. Joan's godfather, also testified in Domrémy (28 January 1456), that Joan went two or three times to Vaucouleurs to see Baudricourt.

Three weeks, says Catherine le Royer, but *at intervals*. Did Joan return to Durand's house from time to time? That might account for his statement that she was there for six weeks in all. We see from her own testimony that she made three visits to Robert de Baudricourt. Bertrand de Poulengy reports that she went back between two visits to her father's house, but that seems extremely unlikely. Given her father's outrage at her plans, she must have gone back to Burey, unless her parents had already forgiven her, but if so, when did she write to them?

At all events, it must soon have been clear that persuading Robert de Baudricourt to send her to the Dauphin was not turning out to be a ten-minute nudge. Robert was a tough old soldier, the veteran of many a battle. As captain of the place since before 1420, he had held out grimly in the fortress town of Vaucouleurs, surrounded on all sides by Anglo-Burgundian territory and hostile soldiery. He was hardly going to make himself the laughing-stock of everyone who was anyone by sending a simple peasant girl with a message to Charles VII, to say that here was the saviour of France and of the throne of the Valois, a girl with no knowledge of royal courts or power politics, no idea of army life, military strategy, weaponry, tactics or anything else about warfare, someone who had never in her life been out of her village before and who, into the bargain, was given to 'hearing voices'. True, other peasants had on occasions been granted audiences with French royalty, claiming that they had urgent prophetic messages to impart, but none had claimed that he (or much less *she*) would personally undertake the task of righting the situation. Durand Laxart tells us that Baudricourt gave Joan very short shrift to begin with: 'Robert told me several times to give her a good box around the ears and take her back to her father' (testimony of 31 January 1456).

In the second session of her trial, on Thursday 22 February, Joan described briefly her encounters with the captain of Vaucouleurs:

When I came into the town of Vaucouleurs, I recognised Robert de Baudricourt, although I had never seen him before, I recognised him through the Voice, which told me it was him. I told him that I had to go into France. He refused me on two occasions, the third time he received me and gave me an escort. The Voice had told me that was how it would be.

People were talking. Stories and rumours became rife about the girl who had appeared from nowhere and was claiming that she must bring the Dauphin an urgent message and that she was sent to save France. Seeing curiosity about Joan's mission spreading among the population and maybe unsettled by her persistence, Baudricourt had evidently become uneasy about his refusal to help her. He had to settle the matter one way or another. One day, Catherine Le Royer found the military commander of the town walking unannounced into her house with the local parish priest in tow, complete with stole and crucifix:

> One day I saw Robert de Baudricourt, at that time captain of Vaucouleurs, entering my house, along with Father Jean Fournier. The priest had brought a stole and exorcised her in the presence of Baudricourt, saying that, if she was possessed of an evil spirit, she should depart and if it was a good spirit she should approach them. Joan went upon her knees to the priest and clasped hm about the knees. She said that he hadn't acted well, although he had heard her in confession.

Joan evidently felt that her confessor should have been convinced of her innocence. Still Robert had his doubts. Catherine continues:

> When she saw that Robert was unwilling to send her, Joan told me that she simply had to go to where the Dauphin was. She said, 'Don't you know that there's a prophecy that France will be ruined by a woman and saved by a maiden from the marches of Lorraine?' Then I remembered having heard it and I was completely astonished. Joan was full of impatience. As she couldn't get to the Dauphin, the time weighed on her as it does on a woman with child.

As we have seen, Joan had already quoted the old prophecy about the ruination and restoration of France to convince Durand Laxart to take her to Vaucouleurs and no doubt it was well-known throughout France, to the detriment of Queen Isabeau's reputation. As some historians have pointed out, it is in fact an adaptation of the biblical story of mankind's Fall, brought about by Eve and redeemed through the Virgin Mary.

'After that,' says Catherine, 'I and many others believed what she said.' But still Baudricourt was not sufficiently convinced. Then one day, tired of pleading in vain, Joan decided to head off without his help. Durand: 'When the Maid saw that Robert was not willing to take her to the Dauphin, she borrowed some clothes from me and said she was going to set out. I took her (to Saint-Nicolas).'[3]

Saint-Nicolas has been identified as either as Saint-Nicolas-du-Port, a popular pilgrimage-centre about thirteen kilometres from Nancy, or

Saint-Nicolas-de-Septfonds, a hermitage a few miles from Vaucouleurs, which seems much the more likely, as it is on the way to Chinon.[4] Durand and a friend of his decided to accompany her thus far. No doubt they all regarded this initial stretch of her proposed long march as a pilgrimage to pray for her safety and the success of her mission. Probably Durand thought it safer for her to be dressed as a boy, given her declared intention to continue to walk the whole way to Chinon through 'bandit country'. Later she would say that she was determined to reach the Dauphin, 'should I wear my legs out up to the knees'. Her determination must have appeared both incredibly brave and staggeringly foolhardy. The length of the walk alone, nearly four hundred miles, would have been a major challenge; her eventual trip took eleven days on horseback. One way or another, her companions must have finally persuaded her that it would be foolish to attempt such a feat, for she turned back, because, as Catherine le Royer was told, she felt it was unseemly (*'pas honnête'*) to continue like that. Probably Laxart and hs friend pointed out to her that such a journey would give rise to malicious gossip, which would certainly do her cause no good.

One of those whose somewhat sceptical curiosity about Joan was aroused was a young squire by the name of Jean de Nouillompont (also known as Jean de Metz). Seeing her one day walking through Vaucouleurs, he went up to her and greeted her with good-natured banter. Testifying at Vaucouleurs, on Saturday, 31 January 1456, he recounted that first meeting with her, when his friendly, teasing greeting received a serious, anxious answer:

When Joan the Maid came to the town of Vaucouleurs in the diocese of Toul, I saw her, dressed in a shabby worn red dress. She was staying with Henri le Royer of Vaucouleurs. I went up to her and said, 'Well, m'dear, what are you doing here? Is the king to be chased out of his kingdom and must we all be English?' The Maid replied: 'I have come to this royal town to speak to Robert de Baudricourt, to ask him to take me to the king or to send me to him. But he pays no attention to me, or to anything that I say. But before mid-Lent I have to get to the king, should I wear my legs out up to the knees. Nobody in the world, neither kings, nor dukes, nor daughter of the King of Scotland, nor any other can restore the kingdom of France. There is no help but in me. And yet I would far rather be sitting spinning beside my poor mother, for this is not my state in life. But I have to go and do it, for such is the will of my Lord.' I asked her who was her Lord, and she replied 'God'.

Nouillompont was dumbfounded by this reply, by its urgency and sincerity. He goes on:

And then I, Jean, putting my hand in hers as a sign of faith, I promised her that with God's help, I would take her to the king. I asked her when she wanted to leave and she replied, 'Rather today than tomorrow, rather tomorrow than later'.

Then the young man asked her how she intended to be dressed:

> I asked her if she wished to go dressed in her own clothes. She replied
> that she would like to have men's clothes. So I supplied her with hose
> and a costume belonging to one of my servants. After that, the people
> of Vaucouleurs got a man's outfit made for her, complete with hose,
> leggings and all the rest. They gave her a horse worth round about
> sixteen francs.

It is interesting to see that Joan is *au courant* with the news about the
Dauphin's attempt to enlist the help of James I of Scotland. Did she
hear about it in Vaucouleurs or in Domrémy? We know that there were
Scottish troops in the region.

By this time, the rumours about Joan had reached the ears of
Charles II, the powerful Duke of Lorraine. who had transferred his
allegiance from Burgundy to the French party after the assassination of
John the Fearless. This alliance was strengthened in 1420 through the
marriage treaty between the Duke's ten-year-old daughter Isabelle and
the thirteen-year-old René d'Anjou, brother of Marie d'Anjou and so
brother-in-law of the Dauphin. The protection of the Duke of Lorraine
extended over Toul and Vaucouleurs and was invaluable to Baudricourt
in his outpost deep in Burgundian territory, so when the duke sent
a safe-conduct and requested that Joan be sent to him, she left with
Baudricourt's blessing. Jean de Nouillompont accompanied her as far
as Toul.

This was her second outing in male clothing and this time she rode
the horse which the people of Vaucouleurs had given her. The rapidity
with which, in the time between this visit and her arrival at Orleans,
she acquired the equestrian skills necessary to ride a warhorse while
holding aloft her standard is not the least of the astonishing things
about her. Some historians remark that she may have ridden farm horses
in Domrémy. I find this unconvincing, a carthorse and a warhorse are
two very different animals. In any case, the daughter of a strictly
respectable family is unlikely to have ridden astride a carthorse. Maybe
the practice she had on the ride to Chinon helped. The medieval saddle
on warhorses was specially adapted to hold the rider in the seat; but
all the same, young nobles had to practise the skills of horsemanship
from early childhood in order to achieve competence. At all events,
her contemporary, the young duke of Alençon, was astonished and
filled with admiration at her skill from the first moment he saw her in
Chinon.

Possibly Charles II was at the time in residence in Toul, so she would
not have needed to travel on to his ducal seat in Nancy. The Duke's
curiosity was partly self-interest. Old and in bad health, he seems to
have hoped that she might be some sort of faith-healer. But Joan was

neither a would-be miracle worker nor an over-awed peasant. Here is her account of the meeting, given in the court in Rouen on Thursday, 22 February 1431:

> The Duke of Lorraine sent for me. I went and told him that I wanted to go into France. He questioned me about how he might recover his health and I told him I knew nothing about that. I didn't talk much about how I would get there [to the Dauphin] but I asked him to give me his son-in-law [René d'Anjou] and men-at-arms to take me into France and I said that I would pray for his health. I had gone with a safe-conduct from the duke and then I returned to Vaucouleurs.

Joan was demanding the moon! René d'Anjou, now aged twenty-two, was not only brother-in-law to the Dauphin Charles, heir to the duchies of Anjou, Bar and Lorraine, but heir also to the thrones of Sicily and Naples and future father-in-law of Henry VI of England. He would one day become *le bon roi René*, writing poetry, adorning his court with priceless works of art and remitting taxes.

According to a witness at the Nullity trial in 1456, Joan was even more forthright in what she said to the Duke. Marguerite La Tourolde, the wife of the *receveur du roi*, (the official in charge of the royal accounts), in whose house at Bourges Joan was lodged when Charles VII and his court returned there after his coronation in Rheims, claimed that Joan had told her about the visit to the Duke of Lorraine:

> I heard Joan saying that the Duke of Lorraine, who had a health problem, had wanted to see her. She had spoken with him and told him that he was behaving badly and that he wouldn't recover if he didn't amend his ways and she urged him to go back to his good wife.[5]

It was public knowledge that the Duke was living with a mistress. If Joan did in fact rebuke him, she was much too discreet to disclose the fact to the court at Rouen. To the duke's credit, he did not take umbrage at the audacity of her approach and, while not giving her his son-in-law as an escort, he gave her instead a grey horse, no doubt more valuable than the one she had been generously given in Vaucouleurs, and a sum of money to help her on her way.

Joan returned, no doubt somewhat disappointed at her failure to secure any substantial help. But Jean de Nouillompont and another squire, his friend Bertrand de Poulengy, were waiting for her. Both men were around thirty years old. Although he had only became acquainted with Joan after she arrived in Vaucouleurs, Bertrand was no stranger to Domrémy, having been there several times. He had even visited the d'Arc household. Was he there on some sort of official business with Jacques d'Arc, the *doyen* of the village? He said he didn't know the name of Jacques's wife, so we may deduce that such was the case. He gave the following testimony at Toul on 6 February 1456:

> I saw her [Joan] speaking to Robert de Baudricourt, who was then the captain of the place. She said that she had come to him from Our Lord and that he should tell the Dauphin to hold fast and avoid any engagement with his enemies, because her Lord would send him help before mid-Lent. She said that the kingdom didn't belong to the Dauphin, but to her Lord, However, it was her Lord's will that the Dauphin should become king and take command of the kingdom. In spite of his enemies the Dauphin would be king and she would lead him to his coronation. Robert asked her who was her Lord and she replied: 'The King of Heaven'.

Maybe Baudricourt received word from the Duke of Lorraine that he should send Joan off to Chinon, maybe Nouillompont and Poulengy succeeded in persuading him to allow them to take her there, or maybe a message came from the court at Chinon that she should be sent there so that her case could be looked into. No doubt, after the visit to the duke of Lorraine, rumours about her had reached the royal entourage and curiosity, sceptical or otherwise, had been aroused. It is interesting that among Joan's small escort was Colet de Vienne, described as a 'king's messenger'. At all events, Baudricourt finally relented. At least he would be rid of the talk of the town and able to turn his attention to more important affairs. It would be up to the Dauphin and his advisers to decide what to do with the girl.

Durand Laxart describes how the citizens of Vaucouleurs fitted Joan out for her journey:

> After Joan returned to Vaucouleurs, the inhabitants of the town paid for men's clothes for her, hose, leggings [6] and everything that was needed. Jacques Alain from Vaucouleurs and I bought a horse for her which cost twelve francs, however Robert de Baudricourt later reimbursed me. After that, Jean de Metz [Nouillompont], Bertrand de Poulengy, Colet de Vienne and Richard l'Archer, together with two servants of Jean de Metz and Bertrand, took Joan to the place where the Dauphin was.

Why did Durand have to buy a horse? It is unclear what had happened to the duke's grey. Did Baudricourt requisition it? At any rate, Poulengy's account at the Nullity trial confirms Durand's:

> Jean de Metz and I, with the help of other people in Vaucouleurs, arranged for her to exchange her woman's red dress for clothes they had got ready for her: a tunic and male clothing, spurs, leggings, a sword and other such things, as well as a horse. Then we set out to go to the

Dauphin, with Joan, my servant Julien, Jean de Honnecourt, the servant of Jean de Metz, Colet de Vienne and Richard l'Archer.

Nouillompont gives the same account (30 January 1456), saying that the inhabitants had a man's costume made for her, 'with hose, leggings and everything necessary and a horse worth about sixteen francs'. But the chronology is a little confused here, since he seems to make all this precede Joan's journey with him to Toul, for which he has just said that he had given her some hand-me-down clothing belonging to one of his servants. He continues:

I and Bertrand de Poulengy, with two of his servants, also Colet de Vienne, a king's messenger, and a certain Richard l'Archer, accompanied the Maid to the king at Chinon, at my expense and Bertand's.

Henri Le Royer's testimony also corroborates that of the previous witnesses:

On arriving at my house, she was wearing a red dress, later she was given a man's outfit, hose and so on. Mounted on a horse, she was taken to the Dauphin by Jean de Metz, Bertrand de Poulengy and their servants, also Colet de Vienne and Richard l'Archer. I saw them leaving. When she was about to leave, she was told what route to follow in order to avoid the soldiers who were occupying the countryside. She said that she wasn't afraid of the soldiers, that her way was clear, if there were any soldiers on her route, God was her Lord and He would clear the way for her to reach the Dauphin. She had been born into the world for that.

Joan gave a very brief account of her departure from Vaucouleurs during the second session of her trial (22 February, 1431):

When I left Vaucouleurs I was wearing men's clothing and carrying a sword given to me by Robert de Baudricourt, but no other arms. I was accompanied by a knight, a squire, and four servants. We went as far as the town of Saint-Urbain, where I spent the night in the abbey.

Nouillompont and Poulengy not only took Joan to Chinon, but served with her throughout her campaign.

Joan was by no means the first woman to ride to war dressed as a soldier. None of her predecessors had been condemned on that account. Theologians, among them the pre-eminent Aquinas himself, were of the opinion that necessity and circumstances could justify such exceptional clothing and behaviour. Contamine names some of the noble 'dames' and 'baronesses' who, mounted and armed, led men into battle, from at least the twelfth century onwards. Women, remarks the historian, fought in the armies of the Franks during the crusades. Less exalted females also rode out to war, Contamine mentions one such fighting in Flanders in 1382 and another in Hainaut in 1396.[7] None of them however claimed divine inspiration or appeared to turn the tide of war. Joan was indeed unique, not a great lady ready to assume a position of leadership, not an adventuress drive by a thirst for a life of action, glory and profit, but a peasant girl taking up arms reluctantly, driven by a conviction that such was the will of God himself.

Perched on her horse in her male garments, her newly cropped hair hidden under a cowl or turban, Joan must have been satisfied that she had shed all outward appearance of feminity and would therefore be in little danger of attracting unwelcome attention from her future companions-in-arms. The cutting of her dark hair represented not only the rejection of all feminine arts and seductions, but also, as for a nun entering the convent, her vow of chastity. The military haircut of the day was one of the most severe since the Romans. The hair was cut pudding-basin style to form a flat round cap sitting atop the head above the nape of the neck and the ears. No hairstyle was ever less attractive.

The clothes that the people of Vaucouleurs had provided would have included a close-fitting doublet with long sleeves and a high, stiff collar, worn over a loose, coarse linen vest or under-garment and hidden in its turn by an ample belted surcoat (*huque*) reaching to the knees. Only the collar of the doublet could be seen. Joan's lower body and legs would be encased in *chausses*, woollen stockings something like long johns. This garment was worn over the *braies* or underpants and fastened to the doublet by twenty sets of strings or laces, the whole being as difficult to get past as the chastity belt of Victorian imagination. It has been pointed out that the number of laces was very unusual, but then so was Joan and her reasons are and were perfectly clear. Over these *chausses* she would pull on a pair of thigh-length black leather leggings ending in a bootee and laced up on the outside of the calf. This was standard military-style riding equipment.

In this sober dark clothing, Joan with her companions took her leave of the people of Vaucouleurs. Six armed men and a girl dressed as a boy: not enough to fight off a gang of marauding soldiers, but enough to be conspicuous. Baudricourt saw them off with much misgiving, he didn't know what to think of the girl and he feared the worst for the intrepid little band now setting out. In the second session of her trial, Joan recalls his farewell: 'Robert de Baudricourt made those who were accompanying me swear to guide me well and safely. And as I was leaving he said: "Off with you! And come what may!"'.

On a winter's day in February, probably on, or a day or two after, the Sunday Jean de Nouillompont calls in his deposition the *dimanche des Bures,* and which that year fell on the thirteenth of the month, the little group of horsemen and Joan rode out of Vaucouleurs through the Porte de

France. So began their eleven-day trek, well over half of it through hostile country, travelling mostly at night. Colet de Vienne, the king's messenger, was surely riding with them on the orders of Baudricourt, for he would have had a good knowledge of the ways and byways, where it was safe to halt and where danger must be avoided. On the first night they arrived at the town of Saint-Urbain and were given shelter in the abbey. Perhaps it is significant that the abbot was related to Baudricourt's mother. Bertrand de Poulengy, testifying at the Nullity trial (6 February 1456), described the journey:

When we set out, on the first day, we were afraid of meeting bands of English and Burgundian soldiers, for they were everywhere at the time. We journeyed through the night. Joan the Maid said to me and to Jean de Metz and the others that it would be good if we could go to Mass, but we weren't able to do that as long as we were in the war zone, for fear of being recognised. She slept every night beside Jean de Metz and me, but she slept in her clothes, with her hose well attached with laces. I was young at the time, but I experienced no physical desire and I wouldn't have dared to proposition Joan, because of the goodness I saw in her. We were eleven days travelling to the king, who was Dauphin at the time. We were very anxious on the way and Joan kept telling us not to be afraid, that once we got to Chinon, the noble Dauphin would make us welcome. She never used swear words and I was very enthused by what she said, for it seemed to me that God had sent her.

Jean de Nouîllompont's account (31 January 1456) is similar:

Leaving the town of Vaucouleurs to go to the king, we travelled sometimes by night, fearing the English and Burgundians who were round about us. We rode for eleven days on the way to Chinon. While I was riding with her, I asked her if she would really be able to do what she had said. She told me not to be afraid, this was her mission, her heavenly patrons were telling her what to do, for the last four or five years they and her Lord, that is to say God, had been telling her that she had to go to the war in order to save the kingdom of France. During the journey, Bertrand and I slept beside her every night. She slept beside me fully clothed and I was so in awe of her that I would never have propositioned her. I declare on oath that she never inspired carnal desire in me. During the journey she would have liked to hear Mass. She would say, 'If we could hear Mass, that would be good.' But we were only able to hear Mass on two occasions, because we were afraid that she would be recognised. I firmly believed in all she said. I was filled with enthusiasm by her words and by her love of God.

Joan was charismatic, as we would say today. People were convinced and inspired by her. Albert d'Ourches, a knight who had been acquainted with Joan at Vaucouleurs and later, remembered how she had asked to be taken to the Dauphin, adding that 'she spoke very well, that girl'.[8] Perhaps he was present at one or other of her interviews with Baudricourt.

So the litle company set off bravely across country on a wintry day in February 1429, through hills and forests and past desolate, deserted farms, a region controlled by the Anglo-Burgundian troops but bristling with robbers brigands and the pillaging soldiers themselves. They had in all half a dozen rivers to cross, including the Marne, the Aube, the Seine and the Yonne that were in enemy territory. The rivers were swollen by the rains of that particularly wet, cold winter. Where it was not safe to cross the bridges because of the sentinels, they had to find places that they could ford with the horses without being noticed, perhaps when the light was fading. At night they travelled, by day they snatched sleep where they could, dossing down in their bedraggled clothes in the woods or fields. Obtaining food supplies en route must have been a problem as long as they were in Burgundian territory, that is to say during the six days or so it took them to reach Gien, for they could not approach castles or garrisoned villages to seek provisions and must have relied on finding outlying inhabited farms, few and far between in those war-torn times. They do not seem even to have dared approach monasteries, the other places of help for travellers.

We cannot be certain of their exact route, for they would have prudently skirted certain places, but after four or five days they reached the ancient city of Auxerre, a town on the river Yonne which had suffered much in the wars and was now held by the Burgundians. It was a substantial place. With its bustling streets, its markets, its churches, its throngs of strollers, tradesmen, hawkers, vendors, itinerant entertainers, it couldn't fail to impress a country girl like Joan. Despite the risks of detection, they passed through the city gates, perhaps separately, so as to pass unnoticed, and rode into the walled town. Alone or accompanied, Joan made her way to the great cathedral of St. Stephen (*Saint Étienne*) to attend Mass. It may have been the Sunday after Nouillompont's *dimanche des Bures*, and she would have been anxious that they should all attend Mass. Was one or more of her companions obliged to stay behind, within the city walls or outside, to tend the horses? As to Joan herself, she showed no fear, for her trust in her 'Voices' was absolute. At her trial, on Thursday, 22 February 1431, she declared: 'On my way (i.e. from Vaucouleurs), I passed through the town of Auxerre and heard Mass in the great church. I heard my Voices frequently then.'

The town of Auxerre was Burgundian-held, so the travellers were taking a risk. Having crossed the Yonne, the little party rode on to the town of Gien, a town on a hill above the Loire, some forty-four miles from Auxerre as the crow flies. There was no broad highway, for only scattered villages lay on the route. Their hearts must have lifted when they sighted the castle overlooking the Loire and crossed the river, for at last they were in French-held territory, although bandits and robbers were still to be avoided, as everywhere.

After crossing the Loire at Gien, the travellers still had about a hundred and twenty miles to cover in order to reach the court at Chinon. On they went for several days, past Romorantin and Loches, until they reached Sainte-Catherine-de-Fierbois, a little place of pilgrimage a few miles from Chinon. There they rested for at least a day and Joan sent a messenger with letters requesting an audience with the king. We hear no more of her friends Nouillompont and Poulengy after the arrival at Fierbois. However, from the accounts of the king's finance officer for the year 1429, we know that they were in Orleans later when she was there to raise the siege. They received expenses for their stay in Chinon and also for 'the journey that they intend to make to serve the said lord (i.e. the king) in the army ordered by him for the relief of Orleans'. In Orleans the two young men and their servants were lodged in the same house as Joan and her brothers, Pierre and Jean. It was the house of Jacques Boucher, treasurer of the Duke of Orleans. [9]

Joan was questioned about Fierbois during the fourth session of her trial in Rouen, on Tuesday, 27 February, 1431, and gave the following account:

> Yes, I was at Sainte-Catherine-de-Fierbois, and I attended three Masses on the same day. Afterwards I went to Chinon. I sent letters to the king asking if I could enter the town where he was and saying that I had travelled a hundred and fifty leagues[10] to see and help him and that I had a lot of good news for him. I think I told him in the same letters that I would recognise him among all the others.

Beaupère, who was interrogating her, next asked her about the sword which had been found in the church at Fierbois and which she had sent for while she was in Chinon. How did she know it was there?

> Joan: It was in the earth, all rusty and had five crosses engraved on it. I knew it was there by my Voices. No, I had never seen the man who found it. I wrote to the clergy of the place to ask them to please send it to me and they did so [...] I think that I wrote that it was behind the altar. As soon as they found it, the clergy gave it a rubbing and immediately the rust easily fell off. It was an armourer from Tours who looked for it and the clergy gave me a sheath for it, the people of Tours also. There were two sheaths made, one in red velvet and the other in cloth of gold. I had another one made of strong leather. When I was captured, I didn't have the sword. I carried it all the time, from the day I got it until I left Saint-Denis after the assault on Paris.

Beaupère: What blessing did you say or have said over the sword?
Joan: I never said or had any blessing said over it, I wouldn't have known how. But I was very attached to it, because it had been found in the church of Saint Catherine and I was very fond of that church.

There are a number of points to be made about this exchange. Joan was fond of the church of Fierbois because she was convinced that Saint Catherine was guiding and protecting her. Moreover, Saint Catherine was popularly believed to be the patron saint of soldiers, a sword was therefore an appropriate present from her. The church at Fierbois, being a place of pilgrimage, naturally had a number of *ex voto*, objects left there in thanksgiving for cures and other favours received through the intercession of the saint. Probably there were a number of swords among them. It is quite probable that Joan would have noticed such an object, and recalled it later, at Chinon, ascribing her recollection to the promptings of her Voices. The question about the blessing is devious, for it is an attempt to ascribe to Joan superstitious practices or worse, sorcery or fraud, as we see clearly from the seventy articles of accusation used as the basis of the interrogations. Article XX is as follows:

Joan cast a spell on her ring, her standard, and certain pieces of cloth and pennants which she was accustomed to carry or have carried by her men, and also on the sword found, she said, by revelation, at Sainte-Catherine-de-Fierbois, saying that it was 'charmed'. She put numerous curses and spells on them in various places, publicly asserting that great things would be accomplished through them and victory achieved over her enemies and that no harm could come to those who carried these banners in their attacks and exploits and that they couldn't suffer any misfortune.

So it goes on. These and other such rants were finally boiled down to the twelve more plausible articles sent to the University of Paris for its considered opinion. It was on the twelve articles that Joan was condemned. Legends grew around the sword of Fierbois, but they were certainly not propagated by Joan, who always dismissed anything smacking of superstition with good-humoured common sense. At the Nullity trial, on 30 April 1456, Marguerite La Touroulde, the well-to-do lady in whose house in Bourges Joan was lodged for three weeks by order of the king after his coronation at Rheims, gave the following testimony:

Several women came to my house when Joan was with me. They brought rosaries and medals to get her to touch them. Joan laughed at that and said to me, 'Touch them yourself. Your touch is every bit as good as mine!'

Simon Beaucroix, who had been a young squire when Joan arrived at Chinon and was for a long time in her company, helping to arm her on occasions during her campaigns, declared likewise on 20 April 1456: 'Joan deplored and regretted seeing pious women coming to greet her, because it seemed to her to be a sort of religious devotion, which annoyed her.'

Another witness, the lawyer Jean Barbin recounts hearing from a colleague, Pierre de Versailles, that people would grab at Joan's horse as she rode by and try to kiss her hands and feet. Versailles had urged her not to allow such idolatry, whereupon Joan answered, 'Truth to tell, I couldn't protect myself against such things if God wasn't protecting me.' Today's celebrities are protected by bodyguards, but Joan had no such firewall.

With humour, with irritation or with resignation, depending what mood she was in, Joan waived away any such manifestations of a pious personality cult.

7

Chinon

Gentil Daulphin, j'ay nom Jehanne la Pucelle; et vous mande le roy des cieulx par moi

Joan of Arc

Dunois tells us in his deposition that Joan had to wait a couple of days at Fierbois, before she received permission to come into the presence of Charles VII. Many discussions took place before she was admitted to the court. Thomas Basin tells us that he had it from Dunois himself that he, among others at Chinon at the time, advised the king to grant an audience to Joan, saying that 'he ought to hear Joan the Maid and having heard her, prudently determine whether what she had to say was the product of her imagination and to be dismissed as such, or whether the message was in fact a divine warning or command, to be humbly received and heeded.'[1] In the court hearing of 7 May 1456, Sir Simon Charles corroborates this testimony. He had been in Venice with an embassy at the time of Joan's coming, but on his return to Chinon he learnt that she had arrived and had been at first refused an audience with Charles himself and closely questioned at a meeting of the king's Council as to why she had come. She had been unwilling to talk to anyone other than the king, but was finally obliged to say that she had two God-given missions: to raise the siege of Orleans and to lead the king to Rheims to be to be crowned. Sir Simon continues:

> Having heard that, certain of the king's councillors said that the king should have no confidence in her. Others, since she said she was sent from God and had certain things to tell the king, said that he should at least hear her. However, the king decided that she should first be examined by clerics and churchmen, and this was done.

Cautious scepticism was an eminently sensible intial reaction. Sir Simon goes on to describe the audience with Charles, saying that 'She talked with him for a long time. When he had heard her, he was seen to be full of joy.' After that, the king sent her to be examined by the eminent doctors of law and theology now gathered at Poitiers, where they would later staff the university to be established in 1432.

During her time in Chinon, Joan was lodged in the tower of the fort of Coudray, where she had the company of the fifteen-year-old Louis de Coutes, who would be appointed her page after she had been interrogated at Poitiers and who remained with her throughout her campaigns, until Paris. She had women around her also, who remained with her at night. In Chinon, as at Vaucouleurs, nobody had known what to think of her. It was essential to protect Charles from becoming the dupe of a fraudster or a girl suffering from hallucinations, or, worst of all, an individual possessed of the devil. If such a thing were ever shown to be the case, the king might as well give up immediately and hide in ignominy in far-off Scotland or Spain, where he was rumoured, in any case, to be thinking of seeking refuge.

To this day, the Catholic Church treats all claims of visions and miracles with prudent scepticism. While the Church never imposes any private revelation as a matter of faith, everyone being free to believe it or not, it does condemn those revelations which are contrary to its theology. *The Independent*, for example, reported on 13 January 2009, that the pope had instructed the Congregation of the Faith (formerly the Holy Office of the Inquisition) to draw up new guidelines aimed at eradicating false claims of visions of the Virgin Mary and other miraculous phenomena. No such claims may be made public until the claimants have been examined by a team of psychiatrists, of any or no religious persuasion, in order to establish the mental health or otherwise of such visionaries and to ascertain whether or not there is any question of a hoax. A team of theologians is also to examine the content of any so-called *heavenly message* to ascertain whether or not it is compatible with Church doctrine. The fifteenth-century *rationale* for both trials of Joan was exactly that.

After much discussion, it was decided that the king should at least see the girl. As she was being brought into the royal castle, an incident occurred which Brother Pasquerel, her chaplain, says she told him herself:

> That day, as she was going in to speak to the king, a man on horseback shouted: 'Isn't that the Maid?' swearing by God that if he had her for a night, she wouldn't come out a maid! Joan called out to the man, 'Ah! In God's name, you are denying Him, and you so near death!' Within an hour, the man fell into the water and was drowned.[2]

It sounds as if the man was drunk and fell into the moat.

A crowd of courtiers, agog with curiosity, resplendent in rich velvets, furs and cloth of gold, some of them, says the chronicler Chartier, 'more sumptuously dressed than the king himself', filled the hall as the girl was led in by the king's cousin, Louis of Bourbon, Count of Vendôme, Master of the King's Household.[3] Joan said at her trial that there were 'more than three hundred knights and fifty torches' in the room the first time she saw the king.[4] In their arrogance, they no doubt expected to see either an over-awed and somewhat bewildered peasant lass or a rather brassy country girl with little idea of the manners current at court. They were confounded in this, for she approached the king, with 'great humility and simplicity', said Raoul de Gaucourt, the former captain of Orleans, who had been present.[5] With humility and simplicity, but also calm and confidence, 'She made all the acts of courtesy and bows which it is usual to make before a king, as if she had been brought up in his court,' writes Charles VII's official chronicler, Jean Chartier.[6] No doubt Nouillompont and Poulengy had coached her, but she must have been a quick and ready pupil, with the natural good manners of a well brought-up village girl.

It had already been decided how a preliminary test of her would be made and we may take the account in the registers of the Town Clerk of La Rochelle as reliable, for he filled this post during the two years of Joan's career and would have therefore been receiving and recording official information:

On the 23rd. day of February, there came before our Lord the King at Chinon a maiden of sixteen or seventeen years of age, born at Vaucouleurs[7] in the duchy of Lorraine. Her name was Joan and she was dressed as a man, that is to say, in a black doublet, hose, a short black robe of coarse linen, her black hair cut round and wearing a black hat on her head. She was accompanied by four squires. When she arrived in the court, she asked to speak to the king. They pointed out Charles de Bourbon to her, telling her that he was the king. But she said at once that it was not him and that she would know him as soon as she saw him, although she had never seen him before. Then they brought on a squire, saying again that he was the king, but again she saw at once that it was not him. The king then emerged from a room and as soon as she saw him, she said that it was he and that she had come to him from the King of Heaven and wished to speak to him. And they say that she told him certain secret things which astonished him extremely.[8]

No-one knows what Joan said to the Dauphin, but all agree that he was visibly astounded and overjoyed by it. It was a major object of the questioning at her trial in Rouen and she determinedly refused to divulge it, at last trying to cover it under a veil of allegory, which we shall look at later. It has remained a mystery ever since. Why was he 'full of joy'? If she had merely repeated that she felt herself to be on a mission ordained by God he would have had no more reason to be convinced than had Baudricourt.

In the deposition of Brother Pasquerel there is perhaps a clue as to what the 'secret' was. He quotes her as saying publicly to Charles during that first interview: 'I tell you, from Our Lord, that you are the true inheritor of France and son of the king.' This of course is an easy enough statement to make. However, it is highly probable that for Charles VII it was the assurance he craved most, tormented as he was by doubts about his legitimacy, given the propaganda onslaught against his mother, together with her own damning verdict on him in the treaty of Troyes. Although certainly no saint and by nature of 'a remarkable sensuality', as one historian puts it,[9] he was introspective and religiously deeply convinced, so that we may well believe that he was plagued by anxieties about his right to the throne or the morality of pursuing a war in defence of it.

Pasquerel's story can be complemented by a second interesting story, recounted much later in a work entitled *Hardiesses des grands Rois et Empereurs*, presented in 1516 to the king of France, François I, by Pierre Sala, then aged sixty-three. Sala had served in various high-ranking capacities under three kings of France, Louis XI, (son of Charles VII), Charles VIII and Louis XII. He claimed to have had the story from a certain Guillaume Gouffier, Lord of Boisy, who had in his youth, as he said, been on terms of close amity with Charles VII. Charles had confided to him, said Boisy, that one day, 'when he was brought so low that there was nowhere for him to retire to in his kingdom but Bourges or some nearby castle, Our Lord sent him a simple maiden by whose counsel his kingdom was entirely restored to him and he ruled thereafter in peace'. What had convinced the king to put his trust in the girl was, said Boisy, 'the fact that she brought him a message from God, in which she revealed to him a secret hidden in his heart, which he had never revealed to any living soul, except in his prayer to God.' What was this secret of which Joan alone was cognisant? Sala goes on:

> One day, the king went into his oratory, all alone, and there made in his heart a humble request and prayer to Our Lord, not saying a single word aloud. He prayed devoutly that if he were the true heir, truly descended from the House of France, and if the kingdom rightly belonged to him. it would please Our Lord to preserve and defend it for him or that if the worst came to the worst, God would grant him the grace to escape death or prison, so that he might seek sanctuary in Spain or Scotland, countries which from of old had been brothers-in-arms and allies of the kings of France, which was why he chose them for his last refuge. [10]

The king does not ask God for any sign, or miracle, it is simply a prayer for help and mercy. This story is taken very seriously by the great historian of Joan, the anticlerical Jules Quicherat, not one to indulge in hagiography. 'We include it here,' he writes, 'because it confirms what we read in earlier chronicles relative to the secret.' It certainly would explain why Joan so stubbornly refused to reveal the secret to her judges in

Rouen. To reveal that the king himself had doubted his legitimacy would have been disastrous to his standing and his claims.

The modern historian and editor of the 1431 trial documents, Pierre Tisset, disagrees with Quicherat and believes that the 'sign' given to the king by Joan was simply the double promise of the relief of Orleans and the coronation and was therefore validated when she raised the siege, but if this was so, it is difficult to see why she so stubbornly refused to reveal such a 'secret' to her judges. The facts were after all common knowledge. However, except for the king, to all who asked her to provide a sign, she answered that the only sign she would give would be the relief of Orleans.

At the Nullity trial, on 3 June 1456, the Duke of Alençon, cousin of Charles VII, gave a full account of Joan's stay at court after this initial interview. Twenty-three years of age, married to a daughter of the captive Duke of Orleans, he was well acquainted with war already. When he was six, his father had been killed at Agincourt. He had himself been found for dead among the corpses on the battlefield of Verneuil, where he was taken prisoner and held at Crotoy, before being released three years later on payment of a ruinously huge ransom. Throughout he had refused the Duke of Burgundy's blandishments and remained faithful to the cause of the Dauphin. This is his deposition:

> When Joan came to see the king, who was in Chinon, I was in the town of Saint-Florent. While I was out hunting quail, one of my stewards came to tell me that a girl had arrived with the king, saying she was sent by God to expel the English from France and raise the siege of Orleans. I went to Chinon the very next day and found Joan there speaking with the king. When I entered, she asked who I was and the king told her I was the Duke of Alençon. She then declared. 'You are most welcome! The more there are together of the Blood Royal of France, the better it will be.' The following day, Joan went to the king's Mass and made a bow when she saw him. The king took her, together with me and the Sire de la Trémoille, into a room and ordered the others to leave. Then Joan made several requests to the king, among other things, that he should make his kingdom over to the King of Heaven. She said that after that donation the King of Heaven would treat him as he had treated his predecessors and restore him to his proper estate. There were a lots of other things which I don't remember now, but the talking continued until we went in to eat. After the meal, the king went for a walk in the meadows. Joan was practising with the lance,[11] When I saw how she could handle it, I made her a present of a horse.

We should note that the lance was the weapon reserved to the aristocracy, as was the horse. Joan was claiming her place among the elite and Alençon was clearly welcoming her in:

The king next decided that she should be examined by the clergy. He appointed the bishop of Castres, who was the king's confessor, and the bishops of Senlis, Maguelonne and Maître Pierre de Versailles, later bishop of Meaux, also Maîtres Jourdain and Morin and many others whose names I have forgotten. They asked Joan, in my presence, why she had come and who had sent her to the king. She replied that she had come on behalf of the King of Heaven and that she had Voices and Counsellors to tell her what she should do. I don't remember all that exactly. But later on, Joan, who was having a meal with me, told me that she had been closely questioned, but that she knew and could do more things than she had told the interrogators. After hearing the reports of the commission, the king decided to send her to Poitiers, where she was again be examined.

Charles may have been convinced, but his council and clergy had to make a careful examination of Joan's claims, for everyone's sake. Her claim to virginity, her wish to be known as *Joan the Maid*, was an essential proof of the blamelessness of her life as a young unmarried girl. If she was found to be lying about that, she was unfit to be the bearer of a divine message and her mission was nothing but a sham. At some point in Chinon therefore, before being sent to Poitiers, she was subjected to a physical examination, according to Brother Pasquerel, her confessor. 'I heard that when Joan came to Chinon, she was physically examined by two ladies, *la dame de Gaucourt*, and *la dame de Trèves*, to ascertain whether she was male or female and if she was a virgin.'[12] Jean d'Aulon, Joan's Chief of Staff, who fought beside her throughout her campaigns, says he was present when Charles VII's mother-in-law, Yolande of Sicily, presented him with the report confirming that Joan was indeed, as she claimed, a virgin.[13] Joan was then sent off to Poitiers, to be examined on her mental stability and her orthodoxy.

Poitiers was the intellectual capital of what was left of Charles's kingdom, the town to which the king's Parlement had moved from Paris after the massacres of 1418, as had those members of the University of Paris who had remained faithful to Charles VII. A university was about to be set there up very shortly after Joan was called to appear; already she is described as being examined *per clericos universitatis Pictavensis*.[14] The king himself and a number of his councillors adjourned to Poitiers and Joan was lodged in the house of Jean Rabateau, the king's procurator general in the Parlement. A board of examiners was convened, including several bishops, among others Gérard Machet, the bishop of Castres and confessor of Charles VII, Pierre de Versailles, afterwards bishop of Meaux, and the bishop of Poitiers. Altogether the examiners numbered close on twenty. Deborah Fraioli calls them 'the flower of the Valois clergy'. The university of Poitiers, soon to be set up, was created around this group of scholars. Their task was what Gerson called the 'discernment of spirits', an examination of the orthodoxy of what she claimed about her visions and the orthodoxy or otherwise of religious concepts which she affirmed they had given her.

At the Nullity trial, on 5 April 1436, one witness, Gobert Thibaut, one of the king's equerries, remembered Joan being interrogated in Rabateau's house in his presence by Pierre de Versailles and Jean Érault, a professor of sacred theology. 'Joan came up to us as we entered,' he said, 'she slapped me on the shoulder and said she'd like to have a lot of men like me with her. Then Versailles said to her that the king had sent them to her. She said, "I know that you have been sent to interrogate me," adding, "I don't know A from B." The minutes of Poitiers have been lost and we have only a summary of the findings. Quicherat writes, 'Posterity will forever mourn the loss of the minutes of Poitiers, the finest document, I have no hesitation in saying, that we could ever possess on Joan of Arc, since that immortal young woman showed herself there in all her freshness and inspiration, full of gaiety, vigour, enthusiasm, replying spontaneously to unbiased judges that she was sure to win over.'[15]

However, we know something of what went on from the eye-witness account of Brother Seguin de Seguin, a Dominican and Professor of Sacred Theology, later Dean of the Faculty of Theology in Poitiers, who gave evidence at the second trial on 14 May 1456. He recounts several titbits, showing Joan in somewhat impatient mood. One such is the exchange between Joan and another Dominican, Guillaume Aymeri, who interrogated her thus:

> You have declared that the Voice told you it was God's will to deliver the people of France from the misery they were in. If God wishes to deliver them, he has no need of men-at-arms.' Joan replied, 'In God's name, the men-at-arms will fight and God will give the victory'.

Or again, Brother Seguin tells a story against himself:

> I asked her what language the Voice spoke to her. 'A better language than yours!' she replied, for the way I speak tells you I come from Limoges. Then I asked her if she believed in God. 'Yes,' she said, 'and better than you.'

No frivolous questions, please! Joan certainly wasn't trying to win her interrogators over with feminine wiles and charm. There is also here an impatience with the questioning which is holding up her mission, an assertiveness one might not have expected to see in the quiet and reserved girl from Domrémy. Joan's transformation from an unremarkable village girl into a determined and forthright public figure, endowed with a good deal of wit and intelligence, is now complete. There had been earlier portents, of course, the girl who took herself to Toul and conducted her own defence against the charge of breach-of-promise had not been lacking in courage or independence of spirit.

Brother Seguin continued his questioning:

Then I said to her that God didn't want anyone to believe her if there was nothing to show why they should, and that unless she could show something more the counsellors would not recommend that the king should entrust men-at-arms to her and put them in danger on her simple affirmations. She replied, 'In God's name, I have not come to Poitiers to give you signs, but take me to Orleans and I will show you signs to prove why I have been sent.' She asked that men should be entrusted to her, as many as she would think necessary, and she would go to Orleans. Then she announced to me and to all present that there were four events to come, first, that the English would be beaten, the town delivered, and that she would give the English something to think about. Second, that the king would be crowned at Rheims. Third, that Paris would return to the obedience of the king of France and last, that the Duke of Orleans would return from England.

She did not claim that she would personally see all these predictions fulfilled, but neither did she affirm the contrary. The future retained its mystery. She put no dates on her predictions and, as it happened, she would not live to see the last two fulfilled.

'I have seen all these things come to pass,' said Brother Seguin. He added that he and other delegates had investigated Joan's life and morals:

We found that she was a good Christian, living as a Catholic and never lazy. For better information as to her conduct, some women were attached to her who gave an account of her behaviour to the council.

Brother Seguin remembered also that some of the delegates had asked Joan why she had a standard and she had replied that she didn't want to use her sword to kill anyone.

The examiners sent a report to the king and his council saying that 'they had found nothing in her contrary to the Catholic faith and, given the state of urgency, the king could have recourse to her'. Some commentators regard this as a sign that they were reluctant to endorse Joan or that they were hedging their bets, or that the whole thing was a set-up by Charles VII, but it should be realised that no commission could have given any more positive report. What more could they have said? Visions cannot be declared to be divinely inspired during the life-time of the visionary (nor indeed thereafter, belief in them always being optional), nor can the visionary be canonised before departing this vale of tears. Judgement can only be made on conformity to orthodoxy and on that score Joan had been approved. Her life had been found blameless and this was the other element in deciding whether or not she was worthy of confidence. Deborah Fraoli, at the end of her volume on the early debate about Joan and her Voices, concludes that the approbation of the Poitiers clerics was neither military nor political, but quite straightforwardly theological and religious. They had completed their task, the military and political aspects of Joan's mission came after this all-important preliminary and were not the business of the Poitiers judges.

It was while Jeanne was in Tours, after Poitiers the next stop on her way to Orleans, that we hear again of her mother, Isabelle, who had now made the pilgrimage to Puy-en-Vélay, the Lourdes of its day. It was (and still is) on the pilgrimage route to St. James of Compostela. 1429 was a Jubilee year, the feasts of the Annunciation and Good Friday falling on the same day, 25 March. The Jubilee is a rare event, in 2016 the two feasts fell on the same day, but now we will have to wait nearly a century and a half for another such event. In 1429 the town was chock-a-block with the bustle and fervour of pilgrims. The excited throng was so great on these occasions that people had sometimes been crushed to death. We do not know how Isabelle travelled, but no doubt it was a tiring and challenging journey for a countrywoman of a certain age, given the hardships of the road and the risks of robbery on the way, as bandits preyed upon the pilgrims. Her intention was no doubt to pray devoutly that God would guide and protect her daughter. Her husband too must by now have accepted the fact that Joan had not 'gone off with the soldiers' to become a camp-follower, but was following a very different path.

It was in Tours that Joan made the acquaintance of Brother Pasquerel. Here is his account, given on 4 May 1456:

> I had my first news of Joan and how she had come to see the king while I was in the town of Puy, where Joan's mother was with some of those who had taken her daughter to the king. They knew me and told me I should come with them to see this Joan and that they wouldn't leave me until I got to her. I went with them to the town of Chinon and from there to the town of Tours, where I was the reader in a friary of the town. In that town, Joan was lodged in the house of a citizen, Jean Dupuy. We found her there and those who had brought me said to her, 'Joan, we have brought this good Father to you. When you know him, you'll like him a lot.' Joan said she was very pleased to meet me, that she'd already heard of me and that she would make her confession to me the following day. The next day, I heard her confession and said Mass in her presence. From then on, I was with her always and accompanied her to the town of Compiègne, where she was captured.

Brother Pasquerel was later asked by Joan to be her confessor. She also had another chaplain, her cousin Nicolas, the Cistercian monk. One historian, Andrew Lang, suggests that Joan's brothers may have escorted their mother to Le Puy and gone on from there to join their sister at Tours. They certainly entered Orleans with her.

Before leaving Poitiers, having received permission to proceed, Joan composed and sent a letter addressed to the child-king, Henry VI, the Regent Bedford, and to the English captains at Orleans. She dictated it to one of the eminent personages who interviewed her in the house of Jean Rabateau. It is now quite clear that she is ready to take on the role of personally leading and inspiring the troops. The letter is in accord with the standard practice between Christian opponents of issuing a summons to the adversary to make peace and threatening dire consequences should he refuse to do so. However, the claim of a God-given mission authorising a chosen individual to act against the said Christian opponent was unheard of and bound to cause outrage.

Here is the text of the letter, written on 22 March 1429, and included in the seventy-two articles of accusation read out to her in the court at Rouen on 28 March 1431 (Article XXII):

+Jesus Maria +

King of England, and you, Duke of Bedford, who call yourself Regent of France, you, William Pole, Count of Suffolk, you, John Talbot, and you Thomas, Lord Scales, who call yourselves lieutenants of the Duke of Bedford, obey the King of Heaven, hand over to the Maid who is sent here by God, the King of Heaven, the keys of all the good towns which you have taken and violated in France. She has been sent here by God, to claim what belongs to the Royal line of France. She is quite ready to make peace if you will see reason and leave France and pay for what you have held. And all you archers, men-at-arms, noblemen and others who are surrounding the town of Orleans, in God's name, go back to your own country. If you do not, you can expect news from the Maid, who will shortly come to find you, to your very great hurt. King of England, if you do not do this, I am *chef de guerre* and in whatever place I find your men in France, I shall make them leave, whether they want to or not. And if they won't obey, I will have them all slain. I am sent by God, the King of Heaven, to drive you out of France. If they obey, I will be merciful to them. Do not think otherwise, for God, the King of Heaven, son of the Virgin Mary, will not give you the kingdom of France, but King Charles, the rightful heir, will have it. It is the will of God, the King of Heaven and has been revealed by the Maid to King Charles, who will enter Paris in good company. If you will not believe this news sent by God and the Maid, wherever we find you, if you will not comply, we will strike you and make a great hahay [tumult] the like of such has not been seen in France for a thousand years. And you may well believe that the King of Heaven will give more force to the Maid and to her good men-at-arms than you can muster with all your assaults, and by the blows struck we shall see who has the better right in the sight of God. You, Duke of Bedford, the Maid implores you not to get yourself destroyed. If you will agree with her, you can come in her company to where the French will achieve the finest feat of arms which ever was made for Christendom. Reply to this if you are willing to make peace in the city of Orleans. If you do not do so, you will shortly suffer damage that you will never forget.

Written this Tuesday of Holy Week [22 March 1429].

At her trial, Joan affirmed that she had not written 'hand over to the Maid', but 'hand over to the king'. She also denied using the term 'chef de guerre'. (It does not in any case signify *commander-in-chief*, but simply a commander). She recognised that she was being implicitly accused of setting herself above both her king and the àrmy commanders.

The letter, which was apparently sent along with others, was received with fury by the English. They arrested the herald, in flagrant breach of all the conventions of chivalry, and refused to let him go. The *Journal du siège* gives this account of their reaction:

> When the English lords and captains read the letters they were furious and because of what she had written, they fulminated against her, calling her a strumpet, a cowherd, and threatening to have her burned alive. They detained the herald who had brought the letters and made mock of all she had written.[16]

Already the idea of having her sent to the stake! The clumsy sentences, the repetitions ('King of Heaven' six times), the unsophisticated threats and challenges, detract nothing from the directness of the message, but are clearly the voice of an unlettered young person desperately anxious to make her points as forcefully as possible.

One or two points arise in this missive: as was standard in all such communications, Joan first pleads for peace and otherwise threatens war. She does not predict miracles, the message is the same as that which she had given to Aymeri: 'In God's name, the men-at-arms will fight and God will give the victory.' God helps those who help themselves. She predicts that Charles VII will recover Paris, but neither here nor anywhere else does she say that she will be there with him. Finally, she invites the English to take part in a joint venture, by which she means a crusade to save Christendom from Turkish domination.

The Turkish empire was aggressively expansionist. In June, 1400, the Byzantine emperor, Manuel Paleologue II came to Paris to seek Charles VI's help against the Turks. Sofia had been captured in 1385 and the Bulgarian Christian kingdom disappeared completely after the battle of Nicopolis in 1396. The battle of Kosovo doomed Serbia. Albania, Anatolia and Hungary were invaded, war was declared on Venice in 1423; Constantinople had already been besieged in 1423 and would fall to the

Ottomans in 1453, to become Istanbul. As has already been remarked elsewhere, Bayezid boasted that he would take Rome and conquer France, while Henry V's last regret was that he had not had time to lead a crusade to Jerusalem. It was a scandal to all that Christian nations should be fighting one another. The ideal of the international crusade was at this time the medieval version of the League of Nations or United Nations – with a sharper sword. Perhaps Joan hoped that such an idealistic alliance would appeal to Bedford more than the conquest of France. Did someone suggest the idea to her, or was it her own?

In a careful analysis of the letter, Deborah Fraioli points out its four essential differences from the standard such missive of the time, which latter she describes as 'no more than a declaration of war', and which was usually accompanied by a bloodstained glove ('throwing down the gauntlet'). She picks out the firm assurance of victory in Joan's letter, the repeated ouvertures for peace, the affirmation of God's will and of the Maid as His messenger, and the broad scope of the demands, addressed not only to the captains at Orleans, but to the young king of England and his regent, Bedford, and requiring not only the lifting of the siege of Orleans, but the restoration of all occupied French territory. As Fraioli puts it: 'The letter reads more like Joan's theological and political platform' than the usual pre-battle missive.[17]

About six weeks had passed since Joan had arrived first arrived at Chinon. Meantime the king had mobilized a body of soldiers and captains at Blois to accompany a convoy of supplies to Orleans. The Duke of Alençon was dispatched to Charles's very capable mother-in-law, Yolande of Aragon, Queen of Sicily, to organise the supplies and finance for the enterprise, but he did not thereafter go to Orleans because, under the terms of his release from captivity, he was barred from fighting until his ransom was fully paid, which at the time it was not. The report from Poitiers made it possible for Charles to send Joan off to join the army. She was escorted by the Archbishop of Rheims, Regnault de Chartres (of whom we shall hear more) and Raoul de Gaucourt. They went via Tours, where Joan was lodged in the house of one of Yolande of Sicily's counsellors, Jean Dupuy. Her suit of 'white armour' had been ordered for her by royal command and made in Tours, a city famous for its smiths and armourers. Her standard and banner (*pennon*) were painted there by the king's painter, a Scotsman by the name of Heuves Poulnoir (at any rate, that is what the local town council made of his Scottish name. Was he Hugh Power?). The sums paid to the master armourer and the painter are recorded in the registers of the king's Treasurer for War, Hémon Raguier.[18]

In Tours, Joan was given her own staff. Jean d'Aulon, a squire aged about forty, who had been present at Poitiers, was appointed her *maître d'hôtel* or military chief of staff. Dunois praises him in his deposition in 1456: 'I often had conversations with Sir Jean d'Aulon, now the seneschal of Beaucaire, appointed by the king to accompany the Maid and protect her, for he was prudent and of exemplary honesty.' This wise and honest knight was with Joan throughout her campaigns and was captured with her at Compiègne, but ransomed not very long afterwards. He would rise to very prestigious positions and gave evidence in 1456. She was given two pages, Raymond (killed in the attack on Paris) and Louis de Coutes, also two heralds, Ambleville and Guyenne, so called because heralds were always given titles pertaining to duchies or provinces. Joan was thus given the same status, equipment and staff as the other captains and had the same authority over her company.

Joan's two brothers Jean and Pierre, having joined her at Tours, served in the army throughout her campaigns. Jean rose to become captain of the town of Vaucouleurs in 1457. Both lived into the 1470s. Pierre was captured with his sister at Compiègne and had to pay a ransom which practically ruined him for a long time. He received various gifts of money from the Duke of Orleans in recognition of the services which his sister had rendered to the kingdom and in particular to the city of Orleans, also a royal pension (which his son later inherited) and a knighthood, taking the name of Pierre du Lys.

La Pucelle: Joan the Maid

*Dixit etiam quod ipsa Johanna in omnibus factis suis, extra factum
guerre, erat simplex et juvenis*
Apart from the business of war, Joan was young and simple in all that
she did
Duke of Alençon, testimony of 3 May 1456

As Joan sets out on her military career, we can pause to consider what
sort of a person she was in this new life and what sort of war she wanted
to wage. Did she reveal herself to be an exultant Amazon at heart, as she
is represented in later Renaissance paintings and illustrations? Or perhaps
a heroine on the Old Testament model, a new Judith ready to sleep in
the tent of Holophernes and strike his head off? A *grande dame* of the
seventeenth-century imagination, dressed in a long robe under her heavy
breastplate, raising aloft a sword and crowned with a voluminous plume-
bedecked headdress atop her long ringlets? Of course not. These images
are even more mistaken than the image of the *petite bergerette*, the 'little
shepherd girl', propagated by the contemporary chroniclers and upper
classes, as also by the sentimental paintings of the nineteenth century.
Joan simply continued to be an intelligent, pious country girl, but not one
to be trifled with; blessed moreover, as long as she lived, with good sense
and a lively wit.

Although when she arrived in Orleans, Joan had no official position
of command (but she is referred to in official documents, in November,
1429, as one of the two commanders of the French troops), she had all the
accoutrements of knighthood: her made-to-measure armour, her sword,
her lance, her horse. The most prized object in her armoury however,
was her standard, the rallying point for the troops. She was questioned
closely about it in the fourth session of her trial, for after Orleans it had
terrified the superstitious English soldiery who believed it to be bewitched,
dedicated to Satan himself. This is the account she gave of it at her trial
in Rouen on 27 February 1431:

Beaupère: When you went to Orleans, did you have a standard or
banner, and what colour was it?

Joan: I had a standard. The field was sewn with fleur-de-lys. The globe was painted on it[1] and there were two angels on each side. It was white, made of white linen, and the names Jesus Maria were inscribed on it, I think, and it had a silk fringe.
Beaupère: Do you prefer your standard or your sword?
Joan: I much prefer my standard, forty times more! I have told you often enough already that I have done nothing but by God's command [...] I carried the standard myself when I was attacking the enemy, in order to avoid killing anyone, I have never killed anybody.

Her assertion that she had never killed anyone, that she carried the standard and not the sword into battle, is supported by Alençon's statement, made at the Nullity trial, describing her action at the walls of Jargeau during the storming of that town:

Joan was on a scaling-ladder, holding her standard in her hand. It was hit and she herself was struck on the head by a rock which broke over her helmet [...] She was knocked to the ground, and picking herself up again, she shouted to the men-at-arms, 'Friends! Friends! Forward! Forward! Our Lord has condemned the English! Now we have them! Courage!'

That tells us all we need to know about Joan's leadership in the field. It was not that she thought herself invulnerable. Marguerite La Tourolde testified that when Joan heard that people were saying such a thing, she said: 'I have no more guarantee than any of the men-at-arms'. Alençon says he had heard her telling the king that she would last 'about a year, not much more'.

She was questioned again about the standard in the first non-public session of her trial, held in her prison cell on 10 March, with only Bishop Cauchon and five assessors, and of course the notaries, present. The interrogator was Jean de la Fontaine:

La Fontaine: What was the meaning of the painting of God holding the world in His hand and accompanied by two angels?
Joan: Saints Catherine and Margaret told me to have a standard and to carry it boldly. I had the King of Heaven painted on it. I told my king about it, but very reluctantly. I don't know anything else about the meaning.

Some item of the questioning seems to be omitted here in the minutes. Why does she say she told the king *reluctantly*? Was she reluctant to describe the standard because the king might think it a piece of vanity on the part of a peasant girl? Is this why she insists that she was only doing the bidding of the saints? Did she guess that the judges were seeking to accuse her of vainglory? Indeed, such is the allegation in Article LVIII of the seventy articles of accusation. After a description of the standard and its appearance at the coronation at Rheims, it is alleged that 'All that seems to be pomp and vanity rather than religion and piety. To attribute such vanities to God and the angels is contrary to the reverence due to God and the saints.' When the seventy articles were finally condensed to twelve, the accusations concerning the standard were dropped. Clearly they were not felt to be a strong enough piece of damning evidence.

Clément de Fauquembergue, clerk of the Parlement of Paris, also speaks of her in his official register, describing her, both at Orleans and at Jargeau, as *une pucelle portant bannière* (a girl carrying a banner).[2] He has drawn a little doodle of her in the margin of the register, showing her with long flowing hair, wearing a long dress, her sword held down by her side in her left hand and her standard in her right hand. He had, of course, never seen her, but the prominence given to the standard is interesting.

Her intelligence, although she declared that she 'didn't know A from B', is clear enough from the answers she gave to her interrogators at Rouen. In his deposition in 1456, Jean Marcel says that he heard the Dominican friar, Jean le Sauvage, who had been present at some of the sessions in Rouen (but not as judge or assessor), say that 'he had never seen a woman of that age give so much difficulty to those who were interrogating her and he greatly admired her replies and her memory'. Jean Barbin, a lawyer who had been present at Poitiers, testified in 1456 that the theologians and lawyers who questioned her there said that 'she had replied very intelligently, as well as if she had been a good cleric.'

All her companions bear witness to her piety. Again it is Jean Barbin who tells us that he had heard the wife of Jean Rabateau, in whose house Joan was lodged during her stay in Poitiers, say that 'Every day, after meals, Joan would kneel for a long time, even at night. She often went into the little chapel in the house and prayed there for a long time also.' Dunois's testimony is similar:

> Every day, at the hour of vespers or twilight, she would withdraw into a church and have the bells rung for half-an-hour. She would assemble the mendicant friars who followed the royal army, say a prayer and have the friars sing a hymn to the Blessed Virgin, the Mother of God.

As well as private prayer, she heard Mass as often as possible, three Masses in one morning, as we have seen, for example, at Fierbois. In this she was not unique, Henry V also on occasion heard three Masses in succession, while Charles VII heard two Masses daily, one with music, the other a Low Mass, made his confession every day and received communion on the feast days of the Church.[3] Like him, she was in the habit of frequent confession. Brother Pasquerel, her confessor, gave the following testimony (4 May 1456):

> She was very pious towards God and the Blessed Virgin, she went to confession nearly every day and frequently went to communion. When she was in a town where there was a friary of the Mendicants (i.e. Franciscans), she asked me to remind her on which days the young children received communion, so that she could receive it with them.

In this frequent recourse to the sacraments, particularly of confession, some critics see a pathology, but they fail to understand the mindset of the time. There is an illuminating exchange during the trial at Rouen, on the afternoon of 14 March 1431:

> Jean de la Fontaine: Do you need to go to confession, since you have a revelation from your saints that you will be saved?
> Joan: I don't know that I have committed a mortal sin, but if I was in a state of mortal sin, I think that Saint Catherine and Saint Margaret would abandon me immediately. I think it is not possible to overdo the cleansing of one's conscience.

The reason for taking a daily shower is not because one is filthy! She was devout, but no solemn kill-joy. She laughed at the idea that people were bringing rosaries for her to touch. In concluding his testimony, Dunois remembered her cheerful good humour:

> Joan used to joke about military exploits to cheer up the soldiers, or about lots of things to do with war, which we hadn't perhaps got around to doing. But when she spoke seriously about the war and her own actions and vocation, she never said anything other than that she had been sent to raise the siege of Orleans, to help the sorely oppressed people of that town and its surroundings, and to lead the king to Rheims to be crowned.

With her vow of chastity, which, she said, did not rule out her getting married at some future date, she was in fact committing herself completely, for as long as necessary, to the vocation to which she was convinced God had called her. Dunois testifies that d'Aulon, who had been with Joan throughout her campaigns, had told him he didn't believe there was a woman alive more chaste than her. Dunois himself testifies that neither he nor any other felt any temptation in her presence.

Jean d'Aulon, appointed by Charles VII to serve as her personal attendant, made the following written deposition in 1456 (dated Lyon, 28 May):

> Despite the fact that she was a good-looking girl, with a good figure, and although several times, in helping her to get armed or such like, or

when her wounds were being dressed, I saw her breasts and sometimes her bare legs, and although also I was physically close to her on many occasions and I was a strong young man in my prime, yet whatever contact or sight I had of her, never ever did I experience any carnal desire, nor did any of my men or squires, as I heard them say a number of times.

Alençon's testimony is similar:

Sometimes on campaign, Joan and I and the men-at-arms slept rough. Occasionally I saw her getting dressed and I glimpsed her breasts, which were beautiful, but I never had any carnal desire concerning her.

One or two other remarks were made at the Nullity trial about Joan's physique, remarks in which some authors have exerted themselves to find abstruse medical or psychological significance. D'Aulon said that he had heard from some ladies 'who had seen the Maid unclothed several times and knew that she had never had the secret malady of women and that nobody had perceived or known of any such thing, from her garments or otherwise.' Unusual, but by no means miraculous or necessarily pathological. Menstruation sometimes did not start until the age of seventeen or so for many young women in the nineteenth century, for example. In any case, Joan was essentially a very private and discreet person.

Sir Simon Charles was struck by another oddity:

While she was armed and mounted, she never needed to dismount for natural physical needs. All the men-at-arms admired her ability to stay so long on horseback.

Once again, exceptional, but nothing more. As she ate and drank very frugally, perhaps that helped. At Orleans, on 7 May 1429, for example, after the taking of the fortification of Les Tourelles, during which she had been wounded, Dunois affirms that 'after the surgeon had dressed her wound, she took some refreshment in the form of four or five little bits of bread soaked in wine diluted with a lot of water, and she took no other food or drink that whole day.' The *Journal du Siège d'Orléans* describes in identical terms her endurance on the day of her arrival in Orleans. Gaucourt testifies that 'Joan was frugal in eating and drinking'. Louis de Coutes, her page at Orleans, gives this account in 1456 of her on the evening after the taking of the *bastille* of Saint-Loup:

In the evening, Joan dined in her lodgings, she was very frugal and several times, during a whole day she only ate a bit of bread. People were astonished that she ate so little. And when she was in her lodgings, she only ate twice a day.

As a rule, Joan slept in the company of women. Louis de Coutes goes on to say: 'Always at night she had a woman sleeping beside her, if she could find one. If she couldn't find any, being at war or on campaign, she slept fully clothed.' Sometimes she even slept in her armour, for the same witness says that, on arriving at Orleans, 'she was all bruised, for she had slept in her armour the night before her departure from Blois.'

D'Aulon and others felt that the chasteness of their reaction to her was so extraordinary that there must be something supernatural about it and it is clear enough that her companions' lack of libido cannot be attributed to any unattractiveness in her person. However, it is equally clear that Joan's courage and piety simply commanded a huge respect among her troops. At her trial in Rouen, on 4 March 1431, she describes her style of leadership: 'Sometimes I said to my troops, "Go in boldly among the English", and I went in myself.'

Her wish to be known as Joan the Maid, her piety, her humanity and simplicity, the enormous enthusiasm of the common people who adored her, the admiration of the soldiers for her bravery in battle, her skill with artillery, her excellent horsemanship, all that added up to what we call charisma and demanded respect from the roughest of men.

All the same, after her capture, she was more vulnerable, the spell was broken. In her prison, especially in Rouen, where she was alone and guarded by hostile soldiers all around her, she had more need than ever of the protection of her male clothing.

We get a glimpse of her private life from Dame Marguerite La Tourolde, the lady we have met already as the mistress of the house in which Joan was lodged at Bourges. Dame Marguerite was a lady of some importance and quite aware of it. Her husband was, after all, as she mentions with pride, the *receveur du roy*. During the three weeks that Joan spent in her house, she had observed that Joan always behaved 'like a respectable Catholic woman, she went to confession frequently and liked to go to Mass. Several times she asked me to go to Matins, and I went with her on several occasions.' She fills in one or two interesting details about Joan's life at the time. Joan, she says, hated dice and gambling. 'She was very generous in alms-giving, liking to help the indigent and saying that she had been sent for their consolation'. She adds that she had seen Joan several times in the public bath-house, *les étuves*, and was sure that she was a virgin (how she could tell this from Joan's appearance is unclear).

This information has raised some eyebrows. What were these public bath-houses? A word here about medieval hygiene: medieval people in general, from at least the twelfth century onwards, were as concerned as any about personal cleanliness and when they could afford it, they enjoyed all the luxuries of bathing in warm water, as well as the herbal rubs and massages which were on offer at the public bath-houses.[4] Medical treatises advocated frequent bathing for one's health. It was recommended, for example, that infants be bathed three times a day. Palaces and monasteries had their own baths. Otherwise, as there was no indoor plumbing, the public baths were, as in Roman times, places of relaxation, sociability and pleasure. People bathed naked and communally in large round tubs or vats. There were steam baths and hot and warm water baths (steam baths were cheaper). The men who serviced the baths were members of guilds and their duties included seeing to the cleanliness of the pipes and conduits, evidently they were aware of the dangers of water pollution.

From the early fifteenth century onwards it had been found necessary to enforce regulations to safeguard public decency, setting aside separate times or days for women's and men's bathing, since some of the bathhouses (or 'stews' in English) had become notorious as places of ill fame. We may be sure that the baths visited by Joan were not in this category, since that very respectable lady, the Dame La Tourolde, had no hesitation in stating that she, as well as Joan, frequented them. Raoul de Gaucourt, when he had a fall from his horse and dislocated his arm early in the siege of Orleans, was taken to the *étuves* to be attended to.[5]

It was later, in the sixteenth century, that the age of the great unwashed set in, possibly because of the fear that any water, especially warm water, was conducive to the spread of disease particularly the syphilis which voyagers had by then brought back from America. Henry VIII ordered the closure of all public bathhouses in 1546.

Marguerite concludes her testimony by saying that Joan was naïve and innocent, 'except for military affairs. She rode carrying the lance as well as the best men-at-arms and the soldiers admired her greatly for that.'

Alençon also testifies to Joan's military skill:

Apart from the business of war, Joan was young and simple in the way she behaved. But she was very competent in things to do with war, carrying the lance, gathering together the army, planning the battle and preparing the artillery. Everyone was full of admiration for the skilful and prudent way she acted in military engagements as if she had been a captain with twenty or thirty years experience, and especially in all that was to do with the preparation of the artillery. She excelled at that.

Was her *beau duc* exaggerating? Be that as it may, Joan certainly had a competence which aroused surprise and admiration.

She was anxious that her soldiers should be in a state of grace as well as herself, that they should use no profane language, should not pillage, should have nothing to do with camp-followers, and should clear their consciences in confession.

Brother Pasquerel describes how the army set out from Blois for Orleans:

When Joan left the town of Blois for Orleans, she gathered all the priests around her standard and they walked in front of the men-at-arms. They proceded along the Sologne side of the Loire, singing the Veni creator Spiritus and many other hymns.

Canon Pierre Compaing, a priest of Orleans, testified in 1456, that he had seen La Hire and several men of his company make their confession 'at Joan's request and instigation'. To get La Hire to confession must have been quite a feat. Another canon of Orleans, André Bordes, says that he heard Joan reproving certain soldiers 'when they blasphemed the name of God. In particular, I saw certain men-at-arms who had led very dissolute lives, whom Joan persuaded to change their ways and cease to do evil.'

Guillaume de Ricarville, who had been in Orleans at the time of the siege, says that Joan 'reproved the men-at- arms when they blasphemed the name of God or swore. She reproved them also when they committed misdeeds or acts of violence.'

Joan made no distinction of rank or power. A woman of Orleans, named simply as Renaude, widow of J. Huré, testified in March 1456:

One day I saw and heard a great lord who, walking down the street, was swearing and blaspheming horribly. Joan saw and heard him and was very upset. She went straight up to this nobleman who was swearing and put her hands around his neck and said, 'Oh! my lord, do you dare to deny Our Lord and Master? In God's name, you will retract all that before I leave you!' Then, as I myself saw, the nobleman repented and amended his ways at the request of the Maid.

For how long he amended his ways, we can't be sure, but no doubt, in his astonishment at what was happening to him, he made his lordly apologies to Joan. La Hire, too, was, as we may expect, addicted to profanity. He also was taken to task by Joan and told that if he must swear, he should swear by his *bâton*, as Brother Seguin de Seguin testified at the Nullity proceedings in 1456. And in future, when Joan was around, he did so.

Alençon had a habit of swearing. However, he couldn't have been the 'great lord' of the Orleans story, since he was not present at Orleans, but he does say, when he testifies:

(Joan) was very annoyed when she heard the men-at-arms swearing, she scolded them a lot, and particularly me, for I swore sometimes, but when I saw her about, I refrained from doing so.

Another problem for Joan's desire for a Christian army was the presence of prostitutes or camp-followers. At Orleans, says Pasquerel, she ordered that 'women of easy virtue should not follow her (i.e. the army), because God would then allow the war to be lost because of their sins.' This conviction was enough to reveal another character trait – she was capable of impatience and anger. Alençon:

Joan was chaste and detested those women who follow the armies. In fact, I saw her at Saint-Denis, after the king's coronation, chasing a woman living with the soldiers, her sword drawn out of the scabbard, and in her chase she broke it.

She must have been on foot, the lady in question could hardly have outrun a horse, perhaps Joan tripped over something and broke the sword in her fall. Alençon does not say that she broke the sword over the woman and indeed that would be out of character with what we know of her, although she did say somewhat defiantly at her trial, that the sword with which she was captured was 'a good sword for war and good for giving thumps and smacks'! (*bonnes buffes et bons torchons*).[6]

She was despondent and exasperated at Saint-Denis, the attack on Paris having failed, largely because of Charles VII's unwillingness to engage fully with it, so perhaps she was blaming the women and their sinful lives for the setback. At all events, she no doubt put the fear of God into the object of her wrath.

Jean Chartier says that she broke the sword earlier at Gien, when she used it to pursue two or three 'women of ill fame' who were dissuading her men-at-arms from taking part in the march on Rheims, The king told her she ought to have used a good stick for the job! Louis de Coutes has a similar but gentler story:

Once, indeed, near the town of Château-Thierry, seeing a woman on horseback, the concubine of a soldier, Joan pursued her with her sword out of its scabbard. However, she didn't hit the woman, but told her, gently and mildly, not to frequent the men-at-arms, or she would be in trouble.

Simon Beaucroix, a squire who was with her at Orleans, testified at the Nullity trial:

She never wanted to see a woman of ill-fame accompanying the troops. None of them dared to show themselves when she was about and Joan forced any that she came upon to depart, unless the men were willing to marry them.

Joan would not eat anything that had been pillaged, and she could lose her temper on that subject. Beaucroix:

On campaign, she never allowed that any of her company should pillage, she would never eat food that she knew had been stolen. One day a Scotsman told her that that she had just eaten stolen veal, she was very angry and was going to hit him.

Who stopped her hitting him? Of course, we don't know if the Scot was deliberately provoking her! 'When the army was campaigning,' says Pasquerel, 'sometimes the necessary provisions could not be found. But Joan would never eat supplies procured through pillage.'

Like Henry V, like many of her contemporaries, Joan was convinced that the misfortunes of the people, French or English, were a consequence of sinfulness. Towards the end of the trial in Rouen, on Saturday, 17 March, several very tricky questions were put to her concerning the Almighty's disposition towards the French and the English, She shows considerable prudence and intelligence in her answers:

> La Fontaine: Do you know whether Saints Catherine and Margaret hate the English?
> Joan: They love what God loves and hate what God hates.
> La Fontaine: Does God hate the English?
> Joan: I know nothing about the love or hate that God has for the English [...],
> La Fontaine: Was God on the side of the English when they were prospering in France?
> Joan: I don't know whether God hated the French, but I believe that He allowed them to be beaten on account of their sins, if they were in a state of sin.

In the afternoon session of that Saturday a leading question was put to her about Charles VII:

> Jean de la Fontaine: Do you think and believe firmly that your king did well to kill the Duke of Burgundy?
> Joan: It was a great disaster for the kingdom of France, but, whatever there was between those two princes, God sent me to help the King of France.

She does not pronounce on the guilt or innocence of Charles VII. Nor does she pass judgement on the state of men's souls. She was capable of compassion for all the afflicted, whichever side they were on. Orleans was her first taste of the horrors of war and she reacted with distress to it. Describing the taking of the fortification of Saint-Loup during the siege of Orleans, her chaplain Pasquerel remarks, in his depositon, 'Many of the English were killed. Joan was greatly distressed, for she said that they had died without confession. She pitied them greatly'.

The greatest misfortune that could befall anyone in the ages of faith, was to die *unshriven*, without the consolation of confession and absolution, 'unhouseled, disappointed, unaneled', like Hamlet's father. 'She greatly pitied the poor men-at-arms, even if they were fighting on the English side,' says Pasquerel again, 'and when she saw them wounded or dying, she got a priest to hear their confession.' As for the French dead, Pasqerel remembers Joan's wish:

> Joan said to me several times, that if she died, Our Lord the King should have chapels built where prayers may be said for the souls of all those who had died for the defence of the kingdom.

Louis de Coutes, Joan's pageboy at the time, remembers how shocked she was by the brutality of war. Here is his testimony in 1456:

> She felt great pity for so much massacre. One day, a Frenchman who was in charge of certain English prisoners, struck one of them such a blow on the head that he left him for dead. When Joan saw that, she got off her horse, sent for someone to hear the Englishman's confession, held his head and did her best to console him.

Joan had her forebodings or premonitions, Alençon remembers hearing her telling the king that 'she would last a year, not much more and that during that year it would be necessary to plan and work hard. She claimed that she had four tasks: to chase the English away, to have the king crowned at Rheims, to deliver the Duke of Orleans from the hands of the English and to raise the siege of Orleans'.

Dunois does not mention Joan's goal of delivering the Duke of Orleans from captivity, whether he never heard her state it or whether because she herself never achieved it. It is certain that she desired to do so. Tisset suggests that regard for the House of Orleans was particularly high in Lorraine because Duke Louis of Orleans had maintained the prestige of the monarchy there during the unfortunate reign of the mad King Charles VI. At the second session of her trial in Rouen (22 February 1431), Joan declared: 'I know that God loves the Duke of Orleans, and I have had more revelations about him than about any other living soul except for my king.'

Again on 12 March, when asked how she would have gone about freeing the duke, she replied that she would have taken enough English prisoners to ransom him and if that didn't suffice, she would have crossed the sea to go and fetch him. To do that, she said, she would have needed between one and three years.

With these goals in mind, after the coronation of Charles VII at Rheims Joan was eager to keep up the impetus of her successes at Orleans and the subsequent astonishing victories. She was anxious to advance immediately on Paris, but the king, engaged in slippery negotiations with Burgundy, was dragging his feet under the influence of his devious minister La Trémoille, who had his own agenda. Dunois, in his testimony of 1456, recalls a melancholy remark which she made at that time while riding with him and the Archbishop of Chartres. 'May it please God, my Creator,' she said, 'to allow me to retire, abandoning arms, and let me go and help my father and mother, keeping their sheep.' Even if the bit about *keeping sheep* strikes one as being supplied by Dunois's aristocratic imagination, which stubbornly held on to the fixed idea that the extraordinary girl was really a little shepherdess, we need not doubt that she did express some weariness at this point in her career.

The tone is quite different from that of a remark which Alençon recalls her making before the assault on Jargeau, a few days after the lifting of the siege of Orleans:

> There was a debate among the captains, some wanted to launch the attack, others were against it, saying that the English were there in force and great numbers. Joan, seeing this dissent, told them not to fear the number and not to hesitate to attack, because God was leading their campaign. She added that if she hadn't been sure that God was in charge, she would have preferred to look after the sheep and not expose herself to such perils.

Is the remark about sheep again an aristocrat's preconception, colouring his version of what was actually said, or was Joan playing up to the popular image? At any rate, her confidence was total at that stage, but what is clear from both remarks is that her preferred way of life was not warfare. She was a soldier only because of a compelling conviction that such was her inescapable duty.

Certain historians, most notably Anatole France, have maintained that she was merely a useful mascot, or standard bearer. That is unsustainable. To achieve her purposes, she had to overcome the initial disdain of the experienced aristocratic captains as well as pushing constantly for action against the private agendas of courtiers such as La Trémoille and others around the king. She it was who recognised the supreme importance of having Charles crowned before Bedford could bring the child Henry VI to Rheims for his coronation. She it was who, after Orleans, hastened with Dunois and other captains to see Charles at Loches, to urge him to set out across the hostile Burgundian territory, to impress upon him the necessity of providing men and arms for a campaign to take the towns and castles blocking his way on the Loire, chiefly Meung, Beaugency and Jargeau: 'She urged the king very insistently and repeatedly, to make haste, not to wait longer,' as Dunois affirms.

At all times throughout the year of her military career, it was she who recognised that rapid direct action was desirable before the other side could strengthen their positions, but she was increasingly handicapped by the passivity of Charles VII, very much at that period of his life under the influence of his favourites. The earliest mention of her in a contemporary chronicle says that, when she spoke to the king and his council in Chinon 'she dealt marvellously with the tactics for getting the English out of the kingdom. No other military leader so well expounded the ways to fight the enemy, which amazed the king and all his council.'[7] Allowing that the anonymous author is partisan, nonetheless he is echoing the popular perception of Joan as a leader. Her example and courage powerfully inspired the troops and tribute has been paid to her on that account by the military leaders of her time, Dunois, Alençon, D'Aulon and others, and by military men ever since. Dunois declared that he believed that her exploits were so extraordinary that they were achieved 'by divine inspiration rather than human talent'. She took decisions. It is Joan, for example, who decides that the English should be allowed to march off from Orleans unimpeded, the morning after the successful assault on the *bastille* of Les Tourelles, a success due, incidentally, to her refusal to give up the assault because night was falling.

Certainly those on the Anglo/Burgundian side thought she was more than a mascot. Clément de Fauquembergue describes her as 'a woman called the Maid, who led the army, together with other captains of the said Messire Charles de Valois'[8] (Charles VII, who was, of course, not given his title of *King* under the English administration). The registers of the Parlement were the Hansard of the day, recording political and military affairs. In the articles of condemnation drawn up for consultation at the end of her trial in Rouen, Article LIII accuses Joan as follows:

> Contrary to the commandments of God and the saints, Joan assumed with presumption and pride domination over men, constituting herself chief and leader of an army sometimes numbering 16,000 men, among whom were princes, barons and many other nobles, whom she obliged to serve under her as under a principal captain.

This item of indictment was dropped from the final twelve articles on which she was condemned, but we see that one of her chief sins was that she stepped out of the role of a woman and scandalously *dominated men*. Joan maintained at her trial that she had never styled herself *chef de guerre*. Of course she did not replace the experienced captains, but she often got her own way, in particular at Orleans and on the campaign to reach Rheims, while her personal bravery, fervour and military competence turned the morale of her whole army around.

9

Orleans

In victory, magnanimity

Winston Churchill

Joan remained in Blois for two or three days, while supplies for Orleans were loaded onto boats on the river. In the town she met such important military personages as the Sire de Boussac, Marshal of France, Louis de Culant, Admiral of France, La Hire, and the Breton Gilles de Rais. De Rais is infamous in history as the prototype for the story of Bluebeard. After 1432, he left military life, squandered a fortune, indulged heavily in occultism and in 1440 was tried and found guilty of innumerable unspeakable murders of children, dating back to 1432. A great number of these heinous crimes were committed in his castle at Machecoul. He was hanged, with two accomplices, at Nantes in October 1440.

It was in Blois, according to Brother Pasquerel, that Joan had another banner made, smaller than her standard, around which she was to gather the priests accompanying her soldiers. It bore an image of the crucified Saviour. Before setting out for Orleans, as the Nullity trial witness Sir Simon Beaucroix remembers, 'Joan recommended all the soldiers to go to confession, to put their souls in order, assuring them that God would help them and that, if they kept themselves in order, they would obtain victory with the help of God.' Acting on this conviction, Joan tried her best to outlaw swearing and pillage and other excesses and to banish prostitutes from the camp. Needless to say, making saints out of sinners is literally a superhuman struggle and success is not guaranteed.

It was high time that help should come to Orleans.

On 27 April 1429, Joan, who had as yet no official command, started out from Blois, some thirty or so miles down the Loire south of Orleans, at the head of an army led by a procession of priests chanting the *Veni creator spiritus* and other hymns, together with a convoy of cattle, on their way to re-provision the town of Orleans and raise the siege. When asked at her trial how many men the king had given her at the start of her campaign, she answered, 'ten or twelve thousand', but to many historians the figure seems implausibly high. We read in Chartier's *Chronique de Charles VII*, that 'Some difficulty was raised about bringing into the town of Orleans so many men, for there were not enough provisions'.[1] It would have been impossible to billet and feed that number in the town for more than a day or two, but then this was probably the time-scale Joan had in mind and she was, of course, bringing copious supplies with her. Several other sources support her statement and perhaps it is worth noting that, for example, when she returned to Orleans after the siege, on 9 June, for a couple of days, she was accompanied by an army of around eight thousand men who would have had to be billeted and fed, no-one making any objection to the number.

It has been suggested that Joan was talking of the army which arrived before the town of Orleans on April 29, since those who returned four days later were three times fewer, according to Chartier,[2] the majority having been persuaded to return to their garrisons, which perhaps it would not have been wise to leave under-manned in the case of a long drawn-out battle for Orleans. A letter sent on 10 May 1429, from Pancrazio Giustiniani in Bruges to his father in Venice, states the original figure (twelve thousand) as representing *tuto el sforzo che pote far el dolfin*, 'the total army which the Dauphin had been able to muster'.[3] Brother Pasquerel says that the number of men she brought into Orleans was very inferior to the number of besiegers, who, as we know, numbered in total about ten thousand. Bedford, in his famous letter addressed to the child Henry VI towards the end of July, 1429, speaks of 'all your people (soldiers) assembled there (at Orleans) in great number'.[4] Monstrelet, the Burgundian chronicler, puts the number of Joan's men in Orleans at seven thousand. Other sources put the numbers much lower, the *Chronique de Tournay* gives an estimate of three thousand troops, with sixty cartloads of food and munitions and four hundred and thirty-five carts laden with livestock. This indeed would be three times fewer than Joan's estinate of twelve thousand and some historians consider it to be the most probable number to have arrived with Joan on the left bank of the Loire on on the morning of 29 April 1429.[5]

When Joan arrived before Orleans, mounted on her charger, in her hand her standard fluttering in the breeze, followed by a troop of chanting priests heading the long column of soldiers and the convoy of provisions and cattle, she realised she was on the wrong side of the Loire. The river was between her and the town. Here she was, with an army and a huge train of provisions, and the river Loire to cross in small boats. No wonder she was aghast. The commander of the defenders inside the town, Dunois, at that time still styled the Bastard of Orleans, had given instructions for her to be brought by this route in order to avoid the strong English fortifications on the Orleans side of the river. They had also to avoid the English-held fort of Saint-Jean-le-Blanc on the Sologne side. Dunois had moreover given orders for a skirmish to be made outside the *bastille* of Saint-Loup, a mile or so upstream on the right bank of the Loire, in order to distract English attention from the arrival of Joan's convoy. Its garrison numbered about three hundred men, but as usual the exact figure is uncertain, Pasquerel puts it at a hundred, others at a hundred and fifty. The skirmish was a serious enough encounter, several combatants being killed or wounded, as well as prisoners taken, on both sides.

Under cover of these happenings, Dunois crossed the river upstream with a number of his men, out of range of the English guns. He did not find Joan ready for the niceties of polite introductions. She had intended to approach Orleans directly, without any need to ship men and supplies and cattle across the river, which was now turning out to be well-nigh impossible, and she had been totally confident that the Almightily would see the whole contingent safely past the English *bastilles*. Both strategies, hers and Dunois', were risky and Joan's plan may indeed have been the better. At least one historian considers that the English would not have risked leaving their forts to attack such a large force beyond the range of their guns, since they were weakened by desertions and waiting for reinforcements to be brought in very soon by Fastolf.[6] To Joan's dismay however, the situation being what it now was, the great body of the troops had no option but to return to Blois and eventually cross the Loire there, as they would have done in the first place, if her intention had been carried out.

Joan was probably already, before the arrival of Dunois, feeling somewhat sore, mentally and physically, for she had left Blois the day before and camped out overnight *en route* with her troops, spending the night, as D'Aulon tells us, sleeping, or trying to sleep, in her fine new suit of armour. That episode was bruising, in all senses of the word. As he himself tells us, Dunois found himself facing a very irascible young woman:

All of them, with Joan the Maid and the soldiers conducting the convoy, came up in orderly fashion on the Sologne side, directly up to the banks of the Loire, opposite the church called Saint-Loup, where there were a lot of brave English soldiers. So it seemed to me and the other captains that the king's troops, that is to say, the men-at-arms accompanying the supplies, were not sufficient to face them and get the supplies into the town, In particular, it seemed that the boats necessary to transport the supplies, which were difficult to procure, would have to sail against the current and with a completely adverse wind. Then Joan addressed me as follows: 'Are you the Bastard of Orleans?' I answered, 'I am, and I'm glad to see you here.' She replied, 'Is it you who gave the advice that I was to be brought here on this side of the river, and that we were not to go directly where Talbot and the English are?' I answered that I, and others wiser than me, had given that advice, believing that we were acting for the best and in the interest of the greatest safety. Then she said, 'In God's name, the counsel of God, the Lord, is more sure and wiser than yours. You thought you would mislead me, and you are much more misled yourselves, for I am bringing you the best help ever given to a soldier or a city, the help of the King of Heaven. It doesn't come to you for love of me. It comes from God, who, at the intercession of Saint Louis and Saint Charlemagne,[7] took pity on the town of Orleans and would not allow the enemy to have the Duke of Orleans and his town as well.'

Then, at that very moment, the wind, which was very adverse, very contrary to the progress of the boats carrying the supplies for Orleans, changed and became favourable. The sails were hoisted immediately. I got on board, together with Brother Nicolas de Géresme, who is now Grand Prior of the order in France, and we sailed past the church of Saint-Loup, in spite of the English. After that, I had great confidence in Joan, more than before. I begged her to cross the Loire and enter the town, where she was eagerly awaited. She was unwilling to do that, saying she didn't wish to abandon her troops, men-at-arms who had all been to confession, repented their sins, and were full of good intentions. I went to see the captains who were responsible for the soldiers and asked them, for the king's sake, to agree that Joan could enter the town and that they would go with the troops to Blois, from where they would cross the Loire to get to Orleans, for there was no nearer crossing point. The captains agreed to this request and consented to cross the river at Blois. Then Joan left with me, she holding aloft her standard, which was white, with the image of Our Lord holding a fleur-de-lys.[8] La Hire also crossed the Loire with her and they entered the town of Orleans together.

The skirmish ordered by Dunois had not only prevented the garrison of Saint-Loup from calling for reinforcements from Talbot's headquarters in the *bastille* of Saint-Laurent and blocking the entry into Orleans, but had ensured that supplies could be safely ferried across further up the Loire to Chécy on the right bank, island-hopping by barge from one large island in the middle of the river to the next. The provisions were then brought safely into Orleans by the one unblockaded gate, the *Porte de Bourgogne*. Joan and Dunois and others followed, with about two hundred lances (eight hundred or a thousand men), according to the witness Simon Beaucroix at the Nullity trial. The other captains and men returned to Blois, whence they had come, shepherded by the escort of priests and Brother Pasquerel carrying the banner with the image of the crucified Christ. As to Joan and her escort, it was decided that they would wait in the village of Reuilly until nightfall before entering the town. The *Journal du Siège d'Orleans* describes the scene as Joan rode into the town on 29 April 1429:

They all agreed that she would not enter Orleans until nightfall, in order to avoid the tumultuous excitement of the people [...] So at eight o'clock, in spite of the English, who made no attempt to stop her, she entered fully armed, mounted on a white horse, her standard being carried before her. It was white also, and on it were painted two angels, each holding a fleur-de-lys. And she had a pennant, on which was painted an Annumciation, that is, Our Lady with an angel kneeling before her and presenting her with a lily.

So, as she entered Orleans, she had on her left the Bastard of Orleans, fully armed and very richly attired. After them followed other valiant noble lords, squires, captains and soldiers (but not the men of the garrison) and citizens of Orleans, running in front of her. Other soldiers came out to welcome her also, and men and women of Orleans, carrying a great number of torches, as joyful as if God Himself had come down among them, and with good reason, for they had suffered many troubles and difficulties and had greatly feared that no-one would come to their rescue and so they would lose both life and goods. But now they felt themselves completely reassured, as if the siege were already lifted by virtue of the holiness that they had been told was in this simple Maid, whom they all, men, women and children, regarded with great affection. There was such a great throng pressing around her, trying to touch her or even the horse that she was riding, that one of the torches came too close to her standard and the pennant caught fire. But she spurred on the horse and turned towards the pennant and extinguished the flames, as if she had been a long time in the wars. The men-at-arms and the citizens were amazed. They accompanied her through the town with great rejoicing and brought her with all honour to the Regnart Gate and the house of Jacques Boucher, then Treasurer of the Duke of Orleans, where she was welcomed with great joy, as well as her two brothers and the two noblemen and their servant who had come with them from the Barrois.[9]

Jean Luillier, a citizen of Orleans, present in the town when Joan arrived, says in his testimony of 16 March 1456, that 'she was received with as much joy and applause by all, men and women, the great and the lowly, as if she had been one of God's angels!'

In Jacques Boucher's house, Joan shared a bed with the young daughter of the family, Charlotte, then aged about ten. In the Middle Ages, bed-sharing between persons of the same sex was perfectly normal. Indeed, it was considered to be a guarantee that no illicit sex of any kind was going on. Charlotte testified at the Nullity trial in 1456 that she had never seen in Joan anything but 'simplicity, humility and chastity'. Joan later made a present of a handsome hat to the little girl.

Joan and Dunois and their company had entered Orleans by the Porte de Bourgogne on the eastern side of the city. She was lodged at the opposite end of the town, beside the Porte Regnart, almost directly opposite the great English fortress of Saint Laurent, Talbot's headquarters.

Dunois' belief in Joan was now absolute. Seeing all that had taken place, 'It seemed to me,' he said, 'That her conduct of the war was inspired by God rather than by human intelligence.'

On 30 April, now inside Orleans, Joan, with youthful impatience, couldn't wait to start on her task. Her page, Louis de Coutes, who, when he testified in 1456, had become lord of several *seigneuries*, describes that first day in Orleans, 30 April 1429:

> The day after her entry into Orleans, Joan went to see my lord, the Bastard of Orleans, and spoke with him. She was very annoyed when she came back, because, she said, it had been decided that there would be no assault that day.

Jean Luillier:

> She wanted to issue a summons to the English besieging the town before allowing an assault to be made to force them out, and this was done. She summonsed the English by a letter, saying in substance that they had to withdraw from the siege and return to England, otherwise they would be obliged to withdraw by force and violence.

Dunois:

> When I wanted to go and fetch the soldiers to make the crossing at Blois and bring help to those in Orleans, Joan didn't want to wait, she wanted either to summon the English to lift the siege or to launch an assault. That was what she did, for she summoned the English with a letter written in very simple terms in her mother-tongue [i.e. not in Latin] either to lift the siege and return to the kingdom of England, or else she would make such a great assault on them that they would be obliged to depart.

As we have seen, she had already written such a letter from Poitiers. At any rate, she now again entrusted the delivery to her heralds. The enraged English, once more disregarding all the conventions of war and honour, again arrested a herald, Guyenne, clapped him in irons, and threatened to burn him. The other herald, Ambleville, was sent back to take this news to Joan.

Dunois politely describes her letter as being written in 'very simple terms'. Joan had no training in diplomatic letter-writing. The inelegant syntax and vocabulary and the naive pleas and menaces no doubt caused great and scornful merriment among the English lords, but great anger too, which found a voice in the insults hurled at the upstart Maid across the waters of the Loire. A rage so great that the herald was seriously in danger. In the eyes of the English, insult was piled on insult by the fact that the messenger had been given the title *Guyenne*, a duchy which had been English since the mid-thirteenth century.

At some point during that day there was a fierce skirmish outside the walls. It was led by La Hire, Florent d'Illiers and other captains, acting on their own initiative, without consulting Joan or Dunois. The English, says the *Journal*, drew up in battle order and raised their terrible battle cries. There were casualties on both sides.

Joan was hugely frustrated. Wishing to issue her summons before resorting to arms, no doubt she was annoyed by this unauthorised skirmish, which seems to have taken place during the morning, possibly while she was talking to Dunois. Later she went out onto the ramparts in front of the house where she was lodged and found herself within hailing distance of the English in their fortress of Saint Laurent. Had she already written her letter and sent it? That would have done nothing but stoke the fury of the recipients, all the more so if they had just suffered casualties. She got a very rough reception. Louis de Coutes describes at the Nullity hearings what ensued (3 April 1456):

> Joan called over to the English on the fortifications opposite, telling them to withdraw, in the name of Our Lord, otherwise she would chase them away. A certain knight called the Bastard of Granville shouted back insults at her, asking her if she thought they would surrender to a woman and calling the French who were with her filthy pimps ...

Granville was a Norman in the service of the English, so he would have had no difficulty at all in finding the appropriate insults in French. Perhaps on that account he had been delegated by Talbot to shout back at Joan.

Nothing daunted, Joan tried again later in the day. She went down to the bridge of Orleans and advanced along it as far as the arches which had been demolished by the defenders to prevent access. From there she called across to the English in the *bastille* of the Tourelles, asking them to surrender and promising that their lives would be spared. William Glasdale, the commander of the Tourelles, and his men replied again with insults, 'calling her cow-herd, as before,' says the *Journal*, 'and shouting that they would have her burned if they caught her'. The Burgundian *Bourgeois de Paris* confirms this:

> An English captain (i.e. Glasdale) swore at her, calling her a soldiers' trollop and a whore, while she replied that in spite of them all, the English would soon depart, but that he would never see the day and a great many of his troops would be killed. And indeed, so it happened, for he was drowned the day before the massacre.[10]

Massacre is a loaded term for the losses on the English side on May 7, when the Tourelles was taken.

Joan was angry, but contented herself with replying simply that what they were saying about her was all lies, then she went back to her lodgings. She wasn't in the business of slanging matches. The *Journal du Siège* says that towards evening she sent emissaries to Talbot to demand the safe return of the herald who had delivered the letter of 22 March and that Dunois sent a message that he would have the English prisoners executed if they failed to comply, under which threat the heralds (plural) were returned. Possibly the *Journal* confuses Joan's herald with the earlier messenger. Certainly Guyenne was not released, since on 5 May, Joan sent a third message demanding his return. Nor does it seem likely that Dunois would have seriously threatened to punish one war crime by another. There is no record of his ever behaving in such a way. The *Journal*, in a subsequent statement, speaks of more than one herald, and indeed the second herald, Ambleville, had been detained also. At some point, possibly a few days later, he was sent back to deliver the news of Guyenne's plight. A witness at the Nullity trial, Jacques l'Esbahy, a citizen of Orleans, says that Joan told Ambleville to return to the English camp and demand the release of his colleague, assuring him that no harm would come to him. The man bravely carried out the order and Guyenne was released, probably on 6 May. The English had had second thoughts about violating what was at the time the unwritten equivalent of the Geneva Convention.

Sunday, 1 May: in Joan's time, Sunday, like other Church feast days, was a day when fighting must be suspended. Dunois with his companions rode off to Blois to rally and fetch the troops assembled there. Joan, accompanied by an escort of knights and squires, rode through the streets of Orleans to show herself to the people, who in their desire to see her were ready to break down the doors of her host's house. We read in the *Journal*:

> There was such a throng of people in the streets as she passed, that she had great difficulty in getting through. The people couldn't get enough of her. It seemed extraordinary to all, how nobly she sat on her horse. Indeed she conducted herself so superbly in every way that she was the equal of any man-at-arms who had followed the wars from the days of his youth.[11]

Later in the day, Joan went out again and called upon the English to return to England, but she was again met with the same insults.

On Monday, 2 May, while Dunois was still away at Blois, Joan rode out to reconnoitre the English positions, 'a great crowd of people following her, hugely delighted to see her and be with her', says the *Journal*. Still the English did not move. Having satisfied herself, Joan turned back and attended Vespers in the Holy Cross Cathedral in the town. And so to bed.

Tuesday was another quiet day. It was the feast day of the Finding of the Holy Cross, celebrating the finding of the crucifix (or what was believed to be the crucifix) in Jerusalem by that energetic lady,

Saint Helena, the mother of the first Christian emperor, Constantine. A great procession, led by Joan and the captains of the troops in the city, was held to pray for the relief of the town. Reinforcements managed to arrive in Orleans from nearby towns, Montargis, Gien, Château-Regnard. Dunois was still in Blois, having found the troops there somewhat discouraged now that Joan was no longer with them, their captains unsure that it was worth going to Orleans or if the city should be written off as a lost cause. However, their confidence and enthusiasm was at last re-awakened and they set off once more, crossing over to the Beauce side of the Loire and approaching the town as Joan had originally intended. They left, says the chronicler Chartier, 'with a great company and a great quantity of grain and cattle and other provisions', and camped that night half-way between Blois and Orleans. The provisions had been contributed by the towns of Bourges, Angers, Tours and Blois. That day again, Joan called over to the English outside, once more to no effect.

Wednesday, 4 May: Dunois returned with about two thousand troops (as usual, the estimates vary), giving a wide berth to the English *bastilles*, London and Paris, on the west and north sides of the walls, and approaching through the forest behind the town, to make their entry through the Burgundy Gate. Between 'Paris' and the *bastille* of Saint-Loup down by the river on the eastern side of the city, there was a large gap, through which incomers could enter the town if the men in the *bastille* of Saint-Loup were unable to prevent them. Joan rode out to meet the reinforcements, her standard proudly held aloft, with La Hire and other captains and six hundred men. The cavalcade entered the town to great rejoicing from the townsfolk and without any stirring on the part of the English in their *bastilles* as Joan and Dunois and their troops passed by, the priests in procession with them chanting canticles as they went. The arrival of Fastolf, the victor of the *Journée des Harengs*, with his reinforcements was imminent and it would have been foolish for the English troops to sally out of their incomplete circle of fortresses in which they were fairly thinly spread. Their strategy was in any case to force the capitulation of the town, as of many others, through starving it of both food and munitions.

Joan ate with her squire Jean d'Aulon that day, probably around noon. When they were finishing their meal, Dunois came to tell them that Fastolf was now only a day's march away, at Janville, with reinforcements and provisions for the besiegers. D'Aulon says:

> When she heard that, she seemed to me overjoyed. She said to Monseigneur Dunois, 'Bastard, Bastard, in God's name, let me know as soon as you hear where he is, for if he gets in before I know it, I'll have your head off!'. My Lord Dunois said that she shouldn't worry, he'd certainly let her know.

After that, D'Aulon said he felt tired, and he and Joan and their hostess retired to Joan's room and all three lay down to have a siesta after the long march and the events of the morning. D'Aulon:

> I was just falling asleep, when suddenly Joan got up and shouted at me to wake up. I asked her what she wanted, and she said, 'In God's name, my Council (i.e. her Voices) are telling me to go out against the English, but I don't know if I am to go against their forts or against Fastolf who had come to reprovision them.' So I immediately got up and armed her as quickly as I could.
>
> While I was arming her, we heard a great deal of noise and cries coming from the people in the street, who were shouting that the enemy was inflicting great harm on the French. So I got armed as well, and while I was doing so, the Maid rushed out into the street, where she found a page on a horse, she made him dismount, mounted the horse herself and as directly and fast as she could, she made straight for the Burgundy Gate from where most of the noise was coming. I followed her immediately, but however fast I went, she was at the Gate before me.
>
> When we got to the Gate, we saw that that they were carrying in a man from the town, very badly wounded, The Maid asked who the man was, and she was told it was a Frenchman. Then she said that she had never seen French blood spilt but the hair on her head stood on end.
>
> Then she and I and other men-at-arms with her went out of the city to bring help to the French and hold back the enemy as best we could, but when we got out of the town, I thought I had never seen so many soldiers of our party as then.
>
> We next turned our attention to a very strong fortress held by the enemy, it was called Saint-Loup. It was immediately attacked and taken with very little loss on our side. All those in it were killed or taken prisoner and it passed into the hands of the French. The Maid and those of her company then withdrew into the city and took some refreshment and rested.

No-one had alerted Joan in advance of the attack on Saint-Loup, nor does Dunois talk about it in his deposition, although the *Journal du Siège* says that he and Joan led the attack, with about fifteen hundred men. But, given De Coutes' and D'Aulon's eye-witness accounts, that is clearly inaccurate.

The battle had lasted three hours, during which Talbot had ordered those of his troops in the great fortress which the English called Paris on the north side of Orleans, to go to the aid of the men in Saint-Loup. However, the church bells of Orleans rang the alarm and a force of six hundred captains, soldiers and citizens rode out to confront them, so that they were forced to retreat before reaching Saint-Loup.

Louis de Coutes also gives an account of that event which fills in some details, although he places it on the wrong day. He may be forgiven, he is speaking twenty-seven years later. He says that it was he whom Joan found in the street when she rushed out of the house and that she sent him post-haste to fetch a horse. Probably D'Aulon only arrived in time to see her mounting it. She had angrily shouted at the page, 'Ah! You wretched boy, you didn't tell me that the blood of France was being shed!' De Coutes continues the story: 'She told me to go and fetch her standard which was upstairs. I passed it out to her through the window. She snatched the standard and galloped off to the Burgundy Gate.'

He says that Joan saved some English clerics who had come out in their clerical robes to give themselves up:

> She received them, wouldn't let anyone do them any harm and had them sent to her lodgings, the other English having been killed by the townspeople of Orleans.

If that is true, there must have been a frenzied attack by elements of the population on the survivors of the assault. No-one else mentions such a massacre, but D'Aulon does say that all the English were killed or taken prisoner. If indeed a slaughter did take place, it would seem to have been the work of furious mobs, all male citizens having been ordered by Dunois to arm themselves in defence of the city. Possibly the 'clerics' were men who had put on clerical vestments to protect themselves from the mob. Joan saved whom she could.

The bravery of the English soldiers was never underestimated by the French. The *Journal du Siège d'Orléans* remarks that 'the English defended it (Saint-Loup) very valiantly for three hours of very bitter fighting.'

One hundred and fourteen English soldiers were killed and forty taken prisoner, according to the *Journal du siège*. Pasquerel says:

> Many of the English were killed. Joan was deeply distressed, for she said they had died without confession. She pitied them greatly, and immediately made her confession to me. She asked me also to exhort all the men-at-arms to confess their sins and thank God for the victory, otherwise she would not stay with them, but would quit their company.

Did she want to confess immediately because she felt she could have done more to stop the killing? This first experience of the brutality of war had profoundly shaken her, to the point that she was even contemplating abandoning her mission. Never again do we hear of such a threat, such turmoil in her soul. Pasquerel also says that she told him that day the siege would be lifted in five days and that 'not one Englishman would remain outside the town', so no doubt she was comforted by the thought that the fighting would soon be at an end and that the English would depart.

Thursday, 5 May, Feast of the Ascension, a day of truce: Joan sent her third letter to the English by arrow-post (medieval airmail). Brother Pasquerel, who ought to know, having been close to Joan as her confessor, gives us a résumé of the letter:

> You men of England, who have no right to this kingdom of France, the King of Heaven warns and commands you through me, Joan the Maid, to abandon your forts and return to your own country, otherwise I will make an assault on you that will never be forgotten. I am writing this to you for the third and last time. I will not write again. Signed: Jhesus Maria. Joan the Maid.
>
> PS: I would have sent you my letter by the proper channels, but you have detained my heralds. If you will send them back to me, I will send you some of your men captured at the Saint-Loup fort, for they are not all dead.

Those may not be the exact words of the letter, but they are certainly in the authentic spirit of Joan. Pasquerel goes on to tell us how the letter was received:

> When the English received the arrow and the letter, they read it, and then began to shout, 'Here's news from the harlot of the Armagnacs!' When she heard them, Joan began to sigh and weep, imploring the help of the King of Heaven.

Not the reaction of a hardened captain of men. Was she weeping for herself or at the thought of the now inevitable deaths in battle to come? At any rate, as noted above, the heralds were finally returned.

On that same day, 5 May, a meeting of the council of war was held in the house of the Chancellor of Orleans. Dunois, La Hire, Gaucourt, Sir Hugh Kennedy, captain of the Scots, and all the top brass were there, but not Joan. She was to be kept in the dark as to the real plan which would be decided. That plan was to launch a feint attack on the fortress of Saint Laurent on the Orleans side of the river, carried out by the town's citizen militia, so that the English would rush over from their fortresses on the other bank, Saint-Jean-le-Blanc, Les Augustins and the Tourelles *bastille* on the bridge across to Orleans, leaving only small garrisons in them, which would then be attacked by the elite French military. Having decided all this, they sent for Joan. Jean Chartier, in his *Chronique de Charles VII*, tells us what then transpired:

> When she came. they told her what had been decided regarding the attack on the great fortress [i.e. the Saint-Laurent] in which were Lord Stafford, Lord Talbot, Lord Scales, Sir John Fastolf and others. They said nothing about the plan to cross the Loire to the Sologne side [...]

And when she had heard the Chancellor, she replied angrily, 'Say what you have concluded and decided. I can keep a much greater secret than that,' and she paced up and down the room and wouldn't take a seat. Then the Bastard of Orleans said to her, 'Joan, don't be angry. We can't tell you everything at once. What the Chancellor has told you is what has been decided. But if the men on the other side of the river abandon their posts to come to the help of the big fortress and their comrades on this side, we have decided to cross the river and attack their positions. We think that this is a good, profitable strategy.' Then Joan replied that she was satisfied and that the plan seemed good, but that it should be carried out exactly as described.[12]

Chartier goes on to say that this wasn't the last time Joan quarrelled with the men at the top and took a contrary opinion to theirs. If they had thought she was a mere mascot, they were wrong. In this case in question, the plan was not in fact carried out, for, according to Sir Simon Charles, who had it from Gaucourt himself, on the next mornng, 6 May, the military chiefs decided that they wouldn't attack after all that day.[13] Gaucourt was charged with guarding the gates of the town, to make sure that there would be no attempt by the citizens to make a *sortie*. Sir Simon tells what happened (testimony of 7 May 1456):

Joan was not in agreement. She thought the soldiers should leave with the citizens and make an assault on the fortress of the Augustins and many of the soldiers and townsfolk were of that opinion. Joan then called Sir Raoul de Gaucourt a bad man, saying, 'Whether you like it or not, the men-at-arms will come and they will win here as they have won elsewhere.' Against Gaucourt's will, the men-at-arms went out to the assault on the fortress of the Augustins, which they took by force and violence. I heard Sir Raoul de Gaucourt say that he himself was in grave danger.

It sounds as though doughty old Gaucourt was in danger of being lynched. No doubt Joan had to calm the troops. Gaucourt understandably does not mention the incident in his deposition in 1456. The historian Xavier Hélary is of the opinion that Sir Simon's memory of what Gaucourt told him is a little faulty here and that the episode actually took place the day after the taking of the fort of the Augustins, the captains having decided that the attack on the Tourelles would be too risky[14]. He quotes the testimony of Louis de Coutes, who declares that it was on the day after the attack on the Augustins that Joan, 'against the opinion of several commanders, who believed that her decision (to attack the Tourelles) would place the king's men in great danger, had the Burgundy Gate and a little gate near the big tower opened ...' On whichever day the incident took place, it shows that at the time, the military men wished to keep Joan away from the decision-making, and that she was no less determined to refuse the role of figurehead and to enforce her will.

At any rate, on Friday, 6 May, the action went ahead with the attack on the Augustins. The French crossed the Loire by boat, landing first on an island mid-stream, from where two barges were moored to form a bridge out of range of the cannon of the Tourelles. It was also possible to ford the river from that point. Their nearest objective on landing was the fort of Saint-Jean-le-Blanc, which they found abandoned, the English having withdrawn to the bigger fort of Les Augustins, which guarded the great *bastille* of Les Tourelles and its protective *boulevard* at the end of the bridge on the left bank. It seems that Joan and La Hire had not yet crossed when the French lost heart at the sight of the seemingly impregnable fortress and decided to retreat back into Orleans. Seeing the English rushing out of Les Augustins in pursuit of the retreating French, Joan and La Hire hastily mounted their horses with which they had just crossed the river and charged the enemy, lances lowered. Immediately the whole scene was changed. The French troops turned about and fought back and now it was the turn of the English to retreat into their fortress. Among other incidents that D'Aulon vividly remembers, was that of a 'big, strong, powerful Englishman' behind the palisade which crowned the boulevard, who was 'causing great havoc' to the French, totally blocking their advance. He was killed by a shot fired by the famous gunner, Jean le Cannonier, on D'Aulon's instructions. When the mighty Englishman fell, the French poured up their scaling ladders, swarming over the palisade and into the fortress. Many of the English were killed or captured, others were still in the Tourelles. The attack on that great *bastille* could wait until the next day. D'Aulon says that Joan and the captains and their men remained at the Augustins all that night.

De Coutes however declares that she and her men, and he himself with them, returned to Orleans for the night. His recollection is the more accurate in this instance, for it agrees with that of Frère Pasquerel, who says that on the evening after the taking of the Augustins, an important personage (whose name he has forgotten) came to tell Joan that there had been another meeting of the council and captains, who had once more decided it would be wiser not to launch another attack:

> They considered that our men were too few compared to the English and that God had already blessed them greatly with the successes they had won. They added, 'As the town is now full of supplies, we are well able to hold it until the King sends help. The council does not consider it wise that the troops should go out tomorrow.' Joan replied: 'You have been to your council and I have been to mine. You may believe me that the council of Our Lord will be accomplished and will hold good, but yours will perish.' Then she told me to get up early the next morning, for she would have much to do. She said to me, 'Stay close to me, for

tomorrow I will have much to do, greater things than I have ever done. Tomorrow blood will flow from above my breast.'

This prediction of the wound which she was to receive had been made at least a couple of weeks earlier. In the fourth session of her trial in Rouen, Joan was asked whether she had fore-knowledge that she would be wounded at Orleans. She answered:

I knew very well that I would be wounded, and I told my king, but nevertheless, I didn't stop going about my business. It was revealed to me by the voices of the two saints, Catherine and Margaret.

The prediction must have been noised abroad, for one finds it mentioned, before it was fulfilled, along with predictions of the success at Orleans and the coronation of Charles VII, in the letter which a diplomat in Lyons sent to the counsellors of Duke Philip of Brabant, a cousin of the Duke of Burgundy, on 22 April 1429. The *greffier* (clerk) of the Chamber of Accounts of Brabant was struck by it and, after Joan's death, recorded the relevant extract in his register, adding his own note to say that all that had been foretold had indeed come about.[15]

Perhaps the reason for the reluctance of the captains to leave the town may have been that they feared an English attempt to storm it in the absence of the bulk of the French troops, fears which had been aroused by the transfer of the English garrison of a *bastille* on the far left bank of the Loire to rejoin the *bastille* of Saint-Laurent on the right bank.[16]

Joan was up early and in good humour the next morning, Saturday, 7 May. One witness at the Nullity trial, Colette, the wife of a Paris lawyer, Pierre Milet, remembers her in the house of her host, Jacques Bouchier. Somebody had brought her a fish, a shad, for her breakfast. Joan said cheerily to Jacques Bouchier, 'Keep it for this evening. I'll bring you back a *godon* (Englishman) for it and I'll come back over the bridge!' No doubt Colette remembered the remark because it would have seemed impossible to come back into Orleans over the bridge whose arches had been deliberately destroyed to prevent access. But in the end, Joan did so.

Joan and the captains met again and decided to launch an assault on the great defensive earthworks or *boulevard* on the left bank, its defences built high and crowned with a palisade. Its function was to protect the massive fort of Les Tourelles, with its twin towers, constructed at the end of the bridge itself and connected to the *boulevard* by a drawbridge over the narrow arm of the river which flowed between the two. The Burgundian chronicler Monstrelet talks of 'the very strong *bastille* at the end of the bridge', which was held by 'the flower of the best soldiers in England.'

The battle lasted from morning until sunset, amid the deafening roars and the smoke of artillery fire, the whistling hails of arrows, the cries of the wounded on both sides, the shouting from man to man, the vain attempts to scale the defences. Still by evening the French had no advantage. Their men being exhausted, they decided to withdraw. The trumpets were sounded for the retreat. Joan's weary standard-bearer, standing at the *boulevard*, passed the banner over to a soldier known as Le Basque, whom D'Aulon had recognised as a brave man. So D'Aulon asked the Basque (no doubt he was in fact a Basque) if he would follow him with the standard into the *fosse* to reach the wall of the *boulevard*, for he feared that if they all left, they would never dislodge the English from the Tourelles and he knew the electrifying effect Joan's standard had on the morale of the troops. When D'Aulon leapt into the *fosse*, holding his heavy shield over his head as protection against the hail of arrows, the Basque started to follow. At that moment Joan caught sight of her standard in the man's hands and couldn't understand what was happening. D'Aulon:

> The Maid rushed up, grabbed the tail end of the standard and snatched it from him, shouting, "Hey! My standard! My standard!" shaking it at the same time, so I think the others thought she was signalling to them. Then I shouted, 'Hey! Basque, what did you promise me?' And then the Basque pulled so hard on the standard that he snatched it back and rushed up to me with it. At that, all the Maid's company reassembled and rallied again and attacked the boulevard so furiously that they took both it and the bastille of Les Tourelles in no time at all. The enemy abandoned the bastille and the French returned to Orleans by the bridge [...] I had heard her saying that very day, 'In God's name, we'll come back to the town this evening by the bridge.'

The men from Orleans had evidently managed to place long planks over the broken arches of the bridge to make some temporary support.

Dunois says Joan was wounded early in the day and that the arrow entered between her neck and shoulder to a length of about six inches. He confirms, as D'Aulon does also, that the wound was dressed when she returned to Orleans. De Coutes says that it was dressed during the battle. Both accounts are correct, a hasty dressing having been applied at the time to stop the bleeding and a more careful one applied later in Orleans.

After the incident, says De Coutes, 'she re-armed and went with the others to the attack, which went on without a break until evening'. In the fourth session of her trial in Rouen, on 27 February, Joan mentions that she was wounded in the neck during the battle, adding. 'But I was greatly comforted by Saint Margaret and I was cured in a fortnight. It didn't stop me riding and fighting.'

Pasaquerel fills in information about the incident and what followed:

> In the assault, Joan, as she had foretold, was hit by an arrow above her breast. When she realised she had been wounded, she was frightened and

wept, then she said she was comforted [by her Voices]. Some of the soldiers, seeing her wounded, wanted to charm the wound with an incantation, but she refused, saying 'I would rather die than do anything that I knew to be a sin or contrary to God's will.' She added that she knew that she would have to die, but she didn't know where or how or at what time. However, if they could cure her wound without recourse to sinful means, she would let them. Then they put olive oil and lard on the wound and after that Joan made her confession to me, weeping and lamenting. Then she returned to the assault, crying 'Clasdas! Clasdas! Surrender! Surrender to the King of Heaven! You called me a whore, but I have great pity for your soul and for the souls of your men!' Then this Clasdas, armed from head to toe, fell into the Loire and was drowned. Joan, full of pity, wept bitterly for the soul of Clasdas and the others, a great number of whom were drowned.

Clasdas is none other than Glasdale. Dunois says that he and his men were drowned trying to escape back into the tower of the fortress from their *boulevard*. What had happened was that the drawbridge between the *boulevard* and the fortress was on fire, Men had got across from Orleans in boats and had towed underneath it a barge filled with well-chosen stinking, combustible rubbish to set it alight. The *Journal* says that between twenty and thirty men were drowned.

Dunois also testified that he and the other captains had decided to call it a day at eight o'clock in the evening, having given up hope of taking the fortress that night and seeing their troops exhausted:

> Joan came up, and asked me to wait a little while. Then she went off on her horse to a vineyard some way from the troops. She spent a quarter of an hour praying in the vineyard and then came back, took up her standard and placed it on the edge of the fosse (the trench around the boulevard). As soon as she appeared, the English took fright, but the French were galvanised and started to storm the place, attacking the boulevard without meeting any resistance. The boulevard was taken and the English in it were put to flight. They all died.

Figures for the total number of English casualties during these assaults vary of course, with Anglo-Burgundian chroniclers giving lower estimates than the French. Estimates are from between eighteen hundred to three thousand killed and from one hundred to four or even five hundred taken prisoner. On the French side, casualties were remarkably small. One recent historian calls the assaults on the bastilles at Orleans 'the bloodiest military engagement of the Hundred Years War after the battle of Agincourt'.[17]

Dunois' closing remark that the English troops all died may be an exaggeration, but all were agreed that they fought exceedingly bravely. This is the first time we hear of the superstitious fear that Joan inspired in the English troops. Seeing her return after being pierced by an arrow, later seeing Glasdale perish after having insulted her, they became convinced that she was a witch, causing men's deaths and the defeat of armies by diabolical sorcery. Perhaps they had thought to have seen the last of her when she rode off to the vineyard and now she had reappeared as if by magic. As her campaign went on, the problem of desertions from the English military grew ever more serious. Collating D'Aulon's account and that of Dunois, we see that Joan must have ridden back from her pause in the vineyard only to see her standard in the hands of the Basque. If D'Aulon's account is accurate, she reacted in alarm just as the trumpets were sounding the retreat. Perhaps Dunois had decided he could wait no longer for her to reappear. If so, he must immediately have countermanded the order when he saw her return and its effect on the men.

Dunois describes the morning after the taking of the Tourelles, Sunday, 8 May:

> The English came out of their tents and drew up in battle order ready to fight. Seeing this, the Maid got out of bed and pulled on a coat-of-mail. She decided however that nobody should attack the English nor demand anything from them, but just let them depart. And in fact they did depart, without anyone pursuing them. From that moment on, the town was delivered from its enemies.

The testimony of Jean Luillier, a citizen of Orleans, agrees entirely with that of Dunois. Another citizen, Jean de Champeaux, adds some information, saying he saw the men-at-arms of Orleans preparing themselves for a great attack on the English on that day:

> Seeing that, Joan went out to talk to the men-at-arms, who asked her if it was right to attack the English on that day, which was a Sunday. She replied that they should first hear Mass. She sent for a table and the ecclesiastical vessels and had two Masses said, which she and all the army attended with great devotion. When the Masses were over, Joan told them to look and see if the English were still facing the town. They replied that they were not, that they had turned in the direction of Meung. When she heard that, she said: 'In God's name, they are going. Let them go and let us give thanks to God, without pursuing them, for this is the Lord's day'.(Testimony of 16 March, 1456)

Five other witnesses from Orleans contented themselves with saying simply that they agreed with Champeaux's testimony. Simon Beaucroix says that when she saw the English being pursued by some of the French, she said: 'Let the English go. Don't kill them. Let them go. Their withdrawal is enough.'

Another witness at the Nullity trial, Aignan Viole, a citizen of Orleans like the others, said that Joan had her troops drawn up in battle order on that Sunday but forbade them to attack the English, saying that it was God's will to let them go. Jean Chartier puts the number of the retreating besiegers at four thousand, but as we have seen, it is difficult to establish exact figures.

So the English marched off to Meung, a town they had taken in September 1428, trudging along in battle order, banners and standards flying. They took with them their prisoners and all that they could manage, but they were obliged to leave behind heavy artillery, bombards, cannons, crossbows, ammunitions, provisions and the wounded. La Hire and one or two other captains disregarded Joan's wishes and rode out after the English for a few miles with about four hundred of their men. Some skirmishing took place with no very serious result. But it did prove a lucky break for one of Talbot's prisoners who was being marched away. This was a man called the Le Bourg de Bar, a 'very brave soldier', according to the *Journal*, whose leg irons were exceedingly heavy. The English Augustinian monk who had looked after him in his prison (and who was in fact Talbot's peronal confessor) had now been told to bring him along. He had to support the man by holding him under the armpits. The attention of the soldiers was distracted by La Hire's skirmishers. The monk and his charge, trailing behind them, had not gone very far when Le Bourg declared that he could not and would not go any further. He somehow persuaded the good monk (who must have been a big, strong fellow himself) to turn about and give him a piggy-back into Orleans, where no doubt they were both received with much merriment. Jean Chartier recounts the anecdote also and it must have been widely enjoyed.[18]

Needless to say, the rejoicing in Orleans was immense. Joan said that everyone should go to the Masses of thanksgiving that were said, hymns were sung, the streets were thronged with processions and music and celebrating crowds, the city was *en fête*. The soldiers were welcomed into people's houses and wined and dined 'as if they had been their own children', says the *Journal*. But Joan didn't waste time in celebration. Speed was her priority. In four days of battle, she had cleared away a siege which had lasted seven months. At the later trial in 1456, the Sire de Termes, Thibault d'Armagnac, who had been with Dunois and the defenders of Orleans throughout the siege, expressed the admiration of the people and captains for Joan: 'During all of these assaults {on the English fortifications}, she behaved so valiantly that no man could have conducted himself better in battle. All the captains marvelled at her courage.'

The day after the departure of the English, Monday, 11 May, Joan set out with a deputation of captains to see the king (or 'the Dauphin' as she would call him until his coronation). They travelled first to Blois and thence to Tours. Dunois did not want to waste time either, he left the same day with Xaintrailles and other captains and men from towns such as Bourges, Blois and Tours, to lay siege to Jargeau. The town, where Suffolk had now established himself, was only eleven miles up-river east of Orleans. Several skirmishes took place, during which a 'valiant English knight called Sir Henry Bisset', the captain of the town and a veteran of both Cravant and Verneuil, was killed, to the great grief of his men and comrades. However, the deep moat surrounding the town walls was impassable, the waters being high, and so the French withdrew back to Orleans. Without Joan, the determination was evidently not the same.

After Orleans

De pauperibus armatis, esto quod essent de parte Anglicorum, ipsa
multum compatiebatur
She greatly pitied the poor men-at-arms, even if they were on the side
of the English
Friar Pasquerel, testimony of 4 May 1456

News of the relief of Orleans spread like wildfire not only in France and
England, but throughout Europe. Charles VII immediately sent a letter
from Chinon to all his *bonnes villes*, all his loyal towns. The original
of one letter was found in the archives of the town of Narbonne. In it
Charles gives the citizens the good news of the siege of Orleans as it was
reaching him on the evening of 9 May and the morning of the 10th. After
telling them how the town had twice in the past week been amply supplied
with troops and provisions, 'by the mercy of God' and 'under the noses
of the besiegers', he next tells them, as he gets the news, of the taking of
Saint-Loup, 'by force and an assault lasting four or five hours'. Next he
receives a herald, at 'about one hour after midnight', coming with the
splendid news of the taking of the Tourelles, and finally two *gentlemen*
arrive, with a letter from Gaucourt, to inform him that, 'at dawn the
next morning, the English who were still there quit the place so hastily
that they left behind them their bombards, cannon, artillery, and most
of their provisions'. For this, he writes, 'You must praise and think our
Creator, Who, in His Divine Mercy, has not forgotten us. The deeds and
marvels which the herald who witnessed them has reported to us, and also
those of the Maid, who was constantly present during them, can never be
sufficiently honoured.'[1]

Charles must have been agog with excitement all night as the news
came in. He hastened up to Tours for his meeting with Joan and Dunois,
who now urged him to leave for Rheims. However, despite his delight at
the success at Orleans, he was difficult to move. It was a month before
Joan could get him going. The trouble was that Rheims was deep in
Burgundian territory and so, in order to reach it, it was necessary to
embark on a campaign to recapture *en route* the towns on the Loire taken
by the English in 1428. Those around him were less than enthused by the

project, for they would have to get to Rheims also if they wanted to be present at the all-important coronation.

Charles was at this period of his life very much under the sway of favourites, self-interested men of whom the most powerful was the now immensely rich (and grossly fat) La Trémoille, always suspected of having a foot in both camps. Quicherat says of him: 'He had the art of making a name and a fortune for himself by veering about between the parties […]. He maintained suspect relations with his brother and others of his family, all of them serving in the palaces or armies of Philip the Good. When the English subdued the Orleans province in 1428, it was very badly regarded in France that they spared Sully, the domain of Georges de la Trémoille.'[2] Contemporary chroniclers, such as Chartier, Cagny, or the anonymous author of the *Gestes des nobles Francois*, are hostile to him. He detested and was detested by Charles VII's most trustworthy adviser, his very intelligent mother-in-law Yolande of Sicily. On the personal level, La Trémoille seems to have been a thoroughly unpleasant character, particularly if you happened to be his wife. Some modern historians take up his defence, not altogether convincingly.

La Trémoille came of a family which owed its wealth and position to the Dukes of Burgundy. He had been brought up at the court of John the Fearless and later served him as chamberlain. When Philip became Duke of Burgundy after the assassination of his father in 1419, it was necessary to make a choice of allegiances. La Trémoille changed sides and went over to the Dauphin's party, for what precise reason we do not know, but Quicherat tells us that Philip had the good taste to loathe him. However, he kept up his contacts. He fought on the French side at Agincourt and was taken prisoner, but was quickly released. No doubt the funds for the ransom were readily made available. We can be sure that he did not fight out of any ideal of loyalty, nothing really mattered to him but the accumulation of power and wealth. He rose to the important position of Master of the Waterways and Forests and then Grand Chamberlain in 1427. Now he was all-powerful. The Vicar of Bray could not have done better.

Throughout his career with Charles VII, La Trémoille constantly received large gifts of money from the king. In 1427, with little regard for the consequences for the on-going war, he had ousted his rival from the court, none other than the very man to whom he owed his rise, Arthur de Richemont, son of the Duke of Brittany. In 1429, at the time of the siege of Orleans, when Charles could not find the money to finance his army, La Trémoille received a royal gift of ten thousand gold crowns. At the same time, the young Guy de Laval had to write to his mother to ask her to sell his lands so that he himself could find the money to pay his contingent of troops.[3] La Trémoille and the clique around Charles were not, as some historians have described them, a 'peace party', but rather the party of appeasement and greed. The endless futile truces with Philip of Burgundy seemed to them the best strategy for consolidating their own positions. La Trémoille was opposed to Joan from the beginning, probably because he feared that she might detach Charles VII from him and his *côterie*.

The king travelled up with alacrity from Chinon to meet Joan in Tours on 13 May, where Dunois had now rejoined her from Orleans. The *Chronique de Tournay* has a pleasant little vignette of Joan's meeting there with Charles, both of them on horseback:

> [Joan] went to meet him, her standard in her hand, her head uncovered, and bowed as low as she could from her horse. As she approached, the king doffed his hat, embraced her and raised her up. It seemed to many that he would gladly have kissed her, he felt so much joy.[4]

It was an exceptional demonstration from a man who was normally extremely reserved.

Dunois and Joan had a definite campaign plan which they lost no time in putting forward. Dunois explains that they came to ask Charles

> ...to supply men to take the castles and towns on the Loire, that is to say, Meung, Beaugency and Jargeau. This would allow him to proceed more freely and surely on his way to Rheims and his coronation. She urged the king most insistently and repeatedly to make haste, not to wait any longer.

Dunois politely and loyally says that the king proceeded 'with all diligence', but this is something of an overstatement, as is clear from the rest of his deposition. He describes Joan's subsequent desperate effort to persuade Charles of the urgency of the situatuon:

> The king was in his chamber, with Messire Christophe d'Harcourt, bishop of Castres, and Monseigneur de Trêves, the former Chancellor of France. Before entering the chamber, Joan knocked at the door, and as soon as she entered, she knelt at the king's feet and embraced his knees, saying, in these or similar words: 'Noble Dauphin, don't hold any more long deliberations. Come as quickly as you can to Rheims to claim your rightful crown.'

Dunois adds:

> The princes of the blood royal and the captains wanted the king to go to Normandy and not to Rheims. But Joan was unshakably of the opinion that he should go to Rheims. She gave a reason, saying that once he was crowned and anointed, his enemies' situation would go from bad to worse and in the end they would be unable to harm either him or his kingdom. All finally accepted this argument.

Joan was certainly right to stress the urgency of getting to Rheims for the coronation. Bedford also knew very well that coronation was an absolutely priority. Already on 29 April, the council of Henry VI, meeting at Westminster, had received an urgent message from him, asking that the child Henry VI should be crowned king of France and receive the due oaths of allegiance. No doubt Bedford had had news from his informants of the arrival of Joan at Chinon and the talk of getting Charles VII crowned. While it would have seemed unlikely that the Dauphin could present himself either at Paris or at Rheims in the near future, both places being under Anglo-Burgundian domination, the Regent was taking no chances. The Council, however, was in no hurry. The nation's finances were under strain and the most they were willing to do for Bedford was to send him, in response to his next urgent message, half the number of troops he was asking for as reinforcements for the siege of Orleans, in view of the fact that the English military was suffering desertions since the death of Salisbury. They sent four or five hundred men and seven hundred archers on the usual six-month contract. Bedford was right and they were wrong, on both counts. Bedford had now gone from Rouen to Paris, where he established himself in the château of Vincennes. Talbot and Scales were in Meung-sur-Loire.

In Tours, as we read in the *Journal du Siège d'Orléans*,

> [Charles] sent for the nobles, military leaders and other wise members of his court and held several meetings at Tours to decide what he should do regarding the Maid's affectionate and urgent request that he should go to Rheims to be crowned. There were diverse opinions, some advising that he should campaign first in Normandy, others that an attempt should be made to take the principal places on the Loire.[5]

Perceval de Cagny, Alençon's chronicler,[6] says that all the councillors thought the whole project too difficult, if not impossible, given the strength of the English-held places on the Loire and the king's meagre financial resources. Jean Chartier speaks at some length of the doubts and hesitations of the king and the opposition of the Council, given that Rheims itself was English-held, 'as was in general all the country between the Loire and the sea', in other words, all the country north of the Loire. Finally, however, Charles made up his mind to follow Joan's urgent advice. If he was to be crowned, it was necessary to have as many members of the aristocracy as possible present at the coronation and to organise and equip forces for a campaign to clear the way to Rheims, so it is understandable that there was some delay. Nonetheless, in Joan's opinion, things dragged on unreasonably.

Sometime during this interval, Alençon invited Joan back to Saint-Florent, near Saumur, for a few days, to meet his mother and his wife. 'God knows how joyful a welcome his wife and mother gave her during the four or five days she was there,' writes Perceval de Cagny. Afterwards she was always closer to the Duke than to any other, and always referred to him simply as *Mon beau duc*, which perhaps would be best translated by *My dear Duke*, since *beau* in this context is simply a polite way of addressing a friend or relative. More formally, the duke might be addressed as *Noble duke*. Henry V calls John the Fearless *beau cousin* (not without sarcasm), and Charles VII addresses Arthur de Richemont similarly. Richemont, with a great battle-scar across his face, was certainly anything but *beau*.

While Joan was staying at Saint Florent, Alençon's young wife told her that she was very worried about her husband going back to the war. Apart from the mortal danger, he had only just succeeded in paying off his crippling ransom. He recounts the incident himself, on 3 May, 1456, at the Nullity trial:

> My wife said to Joan that she was very afraid for me, that huge sums had been spent for my ransom and that she would have liked to ask me not to go. Then Joan replied; 'My lady, don't be afraid! I'll bring him back to you safe and sound. As good as he is now, or even better!'

On 2 June, the King, now back at Chinon, awarded Joan the right to bear arms, 'a blue shield, on which appear a silver sword with a golden pommel, supporting a golden crown at its tip and flanked by two golden *fleurs de lys*'. The symbolism of the sword, the crown and the lilies is abundantly clear. In 1429 the whole d'Arc family was ennobled and Joan's brothers called themselves thereafter Jean and Pierre du Lys. The name *d'Arc* was, it seems, pronounced *Daly* or *Day* in Lorraine and *Duly* in Orleans, thus making the transition to the noble moniker very simple.[7] Joan herself was not interested in such promotion, as we see from her answers at her trial, at the start of which she gives her name simply as *Jeanne* or *Jeannette* and says she doesn't really know about a surname, although her father was called Jacques d'Arc. At her trial, on 10 March 1431, she was asked by the interrogator Jean de La Fontaine: 'Did you have a shield and arms?' to which she answered:

> I never had any, but the king gave arms to my brothers, a blue shield on which there were two golden lilies and a sword between them and in this town. I described the arms to a painter who asked me about them. The arms were awarded to my brothers by the king, without any request of mine, nor any revelation.

This town is Rouen, and it has been suggested by Pierre Tisset that the painter was a spy sent to her by Cauchon in order to entrap her, or who was in contact with Cauchon's ring of informants.[8] One cannot see otherwise how a painter would have been allowed to visit her in prison.

In the seventy articles of accusation, much is made of the granting of arms and she is accused of 'vanity contrary to religion and piety'.

In France, after Orleans, Joan's fame and popularity were spreading like wildfire. People were talking about prophecies which foretold her coming. One was the saying previously mentioned that 'France will be ruined by a woman and saved by a maiden from the marches of Lorraine', to which Joan had made allusion herself. One witness at the Nullity trial, the lawyer Jean Barbin, speaks of the prophecy of a famous French visionary of the beginning of the fifteenth century, Marie d'Avignon (also known as Marie Robin). She had told Charles VI that France would suffer many calamities, saying that 'she had had many visions about the desolation of the kingdom of France, among others, a terrifying vision of the arms of war, which she feared she would be compelled to take up. But she was told not to fear, that she would not bear the arms herself, but that after her a Maid would bear these arms and liberate the kingdom of France from its enemies.' Another witness at the 1456 trial, Gobert Thibaut, also refers to the same prophecy.

One young military admirer was Guy de Laval, whose grandmother, before her second marriage, had been the widow of the celebrated hero of the Hundred Years War, Bertrand du Guesclin, one whose name is to this day a byword for courage in France. Guy was twenty-three when he went off to join Joan and Alençon's troops at Selles-en-Berry, where they were gathering. On 8 June, after travelling to Loches and Saint-Aignan and meeting various courtiers and Charles VII, he wrote an ecstatic letter to his mother and grandmother, giving a rapturous account of his meeting with Joan:

This Monday [June 6] I left with the king for Selles-en-Berry [...]. The king sent for the Maid, who was already in Selles. Some said it was as a favour for me, so that I could meet her. The Maid gave my brother and me a warm welcome. She was wearing full armour, except for her helmet, and holding the lance in her hand. Then, when we went down into Selles, I went to see her in her lodgings. She sent for wine and told me she would soon have me drinking it in Paris. There seemed to be something divine about her, both when you saw her and when you heard her. She left Selles on Monday, at the hour of vespers, to go to Romorantin [...]. I saw her mounting her horse. She was in her shining armour, except for her helmet, with a little battleaxe in her hand. She had a great black charger, which was caracoling about outside her lodgings and wouldn't let her mount. So she said, 'Take him to the cross,' which was in front of the church. Then she mounted and he stood stock-still, as if rooted to the spot. After that, she turned towards the door of the church, which was close by, and said, in her very feminine voice, 'You priests and clergy, please go in procession and offer prayers for us to God.' Next she returned to the road, saying, 'Let's go! Let's go!' Her standard was deployed and held by a good-looking page, and she had her little axe in her hand. A brother of hers, who has been here a week, left with her. He was also wearing shining armour.[9]

Guy goes on to give other news: the Duke of Alençon had arrived on Monday with a large company, the Constable (Arthur de Richemont) was on his way with six hundred men-at-arms and four hundred archers (that was going to cause some problem, as we shall see) and many others are joining them. Guy tells his mother that the king has no money to pay him and that, for the honour of their family, she is to sell or mortgage his land to raise the necessary funds for his participation in the campaign. Alençon, Orleans (Dunois) and Gaucourt are leaving with the Maid, but as a result of some letters which the king has received, His Majesty has asked Guy to wait behind until the way is cleared for them to go Rheims. No doubt the letters came from Guy's wife or mother or both, but neither he nor his brother will hear tell of such dastardly behaviour. 'We all have such trust in God, I am sure He will come to our aid,' he writes. He also mentions that when he had visited Joan, 'She told me, Grandmother, that three days previously she had sent you a little gold ring. She said it was only a trifle and that she would have liked to send you something more, in thanks for your recommendation.' This last phrase seems to indicate that Guy's grandmother had written to Joan as well as to the king.

Both Laval brothers, Guy and André, followed Joan throughout the campaign on the Loire. At Rheims, Guy replaced the Duke of Burgundy as one of the six lay peers participating in the ceremony. André, the younger brother, went on to Paris with her and later had a very distinguished military career, becoming Admiral of France at the age of twenty-seven in 1437 and then Marshal of France in 1439.

Even before Rheims, Joan was becoming a source of amazement not only in France but throughout Europe. Already on 14 May 1429, an important short treatise on her case had been published by Jean Gerson, the illustrious former chancellor of the University of Paris, now living in exile from the capital, in a monastery in Lyons. He had been contacted and asked for his opinion by one of the examiners at Poitiers, Charles VII's confessor, Gérard Machet, who, no doubt, sent him a copy of the famous *Poitiers book*, which Joan referred to at her trial and which disappeared at some unknown date. All we have of it is a short résumé of the conclusions sent to Charles VII at the end of the examinations in Poitiers. The learned doctors and clerics affirm, 'We find no evil in her, only humility, virginity, religious devotion, honesty and simplicity'. Therefore, they conclude, the king should give her the opportunity to prove the truth of her mission by the *sign* which she has said would be the lifting of the siege of Orleans.

The short treatise is Gerson's last work, he died two months after writing it. It is entitled *Super facto Puellae et credulitate ei prestanda, post signum habitum Aurelianis in depulsione absidionis anglicanae*: 'On the achievement of the Maid and the credibility to be given to be given to her, after the sign given at Orleans and the raising of the English siege'. First of all, on the question of belief in her, Gerson points out that it is not a matter of faith. He quotes a saying in the French of his day: *Qui ne le croit, il n'est pas dampné* (i.e. 'You are not damned for not believing it'). However, he goes on to examine the case and defend Joan on all the points on which the court of Rouen would later condemn her. She has not been seen to have recourse to practices forbidden by the Church, sorcery, superstition or fraud. She is not proclaiming anything contrary to faith or morals. The proof of her genuine and deep faith is that she has exposed herself to great peril. Moreover, she and her soldiers behave with normal human prudence, not putting God to the test (the sin of presumption). She is fighting in a just cause, the restoration of the king to his kingdom. As to the male clothing, Gerson declares that no divine law is transgressed, the Old Testament interdiction being essentially a legalistic matter, not binding under the New dispensation. Circumstances must be taken into consideration, the when, the where and the why of things examined. Joan's military dress is appropriate to her role. It should be noted that this is not a revolutionary opinion, Hildegard von Bingen in the twelfth century and Thomas Aquinas in the thirteenth, had already affirmed that the rules concerning male and female clothing could be overridden in certain circumstances involving necessity.

Gerson also gives a general warning: 'Men's expectations are not inevitably fulfilled after a first miraculous event. So, even if Joan's and our hopes come to nought, we should not conclude that what has been achieved is the work of an evil spirit rather than of God, but rather that the disappointment is a result of our own ingratitude and blasphemies or through some other just judgement of God.' The warning is repeated at the conclusion of the short treatise:

> However, the party whose cause is just must beware of frustrating, through incredulity, ingratitude or other offences, the Divine aid so clearly and miraculously bestowed, as happened, so we read, to Moses and the children of Israel [...], for God, while not changing His view (i.e. of the justice of the cause), can change the judgement according to the change in merits.[10]

The treatise was no doubt circulated largely among the intelligentsia and others whose opinion mattered. Pancrazio Giustiniani, in an enthusiastic letter giving news of Joan to his father in Venice, sent him a copy of the work, naming the author only as 'the Chancellor of the University, a doctor of theology, a very eminent person'. He even quotes from it the statement that belief, in such a case, is not a matter of faith. Nonetheless he himself is clearly convinced that Joan has a mission from God and he asks his father to pass the treatise on to the Doge, who will be very pleased to read it.[11]

Another eminent cleric, Jacques Gélu, Bishop of Embrun, a diocese in the Alps, also sent a short treatise to Charles VII, and also probably in May 1429, very shortly after the raising of the siege of Orleans. He too had received a request from Gérard Machet, via the latter's secretary. Gélu had been employed on a number of diplomatic missions and had played a major role in the Council of Constance. A copy of the Poitiers book must have been sent to him and he would have had a month or so to study it. The treatise is addressed to Charles VII and begins with an outline of the history of the war with England and the misfortunes of the kingdom. The king's cause is deemed just and worthy of divine intervention. Gélu goes on to consider the arguments against Joan, the first of which is the fact that she is a woman. However, says Gélu, God can give a dispensation from the general law, which is that deeds suited to men should be entrusted to men. God nevertheless can entrust them not only to a woman, but to an unlettered girl: 'God can put a Maid in charge of men-at-arms, give her command, enable her to conquer the strongest and most experienced soldiers and to do this in male clothing.' As to the male clothing, living, as she has to, in the company of men, it is fitting that she should dress as they do. As to whether she is diabolically inspired or not, Gélu quotes scripture: 'By their fruits shall you know them'. Joan, he affirms, is a good and faithful Christian, 'honest and honourable in words and in her life in society, avoiding loquacity (in which there can be sin), abstemious in food and drink. There is nothing scandalous in her behaviour, nothing offending female modesty […] and, although she resorts to arms, she is never cruel but feels pity for all […]. She does not thirst for human blood, but offers to allow the enemy to withdraw in peace …'[12]

In Germany, the distinguished theologian, Heinrich von Gorkum, Vice-Chancellor of the University of Cologne, added his voice to the debate. His *Libellus de puella Aurelianensi* was written in June, 1429, after Orleans, but before news of the coronation at Rheims reached him.[13] It is possible that he had been asked for an opinion by the judges at Poitiers or by Charles VII himself. The body of his treatise is favourable to Joan. She dresses, rides astride and has her hair cut in the male fashion, he remarks (although he thinks she puts on feminine attire when she dismounts), but none of this, in the circumstances, breaks the law of God. 'It is said also that she lives chastely, soberly and with moderation. She is devout, she forbids murder, rape and other such violence to all who wish to follow her.' However, as a good scholastic philosopher, he recognises that arguments for and against must be carefully weighed, for there are many false prophets about, so he ends his work with six propositions in favour of Joan, and six others which need to be examined against her.

Another industrious German annalist was gathering information for his *Hausbuch* (Household Book), a chronicle of the reign of the Holy Roman

Emperor Sigismund. This was Eberhard Windecke, a much-travelled gentleman, treasurer of the said emperor, at the time of Joan's appearance living in Mainz and closely in touch with official news and newsletters emanating from France and the chancellery of the court of Charles VII. Also in 1429, probably not long after Orleans and the rapid Loire campaign which followed, an item in the accounts of the town of Regensburg records a payment of twenty-four *pfennig* made for an exhibition featuring 'the picture of the Maid fighting in France'. The exhibition coincided with a visit of the Emperor Sigismund to the town.[14]

A wildly extravagant work, based on the hearsay and gossip circulating throughout Europe at the time, was the *Sibylla Francica*, composed between June and September, 1429 by a cleric of the cathedral at Speyer.[15] It portrays Joan as a prophetess, comparing her to the sibyls of antiquity, those of Delphi and Cumae among others, and has little historical value apart from providing an example of the fame of Joan and the excesses of rumour and fantasy.

About the same time, on 21 June 1429, before the coronation at Rheims, but following the victories of Jargeau (12 June), Meung (15 June), Beaugency (17 June) and Patay (18 June), Perceval de Boulainvilliers, a very important personage at the court of Charles VII, (Seneschal of Berry, councillor and chamberlain of the king), wrote a letter in Latin to the Duke of Milan, for whom his father-in-law was governor of Asti. The first part of the letter describing Joan's early life is a compilation of the current rumours of marvels and wonders. Joan is said to have been born on 6 January, the feast of the Epiphany (the symbolism is obvious). On the night of her birth, the villagers were all filled with a mysterious joy and the cocks crowed for two hours. However, when she arrives at the court of Charles VII (where Boulainvilliers could see her for himself) the narrative becomes a factual account of the lifting of the siege of Orleans and the victories on the way to Rheims, where the king is about to be crowned. The most interesting part of the letter is its description of Joan herself: Boulainvilliers writes:

> The girl has dignity and style. There is something virile about the way she conducts herself. She is not effusive, but remarkably prudent in what she says and does. She has a soft feminine voice. She eats little and drinks less, as far as wine is concerned. She is fond of fine horses and armour and enjoys the company of nobles and men-at-arms. She has no taste for crowds and noisy company. She weeps easily and abundantly. Her face radiates joy. Her stamina is incredible ... And so, in conclusion, illustrious Prince, all is more marvellous than I can write to you or tongue can tell.[16]

Alençon, in his testimony in 1456, puts the number of troops he personally had collected together for the Loire campaign at six hundred lances. With those who came with Dunois, Florent d'Iliers and others, they were about twelve hundred lances, which, with between four or five men to a *lance*, could be something in the region of six thousand men. This is the figure given also by the Anglo-Burgundian soldier and chronicler Jean de Wavrin de Forestel. However, it may be an under-estimate. The *Journal du Siège d'Orléans* puts the number at eight thousand. So at last, after the king's endless consultations and shilly-shallyings with his council and advisers, Joan, Alençon, Dunois and the rest of the captains and army were on their way. They went first back to Orleans, arriving there on 9 June, to a rapturous reception from the citizens. The *Journal du siège*:

> The Duke of Alençon and she (Joan), with all their men, took leave of the King and set out across country in fine order. They made such good progress that they shortly entered Orleans in great state, and were welcomed with huge rejoicing by all the citizens, above all the Maid, they simply couldn't see enough of her.[17]

On 11 June, the army left Orléans for Jargeau, well provisioned with arms and artillery, under the command of Alençon, who had been told by the king that 'that he was to undertake nothing unless he had first consulted her (Joan)'. Joan had no official command in this army, her role was that of advisor.

They arrived at Jargeau, six miles or so up-river, that same day, exactly a month after Dunois' failed attack. The place was held by Suffolk and his two brothers, with a garrison of six or seven hundred seasoned troops. They had had a month since Orleans to strengthen their positions. In 1456, at the Nullity trial, Alençon gave a very full account of the battle. Before they started out, he tells us,

> A dispute arose among the captains. Some were of the opinion that we should attack, others disagreed, because of the strength of the English and their numbers in the place. Joan said: 'Don't be afraid, however many of them there are. Don't hesitate to attack, God is directing us. He will come to our aid. If I were not sure that God is guiding us, I would rather look after the sheep than expose myself to such danger.' At that we set out for Jargeau, with the intention of reaching the outskirts and spending the night there. But the English saw us coming. At first they pushed us back. Seeing that, Joan seized her standard and led the attack, calling to the men to go forward boldly. We did so well that the royal army was able to spend the night on the outskirts of Jargeau.

Cagny says that the *gens du commun*, the common people who had tacked on to the army, rushed rashly into the attack, without waiting for the arrival of the army itself or for any orders, such was their enthusiasm.

The *Journal du Siège* clarifies the dispute which had arisen. Those who wanted to leave thought that the siege of Jargeau should be abandoned and that they should instead march to meet Fastolf, who was 'coming from Paris with a good two thousand men and bringing supplies and artillery'. However, most were persuaded by Joan and the other captains to remain. In fact, most historians reckon Fastolf's reinforcements at about five thousand men. Alençon continues the story:

I really and truly believe that God was watching over us, for that night no watch was kept to speak of, and if the English had made a sortie we would have been in great danger.

We prepared the artillery and at daybreak brought up the cannon and bombards. Then, after a couple of days, we held a meeting to decide what must be done in order to take the town. During the meeting, we heard that La Hire was negotiating with the Duke of Suffolk, which annoyed me and the others in charge of the expedition very much. La Hire was sent for and returned forthwith.

After that, we decided to launch an attack. The heralds sounded the call to arms! Joan called to me, 'Forward, noble Duke, forward!' I thought that the attack was precipitous, but Joan said to me: 'Whenever God pleases, that is the right time to strike! Have no doubt about that! We have to go to work whenever God wills it. Help yourself and God will help you!' A little later she said to me, 'Ah! Dear Duke, are you afraid? Don't you know that I promised your wife to bring you back to her safe and sound?'

Indeed, Alençon did remember. There was another incident during the assault which greatly impressed him:

While I was standing on a certain spot, Joan said to me, 'Move away from there. If you don't move away, you'll be killed.' I moved away, and shortly afterwards, the Sire de Lude was killed where I had been standing. That all made a deep impression on me. I was amazed at Joan's words and how her predictions came true.

Joan went forward to the assault and I along with her. The Count of Suffolk sent word that he wanted to parley with me. Nobody paid any attention to that and the assault continued. Joan was up on a scaling ladder, holding her standard in her hand. The banner was hit and a stone struck Joan on her helmet and sent her tumbling to the ground. She picked herself up and shouted to the soldiers, 'Friends! Friends! Forward! Forward! Our Lord has condemned the English! Now we have them! Courage!' And at that moment Jargeau was taken.

By the fifteenth century, artillery and cannon played a major role in warfare. Alençon and Joan brought to Jargeau cannon lent to them by the town of Orleans, including a mighty piece christened *La Bergère*

('The Shepherdess'). We read in the *Journal du Siège* that 'three shots from one of the Orleans cannon, called *La Bergère*, brought down the biggest tower in the place.' We remember the exploits of Jean le Canonnier at Orleans. We meet him again in the *Journal*, here at Jargeau. Another giant of an Englishman was hurling huge iron bars down from the walls onto the scaling ladders and the men on them, causing devastation. Alençon pointed him out to Maître Jean, who trained the cannon on him and knocked him over backwards, dead, into the town.

Joan was questioned about Jargeau during her trial, in the session of 27 February 1431. She was asked why she did not agree a truce with Suffolk. Joan answered:

> The leaders of my party replied that they would not agree the period of fifteen days that was requested, but said that the English and their horses should leave within the hour. As to me, I said that the garrison of Jargeau, if they so wished, should leave, their lives spared, but divested of their armour, otherwise they would be taken by assault.

The sub-text of the question was clearly to stigmatise Joan as implacably bloodthirsty. It was nonsensical in military terms, for no captain would have agreed the two-week truce Suffolk was asking for. It would have given ample time for the arrival of Fastolf and his reinforcements, five thousand strong, who were believed to be on their way from Paris. Indeed, when they had heard this news, some of the French captains and their troops had left before the siege began. It was doubtless the cause of the initial debate which Alençon mentions.

Cagny's account of the battle gives some additional information:

> At nightfall, the Maid called over to those inside the town, summoning them as follows: 'Surrender the place to the King of Heaven and to our noble King Charles and leave, or disaster will befall you', but they paid no heed. [18]

When the fortified bridge fell, Suffolk and others were pursued by a number of French men-at-arms. The *Journal*:

> In particular, there was a French nobleman called Guillaume Regnault, who was very keen to take the Duke of Suffolk. The Duke asked him if he was a noble, to which he replied affirmatively. Then he was asked if he had been knighted, to which he replied that he had not, whereupon the duke knighted him and surrendered. [19]

The Duke could not, of course, surrender to someone who was not a knight.

Disorder and violence broke out among certain of the French troops after the fall of the town. Despite all Joan had done to forbid pillage, properties were ransacked, in particular the church, a sacrilegious crime like the desecration of the church at Cléry by Salisbury's troops. Worse still, a number of prisoners had to be transported secretly to Orleans at night and by water, as the *Journal* again tells us, 'for fear that they would be massacred, since several had been murdered on the way there, a dispute having arisen among some of the French about their share of the captives'. A sordid affair of ransom money. How many were massacred is not known, 'several' certainly seems to be an under-estimate, for Jean Chartier puts the number of English prisoners taken at between three and four hundred (he is alone in this high estimate) and says that most of them were killed, quarrels having arisen between them and their captors on the way from Jargeau to Orleans. According to Cagny, there were about forty or fifty English prisoners, but perhaps this is the number remaining after others had been murdered. The *Chronique de la Pucelle* says that most were killed while on the way to Orleans as a result of 'quarrels among the French'.[20] The army had swollen in numbers since Orleans; clearly, among a certain element, ferocity and greed had broken through the pious restraints which Joan had sought to impose and which in general her combatants seem to have observed. As we have noted also, her role at Jargeau was that of adviser, she had no official command, which circumstance may have put less restraint upon the troops.

Cagny puts the number of French losses at about twenty killed. On the English side several hundred men at least had died in the battle. The *Journal du Siège* puts it at four or five hundred. Alençon's figure for the English dead is a huge exaggeration. He puts it as eleven hundred, which is several hundred more that the entire garrison. As usual the figures are very unreliable.

Leaving a garrison behind them in Jargeau, Joan and Alençon returned to Orleans on Monday, 13 June, where they were received again with great rejoicing. There she was presented, probably on 14 June, by the aldermen and councillors with a superb gift paid for by the Duke of Orleans from his captivity in England. The gift consisted of two magnificent garments, a robe and a *huque* (the sleeveless surcoat worn over armour or over the robe). Both garments were ample and knee-length. The robe, a belted garment trimmed with expensive fur, was made of the greatly prized and very costly fine *Brussels* cloth, dyed vermilion, the *huque* was of a fine green material, also fur-trimmed. Both garments were lined with satin and richly decorated with the heraldic emblem of the House of Orleans, nettle leaves cut from green cloth and sewn plentifully onto the vermilion and green apparel. Obviously a contrasting shade of green was used for the *huque*. When worn over armour in battle, the *huque* served as a rallying emblem for the troops, like the standard. The tailor of Orleans must have worked overtime to have them ready in time for Joan's visit.

The garments were in all respects such as befitted the leading nobles in the land. After her death, the Burgundian writer of the *Chronique des Cordeliers de Paris* asserted that she dressed like a knight and that when she wasn't wearing armour, she sported fashionable footwear, hose, doublets and hats: 'She wore very noble garments of cloth of gold and silk, trimmed with fur.'

The chronicler was certainly prejudiced, but Quicherat considered that he took Joan seriously and does not insult or denigrate her in his writings, so we in turn can probably take seriously what he says about her taste in clothes.[21] At any rate, if she was to live among soldiers and aristocrats, it was advisable to adopt their sartorial conventions, and if she was to be an inspiration to men, she needed to look the part of a leader. The clothes would have signified that she was the equal of the other captains. The semiotic significance of apparel was supremely important in the age in which she lived. No such excuse was allowed at her trial in Rouen, where she would be accused of culpable vanity for having taken delight in such worldly extravagances. The Archbishop of Rheims, who owed the recovery of his episcopal seat to her, also hastened to condemn her on the same charge, as soon as she was captured. How had this peasant girl dared to set herself up as the equal of the nobility?

They didn't stay long in Orleans, but set out again on Tuesday, 14 June, to take Meung, some dozen miles south-west down-river, then on to Beaugency, a few miles down the Loire. Their army had been swelled by great numbers coming from far and wide, among others Guy and André de Laval, whose contingent had not arrived until after the departure for Jargeau. The king bestirred himself to come to Sully-sur-Loire, some fifty or so miles up-river east of Orleans, to the residence of his favourite, La Trémoille. On the way to Beaugency, Alençon and Joan's army took the important fortified bridge at Meung without difficulty (15 June). The taking of the bridge was important, because it provided access across the Loire to the town and to other places to the south. Thus Fastolf, on his way from Paris with four thousand or more men, would find his way to reinforce Beaugency blocked. A section of the French troops was left there to besiege the town itself, while the rest moved on to Beaugency. Alençon, with a small number of men-at-arms, spent the night encamped in a church near Meung, where he was, he says, 'in great danger'.

When the army arrived at Beaugency on 16 June, the English garrison had retreated into the castle (outside the town walls) and the fortifications on the bridge, so the French were able to enter the town from the other side. Some of the English soldiers had, however, taken cover in houses, from whence they emerged to take the French by surprise. Several skirmishes ensued. In the middle of the bombardment of the castle and bridge, news came to Alençon that Arthur de Richemont, the Constable of France, was imminently arriving with six hundred men-at-arms and four hundred archers. Chartier gives a slightly higher figure: a thousand to twelve hundred combatants. The *Chronique de la Pucelle* puts it also at twelve hundred.

Richemont was *persona non grata* at Charles VII's court, having, as we have seen earlier, been ousted from favour by La Trémoille. He had wanted to take part in the relief of Orleans, but on his way there with the large company he had raised, he had received an order from the king to go no farther or he would be met with force and turned back. After the victory at Orleans, he set out again, coming, says Cagny, despite the fact that Alençon had officially sent word to him, 'that on the advice of La Trémoille, who regarded him as his enemy and who spoke for the whole of the King's government, the King did not wish him to have any part in the war.'[22]

Chartier, in his Chronicle says that not only Richemont, but 'several other lords and captains whom the Sire de la Trémoille disliked' had withdrawn from the campaign, 'greatly to the detriment of the king and his kingdom'. He adds:

> Several people said that if the Sire de la Trémoille and others in the king's council had accepted all those who came to serve the monarch, he would easily have been able to recover everything that the English held in France. No-one dared at the time to speak out against La Trémoille, however clearly everyone saw that he was in the wrong'[23]

The *Chronique de la Pucelle* tells the same story:

> At that time, La Trémoille enjoyed the king's favour, but he was constantly in fear of losing his position and especially afraid of the Constable and his friends. On that account, although the Constable had twelve hundred men-at-arms and personnel and other nobles with him who would gladly have served the king, La Trémoille wouldn't allow it. There was no-one who dared speak against him.[24]

Alençon says that he and Joan and the other captains were displeased at Richemont's arrival and wanted to withdraw, because they had orders not to receive him into their company. 'I said to Joan,' he goes on, 'that if the Constable came, I was going.' However, Joan's displeasure, if she was indeed displeased, was clearly qualified. It is in any case unthinkable that she would have agreed to withdraw at this stage, no-one withdrew in the middle of an assault. After this incident, as Alençon testified in 1456, Richemont arrived:

> In the morning, before the Constable arrived, we got news that the English and Talbot were coming in great numbers. The men-at-arms raised the cry, to arms! Then Joan said to me, since I was talking about withdrawing, that we must accept help.

In the end, the English agreed to surrender the castle, which they considered the best strategy in the circumstances, since Alençon allowed them to leave with a safe-conduct. The garrison probably also knew that Richemont was coming. The *Journal du Siège* says that they left after midnight. By agreement, they took with them their horses and those possessions 'the value of which did not exceed one silver mark'. They also had to take an oath that they would not take up arms again for a period of ten days. 'On these conditions they left the next morning, which was the eighteenth day of June, and moved into Meung. The French entered the castle and put in reinforcements of troops to guard it.'[25]

'They had gone,' says Alençon, 'when a man of La Hire's company came to tell me and the other captains, "The English are advancing on us. We'll have to face them. There's a good thousand of them down there." When she noticed him speaking, Joan asked, "What's the man saying?" So we told her. Then she said to the Constable, "Ah! Constable, you haven't come on my account, but since you are here, you are very welcome".'

The *Journal du Siège* also gives an account of Richemont's arrival, saying that the Constable requested Joan to make his peace with the King, and for love of him, the other *seigneurs* added their voice to his. She agreed to do so, on condition that he would swear before her and the others that he would loyally serve the king. She went further. She demanded that the Duke of Alençon and the other lords would guarantee his loyalty with letters bearing their seals. 'They agreed to this. In this way the Constable remained at the siege with the other lords.' Probably no-one would have had so much power of persuasion with the king as Joan. Little wonder that La Trémoille increasingly detested her.

Alençon continues:

Many of the King's troops were nervous, saying it would be as well to fetch the horses [i.e. to retreat], but Joan said, "In God's name, we must fight them! If they were perched on the clouds, we will get them! God is sending us to punish them!' She declared that she was sure of victory. 'Our King,' she said, 'will today have the greatest victory he has had for a long time. My Council [her Voices] has told me that we have them!'

The great victory was that of Patay. Alençon gives a very brief account of it, saying only that the English were beaten without any great difficulty. A full account is given by Jean de Wavrin de Forestel, himself a well-regarded commander on the Anglo-Burgundian side. His father had been killed at his side at Agincourt and now at Patay he was fighting under the command of Sir John Fastolf. This is how his account begins:

The English captains at Janville were informed that the French had just taken Jargeau by assault with a great force of arms, that Meung had been reduced, and that Beaugency was besieged. This news caused great despondency, but they couldn't do anything about it for the time being.[26]

The captains held a meeting to discuss the situation, during which Talbot arrived with his company of about two hundred and fifty men and forty archers. His arrival was greeted with delight, for he was considered to be, says Wavrin, 'the wisest and bravest captain in England'. After dinner, another meeting was held. Wavrin writes:

> Many things were discussed, for Sir John Fastolf, who was considered to be a very wise and valiant knight, debated many points with Lord Talbot and others, pointing to the loss of men at Orleans, Jargeau and elsewhere, which had greatly alarmed and demoralised those on the English side, while greatly heartening and reinvigorating the enemy. His advice was therefore to go no further, to leave the garrison in Beaugency to get the best terms from the French that they could and, for their own part, to retreat to the towns, castles and fortresses that they held, rather than being in such a hurry to fight. They should wait until their nerves steadied and until the reinforcements sent by the Regent should arrive. This advice, made in full council by Fastolf, did not please some of the other captains, in particular Talbot, who said that even if he had only his own men and some others willing to follow him, he would go out and fight, with the help of God and Saint George.

Fastolf was wasting his breath. The command was given to set out in battle order the next morning, and off they all went, knights on horseback, foot soldiers, archers, banners and standards waving in the early breeze. Fastolf persisted in arguing his case, warning that they risked losing all that Henry V had won. He still wanted to await reinforcements. Wavrin affirms that the English were advancing in good order and were close to Meung and Beaugency when they met the French, who had taken up their position on a low hill, with about six thousand men led by 'Joan the Maid, Alençon, Dunois, La Fayette, La Hire, Xaintrailles and others'. (He puts Joan at the top of the list.) The estimate of the number of captains and men on the hill is as usual very unreliable. The French would hardly have absented themselves more or less *en masse* from their siege of Beaugency. They had probably sent out a party to reconnoitre and they were certainly not at that point seeking confrontation. The English got ready to fight, stakes were fixed in the ground in front of the archers, but the French didn't move from their position on the hill. Two heralds were sent to challenge them to send down three champions to fight three English champions; a caustic reply came back, 'Go to your billets for tonight. It's too late. Tomorrow, please God and Our Lady, we'll see you at closer quarters.'

The English entered Meung and lodged there that night, for it was only the fortress on the bridge that was in French hands. The earlier report of the reduction of the town was unfounded. The French, says Wavrin, returned to Beaugency, which capitulated, as we have seen, during the night. Wavrin says that the town capitulated because

> The Maid's reputation had shaken English morale very badly. It seemed to them that Fortune's wheel had turned sharply against them. They had lost several towns and fortresses, which had gone over to the king of France either through assault or by treaty, principally thanks to the exploits of the said Maid ... So it seemed to them that everyone was very anxious to retreat to the marches of Normandy, abandoning everything they held in the Île de France and thereabouts.

The garrison in Beaugency was largely made up of men who had been defeated at Orleans. Little wonder that they were demoralised. Wavrin describes what happened after the English left Beaugency on the Saturday morning:

> There was no doubt that the English (those in Meung), as soon as they heard that Beaugency had surrendered, would set out across the Beauce to return to Paris. At the instigation of Joan, the French decided to pursue them as they crossed the Beauce, where some advantageous place to fight them would be found.

Wavrin goes on to describe the leadership of the French army:

> Every day, men were arriving from all parts to join the French. The vanguard was made up of men under the command of the Constable, Boussac, La Hire, Poton de Xaintrailles and other captains. Leading the army, close behind them, came Alençon, Dunois and Gilles de Rais.

Wavrin estimates the French army at twelve or thirteen thousand men. In fact, most historians put it at about six thousand, so that the two adversaries were fairly evenly matched. As usual, the chronicler wants to show his own side in the best light, here it is a matter of explaining the crushing defeat at Patay by alleging an imbalance of forces. The account of the events leading up to the battle continues:

> Some of the principal seigneurs and captains asked Joan what she would advise them to do now. She replied that she was absolutely certain that the English were waiting for them and would fight and that the French should advance and they would be victorious. Some asked her where they would come across the enemy and she replied that they should simply ride ahead boldly, they would be well led. So the different

companies of soldiers set out in fine order. The most experienced men, sixty or eighty of them, were sent on ahead to seek out the English. They rode on for most of Saturday.

The English had been billeted overnight in Meung, intending to take the bridge in order to be able to re-provision the Beaugency garrison, which however surrendered that night, unknown to us. That Saturday, at about eight o'clock in the morning, after the captains had heard Mass, it was proclaimed that all should get themselves ready, arming themselves with shields, doors or anything else useful for an attack on the bridge, which had been heavily bombarded by our artillery during the night. When we were all equipped with the necessary and ready to start, a messenger arrived from Beaugency to tell our lords and captains that the town and castle of Beaugency were in the hands of the French, who were starting out, even as he was leaving the place, to come and fight us.

The English immediately abandoned their assault on the bridge and ordered everyone to get into marching order outside the town. Wavrin:

The order was promptly carried out. The vanguard rode ahead, led by an English knight carrying a white standard. Between them and the bulk of the army came the artillery, the provisions and all manner of merchants. Finally came the army, led by Sir John Fastolf, Lord Talbot, Sir Thomas Rampston and others. Behind these rode the rearguard, composed entirely of Englishmen. When we were in open country, we rode on in good order on the road to Patay.

We stopped within two or three miles from Patay, for couriers from the rearguard informed us that they had spotted a great number of men coming up behind them, whom they thought must be the French. So the English lords sent riders to ascertain the facts. These quickly returned to report that a great force of the French was riding hard on their tracks and soon afterwards they could be seen coming. So our captains ordered that the vanguard, the merchants, provisions and artillery, should take up positions behind the hedges near Patay, which they proceeded to do. The army then went forward up to two lines of thick hedges which the French would have to pass through.

Lord Talbot, seeing that the site would be advantageous, said that he would go forward on foot with five hundred elite archers and guard the passage against the French until the rearguard joined up with the army. He took up his position behind the hedges at Patay, with the vanguard which was stationed there. Guarding this narrow passage against the enemy, he hoped to be able to rejoin the army by keeping to the hedges, whatever the French should do. But it turned out quite differently.

It was Talbot's plan to hold back the French advance until his army had time to organise itself properly. Unfortunately for the English troops, the

French managed to find them before this strategy could be completed. Their cover was blown, as Andrew Lang says, by the 'unlucky sporting instinct of the English'! Wavrin continues:

The French were advancing rapidly on us, but couldn't yet come face-to-face, for they couldn't find us. Then, as it happened, the mounted scouts of the French army startled a stag which suddenly leapt out of the woods and headed for Patay. It crashed into the hidden English army and the men raised an almighty hunting cry, not realising that their enemies were so close. Thanks to this view-halloo, the French scouts were certain they had found the English and soon afterwards they were able to see them quite clearly. They sent some of their comrades back to inform their captains of what they had seen and found, telling them to advance in good order, for the time had come to begin the work. Preparations were promptly made and the French rode forward rapidly until they had the English clearly in view.

When the English army saw the French closing in, they made as much haste as possible to get to the hedges before them, but they weren't able to get there in time to join up with their vanguard. The French rushed into the narrow passage where Lord Talbot was stationed. Then the vanguard, seeing Sir John Fastolf galloping up to join them, thought that all was lost and that their comrades were fleeing. That was why the captain of the vanguard, with his white standard, thinking this to be the case, took to flight and his men along with him. They all abandoned the hedges.

Then Sir John, seeing the danger of the flight and realising that all was going very badly, was advised to get away. He was told, in my presence, that he should save himself, for the battle was lost. He wanted desperately to remain in the battle and await the fate that Our Lord would send him, saying that he would rather die or be taken prisoner than to flee so shamefully, abandoning all his men. As he was leaving, the French had already captured Lord Talbot and all his men were dead. They were already so on top in the battle that they could capture or kill whomsoever they liked. Finally the English were defeated. There were very few losses on the French side. On the English side a good two thousand men died and a good couple of hundred were taken prisoner.

So the battle went on, as you have just read. When Sir John saw all that, he departed, very much against his will, with very few companions and in the greatest state of grief I have ever seen in a man. In truth, he would have gone back into the battle if it hadn't been for those who were with him, particularly the Bastard of Thien and some others. He headed for Étampes and I followed him as my commander, whom the Duke of Bedford had ordered me to obey and serve. We arrived an hour after midnight at Étampes, where we slept. The following day we arrived at Corbeil.

So, as you see, the French were victorious at Patay, where they spent the night, thanking Our Lord for their good fortune. The next morning they left Patay, which is half a dozen miles or so from Janville. The battle will be forever known as the battle of Patay. From there, the French went on, with their booty and their prisoners, to Orleans, where they were received with great rejoicing by all the people. Above all others, Joan the Maid acquired such fame and praise, that it seemed plain to everyone that King Charles's enemies had no power to resist him wherever she was present, and that, thanks to her, his kingdom would soon be restored to him despite all the efforts of those who were against him.

The Sire de Termes, who had been present at the siege of Orleans, was also one of the captains who fought at Beaugency and Patay. In his evidence at the Nullity trial, he said that he and La Hire spoke to Joan before Patay:

We said to Joan, 'The English are coming. They are approaching in battle order and ready to fight.' She said to the captains, 'Strike boldly! They will be put to flight.' She added that it wouldn't take long.'

Dunois has another anecdote:

At the news that Beaugency had been taken, all the English companies [i.e. at Meung] joined forces to form one army. We believed that they intended to engage us in battle. We drew up our troops in battle order and prepared to fight the enemy. At that, in the presence of the Constable and myself and others, the Duke of Alençon said to Joan, 'What should I do now?' She replied, 'You'd better all have good spurs!' At that, those present said to her, 'What do you mean? Are we going to turn tail and run away?' 'No,' she replied. 'It's the English who will run. They won't defend themselves and they'll be beaten, and you'd better have good spurs to race after them!'

Alençon's account of the battle is very brief:

The enemy was beaten without any great difficulty. Talbot was taken prisoner, among others. There was a great slaughter of the English. Then we came to the village of Patay. There Talbot was brought before me. The Constable and Joan were present. I said to Talbot, 'You didn't think this morning that this would happen to you!' 'It's the fortune of war,' he replied. We went back to the king and it was decided to push on to Rheims for the coronation.

One must admire Talbot's stoicism and dignity in the face of the cock-a-hoop glee of the younger man. He would be exchanged four years later for the French knight, Antoine de Loré. Scales and other leading English captains were also captured. The Burgundian chronicler Monstrelet puts the number of English dead at two thousand two hundred, much the same as Wavrin. He gives a very short account of the battle, making little mention of Joan, not surprisingly, since the captains had relegated her to lead the rearguard. In his testimony at the Nullity trial of 1456, her page, Louis de Coutes says, 'La Hire was leading the vanguard, which upset Joan a lot, for she very much wanted to be in charge of the vanguard,' and adds, 'She was very upset by the butchery, for she was very compassionate.'

Poor Sir John Fastolf became the scapegoat for the English disaster. Bedford disgraced him and took away his ribbon of the Garter, although later he got it back. But the legend of Fastolf the coward lived on. Shakespeare's *Henry VI, Part I*, opens with the funeral of Henry V, at which a messenger appears with news of the battle of Patay and launches into an ecstatic eulogy of Talbot and a ferocious indictment of Fastolf.

> Here had the conquest fully been sealed up,
> If Sir John Fastolf had not played the coward.

Shakespeare generously overestimates the numbers on the French side, putting it at twenty-three thousand (against only six thousand English!) and has 'a base Walloon' stab Talbot in the back (he survives). But then, as that old jester Shaw remarked, the English are never *fairly* beaten ...

Percival de Cagny and Jean Chartier put the estimated number of English dead at between two and three thousand. Guillaume Gruel, the chronicler of Richemont, affirms that the heralds gave the number of English dead officially as two thousand two hundred. This is also the figure given by the *Journal du Siège*. Dunois and others on the French side give wildly exaggerated estimates. The Burgundian chronicler Monstrelet reduces the number of dead to eighteen hundred and brings the number of prisoners down from two hundred to something between one hundred and a hundred and eighty. But it is clear that Patay was at last the French answer to Agincourt.

11

The Road to Rheims: Coronation

L'an mil quatre cens vingt et neuf
Reprit à luire li soleil

Christine de Pisan

Joan, the captains and the army returned to Orleans to great rejoicing. The citizens festooned the town and made great preparations to welcome the Dauphin Charles, but he lingered on in the château of Sully, under the malign sway of his favourite La Trémoille, now more than ever hostile to Joan, who had promised to restore his enemy the Constable to the king's good graces. Joan, Alençon and others went to Sully to plead Richemont's case, the latter himself not being allowed to appear in person, especially not in the château of his arch enemy. He did however send supplications and protestations of loyalty to Charles, going so far as to send gentlemen to beg La Trémoille to allow him, together with his large contingent of archers and men-at-arms, to serve with the army of the king. All to no avail. Charles condescended to 'pardon' him, but obstinately refused to allow him to take any further part in the campaign to reach Rheims. Another important volunteer not to La Trémoille's taste was similarly rebuffed. This was the Count of Pardiac, son of the late Count of Armagnac, who also offered his services and resources in vain. To refuse such considerable reinforcements in the midst of a war seems sheer folly.

Joan was impatient to move forward and have Charles crowned at Rheims. Janville had opened its gates to the French without resistance, other smaller places followed suit. But there were still English garrisons in the bigger towns. Auxerre, Châlons, Troyes, all barred the hundred and seventy or eighty miles that lay between Gien and Rheims, which was itself held by the English. In fairness, we must say that it is little wonder that Charles and his council were not easily persuaded of the wisdom of the undertaking.

Around 21 June, Joan must have ridden over from Orleans to the nearby village of Saint-Benoît-sur-Loire, about four miles or so from Sully, where she had a meeting with Charles, no doubt intending to urge him to follow up as quickly as possible the victories of Beaugency, Meung and Patay. Her disappointment, must have been acute when instead, he urged her to rest! Our informant is again Sir Simon Charles who describes the incident as follows:

> Joan was very simple in all her ways, except at war, where she was very experienced. I heard many good things about Joan from the king's own mouth, when he was at Saint-Benoît-sur-Loire. When he was there, he felt sorry for her, for all the strain she had been under, and he ordered her to take a rest. Then she burst into tears and told the king that he should not delay and that he would recover his all kingdom and be rapidly crowned.

Joan and Alençon left Orleans on Friday, 23 June, to join the king, who had now moved to Gien, closer to the Burgundian-held territory to the east of Orleans. They were met with great feasting and rejoicing. Cagny describes the general euphoria:

> There was great talk among all the lords, knights, squires, men-at-arms and people of every rank, all of whom held the military exploits of the previous Saturday to be an amazing miracle on the part of Joan and her company.[1]

However, Charles could not make up his mind to move on. He would hover indecisively in Gien for nearly a week, only moving on 29 June. The frustration of Joan and the military leaders was immense. Cagny adds:

> The Maid was extremely vexed by the length of the King's stay in Gien, which was due to some of his household advising him against setting out for Rheims, saying that a number of towns and other places were closed against him and that between Gien and Rheims there were towns and fortresses well garrisoned with English and Burgundians. Joan said that she was quite aware of that and not concerned about it. In her frustration, she moved out and camped with her soldiers in the countryside two days before the king himself set out.

At any rate, Charles had spread the news far and wide of the relief of Orleans and the recent astonishing victories. Messengers were sent with letters, proclamations were made, there were celebrations and revelries and processions of thanksgiving throughout the faithful towns of the kingdom. Envoys were sent to the leading nobility and churchmen and to all the king's vassals, to summon them to Charles's coming coronation in Rheims. Charles's wife, Marie d'Anjou, was sent for and came up from her residence in Bourges to Gien. It was intended that she should be present at the coronation in Rheims, perhaps even that she should also be crowned there; however, more cautious advice prevailed and she returned whence she had come.

Wild and exaggerated rumours of marvellous deeds reverberated across the countryside. Men arrived in great numbers to swell the ranks of the army, although the king hadn't the money to pay them. Chartier says that at Gien Charles made a payment of a mere two or three francs to each man. They volunteered anyway. Cagny:

> Although the king hadn't the money to pay the troops, none of them, were they knights, squires, soldiers or the common people, refused to serve him on his journey [to Rheims] in the company of the Maid. They said that they would follow her wherever she wished to go. She said, '*Par mon martin*! I'll lead the noble King Charles and his company in all safety and he will be crowned in Rheims.'

The *Chronique de la Pucelle* adds more detail:

> More nobles, captains and men-at-arms arrived from everywhere to serve the king. Several gentlemen, not having sufficient means to arm themselves or to be suitably mounted, came as archers or *coustillers* mounted on ponies, for everyone had great hopes that thanks to Joan, great good would befall the kingdom of France.[2]

Alençon, Dunois, the Laval brothers, Gilles de Rais, La Hire, Xaintrailles, and all the other faithful captains were there to lead the army. Two days before she moved out of Gien, Joan herself had written letters, one to the town of Tournai, which, although surrounded by Burgundian territory, had remained stubbornly loyal to the Dauphin, and a second to the Duke of Burgundy. The letter to the duke invited him to be present at the coronation in Rheims. As a prince of the Blood Royal, he had every right and duty to be there. It is now known only because of a reference to it in a later letter of Joan's, written on the day of the coronation. As to Tournai, Joan seems to have had a special affection for the town, a direct dependency of the French crown. This letter also contained an invitation:

> To the noble and loyal French people of the town of Tournai:
> Loyal French inhabitants of the town of Tournai, the Maid sends you news, to say that in a week, by assault or otherwise, she has driven the English out of all the places they held on the Loire. They were defeated in battle, with many dead and captured. The Earl of Suffolk, his brother [John] de la Pole, Lords Talbot, Scales, Sir John Fastolf and a number of knights and captains have been taken. Glasdale and a brother of the Earl of Suffolk are dead. Now, dear loyal French people, I pray and request you to be ready to come to the coronation of our noble King Charles at Rheims, where we will shortly arrive. Come out to meet us when you hear that we are coming. I commend you to God's keeping, may He give you His blessing to pursue the just quarrel of the kingdom of France. Written at Gien, 25 June.[3]

The town, says Quicherat, had held out for the Dauphin because it had a relatively democratic form of government. Joan's letter reached Tournai on 7 July, was discussed in the council, then promulgated in all thirty-six *bannières* or boroughs of the town, before it was finally agreed to send representatives to the coronation.

The first stop on the way to Rheims was Auxerre. This was the Burgundian town in which Joan had heard Mass on her way to see the Dauphin at Chinon. The people apparently wanted to keep on the right side of both Charles and the Burgundians, fearing the wrath of either. Chartier writes:

> The town did not enter into full obedience. Some of the citizens came to parley and it is said that they gave money to La Trémoille in order to obtain a temporary truce. Some of the lords and captains of the army were very unhappy about this and spoke their minds plainly about La Trémoille and some of the king's council.[4]

Monstrelet adds the following:

> The representatives from Auxerre promised that they would render full obedience to the king if Troyes, Châlons and Rheims did so. Then, in exchange for supplying the king's army with provisions, for which they were paid, they were left in peace, the king excusing them for the time being.[5]

The *Chronique de la Pucelle* says that La Trémoille pocketed more than a pretty penny in return for his helpfulness:

> The affair was concluded at the request of La Trémoille, who received two thousand crowns for his services. Several of the lords and captains were greatly annoyed with La Trémoille and with some in the council, as was the Maid, for it seemed to her that the town could have easily been taken.[6]

The *Journal du Siège* agrees with this account:

> It seemed to the Maid and to several lords and captains that it would be easy to take the town by assault and they wished to try and do so. But the people in the town secretly gave two thousand écus to La Trémoille, to save them from attack.[7]

Whether the allegation is true or not cannot of course be proved. At least it demonstrates the way in which many regarded the king's favourite.

At any rate, the arrangement was accepted, despite Joan's urging that the town should either open its gates or be stormed. It was naturally risky to leave in the rear a stronghold held by the enemy and no such arrangement was made afterwards with other towns on the route. Probably a show of strength would have sufficed to persuade the citizens to open their gates, as was to be the case with the next, and all the other, towns on the way.

Three days were spent negotiating at Auxerre, then the king and army moved on to Troyes. The first stop on the route was Saint Florentin, which opened its gates on 4 July without demur. The other small fortresses on the route had done likewise. The next day, the army arrived at Troyes. The king had already on July 4 written to the town, inviting the people to open their gates and to have no fear that he would seek vengeance because of the past, assuring them that all would be forgiven and that he would restore them to his good graces. Joan also wrote to them on the same day:

Dear good friends,
If it all depends on you, nobles, citizens and inhabitants of the town of Troyes, Joan the Maid bids you and urges you, from the King of Heaven, her rightful and sovereign Lord, in Whose royal service she stands each day, that you recognise and enter into the obedience of the noble King of France, who will shortly arrive at Rheims and at Paris, regardless of whoever may oppose him, and he will enter all his good towns of this holy kingdom, with the help of Jesus our Lord. Loyal Frenchmen, come out without delay to meet King Charles. Do not fear for your persons or possessions in so doing. If you do not do so, I can promise you and guarantee on your lives, that with the help of God, we will enter into all the towns that belong to this holy kingdom and make a good and lasting peace, no matter who opposes us. I commend you to God, may He be pleased to help you. Reply promptly.
Written before the town of Troyes, Tuesday, 4 July.[8]

To all appearances, Troyes was a much bigger challenge than Auxerre, better garrisoned. It was under the control of the duke of Burgundy and of course it was the town in which the infamous Treaty of Troyes, disinheriting Charles VII, had been signed. It was strongly fortified, with a Burgundian garrison of about six hundred men, but such a town required the support of the citizens if it was to withstand an assault or a siege.

The brave citizens hastened to protest their loyalty to the Anglo-Burgundian cause. How sincere these protestations were must be open to question, in view of later developments. They sent word to the Duke of Burgundy that they had been informed by a certain friar, Brother Richard (of whom more shortly), that a deputation from Rheims had assured Charles VII that he would be welcomed with open arms in Rheims. On 5 July, they sent to Rheims copies of the letter from Charles (still known as the Dauphin) and Joan, saying they had sworn on the sacrament to hold their town for Burgundy and Henry VI, and that they would die rather than surrender. They begged Rheims to send messengers to Bedford and Burgundy to ask for help in their desperate plight. They sent another letter that same day and mentioned again the letter from 'Joan the Maid', that 'silly loud-mouthed hussy' (*cette coquarde*), that 'crazy wench full of the devil'. Her letter, they declared, had no rhyme or reason to it and they had had a good laugh at it and thrown it on the fire.[9]

The first reaction of the Burgundian garrison of Troyes was to make a sortie outside the walls, but they were speedily forced to retreat into the town. However, although Charles's army was now a considerable force, they were very short of provisions and sufficient siege material and very far from base, not really in a position to undertake a lengthy siege. *The Journal du Siège* describes the situation:

> During the five days they were there, the soldiers were suffering from hunger, for there were five or six thousand of them who had not eaten bread for a week. Indeed, many would have died of hunger if it had not been for the abundance of beans which had been sown at the behest of a Cordelier [Franciscan friar] called Brother Richard, who had preached at various places throughout France during the previous Advent, saying, among other things, 'Sow plenty of beans, good people, for He who is to come will soon appear!'[10]

Brother Richard had preached a series of Advent sermons in Troyes in December 1428, with the theme of the coming of Christ. Why did he advise the good people to sow beans? Colette Beaune reminds us of the parable of the Sower and the Seed in the New Testament, an allegory of the spread of God's kingdom on earth, but the friar's listeners took him literally and sowed beans outside their city, which was a lucky chance for the starving soldiers of King Charles's army.

This Brother Richard was well known to the English and Burgundian authorities. He had preached apocalyptic sermons in Paris during the Lent of 1429, urging repentance and bonfires of the vanities, a veritable Savonarola, indeed, *avant l'heure*. His theatricality, his sense of drama, his charisma were unsurpassed. He preached in Paris to gatherings of five or six thousand at a time from a platform raised ten feet aloft, beside the cemetery of the Holy Innocents, whose wall was decorated, since about 1424, with a long mural depicting the *Danse Macabre*, Pope, Emperor, priest and burgher, knight and peasant, noble and beggar, each hypnotically dancing with his partner Death. The Hundred Years War, plague, starvation, pillage and the other innumerable disasters of that century throughout Europe had seized and darkened the imagination of the multitudes. Pestilence, War, Famine and Death, the Four Horsemen of the Apocalypse, so terrifyingly illustrated at the end of the century in Dürer's woodcut, rampaged across the landscapes. Brother Richard proclaimed the imminent end of the world and the coming of the Antichrist, who, he said, had already been born, according to a number of Jews whom he had met in Jerusalem. His Jewish informants didn't say they were speaking of the Antichrist, of course, but of their long awaited Messiah, which Brother Richard interpreted to mean the Antichrist.

People flocked in their thousands to his outdoor sermons, which he started to preach at five o'clock in the morning and which could go on for five or six hours at a time. The men made bonfires and burned dice, gaming tables, bowls, all the accoutrements of frivolous pursuits, the women brought their finery, their *hennins*, their jewelry, their trinkets, and threw the lot onto the flames. Indeed, says the anonymous *Bourgeois de Paris* in his *Journal,*

> The ten sermons that he preached at Paris and one at Boulogne brought more people back to their devotions than all the sermons which had been preached over the last hundred years.[11]

The *Bourgeois* goes on to say that Brother Richard was obliged to leave Paris in early May 1429, no doubt banished by the authorities, whether on account of his preaching which smacked of heresy or because he was suspected of Armagnac sympathies, as Monstrelet alleges in his *Chronicle*, or both. Word got around that he would preach his last sermon outside Paris (at Montmartre) on Sunday, 1 May. The *Bourgeois* describes what happened:

> More than six thousand Parisians set out in great crowds on the Saturday, so as to have the best places on Sunday morning. They slept in dilapidated hovels in the fields or wherever they could, but his sermon was cancelled, how, I won't say. At any rate, he didn't preach, which greatly upset the good people, nor did he preach any more that year in Paris and he had to leave.[12]

Brother Richard had made a great impression on the good people of Troyes also and he was in that city when Joan arrived with the army. The citizens seem to have been divided as to their best course of action and he played a not-inconsiderable role in helping them to make up their minds.

At some point during the days following the arrival of the royal army, at the request of the town council, he went out to confront Joan, armed with holy water, commissioned as he was to establish once and for all whether she was sent by God, as the French believed, or by the Devil, as the English, the Burgundians and the duke of Bedford believed. Joan gives a brief account of the incident when questioned about it on Saturday, 3 March, during her trial:

Beaupère: Have you ever met Brother Richard?
Joan: I had never seen him until I was at Troyes.
Beaupère: What sort of welcome did he give you?
Joan: The people of Troyes, I think, sent him to me saying that they feared that I wasn't sent by God. When Brother Richard approached me, he made the sign of the cross and started throwing holy water. Then I said to him, 'Come on, be bold! I won't fly away!'.

Joan of course, was mocking the idea that she might be a witch and fly away on a broomstick. Brother Richard, satisfied, went back into Troyes, where no doubt he gave Joan a good report. Afterwards he tagged on to her, which Joan, with her abundant common sense, must have found irksome. He was never one of her chaplains. He was present at the coronation in Rheims and we hear of him afterwards at one or two other places where she campaigned. No doubt she suffered him patiently, until finally, in November or December 1429, she had to have a row with him when he championed a woman called Catherine de la Rochelle, who claimed to have visions of a lady in white. Catherine herself was actually a married woman with a family. The 'lady in white' sent a message to Joan to have the king send heralds and trumpeters throughout the country, demanding that all those who had gold or silver or 'hidden treasure' hand it over, and saying that if they didn't, Catherine would know how to find it. Joan saw her for a fraud, told her to go home and look after her husband and family and reported to the king it was all a load of rubbish, which greatly displeased both Brother Richard and his *protégée*. Catherine had her revenge when she fell into the hands of the English, shortly after Joan's captivity. On trial in Paris, she declared that Joan was in league with Satan and would fly out of her prison by his aid unless she was very well guarded.

Meanwhile, Troyes was not alone in its state of perplexity. Those in the royal army were also of divided opinion as to the best course of action, many being in favour of a withdrawal, given the difficulties ahead. They had been encamped outside Troyes for several days, when on 8 July, the king called a meeting of the chiefs of staff and other important personages (but not Joan). Dunois, in his testimony in 1456, also the *Journal du Siège* and the *Chronique* of Jean Chartier, all give concordant accounts of the deliberations which took place. Chartier's is the fullest:

The King summoned the Duke of Alençon, the Duke of Bourbon, the Count of Vendôme and several other lords and captains, together with other lords of his council, to a meeting to advise him as to how he should proceed. At that meeting, the Chancellor, who was the Archbishop of Rheims, argued that the army could not remain at Troyes for a number of reasons: first, that they were suffering a famine and that there was no prospect of receiving provisions; second, that there was no money left, and third, that it would need a miracle to take Troyes, a well-defended city, well supplied with provisions, whose population, as far as could be seen, had no intention of putting the town into the king's obedience. The army had neither cannon, artillery nor men enough to take the place by force [...]. The Chancellor required each of those present to give the king his honest opinion as to how they should proceed. Almost all were of the opinion that the King and his army should turn back, in view of what had been said. also given the fact that the King had been refused at Auxerre, a town with a smaller garrison than Troyes, and for several other reasons which were put forward by various of those present.[13]

The Chancellor then asked a former councillor, by the name of Robert le Maçon, Lord of Trèves, for his opinion. Robert said that he believed that they should send for Joan the Maid, who was with the army but not present at the meeting. He thought she might well have something useful to say to the King. He said that when the King had started out on the campaign, he had not done so because he had any great armed force, nor because he had a vast amount of money with which to pay his soldiers, nor even because the campaign looked possible, but solely at Joan's insistence that he must go to Rheims to be crowned, that he would meet little resistance on the way, and that it was God's will. Robert said that if Joan's opinion did not differ from what had been said in the meeting, he would abide by the general consensus that the king and army should withdraw. However, if she had a different opinion, the King might well come to a different conclusion.

The *Journal du Siège d'Orléans* gives the same account of proceedings at the council meeting, noting moreover that Robert le Maçon was himself a former Chancellor. Its account of Joan's intervention gives identical information to that given by Chartier, but rather more succinctly:

> She knocked loudly on the door of the council chamber, and when she entered, the Chancellor explained to her in a few words the reasons why the king had undertaken the campaign and the reasons for which he was contemplating abandoning it. Then she replied very prudently, saying that if the king would wait, the town of Troyes would be in his obedience within two or three days. The Chancellor said to her, 'Joan, if it were certain that it would be so in six days, we would wait.' To this she replied that she had no doubts about it. So it was agreed that they would wait.[14]

Given this go-ahead, Joan set about preparing a show of strength. Dunois says, in his testimony at the Nullity trial:

> She advanced with the army, fixed the tents along the ditches and took such admirable precautions that two or three of the most experienced

and famous captains could not have done better. She worked so hard that night, that the next day the bishop and citizens placed themselves in the king's obedience in fear and trembling.

The *Journal* describes the events:

> She mounted a charger, her baton in her hand, and made all preparations very diligently to launch an assault on the town with artillery. This amazed the bishop [of the town] and the people. So, considering that, after all, the king was their rightful and sovereign lord, also taking into account the exploits of the Maid and the rumours that she was sent by God, they asked to negotiate. The bishop went out with a number of respectable citizens, military and civilian, who reached an agreement that the garrison would leave with their possessions and that a general amnesty would be granted to the people of the town. The king was willing for the clergy to retain the benefices granted them by King Henry of England, but under new titles granted by himself. On these conditions, the king and most of the lords and captains, all very handsomely attired, made their entry into the city of Troyes the following morning. The men of the garrison wanted to take with them a number of prisoners-of-war, in accordance with the treaty, but the Maid was opposed to that, so the king paid a ransom to their captors.

The *Chronique de la Pucelle* gives a lively portrait of an indignant Joan standing at the city gate to forbid the departure of the prisoners:

> As they were in the act of taking the prisoners with them, Joan stood at the city gate and declared, 'In the name of God! They shall not pass!' And indeed, the prisoners had to be left behind.[15]

No pasaran! How many prisoners? How much ransom? A letter sent to Rheims on 13 July by Jean de Châtillon, brother of the captain of that town, says they got one silver mark for each prisoner.[16] This seems to have been a standard payment in such circumstances, since the garrison at Beaugency had also been allowed to leave and take with them goods not exceeding the value of 'one silver mark'. How did the king scrape together the money? Certainly they cannot have been high-status prisoners, so perhaps it is all the more to Charles's credit that he rescued them, albeit at Joan's insistence.

Sir Simon Charles remarked, in the 1456 trial, that 'the king entered the town of Troyes with great pageantry, Joan riding beside him, holding her standard'. The sight of Joan riding at the head of the pageant beside the king, clad in her splendidly decorated *huque* worn over her armour and holding her standad proudly aloft, would have thrilled the spectators.

Pageantry has always played an important part in establishing status and popularity.

She was asked at her trial, (on Saturday, 3 March 1431), if Brother Richard had preached a sermon when she entered the town. She answered that she hadn't stayed there long, nor was she lodged in the town, she didn't know anything about a sermon. Then she was asked if she had been godmother to an infant there and at other places. She answered that she had done so there and elsewhere:

> I acted as godmother to a child there. I don't remember doing so at Rheims or Château-Thierry, but I did so on two occasions at Saint-Denis. I liked to give the name Charles to the boys, in honour of the king, and I gave the name Joan to the girls. Sometimes I simply gave the name which pleased the mother.

Next she was asked if the women of the town had touched the ring she wore with their own rings (encouragement of such touching would have served as evidence of culpable superstition or worse). She answered: 'Many women have touched my hands and my rings, but I don't know what they are thinking or what they intend.'

It is clear however, from all this, that many in Troyes regarded her as a saint. The king entered Troyes on 10 July and left again with his army on 12 July.

The next stop was Châlons, a town which, like Rheims, had received letters from Troyes asking for help. They had written to Rheims, stoutly assuring their friends there that they too would resist to the death. They submitted without a squeak. The bishop came out to welcome the king and the army, all of whom made another splendid entry into the town on 14 July. In Châlons, Joan met some of her old friends from Domrémy, among others, Jean Morel, her godfather, and Gérardin d'Épinal, who, before Joan's departure from the village had been its only Burgundian inhabitant. His political opinions seem to have undergone a sea change in the few months since Joan had last seen him. Was it Joan's fame, or the influence of his wife, Zabillette, or both, which had brought this about?

After Orleans, the villagers must have made their way from Domrémy until they met up with the army in Châlons. Gérardin says, in his deposition for the Nullity trial, that there were four of them there from Domrémy. Joan seems after all to have had quite a soft spot for him, for it was to him, so he says, that she confided in Châlons that 'she feared nothing but treason.' What treason was she afraid of? Was it La Trémoille or others in the council? To Jean Morel she gave a red robe, which she had been wearing. Perhaps he had asked her for a souvenir.

On 11 July, Troyes had informed Rheims that they had submitted. Their letter was full of praise now for Charles. They said he had spoken very wisely to their archbishop, who had gone out to parley with him. He had promised them to govern in peace and justice and freedom, like the holy king, Saint Louis. They had therefore recognised the justice of his cause, on condition that he would declare a general amnesty, abolish taxes, except for the *gabelle* (salt tax), and not impose a garrison on them (they must have had enough of the Burgundian garrison). They regretted that it had taken them so long to take this step and recommended that Rheims now follow their example, assuring the citizens that if they did so, it would bring them great happiness. Charles, they said, was 'the most discreet, intelligent and valiant prince that the noble House of France had ever bred'.

Rheims had already received a letter from Charles VII written on 4 July. It informed them of the victories at Orleans, Jargeau, Beaugency and Meung. Charles declared his intention of being crowned in their cathedral and assured them that they had nothing to fear, for he would treat them as his good subjects. At the same time, the people of Rheims were receiving letters from all parts of the Burgundian-held territory, urging them to stand firm. On 10 July, a letter of encouragement was sent to them by the pro-Burgundian *bailli* of Vermandois, telling them that the dukes of Burgundy and Luxembourg were entering Paris and that eight thousand English soldiers had landed in Normandy.

Rheims sent all this correspondence to Guillaume de Châtillon, military commander, or captain, of the town, who had taken himself to Château-Thierry about thirty-six miles away. He had sent messengers, described as 'notable knights and squires', to seek help from Bedford and Burgundy, but had to tell Rheims that he hadn't yet got a reply. He assured them that he was ready to come, but urged them to reply quickly. The seventeenth-century compiler of the letters, Jean Rogier, surmised that he preferred to stay away, shrewdly suspecting that the citizens were intending to welcome Charles and the royal army. However, we are told that he did come back, with several other *seigneurs* and a great number of their men, but only to tell the inhabitants that Burgundy had informed him that his army would not be ready for five or six weeks. At this, the council and citizens refused him and the troops entry into the town.

Jean de Châtillon, the brother of Guillaume, had also written to Rheims on 13 July, as we have seen, telling them that the capitulation of Troyes had been due to the treachery of the bishop and the wiles of a Franciscan named Brother Richard. He reported that Charles and his army had entered the town effortlessly, after being on the point of withdrawing because they had no supplies, and that the garrison had left after being compensated for the loss of their prisoners. He added, snidely, that the squire who had brought him all this news had himself seen 'Joan the Maid' and had declared that, in faith, she was 'the most simple-minded creature he had ever seen and not a patch on a valiant woman like Madame d'Or!' Who was Madame d'Or? A female acrobat and entertainer at the court of the Duke of Burgundy. Some said that her gorgeous mane of golden hair (hence her name, Madame *d'Or*) was the inspiration for the naming, in 1430, of Burgundy's great order of chivalry, the Order of the Golden Fleece.

Other letters urged Rheims to submit. Not only Troyes, but also the inhabitants of Châlons, who in their letter praised Charles as 'mild, gracious, compassionate and merciful, handsome and highly intelligent'. Regnault de Chartres, Archbishop of Rheims, had written to his flock on 11 July, exhorting them to receive their king 'honourably'. He himself had been appointed to the archbishopric some fifteen years earlier, but had never yet been able to enter his own cathedral. The time had now come. On 16 July, Charles received a deputation from Rheims at the *château* of Sept-Saulx, about twelve miles outside the city. They brought him the town's willing submission, he granted them a full amnesty and that very morning the archbishop at last made his ceremonial entry into the town. As he did so, another cleric, Bishop Pierre Cauchon, one-time rector of the University of Paris and signatory of the Treaty of Troyes, unobtrusively slipped out of the gates together with a number of other 'renegade French' (*Français reniés*) who owed their position and prosperity to the Anglo-Burgundian authorities. Bishop Cauchon was to become famous (or infamous) as the judge who condemned Joan of Arc to the stake.

On the evening of Saturday, 16 July, at seven o'clock, according to the *Chronique de Tournay*, Charles VII made his solemn entry into the town, to the ringing acclamations of the populace crying *Noël! Noël!*[17] The Archbishop, accompanied by a throng of mitred bishops, abbots and clergy with their crucifixes, important councillors and citizens, came in solemn procession to meet him. Her standard waving above her, Joan rode behind Charles, high on her white horse, dressed in her silver armour, over which she wore again the splendid green surcoat, the present from the duke of Orleans. The crowds were intoxicated at the sight of their heroine, acclamations rose to high heaven from all sides. Pressing around and behind the king and Joan came the nobles, the *seigneurs*, captains, squires and pages, magnificent in their fine surcoats and robes of every colour, riding in full armour, lances held high, while the heraldic banners and pennants floated above them. Their troops followed in a long, joyful procession, accompanied by the blare of trumpets and the cheers and cries of the excited multitude. Nowhere was there any sign of resistance or ill-will towards Charles and his army. That same evening, the king's army was joined by two more contingents, that of Charles's brother-in-law, René d'Anjou (whom Joan had asked for as an escort on her visit to the Duke of Lorraine, his father-in-law) and that of Robert de Saarbruck, lord of Commercy, the mercenary captain who had once extorted protection money from the villagers of Domrémy.

On Sunday, 17 July, Charles VII was crowned in Rheims cathedral. All was to be conducted in solemn ceremony according to the ancient ritual.

Feverish preparations had to be made by the cathedral clergy and others. The coronation regalia were not kept in Rheims, but in the great abbey of Saint Denis outside Paris, so substitutes had to be found at no notice at all, even a crown and sceptre had to be produced from somewhere. According to one source, Charles arrived at the church to keep his vigil in the middle of the night, at 3am, to be exact. [18] The vigil was that of a king before his coronation, but also of a knight before his dubbing, for by tradition the king was knighted at the end of the ceremony. Other sources suggest that he kept the vigil earlier, went back to the bishop's palace, was awakened in the morning with all traditional ceremony and then returned to the cathedral in procession with the clergy. As the coronation ceremony began, he was kneeling before the great altar, dressed humbly only in his shirt and hose.

Before the service began, four knights, armed and mounted, their banners in their hands, had ridden over to the nearby abbey of Saint Rémy to fetch the sacred *ampulla*, the jewel-encrusted gold vessel in the shape of a dove, which contained the holy oil for the anointing. Legend had it that the precious oil had been brought down from Heaven by an angel for the baptism of Clovis on Christmas Day, in the year 496 AD. Clovis was a pagan convert and became the first Christian king to rule over Gaul and unite the Frankish tribes. Some of the Burgundian garrison had attempted to take this precious oil with them, for without it the king's coronation would lack validity, but this had been prevented by the citizens and the garrison had had to leave empty-handed.

One of the four knights commissioned to fetch the oil was Gilles de Rais, known to history as Bluebeard (as already mentioned earlier) after his execution in 1440 for occultism and child murders dating back to 1432, the year in which he left the army. In 1429, such activities had either not started or no-one was aware of them, for he was admired as an outstanding soldier. The title of Marshal of France had been conferred on him by the king on 21 June 1429, after the relief of Orleans and the extraordinary Loire campaign.

At the abbey of Saint Rémy, the knights were met by the lord Abbot, also on horseback, clad in splendid pontifical vestments, a canopy of cloth of gold held above him and in his hands the sacred vessel with the holy oil. They escorted him back as far as the abbey dedicated to Saint Denis, halfway between his own abbey and the cathedral, where he solemnly handed over the precious vial to the Archbishop of Rheims, Regnault de Chartres, who was waiting for him there, draped also in rich vestments and surrounded by the cathedral canons. They in turn formed a procession and were escorted back to the cathedral by the knights. The assembled clergy, led by the archbishop, then entered through the great west portal, the statue of the Virgin and Child looking down on them in welcome as they approached the entrance, the stone angel of the Annunciation, high in the niche in the porch, smiling benevolently on their right as they filed slowly in. They made their way down the crowded nave to the choir, before which the great nobles were standing, sumptuously arrayed, foremost among them the Counts of Clermont and Vendôme, princes of the Blood Royal, the young Duke of Alençon, and of course the inevitable La Trémoille. Joan, armed and wearing the magnificent surcoat given her by the duke of Orleans, her standard held before her, stood beside the king throughout the ceremony. The *ampulla* was placed on the altar by the archbishop, to lie alongside the insignia of kingship and knighthood: the crown, the sceptre, the ring, the golden spurs, and the symbolic 'Hand of Justice'. Following the clergy, the four knights entered the church, still on horseback, the hooves clattering on the stone flooring as they went.

The cathedral was full. On the parvis outside the great crowd was agog with wonder and pious fervour. Joan's father, Jacques d'Arc, was there in the congregation, as was her 'uncle', Durand Laxart, who had taken her to see Robert de Baudricourt. Her father had now certainly forgiven him for his role in Joan's departure. There is a tradition that her mother was there also, but that is not certain. Her brother Pierre was present among the military, most probably also her brother Jean. Pride and awe, even a sense of incredulity or unreality, must have filled each member of Joan's family as they witnessed the solemn drama being played out in cathedral.

The service had started with the singing of the *Veni, Creator Spiritus,* followed by the chanting of the psalms and scriptural readings pertaining to the morning office of *tierce*. A large number of clergy and altar servers stood around the altar. The choir stalls were filled. Five prelates concelebrated with the archbishop, each of them with his crook and mitre and wearing his rich vestments. Among them was the Scottish John Carmichael, bishop of Orleans. By tradition the king was attended by six lay and six ecclesiastical peers, but on this occasion several of both categories were absent and their places had to be filled by others. Most notably, Alençon had to stand in for Burgundy. Among all the noble company present, however, it was Joan that all necks were craned to see, right up there beside the king, her standard proudly unfurled. In a letter written that very day by 'three gentlemen from Anjou' to the queen and her mother, Yolande of Sicily, we read this: 'During the service, the Maid stood beside the king, holding her standard in her hand. It was a fine sight to see the courteous manners of both the king and the Maid.'[19]

As the Constable, Artur de Richemont, had been refused permission to attend, Charles d'Albret took his place and held the sword of state (or one doing duty for it) before the king throughout the service. Quite a feat, since we are told, in the letter quoted above, that the whole proceedings lasted five hours, from nine in the morning until two in the afternoon.

The first part of the service was the blessing of the insignia and the taking of the solemn oaths by the king, who swore to defend the Church and to maintain peace and justice. After that, it fell to the Duke of Alençon to perform the ceremony of dubbing the king a knight. Charles then prostrated himself on the steps of the altar before receiving the anointing with the holy oil, after which he rose, put on the tunic, the silk cape and the gloves which were presented to him and slipped onto his finger the gold ring that symbolised his union with his people. Thus accoutred, he was led to the throne by the six lay and six ecclesiastical peers who held the crown above his head. Once seated, he was crowned and the bishops and peers did homage to him, to the enthusiastic acclamations and cries *of Noël!* from the congregation inside and outside the church. The letter quoted above goes on to tell us:

> When the king was consecrated and also when the crown was placed on his head, everyone cried Noël! And the trumpets sounded so loudly that you would have thought the vaulting of the church would split open.

The chronicler of the *Journal du Siège* describes what happened next:

> When the Maid saw that the king was consecrated and crowned, she knelt, in the presence of all the nobles, and said, in tears, 'Noble King, now is fulfilled the will of God, Who wished that the siege of Orleans should be raised and that you should be brought into this city to receive your holy coronation, showing that you are the true king, the one to whom this kingdom of France should belong.' All those watching her were greatly moved.[20]

The *Chronique de la Pucelle* gives the same account and says that some among the congregation were reduced to tears.

After the ritual of the coronation, Charles, as his first act of kingship, raised the lands of the Laval brothers to the dignity of a county, thus making Guy a count. The Duke of Alençon and the Count of Clermont then dubbed several more knights, after which a High Mass was celebrated with all solemnity, the King received the Eucharist and the ceremonies were completed. The four knights remounted their horses and delivered the holy oil back to the abbey of Saint Rémy. The king and the chosen twelve peers, followed by Joan and the nobles, walked in procession to the Archbishop's palace, where a great feast was laid out for them. No doubt they were ready for it.

12

After Rheims

Tu, Johanne, de bonne heure née,
Benoist soit cil qui te créa!
Christine de Pisan, *Ditié de Jehanne d'Arc*

The king remained at Rheims for several days after the coronation, leaving on Thursday, 21 July, for the Abbey of Saint Marcoul de Corbény, some twenty-odd miles from Rheims, where he 'touched' for the 'King's Evil' a number of persons suffering from scrofula. This ceremony was a royal tradition which had its origins in the eleventh century, with Edward the Confessor in England and Philip I in France. It continued in England until the eighteenth and in France until the nineteenth century. When the king went on that Thursday, Joan rode ahead of him with her standard, in full armour. When she took off her armour, says the chronicler, she wore the clothes of a knight, shoes laced on the foot, well-fitting doublet and hose, a little hat on her head and rich garments of cloth of gold and silk, with fur trimmings.[1]

When the celebrated woman writer, poet, philosopher and historian, Christine de Pisan, heard the astounding news of the relief of Orleans and the coronation of Charles VII, she was transported with joy in her quiet retreat in the Dominican convent at Poissy, to which she had retired after the terrible events of 1418 in Paris. We have met her already as the historiographer of Charles VI. When left a widow with three children at the age of twenty-six in 1390, and finding herself in financial difficulties, she had not sought security in an advantageous second marriage, but battled her way through numerous lawsuits and set about earning a living by her pen. Soon she was known throughout Europe. Modern scholars regard her as the first professional woman writer and an early champion of women's dignity and the right to education. In 1400, she had taken up arms against the scornful misogyny of Jean de Meun and his continuation of the *Roman de la Rose* and in the ensuing polemic she was supported by her friend, Jean Gerson. After 1418, she did not take up her pen for eleven years, apart from some contemplative spiritual writing. Now she saw in Joan not only the heaven-sent saviour of France but the living ideal of feminine perfection and heroism. *What an honour to womankind!* she exclaims in her long poem, the *Ditié de Jehanne d'Arc*, which begins with an explosion of joy. (My apologies for my translation of the following short excerpts, which in no way does justice to the original):

I, Christine, who eleven long years
In my convent home shed bitter tears,
[...]
Now at last I laugh for joy.
In the year fourteen hundred and twenty-nine
The sun once more rose up to shine,
Bringing back that age serene
Which for so long no eye had seen

After rejoicing at the return of the king, she turns to Joan:

And now you, most blessed Maid,
God has such honour on you laid
That never shall your memory fade.
You did the cruel bonds untie
In which poor France did helpless lie.
Who could too much laud your name,
Since to this land in need you came
And brought it peace and cleansed its shame!

This tribute to Joan was the last poem that Christine ever wrote, for she died a few months later.

Jacques d'Arc seems to have enjoyed his stay in Rheims, We find an entry for 22 September 1429, in the registers of the king's finance officer, Hémon Raguier, showing that the newly crowned king, after his coronation, had made Joan a gift of sixty *livres tournois* to be given to her father. Also the city council's minutes for 9 September 1429 record that 'It was decided to pay the expenses of the Maid's father and to present him with a horse for his departure.' Had he not yet left the city? The expenses were to cover the period of the coronation. Had he some ailment which delayed his departure? We do not know his state of health, but there is a tradition that he died after the death of Joan, some two years later. At Rheims he resided in a hostelry called *L'Âne Rayé* ('The Striped Donkey'), opposite the cathedral. The proprietress was a lady by the name of Alice Moreau, a widow. No doubt Jacques, the respected representative of Domrémy, basked in the reflected glory of his daughter, now at its absolute peak throughout Europe. In France, people regarded her as a saint, a heroine, a miracle-worker, legends sprang up around her, try as she might to dismiss or avoid such enthusiasm, to calm it with good humour or common sense.

Why did Charles VII tarry at Rheims instead of immediately exploiting the aura of his success and pressing on to Paris as had been intended?

His coronation had consecrated him once and for all as the legitimate king of France. His adversaries were panicked. Bedford himself had written to the royal Council in London on 16 July, to impress upon them the urgency of the situation, telling them that he knew it was Charles's intention to march on Paris immediately after the imminent coronation. He demanded that child King Henry VI be crowned in Notre-Dame as soon as possible and bitterly reproached the delays. Charles however, at the insistence of La Trémoille and those around him, was hoping for some accommodation with Philip of Burgundy, whose ambassadors arrived in the city for negotiations on 17 July, the very day of the coronation. An emissary of La Trémoille. had already arrived at Arras on 30 June to begin discussions.

Joan had written to Burgundy on 27 June, asking him to be present at the coronation and to be reconciled with the king, but her letter was ignored. Philip was not one to lower himself by doing the bidding of a peasant, much less a peasant girl. Now she wrote again, on the day of the coronation. No doubt she gave the letter to the ambassadors to be delivered to the Duke. We know that she had an opportunity to speak with them at some point, as we see from her reply to one of the articles of accusation brought against her at Rouen (*Article XVIII*), where she was accused of urging Charles VII to refuse all proposals for peace and inciting him to massacre and bloodshed. She replied:

> As far as peace is concerned, and with regard to the Duke of Burgundy, I asked him, in letters and in speaking to his ambassadors, to make peace. As for the English, the peace that is needed is that they should go home to their own country, England.

This was a plain statement of her consistent view throughout her career. The first step in stopping the bloodshed and getting the English to leave France was clearly to get Burgundy to return to the obedience of Charles VII, for the defeat and departure of the English would follow the loss of their ally. This indeed proved to be the course of events after the signing of the Treaty of Arras in 1435, which restored peace between Charles VII and his mighty vassal. However, as long as Burgundy refused reconciliation, the war would have to go on. Charles was a man who, to his credit, preferred jaw-jaw to war-war, but at this stage in his life he was unable to recognise when jaw-jaw was merely a means of manipulation, serving the ends of Burgundy or the self-interest of the favourites with whom he had surrounded himself.

Joan's letter of 17 July was an ardent plea for peace. It opens with:

> Most High and Mighty Prince, Duke of Burgundy,
> I, Joan the Maid, request you, from the King of Heaven, my sovereign Lord, that you and the King of France make a good and lasting peace.

Forgive each other from your hearts, as good Christians, and, if you must make war, go and fight the Saracens.

We note that she asks them each to forgive the other, not heaping blame on either party. As for fighting the Saracens, we may remember, among other things, Nicopolis and John the Fearless, Philip of Burgundy's father, the Turkish threat to Europe and the praise, in Shakespeare's *Richard II*, for the Duke of Norfolk's valour against 'Black pagans, Turks and Saracens ...'

Joan's letter ends:

I pray and beseech you, my hands joined in prayer, to desist from battle and from waging war against us, you and your people or subjects. Know that, however many men you bring against us, nothing will be gained and it will be a great pity for the blood that will be shed by those who come against us in battle.

I wrote to you three weeks ago and sent letters by a herald, inviting you to come to the coronation of the King, who has been crowned this very day, July 17, in the city of Rheims. I have had no reply, no news of the said herald.

I commend you to God, that He may be pleased to protect you and I pray that He will bring about a lasting peace.

Written at Rheims, 17 July.[2]

Philip was hedging his bets. So far, Bedford had seemed the better choice, but now that Charles was crowned and the English dislodged from their positions on the Loire, things looked decidedly more unstable. Bedford, up in Paris and none too sure of the overall solidity of Philip's loyalty towards his government, was doing all he could to restore confidence and particularly to stir up the general enthusiasm of the population for his ally. Recent rumours that the 'Armagnacs' were about to enter and take the city, together no doubt with the news of Orleans, Patay and the ready capitulation of towns on the Loire, had greatly unsettled the people. By Bedford's order, the fortifications on the walls were strengthened with more cannon and artillery, the provost of the merchants and the échevins (city magistrates) were replaced by men whose loyalty was felt to be more assured, individuals whose rise had followed the events of 1418 and who owed their successful careers and wealth entirely to Burgundy.

Philip himself was invited to pay a visit to Paris. He arrived on Sunday, 10 July and stayed for five days, during which time he received the sum of twenty thousand pounds from Bedford and promised to send military reinforcements to Paris. He was unable to fulfil this promise properly, since on this occasion most of his troops in Flanders and Picardy refused to serve outside their own country, a refusal they were entitled to make under feudal law.[3] Philip's visit was marked by meetings with Bedford and the council and public celebrations culminating in a great religious procession through the streets of the city to the cathedral of Notre Dame, where the citizens were treated to a *moult bel sermon* (a very fine sermon), says the *Bourgeois de Paris*. After that, at the palace, in the presence of the council and Parlement gathered there, a *charte* or letter was publicly and solemnly read out, recounting in great detail the assassination of John the Fearless on the bridge at Montereau, where he had presented himself in obedience to the Dauphin and where 'the said Duke of Burgundy, on bended knee before the Dauphin, was treacherously murdered, as everyone knows'.[4]

At the conclusion of the proclamation, there was a great commotion in the vast crowd of onlookers, with cries of hatred for the Armagnacs (no doubt prompted by agents of the government) and general uproar. Bedford and Philip of Burgundy together had to impose silence on the multitude and Philip then launched into a loud lament for the death of his father, after which all the people were ordered to raise their hands and swear loyalty to the Regent and the Duke and to observe the Treaty of Troyes. The two dukes then solemnly vowed to defend the city and hold it for Henry VI.

This then was the Philip who at the same time was sending ambassadors to the coronation of Charles VII and holding out hopes of peace. While perhaps toying with the idea of coming to some advantageous arrangement with Charles VII, Philip did not wish to alienate Bedford. The real object of the parleying seems to have been to buy time for the regent to get reinforcements to Paris and strengthen its defences. It was clear to all that the city was the next goal on the list of Joan of Arc and the French army. Losing no time, Bedford had been taking further measures. All those in positions of authority had had to renew their oaths of loyalty, which would be demanded also of the clergy in a session of the Parlement on 26 August. It was administered in the churches and monasteries in the days following. As the Parisians could be counted on to be well-disposed to Burgundy rather than to any English overlord, Philip of Burgundy was appointed governor of Paris, although he did not have to be there in person.

Meanwhile an army had been raised in England by Bedford's uncle, Henry Beaufort, Cardinal of Winchester, financed by a loan from the pope, Martin V, ostensibly to fight the Hussites of Bohemia.[5] However, when Winchester arrived in Paris on 25 July with his army of some three and a half thousand archers and men, the objective of the expedition was suddenly no longer the battle with the Hussites, but the fight against the forces of Charles VII. One captain's company had brought with them a great white flag, on which was painted a distaff and its load of linen thread and underneath it, in French, the motto: *Or vienne la belle!* (which can be loosely translated as *Come on, my lovely!*).[6] A French saying makes the significance of the distaff clear: *Donner du fil à retordre à quelqu'un*:

literally: to give somebody a lot of thread to rewind, i.e., to give somebody a lot of problems. The message was clear: 'We're not scared of Joan the Maid! She'll get a lesson she won't forget!' Real men were not afraid of a girl.

However, a letter of Bedford, nominally addressed to the young Henry VI, and written in 1434, clearly expresses the regent's enduring anger at the turn of events after Orleans. The letter, rendered into modern English, is as follows:

> Everything prospered for you until the time of the siege of Orleans, undertaken by God knows what advice. At that time, after the misadventure which befell my cousin Salisbury (God have mercy on his soul), your men, assembled there in great numbers, suffered a great blow, they were struck by the hand of God, so it seems. The blow was due, as I believe, to lack of sound belief and to the unholy fear that they had of a disciple and limb of Satan, called the Maid, who employed spells and sorcery. This blow and the defeat not only greatly reduced the number of your men there, but also terribly lowered the courage of those who were left and heartened you adversaries and enemies to join forces in great numbers.[7]

Leaving Rheims on 21 July, Charles and his army headed north, on their way to Paris, as Joan and the military leaders had insisted. The first stop, as we have seen, was at Corbény, where Charles held the ceremony of 'touching' for the King's Evil. Delegations from Soissons and Laon brought the keys of their towns to be handed over to Charles in Corbény and from there he entered Soissons on 23 July, where again he was welcomed with great public rejoicing. The newly confident French seemed to be carrying all before them. Even in Normandy itself, where La Hire and Arthur de Richemont had been campaigning, the important town of Evreux, the key to the English-held region, had been forced to set a date for its capitulation; which however never happened, since there was no back-up for the besiegers. On 16 July, before the date for the capitulation was up, Bedford had gone from Paris into Normandy with an army to meet Winchester and his contingent on their arrival at Calais. Their combined forces would have been too much for Richemont and La Hire. Between 22 July and 25 July, both Compiègne, some forty-five miles north of Paris, and Château Thierry, fifty miles north-east, were negotiating terms for surrender to Charles VII, as were other towns at the time. From 29 July to 1 August, Charles was in Château-Thierry with its important fortified bridges at the confluence of the Seine and the Yonne. The Burgundian garrison and captains, says Monstrelet,

> ...both because they felt that the greater part of the population was in favour of entering into the obedience of King Charles and also because

there was no hope of any help arriving soon and they were not equipped as well as they would have wished, surrendered the town and castle and left in safety, with their goods and without any attempt to stop them.[8]

It was in Château-Thierry that Charles granted, at Joan's request, exemption from taxation to the villages of Domrémy and Greux, a privilege which was in force until the eighteenth century.

After Château-Thierry, to the dismay of Joan, Alençon and the other captains, Charles decided to turn south and abandon the march on Paris. This decision seems militarily incomprehensible. The tide of war was flowing strongly in his favour. However, negotiations were endlessly on-going with Burgundy, and Charles had evidently been persuaded to put his trust in the good faith of his devious vassal.

On 3 August, Bedford issued a proclamation calling on all his vassals in France to obey his call to arms and on August 4 he left Paris with his troops and went to Montereau, well chosen to remind Charles of the assassination of John the Fearless. Meanwhile, Charles continued to march his army south, intending to cross the Seine at a place called Bray-sur-Seine, about fifteen or so miles to the east of Montereau. There he had to turn back. Chartier recounts the episode:

> The inhabitants of the town had promised Charles obedience and a safe crossing, but during the night before he was to cross, a detachment of English soldiers arrived there first and a number of the French in the advance party were either killed or beaten up and robbed. Thus the crossing was made impossible, which very much pleased the dukes of Bar, Alençon and Bourbon and the counts of Vendôme and Laval, also Joan the Maid and a number of other lords and captains, since the decision to cross had been very much against their will.[9]

So the army turned towards Paris again, However, with Bedford and his army on the march, the towns which had gone over to Charles VII were very understandably nervous. On 5 August, the day following the fiasco at Bray, in response to messages of alarm, Joan wrote to Rheims assuring the inhabitants that they need not fear any Burgundian counter-attack, because she would never abandon them, telling them moreover, 'It is true that the King has made a two-week truce with the Duke of Burgundy who is to hand the city of Paris over to him at the end of fifteen days.. However, she adds, 'I am not happy with all these truces and I don't know if I will keep them. If I do, it will be solely for the sake of the King's honour.'[10] Her tone is high-handed, and for that she has been criticised, not least at her trial, but we must remember that she firmly believed that she answered to a higher authority than the king. Clearly she was sceptical about the supposed promise to hand over Paris and we do not know whether the duke's promise was a fact or whether she had been told such a tale to keep her quiet. She had expressed fears of treason (without stipulating from which quarter) already on her way to Rheims, as we remember, when she met Gérardin d'Épinal and the villagers from Domrémy in Châlons.

On 7 August, no doubt alarmed by news that Charles was again marching on Paris, Bedford sent a very insulting letter from Montereau to the newly-crowned king, accusing him of 'seducing and deceiving the ignorant populace with the aid of a woman of ill-fame in male clothing and an apostate and seditious mendicant friar (Brother Richard)', and denouncing him moreover as the cause, since the death of John the Fearless, of all the appalling ills of France and its unfortunate people. He issued a challenge to 'settle the matter by force of arms', in person or otherwise, if Charles would not recognise his abominable faults voluntarily and come immediately to a peace conference. Charles, of course, ignored this polite invitation and continued, now even more reluctantly, no doubt, on his way with the army towards Paris.

Dunois tells us that when the king finally arrived at La Ferté and Crépy-en-Valois, on 10 and 11 August 1429, the people came out full of joy and acclamations. But Joan evidently had melancholy forebodings. Hopes of a quick capitulation of Paris were fading, Rheims and other towns, now fearing the return of vengeful Burgundians, were unnerved. Here is Dunois' account of the scene, given at the Nullity trial of 1456:

> The Maid, who was riding between the Archbishop of Rheims and myself, exclaimed, 'What good people! I've never seen any other people rejoicing so much at the coming of such a noble king. May I be so blessed, at the end of my days, as to be buried in this ground!' Hearing that, the archbishop said to her, 'Oh, Joan! Where do you hope to die?' She replied, 'Wherever God pleases, for I don't know, any more than you do, the time or the place. May it please God, my Creator, to allow me to retire, abandoning arms, and let me go and help my father and mother, keeping their sheep, with my sister and brothers, who would be very glad to see me.'

The last phrases, those about keeping sheep and returning to her sister and brothers, are probably Dunois's faulty, sentimentalised recall, or invention. She was not a little shepherdess, two of her brothers were in the army with her and her sister was dead. Moreover, there is a document showing that at some point Joan had signed a long lease on a house belonging to the cathedral chapter in Orleans, which would indicate that she intended to retire at some future date to the town where she would be so welcome, rather than settling down in Domrémy.[11] But the note of discouragement rings true enough in the context, as also the longing for home.

The next stop, on Friday, 12 August, was the town of Lagny, and on Saturday, 13 August, the French spent the whole day camped at

Dammartin-en-Goële, a village close to what is now the airport of Roissy. Cagny comments:

> During the time that the King spent in going from Rheims to Dammartin, Joan made great efforts to bring a number of places into his obedience and thanks to her, several towns went over to the French side.[12]

At Dammartin the French army waited for the English to come and do battle, but nobody came. The next day, Sunday, 14 August, the king, Joan, Alençon and the soldiers camped six or seven miles outside Senlis, at Montépilloy. Bedford was camped a mile or so outside the town, between the French army and the town itself, with the little river Nonette at their back. The two armies were estimated to be of roughly the same strength, about eight or nine thousand men.

Cagny gives a very full account of the events at Montépilloy. On the evening of that Sunday, there were a few skirmishes, with casualties and a number of fatalities on each side. Early the next morning, 15 August, a solemn feast day of the Church, the French 'put their consciences in order as best they could', heard an early Mass and advanced in battle order. The English sat tight, but had thrown up their usual defences, a ring of sharp stakes to impale the horses, a barricade of carts and wagons, the whole completed by the river which protected the rear. The French could not entice them out to do battle. Cagny describes Joan's frustration: 'When the Maid saw that they wouldn't venture forth, she took her standard in her hand and rode up to their defences and struck them.'[13]

Still there was no reaction. Joan gave the order to pull back the troops, and she, Alençon and the captains sent a message over to the English camp to tell them that if they would come out to fight, the French would wait for them to get into battle order (shades of the famous courtesy to come in 1745 at the battle of Fontenoy: 'Messieurs les Anglais, tirez les premiers!'[14]). Still nobody moved. Still nothing happened, except for a few skirmishes later in the day. The French went back to their camp for the night and the king returned to Crépy. The next morning, 16 August, the English withdrew from Senlis and headed back to Paris. Their adversaries having left the field, Joan, Alençon and the army set out for Crépy.

On Thursday 18, Charles VII entered Compiègne and would remain there until 28 August. He wished to appoint his favourite, La Trémoille, to the important position of Captain of the town, but the citizens wanted an experienced soldier, one who would stay with them and take over command. They had already chosen Guillaume de Flavy. A compromise was reached, La Trémoïlle had the honour of the title and, more lucratively, also the revenues to be raised from the town, but Flavy was the real governor of the place, with the title of *Lieutenant*. We will hear more of Guillaume de Flavy later in Joan's story. It was from Compiègne also that Charles sent the Count of Vendôme with troops to Senlis, where he was welcomed in the town and accepted as its governor. At the same time news came that Beauvais had opened its gates to Charles's heralds with great rejoicing. The citizens had proclaimed that any who did not wish to accept the king were free to go, along with their belongings. One of the few who left was the bishop of the place, Pierre Cauchon, Joan's future judge, who had already been obliged to remove himself from Rheims.

Meanwhile negotiations with Burgundy dragged on. The duke was playing for time, time to build up the defences of Paris and to allow Bedford to recruit and bring more troops from England. Around 15 August, the duke had received at Arras a delegation led by the Archbishop of Rheims, Regnault de Chartres, who came with offers of excessively generous terms, 'beyond what was fitting for the king's Majesty', says Monstrelet. In return for nothing more than a promise of neutrality, Burgundy was offered every kind of guarantee of his own position. Monstrelet admits that 'most of the people were very anxious to see peace and concord between the king and the Duke of Burgundy' and that many of the 'lower orders' (*de moyen et de bas estat*) even went so far as to hand in to the Chancellor's office at Arras, as if peace were already concluded, a great number of *lettres de rémission* and other favours from Charles VII. In fact, says Monstrelet, most of the favours promised were honoured by the Burgundian chancellor. However, the ambassadors had to be content with a vague answer from Philip: he would take advice and reply in a few days. The few days, needless to say, passed without communication.

Monstrelet, who as a Burgundian loyalist cannot be suspected of exaggerating Charles VII's popularity, speaks of the king's reluctance to move on from Compiègne and gives a long list of places, including towns of importance such as Creil and Beauvais, which had willingly opened their gates to him. The English authorities were more than ever concerned about sedition. They couldn't know who would remain loyal to them. Listing towns and fortresses which had been taken or gone over to the French, Monstrelet describes the taking of the stronghold of Torcy and says it was due to

...some of the local men, who had withdrawn into it with the English, whom they then betrayed and delivered into the hands of their enemies. Thus, in a brief space of time, the four fortresses in the hands of the English became French.[15]

Why was Charles then dragging his feet? Monstrelet thinks he knows:

If with all his army he had come to places such as Saint-Quentin, Corbie, Amiens, Abbeville and others, the majority of the inhabitants were ready to receive him as their sovereign and desired nothing so much as to enter into his obedience and open wide their gates to him.

However, he was advised not to advance so far into the territory of the Duke of Burgundy, both because it was well provided with men-at-arms and because he was hoping and waiting for a treaty.[16]

There's the rub: he was advised (need we say by whom?) not to advance, so as to avoid angering Burgundy and he was hoping for a successful outcome to the negotiations in progress. Many were of the opinion that, if Charles had struck after Rheims, he would have quickly recovered his kingdom. That is, for example, the opinion of the author of the *Chronicle of Tournai*, who thinks the English were so demoralised that they would have put up little resistance. The damage inflicted on the morale of the English soldiers by their defeat after the appearance of this slip of a girl at Orleans had been immense. Joan had immediately become in their eyes a 'limb of Satan', as Bedford called her. She could only have achieved such results by sorcery. Thomas Basin would write:

> Such terror assailed their souls at the very name of the Maid that several of them solemnly swore that simply on hearing her or catching sight of her standard, they lost their fighting spirit and strength and they could by no means bend their bows or hurl missiles or strike as they had been used to doing.[17]

Yet immediately after the coronation, Joan's desire to continue her triumphant campaign was opposed by those around the king: La Trémoille, Regnault de Chartres and others. She wanted to go straight on to Paris, was confident that she could take it very quickly and, says Quicherat, 'Everything leads us to believe that she could have done so.'[18] Burgundy would have been reconciled to Charles VII well before 1435 and the Treaty signed then at Arras, and the wars in France would have ended more quickly. As it was, the negotiations entered into by Regnault de Chartres in mid-August at Arras were continued at Compiègne after 21 August. The Burgundian embassy was led by John II of Luxembourg, Count of Ligny, who was later to play such a baneful role in Joan's destiny.

The fifteen-day truce of which Joan had written in her letter to Rheims was at an end, andt Paris had not been handed over. Even if Burgundy had meant his promise honestly, Bedford would never have allowed such a thing. He had already sent an emissary, Hugues de Lannoy, a Burgundian on the Royal Council of England, to Arras to ascertain what was going on and to remonstrate with Burgundy. Joan's patience was at an end. While she was as anxious as anyone for peace with Burgundy, she was also clear in her own mind that the endless truces were futile, merely Burgundy's ploy of playing for time. Peace with Burgundy would only be won 'at the end of a lance', as she once remarked.[19] As Régine Pernoud points out, Joan was as anxious for peace with Burgundy as any, but realised that now he would have to be made to face a *fait accompli*, a situation in which he had nothing to gain from delaying tactics. The Duke of Alençon's chronicler, Perceval de Cagny, puts the matter plainly:

> When the king was at Compiègne, the Maid was very upset by his desire to stay on there. He seemed to be content with the favour God had shown him, without wanting to undertake anything further. She called the Duke of Alençon and said, '*Beau duc*, get your men and captains ready. *Par mon martin*, I want to go and take a closer look at Paris than I have done up till now.'[20]

Joan's prestige and charisma were such that Charles could not dismiss her from the army, instead he let her go ahead to Paris without any military back-up. Joan, Alençon and their men left Compiègne on 23 August. On Friday, 26 August, they arrived at Saint Denis, where thry were received without demur. However, without the King and the rest of the army, the assault on Paris was of course not possible. Joan and Alençon were putting what pressure they could on Charles.

On 28 August a truce was finally signed at Compiègne with Burgundy, while Joan and the captains and the vanguard of the army were already at Saint Denis, The *Chronique des Cordeliers de Paris* gives us a transcript of the whole document. The reason given for arriving at nothing more than another truce? 'It seemed to the said ambassadors that it was necessary to postpone matters for a suitable period so that during that time they could consider with more ease and pertinence the question of the said peace.'

There follow the terms of the temporary truce, which was to last until 25 December 1429. The English, it was stipulated, were free to subscribe to it if they so wished. All the territory north of the Seine, from Nogent-sur-Seine to Harfleur (i.e. all English and Burgundian territory), with the exception of towns affording passage across the river, was to be covered by the truce, but most importantly, Philip of Burgundy retained the right to 'come to the defence of Paris and resist those who wish to make war and cause damage to that city'.

> During the period of the present truce, none of the parties subscribing to it, within the terms and limits designated above, may take, acquire or conquer any of the towns, places or fortresses covered by it, nor may any party admit to their obedience such towns, places or fortresses, should any such wish to place themselves under the obedience of one of the parties.[21]

So an end was put to Joan's triumphal progress and she, already at Saint Denis, was effectively disowned. Hugues de Lannoy, Bedford's Anglo-Burgundian emissary at Arras, now sent urgent messages to the regent urging him to send a strong English army to France before the expiration of this truce and to stay on good terms with Burgundy, his vital ally. At the end of August, Bedford left Paris for Rouen, his headquarters in France. The herald known as *Le Hérault Berry* says explicitly that Bedford was afraid of a popular uprising in Normandy, following the submission of other towns to Charles VII. At the time, the duchy was increasingly troubled by the resurgence of pro-French elements. He left Paris in the charge of his Chancellor for France, Louis of Luxembourg, Bishop of Thérouanne (of whom we shall also hear again at Joan's trial), together with an Englishman called John Radley and the Frenchman Simon Morhier, Provost of the city. The Paris garrison of two thousand men was under the command of Villiers de L'Ile Adam. Charles VII had still not appeared.

13

Paris and After

*Die schönsten Pläne sind schon zuschanden geworden, durch die
Kleinlichkeit von denen, die sie ausführen sollten*
The finest plans have been ruined through the lack of vision of those
who should have carried them out
Bertolt Brecht, *Mutter Courage*

It was clear that Charles would not willingly give Joan and Alençon
his support. They both sent urgent messages to him, but there was no
response. He remained at Compiègne. Finally, on September 1, Alençon
went back to plead with him and on 2 September, the king set out and
went as far as Senlis. 'He came very reluctantly as far as Senlis. It appeared
that he was being given advice contrary to the wishes of Joan, Alençon
and their people.'[1]

On Monday, 5 September, Alençon had to go back to him at Senlis and
try again. Finally Charles arrived at Saint Denis on 7 September. That
night, with their army of about twelve thousand men, Joan and Alençon
camped at the village of La Chapelle, halfway between Saint Denis and
Paris, and launched their assault on the city the following morning,
8 September. This was an important date in the Church calendar,
celebrated as the nativity of the Virgin Mary, therefore usually a period
of truce, something which would be brought up against Joan at her trial.

Skirmishes had taken place intermittently between the French and the
Anglo-Burgundian defenders of Paris in the days since the arrival of Joan
and Alençon with other captains and their companies. Alençon had had
copies of proclamations thrown into the city, addressed to 'The Provost of
Paris, the Provost of the Merchants and the City Magistrates', calling on
them to welcome the King, but these of course were scornfully dismissed
as an attempt to seduce the population. A fierce campaign of counter-
propaganda raged, rumours being spread that the bloodthirsty Charles
VII intended to abandon the population, men, women and children,
young and old, to the barbarities of his hordes, that he would lay waste
to Paris and 'pass the plough over it'. Clément de Fauquembergue records
these scare stories in his court register in Paris, but feels in conscience

obliged to add that 'quod non erat facile credendum', it was difficult to believe this.[2] The anonymous *Bourgeois de Paris* writes in his *Journal* that Charles and his army had with them 'a creature in the appearance of a woman that they call the Maid. What the thing really was, God only knows'.[3] In addition to the flag with the taunting message, the English soldiers were now parading on the walls, defiantly waving an enormous flag of Saint George. Chartier says that they draped the flag along the stonework.

Joan had personally reconnoitred the place and decided on the best point of assault: the Porte Saint Honoré with its fortified double bridge and the *boulevard* or fortification protecting it. The bridges over the two moats (*fosses*) were connected by a *dos d'âne* (a humpback bridge). The outer *fosse* was more than fifteen yards wide, the inner moat more than thirty. The *fosse* was dry, but a considerable depth of water filled the moat. On the morning of 8 September, Joan, with Gaucourt and Gilles de Rais and their contingents took up position at the Porte Saint Honoré. Alençon and the Count of Clermont stationed themselves on a mound facing the Porte, installing on it their cannon and artillery ready to fire into the town. From that vantage point they could also keep watch for any sortie or counter-attack coming from the Porte Saint-Denis to the north. The Parisians had expected the attack to be concentrated there and in the first week of September they had provided it with long-range cannon.

Both the Porte Saint-Honoré and the medieval Porte Saint-Denis have now disappeared. The former was situated on what is now the Rue Saint-Honoré, towards the Palais Royal, the latter was situated a hundred or so yards from the present Arc de Triomphe. A plaque in the courtyard of 15, Rue de Richelieu (leading from the Palais Royal to the Richelieu site of the National Library) marks the place where Joan was wounded during the assault on Paris. In the nearby Place des Pyramides is the famous equestrian bronze statue of Joan astride her charger, her standard held proudly aloft.

Clément de Fauquembergue claims in his official town register that the attackers were hoping to achieve their aim 'by agitation among the populace rather than by force of arms', and indeed they must have had agents and sympathisers in the city, for there was a 'commotion' when the attack started:

There were people in Paris who were either corrupt or scared and who raised a hue and cry in every district of the city and at the bridges, shouting that all was lost, that the enemy had got into Paris and that everyone should rush home and make haste to take cover. At this alarm as the enemy approached, all the people who had gone to church were coming out of the churches and were terrified. Most of them rushed home and locked the doors. But there was no other real panic among the inhabitants. Those of them who were on guard in defence of the gates and walls of the city remained at their posts and others came to their aid.[4]

The assault began successfully with the taking of the defensive *boulevard*, or fortification. The men-at-arms who had come out through the Porte Saint Honoré had to retreat back inside the walls and the drawbridge was raised. The bombardment from the cannon high up on the city walls rained down incessantly. Joan advanced into the dry *fosse*, but she had not been informed about the depth of water in the moat. Cousinot de Montreuil, in his *Chronique de la Pucelle*, gives the following account:

> Nonetheless she advanced into the fosse with a large number of men-at-arms, among others Gilles de Rais, Marshal of France, and went up to the humpback to test the water, which was very deep, with her lance. While she was doing so, an arrow pierced both her thighs, or at least one. Still she refused to withdraw and made great efforts to have wood and faggots brought up and thrown into the inner moat, hoping to pass over and reach the town walls, which wasn't possible because of the depth of the water. When night fell, they sent for her to withdraw several times, but in no way would she agree to retreat. The Duke of Alençon had to come and get her and take her to his tent. They all then withdrew to La Chapelle where they had spent the previous night. The next day the dukes of Alençon and Bourbon returned to Saint Denis, where the king was waiting with his army. It was said that, for lack of courage, he had never wished to take Paris by assault, and that if they had been there until the morning, there were those who would have attempted it. There were several casualties, but no dead. [5]

Cagny, in his *Chroniques*, makes it clear that Joan was struck in one thigh, by a shot from a crossbow mounted on the walls.

> Because it was night and she was wounded, also because the troops were tired by the long assault, Gaucourt and others took her away from the moat, against her will, and so the attack failed. She was extremely upset at departing like that and said, '*Par mon martin*, we would have taken the place!'[6]

So, either Alençon or Gaucourt took her away. She must have been weakened by the wound, which had not been attended to. Cagny tells us what happened after the return to Saint Denis:

> On Friday, 9 September, although the Maid had been wounded the day before during the assault on Paris, she rose early and sent for the Duke of Alençon, through whom she issued her orders, and asked him to have the trumpets sounded and to get mounted, ready for the

return to Paris. She said, *par son martin!* that she would never leave until she had taken the town. Alençon and others among the captains were willing to do as she wished and to return to Paris, but others were against the idea. While the discussion was going on, the Baron of Montmorency, who had always taken the opposite view to that of the king, came out of the town with fifty or sixty gentlemen to join the Maid. When they saw this, those who were willing to return to the assault were very heartened and encouraged. While all this was happening the Duke of Bar and the Count of Clermont came from the king to order the Maid to return to Saint Denis and go no further. They also required Alençon ad all the other captains to return to the king, bringing the Maid with them. Joan and most of the company were extremely dismayed. Nonetheless they obeyed the king's orders, still hoping that they would find a way of taking Paris from the other side of the city, by crossing the Seine on a bridge opposite Saint Denis, which the Duke of Alençon had had thrown across the river. So they came to the king. The following day, Saturday, some of those who had been at the assault on Paris decided to go early in the morning and cross the river by the said bridge, but this proved impossible, for the king, knowing the plan of Joan and Alençon and others of like mind, had had the bridge demolished during the night. So the crossing was impossible. That day, the king held a meeting of his council, where there was a variety of opinions. He remained at Saint Denis until Tuesday, 13 September, intending all the time to retreat to the Loire, which greatly upset the Maid.

In the second session of her trial in Rouen (Thursday, 22 February 1431), Joan herself told her interrogators that she had been forced to leave Saint-Denis against her will:

> The Voice told me that I should stay in the town of Saint-Denis and I wanted to stay there, but the *seigneurs* took me away by force. But if I hadn't been wounded, I wouldn't have left. I was wounded in the ditches outside Paris, when I arrived there, coming from Saint-Denis, but I was cured in five days.

The injury had healed, or was on the way to healing by the time the king left. Before leaving, Joan sadly hung up her arms and sword before the image of the Virgin Mary in the abbey of Saint Denis. She did not intend to give up the struggle to 'chase the English out of France', but she knew now that she could not count on Charles's full support. During the afternoon session of her trial on Monday, 12 March, she would say that if she had lasted three years, she would have achieved her goal of rescuing the Duke of Orleans from English captivity. She never considered giving up before getting the English out of France and rescuing Charles of Orleans.

The king's haste to get back to his safe retreat on the Loire was anything but dignified:

> [Charles] headed as fast as he could for the Loire, sometimes travelling in complete disorder, without any reason. On Wednesday, 21 September, he arrived at Gien in time to dine. Thus was broken the will of the Maid and the army.[7]

Alençon now gave up and returned home to his young wife. The other captains also left. Joan stayed with the king and court, but was downhearted at the departure of Alençon, who was, says Cagny, 'very dear to her'. Soon, however, the duke got together a company of troops to go and campaign in Normandy. The prospects looked promising, French troops were campaigning there under different captains, several towns had already submitted to the French. Laval was taken without difficulty by French troops on 25 September, Torcy and other towns also submitted, and an attempt was even made to take Rouen. Chartier puts the failure of this attempt down to the total darkness of a moonless night, during which approaching bodies of troops lost contact with each other before they had to face the English at the gates of the city. In December 1429, La Hire would take Louviers, about twenty miles from Rouen.

Alençon requested permission for Joan to join him, but it was refused, although, as Cagny comments, he pleaded

> ...that a number of men would join his company who otherwise wouldn't stir an inch if she wasn't going to be with them. Messire Regnault de Chartres [the Archbishop of Rheims], the Sire de La Trémoille, the Sire de Gaumont, all of whom at the time held sway over the king and the conduct of the war, would never consent to the Maid and Alençon being together nor allow such a thing. [Alençon] was never able to get her back again.[8]

Cagny's tone is bitter and no doubt reflects the resentment of Alençon himself against the king. Brought up at court with Charles after his father's death at Agincourt, Alençon's relations with the monarch deteriorated for a number of reasons in later life and he became involved in seditious plots, including conspiring with the old enemy, the English. He was twice condemned to death, in 1458 by Charles VII and in 1474 by Louis XI. Both times the sentence was commuted to imprisonment. On the accession of Louis XI in 1461, he was released from his prison in Loches, but later he again became involved in plots. He died in 1478, shortly after his release from imprisonment in the Louvre. Joan, who remained touchingly loyal to Charles VII to the very instant of her death at the stake, could never have imagined such treachery on the part of her *beau duc*.

Instead of allowing Joan to campaign with Alençon, she was assigned to campaign with the king's lieutenant-general for Berry, the Sire d'Albret, half-brother to La Trémoille himself. They had the task of raising their own troops.

Bedford returned to Paris during the week following the assault on the city, when Charles VII and his army had left Saint Denis. The full force of the Regent's anger fell on the inhabitants of Saint Denis. The abbey was pillaged by the English troops in Paris, Joan's arms and sword were taken by order of the bishop of Thérouanne, Louis of Luxembourg. The *Bourgeois* writes:

> The Regent and the provosts of Paris and the merchants and aldermen were outraged [at the people of Saint Denis] because they had capitulated so quickly to the Armagnacs, without striking a blow. They were condemned to very heavy fines.[9]

Paris too was suffering, as the towns which had gone over to Charles were able to blockade food and other supplies to the capital. The city had been crowded since before that attack on Paris, for the people of the surrounding villages and countryside had poured in before the advance of Charles's troops. They brought goods and crops with them, but the latter had been harvested while still unripe. It was difficult to feed and provide for the swollen population. The *Bourgeois* complains bitterly of the huge price rises for food and other essentials. Moreover, the countryside was plagued by marauding bands of armed men. According to the *Bourgeois*, 'No man dared to venture beyond the *faubourgs* (districts just outside the city walls) for fear of being murdered or held to ransom for more than he possessed.'[10]

On Friday, 30 September, Burgundy returned to Paris in all his magnificence, bringing with him his sister Anne, Bedford's wife, and preceded by trumpeters and heralds, all splendidly attired in ceremonial dress emblazoned with the arms of each of the great lords whom they served. Bedford, together with the royal counsellors, the two provosts and the city magistrates, came out to greet the prince who would soon style himself the 'Grand Duke of the West'. During the following week, Bedford's uncle, the powerful Henry Beaufort, Bishop of Winchester, arrived and meetings of the Royal Council took place. At the request of the University, the Parlement and the leading burghers, Bedford handed over the position of Governor and Lieutenant of Paris to Burgundy, who also became Governor of nearly all the English-held places in northern France outside Normandy. However reluctantly, Bedford was certainly doing his utmost to retain the goodwill of his mighty ally.

Burgundy and Bedford left Paris on 17 October, Bedford for Rouen and Burgundy for Flanders, there to await the arrival of his future third wife, the daughter of the King of Portugal. He took with him the six hundred or so Picard soldiers he had brought to the city. The Bourgeois saw them go without regret and his few sour comments probably reflect the general opinion. He calls them

> ...as rascally a bunch of thieves as any who had entered Paris since the beginning of this wretched war, as could be well seen in all the houses where they had been billeted. The minute they were outside the gates of Paris, there wasn't a soul they met that they didn't rob and beat up. When the vanguard had left, the Duke had the town criers proclaim, by way of calming down the ordinary folk, that if they should see the Armagnacs coming to attack Paris, they should look to their own defence as best they could, then off he went, leaving the city without a garrison. That shows you how much he did, for the town. The English weren't our friends either, because we had put them out of government.

During this time, much of the country which had gone over to Charles was left by his retreat also at the mercy of free-booters. Jean Chartier describes the situation:

> At that time great pillaging and robberies took place in the areas which the king had recently taken back from the English at almost no cost to himself, as we have recorded above, because they had come from everywhere to enter into his obedience without a blow being struck. These were rich areas, well populated and cultivated, but soon afterwards the cultivated land was laid waste and several towns sacked and impoverished, to such a point that certain areas were deserted and uncultivated.[11]

Charles had disbanded his army when he returned to Gien. It seems that he had no money for them. La Trémoille, however, as is recorded in the royal accounts, continued throughout 1429 to profit exorbitantly from the king's generosity, in large gifts of money, horses, pensions and revenues from towns taken, such as Château-Thierry and Compiègne. Charles, however, soon realised that something must be done. On 23 September, he sent a letter to Troyes to say that he was sending the Count of Vendôme to their aid. Joan added a letter of her own and gave them her news. Vendôme however had his hands full in holding Senlis. Charles had to find a substitute. Chartier writes:

> The king sent the Sire de Boussac, Marshal of France, with eight hundred or a thousand troops, to help to restore order in those parts, something which was extremely necessary, for the English, who held Normandy and other places in France, were making war on the one hand and the Duke of Burgundy on the other.

As usual, the king restlessly moved around with his court from one place on the Loire to another. He went from Gien to Selles-en-Berri and then to Bourges, where the queen joined him. Joan was lodged for three weeks there in the house of Marguerite la Touroulde, wife of René de Bouligny, who held the respected position of king's counsellor. Marguerite, as noted here earlier, would testify in 1456 at the Nullity trial. Charles's peregrinations continued, Montargis, Loches, Jargeau, Méhun-sur-Yèvre. In this latter town he spent a couple of months from mid-November. His Council had already been meeting there and towards the end of September had decided that it was necessary to take the towns of La Charité-sur-Loire and Saint-Pierre-le-Moûtier.

La Charité had been held for the Burgundians since 1423 by the notorious freebooting captain Perrinet Gressart, a redoubtable soldier and adversary, as La Trémoille, among many others, knew to his cost. On one occasion Gressart had seized the well uphostered dignitary and held him to a very fat ransom. It was important to dislodge Burgundy's henchman from La Charité, for it provided a base from which the French could be harassed and French-held towns on the Loire attacked; places such as Lagny, Melun or Sens. These were the towns preventing supplies from reaching Paris and they were thereby fostering increasing discontent and subversion in the capital. Burgundy, who felt himself in no way hampered by any truce from attacking the French, had these places firmly in his sights. Bedford moreover was to arrive with a newly recruited army in the spring of 1430, when he would re-launch his campaigns.

Joan and D'Albret, while at Bourges, were informed of the decision taken at Méhun-sur-Yèvres and set about gathering men and arms. Joan's reputation for invincibility was in tatters. She ardently wished to return to Paris, but at least the campaign proposed was better that the soul-destroying inactivity. She did not feel that she now had any God-given directive to advance on the upper Loire, her mission had been to drive the English quickly out of France, which she understood to mean taking the capital, Paris, but faced with the king's determination to negotiate endlessly and fruitlessly with Burgundy, she could undertake nothing but the subsidiary campaigns which he sanctioned.

Before she left Bourges with the army, an episode took place about which she would be questioned at her trial in Rouen. While she and D'Albret were trying to raise money for their expedition, she met, no doubt by appointment and introduced by the famous Brother Richard, a self-styled visionary called Catherine de la Rochelle. As mentioned earlier, she sent the king a report on the visit, with her conclusions, so she may have been commissioned by Charles himself to go and ascertain whether Catherine was fraudulent, deluded, or sane and honest. Catherine had a wonderful idea for raising funds and no doubt also for attaining fame and fortune for herself. This is the account of the incident which Joan gave at her trial on Saturday, 3 March 1431:

> Catherine told me that a lady in white appeared to her, telling her that she should go into the loyal towns and that the king would have to give her heralds and trumpets to proclaim that anyone who had gold or silver or hidden treasure should bring it out immediately and that she herself would discover any who had such hidden treasure and didn't bring it out. She would know exactly where this treasure was and she would pay Joan's soldiers with it. I told her to go home to her husband and keep house and look after her children. Saint Margaret assured me that Catherine's story was all nonsense. I wrote to the king and told him so, but Brother Richard and Catherine were very cross with me.

Joan was then asked if she had talked to Catherine about her intention to go to La Charité-sur-Loire:

> Catherine didn't advise me to go there. She said she wouldn't go, for it was too cold. She wanted to go to the Duke of Burgundy to make peace, but I told her there would be no peace except at the end of a lance. Then I asked Catherine if the lady in white appeared to her every night. In fact, I shared her bed one night and stayed awake until midnight, when I fell asleep and saw nothing. Catherine said she hadn't been able to awaken me when the lady came, so the next day I slept during the day and shared her bed again, remaining awake the whole night, but still nobody came. I kept asking her if the lady was coming and she kept answering, 'Yes, soon'.

Charles's advisors had probably thought that Catherine could be useful, maybe coached her in her support of the policy of endless parleying with Burgundy. Be that as it may, Joan's report scuppered her attempts to make a career as Charles's new female conduit to God. As for Brother Richard, he was just the sort of apocalyptic firebrand to feel an affinity with such a seer. It is not surprising that he took her part against Joan, who had never treated him seriously ('Come on! I won't fly away!' had been the way she greeted him at Troyes). It was a pity that he was allowed to be a hanger-on, for his presence anywhere near her could only reinforce Anglo-Burgundian suspicion of her as a fraud or a witch.

As to Catherine, the recent editor of the trial documents, Pierre Tisset, tells us that she was a well-known visionary at the time.[12] She was in fact a dangerous woman. In August 1430, after Joan's capture at Compiègne, the people of Tours felt obliged to send letters to Charles VII, refuting certain calumnies which Catherine was spreading concerning them and their town. Soon afterwards, she appears among the Burgundians. Maybe she was captured, or, as Anatole France suggests, she went over to them, perhaps thinking the pickings would be easier and richer there. However, she was arrested and taken before an ecclesiastical court in Paris, where she gave a solemn warning that Joan, now a captive, would escape with the help of the Devil if she wasn't strictly guarded. She made other extravagant claims, saying that sacred mysteries were revealed to her at the moment of consecration of the Host during Mass. Two other visionaries were also tried in Paris in 1430. One was released, but the other, a Bretonne called Peronne, a follower of Brother Richard, stubbornly maintained that Joan 'was good, and that what she did was well done and was of God'. Poor Peronne was sent to the stake on 5 September 1430. Catherine's view of Joan was naturally welcome as confirmation of the Anglo-Burgundian opinion. She was released. She seems to have gone back to the other side, for according to the *Bourgeois de Paris*, in August 1431 she was with the 'Armagnacs'.[13]

Having raised what funds and troops they could, Joan and d'Albret set of for Saint-Pierre-le-Moûtier early in November. It was held by the Spanish husband of Gressart's niece and was obviously part of the latter's power base. The faithful D'Aulon, Joan's chief-of-staff who was always with her, describes the assault on the town:

> There was a strong force of men-at-arms in the town and they put up a stiff resistance, so that the French were forced to retreat. I was made lame by a wound in my foot and I couldn't stand or walk without crutches, but at that point I saw that the Maid was left with only a very small number of troops around her. Fearing that something unfortunate was about to happen, I got myself mounted and rode straight up to her and asked her what she was doing there all alone and why she hadn't retreated with the others. She removed her helmet and said that she wasn't alone, she had fifty thousand of her people with her and that she wouldn't leave until she had taken the town.

This declaration left poor D'Aulon speechless, for he was a practical man and one to take things quite literally:

> Say what she may, I could see she had only four or five men with her. I know that for certain and so do several others who were there. So I told her again that she should give up and retreat like everybody else. Then she told me to have planks and bundles of wood brought up to form a bridge over the moat and allow us to reach the town. She called out at the top of her voice: 'Wood and planks, everyone, to make a bridge!' That was quickly done. I was astounded, for the town was quickly taken by assault, without any great resistance.[14]

The heavenly host (if that is what Joan meant) did not excuse her from the normal methods of fighting a battle, nor did they give her any assurance that she would emerge safe and sound, or even alive. As she had said to Dunois and the Archbishop of Rheims, she didn't know, any more than they did, the time or the place where she would die. She had only ordinary human courage to sustain her in battle.

Regnault Thierry, dean of the church of Méhun-sur-Yèvre, in his testimony in 1456, gives us another vivid glimpse of Joan at Saint-Pierre-le-Moûtier, declaring he had seen her then preventing soldiers entering the church by force to loot it, 'But Joan forbade it, opposing them courageously, and wouldn't allow the smallest object to be taken.'

Next on the list was La Charité-sur-Loire. But the supplies and money had been depleted by the attack on Saint-Pierre. The people of Bourges were asked to raise three hundred gold crowns and did so, although the money never arrived. No-one knows what happened to it. Joan and D'Albret also wrote to two other towns, Clermont and Riom, on 7 and 9 November, asking them to send gunpowder, artillery and other supplies. They did what they could, which was not a very great deal. Faithful Orleans sent gunners, artillery and money. Conditions were not propitious for laying siege, for winter set in early that year. The siege lasted from 24 November until nearly Christmas, when Joan had to give up. Cagny blames the failure on Charles VII's lack of support: 'When she had been there for some time, as the king sent her no provisions or supplies for her troops, she had to lift the siege and departed greatly disappointed.'[15]

She was questioned closely about La Charité during her trial in Rouen (sixth session, Saturday, 3 March 1431). A leading question:

Beaupère: Why did you not enter La Charité, since God had commanded you to do so?
Joan: Who told you that God commanded me to enter the town?
Beaupère: Did the Voice not give you the command?
Joan: I wanted to go into France [the Île de France], but the military said it was better to go first to La Charité.

There is probably something missing between the second of these questions and the answer, but it is clear that Joan was maintaining that she had no divine instruction in the matter.

Joan was back in Jargeau over Christmas. At the end of the month, Charles VII decided to show his gratitude for all that she had done by ennobling her and all her family. The titles of nobility were made hereditary even through the female line of the family, something quite exceptional. No land went with the title, so the family did not become rich, although Jean eventually became captain of Vaucouleurs and the city of Orleans contributed to the support of Pierre and Joan's mother. At her trial Joan described the armorial bearings which were given to her brothers, an azure shield on which were painted two *fleurs-de-lys* (the royal lilies) with a sword supporting a crown between them. She said that there had been no request on her part and no divine revelation in the matter. Her brothers changed their name to Du Lys, but Joan, while appreciating the king's gesture, had no interest in such signs of social elevation, she wished to be known simply as Joan the Maid and she kept the standard and banner which she had had since starting out. She never asked for money, except for the war effort.

The truce with Burgundy was renewed until mid-March (some say mid-April) 1430. The Grand Duke of the West celebrated his marriage to Isabella of Portugal in Bruges on 10 January 1430, with a display of wealth and magnificence on a scale worthy of Croesus, outdoing all the splendour of his two previous marriages. Sumptuous banqueting and celebrations went on for a week, the streets were hung with rich draperies, wine flowed out of ornamental fountains, great jousts took place over several days in the tiltyards. The Duchess of Bedford, Philip's sister Anne, and a throng of other great nobles, splendidly apparelled, dazzled the citizens of Bruges when they appeared in the streets. It was during these celebrations that Philip instituted the famous Order of the Golden Fleece. The festivities, says Monstrelet, 'cost the duke a huge amount of money'.

On 19 January 1430, the town council of Tours deliberated on a request from Joan, asking that they should make a wedding gift of a hundred *écus* (crowns) to the daughter of the Scottish painter who had created her banner and standard and who was a resident of the town. On 7 February, it was decided that the money (which was a considerable sum) was needed for reconstruction in the town. However, 'for the love and honour of the Maid, the clergy, burghers and inhabitants of the town will honour the said bride at her wedding which will take place next Thursday ...'. The records show that on 19 February, the bill had been paid for '4 *jalayes* of white wine and claret given by the town on the IX day of this month to Héliote, daughter of Heuves, who was married that day', also that a generous sum had been given to Heuves Poulnoir (Hugh Power, when in Scotland?), to be spent on bread for the wedding breakfast.[16] It must have been quite a celebration, since the four *jalayes* of wine are the equivalent of sixty litres.

Also on 19 January, Joan was entertained to a municipal dinner in the town of Orleans. The gratitude of the dignitaries and townsfolk was enduring and warm. We can only imagine how the time must have hung heavy on her in this period of trailing around after the king, without any purposeful use of her time. In March she was again with the king and court at Sully-sur-Loire. From there, on 16 March, she wrote a letter to reassure the 'clergy, burghers and other inhabitants' of Rheims, who were apprehensive about a possible vengeful return of the Burgundians:

Dearly beloved friends, Joan the Maid has received your letters saying that you fear a siege. Rest assured that you will have no such thing, if

I can shortly encounter them. If I am not there to confront them and they arrive at the town, shut your gates and I will be with you very soon and they will have to get their spurs on so fast they won't have time to clip them on ...[17]

Joan's style is not elegant according to the lights of the era, but it is certainly heartening, vigorous and arguably, distinctly 'modern'.

She wrote to Rheims again on 28 March, for the clergy and citizens had written letters, first of all to inform Charles VII of rumours of a pro-Burgundian conspiracy in the town, and then a second time to reassure him that the rumours were groundless. Joan writes to tell them that the king has received their reassurances and is very pleased with his loyal subjects:

You are in his good graces, and if you have need of help, he will come to your aid regarding any siege. He well knows that you have a great deal to suffer from your treacherous Burgundian enemies. With God's help, he will deliver you very quickly from them, as quickly as possible, and he asks you, very dear friends, to guard the city well and keep good watch over it. You will soon hear good news from me, in greater detail. For now, I write no more except to say that all Brittany is now French and the duke is to send 3000 troops, paid for two months. I commend you to God's keeping,
Joan.

Joan's faith in the Duke of Brittany was ill-founded; the Breton troops never arrived.

In the interval between the two letters, a letter was sent to the Hussites, purporting to come from Joan, but written in Latin and signed by her chaplain, Pasquerel. One must ask whether the inspiration for the Latin letter came from Joan herself or was the initiative of Pasquerel. Quicherat writes, 'The letter, composed by a cleric, is filled with the spirit of a mind trained in literary exercises and consequently is unlike any other of Joan's letters.'[18] What did she know of the Hussite wars? Probably Pasquerel had told her about them and elicited from her expressions of horror at such impiety, after which he felt himself authorised to write the letter in her name.

The exploits of the Hussites of Bohemia in eastern Europe were arousing concern throughout western Christendom. We remember that the army raised in July in England with finance from the pope to fight the formidable Hussite army had been diverted by Beaufort to join the campaign against Charles VII and Joan. The Hussite wars were at their height. Bloody battles, murderous religious fanaticism, devastation of towns and villages, burning of churches and monasteries, the resounding Hussite victories in Bohemia and as far as the Baltic, all these things were a cause of horror and apprehension abroad. Maurice Keen writes of the Hussites,

> While their victories seemed to threaten all Germany with heretic dominion, and tales of their atrocities were making men shudder in France, the invasions of the Ottoman Turks were pressing into the Balkans and threatening Hungary.[19]

No doubt Pasquerel, a man of the Church above all, hoped to hasten the defeat of Hussitism by threatening its adherents with the intervention of Joan, now famous throughout Europe. The letter fulminates against the Hussites as enemies of the Church, iconoclasts, blasphemers, and has Joan declare:

> Unless I hear that you have amended your ways, I will leave the English and come after you, to destroy, by the sword if necessary, your crazed and obscene superstition ...

The letter is an attempt to exploit Joan's fame for ends totally different from her own. For no other cause on earth would she have considered deserting what she believed to be her God-given mission to expel the English from France.

Meanwhile, towards the end of March, a conspiracy was brewing in Paris. Pro-French conspiracies had multiplied everywhere since the successes of 1429 and the coronation of Charles VII in Rheims. In Paris, as we have seen from the remarks of the *Bourgeois*, the inactivity of Philip of Burgundy on behalf of the starving citizens and the behaviour of his garrison had given rise to disaffection not only towards the English but also towards the Burgundians. Now a plot was hatched, involving a number of leading citizens, to admit into the city a number of Scottish soldiers from the nearby garrison at Lagny (under Kennedy's command), who would support a popular uprising. A letter of pardon granted later in the name of Henry VI to a certain Jean de Calais describes how the plot was to be carried out:

> Eighty or a hundred Scots, disguised as Englishmen and wearing the Red Cross [of Saint George], would arrive in small groups or companies straight from Saint Denis, bringing salt fish or cattle, and would enter unremarked by the gate and then do whatever was necessary to overcome the guards. Then the rest of our enemies, hiding nearby, would come out in force to enter and take the town.[20]

The plot was discovered. Here is the account of the *Bourgeois*:

> At the time, there were a number of prominent citizens, members of the Parlement or the Châtelet, merchants and artisans, who plotted together

to introduce the Armagnacs into Paris, whatever the cost. They were to wear certain emblems when the Armagnacs would come in, and any one not wearing these emblems would be in danger of death. A Carmelite friar, by the name of Pierre d'Allée, carried messages back and forth between the parties, but God did not wish that such slaughter should take place in the good city of Paris, so the friar was arrested. Under torture he revealed many names.[21]

More than a hundred and fifty were arrested, says the *Bourgeois*, six of the leaders were beheaded, others were sewn into sacks and drowned in the Seine, some died under torture, others bought their release, some managed to escape. Paris was in fact hungry and sorely pressed at this time. The towns now held by the French were preventing supplies reaching the city. Saint Denis was re-taken on 23 March, sorties were made from Lagny right up to the gates of Paris, where 'people waited for the Duke of Burgundy from one day to the next, through January, February, March and April, but he never came'. Further afield, the now French-held towns of Melun, Sens, Soissons, Compiègne and Laon were strangling the capital. Paris had to be held; if it was lost, all would be lost, as Burgundy and Bedford well knew.

Burgundy's plan of campaign was to retake the towns that had gone over to Charles VII. With a view to the coronation of the nine-year-old Henry VI, still in Rouen, as king of France and England, it would have been desirable to retake Rheims, but it was judged that the city was too well fortified and that if Anglo-Burgundian forces were tied up there in a long siege, Paris itself could well fall to the French. Burgundy decided to campaign along the river Oise in order to take the important city of Compiègne, the place which, in 1429, had refused to let itself be handed over to him in a pre-Christmas truce (Charles had graciously presented him with Saint-Maxence instead). The capture of Compiègne would give the duke control of the Île-de-France and end the pressure on Paris. The town would not be easy to take, with its thick walls, the river blocking attack on one side, the forest affording cover for supplies on the other. In fact, it was not dissimilar to Orleans. However, Philip of Burgundy had a large, well-equipped army, provided with large and small cannon and plentiful gunpowder.[22]

The nine-year-old Henry VI had landed at Calais with a large army on Saint George's Day, 23 April 1430. However, desertions were becoming a considerable problem. On the following 3 May, an edict was issued by Duke Humphrey of Gloucester, ordering those 'captains and soldiers of whatever status, grade or condition' who had failed to appear according to their contracts, to present themselves at Dover or Sandwich immediately, 'under pain of imprisonment at Our pleasure and confiscation of horses and equipment'.[23] Joan's reputation contributed no doubt to this state of affairs.

Joan meanwhile had been filled with frustration, being obliged to waste her time in Sully, while Charles and his counsellors agreed truces which gave all the advantages to Burgundy and none to the French. At the very end of March or early April, she decided to act. Cagny:

> The Maid, who had seen and heard the way in which the king and his council were thinking of recovering his kingdom, was very dissatisfied with it all and she found a way of leaving. Without the king's knowledge and without taking leave of him, she said she was going out riding, but she didn't return. She went to the town of Lagny-sur-Marne, for the people of that town were fighting against the English of Paris and elsewhere.[24]

She left Sully with a small band of troops. The faithful D'Aulon and her brother Pierre rode with her. She had obviously made preparations for this exit and prepared her men. She was no longer riding with the commanders of the king's army, Dunois, Alençon and the others. She was now simply the captain of a band acting in concert with the garrisons of places such as Lagny. However, Cagny may be mistaken in thinking that she left without as much as taking her leave of the king, for she could after all be useful, the campaign which she now undertook was vital to prevent Burgundy from re-taking the towns on the Oise, of which the most important was Compiègne, and then advancing on Orleans and Rheims. At the time of her capture at Compiègne, she was in possession of a war chest of 12,000 *livres*, which the king had made available to her to pay her troops, as she told her interrogators during the trial. Moreover, the king himself was coming at last to the bitter realisation that the Duke of Burgundy had been stringing him along with the endless truces. At the end of April he had avowed as much in a letter to the Duke of Savoy, Amédée VIII, adding that it was clear also that the English had no desire to make peace. The appeasement had achieved, and would achieve, nothing but the prolongation of the wars, as he informed the people of Rheims on 6 May.

Joan set out for Lagny and it seems that she must have visited it twice, once before Melun and once again thereafter. She had scarcely arrived when she came face-to-face with the foe, a certain Franquet d'Arras, who, while being declared to be a knight and a *gentleman* by the Burgundian chroniclers, was in fact nothing other than an adventurer, the captain of a band of *routiers*, guilty of numerous crimes and murders. He was on his way back with his booty from a pillaging raid with three or four hundred men and archers (not English, but Burgundians, according to Monstrelet, probably Picards), when he encountered Joan. She had about the same number of men with her, including captains and men from the garrison at Lagny, among others Sir Hugh Kennedy and his Scots. The upshot was losses on both sides, with nearly all of Franquet's band being killed or captured and Franquet himself taken prisoner. Monstrelet declares: 'And the said Maid had Franquet beheaded, much to the grief of his own party, for he was a man of valiant conduct under arms.'[25]

Great indignation was stirred up among the English and Burgundians as this tale of a bloodthirsty war crime was circulated. Some versions even had Joan cutting off Franquet's head with her own sword. The truth, however, was different, according to Joan, when taxed with such an outrage during her trial. The interrogation, on the afternoon of 14 March:

La Fontaine: Is it a mortal sin to take a man for ransom and then have the prisoner put to death?

Joan: I didn't do any such thing.

La Fontaine: I'm speaking of Franquet d'Arras, whom you had put to death at Lagny.

Joan: I agreed that he should be executed, if he deserved it, because he had confessed that he was a murderer, robber and traitor. He had a trial which lasted a fortnight and he was judged by the bailli of Senlis and the lawyers of Lagny. I had requested that Franquet should be exchanged for a man in Paris, the owner of the inn called L'Ours [The Bear]. When I learned that this man was dead, and the baillli told me that I would be doing a grave injustice if I freed Franquet, I said to him, 'Since the man I wanted to have is dead, do whatever justice requires you to do with this man.'

The innkeeper of the Bear Inn was Jacquest Guillaume, who had been executed for his role in the recent conspiracy in Paris. His wife, Jeannette, was banished and her property confiscated.[26] The interrogator, La Fontaine, did not return to the attack, nor does the incident appear among the twelve articles of accusation sent to the University of Paris for its opinion. Clearly the prosecution realised that the charge was in no way sustainable.

It was in Lagny, in the skirmish with Franquet's band, that Joan acquired a replacement sword, which had been taken from a Burgundian, for the one found at Fierbois. Nobody knows what became of that one. She declared during her trial, as we have seen, that she had it until she left Saint-Denis after the assault on Paris. She must have hung it up in the abbey, along with her other accoutrements before she left. Had she decided that it was too precious to take into battle and put it safely away somewhere, like a sacred relic? It cannot have been the one she broke when chasing the camp-follower, that one was the replaced by one take from a Burgundian. At any rate, the sword was symbolic, no-one ever said that they had seen her kill anyone. We remember the exchange during her trial, when she said that she preferred her standard 'forty times' more than the sword, and that she carried the standard in battle in order to avoid killing anyone.

In Lagny also, an incident took place which was brought up as a charge against Joan in the sixth session of her trial, on Saturday, 3 March 1430. An infant, who had apparently died before he could be baptised, was brought to the church and a number of girls gathered there to pray for him. Joan was sent for and came to pray with them. The child revived for a few fleeting moments and was baptised. Here is the transcript of the proceedings:

Beaupère: What age was the child that you resuscitated in Lagny?
Joan: The child was three days old. He was brought before the statue of the Blessed Virgin, I was told that the girls of the town were gathered there. I wanted to go and pray for the child's life to God and the Blessed Virgin. So I went and prayed with the other girls. At last he gave a sign of life and yawned three times and then he was baptised, but he died after that and was buried in consecrated ground. People said that there had been no sign of life in him for three days and he was as black as my tunic, but his colour started to come back when he yawned. The girls and I were on our knees, offering up our prayers to Our Lady.
Beaupère: Was it not said in the town that you had brought about this resuscitation and that it was thanks to your prayers?
Joan: I never asked anybody about that.

The story illustrates the awed reverence with which Joan was regarded and the difficulty she found in dispelling miracle stories about herself. However, if there was a miracle, it was an answer to the prayers of all the girls, no need to single out Joan.

It is difficult to work out the exact chronology of Joan's movements at this time. The town of Melun, which had been English- or Burgundian-held for ten years, expelled the occupying garrison in Easter Week, 1430 (17–23 April), and Joan seems to have gone there immediately after the visit to her first port of call at Lagny. She went to celebrate with the people their return to the obedience of Charles VII. The events in Lagny may have taken place just before or just after Easter 1430. Be that as it may, it was while she was at Melun that she had, she said, a shattering revelation, which she spoke of in the session of her trial on Saturday, 10 March 1431, when asked about her capture:

Joan: During Easter Week last year, while I was on the ramparts of Melun, my Voices, the Voices of Saints Catherine and Margaret, told me that I would be captured before Saint John's Day [24 June], that it had to be so. I was not terrified, I accepted it and accepted that God would help me.
La Fontaine: After Melun, were you not told by your Voices that you would be taken prisoner?

Joan: Yes, I was told many times, almost every day. I asked my Voices that, when I was captured, I should be allowed to die, without the long torment of imprisonment. My Voices told me to accept everything, that it had to be so, but they didn't tell me when. If I had known when, I wouldn't have gone out. I asked my Voices several times to tell me when I would be captured, but they never told me.

La Fontaine: If the Voices had commanded you to leave Compiègne, telling you that you would be captured, would you have gone?

Joan: If I had known when I would be captured, I would not have wanted to go, but I would have obeyed the commandment of my Voices, whatever was to happen to me.

At the end of April and in early May, 1430, Joan rode back and forth, visiting the towns vulnerable to attack, strengthening their resolve, reassuring them by her presence. One can only admire the great courage of the eighteen-year-old girl who, despite her dread of the fate which she was convinced lay in wait for her, continued to carry out the task she felt was entrusted to her, breathing no word of her revelation or premonition to anyone.

Towards the end of April she was in Senlis, admitted into the town with her captains, although the troops, now numbering a thousand or so horsemen, were not admitted, the town not having provisions to feed them and the animals. She was in Crépy-en-Valois in early May.

On 14 May she was in Compiègne, whose captain was Guillaume de Flavy. At dawn she rode out with Xaintrailles and a company of three or four hundred men to attack the English-held Pont l'Évêque, a dozen or so miles up-river, close to Noyon, where Philip of Burgundy had established himself. Pont-l'Évêque was important because it ensured the supply of provisions to the Burgundians, important also strategically as providing a bridge over to the left bank of the river Oise. Thus it threatened in the first instance the fortress of Choisy-au-Bac, some three miles above Compiègne, with its important bridge across the river Aisne, just above its confluence with the Oise. The captain of the place was Guillaume de Flavy's brother, Louis de Flavy. After Choisy the way would lie open to the attackers to encircle Compiègne itself.

The attack launched on Pont-l'Évêque failed when the Burgundians at Noyon were alerted and came to the rescue of their English allies. In the fighting, there were about thirty casualties on each side when the French withdrew.

On Tuesday, 13 March 1431, in Joan's prison cell, Cauchon, with his few chosen interrogators, raised the episode of Pont-l'Évêque, clearly intending to trip her up on the subject of her 'Voices'. She was asked whether, on 14 May 1430, she had been instructed by revelation to attack the place. She answered:

After the revelation I had when I was at the fosses of Melun, that I would be captured, I mostly just accepted the advice of the captains on the conduct of the war, but I didn't tell them I would be captured.

There seems to be a gap in the answer, probably a simple initial denial, a *No*, omitted from the French and Latin minutes. Michel Riquet writes, 'We should never lose sight of the fact that what we have here is a legal document which cannot be as perfectly accurate as modern shorthand or a modern recording.'[27] As they were written up conjointly by the clerks of the court from their notes each evening, Tisset warns us that there is the odd omission here and there, inadvertent or otherwise.[28] However, if such an omission occurs here, it may be just due to her own or the clerks' impatience with repetition. She had previously had to answer similar questions concerning the assaults on Paris and La Charité, and had replied emphatically that there was no revelation on those occasions. The interrogators were of course anxious to prove that the 'Voices' were either of diabolical origin, or illusory, or fictitious.

On 16 May, Choisy was forced to capitulate to the Duke of Burgundy. Joan and her troops returned to Compiègne, together with Louis de Flavy, there to join the latter's brother and two other important personages, the Archbishop of Rheims, Regnault de Chartres, and the Count of Vendôme. On 18 May, in the company of the archbishop and Vendôme, Joan rode out with her troops to Soissons, where, once again, only the military leaders and dignitaries were allowed to enter. Soon after they left the place, its captain, a Picard by the name of Bournel, handed it over to Burgundy, for which betrayal he received a handsome sum. On 20 May or thereabouts, Joan arrived at Crépy-en-Valois, from where, hearing that Burgundy was now encamped outside Compiègne, she departed on 22 May with a troop of some three hundred men, leaving towards midnight. Cagny quotes one of Joan's very typical answers to those who would have urged caution on her:

> Towards midnight, she left Crépy, with her company of three or four hundred men. Although her staff told her that she had too few men to get her past the English and Burgundians, she said, '*Par mon martin*! There are enough of us. I'm going to go and see my good friends at Compiègne!'[29]

14

Capture

Finish, good lady, the bright day is done,
And we are for the dark
Shakespeare, *Antony and Cleopatra*, Act V, sc. ii

At the head of a long column of cavalry, archers and crossbowmen, followed by relief horses, pack animals and chariots laden with baggage and equipment, flanked by her chief-of-staff D'Aulon, her brother Pierre and other officers, Joan rode in the wake of a guide, under cover of night, some fifteen miles or so through the forest backing onto Compiègne to the south. She entered the town at dawn on 23 May, the eve of the feast of the Ascension. Perhaps she went first to her previous lodgings. Whether she got much rest during that day, after her long night's journey, we do not know. At some point in the morning, she would have made her way to Mass in the nearby Église Saint Jacques and later she must have had a meeting with Guillaume de Flavy to discuss the situation and strategy. After that, the troops had to be prepared for the *sortie*.

By this date, the Burgundians and the English were encamped at strategic points around Compiègne. The nearest was the Burgundian outpost at Margny, on the northern bank of the Oise, directly opposite the bridgehead with its *boulevard* guarding the town, and linked to it by a causeway across marshland. The English, under the command of a certain Montgomery, were encamped two miles or so down-river at Venette, while John of Luxembourg and his men were a couple of miles up-river at the confluence of the Aisne and the Oise at Clairoix. Further up-river was the important bridge at Pont l'Évêque, held by the English garrison. Burgundy's headquarters were at Mondidier, twenty miles north of Compiègne, but he himself was now established with troops at Coudon, on the Aronde, a tributary of the Oise, about three miles north of Compiègne.

Joan lost no time. Lefèvre de Saint-Rémy, counsellor and King of Arms of the Duke of Burgundy, describes her as she rode out:

That day the town gates were shut until about two hours after noon, when the Maid rode out, mounted on a splendid charger and fully armed, a rich vermilion surcoat of cloth of gold over her armour and her standard carried behind her. She was followed by all the soldiers in the town of Compiègne, in very fine battle order, going to attack the nearest post of the Duke of Burgundy.[1]

Riding with her were D'Aulon, her page Louis de Coutes, her brother Pierre and a company of four or five hundred men. Like her standard, the rich *huque* marked her out, to friend and foe alike, as the rallying point and leader of the assault. At her back were the archers, cannon and culverins on the walls of Compiègne and on the *boulevard*. The first objective was to clear away the Burgundian outpost of Margny.

At first things seemed to be going according to plan, but it was Joan's bad luck that John of Luxembourg was at that very time on his way with a small number of gentlemen to visit the garrison at Margny. When he drew rein to survey the town of Compiègne from the cliff above Margny, he saw the outpost being attacked. He immediately sent back for reinforcements from his camp at Clairoix. As the new troops galloped up, Joan's men were panicked and rushed back to the bridge. Joan remained in the rearguard to hold off the pursuers, when the English suddenly came up from La Venette and she was forced off the causeway and onto the marshland. The soldiers and the men in the *boulevard* retreated across the drawbridge, which was raised as soon as they passed, the town gate was promptly shut, leaving the few in the rearguard abandoned.

The Burgundian chronicler Monstrelet take up the story of Joan's capture:

> In the end, after the skirmish had lasted a fair length of time, the French, seeing the numbers of the enemy rapidly increasing, retreated rapidly towards the town, the Maid always bringing up the rear, making a great effort to protect her men and get them home without loss. However, the Burgundians, realising that they would shortly have reinforcements from all sides, attacked vigorously, striking out with all their might. At last, so I was informed, the Maid was pulled from her horse by an archer, close by the Bastard of Vendonne (Wandonne), to whom she surrendered and pledged her faith. She was immediately taken as a prisoner to Margny.[2]

Burgundian and French chroniclers alike admire Joan's courage. Another Burgundian, Chastellain, writes:

> The Maid made great efforts and performed feats well beyond the nature of a woman in trying to protect her men, staying in the rear of the retreat, as the commander and most valiant of her troops. So it was there, as fortune would have it, that her fame came to an end and she would never more bear arms, for an archer, a tough, strong fellow, greatly incensed that this woman, of whom he had heard so much, should hold back so many valiant men, got hold of her by her huque of cloth of gold and pulled her

to the ground and her men were not able to rescue or help her and get her back on her horse, despite all their efforts. A minor captain, by the name of Bastard of Wandonne, came up as she fell and got the better of her, so that, upon his assuring her that he was a noble, she gave him her faith.[3]

Wandonne's very appearance must have been enough to put the fear of God into a less doughty girl than Joan, for he had been gashed across the face and lamed in a leg and an arm in previous battles. At any rate, more delighted than if he had a king on his hands, he took her quickly to Margny and kept her there, under his guard, until the fighting was over. In Margny, she was divested of her armour, which Wandonne was entitled to claim as valuable booty.

Joan herself gave a succinct account of her capture during the session of her trial on 10 March 1431:

I passed over the bridge and through the boulevard with my men and attacked the troops of Messire John of Luxembourg. Twice we pushed them back as far as the Burgundian camp and again half-way there on the third attempt. Then the English who were there cut us off, and in the retreat I was caught in the fields on the Picardy side, near the boulevard. Between the place where I was taken and the town of Compiègne there was the river and the boulevard with its fosse. There was nothing else in between.

In fact, in the first public session of her trial, Joan denied having 'given her faith' (i.e. promised not to try to escape) to anyone. Her judge, Cauchon, forbade her to make any attempt to escape, on pain of being found guilty of the crime of heresy, but she refused to be intimidated, saying, 'If I escaped, no-one could accuse me of having broken faith, because I have never given my faith to anyone.' She added, 'It is true, that elsewhere I wanted to escape and that I would wish to do so, as is licit for anyone incarcerated or a prisoner.'[4]

Cagny's account is consistent with Joan's statement:

The Maid was left outside and her men with her. When the enemy saw this, they all rushed to capture her. She put up a vigorous resistance, but at last was taken by five or six of them together, some clutching at her, others laying hands on her horse, all shouting, 'Surrender to me, pledge me your faith!'. She answered, 'I have sworn and pledged my faith to another than any of you and I will keep that pledge!'[5]

The Burgundian chroniclers say one thing, Joan and Cagny another. Perhaps there was some misunderstanding about exactly what Joan declared to Wandonne.

Guillaume de Flavy, whose career was not exempt of crimes, has been suspected of treason, of deliberately shutting the gates to deliver Joan up to the enemy. No contemporary makes such an accusation. It appears in a little work entitled *Le Miroir des femmes vertueuses*, which Champion identifies as incorporating the work of Alain Bouchart, who claims to have interviewed in 1498 two very ancient inhabitants of Compiègne (one aged eighty-six, the other ninety-eight!). The two ancients told him that, not long before her capture, they had heard Joan tell children crowding round her in the Église Saint Jacques, 'My children and dear friends, I'm telling you that I have been sold and betrayed and that soon I will be delivered up to death. Pray for me.'[6] The author then goes on to make an accusation of treachery. The date of the statement is unclear, the old men's memories may in any case be coloured by analogies between Joan's tragedy and that of Christ, frequently underlined by those who believed her to be a saint.

However, given the warning Joan believed she had received from her 'Voices' at Easter, that she would be taken before Saint John's Day, 24 June, it would not be surprising that she should feel melancholy at times. Nonetheless, as Quicherat points out, it is unbelievable that she would have made such a demoralising statement publicly just before launching an attack on the enemy. Quicherat surmises that the lament, if it was made, was probably made during Joan's visit to Compiègne after the treachery of Bournel at Soissons.[7] A number of nineteenth-century historians, including the great Michelet, for example, regarded the case against Flavy as proven. Few serious historians nowadays are of this opinion. What could have been the motive? If it was money, surely treachery would have proved even more lucrative if the enemy had been allowed to take Compiègne along with Joan? Like Bournel at Soissons, Flavy could have sold the place sooner or later to the Burgundians. On the contrary, he had already rebuffed the offer of bribes and sturdily defended the town until the besiegers were forced to beat a hasty retreat on 26 October 1430.[8] Joan herself never suspected him. Her ardent desire, after capture, was to escape back to Compiègne, still captained by Flavy, to help prevent its fall. It was for that reason that she made a desperate attempt to escape from the tower of the castle of Beaurevoir, coming close to killing herself when she fell from the height. Alençon's faithful chronicler, Perceval de Cagny, does not in any way blame Flavy, simply stating, 'The captain of the place, seeing the great multitude of Burgundians and English about to rush the drawbridge and fearing the loss of the town, ordered it to be lifted and the gate shut.'[9]

Flavy was merely doing what he saw as his duty to save the town when he ordered that the drawbridge be raised and the gates be shut, regret as he might that Joan was left outside. Only the few stranded on the wrong side of the river had been taken prisoner, but however few, the Anglo-Burgundians were overjoyed, for, says Monstrelet, they 'were more joyous than if they had taken five hundred men-at-arms, for their fear and dread of no other captain or commander was as great as that which the Maid inspired in them.'[10]

Burgundy was sent for in his lodgings at Coudon and hastened to arrive immediately, to be greeted in the 'fields' outside Margny by a multitude of English and Burgundian soldiers in a state of great excitement and jubilation. Monstrelet says that they were

> ...all shouting and rejoicing for the capture of the Maid. The duke went in to see her where she was being held and spoke a few words to her, but I cannot recall anything that was said, although I was present.

Curious lapse of memory indeed, for a chronicler! Nor was Chastellain able to find out what was said: '(The duke) went in to see her and had some conversation with her, but nothing of that has come down to me, despite all my enquiries.'[11]

Could it possibly be that the Grand Duke of the West came off worst in the exchange? He in all his magnificence and the peasant girl standing in her shirt (*gippon*) and hose, divested of her armour? After this interview, which no doubt the duke himself did not forget, Joan was given into the custody of John of Luxembourg, since the Bastard of Wandonne was his liege man.

John of Luxembourg was the younger son of a great feudal family, one which could count kings and emperors among its antecedents, but he himself had been in the service of the dukes of Burgundy since 1411, in the time of John the Fearless. He had had the honour of knighting the twenty-five-year-old Philip of Burgundy as they were about to enter a battle against the Armagnacs in 1421. When Philip later created the chivalric Order of the Golden Fleece, in 1430, he duly enrolled his vassal, John of Luxembourg, as one of its twenty-four eminent knights. From Bedford, acting as regent for the child Henry VI, John received the title of Count of Guise and the fiefs that went with it, which he had however to take by conquest, for they belonged to René d'Anjou, the son of Charles VII's mother-in-law, Yolande of Aragon, Queen of Sicily. Now he stood of course to receive a very handsome ransom for such an important prisoner as the famous Maid. Wandonne and the archer who had pulled Joan from her horse would also receive rewards, although only a small fraction of the pot of gold.

A day or two after her capture Joan was taken to John of Luxembourg's fortress of Beaulieu, seven or so miles north of the city of Noyon, which is itself about fourteen miles from Compiègne, Thus she was removed from the war zone and from possible attempts to rescue her. Her brother and Jean d'Aulon were taken to Beaulieu with her.

No time was lost in making known the capture of the Maid, so famously heaven-sent, as her followers saw her, so infamously diabolical in the eyes of her adversaries. Burgundy immediately announced the good news to his towns. He sent a letter also to the duke of Savoy. We have a copy of the letter to the town of Saint Quentin in Picardy.[12] In it the duke proclaims that the 'foolish credulity' of those who had believed in her is now confounded. With her, the letter goes on, were taken other 'captains, knights, squires', many of the French had died, either killed in the fighting or drowned in the Oise, without any of the English or Burgundians being killed or taken and only less than twenty wounded. A famous victory! Or so he said.

The University of Paris, the Sorbonne, since 1418 entirely in the Burgundian camp, was quick off the mark. On 26 May, three days after Joan's capture, the learned academics had the vicar-general of the Inquisitor for France write to the duke of Burgundy demanding that Joan be handed over to stand trial on charges of heresy. The meaning of the term 'inquisition' is, in fact *enquiry*. The *inquisitio* is, as Dyann Elliott, for example, points out, a borrowing from Roman law with its pattern of interrogation, which in the Middle Ages "became the preferred mechanism for arriving at the truth'.[13] French justice is to this day an *inquisitorial* system, in which it has first to be established that there is a case to answer, by means of a preliminary enquiry carried out by a *juge d'instruction*. British justice, on the other hand, is an *adversarial* system, in which it is hoped that the truth of a case will shine forth as a result of the debate between two adversaries, the prosecutor and the counsel for the defence. Neither system is foolproof.

The minds of these eminent canon lawyers and theologians were of course already made up about Joan, she had sown heresy and error in 'several cities, good towns and other places of this kingdom'. Heresy was considered in the Middle Ages to be a crime subversive of the institutions of both State and Church. It had to be sought out and punished. The task of the Inquisition, working in conjunction with the bishop of the diocese, was to examine those suspected of heresy and pronounce upon their guilt or innocence. If guilt was established, the accused was to be handed over for punishment to the secular arm, meaning the representative of the State. The punishment for heresy was life imprisonment, but if the heretic was impenitent or relapsed, the punishment was the terrible death at the stake.

We should perhaps remember that death by fire was only one of the ferocious methods of execution widely used by governments in Europe until the end of the eighteenth century. Throughout the centuries, from the early Middle Ages onwards, lone voices were raised in various places against capital punishment or torture, but in general these things were accepted, or even enjoyed as a public spectacle. The height of the witch-hunts was reached in the sixteenth and seventeenth centuries, when thousands were burnt for witchcraft throughout Europe. In England, the last burning for heresy took place in Lichfield in 1612 and the last witch was burnt at Exeter in 1684, but forty-two women were burnt at the stake for other offences between 1702 and 1789. The punishment was officially abolished only in 1790. An equally gruesome method of execution in England was hanging, drawing and quartering, not removed from the Statute Book until 1814. Burning was for women, as it was considered to spare their modesty! The other punishment, perhaps even more sadistic, was for men and only for commoners. Aristocrats were beheaded. In

France, the atrocious death by torture and dismemberment by wild horses was inflicted as late as 1757 upon a would-be assassin of Louis XV. In 1791, the National Assembly abolished torture and such barbarous forms of execution and replaced them with the guillotine, considered humane.

Let us now return to events following Joan's capture. On the French side, the cravenly diplomatic Archbishop of Rheims, Regnault de Chartres, hastened to repair the damage done by the loss of Joan, sending a letter to the people of his cathedral town, Rheims, the very place of Joan's great triumph, telling them that he had happily found a replacement for her. We only have a summary of the letter, the original being lost. The archbishop wrote that Joan had incurred divine punishment for her refusal to listen to advice (his and La Trémoille's) and for her pride and the vainglory of her rich clothing. The heaven-sent replacement is a 'young shepherd boy, the guardian of sheep in the mountains of the Gévaudan'. The boy promises to do no less than Joan ever did, and declares that the Maid has been punished for her pride, her rich clothes and her disregard of advice. From this summary, we see that the divinely-inspired young shepherd's opinion miraculously coincides exactly with that of the archbishop.[14]

We learn more about the shepherd boy from accounts in various chronicles of the battle near Beauvais in August 1431, in which he was captured by the English. The *Bourgeois*:

> Among those taken, was a wicked boy called Guillaume the Shepherd, who encouraged idolatry, making people worship him. He rode side-saddle and sometimes exhibited his hands, feet and side, stained with blood, like Saint Francis of Assisi.[15]

Guillaume's suitability for sainthood was considerable. He embodied all the qualities of innocence and purity, being a young shepherd, like King David. Nothing is known about his antecedents – all the better. And he seems to have been a much more manageable saint than Joan. Most importantly, he knew his place as a peasant and never made himself disagreeably independent. We do not hear of him wearing rich clothes or armour (nor of them being given to him), so not only was there no visible sign of him aping his betters, but neither was there any unnecessary expense. He had the advantage of being a boy, so there was no problem of improper dressing or of otherwise overstepping the bounds of his sex. The archbishop never thought it necessary to send him off to Poitiers or anywhere else to be examined by the theologians, nor were his Christ-like wounds (his stigmata) medically examined. Time saved.

Guillaume was captured in August 1431, as we have seen. The English then took him to Rouen. To judge from what happened afterwards, his treatment must have been harsh. They kept him until December, in order to show him off, like a captive in a Roman triumph, in Paris, on the occasion of the entry of young Henry VI into Paris, when he was paraded tightly bound and perched on a horse in the grand procession. The *Journal d'un Bourgeois de Paris* describes it:

> Before Henry VI walked the nine *preux* and the nine lady *preuses*. Behind him came a host of knights and squires. Among them was Guillaume the Shepherd, of whom we have already spoken, but he had little joy of it, for he was tightly bound with strong cords, like a thief.[16]

Poor Guillaume seems to have had had a sorry end, after the pomp and ceremony was over. Lefèvre de Saint-Rémy writes: 'What became of him I don't know, but I have been told that he was thrown into the Seine and drowned.'[17]

Such was the fate of common criminals in the Paris of the time. They were sewn into a sack and thrown into the river, like so much rubbish. The English didn't consider Guillaume worth the trouble of a trial. The bloodstains, if he still had any to show at the time of his capture, failed to impress and were probably washed off. Maybe they were simply red dye. One must feel sorry for the boy, imprisoned for months, under heaven knows what conditions, but certainly with gaolers with whom he could not communicate and not a friend in the world. The archbishop of Rheims, who clearly set him on the path to his destruction, has a lot to answer for.

The people and the clergy on the French side paid little heed to Chartres's lead. The capture of Guillaume perturbed no-one and his later demise went unremarked. In contrast, Joan's capture aroused an outpouring of grief and dismay, as far away indeed as Rome. Jacques Gélu, the Archbishop of Embrun who had sent a treatise on Joan of Arc to Charles VII in 1429, now at once wrote again to the king, reminding him of his great debt to Joan, even asking him to search his own conscience to ascertain whether he himself had lost God's favour by offending Him in some way. He urged Charles to spare no effort to obtain Joan's freedom from captivity, 'neither means nor money, nor whatever price you must pay, otherwise you will be forever convicted of ingratitude'. He requested the king to have prayers said for Joan's deliverance, so that, if the misfortune were due in any way to failings on his part or that of his people, God would pardon them.[18]

The ordinary people loyal to Charles VII had regarded Joan as a saint while she was with them, they were not suddenly going to lose faith in her because of her misfortune. Article LII of the preliminary seventy articles of accusation against her in Rouen, at the conclusion of the 1431 trial, states:

> LII. Item. Joan, by her deceptions, seduced the Catholic people to such a point that many adored her while she was with them and still adore her in her absence, ordering Masses and collects (prayers at Mass) in her honour in the churches [...]. They preached publicly that she is a messenger from God and more an angel than a woman.

Prayers were indeed ordered in the churches. We have the text of three prayers to be said at Mass in the cathedral of Embrun, the first to be recited after the Gloria, the second after the Offertory, the third after the Communion. All ask for the intercession of the Virgin Mary and all the saints for Joan's deliverance and for God's help and blessing on the rest of her mission. The third runs as follows:

> Hear, O Lord, Almighty God, the prayers of Your people. Through the sacrament which we have received and the intercession of the Blessed Virgin Mary and all the saints, break the chains which bind the Maid who, while carrying out the work which You commanded, was captured and now is held in the prisons of our enemies. May Your divine mercy allow her to fulfil safely the rest of her mission. Through Our Lord Jesus Christ, etc.[19]

Masses were said for her, notably at Orleans, of course. Processions were held when news of Joan's capture was received, beseeching the help of God. There is a document of 1430 which records one such at Tours, of which we unfortunately have only the following summary:

> Public prayers were ordered, asking God to deliver the Maid from captivity. The following Wednesday there was a general procession, attended by the canons of the cathedral and the secular and regular clergy of the town, all walking barefoot.[20]

Soon after her death in 1431, there were calls for her beatification, something which was, of course, quite out of the question as long as the condemnation of Rouen still hung over her. She would not be beatified until 1909 and finally canonised in 1920.

To return now to Joan at Beaulieu, where she had an unexpected visit. Philip of Burgundy happened to be passing through Noyon on 6 June with his wife, Isabella of Portugal, now pregnant with their first child. Isabella expressed a desire to meet Joan, and Philip did indeed arrange a meeting, possibly in the palace of the archbishop of Noyon, where the couple would have lodged. Once again, we know nothing of what transpired during the interview, but as Joan always seems to have struck a chord with other women (apart from camp-followers) and as Isabella was intelligent and charitable, it is likely that the princess felt a certain pity or even sympathy for the prisoner, no matter what the official line adopted by her husband. Certainly, Philip did not seem afterwards in any hurry to hand Joan over to Bedford or to press John of Luxembourg to do so. While at Noyon, he had a meeting with Luxembourg, who was accompanied by his wife, Jeanne de Béthune. When Joan was later held in Luxembourg's castle of Beaurevoir, a real sympathy arose between her and Jeanne de Béthune and the two other Luxembourg ladies, John's aunt and his stepdaughter. Who can say what influence all these gentlewomen may have had? Unfortunately, it made no difference in the end.

While still in the forbidding fortress of Beaulieu, Joan made an attempt to escape. At her trial, on Thursday, 15 March 1431, she was questioned by the interrogator on the attempt:

Jean de la Fontaine: How did you intend to escape from the castle of Beaulieu, between two wooden posts?[21]
Joan: I was never a prisoner anywhere without wishing to escape. When I was in that castle, I tried to lock my guards into the tower, but the porter saw me and stopped me. It seems to me that it was not God's will that I should escape at that time and that I had to see the English king, as my Voices had told me and as you have recorded it here.
La Fontaine: Have you got permission from God or from your Voices to escape any time it pleases you?
Joan: I've asked for it several times, but I haven't got it yet.
La Fontaine: If you saw an opportunity, would you escape now?
Joan: If I saw the door open, I'd leave. That would be God's command. I believe firmly that if I saw the door open and my guards and the other English not able to stop me, I would know that I had permission and that God would help me. But without permission, I wouldn't go, not unless I made an attempt, just to see if it was all right with God. You known the French proverb, God helps those who help themselves. I'm telling you all this, so that if I escape, you can't say that I went without permission.

Joan was astonishingly honest here. But certainly, chained as she was day and night, with five guards on duty in and outside her cell, her chances of escape were vanishingly small.

At Beaulieu, her brother Pierre and Jean d'Aulon, her faithful attendant and chief of staff, were imprisoned with her, probably also in the tower, in other cells. When she was moved after the escape attempt, they were not brought with her to the next place, the castle of Beaurevoir. D'Aulon was ransomed in 1432, but Pierre was held until 1435, when his ransom was paid by the king, who made over to him the revenue from a certain number of the tolls on the passage of goods in the bailiwick of Chaumont.[22]

The dates of Joan's imprisonment in Beaulieu and afterwards in the more residential and opulent castle of Beaurevoir, about forty miles away, are not entirely clear. In the sixth session of her trial, she says that she was held in the castle of Beaurevoir for about four months, but that may be an over-estimate. As negotiations for the handover to the English were completed in early November, when she was transferred to Crotoy to be handed over to face trial, she had probably arrived at Beaurevoir in July.

In Beaurevoir, Joan was again housed in the keep of the castle. Conditions do not seem to have been too harsh. There was a trio of ladies called Jeanne: Jeanne de Béthune, whose first husband had been killed fighting on the French side at Agincourt, Jeanne de Bar, her daughter from that first marriage, and, most importantly, Jeanne de Luxembourg, Countess of Ligny, Jean de Luxembourg's elderly aunt. These three showed themselves anxious to help Joan as far as they could. They knew that the University was demanding that she be tried for heresy, and evidently wishing to save her from providing her enemies with a deadly focus of indictment: they pleaded with her to lay aside her male clothing and accept a gown, or to have one made from material of her choosing. They were not the only people who tried to persuade her for her own good; later on even the Duke of Burgundy's chamberlain, Jean de Pressy, would offer her a gown, but she had always replied that she would have considered acceptance of such an offer to be a sin and against God's will. No doubt she would have regarded it as tantamount to apostasy, a betrayal of her mission. An exchange in the session of 3 March 1431:

Question: Do you think that you would have committed a mortal sin in putting on a woman's gown?
Joan: I think that I do better to obey and serve my sovereign lord, that is to say, God. But if I had been obliged to put on a woman's gown, I would have done so at the request of those two ladies (Jeanne de Béthune and Jeanne de Luxembourg) rather than for any other ladies in France, except for my queen.

In Beaurevoir Joan was made reasonably comfortable, given the opportunity to wash or take a bath, provided with clean clothing, comforted by women with whom she was able to have friendly conversations. These were all things which we know were important to her and of which, of course, she was later deprived when surrounded by soldiers and male guards. There were four chaplains at Beaurevoir, so she could probably attend Mass or other devotions, even if under guard. As a prisoner, she was of course lodged in a cell or a room in the tower, with a guard on duty outside the door. Once a day she was allowed to go out onto a sort of platform to take the air.[23] There is no record of any complaint on her part concerning her sojourn in the castle.

Some acquaintances of the Luxembourg family were privileged to visit Joan in her cell, even to visit her without anyone else present. Such a one was a certain Sir Haimond de Macy, who was evidently attracted by the girl and saw no harm in trying to take certain liberties with her. Here is his testimony heard in Paris, on 7 May 1456:

I saw her in prison and spoke with her several times. Several times also I tried to touch her breasts, putting my hands on her chest, but Joan wouldn't stand for that and pushed me off as best she could. Her behaviour was very modest, both in words and in deeds.

This was not the only incident of unwanted attention that Joan had to suffer while a prisoner. One other witness heard in Paris (30 April 1456), a certain Jean Marcel, told the following story about a similar incident which occurred when Joan was a prisoner in Rouen:

> I was told by Jeannot Simon, a tailor, that the Duchess of Bedford had ordered a woman's tunic for Joan from him. When he tried to put it on her, he clasped her breast gently. She gave him an indignant slap.

In Article XVI of the seventy articles of accusation drawn up for consideration at the end of the trial, there is an interesting answer of Joan's which does not appear in the minute of the relevant session (17 March):

> She declared that the Demoiselle of Luxembourg requested that Monseigneur John of Luxembourg should not hand her over to the English.[24]

Why was this remark not included in the minute? Was it considered to show the Demoiselle in an undesirable light? As sympathetic to the Armagnacs? During the session, did it arouse the indignation of the assessors and judges? Did they remember that Jeanne de Luxembourg was godmother to Charles VII?

Whatever the sympathy of the three kind ladies, Joan was terribly alarmed at some point during her sojourn at Beaurevoir, by ominous rumours concerning the imminent fate of Compiègne. At her trial, on Wednesday, 14 March 1431, she declared it was these rumours, along with fear of being handed over to the English, that had inspired her attempt to escape from Beaurevoir:

> Jean de la Fontaine: Why did you leap from the tower of Beaurevoir?
> Joan: I had heard that the whole population of Compiègne above the age of seven years old was to be destroyed by fire and the sword, and I would rather have died than survive such a massacre of good people. The other reason is that I knew that I had been sold to the English and I would sooner have died than be in the hands of my enemies, the English.

It is clear that on the French side, the people were ready to believe any horror stories of the English. But who could have told Joan such nightmarish tales? Possibly one of the guards, amusing himself by taunting her? Saint Catherine told her, she said, that God would help her and the people in Compiègne and she must accept this. Moreover, she herself would not be delivered until she had seen the king of England. Joan again replied stubbornly, 'Indeed, I don't want to see him! I'd rather die than be in the hands of the English!'

At all events, despite being forbidden by Saints Catherine and Margaret to do so, she made up her mind to leap, or perhaps somehow attempt to lower herself, from the sixty-foot tower. Did she try to manufacture a rope from something? It would seem unlikely that she had the wherewithal, she slept simply on a straw mattress, there was no need for sheets. Olivier Bouzy suggests that she may have tried to escape through a window in the room in which she was imprisoned and which was probably on a lower floor. If she did jump from anywhere near the top of the tower, did she land in the muddy ditches (*fosses*) and roll down?

The interrogation of 14 March continued. Joan described the results of the fall:

> After I fell from the tower, I couldn't eat for two or three days, I was so shocked by the fall that I could neither eat nor drink. However, I was comforted by Saint Catherine who told me to go to confession and ask God's forgiveness for my leap. And she said that without fail, Compiègne would be relieved before Saint-Martin's Day in the winter [11 November]. Then I began to recover and to eat and I was soon cured.

If she had escaped from the tower, she would still have had well-nigh insuperable obstacles to overcome, some seventy-five miles of unknown country and forest to cross without a guide, before she could reach French-held territory on the other side of the river Oise, and with hostile soldiery alerted and hunting for her everywhere.

No doubt the good ladies of Beaurevoir were concerned at the state they found Joan in, and they saw to it that she was properly cared for. In any case, she was valuable property, negotiations were already underway, as she knew and feared, for her transfer to English custody and a king's ransom was being dangled before her captors. John of Luxembourg however had good reason for not wishing to displease his aunt. She was the heiress to a great part of the family fiefs, titles and fortune and she intended to leave all this to her favourite nephew, John, thereby cutting out his elder brother Pierre. However, wills can of course be changed. This frail brake on John's inclination to keep on the right side of both Burgundy and the English was removed when, at the end of August, the Demoiselle de Luxembourg left Beaurevoir to make her annual pilgrimage to the grave of her younger brother Pierre, who had died in Avignon more than forty years earlier, at the age of eighteen. He had been a pious youth, created a cardinal at that tender age by the Avignon antipope, Clement VII (it was not necessary to have taken Holy Orders in order to receive the red hat). Aunt Jeanne was not in good health and she died on 18 September. Joan's protectress was no more.

John of Luxembourg now came wholly under the influence of his brother Louis, the bishop of Thérouanne, a career cleric totally devoted to the English cause. After Joan's failed attack on Paris, he had been left in charge of the city, as noted earlier, as Bedford's Chancellor for France. He would play a role in Joan's trial in Rouen. He died in England as bishop of Ely in 1443, but seems never to have bothered to visit the place.

It was clear well before Joan's capture that the English and the Burgundians would have Joan tried as a heretic and sent to the stake if they could get hold of her. Pancrazio Justiani, wrote to his father from Bruges on 20 November 1429, with the following news, which he says he had from 'some men in religious orders' around the Burgundian court:

> I understand that the University of Paris, or rather the king's enemies, have sent to the pope in Rome an accusation of heresy against her and not only her, but all those who believe in her. They assert that she contravenes the Faith, in that she wishes people to believe in her and she knows how to foretell the future.[25]

What of the reaction, or lack of reaction, of Charles VII to Joan's capture? In particular, why did he make no attempt to ransom her? Could he not have attempted to bargain with John of Luxembourg? After all, there were several months between her capture at Compiègne and her being handed over to the English at the end of October. It was always clear enough that, if he could get hold of her, Bedford would have her tried as a sorceress or heretic and executed. From 26 May 1430 onwards, the numerous letters sent by the University of Paris and Cauchon to Burgundy and Luxembourg could have left no doubt as to the intentions of the government of Henry VI. Bedford's letter, in the name of the child king, dated 3 January 1431, shortly after Joan finally arrived in Rouen, damns her before the trial even begins:

> It is common knowledge that a woman calling herself Joan the Maid, leaving aside the dress and clothing of a woman, which is a thing against Divine law and abominable to God, forbidden by and repugnant to all law, thus clothed and armed in men's apparel, has committed cruelties and murders and, as is said, has given the common people to understand, in order to deceive and seduce them, that she was sent by God and had knowledge of His divine secrets, as well as making other very dangerous and prejudicial assertions, scandalous for our Catholic faith.[26]

The letter ends by affirming that, should she be cleared of any of the charges, she will be taken back into English custody. She is only on loan to the Inquisition.

Did Charles lose faith in her after Paris? Was he over-influenced by the party opposed to her, the archbishop of Paris, La Trémoille and others around them? His silence regarding her after her capture is contrasted with her unshakeable loyalty and devotion to him throughout her trial. Modern historians such as Pierre Tisset consider that Charles's faith in Joan was shaken, or that there must have been a serious disagreement between them in the months before her capture.[27] However, Pierre Duparc, the modern editor of the appeal trial (the *procès en nullité* of 1452–1456), is of a quite different opinion. He points out firstly that Charles knew very well Bedford and the English administration were determined to have Joan and that any approaches to ransom her would be futile. In support of his view, Duparc instances the evidence of the king's admiration for Joan, culminating in her place of honour at the coronation, the tax exemption for the villages of Domrémy and Greux and the ennoblement of the whole family. These however all preceded the failure at Paris and the capture. There is one piece of evidence which shows Charles VII in a better light. The Venetian Antonio Morosini, in his *Chronicle*, (or *Diario*) states that on 15 December 1430 he has had news from his kinsman Niccolo Morosini, who had left Bruges for Venice. Bruges was the capital of Flanders, famed for its cloth industry and immensely prosperous and wealthy. Philip the Good had set up his court there, and it was there that he was married in January 1430. The Venetian nobleman Niccolo Morosini was excellently placed in Bruges society to hear all that was going on, politically or otherwise. Here is the relevant extract:

> We heard first that the young woman [Joan] was in the hands of the Duke of Burgundy and many people there [in Bruges] were saying that she was going to be sold to the English. They said that at that news the Dauphin sent an embassy to the Burgundians to tell them that on no account were they to agree to such a bargain, otherwise he would treat his Burgundian prisoners likewise.[28]

This is hearsay evidence and the solitary report of any positive action on the part of Charles VII. The threat of retaliation remained an empty threat, if indeed it was made. However. Morosini was generally well informed, his news came straight from court circles at Bruges and he was writing it as he received it, not years later. Some support might be sensed for his assertions in the two letters which the University sent with their negotiator, Cauchon, to Burgundy and Luxembourg in mid-July 1430. Both letters express deep unease at the lack of response from the duke and the count and a fear that Joan could be rescued or ransomed. To Burgundy they speak of the 'malice and cunning of persons, your enemies and adversaries, who, it is said, are making strenuous efforts to deliver this woman out of your hands by crafty schemes …' To Luxembourg, they wrote: 'God's Majesty would be intolerably offended should this woman be freed or if you should lose her, something, it is said, that the enemy are seeking to bring about by all sorts of crafty schemes and, what is worse, by money or ransom.'[29] Georges Bordonove asks pertinently, 'Who do they really mean? What secret deals are they alluding to? […] What mysterious missions were entrusted to La Hire, who took Louviers, near Rouen, in December 1430?'[30] Among other notable historians, Olivier Bouzy also believes that Charles did whatever he could.[31]

There is some evidence that Charles, that most tight-lipped and tormented of monarchs, was deeply affected by Joan's capture. Pierre Sala, writing much later, but in possession of testimony from a contemporary source, says that Charles was very distressed by Joan's death, but that there was nothing he could do about it.[32] Aeneas Sylvius Piccolomini, who had met representatives from all sides, Burgundian and French, when he attended in 1435 both the great Council of Bâle and the peace conference held at Arras and later became Pope Pius II (1458-64), remarked in his *Memoirs* that 'Charles was bitterly grieved by the death of the Maid.'[33] It is worth noting that Jean Jouffroy, Bishop of Arras and Apostolic Legate of Philip of Burgundy, delivered an impassioned oration in praise of the duke at the Congress of Mantua convoked by Pius II in 1459, in which he bitterly denounced Joan as a fraud, repeating all the old slanders against her, but declared sourly at the end of his invective that he would say no more, seeing that 'Charles VII, now King of France, praises her to the skies.'[34]

We should understand that Charles VII's position was difficult. If Joan was tried for heresy and found guilty, as the University was immediately demanding, he himself would be guilty, by association, of promoting his cause and owing his crown to a convicted heretic, maybe even a sorceress or a fraud. His name, it seemed, would be blackened not only in France but throughout Europe and he would be considered unfit to rule. That, in fact, was the object of the whole exercise. Having approached Burgundy in vain, if we accept Morosini's report, Charles possibly believed that his best tactic was to wait and see the outcome of the inevitable trial, hoping that the judges would be impartial enough to find Joan innocent when they actually had her before them. If she was condemned, once again there was absolutely nothing he could do. He would have to wait until he could re-take Rouen, get possession of the trial documents and ask the pope to agree a new court case into the impartiality and legality of the 1431 proceedings. As 1431 had been a tribunal of the Inquisition, it was necessary first of all to seek papal consent to the re-trial, which was quite a lengthy business.

On 15 February 1450, almost immediately after his army entered Rouen in November 1449, Charles commissioned his counsellor, Guillaume Bouillé, to set up an enquiry into the 1431 trial. Such an enquiry was undertaken in 1450 and the Nullity trial, as it is now called, finally got underway in 1455. To ensure that all witnesses could come forward and testify without fear, Charles granted an amnesty in advance to all who had participated in the 1431 trial, save only the three principals, but since two of them were dead (Cauchon and D'Estiver) and the third (Lemaître) had mysteriously disappeared, that was hardly an onerous exception.

15

The Road to Rouen

La Poncela de certo quela è sta mandada a Roan ... veramente queste
son stranie e grande cose
The Pucelle has been sent to Rouen ... Truly these are great and
terrible events

Pancrazio Giustiniani

There was no let-up in the strenuous efforts of the University to have
Joan handed over. As already mentioned, immediately after the dispatch
of the first letter, officially signed by the Inquisitor, Bishop Cauchon in
person arrived at the camp at Compiègne with two more letters (already
mentioned above) demanding that Joan be handed over to the Inquisitor
or to himself. Favier remarks that Cauchon had no justification for his
intervention as the representative of a university in which he had for a
long time held no post, while Tisset affirms that the English government
was 'taking the necessary steps to have Joan, but acting through a third
party'.[1] Cauchon's only official position was that of counsellor of the king
of England, Henry VI. As he will henceforth play the major role in Joan's
story, what do we know of him?

Pierre Cauchon attained immortality as the judge of Joan of Arc. When
in 1431, he presided over the court which tried Joan, he was sixty years of
age and had behind him a long and hugely successful career in the political
and diplomatic service of the two Dukes of Burgundy, John the Fearless
and Philip the Good. He was not an outstanding theologian or canon
lawyer, but a career churchman, an indefatigable and invaluable servant
both of the University of Paris and later of Bedford's administration. In
return, he accumulated lucrative ecclesiastical benefices spread all over
the English-held territories, from Bayeux to Toulouse. Coming from a
well-established family of the prosperous bourgeoisie of Rheims, for many
years he was a student of law and theology at the Sorbonne. In 1397, at
the early age of twenty-six, while still a student, he had been elected to
serve a term as rector of the university (the mandate was limited to three
months). He was twice re-elected to the rectorship, in 1403 and 1409.
Three other important judges at Joan's trial also served as rectors. We
shall meet them again in Rouen, they were Cauchon's contemporary, Jean

Beaupère, and two younger men, Nicolas Midi (in 1418) and Thomas de Courcelles (in 1430). In 1407, during the time of the Great Schism in the Church, Cauchon was a member of the very important delegation sent by royal authority to Rome to negotiate between the two rival popes, Benedict XIII and Gregory XII.

After the assassination of the Duke of Orleans, he became a devoted servant of John the Fearless of Burgundy and a fervent defender of Jean Petit's notorious *Apologia* or *Justification du Duc de Bourgogne*, justifying the murder of Louis d'Orleans, the arguments of which were condemned by the bishop of Paris and the Inquisitor of the Faith in 1414. By their order, all copies of it had been burned. In January 1415, Burgundy sent Cauchon to head a delegation to the great church Council of Constance, where he was to seek the annulment of the condemnation. We find Jean Beaupère there in his company, as a member of the delegation. They were opposed by the very eminent Gerson. Nonetheless, after long drawn-out argumentation and invective, which no doubt wearied all except the French delegates, the condemnation was annulled by a commission of the Council on 16 January 1416. Cauchon had managed to carry the day by distributing largesse from the Duke of Burgundy to those who mattered, including several cardinals. 'The verdict of 16 January was handsomely paid for,' remarks François Neveux, a biographer by no means hostile to his subject, the bishop.[2] Cauchon remained at the Council until 1418. He was by this time someone who needed to be cultivated if one wanted a favour at court. The Duke of Burgundy promoted this upwardly-mobile ecclesiastic to the highest social level and church benefices were showered upon him. After the massacres of 1418, he entered Paris in the train of the duke. Thereafter he was constantly travelling here, there and everywhere as the duke's man on diplomatic and political missions.

In 1419, John the Fearless was assassinated. Cauchon was probably present at the event as one of the duke's counsellors. With Philip the Good, the cleric's career rolled on, his benefices continued to accrue, canonries, prebendaries and other lucrative holdings were his, from Bayeux to Toulouse, from Rheims to Beauvais. In April 1420, he and Jean Beaupère both represented the University of Paris at the Treaty of Troyes, negotiated largely by Cauchon himself. In 1420 also, the University recommended him for the bishopric of Beauvais, to which he was appointed in August. Philip of Burgundy was present in person at his consecration in January 1421. Less than three months before the death of Henry V, in June 1422, he became a member of the royal council of England. His relationship thereafter with the regent, Bedford, was excellent. However, he was unpopular with the clergy of Normandy, who had to suffer greatly increased taxation 'for the defence of the realm', which meant in the first instance the attempted taking of Mont-Saint-Michel, which had held out since 1417. In July 1429, an assembly of the clergy of Rouen protested against Cauchon's high-handed methods of levying these taxes and in early 1430 it was the turn of the Bayeux clergy to complain. Cauchon was even going as far as to excommunicate those who refused to pay up.

In the course of 1429, the bishop had of course grievances of his own, having had to slip out of Rheims as Joan of Arc came in and subsequently having been shown the door by the good citizens of Beauvais. These events, however, did him no harm with those on whose favour he depended. In September 1429, he left for England with the powerful cardinal of Winchester, Henry Beaufort, and Robert Jolivet, the abbot who had abandoned the Mont-Saint-Michel. Their mission was to raise money and troops. Cauchon spent several months in England, returning to France in January 1430. When the eight-year-old Henry VI landed at Calais on 23 April 1430, with Winchester and the Earl of Warwick, it was Cauchon who was there to greet him as the official envoy of the regent.

Cauchon had spent June in Paris, returning to Calais at the beginning of July, no doubt to confer with Bedford, who was there with the child Henry VI, concerning the offers to be made for the purchase of Joan of Arc. It was decided that the first offer would be for six thousand *livres tournois,* the ultimate offer of ten thousand *livres tournois* would be made if the first offer was rejected. The Bastard of Wandonne was also to receive a pension of two or three hundred *livres.* Larger ransoms were indeed paid at times, but the sum of ten thousand livres was nevertheless enormous, the equivalent of a king's ransom, since for that amount the monarch was entitled to make a compulsory purchase of any prisoner 'of note', be he king, prince or duke. However, the money was not to be referred to as a *ransom.* Ransoms bought the freedom of prisoners of war, not their trial and death. The rules of war and chivalry prohibited the sale of prisoners of war from hand to hand like so much prize cattle. Nor was it customary for a bishop to negotiate the purchase of a suspected heretic (nor indeed of anyone else), but this oddity raised no comment. In September 1430, the letter of Thomas Blount, the royal treasurer and Pierre Sureau, officer in charge of finance, setting out the apportioning of the 120,000 *livres tournois* raised in taxes for Henry VI in Normandy, will refer to the ten thousand *livres tournois* price for Joan as 'payment for the purchase of Joan the Maid'.[3]

Cauchon set off for Compiègne on 7 July and arrived there a week later. He brought with him the two letters, one for Burgundy and one for Luxembourg, setting forth the terms agreed. He also brought a third letter, addressed to both noblemen and headed 'The Summons made in the name of the King of France and England by the Bishop of Beauvais to the Duke of Burgundy and Messire John of Luxembourg'. The tone was peremptory: 'This woman, commonly called the Maid, now a prisoner, should be sent to the King to be handed over for trial to the Church [...] The said bishop [...] requires that she be handed over to him to be tried.'[4]

The letter, after setting out again the terms of purchase, has a final paragraph to the effect that if those concerned are not satisfied with the first offer, it can be improved (how anyone thought that the first offer would be accepted in those circumstances is beyond comprehension). The postscript states that 'Although the capture of this woman is not the equivalent of the capture of a king, prince or others of such high estate', nonetheless the king is willing to raise it to ten thousand francs, 'in accord with the law, usage and custom of France'. The money is not referred to as a ransom, since Joan, as stipulated in Cauchon's letter, 'is not to be considered a prize of war'.

In his letter, Cauchon claimed Joan as having been captured within his diocese. A cross erected in the middle of the bridge over the Oise marked the limit of the diocese. If she had been taken over the bridge, beneath the walls of Compiègne, she would have been in the diocese of the bishop of Soissons and there has been some debate arising from this point. However, the deadly machine which would destroy her would doubtless have rolled on, since the bishop of Soissons, Renaud de Fontaines, while maybe not as compliant as the bishop of Beauvais, was also a Burgundian and until 1428 officially vice-chancellor of the University of Paris. Jean Beaupère was one of the two men whom he had had appointed to deputise for him in that office after 1423, when he was appointed bishop of Soissons, no doubt with the approval of Bedford.[5]

On 14 July Cauchon had interviews with Burgundy and Luxembourg. From the time he arrived, says Favier, it was clear that he intended to take over the eventual trial, with the Inquisitor's role reduced to that of assistant. It was not only the plight of Compiègne, but some inkling of these negotiations that drove Joan to make her desperate leap from the tower of the castle of Beaurevoir. After his interviews with the duke and the count, the bishop made a visit to the latter's *château*. Was he invited on that occasion to see the famous prisoner for himself? How was he received by the three Luxembourg ladies? We may imagine a polite but frosty reception. If Cauchon felt that John of Luxembourg's aunt was a factor in the sluggish progress of his negotiations, he may well, after his return to Rouen at the end of July, have solicited the bishop of Thérouanne's assistance in persuading the latter's brother of the profits and virtues of the proper course of action.

Once back in Rouen, Cauchon was able to report to Bedford that negotiations were on-going. He had to set about finding the necessary funds for the price he had offered; it was of course the full amount of ten thousand *livres tournois*. By the beginning of September it had been agreed that the funds should come from taxes raised in Normandy. The total sum was not amassed until 24 October. Cauchon himself was paid seven hundred and sixty-five *livres tournois* for his efforts and expenses.[6] The Inquisitor Lemaître received twenty *saluts d'or* for his trouble. No inquisitor had ever previously been paid in this manner.

Meanwhile, throughout August, Joan's life at Beaurevoir continued as before, her anxieties weighing ever more heavily upon her, relieved only by the kindness of the ladies of the castle and the occasional visitor that she was allowed. Cauchon's negotiations with Luxembourg and Burgundy dragged on. Before leaving for Avignon, Jeanne de Luxembourg had added a codicil to her will asking her nephew to refuse to hand Joan over to the English. Luxembourg found a clever way of getting round his aunt's objections, he would hand the prisoner over not to the English but to Burgundy, who could then send her on. She would be taken first to Arras, the nearby Burgundian town, and from there be sent to Rouen.

One day, at the end of August or in early September, Joan had two visitors from the town of Tournai, that haven of stubborn loyalty to Charles VII, holding out against the odds in the middle of Burgundian territory. She had a soft spot for the town and, as we may remember, had written to invite the counsellors to send representatives to the coronation at Rheims, an invitation which they had accepted. On this occasion she made a very curious request, a plea for money such as she had never made before on her own behalf. She asked, as a favour, that the visitors should take a letter from her to the town, requesting a sum of 'twenty or thirty gold crowns' for her 'necessities'. This was the equivalent of the annual income of a mounted man-at-arms. Why did she need this money? She knew that she would soon be sent from Beaurevoir into a much harsher prison, guarded not by polite and considerate ladies, but by rough-and-ready English soldiery. Did she believe she would be allowed to pay for what she considered basic 'necessities' with which she might otherwise not be provided? Or was she hoping to be able to escape somehow and make her way across country, paying for food and shelter, perhaps even a horse, as she went? The town sent her the money, but she only received it after leaving Beaurevoir, when a halt was made in Arras on her way to Rouen.

Joan left Beaurevoir probably in late October, around the time when John of Luxembourg and the Burgundians had to raise the siege of Compiègne (26 October). The failure of the siege was very bad news for Philip the Good, on a par with the failure of the English at Orléans. Compiègne was the key to the success of his whole campaign, the gateway to the region he wished to control. It must however have been very good news for Joan. The prediction of her 'Voices' had come true. Otherwise there was nothing to comfort her.

The distance by road from Compiègne to Arras is around seventy miles. Joan and her escort of Burgundian soldiers, all mounted, would have made the journey in two stages, taking a route through sure Burgundian territory. They spent the night probably in the fortress (now vanished) of the little town of Bapaume, not far from the Somme, an ancient juncture since Roman times for roads across the plains of Flanders and on to Amiens and the sea in one direction and down to the Seine valley and Paris in the other. After the fatigue of that day's hard ride, Joan would have reached Arras at the end of the following morning.

There is no documentation to tell us much about Joan's imprisonment in Arras, neither the length of her stay, nor even where exactly she was

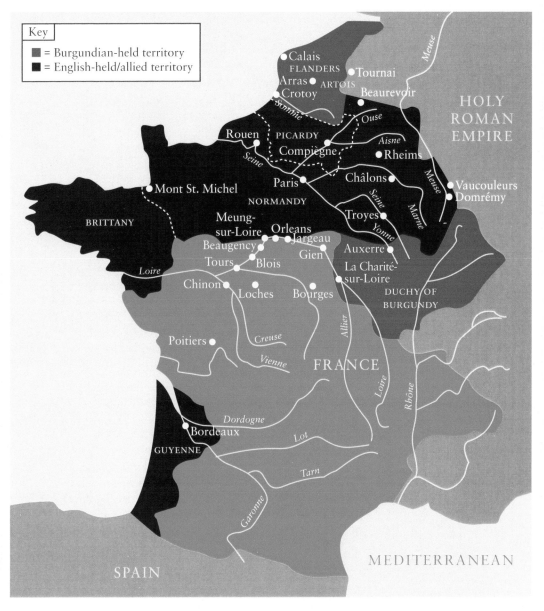

A map of France with English-, Burgundian- and French-held areas at the time of Joan's appearance. The Loire campaign and two of her journeys can be traced as follows:

Vaucouleurs to Chinon: No clear route, as Joan and her companions had to travel by night, avoiding places held by hostile troops. They reached Auxerre, finally making it to French-held territory at Gien, and so on to Chinon. The whole journey took eleven days.

The Loire campaign: Orleans, Auxerre, Troyes, Châlons, Rheims.

Her journey in captivity: Compiègne to Beaurevoir, later to Arras, Crotoy and Rouen.

Above left: Domrémy (now Domrémy-la-Pucelle), birthplace of Joan of Arc, photographed *c.* 1900. The statue is no longer there. The citizens were granted exemption from taxes 'forever' by Charles VII. The enviable perk survived until the French Revolution. (Courtesy of the Rijksmuseum)

Above right: Charles VII receiving the astonishingly wealthy merchant Jacques Coeur. The trader and diplomat helped to oust the English from Normandy. (Wikimedia Commons)

A groat bearing a representation of the young Henry VI, minted some time between 1422 and 1427. (Courtesy of the Metropolitan Museum of Art via Assunta Sommella Peluso, Ignazio Peluso, Ada Peluso and Romano I. Peluso)

John Talbot before
Margaret of Anjou
and Henry VI in the
Talbot Shrewsbury
book, 1445–45.
Talbot can be
identified by the
inclusion of the
Talbot dog at his
side. (Courtesy of
the British Library)

Charles VII and his Queen, Marie of Anjou in the Abbey St. Denis, Paris. The crowns broken off during the Revolution have here been replaced. See note 1, chapter 4. (Wikimedia Commons)

A seal, possibly from the Netherlands, from 1358 depicting St Margaret. (Courtesy of the Metropolitan Museum of Art via H. P. Kraus)

Joan's second 'Voice', a depiction of St Catherine c. 1380 by Cenni di Francesco de ser Senni. (Courtesy of the Metropolitan Museum of Art via Jean Fowles)

Joan of Arc depicted by Albert Lynch in *Figaro* magazine, 1903. The epitome of the received Joan image; anyone would recognise this figure, despite the fact that no portrait from life of the Maid exists. (Author's collection)

Right: The 1429 Siege of Orleans in Martial d'Auvergne's *Vigiles du roi Charles VII*, 1493. (Wikimedia Commons)

Below: Letter from Joan, 1429, to the citizens of Riom, capital of the province of Auvergne, asking for 'war materials'. (Wikimedia Commons, courtesy of the archives of Riom)

Left: An 1824 depiction by Paul Delaroche of Joan being interrogated by Cardinal Henry Beaufort. It is entirely inaccurate. He never interrogated Joan and did not even attend the trial, putting in an appearance only once, in the cemetery of Saint-Ouen. (Courtesy of the Rijksmuseum)

Below: A more imperious Joan. *Joan of Arc imprisoned in Rouen* by Pierre Henri Revoil, 1819. (Courtesy of the Metropolitan Museum of Art via the Isaacson-Draper Foundation)

Right: A 1905 photograph of the keep of Rouen Castle, which is now known as the Tower of Joan of Arc. This tower, with walls four metres thick, is the only remaining part of the castle of Rouen, dismantled in 1591. Joan was imprisoned in one of the other six towers, but was taken here and threatened with the instruments of torture on 9 May 1431. (Courtesy of the Library of Congress)

Below right: One of many equestrian statues of Joan, this one at the entrance to Reims Cathedral. (Courtesy of the Library of Congress)

Below: A medal created at the end of the First World War by Pierre Roche commemorating Joan's sacrifice. (Courtesy of the Metropolitan Museum of Art via David and Constance Yates)

Above left: Lia Félix as Joan of Arc in a production of Jules Barbier's play *Jeanne d'Arc* in the 1870s. The hair is longer than in Albert Lynch's depiction. (Courtesy of the Rijksmuseum)

Above right: Alphonse Mucha's 1909 painting of American actress Maude Adams as Joan in Friedrich Schiller's *The Maid of Orleans*. No bob for Maude, full tresses. (Courtesy of the Metropolitan Museum of Art via A. J. Kobler)

Below: A modern view of the house in which Joan was born. (Courtesy of Thiemo Gamma)

held. Rocolle thinks it unlikely that she was held in the fortress outside the town walls or in the *château* which was the town residence of the Duke of Burgundy. He considers it most likely that she was held in a tower of the fortifications at the Porte Ronville, on the town walls (the ramparts of Arras were demolished in 1890).[7] Joan seems not to have been harshly treated at Arras. She had visitors, no doubt curious grandees. It was there that Burgundy's treasurer and chamberlain, Jean de Pressy, urged her, out of kindness and for her own good, to accept a gift of women's clothing, an offer which, as we have seen, she felt bound to refuse. We know that a Scottish painter came to see her there and showed her a painting of herself. During her trial, on Saturday, 3 March, when asked if she had not had images or pictures of herself made, she made the following reply:

> At Arras, I saw a painting in the hands of a Scotsman. It showed me fully armed, presenting letters to my king on bended knee. I never saw nor caused to be made any other image or painting of myself.

How long Joan was held at Arras is not certain. The English having at last got together the money to purchase her, it was agreed that she should be sent on from Arras to Crotoy, on the coast, at the estuary of the Somme. There she would be handed over to Bedford's officials and the English garrison until Cauchon could arrive with the money.

A letter from Bruges, written by Pancrazio Justiniani and dated 24 November 1430, mentions the latest news of Joan:

> It is certain that the Maid has been sent to Rouen, to be handed over to the King of England, and that Messire Jean de Luxembourg, whose prisoner she was, has received ten thousand crowns on handing her over to the English. What will happen to her now, nobody knows, but it is feared that she will be put to death. These are truly great and terrible events.[8]

Pancrazio goes on to say that he has spoken with a number of people about Joan, and that all agreed that her way of life was truly good and decent. Such was the general opinion outside English and Burgundian circles.

It would appear from this letter that Joan was moved to Crotoy about a month after she arrived in Arras. Allowing time for the news to reach Bruges, she must have left around November 20. Was she told exactly where she was going? With her military guard, she probably made a couple of overnight stops on the way to Crotoy, one of them at the castle of Drugy, altogether about sixty or sixty-five miles by road. They rode through open country and forests, past châteaux and villages, churches and abbeys. Perhaps she heard the ringing of church bells, which she had so loved as a child in Domrémy. As winter was now setting in, she would have needed extra clothing and must have been provided with a hood to cover her head and shoulders, a warm doublet and a cape or surcoat, a far cry from the knightly garments she had worn on campaign. That however would not have had any importance for her, she no longer needed to present an inspiring presence to the troops. She must have caught her first glimpse of the sea as she approached Crotoy. The sight of the sea and the ships at anchor would have deeply impressed the country girl. But with whom, in the guard, could she share her amazement? She was alone. The little company rode on past the ramparts and arrived at a fortress defended by strong towers at each of its four corners, the whole surrounded by massive walls bearing four watchtowers. This would be her abode for maybe as long as a month.

Kelly DeVries describes Joan's journeyings from Beaurevoir to Rouen, via Bapaume, Arras, Drugy, Crotoy and various other villages and places *en route*, as a sort of victory parade by her captors, Joan being on display to the populations along the way. We do not know if this was a via dolorosa for Joan. The sightseers were probably more curious than hostile, perhaps many of them were silently sympathetic to her in her misfortune.

On the way to Crotoy, an overnight stop was made at the castle of Drugy. A history published in 1657, but whose author, a Jesuit priest, seems to have had at his disposal documents now lost, gives a curious account of that interlude. From Beaurevoir, he says,

> She was taken to the castle of Drugy, near the abbey of Saint Riquier, where the provost and the almoner of the abbey came to visit her and pay their respects. They were Dom Nicolas Bourdon and Dom Jean Chappelain. They were accompanied by leading personages of the town. All were saddened to see her, so innocent, thus persecuted.[9]

After Drugy, Joan was held for at least a month at Crotoy, where she was reasonably well treated. The governor of the castle was Ralph Butler, a relative of Bedford. The same early historian continues:

> From the castle of Drugy [...] she was taken to the castle of Crotoy, where, by God's providence, she frequently heard the holy sacrifice of the Mass, which was celebrated in the chapel of the castle, by the chancellor of the cathedral of Our Lady of Amiens, Nicolas de Gueuville, doctor of Law, a notable person, held prisoner at the time. He administered the sacraments of confession and the Eucharist to her and spoke highly of this very virtuous and chaste girl. Some ladies of quality and some young ladies and wives of citizens of Abbeville came to see her, regarding her as a marvel of their sex, a noble soul inspired by God for the good of France.

We notice once again, how women always seem to have been well-disposed toward Joan (except of course for a charlatan such as Catherine de la

Rochelle). Perhaps, nonetheless, we should regard some elements of this account with caution, since we do not possess the documents on which it draws. Corroboration can be found however in the testimony of Haimond de Macy at the 1456 trial and it may be that the later account is largely based on that:

> Joan was taken to the castle of Crotoy, where a very important prisoner was held. He was Maître Nicolas d'Ecqueville, chancellor of the church of Amiens, doctor of canon and civil law. He often celebrated Mass in the prison and Joan was frequently present. Later I heard Maître Nicolas say that he had heard Joan's confession and that she was a good Christian and very pious. He spoke very highly of her.

Ecqueville (whose name appears variously as *Gueuville, Queuville, or Quiefdeville!*) was a political prisoner. While, on the one hand, Hugues Cuillerel, the abbot of Saint-Riquier, his superior, was a member of the higher clergy who had espoused the Anglo-Burgundian cause, on the other hand, Gueuville, like a fair number of clergy in Burgundian or English-held territory – such as the monks of the Mont Saint Michel or of Fécamp – had rejected his example. Gueuville had been somehow involved in a plot to deliver Amiens to the partisans of Charles VII. When the plot was discovered, probably in early November 1430, he was imprisoned first at Amiens and then at Crotoy. After Crotoy, Joan would never be allowed to hear Mass again and she would receive communion only *in extremis*, on her way to the stake.

16

Preparations for Bishop Cauchon's 'Fine Trial'

Ils ne se servent de la pensée que pour autoriser leurs injustices
Voltaire, *Dialogues*

There is no documentation of Joan being in Rouen until 28 December, when the chapter of the cathedral of Rouen, no doubt at the bidding of Bedford, granted Cauchon 'letters of territoriality', allowing him to try her in their diocese, as he could not return to his own. This was in itself an exceptional measure, for a heretic was supposed to be tried in the diocese where he or she lived or in the diocese in which they had been active in promoting heresy. The English certainly intended to entrust the trial of Joan to Cauchon and to no-one else. On 3 January 1431, he was officially appointed by the English authorities as judge for the forthcoming proceedings. As his career seems to have been at a standstill for some time after his consecration in 1420 as bishop, Joan's trial was his big chance for advancement. He had his eye on the greater bishopric of Rouen, vacant at the time, but even his best efforts did not eventually get him there.

While Joan had been in Crotoy, the bishop had had to take his time about things. First, there was the lengthy business of raising the money from taxation and waiting for it to come through, then administrative matters such as the question of territoriality, of selection and appointment of assessors for the trial and other necessary preparations. The whole affair was dragging on too long in the opinion of the University of Paris and they wrote two letters on 21 November 1430, one to Henry VI (i.e. to Bedford) and another to Cauchon. In the first letter they asked that Joan should be sent to Paris for trial. Bedford was certainly not going to accede to such a request. Paris was too unstable as far as the English were concerned, even the Burgundians were no longer really welcome there, plots had been uncovered, the population was unpredictable and it was not unthinkable that the city could be attacked by forces loyal to Charles VII.

In their letter to Cauchon, the eminent academics of the Sorbonne made their displeasure at the slow progress of the affair abundantly clear. It constituted, they roundly declared, 'an offence to the faith and the ecclesiastic jurisdiction'. They demanded that Cauchon see to it that she be handed over to himself and the inquisitor promptly, and thereafter brought to Paris to be examined and judged more diligently and surely 'for the edification of the Christian people and in honour of God'.[1] In the event, of course, the Sorbonne had to make do with sending its own men down to Rouen as assessors at the trial. It sent down six picked theologians, who arrived in Rouen on 13 February 1431, among them Beaupère (former rector of the University in 1412 and 1413), Midi (rector of the University of Louvain in1433) and Courcelles (rector of the University in 1430, later in 1431 and 1435). This group played a leading role in the proceedings, although one, Gérard Feuillet, another emissary of the University, did not appear after April 18, for what reason we do not know. Perhaps he had qualms of conscience.

We do not know exactly how long Joan was held at Crotoy. It has been estimated, from a study of winter tides in the Somme estuary, that she, together with the bishop and her escort, probably left the fortress on the morning of 20 December. Joan and a small number of guards would have been ferried across the bay of the Somme to Saint Valéry, the greater number of men and horses crossing over by the bridge at Abbeville, further upstream. From Saint Valéry, the little company travelled via Eu, passing close by Dieppe and so on to Rouen, arriving on 23 December. Whether she was bound with ropes for the journey on horseback or not, it must have been tiring and cold, she was beset with anxieties, and we can only hope that during the overnight stops in fortresses along the way she was allowed to stretch her limbs and share the meals provided for her escort, also to warm herself during that time at the hearths.

On her arrival, Joan saw nothing Rouen, for she and her guard entered the mighty fortress of Bouvreuil through a postern gate facing the countryside, without having to pass through the maze of busy narrow streets of the cityn, with its great cathedral, its forest of spires, its multitude of churches, monasteries and convents. The fortress of Bouvreuil, a complex of six massive towers linked by walls and surrounded by outer walls and moats, stood at the north-west corner of the town walls with their sixty towers and the great fortified gates facing the fields or the Seine. It was built at the beginning of the thirteenth century under King Philip II Augustus. Nothing of it remains now except the keep, restored in the latter half of the nineteenth century. Known today as the *Tour Jeanne d'Arc*, this is not in fact the tower in which Joan was imprisoned, demolished along with the rest of the complex at the end of the sixteenth century.

At the time of Joan's arrival, the château was the residence of the child Henry VI and his 'governor', Richard Beauchamp, Earl of Warwick (later father-in-law of Warwick the 'Kingmaker'). Did Joan indeed at some point during her imprisonment catch a glimpse of the child king, as her 'Voices' had warned her? He had been brought over from England to Calais at the beginning of the previous July and escorted from there to Rouen by his great-uncle Henry Beaumont, Cardinal of Winchester, together with Warwick and other great lords. The earl and his family had taken over Bedford's apartments in the castle in the absence of the regent himself. As a prisoner-of-war, Joan was Warwick's responsibility and as a prisoner of the Inquisition, she was, during the sessions of her trial, in Cauchon's charge. The bishop had his own place of residence in Rouen, outside the precinct of the castle, a house belonging to a local cleric, where he could have meetings with those he wished to see. Between them, these two men had the power of life and death over the prisoner.

Warwick certainly wanted her death, Cauchon was there to deliver it. She had said that she was sent by God to chase the English out of France, therefore even more important than her death, of course, was that she should first be made to admit that her visions and 'Voices' were illusions or a deceit and that she had erred grievously. Only then could it be demonstrated that Charles had been crowned with the help of a sorceress and a heretic and the claim that God was on his side was a shameless fraud. Without such an admission, death would only make a martyr of Joan in the eyes of the French. Both men may well, like Bedford and indeed every English soldier, have been convinced of the rightness of their view of Joan, Warwick probably until the end, but it is difficult to see how Cauchon, as her judge, could have maintained such an opinion of the prisoner throughout the trial.

On that cold December afternoon, Joan faced a bleak Christmas, one during which she would be kept in chains in a gloomy cell on the middle floor of one of the towers. Massieu, the priest who had the responsibility of bringing her daily from her cell to the chapel where the court was sitting, described the conditions of her imprisonment in his testimony at the Nullity trial:

> Joan was held in the castle of Rouen in a room reached by eight steps on the second level. There was a bed and a great plank to which was attached an iron chain to hold Joan, who in shackles. You locked the chain to the plank by an iron lock. There were five English guards of the roughest sort, who wished her dead and very often insulted and mocked her. She complained of it.

From what evidence there is, in the trial and otherwise, her biographers have concluded that there would have been, in addition to the door, three recesses in the thick stone walls of her cell in the tower. One would have been a barred window, to allow some light to enter, another would have served as the usual privy in such towers (with what *privacy* we had better forbear to conjecture), and the third must have been a narrow slit opening onto the spiral staircase outside the room. It is from this vantage point that her conversation with any interviewer or interrogator could have been overheard. This elementary of form of bugging is mentioned several times in the evidence of the witnesses in the Nullity trial of 1452. In charge of security arrangements in the prison was John Grey, squire to Henry VI, assisted by two other Englishmen, John Berwoit and William Talbot. They were sworn in to guard her faithfully and to allow no-one to speak with her.

Manchon, the principal notary who took the minutes at the 1431 trial, and whose honesty was attested by numerous witnesses in 1452 and 1456, gave evidence concerning the conditions in which Joan was held:

> The Bishop of Beauvais supported the English party. I saw that even before he started the proceedings, Joan was held in chains. After the opening of the trial, still in chains, she was guarded by four English soldiers, under orders from the bishop and the inquisitor to guard her well. She was treated cruelly, towards the end of the trial they showed her the instruments of torture. She was wearing male dress and complained that she didn't dare to undress, for fear that during the night, the guards would assault her. Once or maybe twice, she complained to the bishop of Beauvais, to the deputy inquisitor and to Maître Nicolas Loiseleur that one of the guards had tried to rape her. So when the bishop, the inquisitor and Loiseleur had reported the affair to the Earl of Warwick, he threatened the guards with severe punishment if they made another attempt and two more guards were added to their number.[2]

Joan could expect no compassion from her guards or indeed from any of her English adversaries. She had inspired too much fear. One witness at the Nullity trial of 1456, Pierre Miget, declared that he had been told by a certain English knight that the English feared her more than a hundred men-at-arms. The remark had evidently impressed him, for he had already made the same assertion when convoked to testify at the preliminary investigations in 1452. At those early hearings of witnesses, both Brother Isambard de La Pierre and the clerk of the court, the notary Manchon, affirmed that it was widely believed in Rouen that the English would not have dared to lay siege to Louviers while Joan was still alive.[3] The ordinary soldiers had a superstitious fear of her, desertions, as noted earlier, had become a serious problem. The English high command regarded her with contempt and loathing, either as the half-crazy tool of who knew what forces behind Charles VII, or as an ignorant and heretical upstart peasant exploiting the credulity of her fellow-countrymen and women with tales of miracles and visions, making herself the willing tool of the aforesaid forces and achieving high rewards thereby. The ordinary soldiers regarded her with superstitious dread. She could not try to dispel their prejudices or communicate in any way with them; there was no common language.

In the documents of the two trials, that of 1431 and that of 1456, we find Joan's complaints and fear of her guards and many witnesses' testimony concerning these soldiers' mistreatment and mockery of her. In their eyes, she was an evil sorceress, the cause of many defeats and deaths in battle. The murderous anger which the soldiers around the castle visited upon anyone suspected of trying to help her is also well attested. The notary Manchon testified on 12 May, 1456, that when he and the other notaries were summoned by the earl of Warwick and bishop Cauchon to the castle four days before Joan's execution, there were about fifty armed English soldiers in the courtyard who hurled abuse at them, calling them traitors and accusing them of not acting properly at the trial. The soldiers were furious because Joan had apparently recanted and therefore had not been condemned to the stake. Manchon:

> We got past the mob with great difficulty and fear, I believe they were angry because Joan had not been burnt after the first sermon and sentence.[4] On the Monday, I was called again to the castle by the earl and the bishop. Because of the fright I and my friends had had, I wouldn't have dared to go without the protection of the earl of Warwick, who took me personally to Joan's prison.

Joan had chosen to be known as Joan the Maid. Whether she was indeed a maid, was crucial to her credibility. If she could be shown to have been unchaste, no further proof would be needed to discredit her completely, her lack of sanctity would be crystal clear. Once again, in December or early January, she was subjected, as at Poitiers, to a physical examination by a deputation of respectable matrons. Massieu, whose testimony was taken on 17 December 1455, and again on the following 12 May, gave the following account:

> I know that on the orders of the Duchess of Bedford, she was examined by certain matrons or midwives, in particular by Anne Bavon and another whose name I can't remember. They reported that she was indeed *virgo intacta*. I heard that from the said Anne. After that, the Duchess of Bedford forbade the guards and any others to do her any violence.

The pious duchess, Anne of Burgundy, like other women, took it upon herself to do what she could for Joan.

The guards were posted both inside and outside the cell day and night. She would have no privacy, no woman near her and she had not even the consolation of attending Mass. The conditions were harsh beyond all comparison with anything she had known previously.

During the preliminary enquiries at Rouen for the Nullity trial, a citizen of Rouen, Pierre Cusquel, testified on 3 May 1452, that he had seen Joan twice in her prison, thanks to the grace and favour of Maître Jean Son, in charge of building works. He had seen Joan 'wearing iron shackles and chained by a long chain fixed to a wooden beam'. He adds, 'At work, we had measured an iron cage, in which it was said she was to be held, but I never saw her in it.' No doubt the shackles, chain and omnipresent guards were finally considered security enough. Important prisoners were sometimes held at night in iron cages, to prevent any attempt at escape. Joan might well have welcomed the idea of the cage as a protection against any possible violence on the part of her guards.

As a prisoner-of-war, however, Joan could have expected more humane treatment. Prisoners of rank, such as awaited ransom, often lived in considerable comfort and style. In August, 1431, a few months after Joan's death, Xaintrailles was captured in the encounter in which Régnault de Chartres's 'little shepherd boy' was taken. Like Joan, he was imprisoned in Rouen, in the same castle of Bouvreuil, but he, unlike Joan, was invited to dine with Bedford, Warwick, Cauchon, Henry VI and other notables, while Warwick's daughter, Margaret, the wife of Talbot (a prisoner of the French at the time), played the role of hostess. The conditions under which Joan was held were enough to break the will of a prisoner much older and tougher than she, and that, no doubt, was the intention.

Haimond de Macy, the same who had, as we would say nowadays, sexually harassed Joan at Beaurevoir ('playfully', of course), testified also that he had accompanied John of Luxembourg to Rouen some time after Joan's capture, probably towards the end of the trial, since, on his own testimony in 1456, he was in Rouen at the time of Joan's forced abjuration on 24 May 1431. He goes on:

> One day, the Count of Ligny [Luxembourg] asked to see her and came to her in the company of the counts of Warwick and Stafford, together with the Chancellor of England, the brother of the Count and at that time Bishop of Thérouann [Louis of Luxembourg]. I was there also. He spoke to Joan and said, 'Joan, I have come to get you your freedom against a ransom, on condition that you promise never again to take up arms against us.' She replied, 'In the name of God, you are making mock of me! I know very well that you have neither the desire nor the power to do so.' As he insisted, she repeated this twice, adding, 'I know very well that these English will put me to death, hoping after my death to conquer the kingdom of France, but if they were a hundred thousand *godons* they will never have the kingdom!' The Count of Stafford was outraged and drew his dagger out of its sheath to strike her, but the Count of Warwick stopped him.

Stafford seems to have been particularly irascible. Perhaps he had been nursing his anger ever since the siege of Orleans, where he had been with Talbot and others in the Saint Laurent fortress, the siege headquarters. Manchon recounted, in his testimony of 1456, another incident involving the earl:

> Once a man, whose name I forget, said something to do with Joan which annoyed Lord Stafford. He drew his sword and rushed after the man, who took refuge in a place of asylum, where Stafford would have struck him, except that they told him it was holy ground and a place of asylum.

The episode with Joan may have taken place on the occasion of the grand dinner which Warwick gave on Sunday, 13 May, and to which Cauchon and Jean de Mailly, bishop of Noyon and others were invited. What was Luxembourg thinking of? Did he now really believe it possible to ransom her, after all the effort of persuasion and money which had been made by the English government to obtain her and have her tried? Was he stricken with remorse at having sold her into such captivity? She would be sent to her death less than three weeks later.

Joan was condemned on charges of heresy. The sentence which Cauchon read out immediately before she was led to the stake declared that she was 'relapse in (her) errors and heretical'. Initially, it was intended to bring charges of sorcery against her also, as can be seen in the summons which Cauchon delivered to Burgundy and Luxembourg. That letter does not speak of heresy, but states that Joan is 'strongly suspected and widely regarded as guilty of a number of crimes, such as spells, idolatries, invocations ...'[5] English soldiers widely feared Joan as a witch, a view which evidently seemed to the bishop of Beauvais to be the surest for a trial. In 1452, on Tuesday 9 May, at the preliminary investigations held in Rouen for the Nullity trial, Thomas Marie, prior of the Benedictine priory of Saint-Michel, near Rouen, declared:

> Joan had worked wonders during the war and since the English in general are superstitious they thought that there was something diabolical about her. So, in my opinion, in all their deliberations and elsewhere, they sought her death.
> Question: How do you know that the English are superstitious?
> Thomas Marie: People say so. It's proverbial!

Drunkenness and superstition, the general French view of the English soldiery was not flattering! Accusations of using spells and invoking demons were included in the seventy articles of accusation drawn up against Joan for consideration at the end of her trial, but they do not figure in the final twelve articles sent to Paris for the opinion of the learned gentlemen of the great University, no doubt because they were insufficiently credible. It is interesting that the letter written at the behest of the University by the Vicar-General of the Inquisition on 26 May to the Duke of Burgundy speaks more guardedly only of Joan being "strongly suspected of several crimes savouring of heresy'.

The theologians and lawyers of the Middle Ages were more sceptical of witchcraft than popular fiction would have us believe and the medieval period was by no means the great age of witchcraft trials. In 1450, when Joan's interrogator Jean Beaupère, was interviewed as a witness in the preliminaries of the Nullity hearings, he gave exactly the opinion of any modern sceptic concerning Joan's visions, ascribing them to 'natural causes and human intent' rather than to any supernatural origin. What did he mean exactly by 'natural causes and human intent'? Delusion?

Imposture? As far as her innocence was concerned, he declared that she was 'very wily, with a woman's wiliness'.[6] No doubt the academic Beaupère could only explain to himself in this way, as evidence of low cunning, the peasant girl's ability to cope with abstruse questions.

Until the end of the thirteenth century, there were few sorcery cases in Europe, while in the fourteenth and fifteenth centuries sorcery was principally a pretext for political 'show' trials, as in the case of Joan or the Templars. A small number of celebrated sorcery trials did in fact take place, that of Gilles de Rais, for example (1440), or that known as the Vauderie of Arras (1459-60), in which about thirty persons were arrested and accused of abominable crimes of devil-worship, including the ritual murder of children. In that affair, a dozen of the accused were executed, others imprisoned. However, it is interesting that public opinion was sceptical as to the guilt of the accused and hostile to the executions. The condemnations were finally overturned by a decree of the Parlement of Paris in 1491. Even in its heyday, the notorious Spanish Inquisition concerned itself mainly with not with sorcery but with heresy. Throughout Europe, from Scandinavia, through England, France, Germany and Italy, the great age of the persecution of witches and wizards was a post-Reformation phenomenon, with secular judges taking over from the clerics and showing themselves to be more severe. Jean Palou writes, 'The seventeenth century, the age of triumphant Reason, is that of the greatest number of stakes laden with witches and sorcerers.'[7]

As she was on trial for heresy, Joan should by law have been in a church prison. It was her greatest desire to be transferred to one. We may be surprised to learn that, in her time, the prisons of the Inquisition were more civilised places than secular prisons. As Olivier Bouzy writes, 'There were, in the justice system of the Church, for all its fearsome reputation, measures for the protection of the accused which did not exist in civil courts. It was felt to be essential to avoid punishing the innocent, because that would only be counter-productive.'[8] The anonymity of accusers was preserved to avoid revenge attacks by the accused's family or friends, but the accused was asked to name his or her enemies and accusations made by such persons were dropped. Perhaps it is all the more ironic then, that Joan's judges themselves were all politically her enemies. In a church prison she would not have been chained and most importantly of all, she would have been surrounded and guarded by women. She would not have lived in constant fear of being raped, a compelling reason for clinging to the protection of the male garments, for which she was finally sent to the stake. At the retrial, on 12 May 1456, the notary Manchon testified:

Several times before the beginning of the trial and often during it, Joan asked to be taken to a Church prison, but they took no heed of her and did not grant her request, for, as I believe, the English would not have handed her over and the bishop would not have wanted her to be held outside the castle...

During the trial, I heard Joan complain to the bishop and the Earl of Warwick, when they asked her why she would not wear women's clothes, since it was indecent for a woman to wear a tunic and tightly laced hose. She replied that she didn't dare to remove the hose and she had to tie them on tightly, because, as the bishop and the earl well knew, the guards had several times tried to rape her and once, when she had shouted for help, the earl had come to help her. Without him, the guards would have raped her.

Throughout the trial, Joan remained a prisoner not of the Inquisition but of the English authorities, who stipulated that she was only on loan to the court, must remain in the castle under English guard and that, if she were acquitted, they would reclaim her as their prisoner of war.[9]

The trial officially opened on 9 January 1431, when Cauchon met with eight 'assessors and consultants' in the house designated for official meetings near the castle. In all, eighteen prelates (seven bishops and eleven abbots) attended as assessors, some fairly assiduously, others only once or twice. None of Cauchon's fellow bishops appeared at more than three sessions. The three other bishops of French dioceses were Louis of Luxembourg, bishop of Thérouanne, Jean de Mailly, bishop of Noyon, and Philibert de Montjeu, bishop of Coutances. Two bishops represented England, Henry Beaufort, great-uncle of Henry VI and Cardinal of Winchester, normally referred to as the 'Cardinal of England', and William Alnwick, bishop of Norwich. Both appeared only once, in the cemetery of Saint-Ouen, on 24 May 1431, to hear Joan publicly 'preached at', and to witness her forced abjuration. Apart from these two, only six Englishmen put in an appearance, none of them on more than three occasions.

By far the two most powerful members of the clergy were Beaufort and Louis of Luxembourg. Beaufort, like Warwick, remained in the background, keeping a silent and ominous watch, hawk-like, above the pantomime. Luxembourg would end his days in England as Bishop of Ely, where his recumbent effigy can be seen in the cathedral. He appeared only at the session of 23 May and at Joan's execution on 30 May. Among the 'great and celebrated persons', as Cauchon designated those present, were Gilles de Duremont, abbot of Fécamp, Nicolas Le Roux, abbot of Jumièges, Nicolas de Venderès, the acting vicar in the *sede vacante* of the bishopric of Rouen. At that first meeting the bishop also appointed Jean d'Estivet as prosecutor, *promoteur*. D'Estivet would show himself to be particularly abusive towards Joan in the course of the trial. Numbers of assessors and consultants present at the hearings varied. A few came only once. Some more important individuals, reluctant to attend or otherwise stepping out of line, Houppeville and La Fontaine, for example, were subject to pressure and threats. The Domican friar, Isambard de La Pierre, who was with Joan until her death at the stake, declared in 1450 and again in 1452, as a witness at the Nullity trial, that the aged

Bishop of Avranches, Jean de Saint-Avit, had been threatened by Jean d'Estivet, Cauchon's prosecutor, because, when asked for his opinion, he had declared that the case ought to be sent to Rome or to the General Council. His opinion was not included in the documents of the trial.[10] In the first six 'public' sessions the average attendance was over fifty. The English treasury paid a daily rate for attendance, twenty *sous tournois*.

There was an important proviso in canon law, which in fact allowed the Inquisition to bring a prosecution only if solid evidence could be gathered beforehand that the accused had an evil reputation (defined as *diffamatio*) among respectable persons willing to testify against him or her. Did Cauchon gather such evidence and fulfil this requirement? It is evident that many questions concerning Joan's life before and after she left for Vaucouleurs can only have come from information gathered in Domrémy and other places associated with her earlier life: the Fairy Tree, how she left home, the case brought against her in Toul for breach of promise, and so on. In fact, the documents of the 1431 trial show that, prior to the public sessions, this information was read out in a session held in Cauchon's residence on the morning of 19 February 1431, in the presence of twelve chosen assessors, among them Beaupère, Midi, Jean de la Fontaine, Courcelles and Loiseleur, all major players in the drama. The slippery Thomas de Courcelles, whose memory is so defective in 1456, categorically denied at that trial that he had ever heard such information and maintained his denial even when the minutes of 19 February 1431, confirming his presence at the meeting in question, were read out to him. However, he did manage to recall what the eminent lawyer Jean Lohier had said to him in 1431:

> Maître Jean Lohier came to Rouen and orders were given for the trial documents to be handed over to him. Lohier, when he had seen them, told me that in his opinion Joan should not be proceeded against without preliminary information having been taken concerning her reputation and that such an investigation was required by law.

The trouble is that no-one outside those present on 19 February seems to have even heard of this information. Manchon, the clerk of the trial court, giving evidence on 12 May 1456, says he never saw any such documentation and that if he had done so, he would have included it in his records of the trial. His colleagues Colles and Taquel also say they never saw such a thing. It is clear, from the evidence of Courcelles and Manchon, that Lohier himself had neither seen nor heard of this information either. Yet it did indeed certainly exist. The lawyer Nicolas Bailly from Andelot, who had carried out the investigation in advance of the Rouen trial, was still alive in 1456 and gave evidence at Toul on 6 February of that year. He declared that in 1431 he had been sent by the *bailli* of Chaumont, together with the now deceased Gérard Petit, provost of Andelot, to enquire into the life and reputation of Joan, at the time a prisoner in Rouen. He mentioned that he had seen Joan several times previously, when she was still at home. Perhaps he had then been seeing her father on some business? His statement continues:

> She was always a good girl, well behaved, a good Catholic. She loved going to churches and holy places, she went on pilgrimage to Notre-Dame de Bermont, for example, and she went to confession nearly every month. I heard that from many of the people of Domrémy and also in the investigation I made with the provost of Andelot.

Nicolas Bailly says that he and his colleague interviewed ten or fifteen people, but the *bailli* of Chaumont was very displeased with them and their findings, and declared that they were 'Armagnacs in disguise'.

One witness at the later Nullity trial in 1456, a citizen of Rouen by the name of Jean Moreau, declared that he had met one of the investigators, because they both came from Lorraine. This man, whom he doesn't name, told him that when he handed in his report to Cauchon, expecting to be paid and to get his expenses, the bishop told him that he was a traitor and that he had not done what he had been told to do. So the man was not paid for his report because it didn't suit the bishop. He had heard nothing about Joan that he would not have wished to hear about his own sister.

One or two witnesses from Domrémy had some vague memory of the investigation. Jean Jaquard, a peasant farmer from Greux, recalls seeing investigators. He made the following declaration on 11 February 1456:

> I saw Nicolas Bailly from Andelot and Guillot the sergeant, and some others who came to Domrémy to carry out an investigation, so people said. As far as I know, they didn't force anyone to give evidence. I think that Jean Morel, and my own father, Jean Guillemette, also Jean Colin, all still alive, the late Jean Hennequin from Greux and several others, were interviewed. When they had finished, the commissioners left quietly, for fear of the people of Vaucouleurs. I think that this investigation was carried out at the demand of the bailli of Chaumont, a partisan of the English and Burgundians.

Jean Morel says he knows nothing about an investigation, neither does Guillemette nor Jean Colin. However, Michel le Buin, another peasant farmer from Domrémy, giving evidence on 31 January 1456, declared also that he remembered Nicolas Bailly and some others coming to Domrémy, by order of the *bailli* of Chaumont, to make an investigation into Joan's life and reputation:

> They didn't dare to force anyone to give evidence on oath, because they were afraid of the people of Vaucouleurs. Jean Begot from our village was interrogated, because they were lodged in his house. They found nothing bad about Joan in their investigations.

No doubt that is why the information was not made public at the 1431 trial, it was too favourable to Joan.

Under the statutes of the Inquisition, which was set up in the thirteenth century in response to the Albigensian (Cathar) heresy, at the time spreading in France, northern Italy and Germany, trials were conducted by the inquisitor in conjunction with the bishop in whose diocese the accused had been arrested. Heresy was seen as dangerous to society as much as to religion, therefore, if found guilty, the accused was handed over to the 'secular arm', the civil authorities, for formal condemnation and punishment. Thus the Church washed its hands (like Pontius Pilate) of the blood of the condemned. If guilty but repentant, the sentence was life imprisonment. If obdurate, the sentence was the stake. The final judgement had to be agreed by both bishop and inquisitor, a verdict pronounced by either alone was invalid. The Inquisitor of France, the Dominican Jean Graverent, pro-English though he was, found a pretext to absent himself from Cauchon's proceedings. Was he wary of any involvement in them? After Joan's death, however, on 4 July 1431, on the occasion of a religious procession to a church in Paris, the *Bourgeois* reports that 'a friar of the order of Saint Dominic', who was an inquisitor, delivered a sermon denouncing Joan violently as a homicidal limb of the devil.[11] It is not certain that the said friar was Graverent, the 'Grand Inquisitor of France', it could have been his vicar general, Martin Billorin, who in 1430, at the behest of the University, had written to Philip of Burgundy demanding that Joan be handed over to the Inquisition.[12]

On 19 February 1431, Cauchon reported to a group of his chosen assessors, Beaupère, Midi, Courcelles and others, that he had demanded the Inquisitor appoint a deputy, or 'vicar'. That same afternoon, he sent for the local inquisitor of the Rouen diocese, Jean Lemaître, and demanded that he take on the office of Inquisitor during the trial. Lemaître replied diplomatically that if Graverent should be willing to appoint him, he would of course agree to act, but that he really did not think his competence extended beyond the diocese of Rouen and therefore he would not be able to act in Cauchon's 'territoriality'. The bishop, no doubt much displeased, then required him to re-appear the following day, when, after consultation with his learned associates, he would have the answer for him. On 20 February, again in Cauchon's residence and in the presence of certain assessors, Lemaître was informed that the Inquisitor's commission fully covered him to act in the said trial. The unfortunate Lemaître protested that 'for the peace of his conscience and the proper conduct of the trial', he did not wish to be involved in the case without certainty as to where and how far his commission extended.[13] He asked Cauchon to proceed without him until such firm assurance could be obtained. At that, the bishop immediately went ahead and issued the summons for Joan to appear the next day, Wednesday, 22 February. On that day also, he sent an acerbic letter to Graverent, asking him to come in person without delay, or, if his absence was due to pressure of work or 'any other reasonable cause', to confirm quickly that Lemaître was competent to act in the case, lest Graverent's own dilatoriness be blamed for 'the prejudice caused to the Faith and the scandal given to the Christian people'.

Lemaître sat among the assessors at the first sessions of the trial, taking his place as judge alongside Cauchon only from 13 March, the third session in Joan's cell (actually the ninth interrogation) onwards. At a meeting in Cauchon's residence on the morning of Monday, 12 March, the Inquisitor of France's letter, written on 4 March and authorising Lemaître to act, was read out to Lemaître by Cauchon. He still feebly quibbled, saying he would give his response later, after seeing all the letters, but Cauchon peremptorily ordered him into line, saying he could have all the documents he needed and reminding him that he had already been present at a large part of the trial. In the event, Lemaître found himself completely overshadowed by the bishop. On 12 May, after Joan had been threatened with torture, he evaded the question put to the twelve assessors present in Cauhon's residence, as to whether torture would 'benefit' her or not, and opined merely that she should be questioned again. Only three out of the twelve others voted for torture. The rest evaded the question in the same way as Lemaître.

Nicolas de Houppeville, who, as we shall see, had had serious problems of his own as a result of voicing opinions unwelcome to Cauchon, testified in 1452 at the enquiries made in preparation for the Nullity trial and again in 1456 at the trial proper, that the inquisitor had acted under duress. He made the following statements:

> (8 May 1452, in Rouen): I know with absolute certainty that the vice-inquisitor was very fearful and I saw him extremely worried during the trials.
> (13 May 1456): The vice-inquisitor, Brother Jean Lemaître took part under duress. He was full of fear and I saw him extremely worried during the trial.

At the Nullity trial, on 12 May 1456, Massieu, the court usher, testified that Lemaître went in fear of his life: 'Lemaître said several times to me, "I can see that if we do not act according to the will of the English in this matter, we'll soon be dead."'

The first 'public' session took place on Wednesday, 21 February, the last on Saturday, 3 March. At each of these six sessions, the average number of assessors attending was in the mid fifties, some attending more assiduously than others. Thereafter the sessions took place in Joan's prison, with a greatly reduced numbers of assessors, never more than a dozen, apart from the bishop and the vice-inquisitor, sometimes fewer than six. During the week beginning Sunday, 4 March, Cauchon deliberated in his own residence, with a half a dozen or so of his experts in theology and canon law regarding Joan's testimony. They drew up a list of points on which she should be further examined. Among these eminent experts were Beaupère, Courcelles, Nicolas Midi and Nicolas Loiseleur. This latter, aged over forty, with a modest degree of Bachelor of Theology gained only in 1431, played a particularly odious role on the whole affair, as we shall see, no doubt anxious to ingratiate himself with the powers that be and with Cauchon in particular.

The minutes of the trial were taken down in French by two notaries who acted as clerks of the court, Guillaume Manchon and Guillaume Colles (also known as Boisguillaume). They collated their notes each evening. In the hearings of 1452 and 1456 for the Nullity trial, all witnesses who had been present at the original trial testified to the entire honesty of Manchon and Colles. Manchon would declare in 1456 that he had taken part unwillingly in the trial: 'I was obliged to act as notary against my will, for I wouldn't have dared to refuse to obey an order of the lords of the Royal Council.'

We may well believe that he was a reluctant participant, for he would not allow himself to be overly bullied by Cauchon. He refused, for example, to co-operate in the matter of the spying operations of Loiseleur or to sign the very questionable document drawn up after Joan's death, known as the *information posthume*, on the grounds that he had not been present at the interrogation of Jeanne which it purported to minute. A third notary, Nicolas Taquel, Beaupère's secretary, was appointed to the post by inquisitor only on 14 March. He had therefore not been present at any of the public sessions, but only at those held with a very small number of persons present in Joan's cell. Taquel's function was simply to listen attentively during the proceedings and to discuss the minutes afterwards with the others. If there was a doubt anywhere in the minutes, it was noted and read over to Joan at the next session. She either agreed the text or asked that it be emended. Her memory for what had been said or dealt with was remarkably clear and exact. Colles, giving evidence on 12 May 1456, at the Nullity trial, described her reactions:

I remember that Joan answered very prudently, for sometimes she would reply, if she was questioned about a point on which she had been interrogated previously, that she had already given her answer to that and that she would not answer again. Then she had her answers read out by the notaries.

Pierre Daron, the lieutenant of the *bailli* of Rouen, testifying on 13 May 1456, told what he had heard of Joan's extraordinary memory:

If she was interrogated on a point raised even a week before, she would reply, 'I was asked about that on such and such a day', or 'I was asked about that a week ago and I said so and so'. When Boisguillaume [Colles] once said that she hadn't replied, certain of the assessors insisted that she had done so. The reply in the minutes for the day mentioned was then read out and Joan was shown to be right. She was delighted and said to Boisguillaume that if he made another mistake, she'd box his ears!

Here is the real Joan! Some of her answers seem to be non sequiturs, or to be a reply to a subsequent question. As Pierre Tisset points out, the *minute française* is not verbatim, but a *résumé* or collation of Joan's answers.[14] Where there appears to be incoherence or contradiction, we may assume that this is because the minute-takers have somewhat condensed what seemed to them inessential, leaving out supplementary questions and conflating replies. There is no suspicion of tampering with evidence. In 1456, all those who had been present at the first trial agreed that Manchon and Colles had fulfilled their task irreproachably.

The French minutes were translated into Latin after Joan's death by Thomas de Courcelles, with Manchon present during the work.[15] This Latin translation shows, as Tisset points out, an occasional discrepancy when compared with the French.[16] In the minute for the afternoon of Saturday, 14 March, for example, where the French record of the interrogation about Franquet d'Arras, reads '(Franquet) was put to death at Arras', the Latin imputes his death to Joan herself: '(Franquet) whom *she had put to death* at Arras' (my italics). Such discrepancies are not accidental. Courcelles' command of Latin was not shaky. The five copies were made and signed by all three notaries, one copy each for Cauchon, Lemaître and Henry VI (i.e. for Bedford). Three of the five copies have survived, all now in Paris, one in the library of the Assemblée Nationale and the other two in the Bibliothèque Nationale de France. The French minute has come down to us in two manuscripts. The first is a fifteenth century copy of the original minute from which Courcelles worked. It is referred to as *U* and it is now in the Bibliothèque Nationale in Paris. It is regarded as the more reliable of the two, but is unfortunately incomplete, the first five sessions having been somehow lost. It now starts only with the sixth session, that of 3 March. The second manuscript, today in the municipal library of Orleans (and referred to as *O*), is a copy of the French minute made before 1515. It is evidently a transcription of *U* (or of the original of which *U* itself is a copy). It contains a number of omissions and a certain muddle in the order of things, but Tisset considers it to be of value and reproduces it beneath the Latin for the first five sessions.[17]

From Saturday, 10 March onwards, the venue was changed. While the first six sessions had been attended by over fifty assessors on average, Joan was henceforth to be interrogated in her prison cell, with only the bishop and Lemaître and half a dozen or fewer assessors present, as well of course as the notaries, Colles and Manchon. Why did Cauchon abandon the public sessions? In the articles which the plaintiffs drew up and presented in 1455 when demanding a retrial, it is alleged that Cauchon's motive was to restrict the proceedings to those assessors and counsellors on whom he could rely to deliver the desired hostile opinions:

Article XII: The said accused [i.e. Cauchon and Lemaître], to achieve more easily their ends and all that they planned against Joan, excluded from the sessions all those counsellors and lawyers mindful of God and justice. They changed the time and place of the interrogations and decided that she would in future be examined in the prison ... [18]

It is, as Tisset says, difficult to decide whether or not this accusation is fully justified.[19] However, it is difficult also to think of another compelling reason for the change. Cauchon had had problems with several of his assessors and counsellors. The most convincing testimony in this matter is that of the aforementioned Houppeville, who testified in 1452 and again in 1456 that Cauchon had had him thrown into prison:

(Houppeville, 13 May 1456): Towards the beginning of the trial, I took part in certain deliberations. It was my opinion that neither the bishop nor those who were to be in charge of the trial could act as judges. It did not seem to me to be correct legal procedure that those belonging to the party opposed to Joan should act as judges, given also that she had already been examined by the clergy at Poitiers and the archbishop of Rheims, the metropolitan of the bishop of Beauvais. As a result of this opinion, I incurred the furious indignation of the bishop and was summoned before him. I appeared before him and affirmed that I did not come under his jurisdiction but under that of the diocese of Rouen and so I withdrew. However, after that, while I was about to bring this affair before the Rouen diocesan court, I was arrested, taken to the castle and from there to the royal prison. When I demanded why I had been arrested, they told me it was at the request of the bishop of Beauvais. I believe it was because of the opinion which I had given, for my friend, Maître Jean de la Fontaine, sent me a note telling me that I had been detained because of that and that the bishop was very angry with me. However, at the request of the Lord Abbot of Fécamp, I was released from prison. I then heard that, on the advice of some persons brought together by the bishop, I was to be sent into exile in England or elsewhere, far from Rouen. The abbot of Fécamp and some of my friends prevented that.

This is a slightly more detailed account of the episode as told in Houppeville's evidence of 8 May 1452. At that earlier session, he had also said that he did not believe the Cauchon had been acting under pressure. In particular he spoke of once occasion when he saw the bishop conversing with Warwick:

After Joan had been taken away, I saw him coming back and speaking of his mission to the king [i.e. little Henry VI] and my lord of Warwick. All joyful and exultant, he was saying certain things which I couldn't hear. After that he spoke in private with the earl of Warwick, but I don't know what he said then.

Another dissident was the eminent canon lawyer Jean Lohier, who was in Rouen at an early stage of the trial and whom Cauchon asked to pronounce on the legality of the proceedings. The bishop was determined, as he declared more than once, that no-one should be able to find fault with his *beau procès*. However, here also he had asked the wrong man. Lohier was no longer alive at the time of the Nullity trial, but Manchon gave evidence concerning him on no less than four occasions, during the preliminaries of the trial in 1450, 1452 (twice) and again in 1456. His first and fullest statement was made on 4 March 1450. It is not included in the trial documents proper, as the actual proceedings, approved by the pope only got underway in January 1456, but Quicherat includes it his great work. Manchon testified that Lohier, having been given the trial documents by Cauchon while he was visiting Rouen and asked for an opinion, declared after studying them that the proceedings were invalid. He gave his reasons, firstly, that the trial was not held in a neutral space, where the assessors and judges had a guarantee of freedom to express their opinions, second, that it touched on the honour of the king of France in his absence, neither he nor anyone representing him being called third, that the accused was an unlettered girl and had no defence lawyer to advise her how to reply to the questions of the learned doctors in such weighty matters, especially concerning what she described as her revelations.

The outraged Bishop Cauchon told the unaccommodating lawyer to stay until the end of the trial, but Lohier had already decided that the best course was to leave at once. Cauchon left him in a rage and went straight away to find more congenial company, Jean Beaupère, Jacques de Touraine, Nicolas Midi, Pierre Maurice, Thomas de Courcelles, all luminaries of the University, and Loiseleur, who was already playing the role of spy and informer at the bishop's behest. To these faithful, the bishop gave vent to his anger, saying, according to Manchon,

> Here's Lohier who wants to hold up our proceedings! He's trying to defame the lot, saying it's all null and void. If he were to be believed, we'd have to start all over again, that all we've done so far would be rubbish! You can see where he's coming from! By Saint John! We'll take no notice and go on as we've started! [20]

That was on a Saturday in Lent, sometime before Easter Sunday which fell on I April in 1431. Several sessions of the trial would have taken place already. The next day, Sunday, Manchon happened to meet Lohier in church and asked him what he thought of the trial and of Joan. Lohier said,

> You see how they are proceeding. They will condemn her, if they can, through what she says, I mean the declarations in which she says, 'I know for certain' about things relating to the visions. If she would say, 'It seems to me that ... .' I think no-one could condemn her. It seems they

are acting from hatred rather than anything else. That's why I won't stay here any longer I don't want to be here any longer.

Manchon added that Lohier went straight away to Rome and remained there permanently, ending his days as dean of the appeals tribunal (the Rota) in the papal courts.

Manchon's testimony did not vary in the later sessions of 1452 and 1456. It was supported by other witnesses. His colleague, Massieu, gave testimony on 12 May 1456, declaring that many of the counsellors were very afraid and that Nicolas de Houppeville had been unwilling to participate in the deliberations and was banished (of course, as we have seen, he left for his own safety, rather than being banished). Massieu's evidence is less reliable than Manchon's, more based on hearsay, but he does recount one incident concerning himself personally:

> I myself was in great danger, because once, when I was taking Joan to or from the hearings, I met an Englishman called Anquetil, the cantor of the royal chapel, who asked me what I thought of Joan. I replied that I saw nothing but good in her, she seemed to me to be a good person. The cantor reported this to the Earl of Warwick, who was very annoyed. I got into a lot of trouble and at last was let off after making my apologies.

Massieu had given a slightly different version of this incident in his testimony of 8 May 1452. There he calls the Englishman Turquetil (or was the name taken down wrongly by the minute writers?) and it is Cauchon who tells him that only his friends have saved him from being thrown into the Seine. It is indeed probable that both Warwick and Cauchon wished to scare him. He was probably greatly exaggerating his danger, but the story does illustrate the tense atmosphere under which the trial was taking place.

Another witness in 1456 was Guillaume de la Chambre. With a colleague, Jean Tiphaine, he was one of the two young doctors sent to examine Joan when she became seriously ill in the prison. He was present at only three of the trial sessions, that of 3 March (the last public session), and then at those of 27 and 28 March, when the seventy articles of accusation were read out to Joan. On 2 April 1456, he was interrogated in Paris, where he declared that Jean Lohier and Nicolas de Houppeville had been threatened with drowning. Houppeville himself, in his 1452 statement, says nothing of such a threat. De la Chambre however declares that on 30 May 1431, he himself was coerced into signing the final document which sent Joan to her death:

> I signed the document. I did so because I was coerced into it by the bishop of Beauvais. I had several times tried to excuse myself to the bishop,

saying it was no part of my profession to give an opinion on such a subject. Finally I was told that if I didn't sign like everyone else it would be the worse for me in that town of Rouen and for that reason I signed.

Who told him that he had better add his signature? No doubt in 1456 he wanted to explain his conduct of twenty-five years earlier in the best possible light, but that does not mean that he perjured himself. Nor was he under any threat of prosecution for his part in the first trial, all participants therein being covered by an amnesty granted by Charles VII. Guillaume de la Chambre had been a very young man in 1431, aged about twenty-three and freshly qualified as a doctor only the year before. He was an individual of no account in that assembly of the eminent and learned and no doubt easily intimidated.

Houppeville, in 1452, gave it as his opinion that most of those who took part in the trial did so of their own free will, but that others were fearful:

(*Houppeville, Monday 8 May 1452*): In my opinion, most of the judges and assessors were acting voluntarily. There were others who were afraid, especially after what I heard about Maître Pierre Minier, whose written opinion did not please the bishop of Beauvais. He rejected it, saying that in his opinion Maître Minier should not mix up canon law and theology and that he ought to leave canon law to the lawyers. I heard that threats were made by the Earl of Warwick against Brother Isambard de la Pierre of the Dominican Order, who was attending the trial. It was said that he had been threatened with drowning if he didn't keep quiet, for he was guiding Joan in what she should say. I think I heard that from Jean Lemaître, the vice-inquisitor.

This is of course hearsay evidence, but it illustrates again the atmosphere of unease which hung over the proceedings. Houppeville repeated this evidence in his deposition of 13 May 1456, when he again appeared before the investigators, He said then also that he considered that Cauchon had pursued the trial not out of zeal for the faith or for justice, but because of the hatred Joan had aroused, being of the party of Charles VII.

On 12 May 1456, Manchon enlarged upon the deposition he had already made on 8 May 1452. He declared that Cauchon and Warwick had planned, with the help of Nicolas Loiseleur, to find a way to listen in to Joan's private conversations and had given him and his colleague instructions with a view to that end:

The Earl of Warwick, the bishop of Beauvais and Maître Nicolas Loiseleur spoke to me and my colleague [Colles]. What they said was that since Joan spoke so amazingly about her visions, they had decided, in order to get more fully at the truth, that Maître Nicolas Loiseleur,

claiming to be from Lorraine, Joan's part of the country, and saying he
was loyal to the king of France, would go into her prison dressed not
as a cleric but in ordinary clothes, the guards would withdraw and he
and Joan would be alone. In a room next to the cell an aperture had
been made in the wall, and I and my colleague were ordered to place
ourselves there, to hear what Joan would say. The earl was there also,
unseen by Joan. Loiseleur started to put questions to her, pretending to
give her news of the state of the kingdom and about her revelations.
Joan spoke with him, believing that he was from her part of the country
and loyal to her king. But when the bishop and the earl told me and my
colleague to record her replies, I replied that I couldn't do so and that
it was dishonest to start the trial that way, but that if she said the same
things in court I would be ready to record them.

Did Manchon in fact refuse to act before the plan was ever put into action?
Favier finds the idea of a 'hole in the wall' implausible,[21] and possibly
Manchon was embroidering on some such scheme which had been mooted
but dropped as unhelpful. It must be more than doubtful that he dared
to speak so bluntly to the bishop, although we may well believe that he
maintained he could not legally record such conversations. Perhaps all
concerning the eavesdropping should be in the conditional tense. It is
unlikely that Manchon would have refused immediately before, during or at
the end of Joan's conversations (by which time it would have been too late
to take notes!). In fact, in his earlier deposition, he says that he had *heard*
that Loiseleur had had confidential talks with Joan. Such conversations
could well have taken place following the interview with Cauchon and
Warwick and in the absence of note-takers and spies in the wall.

Manchon's associate clerk of the court, Guillaume Colles, told the
same story about Loiseleur in his deposition of 12 May 1456, saying
that Loiseleur pretended to be a shoemaker from Lorraine. Already, on
Monday, 8 May 1452, Massieu had testified similarly:

I heard that Maitre Nicolas Loiseleur, pretending to be a French prisoner
of the English, went sometimes secretly into Joan's prison to persuade
her not to submit to the judgment of the Church, or else she would find
she had been duped.

If that was all Loiseleur was commissioned to do, he had an easy task,
for Joan had no intention of accepting her enemies as the judges of her
spiritual experiences. With the refusal of the clerks of the court to record her
conversations, the great scheme seems to have been dropped. Tisset thinks
that in fact it was probably only tried once. Perhaps the ruse was all along
Warwick's idea rather than Cauchon's, who might well have judged it unwise
for his *beau procès*, especially if the notaries were unwilling to co-operate
and keep the matter secret. It is in any case difficult to see how Joan could

have been duped by Loiseleur after the third public session of her trial (Saturday, 24 February 1431), when he sat among the sixty-three assessors. Was it possible that he could have been hidden somewhere in the back rows, among the 'very numerous reverend fathers, doctors and *maîtres*'?

At the end of the sessions of the trial, when the seventy articles of accusation were read out to her, Article IV affirmed that, as a child, Joan had been badly instructed in her faith and encouraged to believe in magic and superstition by '*several old women*' and her godmother. Joan indignantly denied that and when she was then asked to say the Creed and other prayers, she replied, 'Ask my confessor, to whom I have said them'. Who was the confessor? Is it possible that she meant Loiseleur? If so, when did he reveal his identity as a priest to her? It seems improbable that Joan ever made her confession to him, although Manchon and Thomas de Courcelles believed she had done so. Did Loiseleur boast of such a thing to them?

It appears that the bishop had a second plan for procuring alternative minutes to those officially approved. Manchon makes a further revelation in his testimony of 12 May 1456:

When Joan was being interrogated [i.e. in court], there were notaries hidden behind curtains over a window seat. I believe that Loiseleur was hidden there with them, supervising what they wrote. They wrote whatever they liked, omitting what Joan said in her defence. I was sitting below the judges, with Guillaume Colles and Maître Guillaume Taquel [i.e. Beaupère's clerk]) and we were taking the minutes. But there were great discrepancies in what was noted, all of which ended in a serious quarrel. That was the reason why, as I said, we marked the disputed points so that Joan could be questioned about them later.

It appears from this that all the note-takers, official and unofficial, got together on at least one occasion to collate their minutes. However, the supplementary hidden minute-writers seem to have quickly disappeared from the scene, no doubt again because of the protests of the three official clerks of the court. On 8 May 1452, Manchon had already mentioned the existence of these hidden note-takers, affirming that when it was suggested to him that he should change his notes to bring them into line with the others, he refused to do so, 'saying that he had written faithfully and would change nothing, and that he did not change anything, but wrote faithfully'. His honesty as the recorder of the minutes is, as we have seen, recognised by all the witnesses who had been present at the 1431 trial.

17

Joan before the Judges

Ils croient dur au diable, mais ils ne veulent pas croire en Dieu
Claudel, *Jeanne d'Arc au Bucher*

All the legal formalities of the trial having been gone through, the first public session, at which forty-two assessors and consultants were present and Joan appeared for the first time, took place on Wednesday, 21 February 1431, at 8 o'clock in the morning, in the Royal Chapel of the castle. The subsequent five 'public' meetings would be held in a room off the Great Hall. Some time before 8 o'clock on that wintry morning, Joan was unchained in her dark room and Massieu came to fetch her, to lead her down the stairs, out into the courtyard and across to the Royal Chapel. She had requested permission to attend Mass, but before her *entrée en scène*, the bishop announced that this request had not been granted, in view of the serious crimes of which she was accused and her indecent clothing. What exactly was this indecent clothing for which, in the end, Joan will be burnt at the stake? It was described in the twelve articles of accusation sent to Paris for consultation by the learned doctors of the University: a short tunic, doublet, and hose tightly attached by many pointed laces. It was an outfit in which Joan felt to some extent protected against sexual assault.

Of course, none of those who had known Joan before her capture could be called as witnesses, Baudricourt, Dunois, Alençon, La Hire and all the others, least of all the key witness, Charles VII himself, who alone could tell them what they so insistently desired to know, the secret which Joan had revealed to him. Apart from the masculine clothing (which they took it upon themselves, heedless of other opinions, to declare to be sinful in all circumstances), their evidence was all rumour and hearsay, therefore Joan had to be made to condemn herself out of her own mouth. Throughout the trial, she was constantly put under pressure, subjected to a torrent of often tricky questions, interjections and interruptions. When he testified on 12 May 1456, at the Nullity trial, Manchon described this first session:

> During the first sessions and on the first day, in the chapel of the castle of Rouen, there was a great uproar and Joan was interrupted at nearly every word when she spoke of her visions, In fact, two or three secretaries of the king of England were there, writing down Joan's words and testimony, whatever way they liked, omitting anything that would clear her. I complained then and said that if order was not restored, I would resign as minute-writer. On account of that, the venue was changed the next day, we met in a room off the great hall, with two English guards at the door.

In the same deposition, he goes on to say:

> During the trial, Joan was exhausted by the number and diversity of the questions. Nearly every day there was a morning session lasting three or four hours, and sometimes they picked out several difficult and thorny questions arising from her answers and interrogated her on them again in the afternoon for two or three hours.

Massieu had give similar testimony on 8 May 1452:

> Often several people at a time would put disjointed or devious questions to Joan, so that before she could reply to one the next would follow. She was upset by that and would say, 'Please speak one at a time!' I admired the way she could deal with certain subtle and tricky questions that a well-educated man would have found difficult.

Jean Monnet, Beaupère's clerk, who took notes during the trial, speaks in his testimony of 3 April 1456, of the difficult questioning, saying that she seemed to him to be very worn down by it.

That first session opened with Joan being required on oath to answer truthfully all questions which would be put to her. With good reason, she was on her guard:

> Joan: I don't know what you are going to question me about. Perhaps you will ask me about things that I will not tell you.
> Cauchon: You will swear to tell the truth on all that you will be asked concerning the faith and on all that you know.
> Joan: I will willingly take the oath on all that concerns my parents and on what I have done since leaving for France, but as to the revelations which I have from God, I have never told or revealed them to anyone, except to my king, Charles, and I wouldn't reveal them if my head was going to be cut off. I have it from my visions that I should not reveal these things to anyone. In another week, I'll know if I may reveal them.

Cauchon insisted, and finally Joan, on her knees, her hands on a missal, swore to tell the truth on all that would be demanded of her concerning the faith. Significantly, the Latin minute says that she did not make any restriction, but the French minute says explicitly that she swore only to answer on matters of faith and repeated that she 'would tell no-one anything concerning her revelations'.[1] She continued to insist on this restriction throughout the trial.

At all five public sessions which followed and at the first session in her prison (10 March) Cauchon persisted in demanding that Joan swear an unconditional oath to answer truthfully any questions put to her. She steadfastly refused to answer any questions outside those relating to faith and to her career. She had never made public the private nature of her revelations, which therefore could not be seen as instruments of heretical teaching and she well understood that the major aim of the trial was not only to condemn her, but through her to destroy Charles VII and his claim to be the rightful king of France. Joan was repeatedly interrogated about her 'Voices' during her trial. Their political importance was momentous, for if they could be shown to be fraudulent or diabolical or even simply illusory, Charles VII's whole war operation would be discredited. He would at a vital point have accepted that his troops be led by a dabbler in black magic ('the witch of the Armagnacs' as Joan was in the minds of the English), or a charlatan, or a deranged female. There was no lack of half-crazy or fraudulent prophets (mostly prophetesses) and visionaries about in those troubled times. Colette Beaune remarks that the frequency of their appearance was strongly connected to the political situation and that it eased off in periods of peace. At all events, if Joan were discredited, it would be most definitely shown that the Almighty was not on the Dauphin's side. In any case, how could the Anglo-Burgundians possibly allow that He might indeed be in favour of the opposite camp? They might as well pack up and go home at once. The prejudice of the judges, conscious or unconscious is easily understood. Less forgivable is the deliberate misrepresentation of the evidence in the seventy articles of accusation and the final twelve articles on which Joan was condemned.

Pierre Miget, prior of the Abbey of Longford-Giffard, who had been, as Tisset points out, 'very assiduous at the trial', commented in 1452, at the Nullity trial, that Joan's judges 'wanted to prove that she was a heretic, in order to discredit the king of France'. We may regret that he hadn't had the courage to make that point in 1431. Joan's loyalty to Charles VII would be total throughout the trial. In particular she was determined that under no circumstances would she reveal to them what she had told Charles at Chinon. If credence is given to the story recounted by Pierre Sala in *Les Hardiesses des grands Rois et Empereurs,* we can fully understand why she could not reveal it, for to let his adversaries know that Charles himself had had doubts about his legitimacy would have been to hand them a trump card in the political game.

The opening of that first session was taken up with establishing Joan's identity, age and background. Then she was asked about her religious education. She replied that her mother, and no-one else, had taught her the Our Father, the Hail Mary and the Creed. At that, the bishop asked her to recite the Our Father. She replied that she would only do so if he would hear her in confession. The most likely explanation for this demand is that she hoped that in the sacrament of confession Cauchon could not fail to be convinced of her innocence. The bishop was not however obliged to hear her confession and he proposed other clerics who would hear her say her prayers, but these she refused to accept unless they would actually hear the confession. The bishop then closed the session, warning Joan not to try to escape under pain of being convicted of the crime of heresy, a quite preposterous threat, since escaping had nothing to do with unorthodox belief. Joan answered:

> Joan: I do not accept this prohibition. If I were to escape, no-one could accuse me of having broken faith, since I have never given my faith to anyone. I protest moreover at being held in chains and with iron shackles.
> Cauchon: You have already attempted to escape from other prisons, that is why we have ordered you to be held in shackles and chains, so that you can be more securely guarded.
> Joan: It is true that I tried and that I would try again to escape, as is the right of any prisoner.

We see from this exchange that Joan's spirit was still unbroken after the couple of months of grim captivity. She will grow wearier, worn down in body and mind as time goes on, but steadfast to the end. Cauchon concluded the session by handing her over to the custody of Sir John Grey, John Berwoit and William Talbot, the three in charge of security.

In the second session (Thursday, 22 February), Joan was questioned about her visions, about leaving home, about Baudricourt, about her visit to the duke of Lorraine, about the journey to Chinon, about the meeting with Charles VII, who; she declared, had also had revelations, about the attack on Paris and the fact that it took place on 8 September, a major feast-day of the Church. She wearily refused to make any comment about this last point and Cauchon wound up the proceedings, considering that he had covered enough ground for that day. It was in the course of this session that for the first time, she was asked if, when she met the king and recognised him, she saw an angel hovering over him, to which she answered: 'I'm sorry, pass!'. In the fourth session, on 27 February, the question was raised again, this time by the interrogator, Beaupère. When later Joan would construct an allegory in answer to persistent questioning about what she had privately told the king, questions which she was unwilling to answer, it will be worth remembering that it was Cauchon and Beaupère themselves who first introduced the idea of an angel into her account of her meeting with Charles.

The third session, on Saturday, 24 February, opened as usual with Cauchon demanding an unconditional oath. Joan spoke up:

Allow me to speak. In faith, you could ask me to tell you things that I would refuse to tell you. You could ask me a lot of things about which I wouldn't reveal the truth, things concerning my revelations, or you might compel me to tell you something which I have sworn not to tell, and then I would be guilty of breaking my oath and you shouldn't want that. I'm telling you to be very careful when you call yourself my judge, for you are taking on a heavy responsibility and you are oppressing me with these charges.

Cauchon warned her that she was putting herself in great danger, but again she would only swear to tell the truth on matters concerning the trial.

At this point, Beaupère took over the interrogation.[2] In her answers, Joan stated that the Voice came to her every day, very often on numerous times during the day, that she had heard it the previous day at the hours of matins, vespers and the evening Angelus. She had been wakened by the Voice, which had told her to answer boldly and that God would help her. Again she warned the bishop: 'You say you are my judge. Be careful what you do, because in truth I have been sent by God and you are putting yourself in great peril'.

The questioning continued:

Beaupère: Is God displeased when you tell the truth?
Joan: The Voices told me to tell certain things to the king, and not to you.

Then she declared, suddenly elated:

Last night, the Voice told me many good things for my king, which I would like him to know at present, even should I not drink wine from now till Easter! It would make him merrier at his dinner!

When asked if she couldn't tell her Voice to bring this good news to her king, she replied that if God wanted him to know it, He could convey the message Himself! A ready wit and common sense were a large part of her armour.

More interrogations on the same topic followed and then Beaupère put the sixty-four million dollar question:

Beaupère: Do you know whether you are in a state of grace?
Joan: If I am not, may God put me there, and if I am, may He keep me there. I would be the most unhappy person in the whole world if I knew that I was not in God's grace.

In 1456, the notary Colles, testifying at Rouen on 12 May, would remember this electrifying reply. He declared that those hearing it were simply astounded. That a simple peasant girl could avoid the pitfall laid for her with such an answer, admirable in its humility and flawless in its orthodoxy, sent a tremor through the court. At the Nullity trial (1456), Jean le Fèvre (later to become bishop of Démétriade) said he had protested that the question was too difficult, whereupon Cauchon had rebuked him, saying, 'It would be better for you to hold your tongue.' The question was, of course, of the catch-22 variety: if Joan had claimed to *know* that she was in a state of grace, she would have committed the sin of overweening pride (by which the very angels fell!), but if she said that she was not in such a state, she was damning herself out of her own mouth.

It has been pointed out that a prayer along similar lines existed around the time,[3] however, even if Joan found her inspiration there, she certainly used it at the right moment and to the greatest effect. Régine Pernoud suggests that Joan's reply could itself have been the inspiration for a prayer composed at some later date, adding that the astonishment of the assessors is implausible if they had any knowledge of a current prayer of the sort. Be that as it may, it was perhaps this answer to his clever question which caused Beaupère to comment sourly that she was indeed 'very wily, with a woman's wiliness'.

After further interrogation concerning her childhood, in particular on such topics as the folklore of Domrémy, the Fairy Tree and the Oak Wood (*le Bois Chenu*), all of which could serve as the elements of a charge of sorcery, she was asked if she wanted to have a woman's dress. Once again she gave a no-nonsense reply: 'Give me one. I'll put it on and leave. Otherwise I won't take it. I am content with what I have since it pleased God that I should wear it.' The judges had had enough, the session was concluded for that day.

Curiously enough, during that session of 24 February, Joan asked that she be given a written record of the points on which she had been questioned but had not at present replied. She certainly could not write, except possibly to sign her name, and it seems very unlikely that she could read. If she had not by this point totally lost faith in Loiseleur, perhaps she hoped that he would advise her on the points. As to writing, it was not a skill highly prized by the nobility. Not writing was not a proof that one could not read. As far as writing was concerned, there were secretaries and clerics for that.

The fourth session took place on the following Tuesday, 27 February. She had been unwell over the weekend. Beaupère began his interrogation by asking her politely how she had been since the previous session. She answered wearily, 'You can see for yourself how I have been. I've been as well as I could manage to be.' Once again she was subjected to lengthy questioning about the apparitions, the appearance of saints Catherine and Margaret, how they were dressed, how she could recognise them.

Beaupère: Was it the voice of an angel which spoke to you, or was it the voice of a saint, or of God directly?

Joan: It was the voice of Saint Catherine and of Saint Margaret. Their faces are crowned with beautiful crowns, very rich and precious. I have our Lord's permission to tell you that. But if you doubt it, send to Poitiers where I have been already interrogated.

She would ask twice more in the course of this interrogation that they should send for the book of Poitiers, for, she said, 'It is recorded in the register of Poitiers'. Of course, they were not interested in the book of Poitiers, which had found no suspicion of heresy or sorcery in her. Other apparently puerile questions followed: were the saints dressed in the same clothes? What age were they? Did they speak at the same time or one after the other? To all of which Joan wearily replied that she can't say.

Jean Guitton makes clear the point of so many apparently silly questions during the interrogations. For the medieval mind, as he says, there was no problem in believing in the reality of the supernatural, of spiritual beings. The question was simply to discern whether such spirits were good or evil in origin. 'The judges knew that the persons seen in visions or in an ecstasy do not have the same kind of reality as the objects of natural perception, because they are not natural, but supernatural. They are objects of revelation, not of perception. For them to condemn her, therefore, it sufficed that Joan should say that the objects of her mystical experiences were similar to physical things'.[4] Hence all these crafty questions about physical traits, hair, dress and the rest. Joan knew nothing of these metaphysical distinctions and answered the questions as best she could or said that she hadn't permission to answer them. The wrong answer would serve as proof that her visions were not heavenly, but diabolical. Guitton writes, 'Joan never gave a coherent account, she was unable to harmonise the details. She was replying to crafty questions, thrown at her at random, often puerile or devious. Sometimes, through weariness or lack of experience and learning, she came close to falling into the trap laid for her'.

Essentially, it seems from what she said, that Joan was only aware of a light, a voice or voices and a vision of faces. She could say nothing about hair, clothes, body or limbs. She declared that she knew they came from God because they comforted her and because the doctrine they taught her was orthodox (although of course she did not use that word).

She said that the first apparition was Saint Michael, whom she saw when she was aged about thirteen: 'I saw Saint Michael before my very eyes. He wasn't alone, but accompanied by angels from Heaven. I came into France only at God's command.' She would add, later in the session: 'I would rather be torn apart by wild horses that to have come into France without the permission of God.'

Beaupère asked her what sign she could give them that her revelations were from God? Her answer shows clearly how tired she was:

Joan: I have told you well enough that they are Saint Catherine and Saint Margaret. Believe. me or not, as you like.

The cross-examination moved onto another topic:

Beaupère: Were you told to put on men's clothes?
Joan: The clothes are of no consequence, nothing at all. I didn't take men's clothes on the advice of anyone in the world. I didn't take these clothes or do anything except at the command of God and His angels.
Beaupère: Do you think that the command to take men's clothing was lawful?
Joan: All that I have done was at Our Lord's command. If He had commanded me to take different clothing, I would have done so, since it would have been God's command.
Beaupère: Did you do it by order of Robert de Baudricourt?
Joan: No.

After that, the questions moved on to the subject of Charles VII and the revelations:

Beaupère: Was there an angel on the head of your king when you saw him for the first time?
Joan: By Our Lady! I don't know if there was and I certainly didn't see one!

Ask a silly question! The old flash of repartee had not been extinguished.

The spotlight of the questioning turned then onto Charles VII. Joan again refused to reveal what she had told him and once more referred the judges to the records at Poitiers. In answer to other questions, she spoke about the sword found on her instructions at Fierbois, about the army at Orleans, about the wound that she suffered there, She was asked if she had known in advance that she would be wounded and replied in the affirmative, adding that her two saints had revealed it to her.

The fifth session was fixed for two days later, Thursday, March 1. Again the demand for an unconditional oath, again the same steadfast refusal and the declaration that she was perfectly willing to tell 'Everything that I know which truly concerns this trial.'

The session kicked off with a trick question:

Beaupère: Who do you believe to be the true pope?
Joan: Are there two?
Beaupère: Didn't you receive letters from the Count of Armagnac asking you which of three popes he ought to obey?

Joan: He did send me letters on that subject, and I answered, among other things, that when I would be in Paris or somewhere and had more time, I would answer him. I made that reply as I was getting onto my horse.

Cauchon then had Armagnac's and Joan's letters read out, and asked her if she recognised her own reply, to which she replied that she recognised part of it, but not all. Did she say that she knew by revelation from God what the Count should do? She answered as follows:

I didn't know what to say to him about whom he should obey, for the Count wanted to know what God wanted him to do. But as for me, I believe firmly that we should obey our lord the Pope who is in Rome. I told the count's messenger other things which are not in your copy of the letters. If the messenger hadn't left at once, he would have been thrown into the river, but not by me. I told him I didn't know what God wanted and I sent messages about other things which were not written down. As for me, I believe firmly in our lord the Pope who is in Rome.

The Count of Armagnac had had his own reasons for asking Joan's advice. The Great Schism had been brought to an end in 1417 with the election of Martin V as pope, but there were still obstinate claimants to the papacy, the anti-pope Clement VII in Spain, who in fact gave up his pretentions in July 1429, and the elusive self-styled Benedict XIV, to be found nobody knew where. The Count of Armagnac had been a supporter, for political reasons, of this latter. Pope Martin V excommunicated him in March 1429. This had serious consequences for his rights over his domains, since it released his subjects from their oath of fidelity and gave his lands over to the king of France. In August 1429, he believed he had found a (literally!) heaven-sent opportunity to change sides without loss of face and to give his allegiance to Martin V and Charles VII. His excommunication was in fact revoked in 1430.

His letter was a serious embarrassment for Joan, who had obviously given a hasty reply, not fully understanding what the whole thing was about. In Article XXX of the seventy articles of accusation, the prosecutor, D'Estivet accuses Joan of having cast doubt on the papacy of Martin V and of having had the presumption to put her own authority over that of the Church, claiming direct communication with God. This would have been a major charge against her. It is very significant that the whole affair is omitted from the twelve final articles of accusation which were sent to the University of Paris and on which she was condemned. Tisset strongly suspects that the copy of the letter which D'Estivert inserted into his seventy articles contained damning interpolations and that the whole charge had to be dropped. Tisset is all the more sure that the letter from Joan has been doctored, since the matter is never referred to again in the trial after 27 March, when the articles were read to Joan.[5] To this article, as well as to others, she simply and wearily answered that she had already replied. We may recall that she said that she recognised parts of the letter, but not all.

Other letters were brought up as charges against her. Why did she put the names *Jesus Maria* in the letter heading, followed by a cross? She said that sometimes the cross was put there to indicate that what was in the letter was not to be obeyed. It was in fact a code to mislead the enemy. Article XXIV accuses her of abusive use of the holy names. The letter to the duke of Bedford was read out to her. She recognised it, apart from a couple of significant details: instead of the words *give to the Maid* (i.e. give the keys of all the good towns), it should read *give to the king*, moreover she had not styled herself 'chief of staff' (*chef de guerre*). In Article XXIII, d'Estivet writes:

> From these letters, it is clearly evident that Joan has been deceived by evil spirits and that she frequently consults them on what she should do, or else that, in order to seduce the people, she wickedly and mendaciously invents such fictions.

After the reading of the letter to Bedford, Joan made an astounding statement:

> Joan: I know by revelation that before seven years are out, the English will lose a greater prize then they did at Orleans and they will lose all in France. They will suffer a greater loss than they have ever had in France, through a great victory which God will give to the French. I know that by revelation as clearly as I know that you are here in front of me.

It was a bold prediction and, like all predictions, veiled in a certain aura of mystery. What is certain, however, is that on 17 April 1436, Paris was taken by French troops under the command of the Constable, Arthur de Richemont, together with Dunois, La Hire and others, aided by the citizens in revolt. The English garrison was given a safe-conduct and allowed to leave by the river. An amnesty was promised by Richemont on behalf of Charles VII to all citizens, whatever their allegiance had been. Was Paris the great prize? After Paris, Normandy still had to be recovered, but Joan does not say that the loss of all in France would occur simultaneously with the loss of the great prize.

Under further questioning on 1 March, Joan again named saints Catherine and Margaret as her informants and maintained that they spoke to her every day. There followed more demands for physical descriptions of her visions, and again she could only say that she was aware of faces and that the two saints spoke very beautifully to her. Beaupère asked her to describe the voice:

Joan: The voice is beautiful, gentle and humble and speaks the language of France.
Beaupère: Does Saint Margaret speak English?
Joan: Why would she speak English, since she is not on the side of the English?

One hopes there was a ripple of amusement in court here at Beaupère's discomfiture. One would like to think that some at least of the assembly had a sense of humour. Speaking English to Joan would not have been particularly helpful. On 12 March, she was asked a similarly ludicrous question: Did she receive letters from Saint Michael or her Voices? Even if the angels were in the habit of writing letters, it is unlikely that Joan could have read them. Probably the agenda behind the question was to discover whether she had been coached by some hidden agency.

Next she was asked whether the saints had earrings, Joan replied that she didn't know.

Beaupère: Have you yourself got any rings?
Joan *(looking straight at the presiding judge, Bishop Cauchon)*: You, Bishop, you have a ring of mine. Give it back to me!

Rings were regarded with suspicion as being amulets used in superstitious practices, divination or witchcraft. In answer to the question about rings, Joan now mentioned a ring given to her by her parents at Domrémy, which the Burgundians had taken from her, and another given to her by her brother Pierre and which she asks should be given to the Church. She denied that she had ever tried to cure anyone by means of the rings. She was asked what promises the Voices had made to her:

Beaupère: What promises did they make?
Joan: That has nothing to do with your trial.
Beaupère (insists): What promises?
Joan: They said that the king would be re-established in his kingdom whether his adversaries wished it or not. They promised to take me to Heaven, as I had asked them.
Beaupère: Was there any other promise?
Joan: Yes, there was one other. But I won't tell you what it was, because it has nothing to do with this trial. But before three months are out, I will tell you.
Beaupère: Did the Voices tell you that before three months were out you would be delivered from prison?
Joan: That has nothing to do with your trial. However, I don't know when I will be delivered.
Beaupère: Did your Counsellors not tell you that you would be delivered from your present captivity?
Joan: Ask me again in three months, I will tell you then.

But in three months she would be dead.

The ring given to her by her parents, the spring near the fairy tree at Domrémy, anything which could be construed as sorcery, was brought up again. Then, like a bolt from the blue came the next leading question:

Beaupère: What did you do with your mandragore?6
Joan: I don't have a mandragore. I have never had one.

She must next have been asked a question which is not recorded, and to which she gave the following answer:

Joan: I have heard that it is a dangerous, wicked thing. But I don't know what it is for.
Beaupère: Where is the mandragore you heard about?
Joan: I've heard it said that it is buried in the ground, near the tree you mentioned. I don't know the exact place. I heard people say that there is a hazel tree over it.
Beaupère: What use is it?
Joan: They say it brings money, but I don't believe any of that.
Beaupère: Did your Voices tell you about it?
Joan: No, my Voices never said anything at all about it.

Article VII accuses Joan of being 'sometimes in the habit of carrying a mandragore in her bosom, hoping by this means to acquire a fortune in wealth and worldly acquisitions ...'. It had to be dropped, like a great many others, from the final list of twelve accusations. It was simply too preposterous.

Next, Beaupère came back to Saint Michael:

Beaupère: How did Saint Michel look when he appeared to you?
Joan: I didn't see any crown. As for his clothes, I don't know anything about them.
Beaupère: Was he naked?
Joan: Do you think Our Lord hasn't the wherewithal to clothe him?
Beaupère: Has he got hair?
Joan: Why would they have shaved it off?

The attempt to find the girl fantasizing about a naked man is obvious. But here again Beaupère drew a blank. This theme of the bodily attributes of the visions was taken up again near the end of the trial. On 17 March, the second interrogator appointed by Cauchon put the following questions to Joan:

La Fontaine: Did you kiss or embrace saints Catherine and Margaret?
Joan: I embraced both of them.
La Fontaine: Did they have a good odour?

Joan: It's a good thing to know that they had a good odour!
La Fontaine: When you embraced them, did you feel any heat or
anything else coming from them?
Joan: I could hardly embrace them without feeling and touching them!
La Fontaine: Did you embrace the upper or lower part of their bodies?
Joan: It is more correct to embrace the lower than the upper part.

Joan has never been able to describe anything but a great light and a vision
of celestial faces and here, if we look at the statement closely, she does
not say that she embraced the knees of her visions, but merely states that
the honour due to them is the honour due to royalty, which is to kneel
and embrace the king's knees, as she herself had done when admitted to
Charles VII's presence after Orleans (Dunois' depositon). The interrogator
has asked for a physical description, is she trying to portray the experience
in terms which he will understand, to put an end to the wearisome
questioning? And is she thereby thereby falling into the trap which Guitton
sees, attributing corporality to what she alleges are mystical experiences?
    The interrogator switched ground again:

La Fontaine: When you make your confession, do you believe you are
in a state of mortal sin?
Joan: I do not know whether I have ever been in a state of mortal sin,
I don't believe I have ever committed sins of that sort. May God forbid
that I should ever have been in such a state or that I should do, or cause
to be done, things which would so burden my soul.

They then turned from that subject to hark back to her refusal to take
an unconditional oath, and to demand that she reveal the 'king's secret'.
Did she see a crown on the king's head when she showed him the 'sign'?
Again she refused to answer, Andrew Lang points out that it is again the
interrogators who first introduce the idea of a mystical crown, another
symbol that Joan will weave into her allegory. The questioning was
persistent, but again Joan declared that she had promised her saints to
keep silence and that she could not break that promise without perjuring
herself. The session was then drawn to a close.
    The final public session took place on Saturday, 3 March. After the
usual demand for an unconditional oath and Joan's refusal to reveal
anything outside the scope of the trial, the attack was launched yet again
on the old grounds, the Voices, the appearance of her saints, the male
clothing, anything which could be adduced as superstition or smacking of
sorcery. Early in the session she was asked if she knew by revelation that
she would escape, the dialogue went as follows:

Beaupère: Do you know by revelation that you will escape?
Joan: That doesn't concern this trial. Do you want me to speak against
myself?

Beaupère: Haven't your Voices said anything about it?
Joan: It doesn't concern this trial. I trust in God. If it concerned the trial, I would tell you, but by my faith, I don't know the day nor the hour when I will escape.
Beaupère: Haven't the Voices told you anything about it in general?
Joan: Yes, indeed. They have told me that I will be liberated and that I must keep my courage up boldly, but I don't know the day nor the hour.

The pronouncement of the Voices is sibylline indeed. Joan was next questioned about her male clothing:

Beaupère: do you remember whether the clerics of your party who examined you, some for a month, the others for three weeks, asked you about your change of clothing?
Joan: I don't remember. They did ask me where I had first worn it and I told them it was in Vaucouleurs.

Her judges and interrogators were well aware that Joan had been exhaustively examined by clergy already and that no fault had been found in her. No condemnation had been made of the male garments. In reply to more questions, she repeated that the ladies of Beaurevoir had offered her a dress or to have female garments made for her, but she had not yet God's permission to change her apparel.

She was asked after that whether her men-at-arms had banners made in imitation of hers? Some may have done so, she answered, but only to distinguish them from other troops. Did she tell them that the banners would be lucky? The exchange here seems to have some gaps in the minutes, for the only answer given is: 'Sometimes I said, "Go in boldly among the English," and I went in like that myself.'

So it went on:

Beaupère: Did your men have the names Jesus Maria painted on their banner:
Joan: By my faith, I know nothing about that.

Then an enigmatic, apparently idiotic question:

Beaupère: When you were outside the town of Jargeau, what was it you carried behind your helmet? Was it something round?
Joan: By my faith, there was nothing!

Joan's exclamation shows that she was as mystified as any of us by the question. They then asked her about Brother Richard, did he preach when she arrived, did she have images of herself painted, were Masses or prayers said in her honour? To this last she replied:

Joan: I don't know anything about that. If they were, I didn't order any such thing. But if people have prayed for me, it seems to me that they were doing nothing wrong.

Beaupère: Do those of your party firmly believe that you are sent by God?

Joan: I don't know if they believe that, it's their business. But whether they believe it or not, I am indeed sent by God.

Beaupère: Do you think they are right to believe you are sent by God?

Joan: If they believe I am sent by God, they are not mistaken.

Beaupère: do you know what they were thinking of when they kissed your feet, hands and clothes?

Joan: Many wanted to see me and I stopped them kissing my hands as best I could. But the poor liked to come to me because I brought them no trouble, but helped them as best I could.

Joan did not forget that she was of the people herself and she understood their sorrows and problems. The interrogation continued:

Beaupère: Did you hold any infants at the baptismal fonts?

Joan: I held one infant for baptism at Troyes. I don't remember doing so at Rheims or Château-Thierry. But I did so twice at Saint-Denis. I liked to give the name Charles to the boys in honour of the king and the name Joan to the girls. Sometimes I just gave whatever name pleased the mothers.

Beaupère: Did the women in the towns touch your ring with their rings?

Joan: Many women touched my hands and my rings, but I don't know what they were thinking or what they intended.

The questions jumped from one topic to another. More questions sought to show that she had claimed to have the powers of a seer. In Rheims, what did she do with the gloves which the king used at his coronation? She answered that all the nobles had been presented with gloves and that somebody had lost his, but she had never said that she knew where to find them. Next question, please!

Beaupère: Have you received the sacraments in male clothing?

Joan: Yes. But I don't remember doing so under arms.

Beaupère: Why did you take the bishop of Senlis's horse?

Joan: The horse was bought for two hundred saluts d'or. I don't know if he received the money or not. However he either had a credit note or he was paid. I even wrote to the bishop to tell him that he could have the horse back, if he wished, because it wasn't suitable, it wasn't fit for the work.

With all these questions, Cauchon was failing to get the damning responses he required.

The interrogation continued relentlessly: had she claimed to resurrect a child at Lagny? What had happened with Catherine de La Rochelle? Had she not gravely sinned in jumping from the tower at Beaurevoir? Did she blaspheme the name of the Lord after that incident? We are already acquainted with her answers to all those questions.

The session came to an end. Joan was led back to her prison. Cauchon announced that he was going to call a commission of experts to consider Joan's answers and decide on the points which required further investigation. Joan would in future be interrogated by a small number of persons deputed by the bishop himself, without bothering the hitherto large number of assessors, who were however forbidden to leave Rouen without his permission.

The first session in Joan's cell took place on Saturday, 10 March. La Fontaine had been appointed by Cauchon as interrogator. Besides Cauchon and La Fontaine, only three others were present, plus Massieu and of course the two minute-takers, Manchon and Colles. These sessions would concentrate on five capital points: her motivation, whether mercenary or delusion, the visions, whether delusion or fiction, the king's secret, the male clothing, in general her reputation, and finally, whether she had encouraged the people to worship her. The interrogations were all directed towards discrediting her on these counts.

La Fontaine started the proceedings with close questioning about Compiègne and her capture. We have read earlier how she spoke of her extraordinary experience at Melun, when she had the revelation that she would be captured before Saint John's Day, and her continuation with her campaign, despite that knowledge. La Fontaine asked if she had gone out on the day of her capture in obedience to the 'Voices' and she answered: 'I didn't know I would be captured that day and I had no revelation or command from my Voices to make the sortie, but I had always been told that I would be captured.'

La Fontaine then turned to questions about the standard and her escutcheon and coat of arms. She gave the following information:

I never had an escutcheon and coat-of-arms. The king gave an escutcheon and arms to my brothers, an azure shield with two gold lilies and a sword between them. I described them to a painter in this town who asked me about them. The arms were given to my brothers by the king, without any request on my part nor any revelation. 7

Next she was asked what rewards she had received from the king. The object of the questioning was of course to establish whether her whole epic had been essentially a money-making enterprise:

La Fontaine: When you were taken did you have a horse, a charger or a trotter?

Joan: I was mounted on a charger.

La Fontaine: Who gave you the horse?

Joan: The king, or else his men gave me money from the king. I had five chargers, paid for by the king's money and seven trotters.

La Fontaine: Did you ever receive any other valuables from the king?

Joan: I never asked for anything except good weapons, good horses and money to pay my staff.

La Fontaine: Did you have funding?

Joan: I had 10,000 or 12,000 crowns, it was not a huge fund for conducting a war, in fact it was quite modest. My brothers have it now, I think. Whatever I have is the king's money [i.e. not hers].

Now La Fontaine came to the third vital point for investigation. Two crucial topics had been raised, the Voices and the question of a mercenary motivation, but no damning evidence had been uncovered. Now the king's secret must be probed:

La Fontaine: What was the sign you gave your king, when you came to him?

Joan: It is a good and honorable sign. Credible and good and the most precious sign in the whole world.

Clearly she is hoping to put her interrogator off with this vague answer, When he persists, she will have recourse to allegory, as she admitted on the morning of her death. Medieval people were of course much better acquainted with allegory and delighted by it than is our modern more prosaic world. The interrogation continues:

La Fontaine: Why won't you show us this sign, just as you wanted to see Catherine de la Rochelle's sign?

Joan: If Catherine de la Rochelle's sign had been shown to me in the presence of important churchmen and others, bishops and archbishops, the archbishop of Rheims and others whose names I don't know, also Charles de Bourbon, Monseigneur de la Trémoille, the Duke of Alençon and others, noblemen who saw and heard as well as I can see you in front of me, speaking to me, I wouldn't have asked any more about her sign.

Does she actually mean that all these people were persuaded by Charles's very evident joy immediately he had spoken with her in Chinon? Was his joy the sign for them?

Then she was asked if the sign was made of gold or silver, was it a jewel or a crown? She answered:

Joan: I won't tell you any more. No man could describe anything as rich as the sign. But the sign you need, is that God should deliver me out of your hands, that's the surest sign He could give you.

La Fontaine: Did the churchmen of your party see the sign?

Joan: When my king and those with him saw the sign and the angel who brought it, I asked him if he was content. He replied that he was. Then I left and went into a nearby chapel and I heard that, after I left, more than three hundred people saw the sign. For love of me and so that the interrogations would cease, those of my party who saw the sign were allowed by God to see it.

La Fontaine: Did your king and you bow down to the angel when he brought the sign?

Joan: Yes, we did so.

It has been pointed out that since her revelations concerned a political personage, Charles VII, and not a cleric, the judges and interrogators in Rouen were clearly and radically exceeding their rights in such demands. Joan is refusing 'to involve ecclesiastical authority in a political cause', says the Carmelite commentator, Jean-Marie Lethel. It raises the question of how far the authority of the Church can extend. The attitude of her judges is 'a veritable ecclesiastical totalitarianism'. as Lethel goes on to say, 'Theology has unfortunately degenerated into ideology in other cases, but the degradation has rarely attained such a degree of perfection'. In this light, the whole trial is 'an extremely radical attempt to nullify what is most precious and sacred in the personality', in other words, the individual conscience. [8]

The interrogation ended at that on this first occasion. It finishes with what is clearly Joan's initial attempt to construct an allegory in order to put an end to the questioning about her revelations concerning Charles VII. The angel is Joan, the churchmen are the judges at Poitiers as well as those present when she met the king. When all these people 'see the sign' it is God who operates this conversion in them, allowing them to 'see the light'. The crowd of people who witnessed these wonders are those present at the meeting between Joan and Charles (Joan is not quite clear about who was actually there). The allegory is somewhat confused, for Joan, very tired no doubt, was making it up as she went along, using the motif of the angel, earlier introduced by Cauchon and Beaupère. La Fontaine's introduction here of a mystical crown will be an element that she will use in the session of 13 March.

The second interrogation in Joan's cell took place on Monday, 12 March, in the presence of Cauchon and six assessors. Jean de la Fontaine took up the questioning on the visions:

La Fontaine: Was the angel who brought the sign to the king the same angel who first appeared to you?

Joan: Yes, He has never failed me.

La Fontaine: Did he not fail you when you were captured?

Joan: I believe, since such was God's will, that it was all for the best that I was captured.

Other questions followed. Joan declared that Saints Catherine and Margaret came to comfort her every day, they never failed to come when she had need of them. The questions then abruptly change course. We abandon the angels and saints and the spotlight now turns on Joan's character. La Fontaine suddenly puts to Joan this question of the type *When did you stop beating your wife?*:

> La Fontaine: Why did you summon a man to appear in a breach of promise case at Toul?'
> Joan: I didn't summons him, it was he who summonsed me and I swore before the judge to tell the truth. I never made him any promise. The first time I heard the Voice, I made a vow to remain a virgin as long as it would please God. I was about thirteen then. The Voices assured me that I would win the case in Toul.

In the seventy Articles of accusation it is stated that the young man died before the end of the case, thus two awkward facts are avoided: the young man brought the case and Joan won it. But if, as the article states, Joan brought a case against him, why was he unwilling to marry her? An ingenious explanation is found for that question. As we remember, during the troubled period of the Burgundian siege of Vaucouleurs, the villagers of Domrémy had taken refuge in the neighbouring town of Neufchâteau and Joan's family had lodged in 'the house of a woman called La Rousse', as Joan herself declared later in the same session. However, Article VIII tells a very different story, stating that, 'in the house of a woman called La Rousse', a woman of ill-repute running a hostelry for prostitutes and soldiers, Joan had worked as a serving wench. Discovering her shocking past, the young man refused to marry her. No doubt these slanders had been gathered from unnamed sources before the trial began, in the 'preliminary investigations' which La Fontaine refers to.

This calumny was refuted by the testimony of witnesses at the Nullity hearings in 1456. The first three testified in Domrémy on 29 and 30 January. Étienne de Syonne, a priest of Neufchâteau stated that he had been told by a number of people 'that Joan went to the house of a woman in Neufchâteau because of the bands of armed men. And she was always in the company of her father and others of her village who had taken refuge there'. Gerard Guillemette, a *laboureur* aged about 40 (therefore a little younger than Joan), remembers being in Neufchâteau with the other refugees. He always saw her with her parents and remembers that she helped the *hôtesse* of the inn, a 'decent woman called La Rousse', about the house. Colin, another *laboureur*, aged about fifty, the son of Jean Colin of Greux and widower of Joan's sister Catherine, testified that everyone had fled to Neufchâteau and that Joan was there 'with her parents'. Husson Lemaistre, native of a village near Domrémy and by profession a coppersmith, gave evidence in on 11 May 1456 in Rouen, where he was living at that time. He said that he and his wife had known

Joan's family well and that on the occasion of the coronation of Charles VII they had met up with Joan's father and brother Pierre in Rheims. He testified that at Neufchâteau Joan had stayed in the house of 'a virtuous woman called La Rousse' and that when the danger from the armed bands was over, Joan returned with her father and mother to Domrémy.

When the seventy articles had to be boiled down to twelve for transmission to the University of Paris for its learned opinion, these allegations were dropped. No doubt it was realised that it would be impossible to sustain them, should they ever be contested. Aware that some day his trial could be subjected to critical scrutiny, Cauchon was very anxious that it should appear irreproachable.

Two other interesting points emerge here: first, the court case took place some time after the family's brief sojourn in Neufchâteau, that is to say when Joan was about sixteen years old, of an age where she was able to defend herself in court and attractive enough to have a young man keen to marry her. Secondly, the marriage was something her parents desired for her, as she says explicitly that she went against their wishes in the matter. That too would immediately serve as an accusation against her. It was the sin of disobedience, the same sin which she committed in leaving home:

> La Fontaine: Do you think you did well to set out without the permission of your parents, in spite of the fact that we are told to honour our parents?
> Joan: In everything else I obeyed my parents, except in the matter of my departure. But afterwards I wrote to them and they forgave me.
> La Fontaine: Did you think you were committing a sin when you left them?
> Joan: Since God commanded it, I had to do it. And since God commanded it, even if I had had a hundred fathers and mothers, even if I had been a king's daughter, I would have gone.

She was asked if she had spoken to her parish priest or any other churchman about her visions. She replied:

> No. I spoke only to Robert de Baudricourt and the King. I was not told by my Voices to keep them secret, but I was very afraid to reveal them for fear of the Burgundians and that they would stop my journey. I was especially afraid that my father would stop me going.

Again a wily question, for if she answered in the affirmative, she could be suspected of having been coached for her role in a scheme thought up by some military coterie to re-ignite the drooping morale of Charles VII's army, if in the negative, she had not deigned to consult those who could properly advise her, the spokesmen of the Church. This accusation appears in Article XI of the twelve articles sent to Paris, 'She asked no-one for advice, neither father, mother, priest nor prelate, nor any other ecclesiastic'.

More questions followed on the subject of the saints and visions. Finally she was asked why she had refused to say the Lord's Prayer, She answered: 'I am quite willing to say it. When I refused, I did so because I wanted the bishop to hear me in confession.'

The session was interrupted for lunch and resumed the same afternoon, Cauchon presiding and the six others again being present. The questioning about her parents and their reactions to her departure took up again. She said they nearly went out of their minds with grief. Did she put on men's clothes at the behest of Baudricourt or was it her own idea? It was entirely her own doing. Did she think she was doing wrong? No, and she would do the same again. How would she have liberated the Duke of Orleans? She would have exchanged him for a large number of English prisoners and if she hadn't enough prisoners, she would have crossed the sea to get him. After this bit of innocent daydreaming, the session closed.

On Tuesday, 13 March, Lemaître made his first appearance as co-judge with Cauchon and fulfilled the formalities of his office as inquisitor, swearing in the two Englishmen in charge of Joan's guards, John Grey and John Berwoit, also Massieu, whose charge included convening witnesses. Among the five assessors present was Friar Isambard de la Pierre, a Dominican friar, assistant to Lemaître, of whom we shall hear more at the later Nullity trial.

The session opened with more questions about the angels and the 'sign' brought to the king. Joan was obliged to elaborate at length on her allegory:

> Joan: The sign was that the angel brought the crown to the king and assured him that he would have the whole kingdom of France with the help of God and through my labours, and that he should put me to work, that is, that he should give me men-at-arms, otherwise he would not so quickly be crowned and consecrated.

After further interrogation, the following question was put to her:

> La Fontaine: What sign did your king have, also you yourself and those who were with him, to make him believe that it was an angel who had brought the crown?
> Joan: The king believed it because of the opinion and teaching of the churchmen who were there and because of the sign which was the crown.

This answer should have made it crystal clear to all but the most obstinately obtuse that Joan was talking allegorically. It appears however, even in the final twelve articles (Article II), as a story intended to be taken literally, thus, by implication, either a fiction or a delusion.

In conclusion, she was asked if she had been following the advice of her Voices when she had encountered setbacks after Rheims. She replied that she had not been acting under revelation, but that she had undertaken the attacks on Paris, La Charité and Pont-l'Évêque at the request of the military and that after the revelations she had had on the ditches of Melun (predicting her capture) she mostly relied on the advice of the captains, without telling them of the prophecy.

A final question:

> La Fontaine: Were you right to attack Paris on the feast of the Nativity of the Blessed Virgin?
> Joan: It is right to keep the feast-days of Our Lady, it seems to me that it would be right to keep them all.

Here again it seems that something has been lost between the question and the reply. At any rate, no accusation based on this answer appears in the seventy or in the twelve articles. Perhaps it was felt to be unsustainable, given that a theologian as eminent as the great Saint Thomas Aquinas himself had been of the opinion that in a just war it was legitimate to fight even on the most solemn of holydays if necessary.[9]

On Wednesday, 14 March, the session started immediately with questions about the leap from the tower of Beaurevoir. Why did she leap? She replied, as we have noted earlier, that she had heard that there was to be a terrible massacre of the whole population of Compiègne and that she wanted to die rather than live after such an event, also that she knew she had been sold to the English and preferred death to such a misfortune. The interrogation went on:

> La Fontaine: Did you make the leap on the advice of your Voices?
> Joan: Saint Catherine told me nearly every day not to leap and that God would come to my aid and to that of the people of Compiègne. I said to her, that since God was going to help them, I wanted to be there with them. Saint Catherine to me, ' You must accept all that. You will not be delivered until you have seen the king of England.' I said to her, 'Indeed, I don't want to see him. I would rather die than be in the hands of the English.'

Joan was then asked if she had intended to kill herself. She replied that she had not done so, but entrusted herself to God. The interrogation continued:

> La Fontaine: When you were able to speak, afterwards, did you deny God and His saints, as has been established in our preliminary investigations?

Joan: I do not recall ever having denied or cursed God and His saints, neither there nor anywhere else.
La Fontaine: Would you like to appeal to the evidence of the investigation which has been made or which is to be made?
Joan: I appeal to God and to no other and I rely on good confession.

Who can have made such a spiteful allegation? Suspicion must fall on Catherine de la Rochelle, who, as noted previously, while on trial in Paris after Joan's capture, had declared that the Maid was in league with the devil and would fly out of prison with his help if she were not closely guarded. Next question:

La Fontaine: Have your Voices asked for time to give you a reply?
Joan: Sometimes Saint Catherine replies and I can't understand what she is saying for the noise in the prison and the guards.

After more questions about the saints and the visions, Joan declared that she prayed for three things:

I ask my Voices for three things. The first is that I should be freed, the second, that God should help the French and watch over the towns now in their obedience, and the third is the salvation of my soul. I would ask also, that if I am to be sent to Paris, you would give me a copy of these interrogations and my replies, so that I can give it to the judges in Paris and tell them, 'These are the interrogations at Rouen and my replies,' so that I won't be tormented any more with so many questions.

Clearly she was finding the endless questioning and the noise and interruptions wearing. Cauchon now asked what she had meant by saying that he was putting himself in great danger in acting as her judge. Her warning of 24 February must have rankled with him. She gave this reply:

You say you are my judge. I don't know if you are or not. But take care not to judge unjustly, because you would be putting yourself in great danger. I am warning you, so that if God punishes you, I will have done my duty in telling you.

God must have saved the punishment for the hereafter, for Cauchon died as bishop of Lisieux, in December 1442, at the age of seventy-one. Guillaume Colles, in his deposition for the Nullity Trial on 12 May 1456, declared that the bishop had died suddenly, while he was having his beard trimmed. Colles however relies heavily on hearsay, in his desire to show that all Joan's judges came to a bad end.

At the end of that morning's session, Joan spoke again of her Voices:

Saint Catherine told me that I will receive help. I don't know if that means I will be freed from prison, or if there will be some disturbance when I am being judged, thanks to which I could be freed, but I think it will be one or the other. Mostly the Voices have told me that I will be freed by a great victory and then they say: 'Accept all willingly, don't fear your martyrdom. You will come at last to the kingdom of paradise.' The Voices have told me that simply and absolutely, quite clearly. I take 'martyrdom' to mean the pain and adversity I suffer in prison. I don't know if I will suffer even greater pain, I place my trust in God.

La Fontaine: Since your Voices have told you that in the end you will go to heaven, are you certain that you will be saved, that you will not be damned?

Joan: I believe firmly what my Voices have told me, that is, that I will be saved. I believe it as firmly as if I were there now.

La Fontaine: After this revelation, do you believe that you cannot commit a mortal sin?

Joan: I don't know anything about that, but I place my trust in God.

La Fontaine: Your reply is of great weight.

Joan: Indeed, and I consider it to be a great treasure.

Such was her last reply for that morning. There is unmistakeably a sense of awe in La Fontaine's final comment here. No doubt he later pondered on what Joan had said.

The interrogations resumed the same afternoon. The case of Franquet d'Arras was brought up and Joan was accused of having him put to death. As we have seen earlier, she denied the charge, and explained that he had been handed over to the *bailli* of Senlis and the lawyers of Lagny for trial, as she had not been able to exchange him for a prisoner in Paris. The well-worn topics of the bishop of Senlis's horse, the leap from the tower of Beaurevoir, the male clothing were brought out again, to all of which she wearily repeated the explanations she had given already.

The session of Wednesday, 15 March, began with the demand that she submit to the judgement of the Church, meaning of course, the partial court in which she found herself. This was the first time the demand had been made and it was of course the crux of the whole proceedings. She must accept the judgement of her adversaries. They would repeat the demand frequently after this point. She declared that she would not wish to maintain anything contrary to faith and asked that the theologians should examine what she had said and done and point out to her anything heretical. They then explained to her that there was a difference between the Church Triumphant (the saints in heaven) and the Church Militant (on earth). She seems to have found their explanation somewhat opaque, and simply replied that she did not wish to give an answer for the present. As was pointed out by the Dominican Jean Bréhal, the Inquisitor for

France consulted for the Nullity Trial, Joan's judges had no right to identify themselves as representing the universal church.

The old reproaches were dragged up again. Would she escape if she saw the opportunity? Yes, she would see it as God's permission., 'God helps those who help themselves,' she said, adding, 'I'm telling you this, so that if I go, you won't be able to say I left without permission.' She pleaded to be allowed to hear Mass. La Fontaine objected to the male costume:

La Fontaine: You will have to put on women's clothes, once and for all.
Joan: Give me a dress such as is worn by a woman in town, a long gown, and I will wear it to go to Mass.

But again she asked insistently: 'Please let me hear Mass in the clothes I am wearing.'

Her pleas were in vain. Endless questions followed again concerning her visions, how she recognised saints Catherine and Margaret, whether she had lit candles to them, had she not disobeyed them and committed a mortal sin in leaping from the tower of Beaurevoir, what doctrine had the angel Saint Michael taught her? To this last she gave the following answer:

He told me to be a good girl and that God would help me. Among other things, he told me to come to the aid of the king of France [...] And he told me about the distress in the kingdom of France.

Such indeed was the inspiration for her whole mission, the distress of the poor in the kingdom.

After a day's pause, the interrogations recommenced on Saturday, 17 March. Again she was asked to describe the appearance of Saint Michael. She gave no detailed description, but declared that she knew it was him because of the good advice, the consolation and the good doctrine which he taught her. She believes as firmly it is him as she believes in Our Lord and His Passion. They explained again to her the difference between the Church Triumphant and the Church Militant. She declared that she submitted everything she had said or done to the former and refused to give an immediate answer as to the latter. She then again made an unwelcome prediction:

You will see that the French will soon have a great success which God will send them and the whole kingdom of France will be shaken up. When that happens, remember that I told you about it.

Was this the same prediction as that concerning the 'great prize'? Or could it be seen as a prediction of the Treaty of Arras, signed in 1435 between Charles VII and Philip of Burgundy, which effectively signalled the end of hopes for English rule in France?

When they turned again to the question of the male clothing, she made the following declaration:

> Joan: As for a woman's dress, I won't put it on yet, as long as it pleases God. If indeed I have to be condemned to death, I rely on the clergy to grant me the favour of having a woman's dress and a covering for my head. I would rather die than renege on what God has made me do. I believe firmly that God will not yet let me come to such a pass without help or a miracle.
> La Fontaine: Since you say you wear the clothes you have by God's command, why are you asking for a woman's dress in *articulo mortis*?
> Joan: It is enough that it should be long.

Poor Joan. This is the first time that she has openly recognised that she may well be sent to the stake, although she has known all along that her enemies want her dead. The prospect of the worst has forced a way into her mind, but she still cannot bring herself to give up hope.

The interrogation continued. Then:

> La Fontaine: Do saints Catherine and Margaret hate the English?
> Joan: They love what God loves and hate what God hates.
> La Fontaine: Does God hate the English?
> Joan: I know nothing about the love or hate God might have for the English, or what will happen to their souls, but I know that they will be chased out of France, except for those who die there and that God will give victory to the French against the English.
> La Fontaine: Was God for the English when they were prospering in France?
> Joan: I don't know whether God hated the French, but I believe that he allowed them to be beaten for their sins, if they were in a state of sin.
> La Fontaine: What guarantee or help do you expect to have from the Lord for wearing men's clothing?
> Joan: As far as the clothes are concerned, and also for everything else I have done, I hope for no reward but the salvation of my soul.

She was questioned on the arms she had hung up in the great abbey of Saint-Denis. Had she hung them up to be worshipped? She replied firmly that she had not. She has done so because such is the pious custom of soldiers who have been wounded and because the name of Saint Denis is the battle cry of France. More questions about her standard, the sword of Fierbois and the way the angels were painted on her standard concluded the morning's session.

The afternoon session opened again with a series of questions concerning the standard and what was represented on it. Was her hope of victory rooted in herself or in the standard? *Answer*: it was rooted in

God alone. Why did she head her letters with the names Jesus Marie? Had it been revealed to her that if she lost her virginity she would lose her good fortune and her Voices would no longer come to her? She said she had no revelation about that. No doubt she feared that she could be raped. Would the Voices come to her if she were married? *Answer*: 'I don't know. I leave that to God.'. Next question:

La Fontaine: Do you believe firmly that your king did well to kill the Duke of Burgundy?
Joan: That was a disaster for the kingdom of France, but whatever happened between the two princes, God sent me to help the king of France.

At this point Cauchon himself took over from La Fontaine:

Cauchon: You said earlier that you would answer me and those appointed by me to interrogate you, as fully as you would answer our Holy Father the Pope, but there are numerous questions which you have not answered. Would you not reply more fully to the Pope than you have done to us?
Joan: I have replied as truthfully as I am able. If I could remember something I should have said and have not done so, I would gladly tell you.
Cauchon: Do you not think that you are bound to tell the truth to our lord the Pope, the Vicar of Christ, on everything concerning the faith and the state of your conscience, more fully than you have replied to us?
Joan: I ask to be taken before our lord the Pope and then I will answer him as fully as I ought to.

This last reply, which in fact constituted an appeal to the pope, was the very last thing Cauchon wanted to hear. He had been hoist with his own petard. The is no record in the minutes of his reaction, we can only imagine his anger. At any rate, he was silenced. Abruptly La Fontaine takes over again and the questioning moves on to another totally unconnected topic, the names *Jesus Maria* engraved on one of Joan's rings.

Cauchon and Warwick would certainly not have tolerated Joan appearing before a different, impartial court, whether in Rome or at the great ecclesiastical Council then about to open in Bâle.[10] Was it at this point in the proceedings that Friar Isambard de La Pierre prompted Joan to appeal to the Council? In his testimony at the preliminaries for the Nullity trial, on 9 May 1452, he described what happened:

When Joan was asked if she would submit to our lord the Pope, she said yes, if they would take her to him. But she refused to submit to those present, or at any rate to the bishop of Beauvais, because they were her mortal enemies. When I urged her to submit to the general Council then assembled, in which there would be many prelates and doctors from the party of the king of France, Joan said she would submit to the Council. Then the bishop of Beauvais flew into a rage at me, shouting, 'Be quiet, in the devil's name!'. Hearing that, Maître Guillaume Manchon asked the bishop if he should record her submission. The bishop said no, that it wasn't necessary. Then Joan said to him, 'Ah! You write down what is against me and you don't want to write down what is for me!'. I believe that it was not recorded and there was great discontent in the assembly.

The notary, Manchon himself, had already mentioned this incident in his deposition of 8 May 1452:

> When Joan was being pressed to submit to the Church and Friar Isambard de La Pierre persuaded her to submit to the general council, I heard the bishop of Beauvais shout at him: 'Be quiet, in the devil's name!'.

Isambard had said in a previous statement that he was threatened by the English after this and other incidents and told that if he did not keep quiet he would be thrown into the Seine.[11]

Joan seems to have asked several times for her case to be referred to Rome. On May 24, when she was publicly 'preached' at in the cemetery of Saint-Ouen in Rouen and forced to make some sort of abjuration (which we will look at later) under threat of being immediately burnt at the stake, she affirmed that she had already appealed to Rome, but there is no record of this in the minutes. She then repeated the request that all that she had said and done should be sent to the pope. This time her statement is recorded, but no notice was taken of the demand on that terrible day.

After that incident and Cauchon's outburst, the questioning continued with variations on the old themes. Had she ever kissed or embraced saints Catherine or Margaret? (*Answer*: Yes, she had). What kind of odour had they, did they feel warm, on which part of their bodies did she embrace them, did she give garlands to them, did she kneel or bow to them? All this is clearly to see if she will admit some sort of erotic or pornographic imaginings which would prove that she was mentally unbalanced or that the visions were the work of Satan.

At the end of the session, the following question was put to her:

> La Fontaine: Why was your standard carried more prominently in the church at Rheims at the coronation of your king than the standards of the other captains?
>
> Joan: It had shared the toil, it was right that it should share the honour.

This concluded the sessions of Joan's interrogations.

On Passion Sunday, 18 March, a meeting was held in Cauchon's residence, at which numerous assertions extracted from Jeanne's responses were read out to the dozen assessors present. These included the heavyweights such as the abbot of Fécamp, the prior of Longueville, La Fontaine and the University's men, Beaupère, Courcelles, Midi, Venderès and Feuillet. Those present were asked to deliberate on the written record of the trial and each was asked to bring his conclusions to Cauchon on the next Thursday. Meantime the final articles of accusation would be drawn up 'against the said Joan'.

On Thursday, 22 March, the two judges, Cauchon and Lemaître, together with twenty-two assessors and the notaries, gathered in Cauchon's residence. Midi, Fécamp and Feuillet were now absent and among the others present were now Loiseleur and Isambard de La Pierre. Extracts and notations from Jeanne's 'confessions' were read out and discussed, after which it was decided to reduce them to a certain number of articles, to be handed to each of those present, for their further consideration.

The next meeting took place on Saturday, 24 March in Jeanne's prison. Only seven of the assessors were now present, including La Fontaine, Beaupère, Midi, Feuillet and Courcelles. The register of Joan's interrogations was read out to her by Manchon and she stated that she believed that she had given the answers that it contained.

On Palm Sunday, 25 March Cauchon entered Joan's prison to ask her if she was willing to put on women's clothes to hear Mass on this solemn day. Only four assessors were present, Beaupère, Midi, Courcelles and Pierre Maurice. Also present were the prosecutor, D'Estivet, Henry VI's secretary Adam Milet (he appeared only on this occasion), and the Englishman William Brolbster, a priest from the diocese of London, who was present only on these three days, 25, 27 and 28 March .

Joan asked to be allowed to hear Mass in men's clothes and also to receive communion in that garb at Easter. The bishop told her sharply to reply to the question, would she leave off the men's clothes if she was allowed this privilege? (it's not quite clear whether he was asking her to renounce men's clothing *permanently*). She replied that she hadn't yet received counsel on this point and couldn't yet take women's clothes. When pressed she said the decision was not hers to make and she desired most earnestly to hear Mass. Then, seeing 'the devotion that she seemed to have', they all exhorted her to put on women's clothes, She replied that if it was her own decision, it would be done at once, but she couldn't do it. She pleaded again to be allowed to receive communion in her present dress, 'saying that this dress was not against her conscience nor was wearing it contrary to the teaching of the Church'. The session was then closed.

As far as the male garments were concerned, Joan had already been cleared by the theologians of Poitiers. Gerson, quoting the opinion of various theologians, including the great Thomas Aquinas, had also pointed out that Deuteronomy, 22.5 simply prohibits indecent costume, the indecency or otherwise depending on circumstances.[12] As far as Joan herself was concerned, it was imperative that she obey God's command, the order she had received to wear such clothing, and this explains her refusal it abandon it even at the request of the kind ladies of Beaurevoir. For her judges, obtaining her agreement to abandon her male outfit would have constituted clear proof that she had disowned her visions and thus discredited her whole mission.

Her ardent desire to hear Mass ought also to have been evidence in her favour. A genuine heretic could be identified, according to the guidelines of the Inquisition, by indifference or downright hostility to the Mass.

On Monday, 26 March it was decided at a meeting of Cauchon, Lemaître and a dozen assessors in Cauchon's place of residence, that the preliminary sessions as laid down by the procedure of the Inquisition were now complete and that the first session of the *procès ordinaire* (the trial proper) should be held on the following day, 27 March.

The Triumph of the Judges

Le sommet de la vie de Jeanne d'Arc, c'est sa mort, c'est le bûcher de Rouen

Paul Claudel

Et Jehanne la bonne Lorraine
Qu'Englois brulèrent à Rouen.

François Villon

The hearing on that Tuesday, 27 March, in the room off the great hall of the château of Rouen, was as usual presided over by Cauchon and Lemaître, in the presence of some thirty or so assessors, together with two friars (one was Isambard de la Pierre), two medical doctors, one of whom was Guillaume de la Chambre who would later testify at the 1456 earings, and two English priests, William Brolbster and John Hampton. Joan was led in as usual by Massieu. The prosecutor D'Estivet came into his hour of glory. The proceedings were opened, as was standard practice, with the presentation of his letter of accusation. In it, Joan was threatened with excommunication if she would not reply without reservation to the accusations now to be put to her. She must either accept them unequivocally by answering 'Oui, je le crois' (*Yes, I believe so*) or deny them by 'Non, je ne le crois pas' (*No, I do not believe it*). This was the usual procedure of the inquisition. What the accused recognised as true was regarded as settled and only what was denied was the basis of cross-examination, the burden of proof being on the prosecutor.[1]

The assembled assessors were asked to pronounce immediately upon the question of excommunication, should Jean refuse to comply with the requirements. Practically all demurred, saying that before they gave a definite answer, the questions should be put to Joan and that she should be given time to consider her replies if she needed it. One brave soul, the prior of the monastery of Longueville, although by no means favourable to Joan in general, declared that she should not be compelled to answer with a simple 'Yes' or 'No' if she was in any doubt.

After due debate in the court, it was decided that the prosecutor should proceed. The seventy original articles of accusation would be read in French to Joan. If she asked for time to consider her reply, adequate time would be granted. She was invited to choose one or more counsellors among those present. If she did not know who to choose, Cauchon and d'Estivet would appoint counsellors. Joan politely thanked the bishop and all the company for their concern, but refused to accept their nominees, because, she said, 'I have no intention of departing form God's counsel'. She took the oath to tell the truth on everything 'touching your trial'.

That day and the next, the articles were read out to Joan, the first thirty accusations on Tuesday, 27 March, the other forty on the Wednesday, seventy in all. The first article stated that it was the remit of the judge and inquisitor to extirpate all heresies, sorcery, superstitions and other crimes and to punish or correct all who held or practiced such things. In her reply, Joan acknowledged that the pope and bishops had such a sacred trust, but as for herself, she said:

I will only submit to the Church in Heaven concerning what I have done.
I mean to God, the Virgin Mary and all the saints. I believe firmly that
I have not sinned against our faith, nor would I wish to do so.

The French manuscript of D'Urfé adds two more words to this declaration, which are not included in Courcelles's later Latin translation. The words are *et requiert (and she demands ...)*. What did she demand? Andrew Lang suggests that it was a demand to be taken to the pope, which the notaries were forbidden to register. [2]

It would be wearisome to analyse each of the seventy articles in detail. We have already looked at some of the most ludicrous accusations in the course of the earlier interrogations. There were still more: she has told Robert de Baudricourt that she would have three sons, one a pope, the other an emperor, the third a king and Baudricourt has said he would like to father one of them, she has poured wax on children's heads to tell their fortunes, she has lived among women of ill-repute, she has consulted demons about the sword of Fierbois and put spells on her sword, ring, standard and other objects. To all this pernicious nonsense she simply made a flat denial. In regard to the other, more believable accusations, she wearily referred back to the answers and explanations she had given in the course of the interrogations. She is accused of the reprehensible crime of lording it over men, as we have seen earlier.

Many of the articles concerned her visions. She has committed murder and terrible crimes, causing her king to refuse peace and spill rivers of blood and she claims she has done all this by command of God and the saints. The visions were fictitious or diabolical on the one hand, but on the other, she had apparently committed a mortal sin when she disobeyed them, for example in jumping from the tower of Beaurevoir. She has worshipped these diabolical apparitions. She is nothing but an ignorant village girl, indoctrinated with such superstitions by her godmother and a lot of old women. She has said that the saints don't speak English and that God hates the English, a pious Christian nation! She refuses to reveal what the sign was that she brought to her king. Clearly her story is either a fiction or the whole thing has been a diabolical illusion. In all of this she refuses to submit to the judgement of the Church Militant. She has been an associate of the notorious Brother Richard (at Troyes), and lived indecently among men, allowing them to be with her constantly and refusing the company of women (the articles can only hint broadly at unchastity, since it was impossible to claim outright that she was not a virgin). She is a monster of vanity and presumption, writing to the King of England, the Duke of Bedford and other lords and captains a disgraceful letter containing numerous pernicious things contrary to the Catholic faith (the letter is read out to her). She had her standard carried before all others in the cathedral of Rheims, She has misused the names Jesus and Maria blasphemously. In addition to attacking Paris on a religious feast day, she had declared that Jesus had not kept His promise on the occasion when she was wounded and lost tmany of her men. She has allowed herself to be worshipped. By all her lies she has made herself and her brothers and parents immensely wealthy, acquiring arms, horses, revenues and honours. She has lied throughout the trial, cursing lords and nobles and a whole nation.

On the second day of this interrogation, she was asked in what words she addressed God (Article XLIX). We may be sure that the prayer she repeated for them is quoted *verbatim*, since it appears both in the original French minute and in French again in Courcelles' Latin transcipt. Here it is:

> Dear God, in honour of Your Holy Passion, I beseech You, if You love me, to make known to me how I am to answer these churchmen. As far as what I wear is concerned, I know very well the command which I received, but I don'tknow how I should put it. May it please You to instruct me.

All the terrible weariness of the prisoner is there.

At the end of these two exhausting and vindictive sessions, Joan was led back to her cell to be chained up and left to the company of her boorish guards for the next couple of days. On one of those days, she was visited by La Fontaine and the two Dominican friars, Isambert de la Pierre and Martin Ladvenu. They had come to try to persuade her to save herself by making an unconditional submission to Cauchon and his court. In fact, we hear no more of La Fontaine after this visit, for, according to the testimony of Manchon and others in 1456 (Massieu, Houppeville, Isambard de la Piere), he incurred the wrath of Cauchon and Warwick. As interrogator he had tried to do a competent job, free of malice, but Joan's answers no doubt troubled his conscience. He didn't have the makings of a hero, much less a martyr, and on 27 March he had cravenly endorsed the opinion that Joan should be excommunicated and *dealt with according to the law* if she did not agree to all the tribunal's demands. Nevertheless, D'Estivet's venomous accusations were more than he could stomach, he had to try to get her to save herself. When, after the visit, the irate Cauchon summonsed him and expressed his displeasure, he remembered the earlier imprisonment of his friend, Houppeville, whose sin was to have voiced an unwelcome opinion, and decided that flight was the better part of valour. He slipped away just before Easter Sunday, 1 April. We hear of him again in 1436 in Paris, but he must have died before the trial of 1456, since he was not called then.

On Easter Saturday, 31 March, Joan was interrogated in her prison by Cauchon, accompanied as always by Lemaître, and in the presence of seven assessors, among them Beaupère, Midi, Feuillet and Courcelles. John Grey was also there as a witness. They pressed her repeatedly to submit to the judgement of the Church and she obstinately refused to revoke any of her acts and revelations. Finally:

Cauchon: Do you believe that you are subject to the Church on earth, that is to say, the Pope, cardinals, archbishops, bishops and other prelates of the Church?
Joan: Yes, God being served first (*Dieu premier servi*).
Cauchon: Do your Voices order you to refuse to submit to the Church Militant on earth, to refuse its judgment?
Joan: I am not making just any reply that has come into my head, what I am saying is by the command of my Voices and they certainly do not command me to disobey the Church, God being served first.

After that, one final rather odd question: Did she have *files* when she was in the castles of Beaurevoir or Arras? To which she replied, again somewhat enigmatically, that if they had been found on her, why would she need to answer? We may wonder whether they suspected that she had found a sympathiser. Was she in fact protecting someone who had tried to help her? Having achieved nothing, Cauchon and his party now left her.

Easter Sunday came and went, Joan was deprived of Mass on the greatest feast day of the Church's year. On the Monday, Tuesday and Wednesday of Easter week, Cauchon and Lemaître, with a number of chosen *seigneurs et maîtres* met to draw up articles, based on D'Estivet's seventy, to be sent to Paris for consultation. They managed to reduce the number to twelve. These articles were sent on the Thursday 5 April to 'the doctors and experts present in this town' for their learned opinion as to whether Joan's assertions or any of them, as presented therein, were 'contrary to the orthodox faith, or suspect therein, contrary to Holy Scripture, to the teaching of the Holy Roman Church, to the judgement of the doctors approved by the Church and to canon law, scandalous, rash, noxious to society, offensive, encouraging crimes, harmful to morals or offensive in any way'. The doctors and experts were asked to submit their erudite opinions to the bishop in writing.

The first of the twelve articles was a long disquisition on Joan's visions, presented tendentiously in conjunction with the Fairy Tree of Domrémy and other local superstitions. By command of these apparitions she has put on male clothing, left her father's house, gone to see 'a prince of our times' (Charles VII is of course not named), promised him a kingdom and lived in the company of a multitude of soldiers, night and day, having no woman with her except on rare occasions. She is said to have boasted that she had recognised by revelation 'certain men whom she had never seen before and that she had revealed where a certain sword hidden in the earth was to be found'. She refuses to obey the Church and declares that she is certain of her own salvation.

The final article, *Article XII*, turns on the crux of the whole matter, Joan's obstinate belief in her saints and visions and her firm refusal to submit on that point to the authority of the Church.

All the articles touch in some way on the question of the visions and Joan's stubborn belief in them. The second article deals with the king's 'sign', reducing Joan's allegory to a fiction which she presents as fact. Other articles deal at some length with the following points:

Article III: Joan's descriptions of the appearance of her saints;
Article IV: She boasts that, thanks to her revelations, she has the gift of prophecy, and predicts that she will be delivered from prison and that the French will, *in her company*, perform the finest feat of arms ever seen in all Christendom (my italics);
Article IX: The saints have promised her paradise on condition that she remain a virgin; moreover, she says that she cannot ever have committed a mortal sin, for if she had done so the saints would not come to her;
Article X: The saints speak French and don't speak English, they say that they are not on the side of the English, but are for the aforementioned prince, since which revelation Joan dislikes the Burgundians;
Article XI: Joan bows the knee to these apparitions, kisses the ground they walk on, vows her virginity to them, has consulted no clergy about them, obeys all their commands, believes in them as firmly as in Christ himself.

Other articles deal with her predictions (seen as empty boasts), the male clothing, in which she has dared to receive communion; her sacrilegious misuse of the names Jesus and Mary in letter headings; her departure from home against the will of her parents; her dealings with 'a certain squire' (Baudricourt), who gave her men's clothing; her arrival at the court of 'the above mentioned prince', to whom she announced she would conquer his enemies and establish him in 'a great domination' because she was sent by God; her suicidal leap from the tower of Beaurevoir.

What could any reasonable person conclude after reading such a *exposé*, other than that the girl was deluded or fraudulent, or (if the reader happened to believe in such phenomena) that she was the victim of sinister occult forces? These articles were never read out to Joan, as Manchon tells us in his testimony of Wednesday, 12 May 1456, at the Nullity trial.

On that day, Manchon was closely questioned about the twelve articles. He was asked how the seventy articles could have been reduced down to twelve, 'particularly in a form so far from Joan's declarations', and by whom. He replied that he had faithfully written up the French minutes of the interrogations and the seventy articles with Joan's replies, but as to the twelve articles, 'he referred us to those who drew them up and said that neither he nor his associate would have dared to contradict them'. Then he, together with the other notaries, Colles and Taquel, were shown a little note in his handwriting, dated 4 April 1431, which he and they all recognised. The note read that 'these twelve articles are not faithfully composed, but are at least in part out of line with Joan's declarations and should be corrected'. However, the articles were not corrected as requested. In answer to further questions, the three notaries declared that they did not know who had drawn up the twelve articles and they believe that no corrections were made, citing a note in d'Estivet's hand, showing that he sent the articles off the next day without correction. Manchon then again stoutly declared that he had had nothing to do with the drawing up of the articles and that all the deliberations were based on them alone.

On Thursday, 12 April Cauchon held a public session at which 'sixteen doctors and six graduates in sacred theology' were present, among them some whose names are already familiar to us here: Beaupère, Midi, Feuillet, Courcelles, Loiseleur and Isambard de la Pierre. Three English clerics were also present, William Haiton, Richard Praty, later bishop of Chichester, and John Carpenter. Praty had put in an appearance at only the first two of the sessions of the trial, Carpenter had appeared at only three. Only six of those now asked for their opinion had been present at any of the sessions held by Cauchon in Joan's prison. Deliberations were held on the content of the twelve articles and a statement was drawn up and signed as authentic by the notaries Manchon and Colles. Joan's affirmations were rejected as suspect of heresy and either diabolically inspired or schemingly invented.

The written opinions which had been requested continued to arrive until mid-May. There were twenty-three of them, including one from the Chapter of the cathedral, one from 'eleven lawyers of the Court of Rouen', and several signed by more than one person. Three came from persons who had never been present at any of the sessions of the trial, the bishops of Coutances and Lisieux and a certain Jean de Bouesgue. Theirs are among the most outright of the condemnations. Philibert de Montjeu, bishop of Coutances, considers that Joan 'has a cunning spirit, inclined to evil, inspired by a diabolical instinct and deprived of the grace of the Holy Spirit', while Zanon de Castiglione, bishop of Lisieux, opines that, 'considering the low class of this person' there are only two possible explanations for her experiences, the devil or fraud. He suggests that if she refuses to submit to the pope or the Council or other prelates, she will have to be considered schismatic.

Most of the letters express humble agreement with the superior judgement of the learned judges and consultants, described by the Abbot of Fécamp, in his missive, as 'men whose equals are perhaps not to be found in the whole world'. The letter from the eleven lawyers and also the joint letter of two other lawyers of the court of Rouen are carefully worded. Both letters state that Joan's claim to have been sent by God should not be believed since it has not been substantiated by any miracle, but both stipulate later in the letter that she can be condemned only 'provided that these revelations do not come from God', adding carefully that this, of course, is something that they do not believe. Both sets of writers cover their backs with the clear statement that, as far as the basic question of the source of the revelations is concerned, 'we rely on the judgement of our lords the theologians', by which, as the eleven make clear, they mean the learned doctors of the Sorbonne. Jean Basset, the *Official* of the diocese of Rouen (i.e. the ecclesiastical judge appointed by the bishop to hear cases of litigation), has considerable reservations. Like the lawyers, when he allows that Joan could be divinely inspired, he adds prudently 'something which I do not believe', but he appears less than certain about the whole matter, refers it to the judgement of the theologians and closes his letter with a formal demand that all the documents of the trial be sent to him.[3] He was imprisoned at some time before the trial ended, but we do not know on what charges.

Two letters expressed grave doubts about condemning Joan's declarations. One was from Raoul le Sauvage, who had been present at Cauchon's meeting on 12 April. He must have had misgivings, for his long letter painstakingly reconsiders each of the twelve articles, expressing doubts and disapproval, but always nervously. The wearing of men's clothing, for example is scandalous, except 'if she did so to protect herself from violence, to safeguard her virginity'. He urges that, 'given the fragility of the feminine sex', the accusations should be read over to her again and she should be charitably advised to place no faith in such untrustworthy revelations, 'which *perhaps* have been inspired by the Evil One, *or otherwise*' (author's italics). In conclusion, 'It seems to me, subject to better judgement, that for the honour of His Royal Majesty and your own honour and for the calming and peace of the consciences of a number of people, the said articles and the qualifications on them, together with the signatures of the notaries, should be sent to the Holy Apostolic See.' Who were these others whose consciences were troubled? Cauchon's certainly was not and Raoul le Sauvage's letter must have been most unwelcome. Cauchon, as we know, had no intention of giving Joan the chance to bring her case before pope or Council or any court but his own.

The letter signed by Pierre Minier, Jean Pigache and Richard de Grouchet expresses even greater doubts as to the origin of the visions, because, as they write, 'it has seemed to us, and still does so, that a formal reply regarding the said articles depends [...] on a certitude which we are not able to arrive at and on the discernment of the origin of the revelations mentioned in the articles.' The phrase to be inserted into the brackets is, as always, the inevitable *caveat*, 'subject to better judgement'. De Grouchet testified in 1452, at the preliminaries for the Nullity trial, that he and the other two went in fear because of the threats to which they had been subjected.

After the gruelling sessions of Tuesday, 27 and Wednesday, 28 March, Joan had been interrogated again in her prison cell on Easter Saturday, 31 March, and we hear nothing of her over Easter. She was not, of course, allowed to hear Mass, which no doubt caused her great grief. Sometime between Easter and 18 April she fell ill. Several doctors were sent to examine her. They had been summoned to attend to her because it was not in the interest of her captors that she should fade gracefully out of their scenario before being branded heretical, deluded or fraudulent. One of those sent was a young man called Jean Tiphaine who was later interrogated in Paris on 2 April 1456, during the Nullity trial sessions. He had been taken to see her by the prosecutor, d'Estivet. Here is his testimony:

> I felt her pulse, to find the cause of the illness, and I asked her where she had a pain. She replied that the bishop of Beauvais had sent her a carp and that she had eaten it and felt that that must be the cause of the illness. Then this d'Estivet, who was still there, rounded on her and told her she was speaking rubbish, he called her a trollop, saying 'You trollop, you've been eating fish in brine and other things that you can't digest!'. She replied that this wasn't true and then she and d'Estivet exchanged angry words. Afterwards, as I wanted to find out more about her illness, I asked some people who told me that she had been vomiting violently.

The other young doctor, Guillaume de la Chambre, whose presence is mentioned in Tiphaine's depositon, gave his evidence on the same day:

> I was sent for by the Cardinal of England and the Earl of Warwick, and I appeared before them with Guillaume Desjardins and other doctors. Then the Earl of Warwick told us that Joan had been ill, as he had been told, and ordered us to examine her, for the king was anxious above all that she should not die of natural causes. He held her dear, in fact, for

he had bought her dearly, and did not wish her to die without being judged and sent to the stake. We were told to examine her carefully, so as to cure her. I and Maître Guillaume Desjardins and others went in to see her. Desjardins and I felt her right side. We found her feverish and concluded that she should be bled. We reported this to the Earl of Warwick, and he said, 'Don't try to take blood, for she is cunning and could bring about her own death.' Nevertheless blood was taken and after that she recovered quickly. Then along came a certain Maître Jean d'Estivet, who shouted abuse at Joan, calling her a whore and a harlot. She was so upset that she became feverish again and had a relapse. When the earl heard that, he forbade this d'Estivet to abuse her in future.

D'Estivet and Tiphaine must have come in after the consultation had begun, which would account for the minor differences in the two accounts. Colles, Manchon's colleague as clerk of the court, in his testimony of 12 May 1456, describes D'Estivet as follows:

He was a nasty man, throughout the trial he was trying to blacken the notaries and those who were trying to proceed justly. He abused Joan terribly, calling her a trollop and a piece of filth.

It is likely that Cauchon's fish had in fact gone off before it got to Joan. She does not accuse him of deliberately trying to poison her. Had the gaolers kept the fish lying around somewhere? Be that as it may, it is clear that, worn down by the conditions and stress of her imprisonment, the healthy, active, buoyant Joan of earlier days was now no more.

Both doctors commented on the profusion and rapidity of the questions thrown at Joan during the trial:

Tiphaine: The is no doctor (i.e. of theology) so learned and subtle that he would not have been perplexed and worn out if he had been interrogated as Joan was, by so many academics and with such an audience.
De la Chambre: I once saw the Abbot of Fécamp questioning Joan, and Maitre Jean Beaupère kept coming in with a lot of other questions, to which Joan couldn't reply all at the same time, to such a point that she told them they were doing her a great injustice and that she had already answered those questions.

Tiphaine remembers an incident which shows a flash of Joan's old spirit. This is his account:

Jacques de Touraine, of the order of Friars Minor, interrogated her on a few occasions. I remember that once he asked her if she had ever been in a place where Englishmen had been killed. She replied, 'In the name of God! Of course. How mealy-mouthed you are! Why don't they leave France and go back where they belong?'. Then a great English lord, whose name I don't remember, exclaimed, 'Struth! What a woman! She ought to be English!'

The twelve articles had been sent off to Paris for consideration by the Faculty of Theology. While waiting for the reply, on Wednesday, 18 April, Joan was visited in her prison, where she had languished for nearly three weeks, by Cauchon and Lemaître, accompanied by six assessors and the notaries. She was still plainly very unwell. Among the assessors were Midi, Feuillet and William Haiton. Cauchon was coming, according to the minute of the visit, to exhort Joan *charitably*, by admonishing her *gently*, and having numerous learned persons of probity, doctors and others, to admonish her likewise, 'in order to bring her back to the path of truth and the sincere profession of our faith'. He also told her that, as she was an illiterate woman ignorant of the scriptures, he was willing to appoint learned men among those present to instruct her. Courcelles' later Latin version of the minute states that he offered her anyone she cared to name, but this is not in the original French minute. The Latin insertion is significant. Cauchon finished his homily by warning her that if she persisted in her error, they would have to abandon her (i.e. to execution).

At the end of this lengthy exhortation, Joan, ever polite, thanked the bishop graciously for his concern for her salvation, adding:

> It seems to me that I am in great danger of dying, seeing that I am so ill. If that be so, if that is God's will for me, I pray you to allow me confession, communion and burial in consecrated ground.

Cauchon replied that unless she submitted to the Church she could not be allowed to receive the sacraments, except for the sacrament of penance (i.e. confession). Joan replied wearily, 'I can't give you any other answer.' Cauchon continued to harass her:

> Cauchon: The more you are in fear of death, because you are ill, the greater is the need to amend your life. You will not have the sacraments unless you submit to the Church.
> Joan: If my body dies in prison I expect you to bury it in consecrated ground. If you do not do so, I await God's mercy.

The interrogation went on and on. Finally she was summoned again to submit to the Church. She gave the same answer: 'Whatever becomes of me, I will not do or say anything different from what I have said previously in the trial.'

Even after that they did not give up, all of them chiming in, harrying her, quoting Saint Matthew, threatening her that she would have to be handed over and sent to her death at the stake. Joan answered:

> I am a good Christian, properly baptised, and I will die a good Christian.
> Cauchon: Since you are asking the Church to allow you the sacrament of the Eucharist, if you will submit to the Church, we will promise to administer the sacrament to you.
> Joan: I cannot give you any other answer. I love God and serve Him as a good Christian, and I wish to aid and support the Church with all in my power.
> Cauchon: Would you like us to order a great procession to bring you back to a proper state of grace, if you are not in one?
> Joan: I would be glad if the Church and the Catholic people would pray for me.

At that they left her.

On Wednesday, 2 May, Cauchon, accompanied as usual by Lemaître, presided over an assembly of the great and the good in the room off the great hall. Over sixty 'reverend fathers and *maitres*' had been convoked. Cauchon addressed them at length, cataloguing his efforts and those of other notable doctors of theology to save Joan's soul and announcing that he is now calling upon a very learned theologian, particularly expert in these matters, *Maître* Jean de Châtillon, to lecture, cajole and charitably warn Joan of the danger she was putting herself in, body and soul. We have heard of Châtillon already, he was the brother of the pro-Burgundian military Captain of Rheims, Guillaume de Châtillon who had left the city for Château-Thierry as Joan led Charles VII to his coronation.

Joan having now been brought in, Châtillon launched into his homily, urging her to amend her attitude. Joan replied, 'Read your book' (i.e. his sermon), 'and then I will reply. I rely on God my Creator, I love Him with all my heart.'

Châtillon's lengthy admonition was structured into six topics: 1) if she would recognise her faults, she would be treated charitably and mercifully, if on the other hand, she persisted in her pride and arrogance, she would be putting herself in great danger; 2) she must submit to the Church's judgement on her visions, otherwise she would incur the grave punishments which such obstinacy entailed; 3) she must abandon the male clothing, which in itself constitutes a grave sin; 4) her affirmations that God and the saints have commanded her clearly sinful behaviour is blasphemous, she must retract such declarations; 5) her story of the sign given to the king, her descriptions of the saints, her prophecies are fictions; Joan must ceased telling such lies and return to the path of truth; 6) she has been led by these imaginings into numerous crimes and idolatries and has never sought the wisdom and teaching of the Church on these matters.

Joan was now called upon to reply. To each of the charges she replied that she had already given her answer and that she referred all her deeds to God who had commanded them. When summoned to say whether she believed that she had no earthly judge, not even the pope himself, she did not answer the question directly, but repeated that she referred all to God. Châtillon then threatened her with death at the stake. She responded: 'I will not change my answer. And if I should see the fire, I would say again all that I have said, I wouldn't change anything.'

When she was asked whether she would submit to the pope, she replied: 'Take me to him and I will reply.'

The questions went on and on, and each time she refused to change her testimony. At last she was asked if she would refer her account of the king's sign to the Archbishop of Rheims, to La Trémoille, La Hire or others. She replied: 'Give me a messenger and I will write to them about this whole trial, otherwise I will refer nothing to them.'

Obviously she felt that she needed to explain her allegory to them, fearing the version that would be sent, even if her interrogators were indeed making her a genuine offer, which was in no way guaranteed. They then asked her if she would submit to the judgement of three or four clerics of her own party if they should be sent for with a safe-conduct, again she replied: 'Bring them here and I will reply. Otherwise I will not refer this trial to them.'

She clearly believes that the offer is not genuine. Similarly when asked if she would submit to the clerics at Poitiers, she answered: 'Do you think you can catch me in this manner and bring me over to your way?'

At last, tired of the threats and bullying, she warned them in her turn:

> You will certainly not do the things you are saying you will do to me without it costing you dear in body and soul.

More of them then joined in the questioning and threats, until the bishop wound up proceedings with a final dire warning to the accused.

A week later, on Wednesday, 9 May, Joan was brought into the great tower of the castle. In fact she found herself in the torture chamber. Torture was an established tool of both criminal and inquisitorial courts throughout Europe, but it was recognised in inquisition law that confessions made under duress were often baseless. To be valid, they had to be confirmed the next day. Moreover, it was not lawful to put a prisoner to the torture a second time. Cauchon and Lemaître were awaiting her, accompanied by eight assessors, as well as the notaries and Massieu. Among those present were Châtillon, Loiseleur, William Haiton and Guillaume Érard, who would be appointed to preach a sermon 'admonishing' Joan a fortnight later in the cemetery of Saint Ouen. The official torturers were also there, ready to fulfil their office.

Joan was immediately accused of having told a pack of lies to the court and informed that if she did not now tell the truth she would be put to the torture. She declared:

> Indeed, even if you were to tear my limbs off and separate my soul from my body, I would not tell you anything different and if I did tell you anything different, I would say afterwards that you had made me do so by force.

This was a weighty statement, for under Inquisition law such a disavowal invalidated the confession. She went on to make further statements:

> On the feast of the Holy Cross [i.e. 3 May] I was comforted by the angel Gabriel, I knew from my Voices that it was him. I asked counsel of my Voices whether I should submit to the Church because the clergy were pressing me very hard to make such a submission. The Voices told me, that if I wanted God to help me, I should rely on Him about everything. I know that God has always been the master of all my actions and that the devil has never had any power over them.

They asked her again whether she would refer her story about the sign given to her king to the archbishop of Rheims. She answered: 'Bring him here and then I will reply to you about that. He won't dare to contradict what I have told you.'

Why did Cauchon pick on Regnault de Chartres as a possible substitute judge? Had he pricked up his ears when Joan mentioned him in her story? What had he heard or known about the archbishop of Rheims which might have inclined him to think he could find an ally there? At any rate, it is clear that he had never had any intention of inviting him to attend Joan's trial in person or to play any impartial role in it. At the most, as Joan evidently feared, Chartres would be sent a letter asking him to condemn her and to urge her to submit.

All exhortations having proved counter-productive, Joan's judges, 'fearing that, given the obstinacy of her soul and the nature of her replies', torture would 'little benefit her', decided to postpone a decision on the use of torture for the moment.

Three days later, on Saturday, 12 May, Cauchon held a meeting in his residence to which twelve assessors were convoked, among them Érard, Courcelles, Loiseleur, William Haiton and Isambard de la Pierre. Cauchon outlined the latest developments and they were asked to vote on the appropriateness of the use of torture. The first response was that of Raoul Roussel, who voted against, 'lest a trial so perfectly conducted as the present should be calumniated'. This reply, says Philippe Contamine, shows that torture was clearly seen to be a last resort and that a competent inquisitor should to be able to do without it.[4] Eight others also voted against. Only three voted for, Courcelles, Loiseleur, and a certain Aubert Morel. In later years, Courcelles, whose memory would be so defective in 1456, managed to prosper under Charles VII and be well regarded by the pope, Aeneas Sylvius Piccolomini, who described him as being of great erudition and 'so modest that he always looked down at the ground and had no wish to attract attention.' Uriah Heep ... Andrew Lang remarks, in his biography of Joan, 'Loiseleur, Estivet, Cauchon and Érard are all great, but the greatest is the modest Thomas de Courcelles...'[5]

A week went by, during which Warwick gave a dinner. On Saturday, 19 May, Cauchon announced, in the chapel of the bishop's palace, to an assembly of more than fifty assessors, that he had now received the opinion of the learned doctors in Paris. The covering letters addressed to Henry VI and to Cauchon are dated 14 May. Both letters acknowledge the information the University has received from Midi, Touraine and Beaupère in addition to the documents they had received. These letters and the University's summary of its deliberations are included in the trial documents. Needless to say, the summaries are a comprehensive condemnation of Joan and her 'scandals, faults and offenses'. She is guilty of lies on all counts. On article VI (on the letter she had sent to Bedford before Orleans), she shows herself to be treacherous, cruel, thirsting for the spilling of human blood, seditious, fomenting tyranny, blaspheming God in His commands and revelations. Article VII (on her departure from home) shows her to be impious, scandalous, blasphemous, errant in the faith and that she has made a rash and presumptuous vow. The condemnation is no less violent in the case of all the other articles.

Appended to the University's missives are the replies of nearly fifty assessors and others in Rouen who had been asked again for an opinion. Almost all those consulted accepted without demur the conclusions of the Sorbonne, while asking that Joan be given a last chance and admonished again. If she is obstinate, she will have to be handed over to the civil authorities. This is the response of Courcelles, Loiseleur and the great majority. Beaupère simply agrees with Paris. Midi considers that a conclusion can be reached and the sentence carried out on the same day. Among the few who had expressed reservations previously, Raoul le Sauvage now had the courage to say that he is standing by his previous submission. He adds that Joan should be admonished again, both in private and in public and that if she persists in her stance, he leaves it to the judges to decide what to do with her. Pierre Minier simply writes that he agrees with Le Sauvage. Isambard de la Pierre makes a similar statement, asking that Joan be admonished again and leaving it to the judges to decide what to do if she is obstinate. They all know that they are powerless to prevent the inevitable. Jean Pigache and Richard de Grouchet weakly hide behind the opinion of the Sorbonne, while, like the majority, asking that Joan be admonished again. There is no letter of opinion this time from Jean Basset, the ecclesiastical lawyer who had expressed reservations and asked that the documents be sent to him, maybe he was already in prison.

On Wednesday, 23 May, Joan was brought before Cauchon and Lemaître and nine others, of whom the most notable were the Chancellor Louis of Luxembourg, bishop of Thérouanne, Beaupère and Midi. Jean de Mailly, bishop of Noyon, was present for the first time. They were gathered in a room near her cell, where, by Cauchon's command, she was addressed at length by Pierre Maurice. He read out to her one by one the twelve articles and the conclusions of the University of Paris on each one. How can she have felt when she heard herself labelled liar, treacherous, blasphemous, avid for human blood and all the rest? Then Maurice urged her, in gently persuasive tones, to forget about human respect, about the shame of losing face and worldly honours, which things were and are, he said, no doubt the reasons why she will not retract her words and actions. Let her disregard such inessentials and return to the bosom of the Church. It is possible that the young man was sincere, he showed signs of sympathy for Joan before her execution, according to the testimony of Colles in 1456. After all this, Joan simply replied that she wished to maintain all that she had said in the course of the trial. Asked again if she did not believe that she was bound to submit to the Church Militant, she replied:

> I wish to maintain what I have always said and affirmed during the trial. If I were condemned and saw the fire lit in front of me, or the bundles of wood prepared and the executioner or whoever lights the fire ready to light it, if I myself were already in the fire, I would still say nothing different and I would maintain what I have said until I was dead.

Cauchon then concluded the session, requiring Joan to be present the next day, when sentence would be pronounced.

On the morning of Thursday, 24 May, Joan was brought out of her prison for the first time and taken on a tumbril through the streets of Rouen to the cemetery of Saint-Ouen, lying in the shadow of its great abbey. Manchon describes, in his deposition of 12 May 1456, how Joan was met and led through a small gate into the cemetery by Loiseleur, who was telling her:

> Joan, believe me, for if you want to be saved, you will be. Put on a woman's dress and do everything you are told, otherwise you are in danger of death. If you do as I tell you, you will be saved, no harm will come to you and you will be given into the keeping of the Church.

Loiseleur seems to have changed his tactics. Why should he have done so? He is no longer urging her not to submit. We can be sure that he would not have dared to defy Cauchon in any way. Is this a new strategy to entrap her and finally destroy her? It is clear that the objective of discrediting Charles VII could not be achieved unless Joan first abjured her revelations and actions. However, even if following Cauchon's directives, maybe Loiseleur sincerely believed that his new advice would save her, for he seems at the end to have been deeply upset by her death.

Then she was taken to a scaffolding or *ad hoc* platform. In the middle of the cemetery stood a monumental crucifix, symbol both of tragedy and of hope. Jean de Mailly, bishop of Noyon, said at the hearings in 1456, that there were three scaffoldings, one was for the judges and chief notables, one for other notables, himself among them, and one for Joan, with the wood for the burning piled up on it. On the first sat Cauchon and Lemaître and the two great and powerful churchmen of the English and Burgundian establishments, the Cardinal of England, Henry Beaufort, uncle of Henry VI, and Louis of Luxembourg, bishop of Thérouanne. Joan was made to mount the platform facing them, on which stood also Loiseleur, the two notaries, Manchon and Collès, also Massieu, Jean Monnet, Beaupère's clerk, and Érard, the cleric appointed by Cauchon to 'admonish' the accused. A crowd of other eminent personages had taken their places also, the bishops of Noyon and Norwich, eight abbots, two priors, and twenty-seven other clerics and doctors, including Beaupère, Midi, Courcelles, William Haiton, and the four who had expressed reservations about condemning Joan, Raoul le Sauvage, Grouchet, Minier and Pigache. Two sentences had already been drawn up, one an abjuration and the other a condemnation.

Crowds had watched her, many from their overhanging windows, as she passed through the narrow streets on the tumbril. A huge multitude was waiting in the cemetery. Among the spectators was Haimond de Macy, who had made unwelcome approaches to Joan at Beaurevoir and had seen her again at Crotoy and Rouen. He speaks of her with admiration in 1456. From Massieu's testimony at the Nullity trial of 12 May 1456, there must have been a good number of English soldiers in the crowd who had come in the expectation of seeing the last of the witch. But there was also a number of townspeople. What would have brought these latter? Curiosity, pity, an obscure sentiment that history was being made? In the 1456 proceedings, many witnesses speak of the widespread view in Rouen in 1431 that Joan would never have been put on trial if she had been on the side of the English and that Cauchon was their willing tool for getting rid of a much feared enemy. Manchon says bluntly, 'It was the English who were behind this trial and it was financed by them. But I believe that neither the Bishop of Beauvais nor the prosecutor (d'Estivet) were forced to conduct the trial, both acted voluntarily'. The Dominican friar, Isambard de La Pierre, one of the two friars who were beside Joan until her death at the stake, stated at the preliminaries for the Nullity trial, in 1452, 'I believe the principal reason behind the trial was to dishonour the king of France'.

Cauchon opened the proceedings by asking Érard to deliver the sermon addressed to Joan. Érard, a cleric of no distinction, had been present at only one of Joan's interrogations, that of 9 May, when she was taken to the torture chamber. Nonetheless, he took part in all the votes on her fate. Taking as his text John, Chapter XV (the shoot and the vine), he launched into a diatribe, which the minute summarises as follows:

> He showed that by numerous errors and grave crimes Joan had been separated from the unity of our holy mother the Church and that she had on numerous occasions scandalised the Christian people. He exhorted her and all the people to adhere to the doctrines of salvation.

Witnesses at the hearings of the Nullity trial give more details of what Érard actually said. Friar Martin Ladvenu, in his testimony of 13 May 1456, says that he firmly believes that the whole trial was launched through 'hatred of the king of France and in order to calumniate him'. To substantiate this statement, he quotes Érard's outburst in the middle of his 'sermon':

> O Royal House of France! Until now you have never housed monsters! But now, harbouring this woman who is given to sorcery, superstition and heresy, you are dishonoured!

At that, Joan interrupted him, exclaiming desperately: 'Don't speak like that of my king, he is a good Christian!'

Massieu, who was standing beside Joan on the platform, gives a fuller version of her interjection, quoting her as follows: 'Your Reverence, what you are saying is not true. I want you to know that there is not a better Catholic alive than him!'

This recall of what Joan said may have become somewhat elaborated over time, but it fits in well enough with what is reported of her unfailing courtesy elsewhere. Manchon and Isambard de La Pierre quote basically the same words of Érard together with Joan's distressed rebuke.

When Érard's rant came to an end, he turned to Joan and repeated that all she had said and done was erroneous and that she must recant. Joan answered:

> I will reply. As far as submission to the Church is concerned, I have answered the judges on that point. All that I have said and done should be sent to Rome, to the Sovereign Pontiff, to whom and to God first I appeal. As far as my words and acts are concerned, they have been inspired by God.

Joan had already appealed to the pope in the session of 17 March. In answer to the next question, she replied:

> I don't put the responsibility for my words or deeds on anyone, neither my king nor anybody else. If there is a fault, it is mine and no-one else's.

She was asked again to recant her deed and words. She replied once more: 'I appeal to God and to our lord the Pope.'

This repeated clear appeal to Rome was dismissed quickly and cavalierly. She was told:

> That's not enough. It's too far to go looking for the Pope at Rome. The bishops are the judges, each in his own diocese. So you have to submit to our Holy Mother the Church and to listen to the clergy and people who know about these things and accept their conclusions about your words and deeds.

Joan was being bombarded with demands that she submit to the judgement of 'the Church'. Loiseleur was still urging her. Tisset considers that she was ignorant about the definition of the Church Militant at the start of her trial, believing that it meant Cauchon, her mortal enemy (as she once called him) and his collaborators. Cauchon and those with him did everything to encourage her in this idea and it was only at the very end of the trial that, having been given some clarification by Isambard and others, she declared her wish to be taken to the pope and her willingness to submit to him. There is some controversy about whether or not Cauchon was obliged to accede to her request. A decree of the fifth century Pope Innocent I laid down that in questions of faith, the bishops should refer to the judgement of the Supreme Pontiff. However later commentators considered that this ruling did not apply in cases where there was no possible doubt about the heresy.[6] Cauchon was certainly (and perversely!) in no doubt whatsoever. Other authors take a less indulgent view of his refusals even to allow such an appeal to be registered. The editor of the trial documents, Pierre Tisset, considers that Joan had the legal right to appeal, but no-one told her that she should ask for an *acte d'appel* or that she should submit her appeal in writing.[7]

In Catholic theology, even well before the Middle Ages, the Church is and was bound to condemn the teaching or messages propagated by revelations when they are contrary to the tenets of Christianity, but otherwise, if the revelations are consistent with Christian doctrine, the individual has the right to decide for her or himself whether or not they genuinely come from God. Régine Pernoud points out that there are a number of Inquisition trials in which an appeal to the pope was sufficient to interrupt the procedure.[8] To say that the pope was too far away was a very flimsy excuse, particularly in a case which aroused huge interest throughout Europe and in which the king of France was himself indirectly accused.

After the brusque dismissal of her appeal to the pope, Cauchon addressed a third admonishment to her and then, on Joan's repeated refusal to abjure, he started to read out the death sentence, to be carried out immediately. Joan, evidently in great distress, suddenly crumbled and interrupted him. She said she was willing to obey, whereupon she was immediately presented with a form of abjuration which was read out to her and which she was required to sign at once. The executioner was standing by with his cart, the wood for the fire was stacked already beneath the stake. At the Nullification poceedings on 3 April 1456, Jean Monnet, Beaupère's clerk, described in some detail what happened:

> I was present at the sermon preached in the cemetery of Saint-Ouen, seated at a desk below Maître Jean Beaupère whose clerk I was. When the sermon was finished, as the sentence was being read out, Joan declared that, if she was advised by the clergy, on their conscience, she would do what had been asked of her. At that, the bishop of Beauvais asked the cardinal of England what he should do, given Joan's submission. The cardinal replied that she should be admitted to do penance. The sentence, which the bishop had started to read, was then laid aside, and he admitted Joan to penance. I saw the abjuration document which was read out then, it seemed to be, about six or seven lines long on a small sheet of paper. I remember that Joan referred all to the conscience of her judges, as to whether she should abjure or not.

Joan seems to have been traumatised. She appealed desperately to the clerics there present to guide her. At the Nullity trial, Haimond de Macy remembered that a certain secretary of Henry VI, by the name of Laurence Calot, then handed her the form to sign, She said that she couldn't read or write. There is some debate as to whether she could actually sign her name.[9] Her letters are signed and the signatures, although ill-formed, are more or less identical. Perhaps she was desperately playing for time or in some way to invalidate the document. When Calot gave her a pen, she traced a circle with it. Calot took her hand and guided the signature. Near to a state of nervous collapse, she seemed to laugh, no doubt a rictus brought on by her distress.

The question is, what did she sign? In the minutes of that day, there is no trace of the short form of abjuration which Monnet describes. What we have is a much longer document, filling about a couple of pages in French, followed by Courcelles' Latin translation. In it Joan is made to confess to everything her judges have accused her of, she has lied about her revelations, blasphemed, seduced the people, thirsted after human blood, despised God and the sacraments, worn indecent garments, invoked evil spirits, and so on. She promises never to return to such errors and crimes.

There can be no doubt that this is not the short document that Joan signed under duress. In total, five eye-witnesses testified at the re-trial in 1456 that the document read to Joan was between six and eight lines long. Massieu had been required to read it out to her. On 8 May 1452, he made the following statement:

> I was on the rostrum with Joan. I read her the formula of abjuration. At her request, showing her the danger she was in, I advised her as to whether she should sign or not, if the articles were not first examined by the Church, Seeing what was going on, Maître Érard, the preacher, asked me what I was saying. I replied, 'I'm reading the abjuration to her and asking her to sign.' However, she said she didn't know how to sign and that she wanted the articles to be seen and examined by the Church. She said that she couldn't abjure what was in the form, and that she wanted to be placed in the care of the Church and not in the hands of the English. Then Érard replied at once that there would be no further delay and that if she didn't abjure the content of the form she would be burnt. He forbade me to speak to her any more or to advise her.

Convoked again on 12 May1456, Massieu declared even more categorically:

> I know that the abjuration I read to her obliged her not to bear arms in future, not to wear male dress, nor to have her hair cut short and round like a man and many other things that I don't remember. I know also that the form was about eight lines long, no more, and I know for certain that it was not the one in the trial documents, for the one that I read and that Joan signed was different.

The things that Massieu doesn't remember cannot have been very memorable, nor indeed very many, given the length of the abjuration as he describes it. Nicolas Taquel testified on 11 May 1456 and declared that he had been present in Saint-Ouen, but not on the platform with Joan. However, he was very close and he could hear and see all that was going on. He remembers the abjuration being read to her by Massieu and that 'it was about six lines of large writing'. Guillaume de La Chambre, the doctor who had attended Joan in prison, also corroborates Massieu's testimony. On 2 April 1456, he declared that he too had been present in the cemetery and that the abjuration was about 'six or seven lines long'. Pierre Miget, the prior of the Cistercian abbey of Longueville-Giffard, testified on 12 May 1456, that he had heard Joan's abjuration (she had had to repeat what Massieu read out to her) and that 'it lasted about as long as an Our Father'.

All that we can know for certain is what Massieu remembers: Joan signed a document committing her not to bear arms, to put on women's clothing and not to have her hair cut short. Nothing about revelations, sorcery or blasphemy. We know what it must have cost her to promise such things, what significance the male clothing had for her, nonetheless she knew that her captors were not going to release her, she had been promised that she would be taken to a Church prison and put in the care of women, so it must have seemed madness to face death at the stake for these secondary things. 'Joan, do what we've been telling you. Do you want to die?', they were saying to her on the platform.[10] Favier suggests that this short formula was a hasty summary of the long document, not actual duplicity on Cauchon's part. However, even if there was more in the document, it is not hard to understand Joan's bewilderment and her panic. Did not Saint Peter himself deny Christ in the courtyard of the High Priest?

When Cauchon paused in his reading of the death sentence and waited for Joan to abjure, uproar broke out in the crowd among the soldiers who had come to see her condemned. An English cleric called the bishop a traitor. Several witnesses at the Nullity trial mention the incident. Jean de Mailly, bishop of Noyon, places the episode immediately after Joan had signed, Manchon, Miget and Massieu place it at the point where Cauchon paused in reading the sentence, waiting for Joan to sign. Mailly however gives the fullest account:

> After the abjuration, a number of them said it was all a farce, that she was only laughing at them. An English cleric among them, belonging to the entourage of the cardinal of England, declared to Cauchon that he was too favourable to Joan, too easy on her. The bishop replied that he was lying and the cardinal of England told him to be quiet. Then several of those present said they didn't give much for this abjuration, it was all a farce.

She was laughing at them ... Joan's anguished face as she signed only increased the fury of the hostile spectators. Massieu in 1456 remembers the anger in the crowd:

> When Joan was told to sign the abjuration, there was a great wave of discontent in the crowd and I heard the bishop [i.e. Cauchon] say to someone, You will apologise to me! He was declaring that he had been insulted and that he would not continue with the procedure until he had received an apology.

Marguerie testified in 1456 that the angry English cleric was reprimanded and told to be quiet by Beaufort. Manchon declared that the man had actually called Cauchon a traitor. Perhaps that shows that the English were never too sure of their Burgundian allies, even one so devoted to their cause as the bishop of Beauvais.

Massieu remembers the fury after Joan had signed and how she was taken away:

> Then there was a great outcry in the crowd and stones were thrown. When she had signed, Jean asked Lemaître if she was going to be given into the hands of the Church and where she was to go. He replied that she was going back to the castle of Rouen. She was taken there and dressed in women's clothes.

Joan had been duped. There had never been any question of handing her over to a prison other than that of the castle of Rouen. She was now in a worse plight than ever, condemned to perpetual captivity in a cell guarded by soldiers 'of the roughest sort', as Massieu described them in 1456, and deprived of even the flimsy protection of the masculine garments. We can only imagine her despair.

She was taken back to her cell. The lawyer Jean Fave, a citizen of Rouen, testified on May 9 1452, that abuse and taunts were hurled at her as she entered the castle precincts:

> After that first sermon, when they were bringing her back to prison in the castle, some of the servants taunted Joan and were allowed to do so by their masters. The leaders of the English, as I heard, were hugely indignant against the bishop of Beauvais and the doctors and assessors at the trial because she had not been condemned and executed. I heard also that some of the English, in their anger at the bishop and others coming back from the castle, raised their swords at them, but didn't actually strike them, saying that the king had wasted his money on them. I also heard from certain people that the Earl of Warwick had complained about the bishop and the others, saying that the king had been ill-served, seeing that Joan had got off like that, whereupon one of the doctors said, 'Sir, don't worry. We'll get her in the end.'

With Joan returned to her prison, Lemaître, accompanied by Midi, Loiseleur, Courcelles and Isambard de La Pierre visited her in her cell that same afternoon. Lemaître gave her the statutory lesson about the great grace and mercy she had received and the warning that she must on no account relapse, for in such a case the Church would have to abandon her to the 'secular arm'. They waited while she changed into feminine clothes and then while her hair was entirely shaved off. This done, they went, leaving her with the soldiers.

On Sunday, 27 May, word was sent to Cauchon that Joan had resumed men's clothing. This was what he had been waiting for and he immediately hastened off to interview her in her prison.

Manchon testified on 12 May 1456, that he and the other notaries had been called to the castle on that day by Warwick and Cauchon. However, no interview took place, because the notaries were scared off the premises by angry soldiers. Manchon recounts the incident as follows:

When we arrived in the courtyard of the castle there were about fifty armed soldiers there, who shouted abuse at us, saying we were traitors and had not behaved as we ought during the trial. We escaped with great difficulty and in fear, because they were angry, as I believe, that Joan hadn't been burnt after the sermon.

The next morning, Monday 28 May, Cauchon set off again at once for the castle, accompanied by eight others, among them Venderès, Courcelles, Isambard, and two Englishmen, William Haiton and John Grey, Joan's gaoler. This time the notaries arrived at the prison escorted by Warwick himself. The minutes of Cauchon's interrogation of Joan are as follows:

Cauchon: When and why did you put these clothes on again?
Joan: I put them on recently and left off the women's clothes.
Cauchon: Why did you do this and who induced you to do so?
Joan: I did it of my own accord, nobody forced me. I prefer these clothes to women's clothes.
Cauchon: You took an oath that you would not put on men's clothes again.
Joan: I didn't realise that I was taking an oath never to wear men's clothes again.
Cauchon: Why did you do this?
Joan: I did it because it is more decent for me to wear men's clothing rather than women's while I am among men. Also I did so because you didn't do what you promised me, that I could go to Mass, receive communion and that I would not be shackled.
Cauchon: Did you not in fact abjure and specifically promise not to put on men's clothes again?
Joan: I would rather die than be in irons, But if you allow me to go to Mass and take the shackles away and put me in a proper prison, I will be good and do whatever the Church wants.[11]

This last exchange raises an interesting point: if she was shackled, how and when could she have managed to struggle out of one set of clothes and into another? One can only conclude that there must have been some sort of Machiavellian collusion between the authorities and the guards to make it possible. In his testimony of 8 May 1452, Massieu said that Joan herself had told him that on the morning of Sunday, 27 May, before she rose, the guards had taken away the female clothing and replaced it with a set of men's clothes, which she was finally, in spite of her pleas, obliged to put on in order to get up 'for natural necessities'. There are of course questions here: what was she wearing during the night? She could hardly have been obliged to strip off in the presence of the guards, or to sleep naked beneath a blanket? After she had worn the male clothes all that day, they gave her back her female clothes on the Monday. Although Massieu's deposition is very opaque, this may square well enough with her declaration that she had taken the men's clothes of her own free will, since she must have refused the female costume on the Monday. Had she had some sort of crisis of conscience in the course of Sunday about the abandon of the male clothes, the sign of her mission?

Other questions arise also however. At the Nullity trial, Manchon's testimony of 12 May 1456, reads: 'They asked Joan why she had put on men's clothes. She said she had done so to protect her chastity, because she wasn't safe in woman's clothes with the guards who wanted to rape her.'

How safe was she while she lay in bed? Again we must ask, when and how did the guards take her clothes away? Manchon remembered, in 1456, how on one occasion, when Cauchon and Warwick reproached Joan with wearing male clothing, telling her it was indecent for a woman to wear a tunic and hose 'attached with a lots of laces tied up tightly', she replied that she wouldn't dare to take off the hose or wear them any other way than tied up securely, for the bishop and the earl well knew that the guards had tried to rape her several times. There is ample testimony, for example that of Louis de Coutes, her page, in his testimony before the judges at the 1456 hearings of the Nullity trial, that when on campaign and obliged to sleep rough, Joan slept fully dressed, sometimes even in her armour, as at Blois before her entry into Orléans. In the prison in Rouen, as we are told, she slept fully dressed also, for fear of the guards. So in what manner was she was lying in bed after she was brought back from the cemetery of Saint Ouen? Was she shackled as she lay there? Did she lie awake all night in fear of rape? Who knows what humiliations she was subjected to in those three days and nights. Was it part of a scheme to get her to make the fatal mistake?

At some point, Joan told Friar Martin that 'a great English lord had come into the prison and tried to rape her, and she said this was the reason she had put on men's clothes again'. To Isambard also Joan complained that she had been maltreated in the prison while wearing the feminine clothes. He testified:

> In truth, I saw her in tears, her face all disfigured, so that I felt pity and compassion for her. When she was called an unrepentant heretic, she said. 'If you, the clergy, had put me in your prisons, maybe this would not have happened.'

Joan seems to have believed until the end the only charge on which she was being sent to her death was that of having resumed male clothing. She thought, as she said, that this alone was what she had promised to renounce At the Nullity trail of 1456, the Dominican Jean Bréhal, the

Inquisitor for France, in his lengthy written examination of the trial of 1431, declared categorically that the male costume alone did not constitute sufficient grounds on which to condemn her as a heretic.[12]

To continue now with Cauchon's interrogation:

Cauchon: Have you heard the voices of saints Catherine and Margaret again since Thursday?

Joan: God has sent me the message by saints Catherine and Margaret that the treason which I committed in abjuring in order to save me life was a great pity and that I was damning myself to save my life. Before Thursday, my Voices told me what I was would do that day and I did it. They told me as well, when I was on the rostrum, in front of the people, that I should reply boldly to the preacher. He was a false preacher and he said I had done things which I had not done. If I said that God had not sent me, I would be damning myself, for in truth God did send me. My Voices have told me, since Thursday, that I had done something very bad in confessing that what I had done was not good. Whatever I said on that day, I said and did so solely for fear of the fire.

In the Latin version of the minutes, Courcelles has noted here *responsio mortifera,* 'the fatal reply'.[13] Joan had sealed her own fate. We remember what she had said when threatened with torture: that if she disavowed anything, 'I would say afterwards that you had made me do so by force'.

The long statement quoted above is obviously made up of several replies to questions. There is a naivety about it which is touching and which reminds one of the way so many witnesses at the 1456 trial spoke of her as a very simple young girl. Apart from affairs of war, said Alençon in 1456, she was 'simple and young'.

The minute finishes with more of Joan's answers strung together, in which she bravely maintains the truth of her visions:

Cauchon: Do you believe that the Voices and apparitions are saints Catherine and Margaret?

Joan: Yes, and I believe they come from God.

Cauchon: Tell us the truth about the crown you talked about! (i.e. the king's secret)

Joan: I have told you the truth during the trial as best I was able.

Cauchon: When you were on that rostrum, in front of us, the judges and others and the people, you abjured and said that you had told lies and boasted that the Voices were saints Catherine and Margaret.

Joan: I didn't understand that I was doing or saying that. I didn't say or understand that I was denying my visions, saying that they were not saints Catherine and Margaret. Everything that I did, I did it through fear of the fire. I didn't revoke anything untruthfully. I would rather do my penance in one go, in going to my death, than bear this imprisonment any longer. I have never done anything against God and the faith, no matter what you ordered me to abjure. I didn't understand at the time what was in the abjuration form. I hadn't the intention of revoking anything unless it pleased God. If you wish, I will put on woman's clothes again, but I won't do anything else.[14]

Cauchon had now got all that he needed. Isambard recalled, when he testified to the investigators for the nullity trial, on 5 March 1450, Cauchon's elation on leaving Joan's cell: 'At the end of that session, the bishop of Beauvais left and said to the English waiting outside, "Farewell! Be of good cheer! It's finished."'

He would repeat this testimony when he was called again in 1452:

After she had put on the male clothes again, I saw and heard the bishop, overjoyed, saying to Warwick and a crowd of English and others, 'We've got her!'

The next day, 29 May, Cauchon convened in the chapel of the archbishop's palace a meeting of his assessors and the two friars, Martin Ladvenu and Isambard de La Pierre. The vice-inquisitor, Lemaître was not present. Altogether forty-two persons were present, plus the notaries. He gave them an account of the developments of the previous day and they were then each required to give their opinion on action now to be taken. The first to do so was Nicolas Venderès, who declared bluntly that Joan had to be handed over to the 'secular arm'. Next was the abbot of Fécamp, Gilles de Duremort, who judged Joan to be relapsed, but asked that the formula of abjuration should be read and explained to her again. Evidently he had some qualms about how well she may have understood it or what it contained. All but three of those who spoke after the abbot took refuge in saying that they agreed with his opinion. However, Cauchon was not obliged to act in accordance with their views, their role was merely consultative. He thanked them and announced that 'Joan would be proceeded against as relapsed, in accord with law and reason.' There was to be no last chance and no quibbling about what had been or had not been in the short form of abjuration. Only the long document was consigned to the minutes.

On 12 May 1456, André Marguerie told the judges at the Nullity trial that he had been present at the meeting which Cauchon convoked on 29 May in the chapel of the archiepiscopal palace, to inform the assessors solemnly of the events of the day before. He had incautiously asked in what circumstances Joan had come to resume the male clothing. Then he describes the effect this question had:

The English, furious at hearing of that question, raised a great tumult, so much so that I and many of the others who had come to the castle on this business, had to leave rapidly, in danger of our lives.

The English in question can only mean the soldiers outside, the only Englishman present at the meeting being the cleric William Haiton, hardly the most murderous of Englishmen. Massieu says that Marguerie was threatened by a soldier who made to strike him with a lance, calling him a 'treacherous Armagnac!', which gave him such a fright that it made him ill.[15] The assessors on the whole do not seem to have been made of the stuff of heroes. Who had let the soldiers know immediately what was going on in the meeting? In any case, the question raised by Marguerie must have caused consternation. Marguerie's testimony is also corroborated by Pierre Cusquel, giving evidence on 12 May. Cusquel says that, as he had heard, when *maître* André Marguerie declared that before going any further, they would have to enquire carefully into the truth about Joan's resumption of male clothing, *someone* told him to be quiet, *in the devil's name*! Surely more than a coincidence that this was also the form of words used earlier by Cauchon when slapping down Isambard de La Pierre?

The fullest account of Joan's last hours is given by Massieu (12 May 1456), who went to fetch her from her prison and bring her to the place of the Vieux Marché at eight o'clock on the morning of 30 May. He begins by describing how the Dominican friar Martin Ladvenu had been sent to her earlier and authorised to hear her confession:

> On Wednesday morning, the day of Joan's death, Friar Martin Ladvenu heard her confession and then he sent me to the bishop of Beauvais to tell him she had been heard in confession and that she was asking to receive the Eucharist. The bishop conferred with some others and then told me to tell Friar Martin to give her the sacrament and anything else she wanted. I went back to the castle and told Friar Martin, who gave her communion in my presence.

Joan was about to be executed as an impenitent and relapsed heretic. As such, she should not have been allowed to receive the sacrament. The bishope's off-hand permission was quite out of order and its implications would be an important consideration at the re-trial. Did those he consulted express some unease of conscience and was he in a hurry to have done with hair-splitting arguments and finish the whole business?

Before administering the sacrament, Friar Martin had to tell Joan that she was to die that morning. The young Franciscan friar who had accompanied him, Jean Toutmouillé, at twenty-three years old hardly much older that Joan herself, described her reaction:

> Joan was weeping and exclaiming, 'Alas! They are treating me horribly and cruelly! Must my body, which has never been corrupted, be burned and reduced to ashes! I would seven times rather be beheaded!'[16]

Friar Martin himself described how she received the sacrament:

> On the morning of her death, before the sentence was pronounced, I was authorised by the judges to hear her confession and give her communion. She received it humbly, with many tears and great devotion, more than I can describe.

The communion was brought to her cell by Pierre Maurice, who had 'admonished' her on Wednesday, 23 May, without abusing her as d'Etivet and Midi would do later. In 1452, Massieu described the way the Eucharist was brought as 'very lacking in reverence, on the salver of a chalice, without candle or assistant, without surplice or stole'. No doubt not the fault of Maurice, whom Joan seems to have turned to in this extremity for reassurance. Another witness, Jean Riquier, testifying on 9 May 1452, tells us that after the communion, Maurice spoke a few words to her:

> Joan said to him, 'Maître Pierre, where shall I be this evening?'. He answered, 'Do you not trust in God?' She said that she did and that with God's help she would be in paradise. Maître Pierre told me that himself.

Soon afterwards, Cauchon and several others appeared in her cell. Venderès, Courcelles and Loiseleur were among them. Toutmouillé recounts the scene:

> Then Cauchon himself appeared and she exclaimed: 'Bishop! I die through you!'. He replied, 'Joan, bear it all patiently! You are to die because you have not kept your promise, you have returned to your wickedness'. The poor Maid replied, 'Alas! If you had put me in a Church prison and given me into the care of authorised ecclesiastical guardians, this would not have happened. I appeal to God against you!'

Joan was then made to put on a long woman's dress. On her shaven head they placed a mitre, inscribed in huge letters with the words 'heretic, relapsed, apostate, idolatress'. Massieu and Martine Ladvenu led her out. Manchon estimated the number of armed men escorting them at about eighty, Houppevile puts it at a hundred and twenty. They led her to the place of execution, the Old Market square, *le Vieux Marché*. In 1452, on Monday, 8 May, the priest Nicolas Taquel would recount what he had been told very shortly after she left the castle:

> And afterwards I was told that before being led out to her execution, she said devout prayers to God, the Blessed Virgin Mary and the saints, which greatly touched several of those present, especially Nicolas Loiseleur, who left in tears and was insulted by a group of the English in

the courtyard who threatened him and called him a traitor. He was very frightened and straightway went to Warwick for protection and I believe he would have been killed if the earl had not been there.

Colles testifying four years later, in 1456, also reported that Loiseleur had been upset and would have been murdered by the soldiers had Warwick not been there to protect him, but he places the incident at a different moment, as Joan comes down from her platform and is about to be burned. One or other recollection is a little blurred, but some such incident must have taken place. Did Loiseleur feel remorse for his role in the tragedy? We can't know what went on in his mind.

Nicolas de Houppeville, testifying also that same day, gave the following evidence:

> I saw Joan weeping copiously as she was taken out of the castle to the place of execution and the final sermon, she was led by about a hundred and twenty men, some carrying clubs and others swords. Moved by compassion, I had no wish to follow them.

In 1456, Massieu:

> She was taken in women's clothes by Friar Martin and myself to the place of execution. She lamented so piously that Friar Martin and I were both in tears. She recommended her soul so devoutly to God and the saints that those who heard her wept. She was taken to the Old Market where maître Nicolas Midi, who was to preach the sermon, was waiting.

She was mounted on a platform in the square facing Cauchon and his assembly, seated, as before, on a rostrum opposite. She had to endure another diatribe, this time delivered by Nicolas Midi. 'When he had finished', says Massieu, 'he said to her, "Joan, go in peace! The Church cannot defend you any further and gives you over to the secular authorities."'

Massieu goes on:

> At [Midi's] words, Joan, on her knees, prayed very devoutly and asked me for a crucifix. Then an Englishman who was there made a little cross with a stick, which she kissed and placed on her breast with the greatest devotion. But she still wanted another crucifix from the Church. She was given it, kissed it, clasping it to her in her arms· and recommending her soul to God, Saint Michael, Saint Catherine and all the saints. She clutched the cross to her and bowed to all those present. Then she came down from the platform, accompanied by Friar Martin and was led to the place of execution, when she died very piously.

Called to testify on 9 May 1452, Jean le Fèvre, bishop of Demetriade, who had been present at this last sermon, said that after it, Joan asked each of the priests present to say a Mass for her.

She was handed over to the *bailli* of Rouen. The judges were in such a hurry to finish with the affair, that neither the *bailli*, the ultimate representative of the civil authority, nor Laurent Guesdon, his *lieutenant* at the time of Joan's death, had time to arrange a formal hearing and pronounce the lawful civil sentence, as Guesdon himself and others testified in 1456. That might have delayed the execution by anything up to a day. According to Manchon, Ladvenu and others, the *bailli* had only time to wave his hand and say, 'Take her away! Take her away!'. Did he fear the fury of the soldiers? Or maybe even a tumult to get her away? With so many soldiers around her, such an attempt would have been reckless indeed. However, Colles testified in 1456 as follows:

> The judges and those who had taken part in the trial incurred the greatest hostility among the people. After Joan was burned, the ordinary people pointed out with horror those who had been involved in the trial.

Or was it on Warwick's instructions that she was hustled off immediately, allowing her no time to proclaim again publicly her belief in her mission and therefore, by implication, in the rightness of Charles VII's cause? Could the *bailli* have contravened the legal niceties without some higher authority?

It must have been while Friar Martin was accompanying Joan that Friar Isambard ran into the church to get the crucifix, as he himself described:

> The poor woman asked me urgently and humbly to go into the nearby church and bring her the cross. She asked me to hold it aloft before her eyes until the end, so that the cross on which God Himself was crucified would be constantly in her sight.

Joan climbed onto the platform of the stake. In his entry in the court register for 30 May 1431, Clément de Fauquembergue describes the huge inscription posted prominently in front of her:

> On a board in front of the platform on which Joan was standing, these words were written: 'Joan who calls herself the Maid, a liar, pernicious, deceiver of the people, sorceress, superstitious, blaspheming God, presumptuous, erring in the faith of Jesus Christ, boastful, idolatrous, cruel, dissolute, invoking devils, apostate, schismatic and heretic.' [17]

Fauquembergue was probably informed a day or two after the event by someone returning to Paris from Rouen and must have written up his entry for 30 May at that time. Although he knows only one version of the story, Fauquembergue does not appear totally convinced by the proclamation and its stream of vituperation, his final comment on Joan is inspired by pity: *Deus suae animae sit propitius et misercors*, he writes. 'May God look kindly on her and have mercy on her soul'.

Friar Martin described Joan's last moments as follows:

> When the sentence was pronounced, she came down from the platform and was led by the executioner to the place where the wood was piled up for the fire. When she saw the fire lit, she told me to step down and to raise high the crucifix so that she could see it, which I did.

Had Isambard's arms got tired, holding up the heavy cross? Martin added:

> She maintained till the end that the voices she heard came from God and that everything she had done had been done by God's command and that she didn't believe she had been deceived by the voices, but that her revelations came from God.

He states also that from the stake Joan again accused Cauchon of being the cause of her death. This is unlikely, it is most probably a memory of the accusation she had made in her cell. No such last words are recorded by any other witness. nor affirmed elsewhere. According to Manchon's testimony of 8 May 1452:

> Jeanne prayed very beautifully, recommending her soul to God, to the Blessed Virgin Mary and all the saints, asking pardon of the judges and the English, the King of France and all the princes of the kingdom.

At such a moment she would hardly have been thinking of accusing Cauchon again. Would she in fact have had time to pray and apologise as Manchon says? Once the fire was lit, she would have been dead, suffocated by the smoke in a couple of minutes. If she did ask the forgiveness of everyone whom she could possibly have grieved in any way, it was certainly as a result of her extreme scrupulosity, which we have seen elsewhere illustrated in her frequent sacramental confessions.

Some of the witnesses remember that Joan lamented over Rouen. Guillaume de La Chambre, the doctor who had attended her, testifying on 2 April 1456, declared he heard her lament,

> Ah! Rouen! I greatly fear that you will have to suffer because of my death!' Then she began to cry 'Jesus!' and to call upon the name of Saint Michael, and at last she disappeared amid the flames.

Pierre Daron, in 1456 *lieutenant* of the *bailli* of Rouen, also declared at the Nullity trial that she had cried, 'Ah! Rouen, Rouen, are you to be my last abode?' He adds that there was great pity for her, some people weeping and many angry that she was being executed in Rouen.

The stake had been specially constructed on a plastered platform, raising it above the heads of the crowd, so that all could see her. This exceptional measure prevented the executioner from climbing up behind the accused and strangling her, thus sparing her the agony of the fire, a small mercy which was, according to the man himself, normal practice.[18] Isambard de la Pierre, Ladvenu and others who witnessed Joan's death agree that she called upon the name of Jesus as the flames surged up. Maugier Leparmentier, testifying in 1456, said: 'The wood was already on the stake. She cried out more than six times "Jesus!", so loudly with her last breath that all could hear it and nearly all were in tears.'

Jean Riquier, a parish priest in Rouen, gave evidence in 1456:

After they lit the fire, she called loudly on the name of Jesus repeatedly until her death. After her death the English, fearing that there would be rumours of an escape, told the executioner to push back the fire a bit, so that all those present could see her dead and there would be no talk of any escape.

The clothing had been consumed by the flames and the charred body was allowed no shred of dignity. Then the flames were revived and the body reduced to ash.

Massieu finishes his testimony of 12 May 1456:

I heard from Jean Fleury, the clerk of the bailli and town clerk, that the executioner had told him that when Joan's body was burned and reduced to ashes, her heart remained intact and full of blood. The executioner was told to gather the ashes and all that was left of her and to throw them into the Seine, which he did.

Warwick was determined that there should be no relics which could be gathered to become an object of cult, a rallying point for processions or vigils. As Favier points out, this in itself is evidence of his fear of popular hostility to the trial and execution.

The judges and clergy of the tribunal had left immediately after the reading of the sentence, thus complying with the precept *ecclesia abhorret a sanguine* ('the church abhors the shedding of blood'). Manchon was among those who left, but he tells us:

I was so upset that I was suffering from panic for a month. With the money I was paid for the trial, I bought a missal in memory of her and in order to pray for her.

The terrible scene caused great emotion in the crowd. Many had left when the clergy did so, unable to stand the horror. Only some of the soldiers standing around were unmoved. 'Some people wept, but some of the English laughed,' said Guillaume de la Chambre. Others, even among the soldiers, even the executioner himself, were traumatised. Isambard de La Pierre told the following story on 9 May 1452:

> A certain English man-at-arms, who really hated Joan, had sworn he would put a faggot on the stake with his own hands. When he was doing so, he heard Joan calling on the name of Jesus as she died. He was completely shattered. They had to take him to an inn near the Old Market to bring him round with a drink. When he had had a meal with an English Dominican, as I heard from that same English friar, he admitted he had gravely erred and that he repented of what he had done, saying that Joan was a good woman. It seemed to him that at the moment she rendered up her soul, he saw a white dove rising up from the flames.[19] Then the executioner came that same day to the Dominican friary and told me and Brother Martin Ladvenu that he feared he was damned, for he had burned a saint.

Similar stories were told of other conversions. Pierre Cusquel, the citizen of Rouen who had managed to see Joan in her prison, testified on the same day as Isambard above:

> Maître Jean Tressart, secretary to the English king, leaving the scene of the execution, lamented what he had seen, saying: 'We are all damned, for a good and holy person has been burned', and he believed her soul was with God, since amidst the flames, she invoked the name of Jesus.

Jean Riquier, who was called to testify twice, in 1452 and 1456, spoke on each occasion of the case of Jean Alespée, one of Cauchon's assessors. Alespée's words seem to have been engraved in his memory, for he quotes them in almost identical terms both times: Maître Jean Alépée, a canon of Rouen at the time, was standing beside me. He said, weeping, "If only my soul could be where I believe the soul of that woman to be!"'

Ladvenu claims that Louis of Luxembourg, the Bishop of Thérouanne wept (when? We know that the judges and assessors had withdrawn before the execution), while Isambard says that even Cauchon shed tears, although that seems to sit very ill with the rest of his behaviour. Perhaps he had a cold and a runny nose.

With Joan's death, the story was not yet at a satisfactory end for Cauchon. It had to be made clear once and for all that her claims to have been sent by God were fraudulent and diabolical. Faith in such claims must be destroyed throughout France and Charles VII totally discredited beyond all possible doubt. A week after Joan's death, on Thursday, 7 June 1431, Cauchon convened a meeting, jointly presided by himself and Lemaître, as always, and attended by Venderès, Loiseleur. Courcelles, Pierre Maurice, Jean Toutmouillé, Jacques le Camus and Martin Ladvenu.

Manchon, the official clerk of the court, did not attend. He was entitled to refuse, since the trial was at an end on 30 May and his function ended with it.

A lengthy document was drawn up, now known in French as the *information posthume*. In it, Cauchon declared that he has gathered information from these witnesses who had visited Joan on the morning of her execution and that she then, *in articulo mortis*, totally denied her visions, saying that they were evil spirits who had deceived her, since they had promised her deliverance and now she was to die. It is easy to see how that could be a misrepresentation of what Joan actually said, when we remember how during the trial, on 14 March, she had understood the message given by the 'Voices': 'Mostly the Voices have told me that I will be freed by a great victory and then they say: "Accept all willingly, don't fear your martyrdom. You will come at last to the kingdom of Heaven."'

Taking the word 'martyrdom' to mean her captivity, she had declared then:

> Saint Catherine told me that I will receive help. I don't know if that means I will be freed from prison, or if there will be some disturbance when I am being judged, thanks to which I could be freed, but I think it will be one or the other.

Joan may well have admitted that she had misunderstood this exhortation, thus making it possible to allege that she had disowned her revelations. Looking at the misrepresentations of her declarations in the famous twelve articles, there can be no doubt that this document, unverified by any notary, could well have been edited for the same purpose, the destruction of Joan's claims and thus of Charles VII's reputation. Historians agree that Cauchon would have been astute enough not to concoct a completely fictitious account, but rather one which slanted the truth. Even here, Joan is never reported as denying the reality of the 'Voices' and apparitions, on the contrary she obstinately reaffirms her belief in them. Her obstinacy is quoted *verbatim* in French in this Latin document: *Soient bons, soient mauvais esperils, ilz me sont apparus* ('Whether good or evil spirits, they appeared to me!'). Amidst her terror of the fire awaiting her, she clings unshakeably to this conviction. She also declares that she herself was the angel she had spoken of who brought the crown to the king, and that the crown itself was the promise of his coronation, thus explaining her allegory, but this is presented as an admission of lying. Finally, she is exhorted by Cauchon to make a public confession:

> I exhorted her [...] to disavow publicly the error which she had spread among the people, to confess publicly that she had been deceived and

had herself deceived the people, by believing in such revelations and exhorting the people to believe in them, and that she humbly ask forgiveness for all that.

There then follows what is clearly meant to be an explanation for the fact that Joan never made any such public apology:

> Joan replied that she would willingly do so, but she was afraid she might forget to do so when it was necessary, when she was being publicly sentenced. *She asked her confessor to remind her to do so* (my italics).

Apparently this minor detail must have slipped her confessor's mind also. If she had indeed made such a public confession as is here required of her, this legally invalid document would never have been necessary.

It is of course conceivable the Joan could have suffered some sort of temporary nervous collapse when told to prepare herself immediately for such a horrendous death and that she could, as a result, have in her anguish agreed to all the promptings of Cauchon and others, or made muddled statements. No-one could feel anything but pity for her on that account. But that she should, *sana mente*, 'in her right mind', as the document affirms, have recanted on the morning of her execution everything she had so courageously and strenuously maintained until then, is highly unlikely, if for no other reason than that she knew that nothing was to be gained, that she was about to be burned no matter what. Only two days earlier she had adamantly declared that she had put her eternal salvation in peril by whatever it was that she had abjured and that she would rather do her penance at once than remain in the castle prison. Those statements are authenticated by the notaries, while neither Manchon nor any other clerk of the court signed the *informatio post execucionem*. When the death sentence was publicly read out there was no assertion that Joan had finally repented and renewed her abjuration.

Manchon himself, in his testimony of 4 March 1450, affirmed that he had refused to sign the document in question, since he had not witnessed the proceedings.[20] All witnesses to her very public death confirmed her steadfast faith in her mission and revelations, her prayers to her saints until the very end. At the Nullity trial in 1452 and 1456, the judges pointed out that she was burned as an unrepentant heretic, there was no public declaration of a renewed abjuration nor any public absolution, as required by law in the case of the accused's repentance. Cauchon, a canon lawyer by training, would certainly not have carelessly omitted such a demonstration of the prisoner's definitive recantation.

However invalid the *information posthume*, Bedford's government did not hesitate to make maximum use of it. In fact, they had no doubt demanded that Cauchon produce such a document. The very next day, 8 June, a letter in the name of little Henry VI was sent to 'The Emperor (i.e. the Holy Roman Emperor, Sigismund), Kings, Dukes and other Princes of All Christendom', denouncing the 'deceitful visionary who had arisen recently in Our Kingdom of France' and listing all Joan's wickednesses, made the more heinous because she had rejected the judgement of 'the Sovereign Pontiff, the General Council and the universal Church Militant' (Cauchon and his assessors being the 'universal Church'). She was declared to have, after the abjuration, returned to her errors, but to have retracted them again *in articulo mortis*. A similar letter was addressed on 28 June to 'The Prelates of the Church, Dukes, Counts and other Nobles and Cities of Our Kingdom of France'. The University of Paris sent a letter to the same effect to 'Our Lord the Pope, the Emperor and the College of Cardinals'.

Already on 12 June 1431, 'Letters of guarantee' in the name of Henry VI had been issued to all who had had any part in Joan's trial, no doubt at Cauchon's demand. The document is couched in the usual legal verbosity and the essential paragraph runs as follows:

> If by chance, any who may have benefitted from the errors and evil doings of the said Joan, or who would try or wish to try through hatred or vengeance, or otherwise, to dispute the true judgments of our Holy Mother the Church and to bring a case before Our Holy Father the Pope, the Holy General Council or elsewhere against the said reverend father in God (Cauchon), vicar (Lemaître), doctors, masters, clerks, prosecutors, lawyers, counsellors, notaries or others involved in the said trial, We, as Protector and Defender of our Holy Catholic Faith, will defend and support the said judges, masters, clerks, prosecutor and lawyers, consellors and all others who participated in any way in the said trial, in all that they said and pronounced and in everything concerning the said trial and all its circumstances.

Clearly Cauchon was aware that Joan's condemnation could be challenged. Her suppressed appeals to the pope might, for example, come to light, the warped twelve articles sent to Paris could be examined against what the notaries had actually recorded in the minutes. He naturally had to take precautions.

Included among the documents appended at the end of the trial is the formal retraction of a certain Dominican friar, Pierre Bosquier by name, who had dared to say, in front of witnesses, on 30 May, the day of Joan's death, that she had been wrongly judged and condemned. The Dominican is obliged to say that his words had been 'stupid and seem to show support for heresy' (a very serious charge) and that he had uttered them 'without thinking, inadvertently and after drinking', that he begs the pardon of the judges 'on my knees and with my hands joined' and that he submits most humbly to his punishment and asks for mercy. A second document is the judgement of Cauchon, sentencing him, in all mercy, given his excuses and apologies, to imprisonment in a Church prison, on bread and water, until the following Easter, which would be 20 April 1432. One can understand why other critics kept a much lower profile.

19

After Joan: The War Goes On

'En nom Dé, les gens d'armes batailleront et Dieu donnera la victoire!'
Joan of Arc at Poitiers

A number of the principal personalities of the trial went to the General Council of Bâle soon afterwards or in the next couple of years. No doubt they used the opportunity to disseminate their version of the Joan of Arc affair. Chief among them were Beaupère, Courcelles, Midi, Loiseleur and in 1434, Cauchon himself. By this time he was bishop of Lisieux, any prospect of returning to Beauvais having evaporated and his cherished hopes of succeeding to the bishopric of Rouen having been dashed. His career stalled after 1431. When Henry VI, not yet ten years old, came to Paris on 12 November 1431, to be crowned king of France in Notre Dame in December of that year, it was not Cauchon, but Nicolas Midi who pronounced the oration welcoming him to the capital. Cauchon spent a year in Bâle, during which period he was threatened with excommunication for non-payment of part of the dues payable on his accession to the bishopric of Lisieux. In 1435, he represented Henry VI at the congress of the Treaty of Arras, which brought to an end Philip of Burgundy's quarrel with Charles VII. There, like the other representants of the University of Paris, he would have met the future Pope Pius II, Aeneas Sylvius Piccolomini, at the time a young man in minor orders (not ordained) and of considerable intellect and somewhat scandalous reputation (happily he reformed his free and easy ways some time before becoming pope in 1458). Cauchon may have come across Piccolomini already at the Council of Bâle. As pope, the Italian would write a glowing eulogy of Joan of Arc in his *Memoirs*.

Cauchon left Arras empty-handed, He was not even officially acknowledged as part of the English embassy. The list of official ambassadors comprised eleven names, all English, headed by the Archbishop of York. The Duke of Bedford died in Rouen on 14 September 1435, a week before Philip of Burgundy signed the Treaty of Arras, thus making his peace with Charles VII and effectively putting an end to English hopes of conserving the dual monarchy.

After Arras, Cauchon was appointed one of a quadrumvirate charged with the administration of Paris, the others being Louis of Luxembourg, still Chancellor for Henry VI, and the bishops of Paris and Meaux. It was a thankless task, Paris was in a very depressed state. The English government had run out of funds to pay what we should now call its senior civil servants, the counsillors, the lawyers of the Parlement and those of a similar rank. In 1430 there had been fifty members of the Parlement, by 1435 there were only twenty-one.[1] The aristocrats and the wealthy were abandoning the city to the poor and the starving. On 15 March 1436, Louis of Luxembourg required that all senior members of the Church and government, together with twenty citizens of bourgeois status, representing the population, should take an oath of allegiance to Henry VI. A solemn public ceremony to that end was held in the Parlement. The population did not knock down the doors to get in to witness the proceedings. Neither the parish clergy nor the University were asked to take the oath. The University was still furious at the creation of a rival institution in Caen in 1432 and at Cauchon's support for it. Less than a month later, on 13 April 1436, Paris opened its gates to Charles VII's Constable of France, Arthur de Richemont, together with Dunois and other grandees, accompanied by two thousand knights and soldiers in the service of the king.

Cauchon decamped from Paris on 15 April, just as he had in previous years slipped out of Beauvais and Rheims. He obtained a safe-conduct from the French on payment of a large ransom. He would never see Paris again, residing mainly in his palace in Rouen, interspersed with visits to his cathedral of Lisieux, where he had a chapel constructed in the apse and dedicated to the Virgin Mary. His heraldic arms can still be seen there. On 18 December 1442, he died in his residence in Rouen. According to the testimony of Guillaume Colles in 1456, he expired suddenly while his barber was shaving him, doubtless a heart attack. Although Colles' testimony concerning the unedifying ends of several of the principal actors in the drama of 1431 is based on rumour and hearsay, it seems from other evidence that he may well be right about Cauchon. The story was current at any rate in Rouen. The bishop had expired *unhouseled, disappointed, unaneled*, without any of the rites of the Church. To many, it seemed a suitable fate.

Rouen was the headquarters of English rule in France. After 1429, the Regent visited Paris rarely, it was too volatile, with discontent and disaffection constantly rumbling beneath the surface, sedition lurking around dark corners and in narrow streets. Philip of Burgundy had tired of his office of governor and had resigned the post. He was more interested in his Burgundian territories. The difficulty of getting food supplies into the city was a cause of great distress as the roads and countryside around it were constantly under threat from marauding bands and elements of the French military. La Hire and his men ambushed the food convoys and made it impossible for the peasants of the villages to go out and harvest their crops and vines. The population had had to depend for years on provisions arriving by boat from Normandy along the Seine. On top of the cost of transport, these convoys with their large escorts of armed men were very expensive. The price of corn rose and what came through was of abysmal quality, even peas and beans were priced out of reach of the poor. They could not afford the price of wood to light a fire for themselves in the bitter winters.

At the end of January, 1431, Bedford and his duchess Anne made an exhausting journey by boat from Rouen to Paris, which they had not visited for fifteen months. They were accompanied by a huge convoy of fifty-six boats and twelve barges bringing food, escorted by a strong military force. The weather was very bad, the wind howling and the rain incessantly pelting down on the swollen river. When they arrived, there was great rejoicing and religious processions were held in thanksgiving. It was said that in four hundred years such a plentiful supply of provisions had never before been delivered at one go.[2]

Philip of Burgundy's unconcern for the city showed up badly against Bedford's admirable effort. His popularity was on the way down and people said that 'In truth, he cared not a fig whether they were dying of hunger or thirst, for everything was being lost through his negligence, in Paris and in his own territory, Burgundy'. They added that they didn't believe that he ever kept any of his promises. However, Bedford's supplies could only be a one-off measure. In April, 1431, twelve hundred of the poor and desperate, not counting the children, left the city, 'because there was nothing to eat and they were dying of hunger', writes the *Bourgeois*.[3]

In August, Bedford and Anne, travelled again from Rouen to Paris, narrowly escaping by river an ambush laid at Mantes by Poton de Xaintrailles. Shortly afterwards however, Poton was captured and with him the unfortunate Guillaume the Shepherd Boy. In October, Louviers surrendered to Bedford's forces after a five-month siege. English troops had been deserting in large numbers, some trying to take ship back to England, others living as bandits off the land and terrorising the population. Now however with the witch dead, Louviers taken and the morale of the troops somewhat repaired, things seemed to be looking up. The Duke of Burgundy's campaigns, on the other hand, were not going so well. His withdrawal from the siege of Compiègne in October was followed by setbacks and losses in the Dauphiné and other parts of his territories.

In Charles VII's kingdom, things were in a sorry mess. Charles appeared to be sunk in lethargy. On top of the problem of freebooters and bandits, there was a civil war going on between La Trémoille, grown more obese, wealthy and powerful than ever, and Richemont, who hated and despised him. La Trémoille, who had bought the services of the ferocious *routier* captain Villandrando and his ten thousand mercenaries, now in the early summer of 1430 cunningly invited his adversary to come and make peace with him. Richemont suspected treachery. Three of his friends agreed to meet La Trémoille and parley in his stead. La Trémoille welcomed them, invited them to accompany him on a hunt, had them seized in the forest and then held them captive in various castles. He next brought proceedings against them in the king's parlement at Poitiers, accusing them of plotting against his life and intending to take over the government of the land. On 7 May 1431, La Trémoille obtained from the parlement 'letters of abolition'. This was a document in which he unashamedly recounted all his crimes, including murder and pillage, and awarded himself a general pardon ensuring his untouchability for the future. The list of crimes did not include the snare set for his three unfortunate prisoners, against whom a death sentence was passed by the parlement the next day. Two were executed, the sentence of the third, Louis d'Amboise, was commuted to indefinite imprisonment. To have him executed was undesirable, in the first place because he was the father of the four-year-old girl to whom La Trémoille intended to marry, most advantageously, his own eldest son, and secondly, Louis d'Amboise's sister was married to La Trémoille's brother, Jean de la Trémoille. Georges contented himself with seizing the prisoner's viscounty.[4]

The war and the bloodshed, the misery, the terror, the marauding, continued throughout both French and Anglo-Burgundian territory. In November 1431, six months after Joan's death, Bedford at last took the young Henry VI to Paris to be crowned. The boy was taken from Rouen to Saint-Denis. He passed the nights of 30 November and 1 December in the precincts of the abbey of Saint Denis and was escorted into Paris on Sunday, 2 December, the first day of Advent. No doubt the date was chosen with forethought, the young king's coming mirroring the coming of the Lord.

He was met as he entered the city through the Porte Saint-Denis by the provost and the four chief magistrates (échevins), all splendidly arrayed in red, one of the colours representing both Paris and England. They held aloft a great blue canopy embroidered with the *fleurs-de-lis* of the royal House of France. A huge shield painted with the arms of Paris rose atop the gate, over the boy's head as he entered on his white horse. The goldsmiths, haberdashers and butchers and other guilds took turns to carry the magistrates' canopy. A cortege of heralds and trumpeters preceded the young king, on his route wine and milk were spouting from a great ornamental lily, actors cavorted as 'wild men' to amuse the throngs, set tableaux portrayed scenes from the infancy of Christ and the martyrdom of Saint Denis, while behind the boy king rode Bedford and his duchess in the forefront of the lay and ecclesiastical peers of England and Burgundy. The crowds cried 'Noël!' and waved as they passed. The old queen, Isabeau, as mentioned earlier, was at her window in the Hôtel Saint-Pol with her ladies as the young Henry rode by. He bowed and doffed his hat to her and she turned away, weeping. Who knows what thoughts prompted those tears? Was it pity for the boy whose adored mother, Henry V's widow, the beautiful Catherine of Valois, had had to abandon him in order to live hidden away from the court with her lover, her secret husband, Owen Tudor? Did Isabeau perhaps have some fear or premonition of the tragic future awaiting her grandson?

Young Henry was crowned in Notre-Dame on Sunday, 16 December, the day after his tenth birthday. All had been done to follow the traditional ceremonial for the coronation of kings of France, but for the majority of Frenchmen, it was all a hollow show, Paris was not Rheims and the sacred oil which had anointed Clovis had not been available to Henry VI. France already had its anointed king. Bedford showed little consideration for the susceptibilities of the French, taking for himself the role traditionally fulfilled by a peer of France. Also, it should have been the right of the bishop of Paris, Jacques du Châtelier, to conduct the ceremony in his own cathedral, but instead it was Heny Beaufort, the Cardinal of England, as the people called him, who officiated. Châtelier, loyal supporter of the English though he was, took deep offence. He was reduced to the role of assistant to Beaufort and was accompanied in that role by Louis of Luxembourg, the bishop of Noyon, and by Cauchon. The archbishop of the diocese which included Paris, Jean de Nanton, was conspicuous by his absence. Burgundy did not bother to come, the pope did not send a legate, French peers were few and far between. The canons of the cathedral made a formal complaint about the expense.

Worse was to follow. At the banquet laid on in a nearby palace, there was total disorder, for, says the *Bourgeois*,

> The common people of Paris had pushed in that morning, some to see, others to get anything they could eat, still others to pilfer and steal meats and other things, for with the throng there on that day, more that forty capons disappeared and a great number of purses were cut from their owners' belts and stolen.[5]

When the grandees and aldermen and others of the great and good tried to take their places at the long marble table, they found it taken over by

> ...cobblers, mustard sauce-makers, kitchen boys, wine sellers and navvies. When one or two of these were evicted, the places were at once filled by six or eight more.

The *cuisine* also was very substandard:

> What was served up was so bad that no one was satisfied. Most of the meat, especially that for the ordinary people, had been cooked the previous Thursday, which seemed very strange to the French, for

the English were in charge of the kitchen and they didn't care about their reputation, but just wanted to get it over and done with. Indeed no-one had a good word to say about it, even the destitute sick in the Hôtel-Dieu [i.e. the town hospital]) said that they had never seen such miserable left-overs.[6]

On the day after the coronation, by way of entertainment, there was held what the *Bourgeois* calls *unes petites joutes*, clearly paltry little jousts, and he adds that people were saying they had seen better displays at the weddings of the children of goldsmiths and other merchants.

Henry VI left Paris for Rouen on 26 December and departed for England a fortnight later, never to see the capital city of France again. To the chagrin of the population, none of the customary acts of royal generosity following a coronation were made, no prisoners were pardoned, not even the smallest of the heavy taxes was abolished, and this notwithstanding the right royal welcome which the population had given the boy amidst all their hardships, the miserable wages, the sky-high cost of food and firewood, the exceptionally cold winter, snowing and freezing day and night. The popularity of the English was at an all-time low.

The year 1432 was not a good one for Bedford. Already in Lille, on 13 December 1431, the pope's legate (he who hadn't come to the coronation of Henry VI!) had achieved an agreement to a six-year truce endorsed by the ambassadors of Philip of Burgundy and Charles VII. Bedford was now on his own. The financing of the war was a great problem, hence he had little option but to tax the French population heavily. To add to the miseries of the people, it was still snowing in April. In March there was widespread flooding in Paris, which lasted until the end of the first week in April. The bitter weather continued into May. The fruit crops were ruined. There was no let-up and towards the end of June there were terrible thunderstorms and hailstones pelted down as big as billiard balls in places close to Paris, such as Lagny and Meaux.[7]

In Rouen, on 3 February, a small band of intrepid French soldiers, under the command of one Guillaume de Ricarville, who had fought at the siege of Orléans, managed to scale the walls of the castle and seize the tower, killing or putting to flight the garrison. Ricarville then departed and rode in great haste to Beauvais in order to seek reinforcements. Unfortunately none were forthcoming, the men-at-arms quarrelling bitterly among themselves over questions of booty and their commander dithering as to what he should do. The troops occupying the tower were left to their fate. The English commander, the Earl of Arundel, had managed to escape and returned with troops and artillery and reinforcements called up from among the townspeople. The men in the tower held out for twelve days, but at last were forced to surrender. On 16 and 17 March, they were executed in the Place du Vieux Marché, where Joan herself had died. Ricarville lived to fight another day and to give testimony at the Nullity trial in 1456, where he affirmed that he believed that Joan was divinely inspired.

On Saturday, 12 April, Chartres was taken by a stratagem. Three carts supposedly laden with barrels of fish and salt gained entry through the principal gate of the town, One remained behind on the drawbridge to prevent it being raised, while four soldiers sprang out of the other barrels to keep the gate open. The waiting French troops poured in. The bishop of the town, ardently Anglo-Burgundian in sympathy, issued forth, armed for war and accompanied by a number of Burgundians. He was mortally wounded, the blow having been struck, it is said, by Joan's old comrade-in-arms, Dunois. There were around sixty casualties in the ensuing skirmishes before the town was taken. On 23 April, Charles VII was solemnly recognised as the king of France by the cathedral chapter. In return he issued 'letters of abolition' to all who had been in any way involved with his adversaries. This was a general amnesty which guaranteed their persons and property and the privileges of the town. Chartres remained loyal to him ever after.

In August 1432 Bedford himself had to abandon the three-month siege of Lagny, leaving behind his artillery and large supplies of wine, meats, bread, all of which were in short supply in Paris and reaching sky-high prices. The Parisians were incensed at such a loss of resources, especially as they didn't even dare to go out of the city to get in the wine harvest. The French troops, having been emboldened by their success, were now carrying out raids everywhere. The *Bourgeois* calls Bedford's withdrawal from Lagny shameful. People said that the siege had cost the enormous sum of one hundred and fifty *saluts d'or*. Taxation would of course have to cover the all the losses.

Bedford's skilful use of propaganda, the constant insistence on the barbarism of the 'Armagnacs' and the harping on their atrocities, no longer produced such a powerful effect. Poverty, plague and famine spoke more loudly. The corn harvest had failed and in September there was an epidemic that stuck cruelly at young people and children. Mortality was high. Conspiracies rumbled on below the surface in the capital. On 3 September 1432, the noble lady abbess of the royal convent of Saint-Antoine-des-Champs, Emerance de Calonne, of all unlikely people, together with some of her nuns, was arrested and imprisoned in the Châtelet on a charge of being involved in a seditious plot. She was however later released and returned to her convent. Whatever the truth of the charge, it shows the oppressive atmosphere of suspicion and fear prevailing in the city.[8]

In 1432 also, as already mentioned, a university was set up in Caen, to the fury of the learned doctors and professors in Paris. It was seen not only as a rival institution, but as clear evidence of English mistrust of the political situation in Paris. Jean Favier points out that Bedford, faithful to the dying wishes of Henry V, was making provision for the future English duchy of Normandy, which he was determined to maintain at all costs. The University of Caen would provide that duchy with the necessary elite, the province would not be dependent on Paris for its intelligentsia. The professors of the Sorbonne were deeply anxious at the time about their financial situation, given the decrease in the population of the capital, due to plague, hunger and banishments, with a drop of ninety per cent in house values and rents in the previous ten years. Around Notre Dame well over half the houses stood empty.[9] Where was the University's funding to come from, especially now with the competition from Caen? A great number of its students came from Normandy. Letters of protest were sent to Bedford, the pope, the council of Bâle, the Parlement. Protest proved fruitless, and the University of Caen was formally inaugurated in 1439, its first Rector being an Englishman, Michael Tregury from Cornwall, later Archbishop of Dublin.

At the end of 1432, Bedford was stricken by the death of his wife, Anne of Burgundy. Theirs had been a good and loving marriage. Bedford's devotions, his pilgrimage around the churches of Paris, masses said for Anne's recovery, the exposition in Notre Dame of the relics of Saint Geneviève, the patron saint of Paris, all was in vain. Anne died in Paris, in the Hôtel de Bourbon, on the night of 13–14 November 1432. The *Bourgeois* writes an affectionate obituary, describing her as 'the most gracious of all the ladies then in France, for she was as good as she was beautiful, and in the flower of her youth, being only twenty-eight years old when she died. She was certainly well loved by the people of Paris.'[10] She had shown herself to be kind, generous and charitable, not fearing to visit the sick in the city's hospital, the Hôtel-Dieu. Indeed it was there that she caught the fever of which she died. She had died childless and her death broke the personal link between Bedford and his brother-in-law Philip of Burgundy. She was buried in the church of the Celestines, not far from the tomb of the Duke of Orleans, assassinated by order of her father.

Bedford married again in April, 1433, only four months after his wife's death, but we should not deduce from that a lack of loyalty to Anne. He married the niece of the cardinal Louis of Luxembourg, a pretty and lively seventeen-year-old, but the marriage was widely recognised as political, an opportune strengthening of the alliance with the powerful dynasty of Luxembourg. Bedford knew he was in sore need of trustworthy allies, Philip of Burgundy having shown himself so slippery. Philip had now made a six months truce with Charles VII and had attended neither Henry VI's coronation nor his own sister's funeral. His fury was aroused at news of the marriage, coming so soon after Anne's death. Nor had his permission been sought, as it ought to have been, for the marriage of a daughter of one of his vassals. In late May, a meeting was arranged between Philip and Bedford at Saint Omer. Both arrived there, but then each stubbornly refused to leave his lodgings to meet the other, regarding such a step as a loss of dignity, and each departed in high dudgeon.

In February 1432, the papal legate, Cardinal Albergati, had arrived in Paris to urge peace talks between Burgundy, England and France. A conference was arranged and took place in Auxerre at the end of November, but broke up without agreement. The disappointment in Paris was immense. The people accused the returning delegates of scandalously wasting both time and money. So great was the anger, that, in order to calm it, several of the delegates had to be imprisoned and only later quietly released. Anger was turned against the Chancellor, Louis of Luxembourg, who was now, says the *Bourgeois* in 1434, in sole charge in Paris, Philip of Burgundy never appearing there and having abandoned the post of regent of France.

In 1433, Bedford had to return to England to justify his conduct of French affairs before Parliament, accusations of incompetence swirling about him and emanating from the circles around his brother Gloucester, with whom he was on bad terms. He also desperately needed finance for his army in France, but the parliament and people were less than eager to supply it. This was his last visit to England, perhaps he preferred now to be in France, where he was generally liked and respected by those who knew him. In France it was the Chancellor, Louis of Luxembourg who was, says the *Bourgeois*, 'greatly hated by the people, who said privately and often openly too, that but for him, there would have been peace in France. Because of that, he and his cronies were more hated than the emperor Nero ever was.'. The *Bourgeois* complains that French attacks were carried out right up to the gates of Paris and no great lord made any effort to put an end to the war.[11] The people blamed Bedford and Burgundy, but above all Luxembourg. So it went on, freezing winters, floods, storms, scorching weather at intervals in the summer, crops failing, hunger, epidemics, conspiracies, attacks, marauding bands terrorising the countryside. The people were worn out, famished and despairing.

In 1433 an incident took place in the castle of Chinon which would have a beneficial impact on the character and conduct of Charles VII. While night had fallen and all was shrouded in darkness, the king asleep in his chamber with his wife, three nobles, followed by fifty armed men, entered the castle by a postern gate opened to them by Olivier Frétard, lieutenant for Raoul de Gaucourt, the same who had been captain of Orleans at the time of the siege. The imminent *coup* went ahead of course with Gaucourt's blessing. The party made its way up to La Trémoille's bedroom on the floor above the king. He was awakened by the noise, yelled, was then dealt a blow with the hilt of a sword and stabbed in the stomach. His immense girth was such that the wound missed all the vital organs. Probably his death was no part of the plot, for he was next taken prisoner. He was tied up, bandaged and carried off, down the staircase and out of the castle. The king had been awakened by the shouting and scuffle, but he was calmed by his wife (who had advance knowledge of the plot) and told that Richemont, whom he feared, was not present.

The leaders of the *coup* came in and assured him that they were acting in his best interest and that of the country. So persuaded, he got back into bed and went to sleep again. La Trémoille was taken to a nearby castle. Some time later, after paying a large ransom and taking an oath never to go near the king or court again, he was released. The mighty reign of the 'king's governor' had been brought at last to an ignominious end. Louis d'Amboise, whom we last heard of as La Trémoille's captive in 1431, recovered his freedom and his lands.

For Charles VII it was delivery from a paralysing spell. His determination and confidence in himself would grow steadily thereafter. Those around him now were his mother-in-law Yolande, Queen of Sicily, and others who would serve him with intelligence and loyalty. The Constable, Richemont, would soon be received back into the king's service. The archbishop of Rheims, Regnault de Chartres, repudiated his old crony, La Trémoille, and kept his place on the king's Council. Dunois also had his place on it. He would become the Count of Dunois in 1439 (but remained proud of his title of *Bâtard d'Orléans*!) and *lieutenant-général* of the army ten years later, a post second only to that of Constable. He would play a large part in the reconquest of Normandy in the early 1450s.

The war continued. The historian Vallet de Viriville remarks that it was atrocious. The soldiers were no longer led by a saintly idealist like Joan, insisting on the rules of a 'just war', but by such as Rodrigo de Villandrando, a merciless 'captain of foreign bandits'.[12] The peasantry were the victims of robbers and soldiers or deserters in search of booty on both sides. Bedford had as a last resort decided to arm the peasants against such attacks, ordering them to practice archery on Sundays, but massacres and robberies continued. When he returned at the beginning of 1434 from England he was met by the news of a massacre perpetrated by the Englishman Richard Venables, who styled himself *King of France and England*. With his band of freebooters, he had slaughtered some twelve hundred villagers and peasants who had tried to oppose him near Falaise.[13] To his credit, Bedford had him and his assassins hunted down and executed. But even that lesson was in vain. The badly-paid English soldiers were angered to see the French peasants armed and defending themselves as best they could against the marauders, for no pay at all. It seemed like unfair competition. In August 1434, a large body of the peasant militia was ambushed by soldiers near Saint-Pierre-sur Dives, about twenty miles from Lisieux, and hundreds were 'put to the sword', as the *Bourgeois* describes the killing.[14] It is debatable whether the attackers were regular soldiers or pillaging deserters, the *Bourgeois* simply describes them as 'Englishmen'. Bedford's best efforts could not counterbalance such outrage. The peasants now started to attack those garrisons where numbers were reduced.

So the misery continued. In 1433, Philip of Burgundy was ravaging Champagne and the Beaujolais, while the Mont Saint-Michel repelled another assault from Bedford's forces in 1434. In May, 1435, the Earl of Arundel was defeated when he attacked a fortress defended by La Hire and Xaintrailles at Gerberoy in Picardy. The earl himself was badly wounded in the foot. He was taken prisoner and died of gangrene a few days later. On 1 June that year, a force under Dunois and the captain of Lagny succeeded in taking Saint-Denis. However, after a siege with fierce fighting and heavy losses on both sides, the newly installed garrison had to capitulate and was allowed to leave on 24 September. But by that time events had moved on. After a lengthy illness, Bedford had died ten days earlier, a sad death, for he knew that his dearest hopes were shattered, since the Treaty of Arras was about to be signed by Philip of Burgundy and Charles VII on 21 September, signalling an end to English ambitions for a dual kingdom.

The search for peace had been going on for some time. Charles was always a peripatetic monarch, Chinon and Bourges in the Loire valley, Lyons and Vienne on the Rhone, were among his favourite stopping-off places and it was in Vienne, in 1434, that legates from the pope, Eugene IV, and delegates from the Council of Bâle came to urge the king to renew the effort for peace abandoned at Auxerre two years before. Charles VII had allowed Richemont to come to Vienne, as well as Tanguy du Chastel, he who had saved the young Dauphin from the mobs in 1418 and despatched (or so it was believed) John the Fearless at Montereau. Tanguy had been sent away in 1424, when Charles had had to dismiss him as the price of a truce with Burgundy. Now he was back. The Vienne meeting was however a convocation of the French party alone and it restricted itself to discussions of the conduct of the war. But the climate was changing.

Serious negotiations for peace opened in Nevers in January 1435 and were attended by Philip of Burgundy. Among the French delegates was Charles VII's cousin, the Duke of Bourbon, formerly the Count of Clermont, who had recently acceded to the duchy on his father's death as a prisoner-of-war in England since Agincourt. Bourbon was accompanied by his wife, Agnès, the sister of Philip of Burgundy, and there was a joyful reunion of the brother and sister who had not seen each other for many long years. Splendid festivities and merry-making marked the occasion. Burgundy and Bourbon were reconciled. Philip's natural affinity was in any case with the royal family of France, rather than with the Lancastrians. He was also vain, sensual and pleasure-loving, a very different character from the earnest and severe Bedford, who had hurt the duke's prickly pride more than once. Politically also it was increasingly evident that it would be to Philip's advantage to make peace with Charles VII. It would not do to antagonise the Holy Roman Emperor Sigismond, who was a friend of Charles and opposed to Philip's ambitions for the expansion of his territory. In Flanders, the wool trade with England was becoming less important, merino wool was coming in from Spain and in general an increase in trade with other countries of the continent was now more desirable and the war was an obstacle to it.

Philip of Burgundy had one tricky problem: he had sworn allegiance to the dual monarchy of Henry V and his heirs at Troyes. He prided himself inordinately as a man of honour. Had he not established with great pomp and ceremony the chivalrous Order of the Golden Fleece? How could he now break his oath and sign a treaty with Charles VII? His brilliant chancellor Rolin, depicted for posterity in the famous paintings by Jan van Eyck and Rogier van der Weyden, presented him with the answer: Henry V's death had preceded that of King Charles VI, so in fact the English monarch had never been king of France. Therefore he could not pass on to his heir, Henry VI, any French vassal, in this instance, Philip of Burgundy. Honour thus satisfied, Philip could now happily go ahead.

Burgundy hadn't been seen in Paris since 1431, but when he left Nevers he returned in great style to the city at Easter 1435. He made a spectacular entry, mounted on a magnificently caparisoned horse and accompanied by his wife, whose infant son was carried on a glittering litter. Four of his young illegitimate children rode beside them, all mounted on their splendidly bedecked ponies, and these were followed by a vast 'noble company' of mounted lords and ladies in all their ceremonial finery. Three wagons covered with cloth of gold came behind the nobility, next followed a hundred and twenty wagons carrying arms, artillery and provisions of salted meats and fish, cheeses and wines. The company was not going to be short of provisions in the starving city.

On Easter Sunday, 17 April, Philip held an open court to which all citizens had access, following the royal custom of the kings of France at Eastertide. On the Tuesday he attended a solemn requiem mass for the repose of the soul of his sister Anne in the church of the Celestines, making lavish offerings of money and candles and distributing largesse to all the priests present. The contrast with the tight-fistedness during the coronation of Henry VI was not unintentional. On Wednesday, 20 April, the duchess received a delegation of the ladies of Paris, who begged her to plead with her husband for an end to the war. She answered graciously that this was a thing she greatly desired and that the duke was equally anxious to achieve it. In fact, a peace conference was already in preparation and Philip and his family left Paris the very next day, in order for him to prepare for the Congress of Arras in July.

The Congress opened on 1 July. Burgundy and England were to meet with France to thrash out peace terms under the mediation of the papal mission headed by Cardinal Albergati. The Cardinal of Cyprus was there as the second negotiator, representing the Council of Bâle. Albergati had a large experience in the field of negotiations, in particular in those between the warring parties in France, where he had undertaken several such missions in the period 1430 to 1434. 'The history of the later medieval papacy as a peacemaker in Europe still has to be written,' remarks Jocelyne

Dickinson, adding that 'the papacy was in this sphere the equivalent of the modern United Nations.'[15] The papal mission was no lightweight affair, Albergati's two secretaries would each later become pope, one as Nicolas V, the other as Pius II. The nominal head of Charles VII's legation was the Duke of Bourbon, but the active leader was Regnault de Chartres, the Archbishop of Rheims. There were twelve ambassadors on the French side and a large number of French delegates, including Richemont and Alençon.

The English delegation was led nominally by Henry VI's uncle, Henry Beaufort, Cardinal of Winchester, but he was in no hurry and only arrived at Arras on 23 August. The Archbishop of York, John Kemp, conducted the negotiations on the English side, with Bishop Cauchon as his deputy. The latter's presence and function represented the interests of the 'French subjects of Henry VI' and the English claim to the 'dual monarchy'. Guillaume Érard, who had 'preached' Joan in the cemetery of Saint Ouen in Rouen, was also there as part of the delegation of Henry VI. Paris and the University sent their own independent delegates, among whom we meet again Thomas de Courcelles. Burgundy's ambassadors were led by his celebrated chancellor Rolin. However, as Dickinson tells us, 'The agreement with Burgundy was almost cut and dried before the arrival of the ambassadors at Arras'.[16] Just over a week after the arrival of the English, on 1 September, Philip gave a banquet in honour of Henry Beaufort, at the end of which he picked a quarrel with the cardinal, accusing him of ruining the Anglo-Burgundian alliance by his obstinacy. Beaufort flew into a rage and furious accusations were exchanged. Burgundy had prepared his defection to Charles.

Cauchon put forward the English proposals: their claim to the French crown was non-negotiable. Charles VII was to give up all the towns he had taken, in return the English would pay compensation and recognise his rule over all his territories south of the Loire except for Guyenne. Henry VI would marry one of Charles VII's daughters (shades of Henry V and Princess Catherine?). The French ambassadors rejected the handover, but accepted the marriage proposal. They went as far as they could to meet the demands of the English, proposing that, except for the Mont Saint Michel, Henry VI could keep Guyenne and Normandy, but as a vassal of the king of France. This was rejected and on 6 September, led by the Cardinal of Winchester, the whole English delegation left Arras in a downpour of rain, which must have reflected the prevailing mood of the party.

News was brought to Bedford on his deathbed. He died on 14 September and was buried in Rouen cathedral, where his Norman ancestors had been buried before him. He rested in peace in his black marble tomb until 1562, when it was destroyed by Calvinists on their rampage through the churches of Rouen. A plaque marks the spot where the remains of the Regent of English France still lie, a man with many good qualities, but in a lost cause. He was replaced by the Duke of York and then by Warwick in 1437, both with the title of Lieutenant-General. Warwick died in April, 1439, and shortly afterwards the Duke of York again filled the vacant post.

At Arras, Burgundy drove a hard bargain. Charles VI was however prepared to go to great lengths to achieve reconciliation. On 21 September, after a solemn Mass in the cathedral of the city and in the presence of the ambassadors and delegates, the provisions of the Treaty of Arras were proclaimed from the pulpit, after which Charles VII's aged ambassador, Jean Tudert, walked slowly up the nave to kneel at the feet of Philip of Burgundy seated in the choir and surrounded by his family and knights and retainers. The old man made a humble apology, in the king's name, for the assassination of John the Fearless. The terms of the apology were to be included in the treaty itself, stating that Charles had always disapproved of the murder, but that at the time he had been too young and inexperienced to prevent it. Philip accepted the apology, raised the old man up, kissed him and took a solemn oath, placing his hand on a crucifix, to make peace with the king and never again to bring up the subject of his father's death. A *Te Deum* was sung, the Duke and the great and good of the kingdom processed out of the cathedral to be greeted by ecstatic cries of *Noel!* from the crowd. A whole week of banquets and spectacular celebrations followed.

Under the treaty, the instigators of the murder of John the Fearless were to be punished, Masses were to be said for his soul, a Trappist monastery founded in his memory at Montereau and a memorial erected on the fatal bridge. Great tracts of territories were granted to Philip, who was dispensed for as long as he would live from doing homage as vassal to Charles VII. If Charles should pre-decease him, Philip would then do homage as vassal of the next king. His descendants would re-assume the duty of homage to the king of France and his successors. There were those who felt strongly that Charles had conceded far too much. The faithful chronicler of the Duke of Alençon, Perceval de Cagny, bitterly disapproved of Charles's concessions and considered that, if amends were to be made to the dead, Philip of Burgundy should have apologised for his father's murder of the Duke of Orleans and have founded churches and masses for the repose of that duke's soul. [17] The captive Charles d'Orléans himself and his half-brother Dunois were sorely disappointed that Charles had not insisted on the release of the former as a pre-condition of the treaty. The duke would only be released in 1440, on payment of a huge ransom. His poetry, written in captivity and later, is one of the treasures of late medieval French literature.

When the Treaty was signed, the knell of the dual English-French monarchy was sounded, but the war dragged horribly on. There was fury in England and resentment at new taxes and levies of troops. Philip of Burgundy was execrated as a vile traitor, there were riots in London and the houses of Flemish merchants were burned down. English pirates in the Channel were given official leave to plunder Flemish shipping, previous sanctions against such activity being dropped. On the French side, a large number of soldiers in the pay of nobles and princes were disbanded after the Treaty. To the unemployed mercenaries of assorted nationalities were added desperate men of all kinds, starving peasants, dispossessed nobles, criminals, thus increasing the numbers of greatly feared freebooters. They were known, as we have already seen earlier, as *routiers* or *écorcheurs*. They were popularly referred to also as *bouchers* (butchers), because of their ferocious inhumanity. They burnt villages, extorted ransoms, pillaged, raped, murdered, in a word they committed every crime of which an undisciplined soldiery is capable. The troops of captains such as La Hire or Poton de Xaintrailles had been recruited largely from such desperados, but they had been paid like other troops, discipline had been imposed and under their captains they now served Charles VII, harrying the English, even succeeding in taking towns and fortresses. Others however simply sold their services to whichever side would pay them, be it the English or the French.

Basin recounts how disaffected soldiers on both sides would raze villages and take the peasants to ransom, leaving them to die of 'hunger and vermin' in foul dungeons or the depths of forests, or sometimes at the bottom of ditches if the huge ransoms could not be raised. But despite the best efforts of the English captains to control the situation in Normandy, resistance to English rule grew. Dispossessed nobles returned like 'ravening wolves', says Basin, to incite rebellion on what had been their land, not too difficult a campaign, given the rising hatred of the peasantry for the English soldiers. That hatred was furiously reciprocated, resistance was put down with massacres, such as that at Caudebec where a great peasant rebellion, armed only with farming implements, was slaughtered by a charge of two or three hundred mounted knights in armour wielding steel.

Normandy was now a desert, there was no farming, thousands of refugees were trying to get to Brittany or England in search of work and sustenance. Thousands more died of hunger, epidemics, or fires on board ship. Thomas Basin describes the misery as follows:

> Thus it came about, that in a short pace of time, that once noble land, abounding in population and wealth, fell into total devastation and desolation, all its great farms lying uncultivated and neglected. In that part of the country there was such terrible famine, accompanied by plague, that it is estimated that in a brief interval more than two hundred thousand souls perished by the sword, hunger or disease. Many indeed left for foreign parts, and many of them, taking ship for Brittany or England, found themselves trapped in miserable servitude, others were drowned in storms at sea or died as soon as they reached the shore, having been infected by their companions who had already caught the

plague. So grief and lamentation followed those unhappy multitudes, not only in their native land, but wherever they tried to go.[18]

Basin goes on to describe the bands of men and women begging in the streets, those lying in the hospitals for the poor in Rouen and all the villages of Normandy, so many that it was beyond the means even of the charitable among the rich to help them.

Uprisings continued throughout Normandy after Arras. Dieppe was taken by the French in October, 1435. Harfleur followed, but in 1436 it was retaken by the English, who also managed to recover other places. On 3 May, 1435, the French had taken St. Denis. Anti-English plots were rife in Paris, the small English garrison was underpaid and hungry and had been given leave by the governor of the city to pillage the villages roundabout. By the spring of 1436, Paris was encircled by the troops of Richemont, who held the surrounding places, Melun, Lagny, Saint Germain-en-Laye and others. With the help of a staged riot against the English within the city and that of the guards on the Porte Saint-Jacques, who opened the gate to the French troops, Richemont, Dunois and Villiers de l'Isle-Adam entered Paris on 13 April 1436. Charles VII proclaimed a general amnesty and forbade pillage. The soldiers of the English garrison were allowed to come out of their refuge in the Bastille and leave, never to return. With them departed Louis of Luxembourg, Simon Morhier the Provost, and others devoted to the English government. Charles showed the same forbearance to other English-occupied places as he took them. Was the royal generosity due to the fact that Joan herself, at Chinon, had insisted that he should pardon all his adversaries, whether under arms or otherwise?

The historian Desmond Seward has described the period from 1435 to 1450 as a 'protracted rearguard action by the English in France'.[19] The anger in England at the losses in France is reflected nearly half a century later in Shakespeare's play, *Henry VI, Part II*, where in Act I, scene I, the Duke of York declaims:

Anjou and Maine are given to the French.
Paris is lost; the State of Normandy
Stands on a tickle point now they are gone.
Suffolk concluded on the articles,
The peers agreed and Henry was well pleased
To change two dukedoms for a duke's fair daughter.
I cannot blame them all, what is't to them?

In 1435, Fastolf proposed to the English a desperate plan for total war in France, neither women nor children were to be spared. Happily this idea was never acted upon. The English did however have some successes. In July 1436, Burgundian troops laid siege to Calais, but in August

Humphrey of Gloucester led a campaign into Flanders and in 1437 the Calais siege had to be lifted. Philip of Burgundy, tired of revolts instigated in his territories by the English, concluded a truce with them in 1439. He was well versed in the art of truce-making, as we know. Calais of course remained in English hands until the reign of Henry VIII's daughter Mary. Also in 1436, Dieppe was re-taken from the French and Talbot was successful against the troops of Xaintrailles and La Hire who were besieging Rouen. In 1437, the same greatly feared English general arrived with his troops before the very walls of Paris, instilling terror in the population. However in October 1437, Montereau was taken by troops under the command of Charles VII in person. The introspective and solitary monarch had at last matured into a determined military leader, deciding and tirelessly conducting manoeuvres himself. On the day of the assault, in full armour, he waded with his men into the ditches around the city and scrambled up a scaling-ladder, sword in hand, appearing among the first of the assailants on the city walls.

Charles VII at last made his solemn state entry into Paris from Saint Denis on 12 November 1437. He was now on his way to becoming Charles the Victorious. In glittering armour and mounted on a great horse draped to the ground in cloth of gold, with his son, the fourteen-year old Dauphin, similarly arrayed, riding at his side, he was accompanied by a long cavalcade of his knights and troops, the Scots Guard in the forefront, his archers and his heralds parading behind. Jean d'Aulon, Joan's faithful companion and chief-of-staff, walked beside the king's horse, holding the bridle. Dunois, La Hire, the Count of Vendôme other nobles and the main body of the victorious army followed in the king's wake.

He was greeted by a long cortege of notables, the provost of the city and the provost of the merchants, the aldermen, the representatives of the Parlement and University, the bishop of Paris, a bevy of abbots and friars, the Archbishop of Sens, in his office as metropolitan, all were present to do him homage. In a ceremony outside the Porte Saint-Denis, the keys of the city were solemnly handed over to the king, who then gave them into the keeping of his Constable, Richemont. It was a powerful symbol of the town's voluntary return to the royal obedience. When the cortege reached Notre Dame, it was Nicolas Midi, the same who had harangued Joan before her execution in the Old Market in Rouen, who delivered the speech welcoming Charles VII to Paris. Was it the same speech, made in the same place, no doubt slightly doctored now to fit the occasion, with which he had welcomed young Henry VI to the capital exactly half a dozen years earlier?

The great cathedral bells pealed, the doors of the church opened, cries of *Noël!* resounded on all sides, a *Te Deum* was sung. The rejoicing was genuine, for the outlook of the population had changed, the *Armagnacs* had become the *French*, the town had not been taken by assault, but had been liberated. The citizens had never been pro-English, simply pro-Burgundian for as long as the popularity of Philip of Burgundy prevailed. In any case, Burgundy himself had now gone over to the French side. Burgundian counsillors would henceforth sit alongside Charles VII's representatives in the Parlement. Men appointed to high office by Bedford and others who had served the Anglo-Burgundian government kept their places or were appointed again to positions of importance. The new provost of Paris, for example, Philippe de Ternant, had been a loyal servant of Burgundy.

Charles remained only three weeks in Paris before Christmas, 1437. He never felt any affection for the city from which he had had to flee in 1418. When Paris had been taken in 1436, and for a lengthy period thereafter, it was in a state of economic depression, its industry and commerce wrecked by the preceding decades of war. Its population had fallen by half, whole districts had been devastated. The shops were empty, the population was demoralised, the poor were starving. The *Bourgeois* describes the misery in Paris and the surrounding countryside in 1438. As winter came in, wolves again roamed the streets, killing at least one child and attacking the dogs. Plague and famine ravaged the region. Convoys of supplies could not reach the city, being harassed by English troops, just as the French had previously obstructed Bedford's convoys. Victims of the plague included the sister of Charles VII, Marie de France, who was a nun in the convent at Poissy, and also the highly unpopular bishop of Paris, Jacques du Châtelier. Richemont and the aristocracy abandoned the town. The people lay dying of plague and hunger in the Hôtel-Dieu, the hospital for the destitute. The *Bourgeois* writes,

> Mortality was extremely high, for in this year five thousand died in the Hôtel-Dieu, and in the city more than forty-five thousand, men, women and children. When death entered a house, it carried off nearly everybody, especially the strongest and the youngest.[20]

The figures can be no more than a rough estimate, as are the medieval accounts of the casualties in war, but undoubtedly a very great number perished.

Charles and his government had to set about rebuilding what had been destroyed, re-organising taxes and municipal administration. The great city had somehow to attract again the cosmopolitan flocks of students to its university, to re-establish its coteries of lawyers, its magistrates, its rich merchants, to lure back its aristocracy and their gorgeously liveried retainers to their great town houses and vast gardens within the city walls. Nobody could predict when the many hostelries would again bustle with convivial business, the narrow streets be congested with the passage of mule-drawn carts laden with goods, when the half-timbered houses and shops and markets on the five bridges spanning the Seine would again be thronged with artisans of every trade, the streets be noisy with butchers, bakers and candlestick makers, with crowds sauntering or gossiping with their neighbours, children playing, beggars begging and street entertainers entertaining. The restoration of this happy state would take quite some time. When Louis XI came to the throne in 1461, after the death of his father, he told the pope that it would take a century to repair all that had been destroyed in the Franco-English wars.

Two events marked 1440. One was the release against a huge ransom of Duke Charles of Orleans in November from his twenty-five year captivity in England. The other took place early in that year, when Charles VII had to face a rebellion nominally led by his son, not yet seventeen years old, who could not wait to become Louis XI. In 1439, Charles had given the youth his first important military appointments, against the English in the Languedoc and following that in the Poitou region, with its capital Poitiers. But these honours and appointments did not satisfy the Dauphin. He was persuaded to believe his chance had come when discontent was occasioned among the great nobles by Charles's determination to reform recruitment to the army.

The king was determined to end the nobles' right to employ their own troops under mercenary captains, in fact bands of the rampaging *écorcheurs*. Captains were now to be appointed solely by the king and discipline enforced. At the end of 1439, a decree to that effect had been promulgated after a meeting in Orleans of the Three Estates (Clergy, Nobility and Bourgeoisie). Each captain was limited to six mounted auxiliaries (the unit known as the 'lance') and detachments were billeted in various towns. Their hosts were required to finance their upkeep, paying a fixed rate per man according to the regulations on food rations. Payment for fodder for the animals was regulated also. The captains appointed by the king were given the task of ridding the army of the hangers-on and bandits who had terrorised the countryside. A standing army, properly paid and disciplined was in the process of being born. The great nobles also lost their right to levy taxes (the *taille*) on their peasants. Taxes were to be levied only by the king. It was darkly rumoured however by the discontented nobles, that Charles's intent, in pushing through these reforms, was to make of himself an absolute ruler, a tyrant.

Encouraged by the scheming La Trémoille, now banished, and the Duke of Bourbon, who promised to depose Charles VII and make the Dauphin regent, Louis agreed to become the nominal head of a revolt led by a number of noblemen, including, very surprisingly, Dunois and Alençon, Joan's *beau Duc*. Charles sent Richemont to bring the rebels to heel, a result achieved in a couple of months, for they had no support among the population. Charles forgave all concerned and his son was pardoned when he made his apologies. That would, however, not be the end of the dissent between father and son. After 1445 and the death of the Scottish princess Margaret, to whom the Dauphin Louis had been married in 1436 at the age of fourteen and who was regarded with some affection by her father-in-law, father and son became completely estranged. They never saw each other thereafter. Louis went his own way and in 1461 even refused his father's dying request to come and bid him farewell.

In 1441, Charles laid siege to Pontoise, less than twenty miles from Paris and last of the English-held strongholds in the Ile-de-France. It was taken on 25 October. In 1442, he invaded Guyenne, but failed to take Bordeaux or Bayonne. At the end of May 1444, Suffolk managed to negotiate a truce signed at Tours, the French negotiators being Dunois and Bourbon. Suffolk was obliged to make a secret agreement to hand over Maine to Charles d'Anjou, the Count of Maine and brother-in-law of Charles VII. A marriage was also arranged between Henry VI and the daughter of Charles d'Anjou. They were married in 1445. The truce was to last for two years, but at the end of 1445, Henry VI agreed to surrender Maine and the truce was extended until April 1447. While news of such a truce caused fury in England, the hard-pressed English in France reacted with relief. There had been no break in hostilities for over fifty years.

Meanwhile, the state of English finances progressively worsened while that of the French improved. Charles VII's reforms of the army were also put into effect. By 1445 he had a well-equipped standing army. Instead of being made redundant in times of peace, the troops were now paid regularly. Discipline was enforced and no soldiers now needed to resort to living off the land. As early as 1434, Charles had found himself an artillery expert of genius named Jean Bureau. Bureau had started in life as a lawyer and by 1443 he was appointed Treasurer of France. With his brother Gaspard he had by then branched out into the study of artillery. Their cannon had a longer range than the longbow and gunpowder had become more deadly in the early thirties, so the dreaded English archers found themselves outclassed.

The brothers' artillery played an important role in the ensuing French victories, among others, those of Montereau and Pontoise, and in Charles VII's Normandy campaign of 1449–50. Rouen and Harfleur were taken in late 1449. In some places, in fact, there was no resistance and the gates were simply thrown open to the French. In Rouen, Talbot and Somerset and the English garrison had to retreat into the citadel when the gates were opened by the inhabitants to welcome Charles VII and Dunois into the capital of what Juliet Barker has called the *English kingdom of France*. Somerset and the garrison were allowed to go and retired to Caen, Talbot was held hostage for the payment of a very large indemnity. A general amnesty was granted to all citizens, but all English property and goods were confiscated, reducing many soldiers and others, among them members of the Church and nobility, to dismal poverty.

Following the fall of Rouen, England was awash with ugly rumour and anger. The loss of Normandy must be due to treachery among the great. Who else could it be but Suffolk? News of the secret deal with Charles VII and Charles d'Anjou had leaked out and were sufficient to damn the latter. In Act I of Shakespeare's aforementioned play, York furiously exclaims:

> For Suffolk's duke, may he be suffocate,
> That dims the honour of this warlike isle!

In January 1450 the duke was tried on various counts of treason and corruption. Henry VI, wishing to show him mercy, ordered his banishment for five years, but when he sailed for Calais the ship was intercepted at sea and he was summarily beheaded. His body was flung onto the sands at Dover. Responsibility for the murder is unclear. Later in the same year the men of Kent rose in a rebellion led by a murderous character called Jack Cade. Almost all were peasants or petty shopkeepers, but a handful of squires had joined them. When they reached London in July they stormed the Tower and beheaded the Lord High Treasurer. Cade declared himself Mayor of the city while the rebels looted, murdered and robbed all around them. They were finally routed by the troops and the population on 5 July. Cade was caught and killed as he fled.

The Bureau artillery was also important in the decisive French victory of Formigny, scarcely a dozen miles from Bayeux, on 15 April 1450, when the English were routed by the forces of Charles de Bourbon, Count of Clermont, thanks to the timely arrival of Breton troops under the command of Richemont at the crucial point of the battle. English losses in dead, wounded and prisoners were huge, and Desmond Seward comments that Formigny was the first decisive battle lost by the English since Bannockburn in 1314. In June 1450, Caen capitulated and in August it was the turn of Cherbourg, after a merciless pounding from Bureau's cannon. In Normandy, only Calais and the Channel Islands remained in English hands.

Early in 1451, Dunois marched into Guyenne with Bureau and his artillery. Bordeaux was taken in June and Bayonne in August. However, the arrogance of the French officials and tax collectors quickly made them unpopular with the local population, who sent secret messengers to London to say that they were ready to rise in support of an English army. An army under the command of the doughty Talbot, now in his seventies, duly arrived. The French were taken by surprise, the gates of Bordeaux were opened and Talbot and his men marched in on 21 October. The counter-attack came in the spring of 1453, when the French invaded Guyenne from three sides. On 16 July, Talbot rode out with an army estimated at 10,000 men, to raise the siege of Castillon, about thirty miles inland from Bordeaux. The encounter was a disaster for the English, who were mown down by the cannon. Talbot was among the dead. Bordeaux capitulated on 19 October and Jean Bureau became its Mayor for life.

England was about to be plunged into greater miseries at home. What would become known as The Wars of the Roses erupted in 1455.

20

The False Joan of Arc

'Grand'pitié! jamais personne ne secourut la France si à propos et si heureusement que cette Pucelle, et jamais mémoire de femme ne fut si déchirée'

Étienne Pasquier (1529–1615)

Early on, during all these dramatic events, rumours that Joan had not died, but had escaped or been spirited away or that another had been executed in her place, circulated among the French population. In an age before the printing press and newspapers, hard fact was difficult to establish for the ordinary people. Many could not believe that Joan had been burned, she was after all an internationally famous prisoner of war. By all the rules of chivalry, such were inviolable. Those who thought of her as a saint and a saviour overlooked the fact that for her enemies, Joan was merely an upstart peasant, dabbling in witchcraft to boot. False Joans appeared, just as half a century later Lambert Simnel or Perkin Warbeck would each in turn claim to be the younger of the two unfortunate little princes in the Tower. Even in our own age, we have had many false claimants to fame or fortune, among others Anna Anderson, claiming to be Anastasia, the daughter of the murdered Czar Nicolas. These persons however all claimed to be grown-up versions of children. To impersonate the nineteen year-old Joan only five or six years after her death demanded rather more research, not to mention a reasonably similar appearance.

On 20 May 1436, there appeared in the city of Metz a young woman giving her name at first as Claude, but claiming to be none other than Joan herself. Dressed as a soldier and mounted on a horse which she handled expertly, she had come to meet the notables of the town, who had heard amazing rumours about her. The *doyen* (dean) of the church of Saint Thibaud in Metz tells the story in his Chronicle. When writing his first account, he was convinced by her, but in a later manuscript of the chronicle, he (or a continuator) dismisses her as a fraud. 'In that year' (i.e. 1436), we read, 'there came young woman calling herself the Maid of France, and playing the part so well that several people were taken in, and especially people of the highest rank.'[1]

Joan's brothers, Pierre and Jean, had been sent for and arrived on the same day. Unbelievably, they recognised her as their sister, or at any rate, Jean did so. Pierre was the younger of the two brothers and closer to his sister. During her trial, on 1 March 1431, she had mentioned a ring which he had once given her and which she clearly treasured. He had been with her until they both were captured at Compiègne. If he had any doubts, he did not voice them, but certainly after the first encounter, when both brothers are said by the dean of Metz to have accompanied her to Bacquillon (wherever that was),[2] we never again hear of Pierre having anything to do with her. Jean seems to have had faith in her for several months, from her appearance at least until September 1436. After that, we hear no more of any action of his on her behalf. Perhaps the brothers were overjoyed at this first meeting, where they were rapturously greeted by their supposed sister. The resemblance must have been striking.

The next day, the two brothers took her, says the chronicler, to this obscure place called Bacquillon. She remained there about a week, until Pentecost. The brothers seem to have left her there, or she left them. She spoke inscrutably, says the doyen, 'in parables', which must have neatly fended off any awkward questions. In case anyone should ask her for a 'sign', she took the precaution of declaring that her powers would only become operational a month later, on the feast of Saint John the Baptist (24 June). Midsummer Day is, of course, associated since pre-Christian times with magic, perhaps that is why she chose it. She so impressed the local nobility, that a number of them presented her with costly gifts, a horse, a sword and other items of military equipment. Next she went to the town of Mareville, not far from Metz, where she was given another horse and jewels. Her success there was such that she stayed three weeks. After that she progressed to Arlon in the duchy of Luxembourg, where she was welcomed by the Dame of Luxembourg, Elisabeth of Gorlitz, not to be confused with any of Joan's kind ladies. Here she made a conquest of the young Count of Würtemberg, who, says the *doyen* in his Chronicle, 'was terribly in love with her' and presented her with another costly piece of armour (a cuirass). He took her under his protection to Cologne.[3]

In Cologne she grew ever bolder, dancing, feasting, eating and drinking lustily in public, and performing conjuring tricks to impress the locals. She knew how to tear up a cloth and pull it out again all in one piece, or to throw a glass against a wall and then present it to the public in its pristine state. In the midst of a scandalous clerical squabble, she declared that God had revealed to her which of the two rival bishops was the rightful archbishop of Trier. The Dominican Johann Nider, in his manual on witchcraft entitled *Formicarium* (1439),[4] tells us that this lifestyle and these feats attracted the unwelcome attention of the inquisitor of the diocese, who was not in the least impressed by them, and she was summoned before the church court. Würtemberg hastily removed her from the immediate neighbourhood of the Inquisition and she was excommunicated in her absence.

On her return to Arlon, at the beginning of November 1436, she married a noble gentleman by the name of Robert des Armoises. At the same time, on 7 November, a deed of sale of part of Robert's estate was signed jointly in both their names, Claude is styled 'Jehanne du Lyce, la Pucelle de France, Dame de Thichiemont'.[5] Why the sale at that time? Was it Claude's idea and did it provide her with ready cash? On top of what is now called sex-appeal, she obviously had considerable powers of persuasion. What had happened to Würtemberg? Did she simply send him packing, or did he suspect her credentials? Did his noble relatives gib at the idea of welcoming such an upstart into the family?

Already before her marriage, in July and August 1436, Claude had been busy writing letters. On 9 August 1436, letters from her were brought to Orleans by one of the town's official messengers, as we see from the town's accounts. In October of that year a payment was made to the town's *poursuivant d'armes*, or messenger, for journeys he had made to see 'the Maid' in Arlon and for going to Loches on his way back with yet another letter from her for Charles VII. In all the *poursuivant* had been away six weeks when he returned on 2 September, on which date he had had to be copiously supplied with wine, for it is recorded that 'he said he had a great thirst'.[6] Thirsty work, no doubt.

In August also, her 'brother' Jean also carried letters from her to Orleans and to the king. The king allowed him expenses of 100 francs for himself and his four mounted attendants, but the royal council only paid out twenty francs. Charles VII was still short of money. He seems in any case to have paid little attention at the time to Claude's missives. On Jean's arrival in Orleans, he complained to the town council that he had only eight francs left, quite insufficient to cover his costs, whereupon they provided him with money for his return to his 'sister' and feasted him royally. Jean, also known as Petit-Jean, returned home. He seems to have had no more dealings with on or behalf of Claude des Armoises, perhaps her behaviour disabused him. His career progressed and he finished in 1457 as captain of Vaucouleurs.

Claude des Armoises appeared in Orleans on 18 and 19 July 1436. Neither of Jeanne's brothers was anywhere in her vicinity. She was given what we should call a civic welcome, royally wined and dined. She was there again on 29 July and stayed until 1 August, having once again been royally received and given copious presents of wine, meat and 210 *livres parisis*, a considerable amount of money. There is no further mention of her in the accounts for the town of Orleans until 4 September, but she seems then only to have stayed long enough to collect a present of wine. She didn't stay to dinner that day.

Masses were said every year for the repose of Joan's soul two days before the feast of Corpus Christi, a moveable feast held sixty days after

Easter, usually therefore in early June. There are entries in the town's accounts in 1432, 1435, 1436 and 1439 for the expenses on candles for the anniversary Masses. The gaps do not mean that no Mass was celebrated on the intervening years. In 1439 the Mass was said as usual on 5 June and candles were bought were bought 'for the obsequies of the late Joan the Maid'. [7] Yet less than six weeks later they were wining and dining the new Joan! It looks as if opinion in Orleans must have been divided about the survival of their heroine, or that the councillors were hedging their bets.

We hear nothing precise about Claude's doings from 1436–39. She lived for a time with her husband in Metz and had two sons by him, but seems to have left him before appearing in Orleans in 1439. In Italy, Claude joined the papal army and fought in the revolts and wars then raging in the papal states. Whether before or just after her visits to Orleans in 1439, she appears to have joined a band of mercenaries in the service of the infamous Gilles de Rais, who would be executed for his abominable crimes only a year later.[8] Certainly she was with a band of mercenaries somewhere near Paris in August 1440, when the University and the Inquisition, more successful here than in Metz, managed to find her and bring her before a church court in Paris. The *Bourgeois* gives the details of the story, which is worth telling in full. So here it is:

> At that time, the men-at-armes had with them a woman who was very honourably received in Orleans. When she was in the vicinity of Paris, people fell into the great error of believing firmly that she was the Maid. For that reason, the University and Parlement had her brought to Paris by force and she was shown to the people on the marble stand in the great courtyard of the Palace, and there a sermon was preached about her past and her way of life. She admitted that she was not a Maid, that she had been married to a knight and had two sons, also that she had done something in expiation of which she had to go to the Pope in Rome, a sin such as striking a parent or a cleric. [9] She said she had done so only in defence of her own honour, and by accident, for she had thought she was hitting someone else and would have missed her mother, except she was so angry and her mother was holding on to her as she was going to hit a neighbour of theirs. It was for that reason that she had to go to Rome. She went dressed as a man and was a soldier in the Pope's army and killed two men.[10].

At some stage, probably after the visits to Orleans but shortly before this grand finale, she had succeeded in having an interview with Charles VII. He was campaigning in the Paris region at the time and may, on hearing of the expense and feasting in Orleans have decided that enough was enough, the whole thing was beyond a joke. He himself may have had her brought to Paris. Pierre Sala tells the story of the encounter. He has it again from Monsieur de Boisy, who had been in his youth, the king's *confidant*. This is his account:

> Moreover, the said gentleman [Boisy], told me that ten years later [i.e., after Charles had met Joan in 1429], another Maid was brought to him, who bore a strong resemblance to the first. By spreading rumours, she wanted to have people believe that she was the other come back again. On hearing this, the king ordered that she should be brought to him. Now, at the time, the king had suffered an injury to his foot and he was wearing a yellow boot. Those who had organised this deception told the false Maid about it, so that she wouldn't fail to pick him out from among his courtiers. When the appointed time came for the interview, he was behind a vine arbour in a garden. He ordered one of his courtiers to go and meet the Maid when she entered, as if he were the king, This was done. However, thanks to the information she had been given, she refused to greet him and went straight to the king himself. He was dumbfounded, not knowing what to say, and then, greeting her very politely, he said, 'Maid, my dear, you are very welcome back, in the name of God who knows the secret that we share.' Then, miraculously, on hearing these simple words, the false Maid fell to her knees before the king and begged his pardon, confessing the whole plot, for which certain people were severely punished, as is only right in such a case.[11]

Claude seems to have returned to a soldier's life after Paris. We last hear of her in 1457, when a pardon, or *lettre de rémission* was issued by René d'Anjou, after she had been held for three months in a prison of his duchy for some transgression concerning a quarrel with a woman of noble rank. We see from the document that, her first husband having died, she had at some point married an obscure individual named Jean Douillet. Her days of enthralling members of the aristocracy were over. She was pardoned on condition that in future she dress as a woman and behave accordingly, so her military career had to come to an end.[12]

It has been held that the whole episode of the false Joan of Arc was a plot thought up by members of the Burgundian party, anxious to clear themselves and the English of the accusation of having burnt a saint.[13] How else did she find such ready acceptance from 'people of the highest rank', among them the Dame of Luxembourg, the niece of Philip of Burgundy? Who were these mysterious people who coached her for this encounter with Charles VII? However, if such was the case, they had chosen badly. A physical resemblance and acrobatic horsemanship were not sufficient to make her pass anywhere for more than a short space of time as the real Joan.

The episode of the false Maid, however, changed the image of Joan at least in the eyes of the sophisticated elite in the sixteenth century and later. 'Religious respect, which they had paid her during her lifetime, was not restored,' says Quicherat.[14] Monstrelet provided a source for those who would consider Joan to be a political tool. From that of a pious village girl divinely inspired, she would now be depicted as an Amazon. The literary taste of the time fitted her out with all the trappings of classical epic poetry merged with the Christian *merveilleux* of Ariosto or Tasso. In an inscription he composed for her monument in Orleans, Malherbe, the leading exponent of the classical school of early seventeenth century French poetry, calls her *belle Amazone* and compares her to Alcibiades.

Among those who defended her against sixteenth century disbelief or derision was Étienne Pasquier, historian, lawyer, friend of Ronsard and Montaigne, minor poet. He was deeply convinced of the divine inspiration of Joan's mission and is important as the first notable historian to have undertaken serious archival research instead of relying solely on chronicles. He had studied, he says, a copy of the 1431 trial documents in the library of François I and claims to have had a copy of this and other documents in his possession for four years, quoting at some length from the Latin of the originals.[15]

Du Haillan, the official historiographer of Henry III, gives a fairly full account of Joan in his *Histoire de France* (1576). He leaves the reader to decide for him or herself as to whether Joan was genuinely inspired or whether she was merely the instrument and/or peasant mistress of Dunois, Baudricourt or others seeking to rekindle courage in a demoralised and superstitious population. Some consider her history, he says, to be 'a spurious miracle, thought up by the aforesaid nobles, while the majority consider it, and have done so since the beginning, as an authentic and certain miracle'. He puts her age at twenty-two when she arrives in Chinon and quotes her letter to Bedford, giving it added ferocity with threats of massacre and 'great carnage'. This image of a virago is at odds with the admiration he accords her courage, piety, chastity, and concern for the poor. No less than twenty pages are devoted to her trial, including a summary of the seventy articles of accusation and her refutation of them. She is, he writes, 'One who deserved praise rather than blame and a glorious reward rather than an ignominious condemnation.'[16]

The seventeenth century continued this glorification of Joan as a virago arising straight out of the pages of the admired Ancients. In the *Tragedie de Jeanne Darques* of Jean de Virey des Graviers (1611), *cette Amazone* makes her appearance in the first scene of the second act, bidding adieu to Diane and her nymphs and dedicating herself to *l'homicide Mars*.

Among the luminaries of the literary world, Chapelain brought derision down on his head with his epic poem *La Pucelle ou la France délivrée* (*The Maid, or France Delivered*), published in 1656. He at least had the merit of praising the virtues of women, saying in his preface that their qualities are equal to men's in all respects, including heroism. But, alas, the great epic, long announced and awaited, was a fiasco of monumental proportions. The mixture of allegory and inspiration from Virgil and

Tasso was indigestible. After some initial acclaim in the salons of Paris, Chapelain quickly became the victim of sarcasm and epigrams, the most lethal being those of his younger contemporary Boileau, famous above all as a satirical poet and literary critic.

The apex of derision was reached in the eighteenth century with Voltaire's bawdy mock-heroic epic *La Pucelle d'Orléans*, which he started to write in 1730 and only published in 1762. In the meantime, clandestine versions had enjoyed a *succès de scandale* all over western Europe, from Paris and London to Geneva. In it, Joan's father is a randy local *curé* 'very ardent in bed', and her mother a robust and plump chambermaid. Joan herself is described in equally racy terms, with 'brown nipples, firm as a rock'. She distributes hearty smacks to the impudent customers groping her in the inn where she works. A dissolute English monk and a muleteer are rival lovers and she is saved from being raped by them thanks only to the miraculous appearance of Saint Denis. She comes close to surrendering to the charms of an amorous donkey (like Shakespeare's Titania), but is saved by the intervention of the love-struck Dunois, to whom she surrenders herself in gratitude at the end of the epic. This grand finale is accompanied by a triumphant cry: *Englishmen! She is a Maid!*

It only became intellectually respectable to write seriously about Joan again at the end of the eighteenth century, thanks to the work of painstaking historians such as L'Averdy, who published a conscientious study and extracts from the trial documents in 1790. A counsellor in the Parlement and Controller-General of Finance before the Revolution, L'Averdy went to the guillotine in 1793. The Romantic movement in literature, with its enthusiasm for the Middle Ages, awoke interest in Joan among historians, poets, dramatists and novelists, among others Alexandre Dumas, who published a romanticised biography of Joan entitled *Jehanne la Pucelle* in 1842. But the greatest of these was the historian Michelet, whose heroine is the personification of the People and of France. A Joan very close to that of Bernard Shaw, an individualist Joan, defying the churchmen, whose visions are nothing other than the images projected by her ardent spirit and poetic imagination. It was Michelet who declared however, 'Religiously and patriotically, Joan of Arc was a saint!'. It remained only for the Church to canonise her, which process was completed in 1920.

21

The Last Victory: Forever the One and Only Joan

O Jeanne sans sépulchre et sans portrait, toi qui savais que le tombeau des héros est le coeur des vivants.
André Malraux, Rouen, 30 May, 1964

When Charles VII entered Rouen in 1450, one of the first things he did was to take possession of the documents of the 1431 trial. Many historians have suggested that his alacrity was merely inspired by the need to clear himself of the opprobrium of owing his crown to a heretical witch. I see no compelling reason for such cynicism. Of course there was a political aspect to his action, but that does not exclude a concern for the reputation of Joan herself. Pierre Duparc, the modern editor of the documents of the retrial, defends the king against the charge of ingratitude so often levied at him because of his silence during Joan's captivity, pointing out the favours he bestowed upon Joan's village, her family and those near her – Pierre d'Arc being ransomed with money the king granted – and he quotes also the favourable mentions made by Morosini, Sala and Pius II concerning Charles's attitude after Joan's capture. It was quite evident that the English would never allow Jeanne to return and that all offers of ransom would have been futile, we need only remember the twenty-five-year captivity of the Duke of Orleans and the repeated refusals to allow him to be ransomed. The duke, however, whatever the politics of the refusals, was in no way as great a threat to the morale of the English soldiers as was the *witch of the Armagnacs*. There was nothing that Charles VII could do until he came into possession of the trial documents and had them examined by lawyers and theologians.

On 15 February 1450, Guillaume Bouillé, who had been rector of the University of Paris from 1437–39, was instructed by the king to examine the documents for irregularities or prejudice on the part of the judges. In March 1450, seven sworn depositions were taken in Rouen, the witnesses being four Dominicans (Isambard de la Pierre, Martin Ladvenu, Jean Toutmouillé and Guillaume Duval), also the clerk of the court, Manchon, the court usher, Massieu and Jean Beaupère, who had largely played the role of interrogator. Beaupère had been quick to present himself in order to make sure that his situation as canon in Rouen was secure. He had nothing to lose by speaking his mind plainly, Charles VII having granted letters of pardon in advance to all appearing at the enquiry. As far as Joan's visions were concerned, Beaupère, as we have seen, gave as his opinion that they were due to 'natural causes and human intent' rather than of supernatural origin, and that she was 'very wily, with a woman's wiliness'.[1] The most he would allow was that there was nothing to make him think that she was not a virgin. A beautiful example of sour masculine prejudice ...

Then in 1451, Pope Nicolas V appointed a legate to discuss diplomatic and ecclesiastical affairs with Charles VII, principally the defence of Europe in the light of the Turkish menace and the affair of the Pragmatic Sanction, in which the king was in dispute with the Pope over his royal right to control church matters. The legate appointed was Cardinal Guillaume d'Estouteville, scion of a Norman family staunchly loyal to the French cause. His father had resisted Henry V at Harfleur and had been a prisoner in England for twenty years thereafter, his brother Louis d'Estouteville had been the captain of Mont Saint Michel from 1423–31. He himself had received the cardinal's hat in 1439, and would become archbishop of Rouen in 1453. In the papal conclave of 1458 he was regarded as the favourite *papabile,* but was pipped at the post by Aeneas Sylvius Piccolomini, who took the title of Pius II.

D'Estouteville arrived in France from Rome at the end of 1451, accompanied by two Italian clerics, Theodor de Leliis and Paul Pontanus, both eminent canon lawyers. When he met Charles VII, he was asked to enquire into the Joan of Arc affair and given the documents of the trial of 1431 and the depositions of 1450. The two lawyers examined these documents and submitted written opinions to D'Estouteville. De Leliis scrutinised the twelve articles submitted to the University of Paris and found serious fault with them all. In the first place, he made the important point that since Joan sincerely believed her visions to come from God, even if she were wrong, she could not be found guilty of a crime. Since her apparitions had not taught her anything contrary to the faith, they were at least harmless. The Church can pronounce only on the orthodoxy of the message conveyed by such phenomena, not on the nature of the experience itself, i.e. as to whether it is due to natural or supernatural causes. The faithful are welcome to their own opinions on the matter. The Dominican Jean Bréhal, Inquisitor for France, echoed this point in his final written summing-up of the various opinions:

> As the revelations which Joan affirmed she had, had simply led her to virtue, faith and piety, as is stated, certainly nothing in them can be judged superstitious or dangerous to the Christian faith.[2]

As for the male dress, De Leliis points to earlier saints who had found such garb expedient. Pontanus makes similar points. De Leliis and Pontanus both observe that Joan had indeed made her submission to the Pope and Church in the Cemetery of Saint Ouen and had also made a reference to a previous submission which, however, is mysteriously missing from the minutes. In respect of the 'King's secret', De Leliis writes, 'Joan expressed herself mystically and by metaphor, something she admitted openly at the end.' Basin, in his consultation paper, written in 1450, writes: 'Joan, exhausted by the persistence of her interrogators, replied as best she could, hiding the sign under parables and metaphors.'[3]

Other treatises or memoirs were also obtained, some before the hearings held in 1456, some at their close, when those consulted were supplied with all the relevant documents. Gerson's short work, written in 1429, was seen as extremely important and included in the Nullity documents, together with seven more, among them those of Bouillé and Thomas Basin, both written at the time of the first hearings in 1450. Finally, Bréhal's very lengthy *Recollectio (Recapitulation)*, is what the title suggests, a summing-up of the arguments and points made in the preceding treatises, with supporting references to, and quotations from, the prophets, the gospels, Saint Paul, Saint Augustine, Saint Thomas Aquinas and many other doctors of the Church. It runs to nearly two hundred pages in Volume II of Duparc. The next longest consultation is that of Bishop Élie de Bourdeilles, which runs to some one hundred and seventeen pages. All these works conclude by calling for the annulment of the sentence of 1431.

D'Estouteville embarked formally on the enquiry in April 1452, in conjunction with the Bréhal. Shortly thereafter he had to leave Rouen on other important business, connected with the University and with the Pragmatic Sanction dispute. By 1452, at any rate, sufficient grounds had been found to justify the demand for an appeal. The appeal against a sentence passed by the Inquisition had to be heard by a church court acting on papal authority. It is unclear why the procedure was interrupted after 1452, possibly some of the documents may have been lost or perhaps it was simply that Pope Nicolas V was preoccupied with the disastrous situation for Christendom after the fall of Constantinople to the Turks in 1453. He was anxiously trying to unite Europe in a common defence against the Turkish menace and certainly had no wish to antagonise England, which had supported him through all the stormy sessions of the Council of Bàle. The matter dragged on for some time. Nicolas V was Pope from 1447 until 1455, when Calixtus III was elected. Their pontificates cover the period both of the preliminaries and of the actual hearings of what is now called the Nullity trial.

To avoid the political embarrassment of the involvement of the king of France in a case against a judgement supported by the authority of the king of England, the appeal was entrusted to Joan's family. Her father was dead, probably not long after Joan's execution, so it was her mother and her brothers, Pierre and Jean, who lodged the petition which was sent to the newly elected Pope Calixtus III in 1455. He approved it and appointed three judges or commissioners, the archbishop of Rheims, Jean Juvenal des Ursins, the bishop of Paris, Guillaume Chartier (brother of the celebrated poet Alain Chartier) and Richard Oliver, bishop of Coutance. All three were eminent churchmen, considerably superior in intellectual standing to the late lamented Bishop Cauchon.

On 7 November 1455, in the cathedral of Notre Dame in Paris, the now aged and ill Isabelle d'Arc and her son Pierre made their way slowly up the nave past a great assembly of clergy, nobles and laypeople, to place their petition before the archbishop of Rheims, the bishop of Paris, and the Inquisitor, Bréhal. Wearing mourning and weeping behind her veil, Isabelle presented the petition and the necessary papal document (the *rescript*). She recalled her daughter's piety and her cruel and unjust death and asked for justice. Many in the congregation were in tears. Such was the emotion in the cathedral that the judges and plaintiffs had to retire to the sacristy, only returning to announce that the petition was accepted.

The petition was drawn up carefully. Only the three principals of 1431 were to be actually prosecuted. Two of them could not be called, having opportunely died since then, Cauchon in 1442, D'Estivet in 1438. Lemaître could not be found, either he was also dead or that reluctant vice-inquisitor had successfully hidden himself away. His disappearance has remained a mystery ever since. Other players in the drama of 1431 had also departed this life. Midi had died of leprosy in the same year as Cauchon. The University was cleared of blame on the grounds that the twelve perfidious articles sent by the court of Rouen were the only evidence its academics had had before them.

On 17 November, Isabelle and both her sons, Pierre and Jean, appeared with their lawyer, Pierre Maugier, before the archbishop of Rheims, the bishop of Paris and the inquisitor, now in the great hall of the bishop's palace. There was again a great concourse of clergy and canon lawyers. The papal rescript was read out solemnly and publicly, Maugier delivered a speech detailing the defects of the 1431 trial and asking that subpoenas be issued forthwith. This was done, summonses were posted up on the church doors of the dioceses of Rouen and Beauvais, requiring any clerics with personal knowledge of the 1431 trial to appear, but without result. As the judges were anxious to ensure the impartiality of the court, the legal beneficiaries of Cauchon, D'Estivet and Lemaître, whether by inheritance or succession in office, were convoked to represent them. The bishop of Beauvais, Guillaume de Hellande, surrounded by members of his clergy, refused to accept the subpoena brought to him by the court lawyer on 12 February 1456, declaring that neither he nor any of his clergy were interested parties and that they were happy to leave the matter to the appointed judges. Moreover, he added somewhat tartly, it was not he, but the principal judge himself, Juvenal des Ursins, who was the legal beneficiary of Cauchon, having succeeded to the seat of Beauvais in 1432, when Cauchon relinquished it. Cauchon's grand-nephew, Pierre de Rinel, sent a letter, declaring roundly that none of the family wished to be involved, they had all been too young at the time, or not even born, and that he had no intention of presenting a defence of the previous proceedings and sentence.[4]

On 11 June 1455, the three judges had received from the notaries the original documents of the 1431 trial, including the minutes in French and Latin. Manchon provided the French minute written in his own hand. All the witnesses who had testified in 1450, except Beaupère, had been heard again in 1452, when testimony was taken from seventeen persons in Rouen in the week between 2 May and 9 May. Some of them, like Manchon, testified twice.

Hearings were held in Domrémy between 28 January and 11 February 1456, when thirty-four depositions were taken. The witnesses here included Joan's childhood friends, relatives, neighbours and godparents, people such as Durand Laxart, Hauviette and Mengette, as well as more exalted persons, nobles or companions from the start of her career, Jean de Nouillompont and Bertrand de Poulengy, for example. The enquiry in Orleans began on 22 February 1456, and the first witness was Dunois himself, followed by Gaucourt, in all forty-one witnesses. Hearings were held in Paris and again in Rouen during April and May. The slippery Courcelles was heard in Paris, as were others whose names are now familiar to us, Alençon, Joan's *beau duc*, her page, Louis de Coutes, her confessor, Brother Pasquerel, also some of those who had been assessors at the 1431 trial, the bishop of Noyon, Jean de Mailly, Houppeville who had been arrested by Cauchon's orders, Manchon (now interviewed for the third time), Massieu (again!) and many more. In all thirty-two new witnesses came forward.

Finally Jean d'Aulon, now an important person in the king's household, the *seneschal*, made a long sworn deposition from Lyons, taken down in French (not Latin) by the vice-inquisitor. His testimony is especially interesting, since it was not limited to answering the questionnaire presented to witnesses at the court hearing, but was a response to this letter from Jean Juvenal des Ursins, who wrote to him on 28 May 1456:

> I am writing to you about the trial of Joan the Maid by the English, maintaining that she was a witch and a heretic and that she invoked devils. In this way they hold that the King and those who served him are heretics. As you have a wide knowledge of her life and social life and conduct, I ask you to be so good as to send me a written account, signed by two apostolic lawyers and an inquisitor of the Faith.

Twelve articles were presented to the five witnesses heard in Rouen in the first week of May 1452. In the second week of May, they were heard again, along with twelve others, all of whom had been involved in the 1431 trial. The witnesses were now required to respond to twenty-seven articles, taking the form of statements to be accepted as true or rejected as false, each witness giving reasons to justify his response. The articles cover questions concerning the political motivation behind the trial, that is to say, the perceived intention on the part of Bedford and Warwick's government to ruin the character and reputation of Charles VII, also the fears and animosity of the English troops, the pressure put upon certain assessors, Cauchon's anger and his directive to omit at least one significant response from the minutes (Manchon's testimony), the fact that Joan was not in a church prison, that she was given mendacious advice (Loiseleur), that the questioning was of a subtlety beyond her. Other articles deal with her character, her faithfulness as a Catholic, her imperfect understanding of the demand to submit to the Church militant, since she was given to understand the term as meaning the court around her. The remaining articles return to the defects of the trial, the competence or otherwise of Cauchon and the injustice of the sentence.

A new list of twelve articles dealing with Joan's character and conduct was drawn up for the 1456 hearing in Domrémy, where the witnesses were relatives or neighbours who had known her as child, or others such as Poulengy and Nouillompont who had known her later. Although we do not have lists of articles for other hearings, it is clear from witnesses' statements that articles were certainly drawn up for the hearings in Orleans in February and March, 1456 and again for the hearings in Paris and Rouen in April and May, 1456, where the witnesses were a mixed bag of those who had been concerned in the 1431 trial and those who had known or served with Joan during her campaigns. In Paris, Courcelles, Alençon and Louis de Coutes were among the most notable who appeared, while Ladvenu, Manchon and Massieu appeared yet again in Rouen. The depositions vary greatly in length, depending upon the extent of the witnesses' knowledge. Among the longest are those of Manchon, Dunois and D'Aulon. Dunois' statement is something close to three thousand words, Manchon's final statement is closer to four thousand, D'Aulon's written statement is of a similar length to Manchon's.

We are already familiar with the testimony of these witnesses. It is clear that the enquiries were carried out diligently and that evidence was collected from all who could give valid testimony both about Joan herself and about the trial in Rouen. It is true that some of the latter, such as Courcelles, had astonishing blanks of memory as to what had actually taken in place in 1431 and their own part in it, putting the opprobrium on the dead Cauchon or D'Estivet. But really, what else could one expect?

In any case, the two certainly merited censure. The vanished Lemaître was on the other hand largely regarded as something of a victim. Perhaps the court was anxious to go easy on the Dominican order.

After the end of the hearings, on 10 June 1456, in the hall of the archiepiscopal palace in Rouen, the prosecuting lawyer, representing Joan's family, appeared before the three judges, Archbishop Jean Juvenal des Ursins, the bishops of Paris and Coutances and the Inquisitor, Jean Bréhal, to demand that those representing Cauchon, D'Estivet and Lemaître be declared contumacious. This request was agreed and on 7 July, again in the hall of the archbishop's palace in Rouen and the presence of the three judges and Bréhal, the required declaration was solemnly pronounced.

Joan's image was completely restored by the evidence of the witnesses at the hearings of the Nullity trial. Her simplicity, her innocence, her piety, her amazing courage illuminate the pages of the documents. The testimony of the many witnesses who knew her personally is heartfelt and moving. At the end of the Nullity trial, on 7 July 1456, in the great hall of the episcopal palace in Rouen, the solemn verdict on the 1431 trial and on Cauchon, D'Estivet and Lemaître was pronounced, in the presence of the three judges and Bréhal, as well as that of other notables, among whom were Jean d'Arc, representing Joan's family, the family's lawyer, Maugier, and Brother Martin Ladvenu, who had accompanied Joan to the very end of her calvary. A lengthy *exposé* of all the considerations which had been taken into account and all the serious efforts made to establish the truth was followed by the proclamation:

> We declare and pronounce that the said proceedings and sentences [i.e. of 1431] containing deceit, calumny, contradictions and manifest error in law and in fact, as also the said abjuration, execution and all following therefrom, were and are null, void, without effect and without validity.

Joan's total innocence was proclaimed.

> We order that our sentence be immediately and solemnly proclaimed in two places in this city: in Saint Ouen immediately, with a general procession and a sermon, and tomorrow, in the Old Market, where Joan died in a cruel and horrible death by fire. There shall be a solemn sermon and a crucifix shall be raised in honorable and perpetual memory of her who died and for the salvation of the souls of all the deceased.[5]

The sentence was immediately put into action. Sermons and processions took place not only in Rouen but also in other towns. They were attended by great crowds everywhere. In Orleans, where the ceremonies were celebrated on 27 July, Guillaume Bouillé, who had undertaken the researches for the appeal in 1450, and the Inquisitor Bréhal himself, together with the Bishop of Coutances, presided at the ceremonies. Joan's mother had been living in Orleans since 1440, supported by a pension from the grateful town. Now nearing seventy, she was there among the rejoicing crowds, despite her frailty and age. *Nunc dimittis* ... at last that pious old lady could go to meet her Maker with a quiet heart. She died in November 1458.

Pope Pius II, a man of her own times, wrote a glowing epitaph for Joan of Arc. He allows the sceptics the right to their opinion, but forcefully expresses in his *Memoirs* his own admiration for the Maid of France. After re-telling her story from her arrival at Chinon to the raising of the siege of Orleans, the coronation of the king, her capture and death, he exclaims:

> So died Joan, that marvellous and amazing girl, who restored the kingdom of France which was on the point of collapse and very nearly destroyed, who inflicted so many and such disasters on the English, who, while being a leader of men and living among mounted troops, kept herself chaste, and of whom nothing disreputable was ever heard.

Here he gives a nod in the direction of the sceptics, saying, 'Whether this was divine intervention or human invention is difficult to say' but goes on to add that whatever truth there may have been in theories of 'human invention', what no-one can deny is that:

> It was under the Maid's leadership that the siege of Orleans was raised, by whose arms all the country between Bourges and Paris was retaken, by whose counsel the people of Rheims were brought back to the king's obedience and his coronation celebrated among them, through whose assault Talbot was put to flight and his army cut down, by whose efforts France was rescued from danger.

In conclusion, he salutes her memory: 'All these things deserve to be remembered, even if in future generations they will find more admiration than belief.'[6]

Some five centuries later, at the end of his play *The Lark*, (1952), Jean Anouilh put into the mouth of King Charles VII another radiant tribute:

> The true end of the story of Joan, the true ending which will never end, that people will tell when they have forgotten or confused all our names, is not to be found in her wretchedness in Rouen, like some trapped animal, it is the lark high above in the clear air! It is Joan at Rheims in all her glory! The true end of Joan's story is joy! Joan of Arc, a story with a happy ending!

Perhaps we should conclude on a different plane, with Joan joining her saints in glory. The last word goes to a great poet and a great musician, Paul Claudel and Arthur Honneger. 'The summit of Joan of Arc's life is her death, it is the stake at Rouen,' writes Claudel. In their Oratorio, *Jeanne d'Arc au Bucher*, the poet and the composer portray Joan chained to her stake, high above the city of Rouen. Before her terrified eyes, her past life unfolds in a series of visions. In the ultimate moment her Voices call to her from above:

> Voices: Joan! Joan! Joan! Daughter of God! Come! Come!
> Joan: These chains hold me here!
> Voices: There is joy which prevails! There is love which prevails! There is God who prevails!

And Joan, her terrors forgotten, answers exultantly:

> I'm coming! I'm coming! The chains are broken! I've broken them! There is joy which prevails! [...] There is love which prevails! There is God who prevails!

And so we take our leave of Joan, not in tragedy, but in jubilation.

Bibliography

Primary Sources

In the nineteenth century, Quicherat produced the great scholarly five-volume edition of the documents of both trials and related texts from chroniclers and other sources, which is still indispensible. Today we have the equally scholarly editions of Pierre Tisset (3 volumes, the trial of 1431) and Pierre Duparc (5 volumes, the proceedings of 1452 and 1456).

In references to the condemnation trial of 1431, I simply give the date of the session, and for the second trial, now known as the Nullity trial, I give the the name of the witness. The relevant pasage can then be easily found in any edition, whether in French, Latin or an English translaton. Where the reference is outside the trial documents, whether it be the editor's commentary or other material, I give page references, to Quicherat, Tisset or Duparc, as the case may be. In the case of the chroniclers, the most convenient references for most of them are to Quicherat's extracts, tome IV, where the passage in question is included in the extract. However, I also give page references to the various scholarly editions of the works. The translations from French or Latin are my own.

The indispensable documents are of course those of the two trials, published by Jules Quicherat, Perre Duparc, Pierre Tisset, and Lanéry d'Arc:

Quicherat, Jules-Étienne, *Procès de condamnation et de réhabilitation de Jeanne d'Arc, dite la Pucelle, publiés pour la première fois d'après les manuscrits de la Bibliothèque royale, suivis de tous les documents historiques qu'on a pu réunir, et accompagnés de notes et d'éclaircissements*, par *Jules Quicherat*, Paris, J. Renouard et Cie, 1841–1849. 5 vol.

Quicherat, Jules-Étienne, 'Supplément aux témoignages contemporains sur Jeanne d'Arc et la Chronique des Cordeliers de Paris', in *Revue historique, 7e. année, t. 19*, mai-juin 1882, pp.60-83

Duparc, Pierre, *Procès en nullité de la condamnation de Jeanne d'Arc.* 5 vols. Paris, Klincksieck, 1977-88

Tisset, Pierre, *Procès de condamnation de Jeanne d'Arc.* 3 vols. Paris, Klincksieck, 1960-71

Lanéry d'Arc, Pierre, *Mémoires et consultations en faveur de Jeanne d'Arc. Par les juges du procès de Réhabilitation. D'après les manuscrits authentiques.* Paris, Picard, 1899.

Other older but worthwhile editions of the trials are:

Champion, Pierre, *Procès de Condamnation de Jeanne d'Arc. Texte, traduction et notes.* 2 vols. Paris. Honoré Champion, éditeur Edouard Champion, 1921

O'Reilly, E, *Les deux Procès de condamnation, les enquêtes et la sentence de réhabilitation de Jeanne d'Arc, mis pour la première fois intégralement en français, t.11.* Paris, Plon, 1868

Also in the category of primary sources:

Actes de la Chancellerie de Henri VI concernant la Normandie sous la domination anglaise (1422-1435), publiés par Paul le Cacheux, Rouen, A. Lestringant, Paris, A. Picard, 1907-8, 2 vols.

Basin, Thomas, Histoire des règnes de Charles VII et de Louis XI. Publiée pour la première fois avec les autres ouvrages historiques du même écrivain, pour la Société de l'Histoire de France, par J. Quicherat. Tome premier. Paris, Jules Renouard et Cie. 1855

Cagny, Perceval de, *Chroniques de Perceval de Cagny, publiées pour la première fois pour la Société de l'Histoire de France*, H. Moranville, Paris, Renouard, 1902

Chartier, Jean, *Chronique de Charles VII, roi de France, par Jean Chartier. Tome 1 Nouvelle édition, revue sur les manuscrits.* Publiée avec Notes, Notices et Éclaircissements par Vallet de Viriville, Paris, P. Jannet, 1858.

Chastellain, Georges, *Oeuvres de Georges Chastellain, publié par M. le Baron Kervyn de Lettenhove.* Tome I, Chronique 1419-1422; Tome II, 1430-31, 1452-53, Brussels, F. Heussner, Libraire-Éditeur, 1863

Chronique d'Antonio Morosini. Extraits relatifs à l'histoire de France. Publiés pour la Société de l'Histoire de France. Introduction et commentaire par Germain Lefèvre-Pontalis. Texte établi et traduit par Léon Dorez. Tome troisième. G. Lefèvre-Pontalis et L. Dorez. Paris, Renouard, 1902

Chronique des Cordeliers de Paris, can most readily be consulted in Ayroles III, *La Libératrice,* pp.629-37. The relevant extracts are also reproduced in Quicherat's article listed below and available on the internet site stejeannedarc.net

Chronique de la Pucelle ou chronique de Cousinot, suivie de la chronique Normand de P Cochon, relatives aux régnes de Charles VI et de Charles VII, restituées à leurs auteurs et publiées pour la première fois intégralement à partir de l'an 1403, d'après les manuscrits, avec notices, notes, et développements, ed. Auguste Vallet de Viriville, Paris, Adolphe Delahays, 1859.

Chronique de Tournay, can most readily be consulted in Ayroles III, *La Libératrice*, pp.619-25

'Comptes des dépenses faites par Charles VII pour secourir Orléans pendant le siège de 1428', in *Mémoires de la Société archéologique et historique de l'Orléanais*, t. XI, 1868. There is an appendix entitled 'Extraict du compte de maître Hémon Raguier, trésorier des guerres du Roy nostre sire, depuis le 1er mars 1424 jusques au dernier septembre 1433, rendu par Charles Raguier son fils, et Louis Raguier, conseiller en la Cour du Parlement, aussi son fils, en l'an 1441'

Gélu, Jacques, *Tractatus de Puella,* in Quicherat, t. III, pp. 395-410

Gerson, Jean, *Opusculum magistri Johannis de Jarsonno*, in Duparc, T. II, pp.33-9

Journal d'un Bourgeois de Paris. 1405-1449. Publié d'après les manuscrits de Rome et de Paris par Alexandre Tuetey, Paris, Champion. 1881. It has recently been available also in the Livre de Poche collection of the Librairie Générale, edited by Colette Beaune in 1990. The spelling has been slightly modernised in the Beaune edition. Page references are given to the entry number, rather than the page number, so that the reference can be looked up in either edition.

Journal de Clément de Fauquembergue, Greffier du Parlement de Paris. 1417-1435. Tome II. Texte complet. Publié pour la Société de l'Histoire de France par Alexandre Tuetey, avec la collaboration de Henri Lacaille, Paris, Librairie Renouard. 1909.

Journal du Siège d'Orléans. 1428-1429. Augmenté de plusieurs documents, notamment des Comptes de Ville, 1429-1431, Orléans, Herluison Libraire-Éditeur, 1896.

Juvenal de Ursins, Jean: *Histoire de Charles VI, roy de France*, ed. A. Desrez, Paris, 1841

Le Fèvre de Saint-Rémy, *La Chronique de Jean le Fèvre, Seigneur de Saint-Rémy. Transcrite d'un manuscrit appartenant à la Bibliothèque de Boulogne-sur-Mer. Par François Morand.* Tome Second, Paris, Renouard. MDCCCLXXVI

Letters and Papers Illustrative of the Reign of King Henry VI, vol.1. Edited by the Reverend Joseph Stevenson, M.A.; London, Longman, Green, Longman and Roberts, 1861.

Monstrelet, Engerrand de, *La Chronique d'Enguerrand de Monstrelet. En deux livres avec pièces justificatives. 1400-1444.* Publiée pour la Société de l'Histoire de France par L. Douet D'Arc, Paris, Jules Renouard, MDCCCLXII (6 vols: t. I-VI) For Joan of Arc, see vol. IV

There is a scholarly paperback publication of J. A. Buchon's 1826 edition of these *Chroniques*, published in the BiblioBazaar Reproduction Series, s.d.

Morosini, Antonio: *Chronique d'Antonio Morosini. Extraits relatifs à l'histoire de France. Introduction et commentiare par Germain Lefèvre-Pontalis. Texte établi et traduit par Léon dorez.* Tome III, 1429-1433, Paris, Renouard, 1901

Ordonnances des Rois de France de la Troisième Race. Recueillies par ordre chronologique. Contenant les Ordonnances de Charles VI données depuis le commencement de l'année 1419 jusqu'à la fin du règne de ce Prince, Par M. De Vilevault. Paris, Imprimerie Royale, MDCCLXIX

Quicherat, Jules: 'Supplément aux témoignages contemporains sur Jeanne d'Arc et *La Chronique des Cordeliers de Paris*', in *Revue historique, 7e. Année, t.19, mai-août 1882,* pp.60-81

Relation inédite sur Jeanne d'Arc. Extrait du Livre Noir de l'Hotel-de-Ville de La Rochelle. Publiée par M. J. Quicherat. Orléans, H. Herluison, Libraire-éditeur 1879 (Greffier de La Rochelle)

Stevenson, Joseph: *Letters and Papers Illustrative of the Wars of the English in France during the Reign of Henry the Sixth, King of England,* London, Longman, Green, Longman and Roberts, 1861

Wavrin du Forestel, Jean de: *Recueil des Croniques et Anchiennes Istories de La Grant Bretaigne, à présent nommée Engleterre,* ed. Wm. Hardy, London, Longman & Co., 1879 (reprint Eyre and Spottiswoode, for HMSO)

Secondary Sources

Ayroles, J.B.J. *La Vraie Jeanne d'Arc.* 5 vols., Gaume et Compagnie, Paris, 1890-1902

Barker, Juliet, *Conquest: The English Kingdom of France in the Hundred Years War.* London, Little, Brown, 2009

Beaune, Colette, *Jeanne d'Arc,* Paris, Perrin, 2009

Beaune, Colette, *Jeanne d'Arc. Vérités et légendes,* Paris, Perrin, 2008

Bordonove, Georges, *Les Rois qui ont fait la France.* t.I Charles VI. 1380-1422, fils de Charles V, Paris, Pygmalion, 2006

Bordonove, Georges, *Les Rois qui ont fait la France.* t.II. Charles VII le Victorieux. Les Valois, Paris, Pygmalion, 1985.

Bouzy, Olivier, *Jeanne d'Arc en son siècle,* Paris, Fayard, 2013

Calmette, Joseph, *Les Grands Ducs de Bourgogne,* Paris, Albin Michel, 1949

Carleton Williams, E., *My Lord of Bedford, 1389–1435. Being a life of John of Lancaster, first Duke of Bedford, brother of Henry V and Regent of France*, London, Longmans, 1963

Champion, Pierre, *Guillaume de Flavy, capitaine de Compiégne*, Paris, Honoré Champion, 1906

Clin, Marie-Véronique, *Isabeau de Bavière. Préface de Régine Pernoud*, Paris, Perrin, 1999

Clin, Marie-Véronique, Régine Pernoud: *Jeanne d'Arc*, Paris, Fayard, 1986

Contamine, Philippe, *La Guerre de Cent Ans*, Paris, PUF, edition of 2010

Contamine, Philippe, *La Guerre au Moyen Âge*, Paris, PUF, edition of 1994

Contamine, Ph., Bouzy, O., Hélary, X.: *Jeanne d'Arc.Histoire et dictionnaire*, Paris, Robert Laffont, 2012

Crane, Susan, *The Performance of Self. Ritual, Clothing and Identity during the Hundred Years War.* University of Pennsylvania Press, 2002. See: Chapter 3: "Joan of Arc and Women's Cross-Dress" (pp.73-107).

Defourneaux, Marcelin, *La Vie quotidienne au temps de Jeanne d'Arc.* Paris, Hachette, 1952

Delorme, Philippe, *Histoire des Reines de France. Isabeau de Bavière. Épouse de Charles VI, Mère de Charles VII.* Paris, Pygmalion, 2003

DeVries, Kelly, *Joan of Arc. A Military Leader*, Stroud, The History Press, 2011.

Dickinson, Jocelyne Gledhill, *The Congress of Arras, 1435. A Study in Medieval Diplomacy*, Oxford, Clarendon Press, 1955.

Dockray, Keith, *Warrior King. The Life of Henry V*, Stroud, Tempus, 2007

Duby, Georges, *Le Moyen Age. De Hugues Capet à Jeanne d'Arc* (987-1460), Paris, Hachette, 1987

Dunand, Ph.-H, *L'Abjuration du Cimetière Saint-Ouen d'après les textes. Etude critique*, Paris, Librairie Ch. Pousseilgue, 1901

Dunand, Ph.-H., *Histoire complète de Jeanne d'Arc: Du procès qui l'a condamnée et de sa Réhabilitation. D'après les manuscrits des deux procès, les travaux le plus récents et des documents inédits de la Bibliothèque Nationale.* Toulouse, Édouard Privat, Libraire-Éditeur, 1899

Elliott, Dyan, 'Seeing Double: John Gerson, the Discernment of Spirits, and Joan of Arc' *American Historical Review 107, 1* (February 2002), pp. 26 - 54

Erlanger, Philippe, *Charles VII et son mystère*, Paris, Gallimard, 1945

Fabre, Lucien, *Jeanne d'Arc*, Paris, Tallandier, 1948

Favier, Jean, *La Guerre de Cent Ans*, Paris, Fayard, 1980

Favier, Jean, *Pierre Cauchon, Comment on devient le juge de Jeanne d'Arc*, Paris, Fayard, 2010

Fraoli, Deborah, *Joan of Arc and the Hundred Years War*, Westport CT, Greenwood Press, 2005

France, Anatole, *Vie de Jeanne d'Arc*, 2 vols., Paris, Calmann-Lévy, 1908

Gérard, A.-M, *Jehanne la mal jugée*, Paris, Bloud et Gay, 1964

Goyau, Georges, 'Jacques Gélu. Ses interventions pour Jeanne d'Arc', in *Revue des questions historiques*, 60e. Année, 3e. Série, t. XXI, pp. 302-20, Paris, 1932

Guenée, Bernard, *L'Opinion publique à la fin du Moyen Âge d'après la "Chronique de Charles VI" du Religieux de Saint Denis*, Paris, Perrin, 2002

Guibal, Geoges, *Histoire du Sentiment national en France pendant la Guerre de Cent Ans*. Paris, Gallica, 1875

Guillemin, Henri, *Jeanne, dite Jeanne d'Arc*, Paris, Gallimard, Coll. Folio 1970

Guitton, Jean, *Problème et mystère de Jeanne d'Arc*, Paris, Fayard, 1961

Heer, Jacques, *Le Moyen Âge. Une imposture*, Paris, Perrin, 1992.

Hérubel, Michel, *Charles VII*, Paris, Olivier Orban, 1981

Keen, Maurice, *Medieval Europe*, London, Penguin Books, 1991 (reprint of *A History of Medieval Europe*, Routledge and Kegan Paul, 1968)

Lanéry d'Arc, Pierre, *Le Culte de Jeanne d'Arc au XVe. siècle*, Orléans, Herluison, 1887

Lang, Andrew, *The Maid of France. Being the Story of the Life and Death of Jeanne d'Arc*, London, Longmans, Green, and Co. 1908

Lecoy de la Marche, A., *Une fausse Jeanne d'Arc*, Paris, Victor Palmé, 1871

Lethel, François Marie, "La Soumission à l'Église Militante: un aspect théologique de la condamnation de Jeanne d'Arc". In *Jeanne d'Arc.Une époque, un rayonnement, Colloque d'histoire médiévale, Orléans 1979*, Éditions du CNRS,1982, pp. 182-89

Luce, Siméon, *Jeanne d'Arc à Domrémy. Recherches critiques sur les origines dela mission de la Pucelle*, Paris, Champion, 1886

Lucie-Smith, Edward, *Joan of Arc*, London, Penguin Books, Ltd., 2000

McGuire, Brian Patrick, *Jean Gerson and the last Medieval Reformation*, Pennsylvania State University Press, 2005

Markale, Jean, *Isabeau de Bavière*, Paris, Payot, 1982

Michelet, Jules, *Jeanne d'Arc. Avec une introduction par Émile Bourgeois*, Paris, Hachette, 1902

Mortimer, Ian, *1415. Henry V's Year of Glory*, London, Vintage Books, 2010

Mortimer, Ian, *The Fears of Henry IV. The Life of England's Self-Made King*, London, Vintage Books, 2008

Mortimer, Ian, 'What Hundred Years War?' in *History Today*, October 2009, vol.59, Issue 10, pp. 27-33.

Neveux, François, *L'Évêque Pierre Cauchon*, Paris, Denoël, 1987

Palou, Jean, *La Sorcellerie*, Paris, PUF 2002

Pernoud, Régine, *Christine de Pisan*, Paris, Calmann-Lévy, 1982

Pernoud, Régine, *Jeanne d'Arc par elle-même et par ses témoins*, Paris, Éds.du Seuil, 1962

Pernoud, Régine, *Vie et Mort de Jeanne d'Arc. Les témoignages du procès de réhabilitation, 1450-1456*, Paris, Hachette, 1953

Pernoud, R., M-V –Clin, *Jeanne d'Arc*, Paris, Fayard, 1986

Quicherat, Jules-Étienne, *Aperçus nouveaux sur l'histoire de Jeanne d'Arc*, Paris, 1850

Rocolle. Pierre, *Un prisonnier de guerre nommé Jeanne d'Arc*, Éditons S.O.S., Paris, 1982

Rogers, Clifford J., "The Age of the Hundred Years War", in *Medieval Warfare.A History, ed. Maurice Keen*, Oxford University Press, 1999, pp.136-60

Roux, Simon, *Paris au Moyen Âge*, Paris, Hachette, 2003

Sackville-West, V., *Saint Joan of Arc*, Harmondsworth, Middlesex, Penguin Books, 1955

Schnerb, Bertrand, *Jean sans Peur. Le prince meurtrier*, Paris, Payot et Rivages, 2005

Seward, Desmond, *A Brief History of the Hundred Years War. The English in France, 1337-1453*, London, Robinson, 2003

Verdon, Jean, *(La) Femme au Moyen Âge*, Paris, Éditions Jean-Paul Gisserot, 2006

Verdon, Jean, *Isabeau de Bavière. La mal-aimée*, Paris, Tallandier, 2001
Verdon, Jean, *Les Superstitions au Moyen Âge*, Paris, Perrin, 2008.

Vallet de Viriville, M., *Histoire de Charles VII, Roi de France, et de son époque. 1403 – 1461*, 3 vols., Paris, Renouard, 1862-5. (Vol. II covers the period 1429-44)

Wallon, Henri, *Jeanne d'Arc*, Firmin-Didot, Paris, 1876

Warner, Marina, *Joan of Arc.The Image of Female Heroism*, London, Weidenfeld and Nicolson, 1981

Waugh, W.T., "The Administration of Normandy. 1420-22", in *Essays in Medieval History, presented to Thomas Frederick Tout*, A.G.Little, F.M.Powicke (edited), pp.349-359, 1925 (reprint 1967, Books for Libraries Press)

Williams, E. Carlton, *My Lord of Bedford. 1389 – 1435*, London, Longmans, Green and Co., 1963.

Wright, Nicolas, "French peasants in the Hundred Years War", in *History Today*, vol.23. no.6. June 1983., pp.38-42

The internet site stejeannedarc.net provides copious information on every aspect of the life and career of Joan of Arc and also provides a digital library of Quicherat's volumes and extracts of relevant passages from chronicles and other documents.

Notes

In the text, where I have referred to or quoted evidence or testimony given in the 1431 trial at Rouen, I give the date of the session and name of the witness, the Latin or French source can then be found in Quicherat, t.I or Tisset, t.I. I do the same for testimony quoted from the Nullity trial (1452–6), the source is then to be found in Quicherat II, III or in Duparc I, II. Page references are given for anything outside the trial documents, whether it be commentary or other material. Quicherat IV is a collection of extracts from fifteenth-century chronicles and historians, while the final volume contains letters, acounts and other relevant documents.

All translations from French or Latin are my own.

Prologue

1 Her height has been calculated from the length of cloth purchased for a garment presented to her as a gift from the Duke of Orleans in June 1429.

2 Testimony of Massieu, 8/5/1452

3 Testimony of Nicolas Caval, priest and canon of Rouen, 8/5/1452. Caval was by no means favourable to Joan.

4 See the discussion of Jeanne's speech in Pernoud/Clin, pp.331-3. She pronounced 'j' as 'ch', *e.g.* 'joyeux' became 'choyeux' (her scribe wrote it phonetically thus (and then corrected it) in the letter to the people of Rheims of 16 March 1430; 'En nom Dé', was her exclamation , not 'En nom Dieu', 'Rends-ti', she cried to Glasdale, and not 'Rends-toi'.

5 Étienne Pasquier (1529-1615): see *Oeuvres choisies*, t.1, p.175, Skatkine Reprints, Geneva, 1968.

6 Tisset I, p.40: I have translated the Latin *in partibus suis* as 'at home'. Joan woud have said *dans mon pays* ('in my country'), by which she meant her *part of the country*. The French still often refer to their region as *mon pays*, just as the *vin du pays* is the local wine. *France,* for Joan and her contemporaries, was the Île de France, a region of the *kingdom of France*, lying between the Seine, the Loire,

Bourges and Poitiers, just as today Holland is not the whole country, but a region of the Netherlands. When she went 'into France' she went to see the Dauphin at his court in Chinon. (Tisset II, p.137).

7　Surnames were not common among the people in the 15th century and earlier. Joan's father's name may indicate that the family originally came from the village of Arc-en-Barrois on the Marne.

8　See *Aperçus nouveaux*, pp 46 and 60-1. Please forgive the use of *he* instead of *s/he*, which would be anachronistic!

9　See Basin, p.86.

Chapter 1

1　Rogers, p.151.

2　*Harengue faicte au nom de l'Université de Paris devant le Roy Charles sixiesme & tout le conseil, contenant les remonstrances touchant le gouvernement du Roy et du Royaume ... [par maistre Jean Gerson]*, (ed). par Vincent Sentenac, à Paris, 1561. See pp.33-4.

3　Basin, see pp.44ff.

4　*Richard II*, act IV, sc.i.

5　For a full analysis of the evidence, see Mortimer, *The Fears of Henry IV*, pp. 210-7.

6　*1, Henry IV*, act 1, sc.iii.

7　Mortimer (2010), p.24.

8　Mortimer, 'What Hundred Years War?', (Oct. 2009).

9　Mortimer, (2010), p.453.

10　See Monstrelet, III, p.118.

11　Ibid., p.111.

12　*Vita et Gesta Henrici quinci*, by the anonymous chronicler known now as the Pseudo-Elmham, quoted Dockray, p.21.

13　See Contamine (2010), p.84.

14　Monstrelet III, p.303.

15　Mortimer (2008), p.185.

16　Sermon quoted by Mathieu-Maxime Gorce, *Saint Vincent Ferrier*, p. 152, Paris, 1923.

17　See *Bourgeois*, entry no.591.

18　See Viriville II, p.347.

19　See Monstrelet V, p.188.

20　See Guibal, p.188.

21　See Mortimer (2008), p.257

22　See Markale, p.12.

23　See Froissart, *Oeuvres*, ed. Kervyn de Lettenhove, XV, 216-7. Bayezid's victorious career came to an end in 1402, when Tamburlaine defeated him at Ankara and took control of the Ottoman empire.

Chapter 2

1 See Schnerb, p.252ff.
2 See Juvenal des Ursins, p.438. Juvenal des Ursins was later to later to play an important role as judge in the Nullity proceedings of 1452-6.
3 See Chastellain.I, p.16ff; However, our Burgundian diplomatically clears the now reigning monarch Charles VII of any complicity in the assassination, allowing that he was at the time 'un jeune enfant pour lors [...] lui ignorant, veuille Dieu! et ainsi le croy' (p.22).
4 The whole letter is quoted in Schnerb, p.530.
5 See Calmette, p.139.
6 See Tisset III, p.3.
7 See Chastellain I, passim, and pp.32-3.
8 See Beaune (2009), p.252. Philippe de Mézières was a knight and diplomat, also the former tutor of the young Charles VI. He was possibly the model for Chaucer's Knight in the *Knight's Tale* of the *Canterbury Tales*.
9 See Duparc I, p.289; III, p.277.
10 See Favier (2010), p.356.
11 See Calmette, p.142.
12 See Monstrelet, II, 345-6.
13 See Juvenal des Ursins, pp.485-6.
14 By 1430 both these territories would pass under the control of his son Philip the Good (regent of Holland and Hainaut in 1428, Duke of Brabant in 1430, Count of Hainaut in 1433).
15 Calmette talks of a minute, dating from May 1417, written in the duke's hand and containing these stipulations, specifically that of secret aid, which he believes was actually a secret pact. The reference is to Rymer, *Foedera*, IX, p.394.
16 See Schnerb, p. 661.

Chapter 3

1 Waugh, p.352.
2 Lang, p.18.
3 See *Bourgeois*, entry 259; for the Bourgeois's description of the misery of the refugees and people, see entries 256ff.
4 See Monstrelet III, p.321.
5 Kervyn de Lettenhove quotes this letter in a long footnote to Chastellain I, p.39. Kervyn adds that he considers that John the Fearless did indeed intend to deprive the Dauphin of his liberty (op. cit. p.31, n). an opinion he had already defended in his *Histoire de Flandre*. Viriville I, pp.173-81, is also of this opinion.
6 See Eric Jager, *The Last Duel*, Arrow Books, London, 2006.
7 See Chastellain I, pp.72.

8   Carleton Williams, p.55.
9   See *Ordonnances*, pp. 86,87,88,90.
10 See *Bourgeois*, entry no.279.
11 See Juvenal des Ursins, pp.564.
12 See *Bourgeois*, entries no.294 and 302.
13 See Juvenal des Ursins, p.567.
14 See Ibid. p.564.
15 I am indebted for this information to Rogers, pp,157-8.
16 Juvenal des Ursinsl, p.566; Juvenal says the son was his only child, but in fact, he also had a daughter.
17 See Monstrelet IV, p.110.
18 See Chartier I, p.6.
19 He died in 1416 and is buried in the Cathedral of Saint Étienne in Bourges.
20 See Basin, pp.47.
21 See *Bourgeois*, entry no.389
22 Ibid., entry no. 375
23 See *Actes de la Chancellerie* II, pp.5-10.
24 ibid. pp.35-7.
25 See Champion II, p.lxxxv.
26 See Quicherat IV, p.413; Wavrin, p.284.
27 *Letters and Papers*, p.xliii. I am indebted also to the editor of these papers for the information on this same page.

Chapter 4

1   The bust is the head and shoulders of the recumbent statue which was placed on the royal tomb, along with that of Charles VII, in 1464 or 1465. The tomb was smashed up by revolutionaries in 1793, but parts of the statues were saved by Alexandre Lenoir, and the two busts reinstated in Saint Denis in the 1990s. Some restoration has been carried out, principally the noses. However. both heads are realistic, that of Charles modelled on his death-mask. It is rather better-looking than his portrait by Jean Fouquet. See the website saintdenis-tombeaux. forumculture.net.
2   See Monstrelet IV, p.198.
3   See Basin, p.52.
4   The following lines are from Buchanan's 'Epithalamium' (1558), composed for the marriage of Mary Stuart (later Mary Queen of Scots) and the Dauphin François. 'When all the nations at one solemn call Had sworn to whelm the dynasty of Gaul, In that sad hour her liberty and laws Had perished had not Scotland join'd her cause ...'
5   Chevalier was an important personage in the administration of Charles VII, becoming royal Treasurer in 1452

6 See 'Comptes des dépenses faites par Charles VII pour secourir Orléans pendant le siège de 1428', J. Loiseleur, *in Mémoires de la Société archéologique et historique de l'Orléanais*, tome XI, 1868.

7 See the answer to a Query in *Notes and Queries*, vol.IX, Issue 24, June 23, 1866, pp.513-4: 'Epitaphs abroad: Jean (Carmichael), Bishop of Orleans', by Chas. H.E. Carmichael.

8 See Quicherat, IV, pp.482-4. Andrew Lang, the Scottish biographer of Joan, wrote a novel inspired by this person and entitled *A Monk of Fife* (1896).

9 See Le Fèvre de Saint-Rémy I, p.239.

10 Henry IV of England had fallen in love with Joanna in 1398 during his exile in Brittany. Her stepson Henry V had her imprisoned in 1419. He relented as he lay dying and she lived until 1437 in Nottingham castle. Her recumbent statue lies beside that of Henry IV in Canterbury Cathedral.

11 Philip incorporated Jacqueline's estates into his territories in 1432, the duke of Brabant having died in 1427.

12 Monstrelet IV, p.208

13 The letter is given in Monstrelet IV, pp.213-6

14 Jacqueline had been caught and placed under house-arrest by Philip. John of Brabant died in 1427. In 1432 Jacqueline secretly married without Philip's consent. Her husband, Frank van Borselen, was imprisoned and released only when his wife handed over her estates to Philip. She died in 1436. Eleanor and Humphrey were happy together. They filled their court at Greenwich with poets and musicians. However, Eleanor took to consulting astrologers and trying out magic potions. In 1441 she was tried on charges of treason and witchcraft. She was imprisoned in various castles, and died in 1452. Humphrey had been arrested on a charge of treason in 1447 and died three days later. He is commemorated in an annual Requiem Mass celebrated on 20 February, usually in the Blackfriars Priory Church in Oxford. His library is now incorporated into the Bodleian.

15 *Letters and Papers Illustrative of the Reign of King Henry VI*, vol. I, pp. 403-21.

Part II

Chapter 5

1 These are the opening statements of Joan at her trial. The minutes are in Latin and in indirect speech, but I have put them into direct speech.

2 See Luce, pp.25-7.

3 Clovis came to the throne in 481. His kingdom stretched from the Rhine across northern Gaul to Acquitaine, with his capital at Paris, where he and his devout wife Clothilde were buried in the crypt of the church of Sainte Geneviève. He established equal rights for all his subjects, Latin or Germanic, Arian or Catholic. Most of them were in fact Catholic before his own conversion. The Frankish kingdom thus became the 'eldest daughter of the Church', promoter and defender of Christianity throughout western Europe. Clovis codified the Salic law, the basis for much of European law.

4 See Luce, p.121n.

5 See Wallon, p.28.

6 A *clerc* was not necessarily a cleric (if married, as here, obviously not). The word was also applied to persons able to read and write and earning their living in some profession requiring these skills.

7 See Luce, pp.37-8.

8 Ibid., p.41.

9 The term for a ploughman is *charron*, in the Nullity documents the witness Jean Moen, for example, is a charron.

10 This fortified house and its *dépendances* were farmed out on 2 April 1420 for a period of 9 years by the seigneur de Bourlémont to Jean Biget and Jacques d'Arc. See Tisset II, note, p.64-5.

11 This is pointed out by Beaune (2008), pp.36-7.

12 The vogue would reach its full flowering in the sixteenth century throughout Europe, with such poets and dramatists as Ronsard, Sir Philip Sidney, or Beaumont and Fletcher's drama *The Faithful Shepherdesse*.

13 Joan called him her uncle since he was fifteen or sixteen years older than her, which must have seemed a lot to her as a child. He was married to her cousin Jeanne, daughter of her mother's sister, Aveline.

14 Is this a reference to the raid by Burgundian freebooters which Siméon Luce dates to 1425?

15 This is a harmless exclamation, literally it means *By my staff!* or *By my baton!*

16 See Luce, p.57.

17 Hauviette is particularly unclear about her age and probably thinks she is older than her actual number of years. for she thinks she was 'three or four years younger than Joan', who would by now be forty-four. Perhaps Joan appeared more grown-up to the younger child than she was.

18 *Laetare Sunday* is the fourth Sunday of Lent, a joyful break in the middle of the penitential season, when the Mass begins with the exhortation *Laetare Jerusalem!* (*Rejoice, Jerusalem!*).

19 *Fontaine des Groseilliers*: the Redcurrant Bushes Fountain.

20 See Luce, p.68.

21 Ibid. pp.76-80.

22 The French minute of the trial here merely states that this occurred on a day of fasting, but the Latin translation affirms that Joan says she had not fasted on the day before. Was the Latin an amendment demanded by Joan when the French was read out to her in court?

23 See Quicherat V, p.304, extract from the *Registre delphinal* of Mathieu Thomassin.

24 Those of Pierre Sureau, Financial Controller of Normandy, for the English and those of Hémon Raguier, Treasurer for War of Charles VII for the French.

25 See Quicherat IV, p.303.

26 See *Journal du siège*, p.10; Also *Bourgeois*, entries 447 and 493.

27 Ibid. p.15; Quicherat IV, p.103.

28 Ibid. p.45-6; Quicherat IV, p.126.

29 Ibid., p.18; Quicherat IV, p.105. Maître Jean was firing from the earthworks at the Orleans end of the bridge. Three arches of the bridge had been destroyed to prevent access to the town.

30 Ibid. p.53; Quicheraat, p.131.

31 See Chartier 1, p.65.

Chapter 6

1 Tisset I, p. 49: 'Dixitque tunc prefato avunculo suo quod opportunebat ipsam ire ad praedictum oppidum de Vallecoloris.' (Session of 22 February). The word *tunc* (*then*) is significant. This sentence is missing from the French minute. As Tisset points out (III, p.29), the French minute is not verbatim, but a résumé of Jeanne's replies, compiled each evening from notes taken by the notaries.

2 Concerning Joan's visit to Vaucouleurs, the only witness to give a date is Bertrand de Poulengy, one of the two young nobles who accompanied her to Chinon. According to the minute for 6 February 1456, Bertrand stated: 'I think that Joan the Maid came to Vaucouleurs around the Feast of the Ascension' (i.e. 13 May 13 1428). Tisset (II, p.49n.) suggests that *Ascensionem Domini* is a slip for what should be *Adventum Domini* (Advent).

3 The minute gives *Vaucouleurs* here, but this is certainly an error of the notary. See Duparc I, p.296, III, p.283, and Tisset II, p.51n. There is some controversy about which Saint-Nicolas she would have gone to. Poulengy says in his testimony that she went to Saint-Nicolas before going to see the Duke of Lorraine (Duparc III, p.293)

4 See Olivier Bouzy, in *Jeanne d'Arc. Histoire et dictionnaire*, (Contamine et al.), p.104.

5 See Duparc I, p.378; IV, p.61.

6 This probably refers to the thigh-length leather boots-cum-leggings worn to protect the thighs and hose when riding.

7 Contamine (1994), pp. 394-5.
8 Testimony of 5 February 1456, at Toul.
9 See Quicherat V, p.257, extract from the accounts of Guillaume Charrier; also *Journal du siège*, pp.77-8.
10 A French league was 2.72 English miles.

Chapter 7

1 See Basin, p.69
2 Session of 4 May 1456
3 Louis of Bourbon, cousin of Charles of Bourbon, had been taken prisoner at Agincourt. He escaped from the Tower of London in 1422. He was present at Orleans and Rheims and fought in Joan's campaigns right up to the failed assault on Paris.
4 Session of 27 February, 1429.
5 Session of 25 February, 1456.
6 See Chartier I, p,67; Quicherat IV, p.52.
7 It is easy to see how this error arose.
8 Quicherat believes that this official account was written up after the failed assault on Paris (September 1429), while the couple of paragraphs covering Joan's capture and death were added after May 1431. Quicherat's article and the extracts from the registers of the *Greffier* can be most conveniently consulted on the website *stejeannedarc.net*
9 See Viriville I, p.256.
10 See Quicherat IV, p.277ff.
11 Obviously she was mounted.
12 See Duparc IV, p.71.
13 See Duparc I, p.476; All subsequent quotations from D'Aulon are take from his lengthy written deposition made in French, in the same volume, pp.473-87.
14 See Duparc I, p. 400; testimony of Sir Simon Charles.
15 See Quicherat V, p. 472.
16 See *Journal du siège*, pp.63-4; Quicherat IV, pp.140-1.
17 Fraioli, *The Early Debate*, p.74.
18 See Quicherat, V, pp. 257-8.

Chapter 8

1 The world is represented as a globe decades before Christopher Columbus sets out on his travels!
2 See Quicherat IV, p.452.
3 See Viriville I, p.258.
4 I am indebted for much of this information to an article by the French medievalist Monique Closson, 'Propre comme au Moyen Age', in *Historama*, No. 40, June, 1987.

5   See *Journal du siège*, pp.7-8;. Quicherat IV, p.99.

6   Tuesday, 27 February, 1431.

7   In *Gestes des nobles français*, quoted in Contamine, Bouzy and Hélary, p.1071.This chronicle ends in 1429 and celebrates Joan's successes. It was continued by Cousinot's *Chronique de la Pucelle*, which takes over the 1429 passages, but omits some details, in particular the remark quoted here.

8   See Fauquembergue II, p.323; Quicherat IV, pp.457-8.

Chapter 9

1   See Chartier I, p,69; Quicherat IV, p.54.

2   Chartier I, p.71; Quicherat IV, p.56.

3   See Morosini III, p.24. A major source of fact, rumour, anecdote and gossip at the time is his *Chronique*. Morosini was the nephew of the Doge of Venice. He copied and kept a collection of documents and letters to which he had access as a member of the Council of State, among others, letters from Pancrazio to his father.

4   See Quicherat V, p.136.

5   See *Chronique de Tournay*, in Ayroles III, p. 622. A number of historians, among them Lang and Xavier Hélary, consider this to be the most probable of the estimates. See Lang, p.344, note to p.112, line 11. Also Xavier Hélary, 'La levée du siège d'Orleans', p.123, in *Jeanne d'Arc. Histoire et Dictionnaire*, by Contamine, Bouzy, Hélary.

6   Lang, p.115-6.

7   Is Dunois' memory at fault here? There is no other mention of Joan ever invoking Saint Louis and Charlemagne! It may well be that Dunois' subconscious prompted him to substitute for saints Margaret and Catherine these male saints more experienced in the arts of war!

8   Christ was actually holding the globe of the world in his left hand and blessing with his right hand a fleur-de-lys (the symbol of the royal arms of France) held by an angel.

9   See *Journal du siège*, pp.76-8; Quicherat IV, pp.152-3.

10 See *Bourgeois*, entry 504.

11 See *Journal du siège*, p.80; Quicherat IV, p.155.

12 See Chartier I, pp.74-5; Quicherat IV, pp.58-59. The mention of Fastolf is an error, he was still in Paris.

13 D'Aulon and De Coutes mistakenly say that this attack took place the day after the storming of Saint-Loup, but they had forgotten that 5 May was a religious feast day, a day of truce. Frère Pasquerel (4 May 1456) confirms that Joan declared to him on 4 May that there would be no fighting the next day.

14 Contamine, Bouzy , Hélary, pp,133-4, article by Hélary.

15 Quicherat IV, p.425: '– et quod ipsa ante Aurelium conflictu telo vulnerabitur sed non morietur ...'
16 See Wallon, p.82.
17 Kelly DeVries, p. 81.
18 See Chartier I, pp.79-80, *Journal du siège*, p.90. Quicherat IV has a note (p.63, n.1), telling us that Le Bourg's father, Guy de Bar, had served with the Burgundians and was said to have commanded the Paris massacres in 1418. The son cannot have been on very close terms with his father.

Chapter 10

1 See Quicherat, V, pp.101-4. Charles underestimates the duration of the assault on the Tourelles.
2 See *Aperçus nouveaux*, pp.25-6.
3 Lang, pp.222 and 361, notes to p.222.
4 See Ayroles III, p.225.
5 See *Journal du siège*, pp.93-4; Quicherat IV, p.168
6 Cagny was writing his chronicle in 1436, only five years after Joan's death. In 1436, he had already served the Alençon family, as he says, for forty-six years. Quicherat regarded him as the best-informed of the chroniclers, although more recent historians accuse him of bias in favour of Alençon and prejudice against Charles VII. Quicherat had already defended him against such charges.
7 See Contamine, Bouzy, Hélary, p.511.
8 See Tisset II, p.106n.2.
9 For the complete letter, see Quicherat V, pp.105-11.
10 See Duparc II, p.39.
11 See Morosini III, pp 232ff.
12 See Quicherat III, pp.393-410.
13 Ibid, pp.411-21.
14 See Quicherat V, p.270.
15 See Quicherat III, p.422-68.
16 See Ayroles II, pp.539-42.
17 *Journal du siège*, p.95; Quicherat IV., pp.169-70.
18 See Cagny, p.150, Quicherat IV, p.12.
19 See *Journal du siège*, p.99; Quicherat IV, p.173.
20 See *Chronique de la Pucelle*, p.302 .
21 See Ayroles III, p.631 (*Chronique des Cordeliers*), also Quicherat's comments (article reproduced on stejeannedarc.net)
22 See Cagny, p.153; Quicherat IV, p.14.
23 See Chartier, pp.89-90: Quicherat IV, p.71.
24 See *Chronique de la Pucelle*, p. 313; Quicherat IV, p.249.
25 See *Journal du siège*, p.101-2; Quicherat IV, p.175-6
26 For this and the following account of Patay, see Wavrin, chap. XII and XIII, pp.288-305.

Chapter 11

1 For this and the following quotations, see Cagny, pp.156-7; Quicherat IV, pp.17-8.

2 *Chronique de la Pucelle* p.312., See Quicherat IV, p.248. The *coustiller* was a knight's assistant, armed with a sword and dagger, His status was similar to that of an archer.

3 See Quicherat V, p.125. Fastolf, of course, was not captured. Perhaps another had been mistaken for him, or someone had claimed to be him in order to give him time to get away with the remains of the army. Joan was misinformed.

4 See Chartier, pp.90-1; Quicherat IV, p.72.

5 See Monstrelet, IV, p.336; Quicherat IV, pp.377-8.

6 See *Chronique de la Pucelle*, p.313; Quicherat IV, p.250.

7 See *Journal du siège d'Orléans*, p. 108-9; Quicherat IV, p.181.

8 See Quicherat IV, pp.287-8, in extracts from Jean Rogier's collection and summaries of documents and letters which were still in the archives of the town of Rheims in Rogier's day, at the beginning of the seventeenth century, many of which have since been lost. Rogier states that he has seen the letters and that they are in 'bonne forme'. (pp. 284-99)

9 See Quicherat IV, p.289-90.

10 See *Journal du siège d'Orléans*, pp.109-10; Quicherat IV, p.182.

11 See *Bourgeois*, entry 500; see also entries 497, 499.

12 Ibid, entry 505.

13 See Chartier, pp. IV; Quicherat, pp, 73-4.

14 See *Journal du siège*, pp.110-11; Quicherat, p.182-3. The next quotation from the *Journal* follows on from this.

15 See *Chronique de la Pucelle*, p.319; Quicherat IV, p.252.

16 Quicherat IV, pp, 296-7 (extracts from Jean Rogier's collection).

17 The customary acclamation, Christmas or not!

18 This detail is given in the *Chronique de Tournay*, which is well-informed on the detail of Joan's public career as far as the coronation. See Ayroles III, p. 623.

19 See Quicherat V, p.129.

20 See *Journal du siège*, p.114; Quicherat IV, p.186.

Chapter 12

1 See *Chronique des Cordeliers*, in Ayroles III, p.631.

2 See Quicherat V, p,126-7.

3 He did eventually manage to send six or seven hundred Picards to Senlis, a town in Picardy, where Bedford's army faced the French on 14 and 15 Augustt 1429. See below.

4 See *Bourgeois*, entry no.512.

5 The Hussite or Bohemian Wars had their origin in the execution of the reformer Jan Hus by order of the Council of Constance in 1415 and continued until the 1430s. They were both religious and civil wars. The Hussite army was formidable and had a great number of successes, invading Germany, Silesia, Hungary and other regions and advancing as far as the Baltic.

6 See Viriville II, pp.105-6, also p.106 n.1, quoting the *Chronique de Lille.*

7 See Quicherat, V, pp.136-7. Quicherat dates the letter to July 1429, but Régine Pernoud dates it to 1434 (*Jeanne d'Arc*, 1962, p.116).

8 See Monstrelet IV, p.340; Quicherat, IV, p.381.

9 See Chartier, pp .99-100; Quicherat IV, p,79.

10 See Quicherat V, p.139-40.

11 See Quicherat, *Revue historique* (May-August 1882) pp.66-7

12 See Cagny, pp.161, Quicherat IV, p.21.

13 See Cagny, p,162-3; Quicherat IV, p.22.

14 *Gentlemen of England, I pray you, fire first*! The anecdote is recounted in Voltaire's *Précis du Règne de Louis XV*, and the phrase, supposedly pronounced by the Count of Anteroche at the beginning of the battle (11 May 1745), has become famous in folk memory.

15 See Monstrelet IV, p.351.

16 Ibid., p.354; Quicherat IV, p.391.

17 See Basin I, pp.72-3.

18 See Quicherat, article in the *Revue historique*, 1882, p.70.

19 See *Procès de condamnation*, 3 March,1431).

20 See Cagny, pp.164-5; Quicherat IV, p.24.

21 See Quicherat, article in the *Revue historique*, 1882, pp.70, 77-8.

Chapter 13

1 See Cagny, p.165; Quicherat IV, p.25.

2 See Fauquembergue II, p.324; Quicherat IV, p.458.

3 See *Bourgeois*, entry 519.

4 See *Fauquembergue*, 322-3; Quicherat IV, p.456-7.

5 See *Chronique de la Pucelle*, pp.333-4.

6 This and the following quotation, see Cagny, pp.167-9, Quicherat IV, pp.27-9.

7 See Cagny, p.170; Quicherat IV, p.29.

8 See Cagny, p.170-1; Quicherat IV, p.29-30.

9 See *Bourgeois*, entry 520.

10 See *Bourgeois*, entry 522; the next quotation is from entry 523.

11 This and the following quotation, see Chartier I, p.116; Quicherat IV, p.90.

12 See Tisset II, p.99, n.1.

13 See *Bourgeois*, entry 580.

14 This deposition was given, under oath, in written form, to the Nullity trial judges in 1456; see Duparc I, pp.473-488.

15 See Cagny, p.172; Quicherat IV, p.31.

16 See Quicherat V, pp.154-6, 271.

17 Ibid., this and the following letter, p.160-2

18 Ibid., p.156, also Pernoud/Clin, p.387.

19 Keen, p.294ff.

20 Stevenson, p.41.

21 See *Bourgeois*, entry 529, as also the following short quotation.

22 DeVries, pp.163-4.

23 Quoted Quicherat V, p.162-4. Quicherat found the document in Rymer, *Pacta foedera* X. He gives a heading which Rymer declares to be contemporary with the document: 'De proclamationibus contra capitaneos et soldarios tergiversantes incantationibus Puellae terrifiicatos'. The heading is *not* contemporary with the document, but it is certain that dismay was rife among the superstitious soldiery.

24 See Cagny, pp.173; Quicherat IV, p.32.

25 See Monstrelet IV, pp.384-5, Quicherat IV, p.400.

26 See *Bourgeois*, entry 529; Tuetey's edition, p. 252, n.2, gives information on those who were executed, including the innkeeper.

27 See the *Preface* to R. Oursel, *Le Procès de condamnation et le Procès de réhabilitation de Jeanne d'Arc*, Paris, Denoël,1959 (p.7).

28 See Tisset III, pp.30ff.

29 See Cagny p.174; also Quicherat IV, pp. 32-3.

Chapter 14

1 See Lefèvre de Saint-Rémy II, p.179; Quicherat, IV, pp. 438-9. Actually it was later, about five o'clock in the afternoon, when Joan and her company rode out.

2 See Monstrelet IV, pp.387-8: Quicherat IV, p.401-2.

3 See Chastellain II, p.48-9, Quicherat IV, pp.446-7.

4 See Tisset I, p.42, also Tisset II.p.42.

5 See Cagny, pp. 175-6; Quicherat IV, p. 34.

6 See Quicherat, IV, pp.272-3, See Champion's commentary, *Flavy*, pp.283-5. The passages on Joan of Arc in the *Miroir des femmes vertueuses* are lifted wholesale from Alain Bouchart's *Annales de Bretagne* (1514).

7 See *Aperçus nouveaux*, pp.79-81.

8 See Champion, *Flavy*, p,33 ff, and p.33 n.2.

9 See Cagny, p.175; Quicherat, IV, p.34.

10 See Monstrelet IV, p.388; Quicherat IV, p.402.

11 See Chastellain II, p.50; Quicherat IV, p.447.

12 See Quicherat V, pp.166-7.

13 Elliott, p.36.

14 See Quicherat V, pp. 168-9

15 See *Bourgeois*, entry 581.

16 Ibid, entry 587. The nine *preux* were heroes, three each chosen from antiquity (Hector, Alexander, Caesar), the Old Testament (Joshua, David, Judas Macchabeus) and Christian history (Arthur, Charlemagne, Godefroy de Bouillon). The nine ladies were also models of virtue, including Esther, Judith and Saint Helena.

17 See Lefèvre de Saint-Rémy II, p.264; Quicherat V, p,171.

18 See Ayroles I, p.79.

19 Ibid., pp.79-80, Lanéry d'Arc (1887), pp.25-6.

20 See Quicherat V, pp.253-4.

21 See Tisset I, p.155, Tisset II, p.133.The phrase which I have translated as '*between two wooden posts*' is obscure both in the Latin and in the French minute: *inter duas pecias nemoris, entre deux pieces de boys*. Rocolle suggests that it might mean that she had managed to enlarge an opening in some wooden partition in her cell in the tower, but it is very difficult to imagine.

22 See Quicherat V, p. 210.

23 I am indebted for these details to Rocolle, pp. 63-4.

24 See Tisset I, p.213, Tisset II, p.178.

25 See Morosini III, pp.232-4.

26 For this and the preceding letters mentioned, see O'Reilly II, pp.12-26.

27 See Tisset, III, p11ff.

28 See Morosini III, pp.336-8.

29 See Tisset I, pp.5,7.

30 See Bordonove (1985), p.173.

31 See Bouzy (2013), pp.213ff, for a discussion of the question.

32 See Quicherat IV, p. 281; Sala's informant is again the Chevalier de Boisy.

33 See Quicherat IV, p.518.

34 See Ayroles III, pp. 536-8.

Chapter 15

1 See Favier, p.383; Tisset III, p.6.

2 See Neveux, p.60.

3 See Quicherat V, pp.178ff.

4 See Quicherat I, pp.13-4.

5 See the article of Félix Brun: 'Notes biographiques sur Renaud de Fontaines, Évêque de Soissons', in the *Bulletin de la Société archéologique, historique et scientifique de Soissons*, t. XVII (1910), Soissons, 1912, pp.31-61.

6 See his letter of January 31, acknowledging receipt of this and other related payments, Quicherat V, pp.194-5.

7 See Rocolle, p.85.

8 See Morosini, pp. 332-4. *Crown* and *franc* or *franc d'or* are other terms for the *livre tournois*.

9 See Quicherat V, pp. 360-3.

Chapter 16

1 See Tisset II, p. 14.

2 Testimony of 2 May 1452. Loiseleur was a friend of Cauchon, a cleric of little distinction.

3 Louviers is some 22 miles south of Rouen. It had been taken by the French, under La Hire and other captains, in December 1430. Bedford undertook the siege of the place in May, 1431, very shortly before Joan was executed, and it capitulated at the end of the year.

4 This refers to the public sermon preached on 24 May 1431, before Joan was coerced into signing some form of abjuration, thus escaping the stake that day.

5 See Tisset I, pp.9-10.

6 It is worth quoting this piece of male prejudice in the original French: '...elle estoit bien subtille de subtillité appartenante à femme' Quicherat, II, 21. As the depositions of 1450 did not form part of the actual nullification trial, they were not transcribed into Latin, like all the later depositions.

7 See Palou, p.46

8 See Bouzy (2013), p.223.

9 See Tisset I, pp. 14-5, letter of Henry VI, dated 3 January 1431 (1430 old style). It orders that Joan should be handed over to Cauchon each time he should require her, while stipulating that ' It is Our intention to take back the said Joan into Our custody, should she not be condemned and convicted of any of the above charges or others concerning Our faith.'

10 Quicherat II, pp.5-6 and 348-9; Duparc, III, .209-10; The 1450 deposition is not included in Duparc's volume, since it was a preliminary and not part of the trial hearings as such. Jean de Saint-Avit was pro-French. He was imprisoned in Rouen a year after Joan's execution and died in the prison in 1442.

11 See *Bourgeois*, entry 580.

12 See Contamine *et al.*, pp.738-9.

13 See Quicherat I, p.34. For the whole episode, see pp.31-7.

14 See Tisset III. p.29.

15 The date of the Latin translation is uncertain. For two different opinions, see Tisset I, pp.xix-xx, and Pernoud/ Clin, pp.371-2.

16 See Tisset III, p.40.

17 For a detailed analysis of the surviving copies of the French minutes, see Tisset, I, pp.xxi-xxvi.
18 See Duparc I p.116; III, p.108.
19 See Tisset, III, pp.84-5.
20 See Quicherat II, pp.11-12.
21 See Favier, *Pierre Cauchon*, pp.434-7.

Chapter 17

1 The Latin minute reads *tacendo de condicione antedicta*, while the French minute (O) states specifically that she maintained her refusal to reveal anything of her revelations: *mais que, des revelacions dessusdictes, elle ne les diroit a personne.* (Tisset I.p.39).
2 There was frequently hubbub in the court, with various assessors firing questions at Joan. She herself complained about this. In presenting the interrogations, I place all questions in the mouth either of Cauchon or of one of the two assessors whom he appointed to deputise for himself, Beaupère and La Fontaine. Beaupère acted in the public sessions and La Fontaine in the later sessions in Joan's prison cell and I assume that it is their official questions which are minuted.
3 See Tisset II, p. 63, n.1.
4 See Guitton, p.116
5 See Tisset III, pp.114-7.
6 The mandragore is an evil-smelling plant which resembles the shape of the human body. It was believed to be a powerful instrument in sorcery.
7 Tisset points out (III, pp.118-9) that this reply is inexact in its description of the shield and that Charles had ennobled both Joan and her brothers. However, Joan never herself made use of the ennobled shield or coat-of-arms. Tisset II, p.106, n.2, suggests that the painter mentioned 'in this town' could well have been an agent sent by Cauchon.
8 See Lethel, pp.184, 187-8.
9 See Contamine (1994), p.437.
10 The opening on 3 March 1431, was put back until July, because of the death of Pope Martin V.
11 See Quicherat II, p.5; deposition of 5 March 1450.
12 See Tisset III, pp. 86-89.

Chapter 18

1 See Tisset II., n.1, p.153.
2 See Quicherat I, p.205, n.1; Lang, p.275.
3 See Tisset II, n.1, p.257. Also p.384, concerning Basset's imprisonment.

4 See Contamine, Bouzy, Hélary: their dictionary entry 'Torture', pp.1015-7.

5 Lang, p.259.

6 See Tisset, III, pp.109-13.

7 Ibid., p. 132.

8 Pernoud/Clin, p.207. See Ayroles, pp. 533-4, for an elucidation of the question of divine inspiration from Augustine onwards.

9 Régine Pernoud discusses the question at some length (1962, p,170).
10 Testimony of Jean de Mailly, 2 April 1456.

11 The French minute includes her express desire to have a woman about her (*qu'elle eust une femme*). This is not included in the Latin minute.

12 Duparc II. p.514, *Récapitulation de Jean Bréhal*

13 See Quicherat I, p.456, n.1.

14 Tisset points out (t.II, p.346, n,1) that there is a serious omission in Courcelles latin translation of the French minutes. Joan says specifically that she did not intend *at the time* of abjuring, or *as she was abjuring*, to revoke anything unless it pleased God. Courcelles does not translate the phrase *en l'eure*, meaning *at the moment* (of abjuring).

15 Massieu places the incident before the meeting began, but that must be a slip of memory, as Marguerie was there until the end (his opinion is recorded).

16 Testimony of 5 March 1450, See Quicherat II, p.3-4.

17 See Quicherat IV, p.459-60 and Tuetey III, pp.13-4.

18 See Bouzy (2013), p.249.

19 The Latin has: *exeuntem de Francia*, i.e. rising up from the French-held part of the country. Ayrtoles V, p.133, n.3, argues convincingly that this must be a scribe's error for *de flamma*, 'from the flames'.

20 See Quicherat II, p.14. These preliminaries are not included in Duparc's volumes, as they were carried out at the behest of Charles VII, after the re-taking of Rouen and are therefore not part of the enquiry set up later under the papal *rescript*.

Chapter 19

1 See Favier (2010), pp.526-7.

2 See *Bourgeois*, entry no. 552.

3 Ibid., entry 555, see also entries 553-4.

4 See Viriville.II, pp. 296-9.

5 See *Bourgeois*, for this and following quotes, entries 593-4.

6 Ibid, .entry 594; Beaune's note 269, on the same page 309, explains that left-overs from feasts were sent to the Hotel-Dieu.

7 Ibid. entry no. 609.

8 Ibid. entries 612-14, 617.

9 See Favier (1980) p.535.

10 See *Bourgeois*, entry.620.
11 Ibid., entry 641 and entry 644.
12 Viriville II, p.312.
13 Ibid., pp.334-5.
14 See *Bourgeois*, entry 649. The Bourgeois puts the number of victims at 1200, but that is hard to believe.
15 Dickinson, p.78.
16 Ibid., p.3.
17 See Cagny, p.208.
18 See Basin, p.117.
19 Seward, p. 235.
20 See *Bourgeois*, entry 754.

Chapter 20

1 See Quicherat V, pp.321-4.
2 Anatole France has a note suggesting that Bacquillon may be actually Vaucouleurs (vol. II, p.413, n.1).
3 See Quicherat V, p. 323.
4 Ibid., pp. 324-5.
5 Ibid., pp.328-9.
6 Ibid., p.327.
7 Ibid., pp.274-5.
8 Ibid., pp. 332-3, *lettre de rémission* granted to Jean de Siquemville; see also Lecoy de la Marche, p.12.
9 Jonathan Sumption, in his chapter entitled 'Penitential Pilgrimage', explains the medieval use of pilgrimage as a punishment for various misdeeds. As there were few public prisons, this custom had the advantage of expelling culprits from town for a considerable period. (See Sumption, *Pilgrimage. An Image of Mediaeval Religion*, Faber and Faber, London, 1975).
10 See *Bourgeois*, entry 790.
11 See Quicherat IV, p.281.
12 See Lecoy de la Marche, p.19.
13 Ibid., p.20ff.
14 See *Aperçus nouveaux*, p.157.
15 He worked on his *Recherches de la France* fron 1557 until his death in 1615. Chapter V of Book VI deals with the history of Joan of Arc.
16 *Histoire de France*, see pp.1144ff, and pp. 1167-1187.

Chapter 21

1 Quicherat II, p.20-1. The depositions of 1450 did not form part of the actual Nullity trial and were not translated into Latin.
2 See Duparc II, pp.585-6

3 The papers of De Leliis and Pontanus can be consulted in Lanéry d'Arc, *Mémoires et consultations*, pp. 17-33 and 35-71 respectively. Basin's consultation is included in Duparc II, pp.157-219.

4 See Duparc I, pp.164 and 99-100, (Latin text) and III, pp.156 and 91-2 (French text).

5 See Duparc IV, p.229.

6 See Quicherat IV, p.518.

Index of Persons

For the Rouen trial, with well over a hundred assessors, not all of those in the text are indexed, only the individuals who played a prominent role in the proceedings. Similarly, nor are all one hundred and twenty witnesses at the later Nullity trial, only those who played an active part in Joan's life. This is in order to keep the index to a usable length. All citations from the two trials can be looked up in the indexes of Quicherat's or Du Parc's and Tisset's volumes (see Bibliography and Notes).

Albret, Charles II d' (son of Charles d'Albret, killed at Agincourt), 44, 201, 221, 223, 225-6

Alençon, Jean, Duke of, 63, 74, 108, 122, 129, 131-43 *passim*, 167-82 *passim*, 185, 187-9, 194, 201-2, 209, 211, 214, 216-21, 231, 239, 281, 293, 360-61, 366, 380-81

Amboise, Louis de, 351, 357

Anjou, Louis, Duke of, 35-6

Anjou, Marie d', Queen of France, 48, 61, 108, 188

Anjou, René de, 108-9, 199, 240, 373

Arc, Catherine d', (sister of Joan), 76, 88, 299

Arc, Isabelle d', see Rommée, Isabelle

Arc, Jacques d' (brother of Joan), 76, 94

Arc, Jacques d' (father of Joan), 8, 73-4, 80, 87, 93, 109, 168, 201, 204

Arc, Jean d' (brother of Joan), 130, 201, 226, 370-71, 379, 382

Arc, Pierre d', (brother of Joan), 93, 201, 231, 236-7, 245, 248, 291, 300, 376

Armagnac, Bernard VII, Count of, 14-16, 18, 22, 28, 38, 42, 44-6, 48, 69, 187, 288-9

Armoises, Claude des (the false Joan of Arc), 369-73 *passim*

Arras, Franquet d', 231-2, 274, 304

Aulon, Jean d', 123, 129, 134-6, 143, 146, 152-4, 157, 159, 161, 225, 231, 236-7, 240, 245, 364, 380-81

Avignon, Marie d', (Marie Robin), 169

Basset, Jean, 317, 325, 407

Baudricourt, Robert de, 76, 85,
102-3, 105-13, 120, 201, 281,
284, 288, 300-301, 312, 315,
374
Bavaria, John of, (bishop of
Liège), 31, 37
Bavaria, Louis of (brother of
Queen Isabeau), 33, 38, 42
Bayezid, Sultan of Turkey, 31, 129
Beaufort, Henry, Cardinal of
Winchester, (uncle of Henry V
and Chancellor of England),
56, 67, 207, 221, 228, 254,
268, 326, 331, 352, 360
Beaupère, Jean (interrogator),
73, 78, 84-5, 89-90, 115-6,
131-2, 194, 226, 233, 253,
255, 261, 266-95 *passim*,
298, 309, 314, 316, 319,
324-6, 329, 348, 377, 380
Bedford, John of Lancaster, Duke
of, 40, 55-70 *passim*, 88,
95-101 *passim*, 127-9, 142,
145, 167, 184, 186, 192-3,
198, 205-15, 221, 223,
227, 230, 240, 244, 247-65
passim, 274, 290, 313, 324,
345, 348, 350-60, 365, 374,
381
Benedict XIII, anti-pope, 19, 36,
67, 253
Berry, John, Duke of, 23, 26,
33-9, 44, 56, 65
Béthune, Jeanne de (wife of John
of Luxembourg), 244, 246
Boniface IX, Pope, 19
Bosquier, Pierre, (Dominican
friar), 346
Bréhal, Jean, Inquisitor for France,
304, 334, 377-9, 382-3
Buchan, John Stuart, Earl of, 54,
62-3, 65
Bureau, Jean, 367-8
Burgundy, Anne of (wife of
Bedford), 264, 355

Burgundy, Philip the Bold, Duke
of, 16, 20, 23-4, 28-30, 32
Burgundy, John the Fearless, Duke
of, 15, 18, 20-22, 25-6, 28-61
passim, 64-5, 72-3, 96, 108,
165, 168, 206-7, 209-10, 240,
252-3, 358, 361
Burgundy, Philip the Good, Duke
of, 22, 28, 36, 50-52, 55-7,
64-8, 99-101, 141, 165, 170,
189, 191, 198, 201, 205-7,
209, 212-15, 221-3, 227,
230, 234-5, 240, 244, 250,
252-3, 255, 348-50, 352, 355,
360-361, 364-5

Caboche, Simon, 42, 48
Cade, Jack, his rebellion, 368
Calixtus III, Pope, 378-9
Calonne, Emerance de (abbess of
Saint-Antoine-des-Champs),
354
Capeluche, 42, 46
Carmichael, John, (Bishop of
Orleans), 64, 201
Cauchon, Pierre, (Bishop of
Beauvais), 8, 70, 72-3, 92,
132, 168, 199, 212, 234,
238, 249-92, 295-301, 303,
307-349, 352, 360, 379-82
Charles V, King of France, 13,
15-16, 29-30, 39, 43, 63
Charles VI, King of France, 15-16,
20, 22, 26-30, 32-5, 37-8, 43,
45, 49-52, 55, 65, 69, 141,
169, 203, 359, 361
Charles VII King of France (earlier
Dauphin), 9, 14, 24, 26-8, 44,
55, 59, 61-3, 70, 75-7, 82, 94,
105, 109, 118, 121-3, 125,
128, 133-5, 140-44, 155, 158,
164-73, 191, 198-9, 203-16,
220-33 *passim*, 243, 247,
249-51, 256, 259-60, 263,
278, 281-4, 284, 288-90, 298,

300, 315, 321, 324, 326, 343, 348, 353-67, 371-3, 376-7, 381, 383

Chartres, Regnault de, (Archbishop of Rheims), 62, 100, 129, 199-200, 212-3, 220, 235, 242, 265, 323, 357, 360

Chastel, Tanguy du 45, 48-50, 65, 358

Châtelier, Jacques de (bishop of Paris) 352, 365

Clarence, Thomas, Duke of, 18, 40, 53, 55, 62

Clermont, Charles de Bourbon, Count of, 98-100, 201-2, 217, 219, 226, 358, 368

Clisson, Olivier de, Constable of France, 22, 24

Colles, Guillaume (Boisguillaume, notary), 73, 269, 273-4, 278-80, 286, 296, 303, 316, 319, 325-6, 339-40, 349

Courcelles, Thomas de, 253, 261, 269, 271, 273-4, 276, 280, 309, 313-4, 316, 320, 323-4, 326, 329, 332-3, 335, 338, 343, 348, 360, 380-81

Coutes, Louis de, squire of Joan, 119, 130, 135-6, 139, 141, 149-50, 153-4, 156-7, 159, 186, 237, 334, 380-81

Darnley, John Stewart, Earl of, 62, 98-100

Douglas, Archibald, Earl of Wigtown, 62-4

Dunois, John, Count of (Bastard of Orleans), 19, 21, 68-9, 74, 97-101, 118, 129, 133-5, 141-55, 159-70 *passim*, 174, 181-2, 185-6, 189, 194-5, 210, 226, 231, 281, 290, 293, 349, 354, 357-8, 361, 363-8, 374-5, 380-81

Edward III, King of England, 13, 15, 19, 31

Érard, Guillaume, 322, 324, 326-7, 330, 360

Essarts, Pierre, des, 37-8, 41

Estivet, Jean d' (prosecutor at Rouen), 268, 290, 312, 318-9

Estouteville, Guillaume d', Cardinal, 377-8

Fastolf (Shakespeare's Falstaff), 98-9, 146, 152-3, 155, 175-6, 178, 180-1, 183-4, 186, 189, 363

Battle of the Herrings, 96, 98, 100-101

Flavy, Guillaume de, 211, 234-6, 238-9, 404

Gaucourt, Raoul de, 19, 69, 74, 77, 96-7, 120, 129, 135, 137, 155-6, 164, 170, 217-8, 356, 380

Gélu, Jacques, 172, 243

Gerson, Jean, 13, 30, 42, 72-3, 123, 170-71, 203, 253, 309

Giac, Pierre de, 48, 65-6

Giles de Durement (Abbot of Fécamp), 268, 275, 309, 317, 319, 336

Glasdale, Sir William, 98, 150, 160, 189

Gloucester, Humphrey, Duke of 55-6, 66-7, 230, 356, 364

Gorkum Heinrich von, 172

Gorlitz, Elisabeth of, Dame de Luxembourg, 370

Gressart, Perrinet, 59, 223

Grey, John, (Joan's gaoler), 263, 284, 301, 314, 333

Grouchet, Richard de, 318, 325-6

Guillaume (the Shepherd Boy), 242-3, 350

Guyenne, (herald), 130, 149, 151

Guyenne, Louis (Dauphin), Duke of, 36, 38, 41, 43

Hainaut, Jacqueline, Countess of, 66
Haiton, William, 316, 320, 322-3, 326, 333, 337
Hampton, John, 311
Hellande, Guillaume de, (Bishop of Beauvais), 379
Henry IV, King of England, 14, 16-18, 21, 29, 35-6, 39-40, 62, 64, 98
Henry V, King of England, 13-4, 17-8, 27, 37. 39-40, 43-4, 47-9, 51-3, 55-9, 63, 65, 67, 96, 133, 140, 168, 181, 186, 253, 354, 359-60
Henry VI, King of England, 25, 27, 32, 55-6, 60, 99, 109, 127, 142, 145, 167, 186, 192, 205, 207-30, 240, 242-3, 249, 252, 254, 260-1, 263, 265, 268, 274-5, 324, 326, 329, 346, 348-9, 351-3, 359-60, 363-4, 367-8
Houppeville, Nicolas de, 268, 272, 275, 277-8, 313-4, 339, 380
Humphrey, Duke of Gloucester, 55-6, 66-7, 230, 364

Iliers, Florent d', 174
Isabeau of Bavaria, Queen of France, 16, 23-33, 38, 44-6, 48-50, 52-3, 85, 106, 351-2

James I, King of Scotland, 54, 62-3, 99, 108
John II, King of France (John the Good), 15, 64
Juvenal des Ursins, Jean, 36, 42, 53-4, 379-80, 382

Kennedy, Sir Hugh, 62, 99, 155, 231

Kirkmichael, John, (Bishop of Orleans), 100

La Chambre, Guillaume de (doctor during Joan's illness at Rouen), 277-8, 311, 318-9, 330, 341, 343
La Fontaine, Jean de, 92-3, 132, 134, 140, 168, 232-4, 245, 247, 268-9, 275, 292-3, 296-309, 313
La Hire (Etienne de Vignolles), 69-70, 87, 98-100, 138, 144, 147, 150, 152, 155, 157, 162, 175, 180-82, 185-6, 189, 208, 220, 250, 281, 290, 322, 349, 258, 362, 364
La Pierre, Isambard de (Dominican friar), 263, 268, 278, 301, 307-09, 311, 313, 316, 323-4, 326-7, 332, 336-7, 342-3, 376
La Rochelle, Catherine de, 194, 223, 296-7, 303
La Trémoille, Georges de, 48, 65-6, 99, 122, 141-2, 165-6, 178-80, 187, 190, 197, 201, 205, 211, 213, 220-223, 242, 249, 297, 322, 350-51, 356-7, 366
Laval, Guy de, 165, 169-70, 202, 209
Laval, André de, 178, 202, 209
Laxart, Durand, 76, 78, 85, 102-07, 110, 201, 380
Le Bourg du Bar (soldier), 162
Le Cannonier, Jean, 157
Leliis, Theodor de, 377-8
Lemaître, Jean (deputy Inquisitor at Rouen), 92, 251, 255, 271-4, 278, 301, 309-11, 314, 320-21, 325-6, 332, 336, 343, 346, 379, 382
Le Sauvage, Raoul, 317, 324, 326
Lohier, Jean, 269, 276-7

Loiseleur, Nicolas, 263, 269, 273, 276, 278-80, 286, 309, 316, 322-32, 338-9, 343, 381

Lorraine, Charles II, Duke of, 108-10, 199, 284

Louis de Valois, Dauphin, later Louis XI, 61-2, 70, 121, 220, 366

Luxembourg, Jeanne de, Countess of Ligny, 246-7, 256

Luxembourg, John of, 236-8, 240, 244, 247-9, 254-6, 265

Luxembourg, Louis de, bishop of Thérouanne, (Chancellor of France for Henry VI), 215, 221, 248, 255, 268, 325-6, 343

Macy, Haimond de, 246, 259, 265, 326, 329

Mailly, Jean de (bishop of Noyon), 266, 268, 325-6, 331, 380

Manchon, Guillaume (clerk of the court at Rouen), 73, 263-282 *passim*, 296, 308-9, 313, 316, 319, 325-7, 331, 333-4, 338, 340-45, 376, 380-81

Marguerie, André, 331, 336-7

Massieu, Jean, 73, 262, 264, 272, 277-282 *passim*, 296, 301, 311, 313, 322, 326-7, 330-34, 337-9, 342, 377, 380-81

Maurice, Pierre, 276, 309, 325, 338, 343

Mezières, Philippe de, 22, 40

Midi, Nicolas, 253, 261, 269, 271, 273, 276, 309, 314, 316, 320, 324-6, 332, 338-9, 348, 364, 379

Monnet, Jean (clerk to Jean Beaupère) 282, 326, 329

Montaigu, Jean de, 37

Nicolas V, Pope, 360, 377-8

Nouillompont, Jean (Jean de Metz), 93, 107-15, 120, 380-81

Ogilvy, Patrick, Sheriff of Angus, 62, 64

Orleans, Charles, Duke of, 20, 22, 32-3, 36, 95-6, 115, 122, 125, 130, 141, 147-8, 177, 219, 253, 301, 376

Orleans, Louis, Duke of, 16, 23, 26, 32-34, 355, 361

Pasquerel, Brother John (chaplain to Joan), 119-21, 123, 126, 134, 137-8, 140, 144-7, 154-5, 157, 164, 228-9, 380

Petit, Jean, 36-7, 72-3, 253

Philip IV, King of France, 15

Philip VI, King of France, 15

Piccolomini, Aeneas Sylvius, (Pope Pius II), 7, 251, 324, 348, 360, 376-7, 383

Pisan, Christine de, 29, 187, 203

Pius II, Pope, *see* Piccolomini

Pontanus, Paul, 377-8

Poulengy, Bertrand de, 94, 105, 109-11, 113, 115, 120, 380-81

Rais, Giles de, 144, 182, 189, 200, 217-8, 267, 372

Ribes, André de, 59

Ricarville, Guillaume de 77, 138, 353

Richard II, King of England, 16, 18, 22, 31, 34, 40, 206

Richard, Brother (friar), 191-8, 210, 223-5, 294, 313

Richemont, Arthur de, 57, 64-66, 68, 170, 178-80, 186-7, 201, 208, 290, 349-51, 356-8 *passim*

Rommée, Isabelle (mother of Joan), 75-6

Sala, Pierre, 121, 251, 283, 372, 376
Salisbury, Thomas Montagu/ Montacute, Earl of, 95-7, 99, 167, 177
Scales, Sir Thomas, 97, 100, 127, 155, 167, 186, 189
Sorel, Agnès, 61
Stafford, Humphrey, Count of, 155, 265
Suffolk, William Pole, Earl of, 91, 97, 100, 127, 163, 174-6, 189, 363, 367-8

Talbot, John, Earl of Shrewsbury, 70, 97, 100, 127, 146-8, 150-53, 155, 162, 167, 179, 181, 183-6, 189, 263, 265, 284, 364, 367-8, 383
Taquel, Nicolas, 73, 269, 273-80, 316, 330, 338
Tiphaine, Jean (doctor during Joan's illness at Rouen), 277, 318-9
Touraine, John of (Dauphin), 43-4, 48, 64, 276, 319, 324
Toutmouillé, Jean, (Franciscan friar), 337-8, 343, 376

Valois, Catherine de (wife of Henry V), 352
Venables, Richard, 59, 357
Vendôme, Louis of Bourbon, Count of, 119, 194, 201, 209, 211, 222, 235, 364
Villandrando, Rodrigo de, 59-60, 350, 357
Visconti, Valentina, Duchess of Orleans, 29, 35

Wandonne, 237-8, 240, 254
Warwick, Richard Beauchamp, Earl of, 68-70, 96, 254, 261-8 *passim*, 275, 277-9, 307, 313, 318-9, 324, 332-34, 336, 339-40, 342, 361, 381
Windecke, Eberhard, 173
Würtemberg, Count of, 370-71

Xaintrailles, Poton de, 69-70, 99, 162, 181-2, 189, 234, 265, 350, 358, 362, 364

Yolande of Aragon, Queen of Sicily, (mother-in-law of Charles VII), 45, 48, 64, 123, 129, 165, 201, 240, 357